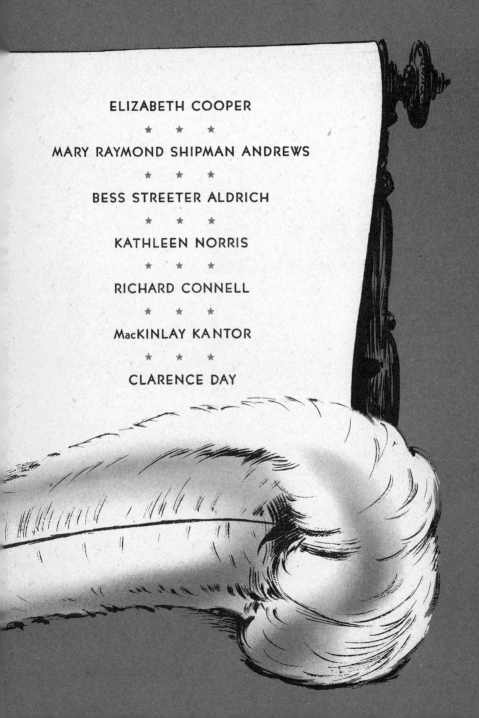

ELIZABETH COOPER

★  ★  ★

MARY RAYMOND SHIPMAN ANDREWS

★  ★  ★

BESS STREETER ALDRICH

★  ★  ★

KATHLEEN NORRIS

★  ★  ★

RICHARD CONNELL

★  ★  ★

MacKINLAY KANTOR

★  ★  ★

CLARENCE DAY

# Authors' Gold

◇◇◇◇◇◇◇◇◇◇◇◇◇◇◇◇◇◇◇◇◇◇◇◇◇◇◇◇◇◇◇◇◇◇◇◇◇◇

COMPILED BY GEORGE EATON

PEOPLES BOOK CLUB
Chicago

# Publisher's Foreword

Authors' Gold is a book of rich and beautiful romance. The editor set out to find pure gold in the writings of some of the world's best-loved authors and those stories gathered here are the result.

Here you will find many novelettes. The novelette is the most readable form of literature today. It contains the fullness and virility of the novel coupled with the very desirable elements of brevity, conciseness and completeness which are characteristic of the short story.

Authors' Gold is a warm and open-hearted book to be read with laughter and tears, and even nostalgia. It is a book to turn to for relaxation and pleasure. Some of the stories are pure, delightful entertainment; in others you will find that plus a solid, substantial quality. Sometimes you will sympathize with the problems of the characters, frequently you will laugh with them and you may even fall in love with them. It is more than just an interesting book—it is like gold, a rich and permanent thing. Certainly no book can offer very much more than the promise of this golden anthology.

v

WE WISH TO THANK the publishers
and authors' agents who allowed us to reprint
material found in this book. For further help
we also thank Fredrika Shumway Smith,
Anthony Lane, and Brant Sterne.

# Contents

PUBLISHER'S FOREWORD . . . . v

| | | |
|---|---|---|
| Neighbour Rosicky | WILLA CATHER | 1 |
| Snow in Summer | HELEN HULL | 29 |
| Night Bus | SAMUEL HOPKINS ADAMS | 93 |
| Monsieur Beaucaire | BOOTH TARKINGTON | 145 |
| Death of a Country Doctor | MARY MEDEARIS | 177 |
| Annie Laurie | ZONA GALE | 199 |
| His Very Successful Wife | MARGARET AYER BARNES | 213 |
| The Revolt of Mother | MARY E. WILKINS | 261 |
| My Lady of the Indian Purdah | ELIZABETH COOPER | 277 |
| The Counsel Assigned | MARY RAYMOND SHIPMAN ANDREWS | 355 |
| Bid the Tapers Twinkle | BESS STREETER ALDRICH | 367 |
| Mother | KATHLEEN NORRIS | 379 |
| A Friend of Napoleon | RICHARD CONNELL | 397 |
| Valedictory | MACKINLAY KANTOR | 415 |
| God and My Father | CLARENCE DAY | 433 |

# Authors' Gold

# Neighbour Rosicky

## WILLA CATHER

*Neighbour Rosicky will linger forever in our memory. Here people dwell with zest and with dignity, people whose courage and serenity and clean pride have not been lost, who are as firmly rooted in the soil as the crops themselves. Here is the great Willa Cather at her best!*

WHEN DOCTOR BURLEIGH told neighbour Rosicky he had a bad heart, Rosicky protested.

"So? No, I guess my heart was always pretty good. I got a little asthma, maybe. Just a awful short breath when I was pitchin' hay last summer, dat's all."

"Well now, Rosicky, if you know more about it than I do, what did you come to me for? It's your heart that makes you short of breath, I tell you. You're sixty-five years old, and you've always worked hard, and your heart's tired. You've got to be careful from now on, and you can't do heavy work any more. You've got five boys at home to do it for you."

The old farmer looked up at the Doctor with a gleam of amusement in his queer triangular-shaped eyes. His eyes were large and lively, but the lids were caught up in the middle in a curious way, so that they formed a triangle. He did not look like a sick man. His brown face was creased but not wrinkled, he had a ruddy colour in his smooth-shaven cheeks and in his lips, under his long brown moustache. His hair was thin and ragged around his ears, but very little grey. His forehead, naturally high and crossed by deep parallel lines, now ran all the way up to his pointed crown. Rosicky's face had the habit of looking interested,—suggested a contented disposition and a reflective quality that was gay rather than grave. This gave him a certain detachment, the easy manner of an on-looker and observer.

*Reprinted from* Obscure Destinies *by Willa Cather, by permission of Alfred A. Knopf, Inc. Copyright 1930, 1932 by Willa Cather.*

"Well, I guess you ain't got no pills fur a bad heart, Doctor Ed. I guess the only thing is fur me to git me a new one."

Doctor Burleigh swung round in his desk-chair and frowned at the old farmer. "I think if I were you I'd take a little care of the old one, Rosicky."

Rosicky shrugged. "Maybe I don't know how. I expect you mean fur me not to drink my coffee no more."

"I wouldn't in your place. But you'll do as you choose about that. I've never yet been able to separate a Bohemian from his coffee or his pipe. I've quit trying. But the sure thing is you've got to cut out farm work. You can feed the stock and do chores about the barn, but you can't do anything in the fields that makes you short of breath."

"How about shelling corn?"

"Of course not!"

Rosicky considered with puckered brows.

"I can't make my heart go no longer'n it wants to, can I, Doctor Ed?"

"I think it's good for five or six years yet, maybe more, if you'll take the strain off it. Sit around the house and help Mary. If I had a good wife like yours, I'd want to stay around the house."

His patient chuckled. "It ain't no place fur a man. I don't like no old man hanging around the kitchen too much. An' my wife, she's a awful hard worker her own self."

"That's it; you can help her a little. My Lord, Rosicky, you are one of the few men I know who has a family he can get some comfort out of; happy dispositions, never quarrel among themselves, and they treat you right. I want to see you live a few years and enjoy them."

"Oh, they're good kids, all right," Rosicky assented.

The Doctor wrote him a prescription and asked him how his oldest son, Rudolph, who had married in the spring, was getting on. Rudolph had struck out for himself, on rented land. "And how's Polly? I was afraid Mary mightn't like an American daughter-in-law, but it seems to be working out all right."

"Yes, she's a fine girl. Dat widder woman bring her daughters up very nice. Polly got lots of spunk, an' she got some style, too. Da's nice, for young folks to have some style." Rosicky inclined his head gallantly. His voice and his twinkly smile were an affectionate compliment to his daughter-in-law.

"It looks like a storm, and you'd better be getting home before it comes. In town in the car?" Doctor Burleigh rose.

2

"No, I'm in de wagon. When you got five boys, you ain't got much chance to ride round in de Ford. I ain't much for cars, noway."

"Well, it's a good road out to your place; but I don't want you bumping around in a wagon much. And never again on a hay-rake, remember!"

Rosicky placed the Doctor's fee delicately behind the desk-telephone, looking the other way, as if this were an absent-minded gesture. He put on his plush cap and his corduroy jacket with a sheepskin collar, and went out.

The Doctor picked up his stethoscope and frowned at it as if he were seriously annoyed with the instrument. He wished it had been telling tales about some other man's heart, some old man who didn't look the Doctor in the eye so knowingly, or hold out such a warm brown hand when he said good-bye. Doctor Burleigh had been a poor boy in the country before he went away to medical school; he had known Rosicky almost ever since he could remember, and he had a deep affection for Mrs. Rosicky.

Only last winter he had had such a good breakfast at Rosicky's, and that when he needed it. He had been out all night on a long, hard confinement case at Tom Marshall's,—a big rich farm where there was plenty of stock and plenty of feed and a great deal of expensive farm machinery of the newest model, and no comfort whatever. The woman had too many children and too much work, and she was no manager. When the baby was born at last, and handed over to the assisting neighbour woman, and the mother was properly attended to, Burleigh refused any breakfast in that slovenly house, and drove his buggy—the snow was too deep for a car—eight miles to Anton Rosicky's place. He didn't know another farm-house where a man could get such a warm welcome, and such good strong coffee with rich cream. No wonder the old chap didn't want to give up his coffee!

He had driven in just when the boys had come back from the barn and were washing up for breakfast. The long table, covered with a bright oil-cloth, was set out with dishes waiting for them, and the warm kitchen was full of the smell of coffee and hot biscuit and sausage. Five big handsome boys, running from twenty to twelve, all with what Burleigh called natural good manners,—they hadn't a bit of the painful self-consciousness he himself had to struggle with when he was a lad. One ran to put his horse away, another helped him off with his fur coat and hung it up, and Josephine, the youngest child and the only daughter, quickly set another place under her mother's direction.

3

With Mary, to feed creatures was the natural expression of affection,—her chickens, the calves, her big hungry boys. It was a rare pleasure to feed a young man whom she seldom saw and of whom she was as proud as if he belonged to her. Some country housekeepers would have stopped to spread a white cloth over the oilcloth, to change the thick cups and plates for their best china, and the wooden-handled knives for plated ones. But not Mary.

"You must take us as you find us, Doctor Ed. I'd be glad to put out my good things for you if you was expected, but I'm glad to get you any way at all."

He knew she was glad,—she threw back her head and spoke out as if she were announcing him to the whole prairie. Rosicky hadn't said anything at all; he merely smiled his twinkling smile, put some more coal on the fire, and went into his own room to pour the Doctor a little drink in a medicine glass. When they were all seated, he watched his wife's face from his end of the table and spoke to her in Czech. Then, with the instinct of politeness which seldom failed him, he turned to the Doctor and said slyly; "I was just tellin' her not to ask you no questions about Mrs. Marshall till you eat some breakfast. My wife, she's terrible fur to ask questions."

The boys laughed, and so did Mary. She watched the Doctor devour her biscuit and sausage, too much excited to eat anything herself. She drank her coffee and sat taking in everything about her visitor. She had known him when he was a poor country boy, and was boastfully proud of his success, always saying: "What do people go to Omaha for, to see a doctor, when we got the best one in the State right here?" If Mary liked people at all, she felt physical pleasure in the sight of them, personal exultation in any good fortune that came to them. Burleigh didn't know many women like that, but he knew she was like that.

When his hunger was satisfied, he did, of course, have to tell them about Mrs. Marshall, and he noticed what a friendly interest the boys took in the matter.

Rudolph, the oldest one (he was still living at home then), said: "The last time I was over there, she was lifting them big heavy milk-cans, and I knew she oughtn't to be doing it."

"Yes, Rudolph told me about that when he come home, and I said it wasn't right," Mary put in warmly. "It was all right for me to do them things up to the last, for I was terrible strong, but that woman's weakly. And do you think she'll be able to nurse it, Ed?" She sometimes forgot to

4

give him the title she was so proud of. "And to think of your being up all
night and then not being able to get a decent breakfast! I don't know
what's the matter with such people."

"Why, Mother," said one of the boys, "if Doctor Ed had got breakfast
there, we wouldn't have him here. So you ought to be glad."

"He knows I'm glad to have him, John, any time. But I'm sorry for
that poor woman, how bad she'll feel the Doctor had to go away in the
cold without his breakfast."

"I wish I'd been in practice when these were getting born." The doctor
looked down the row of close-clipped heads. "I missed some good breakfasts by not being."

The boys began to laugh at their mother because she flushed so red, but
she stood her ground and threw up her head. "I don't care, you wouldn't
have got away from this house without breakfast. No doctor ever did.
I'd have had something ready fixed that Anton could warm up for you."

The boys laughed harder than ever, and exclaimed at her: "I'll bet you
would!" "She would, that!"

"Father, did you get breakfast for the doctor when we were born?"

"Yes, and he used to bring me my breakfast, too, mighty nice. I was
always awful hungry!" Mary admitted with a guilty laugh.

While the boys were getting the Doctor's horse, he went to the window
to examine the house plants. "What do you do to your geraniums to keep
them blooming all winter, Mary? I never pass this house that from the road
I don't see your windows full of flowers."

She snapped off a dark red one, and a ruffled new green leaf, and put
them in his buttonhole. "There, that looks better. You look too solemn
for a young man, Ed. Why don't you git married? I'm worried about
you. Settin' at breakfast, I looked at you real hard, and I seen you've got
some grey hairs already."

"Oh, yes! They're coming. Maybe they'd come faster if I married."

"Don't talk so. You'll ruin your health eating at the hotel. I could send
your wife a nice loaf of nut bread, if you only had one. I don't like to see
a young man getting grey. I'll tell you something, Ed; you make some
strong black tea and keep it handy in a bowl, and every morning just
brush it into your hair, an' it'll keep the grey from showin' much. That's
the way I do!"

Sometimes the Doctor heard the gossipers in the drug-store wondering
why Rosicky didn't get on faster. He was industrious, and so were his

boys, but they were rather free and easy, weren't pushers, and they didn't always show good judgment. They were comfortable, they were out of debt, but they didn't get much ahead. Maybe, Doctor Burleigh reflected, people as generous and warm-hearted and affectionate as the Rosickys never got ahead much; maybe you couldn't enjoy your life and put it into the bank, too.

# II

When Rosicky left Doctor Burleigh's office he went into the farm-implement store to light his pipe and put on his glasses and read over the list Mary had given him. Then he went into the general merchandise place next door and stood about until the pretty girl with the plucked eyebrows, who always waited on him, was free. Those eyebrows, two thin India-ink strokes, amused him, because he remembered how they used to be. Rosicky always prolonged his shopping by a little joking; the girl knew the old fellow admired her, and she liked to chaff with him.

"Seems to me about every other week you buy ticking, Mr. Rosicky, and always the best quality," she remarked as she measured off the heavy bolt with red stripes.

"You see, my wife is always makin' goose-fedder pillows, an' de thin stuff don't hold in dem little down-fedders."

"You must have lots of pillows at your house."

"Sure. She makes quilts of dem, too. We sleeps easy. Now she's makin' a fedder quilt for my son's wife. You know Polly, that married my Rudolph. How much my bill, Miss Pearl?"

"Eight eighty-five."

"Chust make it nine, and put in some candy fur de women."

"As usual. I never did see a man buy so much candy for his wife. First thing you know, she'll be getting too fat."

"I'd like dat. I ain't much fur all dem slim women like what de style is now."

"That's one for me, I suppose, Mr. Bohunk!" Pearl sniffed and elevated her India-ink strokes.

When Rosicky went out to his wagon, it was beginning to snow,—the first snow of the season, and he was glad to see it. He rattled out of town and along the highway through a wonderfully rich stretch of country, the finest farms in the county. He admired this High Prairie, as it was called, and always liked to drive through it. His own place lay in a rougher territory, where there was some clay in the soil and it was not so productive. When he bought his land, he hadn't the money to buy on High Prairie; so he told his boys, when they grumbled, that if their land hadn't some clay in it, they wouldn't own it at all. All the same, he enjoyed looking at these fine farms, as he enjoyed looking at a prize bull.

After he had gone eight miles, he came to the graveyard, which lay just at the edge of his own hay-land. There he stopped his horses and sat still on his wagon seat, looking about at the snowfall. Over yonder on the hill he could see his own house, crouching low, with the clump of orchard behind and the windmill before, and all down the gentle hill-slope the rows of pale gold cornstalks stood out against the white field. The snow was falling over the cornfield and the pasture and the hay-land, steadily, with very little wind,—a nice dry snow. The graveyard had only a light wire fence about it and was all overgrown with long red grass. The fine snow, settling into this red grass and upon the few little evergreens and the headstones, looked very pretty.

It was a nice graveyard, Rosicky reflected, sort of snug and homelike, not cramped or mournful,—a big sweep all round it. A man could lie down in the long grass and see the complete arch of the sky over him, hear the wagons go by; in summer the mowing-machine rattled right up to the wire fence. And it was so near home. Over there across the cornstalks his own roof and windmill looked so good to him that he promised himself to mind the Doctor and take care of himself. He was awful fond of his place, he admitted. He wasn't anxious to leave it. And it was a comfort to think that he would never have to go farther than the edge of his own hayfield. The snow, falling over his barnyard and the graveyard, seemed to draw things together like. And they were all old neighbours in the graveyard, most of them friends; there was nothing to feel awkward or embarrassed about. Embarrassment was the most disagreeable feeling Rosicky knew. He didn't often have it,—only with certain people whom he didn't understand at all.

Well, it was a nice snowstorm; a fine sight to see the snow falling so quietly and graciously over so much open country. On his cap and shoulders, on the horses' backs and manes, light, delicate, mysterious it fell; and with it a dry cool fragrance was released into the air. It meant rest for vegetation and men and beasts, for the ground itself; a season of long nights for sleep, leisurely breakfasts, peace by the fire. This and much more went through Rosicky's mind, but he merely told himself that winter was coming, clucked to his horses, and drove on.

When he reached home, John, the youngest boy, ran out to put away his team for him, and he met Mary coming up from the outside cellar with her apron full of carrots. They went into the house together. On the table, covered with oilcloth figured with clusters of blue grapes, a place was set, and he smelled hot coffee-cake of some kind. Anton never lunched in town; he thought that extravagant, and anyhow he didn't like the food. So Mary always had something ready for him when he got home.

After he was settled in his chair, stirring his coffee in a big cup, Mary took out of the oven a pan of *kolache* stuffed with apricots, examined them anxiously to see whether they had got too dry, put them beside his plate, and then sat down opposite him.

Rosicky asked her in Czech if she wasn't going to have any coffee.

She replied in English, as being somehow the right language for transacting business: "Now what did Doctor Ed say, Anton? You tell me just what."

"He said I was to tell you some compliments, but I forgot 'em." Rosicky's eyes twinkled.

"About you, I mean. What did he say about your asthma?"

"He says I ain't go no asthma." Rosicky took one of the little rolls in his broad brown fingers. The thickened nail of his right thumb told the story of his past.

"Well, what is the matter? And don't try to put me off."

"He don't say nothing much, only I'm a little older, and my heart ain't so good like it used to be."

Mary started and brushed her hair back from her temples with both hands as if she were a little out of her mind. From the way she glared, she might have been in a rage with him.

"He says there's something the matter with your heart? Doctor Ed says so?"

"Now don't yell at me like I was a hog in de garden, Mary. You know I always did like to hear a woman talk soft. He didn't say anything de matter wid my heart, only it ain't so young like it used to be, an' he tell me not to pitch hay or run de corn-sheller."

Mary wanted to jump up, but she sat still. She admired the way he never under any circumstances raised his voice or spoke roughly. He was city-bred, and she was country-bred; she often said she wanted her boys to have their papa's nice ways.

8

"You never have no pain there, do you? It's your breathing and your stomach that's been wrong. I wouldn't believe nobody but Doctor Ed about it. I guess I'll go see him myself. Didn't he give you no advice?"

"Chust to take it easy like, an' stay round de house dis winter. I guess you got some carpenter work for me to do. I kin make some new shelves for you, and I want dis long time to build a closet in de boys' room and make dem two little fellers keep dere clo'es hung up."

Rosicky drank his coffee from time to time, while he considered. His moustache was of the soft long variety and came down over his mouth like the teeth of a buggy-rake over a bundle of hay. Each time he put down his cup, he ran his blue handkerchief over his lips. When he took a drink of water, he managed very neatly with the back of his hand.

Mary sat watching him intently, trying to find any change in his face. It is hard to see anyone who has become like your own body to you. Yes, his hair had got thin, and his high forehead had deep lines running from left to right. But his neck, always clean shaved except in the busiest seasons, was not loose or baggy. It was burned a dark reddish brown, and there were deep creases in it, but it looked firm and full of blood. His cheeks had a good colour. On either side of his mouth there was a half-moon down the length of his cheek, not wrinkles, but two lines that had come there from his habitual expression. He was shorter and broader than when she married him; his back had grown broad and curved, a good deal like the shell of an old turtle, and his arms and legs were short.

He was fifteen years older than Mary, but she had hardly ever thought about it before. He was her man, and the kind of man she liked. She was rough, and he was gentle,—city-bred, as she always said. They had been shipmates on a rough voyage and had stood by each other in trying times. Life had gone well with them because, at bottom, they had the same ideas about life. They agreed, without discussion, as to what was most important and what was secondary. They didn't often exchange opinions, even in Czech,—it was as if they had thought the same thought together. A good deal had to be sacrificed and thrown overboard in a hard life like theirs, and they had never disagreed as to the things that could go. It had been a hard life, and a soft life, too. There wasn't anything brutal in the short, broad-backed man with the three-cornered eyes and the forehead that went on to the top of his skull. He was a city man, a gentle man, and though he had married a rough farm girl, he had never touched her without gentleness.

They had been at one accord not to hurry through life, not to be always

9

skimping and saving. They saw their neighbours buy more land and feed more stock than they did, without discontent. Once when the creamery agent came to the Rosickys to persuade them to sell him their cream, he told them how much money the Fasslers, their nearest neighbours, had made on their cream last year.

"Yes," said Mary, "and look at them Fassler children! Pale, pinched little things, they look like skimmed milk. I'd rather put some colour into my children's faces than put money into the bank."

The agent shrugged and turned to Anton.

"I guess we'll do like she says," said Rosicky.

# III

Mary very soon got into town to see Doctor Ed, and then she had a talk with the boys and set a guard over Rosicky. Even John, the youngest, had his father on his mind. If Rosicky went to throw hay down from the loft, one of the boys ran up the ladder and took the fork from him. He sometimes complained that though he was getting to be an old man, he wasn't an old woman yet.

That winter he stayed in the house in the afternoons and carpentered, or sat in the chair between the window full of plants and the wooden bench where the two pails of drinking-water stood. This spot was called "Father's corner," though it was not a corner at all. He had a shelf there, where he kept his Bohemian papers and his pipes and tobacco, and his shears and needles and thread and tailor's thimble. Having been a tailor in his youth, he couldn't bear to see a woman patching at his clothes, or at the boys'. He liked tailoring, and always patched all the overalls and jackets and work shirts. Occasionally he made over a pair of pants one of the older boys had outgrown, for the little fellow.

While he sewed, he let his mind run back over his life. He had a good deal to remember, really; life in three countries. The only part of his youth he didn't like to remember was the two years he had spent in London, in Cheapside, working for a German tailor who was wretchedly poor. Those days, when he was nearly always hungry, when his clothes were dropping off him for dirt, and the sound of a strange language kept him in continual bewilderment, had left a sore spot in his mind that wouldn't bear touching.

He was twenty when he landed at Castle Garden in New York, and he had a protector who got him work in a tailor shop in Vesey Street, down near the Washington Market. He looked upon that part of his life as very happy. He became a good workman, he was industrious, and his wages were increased from time to time. He minded his own business and envied nobody's good fortune. He went to night school and learned to read English. He often did overtime work and was well paid for it, but somehow he never saved anything. He couldn't refuse a loan to a friend, and he was self-indulgent. He liked a good dinner, and a little went for beer, a little for tobacco; a good deal went to the girls. He often stood through an opera on Saturday nights; he could get standing-room for a dollar. Those were the great days of opera in New York, and it gave a fellow something to think about for the rest of the week. Rosicky had a quick ear, and a childish love of all the stage splendour; the scenery, the costumes, the ballet. He usually went with a chum, and after the performance they had beer and maybe some oysters somewhere. It was a fine life; for the first five years or so it satisfied him completely. He was never hungry or cold or dirty, and everything amused him: a fire, a dog fight, a parade, a storm, a ferry ride. He thought New York the finest, richest, friendliest city in the world.

Moreover, he had what he called a happy home life. Very near the tailor shop was a small furniture-factory, where an old Austrian, Loeffler, employed a few skilled men and made unusual furniture, most of it to order, for the rich German housewives up-town. The top floor of Loeffler's five-story factory was a loft, where he kept his choice lumber and stored the odd pieces of furniture left on his hands. One of the young workmen he employed was a Czech, and he and Rosicky became fast friends. They persuaded Loeffler to let them have a sleeping-room in one corner of the loft. They bought good beds and bedding and had their pick of the furniture kept up there. The loft was low-pitched, but light and airy, full of windows, and good-smelling by reason of the fine lumber put up there to season. Old Loeffler used to go down to the docks and buy wood from South America and the East from the sea captains. The young men were as foolish about their house as a bridal pair. Zichec, the young cabinet-maker, devised every sort of convenience, and Rosicky kept their clothes in order. At night and on Sundays, when the quiver of machinery underneath was still, it was the quietest place in the world, and on summer nights all the sea winds blew in. Zichec often practised on his flute in the evening. They were both fond of music and went to the opera together. Rosicky thought he wanted to live like that for ever.

But as the years passed, all alike, he began to get a little restless. When spring came round, he would begin to feel fretted, and he got to drinking. He was likely to drink too much of a Saturday night. On Sunday he was languid and heavy, getting over his spree. On Monday he plunged into work again. So he never had time to figure out what ailed him, though he knew something did. When the grass turned green in Park Place, and the lilac hedge at the back of Trinity churchyard put out its blossoms, he was tormented by a longing to run away. That was why he drank too much; to get a temporary illusion of freedom and wide horizons.

Rosicky, the old Rosicky, could remember as if it were yesterday the day when the young Rosicky found out what was the matter with him. It was on a Fourth of July afternoon, and he was sitting in Park Place in the sun. The lower part of New York was empty. Wall Street, Liberty Street, Broadway, all empty. So much stone and asphalt with nothing going on, so many empty windows. The emptiness was intense, like the stillness in a great factory when the machinery stops and the belts and bands cease running. It was too great a change, it took all the strength out of one. Those blank buildings, without the stream of life pouring through them, were like empty jails. It struck young Rosicky that this was the trouble with big cities; they built you in from the earth itself, cemented you away from any contact with the ground. You lived in an unnatural world, like the fish in an aquarium, who were probably much more comfortable than they ever were in the sea.

On that very day he began to think seriously about the articles he had read in the Bohemian papers, describing prosperous Czech farming communities in the West. He believed he would like to go out there as a farm hand; it was hardly possible that he could ever have land of his own. His people had always been workmen; his father and grandfather had worked in shops. His mother's parents had lived in the country, but they rented their farm and had a hard time to get along. Nobody in his family had ever owned any land,—that belonged to a different station of life altogether. Anton's mother died when he was little, and he was sent into the country to her parents. He stayed with them until he was twelve, and formed those ties with the earth and the farm animals and growing things which are never made at all unless they are made early. After his grandfather died, he went back to live with his father and stepmother, but she was very hard on him, and his father helped him to get passage to London.

After that Fourth of July day in Park Place, the desire to return to the country never left him. To work on another man's farm would be all he asked; to see the sun rise and set and to plant things and watch them grow. He was a very simple man. He was like a tree that has not many roots, but one tap-root that goes down deep. He subscribed for a Bohemian paper printed in Chicago, then for one printed in Omaha. His mind got farther and farther west. He began to save a little money to buy his liberty. When he was thirty-five, there was a great meeting in New York of Bohemian athletic societies, and Rosicky left the tailor shop and went home with the Omaha delegates to try his fortune in another part of the world.

# IV

Perhaps the fact that his own youth was well over before he began to have a family was one reason why Rosicky was so fond of his boys. He had almost a grandfather's indulgence for them. He had never had to worry about any of them—except, just now, a little about Rudolph.

On Saturday night the boys always piled into the Ford, took little Josephine, and went to town to the moving-picture show. One Saturday morning they were talking at the breakfast table about starting early that evening, so that they would have an hour or so to see the Christmas things in the stores before the show began. Rosicky looked down the table.

"I hope you boys ain't disappointed, but I want you to let me have de car tonight. Maybe some of you can go in with de neighbours."

Their faces fell. They worked hard all week, and they were still like children. A new jack-knife or a box of candy pleased the older ones as much as the little fellow.

"If you and Mother are going to town," Frank said, "maybe you could take a couple of us along with you, anyway."

"No, I want to take de car down to Rudolph's, and let him an' Polly go in to de show. She don't git into town enough, an' I'm afraid she's gettin' lonesome, an' he can't afford no car yet."

That settled it. The boys were a good deal dashed. Their father took another piece of apple-cake and went on: "Maybe next Saturday night de two little fellers can go along wid dem."

"Oh, is Rudolph going to have the car every Saturday night?"

Rosicky did not reply at once; then he began to speak seriously: "Listen, boys; Polly ain't lookin' so good. I don't like to see nobody lookin' sad. It comes hard fur a town girl to be a farmer's wife. I don't want no trouble to start in Rudolph's family. When it starts, it ain't so easy to stop. An American girl don't git used to our ways all at once. I like to tell Polly she and Rudolph can have the car every Saturday night till after New Year's, if it's all right with you boys."

"Sure it's all right, Papa," Mary cut in. "And it's good you thought about that. Town girls is used to more than country girls. I lay awake nights, scared she'll make Rudolph discontented with the farm."

The boys put as good a face on it as they could. They surely looked forward to their Saturday nights in town. That evening Rosicky drove the car the half-mile down to Rudolph's new, bare little house.

Polly was in a short-sleeved gingham dress, clearing away the supper dishes. She was a trim, slim little thing, with blue eyes and shingled yellow hair, and her eyebrows were reduced to a mere brush-stroke, like Miss Pearl's.

"Good evening, Mr. Rosicky. Rudolph's at the barn, I guess." She never called him father, or Mary mother. She was sensitive about having married a foreigner. She never in the world would have done it if Rudolph hadn't been such a handsome, persuasive fellow and such a gallant lover. He had graduated in her class in the high school in town, and their friendship began in the ninth grade.

Rosicky went in, though he wasn't exactly asked. "My boys ain't goin' to town tonight, an' I brought de car over fur you two to go in to de picture show."

Polly, carrying dishes to the sink, looked over her shoulder at him. "Thank you. But I'm late with my work tonight, and pretty tired. Maybe Rudolph would like to go in with you."

"Oh, I don't go to de shows! I'm too old-fashioned. You won't feel so tired after you ride in de air a ways. It's a nice clear night, an' it ain't cold. You go an' fix yourself up, Polly, an' I'll wash de dishes an' leave everything nice fur you."

Polly blushed and tossed her bob. "I couldn't let you do that, Mr. Rosicky. I wouldn't think of it."

Rosicky said nothing. He found a bib apron on a nail behind the kitchen door. He slipped it over his head and then took Polly by her two elbows and pushed her gently toward the door of her own room. "I washed up de kitchen many times for my wife, when de babies was sick

14

or somethin'. You go an' make yourself look nice. I like you to look prettier'n any of dem town girls when you go in. De young folks must have some fun, an' I'm goin' to look out fur you, Polly."

That kind, reassuring grip on her elbows, the old man's funny bright eyes, made Polly want to drop her head on his shoulder for a second. She restrained herself, but she lingered in his grasp at the door of her room, murmuring tearfully: "You always lived in the city when you were young, didn't you? Don't you ever get lonesome out here?"

As she turned round to him, her hand fell naturally to his, and he stood holding it and smiling into her face with his peculiar, knowing, indulgent smile without a shadow of reproach in it. "Dem big cities is all right fur de rich, but dey is terrible hard fur de poor."

"I don't know. Sometimes I think I'd like to take a chance. You lived in New York, didn't you?"

"An' London. Da's bigger still. I learned my trade dere. Here's Rudolph comin', you better hurry."

"Will you tell me about London some time?"

"Maybe. Only I ain't no talker, Polly. Run an' dress yourself up."

The bedroom door closed behind her, and Rudolph came in from the outside, looking anxious. He had seen the car and was sorry any of his family should come just then. Supper hadn't been a very pleasant occasion. Halting in the doorway, he saw his father in a kitchen apron, carrying dishes to the sink. He flushed crimson and something flashed in his eye. Rosicky held up a warning finger.

"I brought de car over fur you an' Polly to go to de picture show, an' I made her let me finish here so you won't be late. You go put on a clean shirt, quick!"

"But don't the boys want the car, Father?"

"Not tonight dey don't." Rosicky fumbled under his apron and found his pants pocket. He took out a silver dollar and said in a hurried whisper: "You go an buy dat girl some ice cream an' candy tonight, like you was courtin'. She's awful good friends wid me."

Rudolph was very short of cash, but he took the money as if it hurt him. There had been a crop failure all over the country. He had more than once been sorry he'd married this year.

In a few minutes the young people came out, looking clean and a little stiff. Rosicky hurried them off, and then he took his own time with the dishes. He scoured the pots and pans and put away the milk and swept the kitchen. He put some coal in the stove and shut off the draughts, so

15

the place would be warm for them when they got home late at night. Then he sat down and had a pipe and listened to the clock tick.

Generally speaking, marrying an American girl was certainly a risk. A Czech should marry a Czech. It was lucky that Polly was the daughter of a poor widow woman; Rudolph was proud, and if she had a prosperous family to throw up at him, they could never make it go. Polly was one of four sisters, and they all worked; one was bookkeeper in the bank, one taught music, and Polly and her younger sister had been clerks, like Miss Pearl. All four of them were musical, had pretty voices, and sang in the Methodist choir, which the eldest sister directed.

Polly missed the sociability of a store position. She missed the choir, and the company of her sisters. She didn't dislike housework, but she disliked so much of it. Rosicky was a little anxious about this pair. He was afraid Polly would grow so discontented that Rudy would quit the farm and take a factory job in Omaha. He had worked for a winter up there, two years ago, to get money to marry on. He had done very well, and they would always take him back at the stockyards. But to Rosicky that meant the end of everything for his son. To be a landless man was to be a wage-earner, a slave, all your life; to have nothing, to be nothing.

Rosicky thought he would come over and do a little carpentering for Polly after the New Year. He guessed she needed jollying. Rudolph was a serious sort of chap, serious in love and serious about his work.

Rosicky shook out his pipe and walked home across the fields. Ahead of him the lamplight shone from his kitchen windows. Suppose he were still in a tailor shop on Vesey Street, with a bunch of pale, narrow-chested sons working on machines, all coming home tired and sullen to eat supper in a kitchen that was a parlour also; with another crowded, angry family quarreling just across the dumb-waiter shaft, and squeaking pulleys at the windows where dirty washings hung on dirty lines above a court full of old brooms and mops and ash cans. . . .

He stopped by the windmill to look up at the frosty winter stars and draw a long breath before he went inside. That kitchen with the shining windows was dear to him; but the sleeping fields and bright stars and the noble darkness were dearer still.

# V

On the day before Christmas the weather set in very cold; no snow, but a bitter, biting wind that whistled and sang over the flat land and lashed one's face like fine wires. There was baking going on in the Rosicky kitchen all day, and Rosicky sat inside, making over a coat that Albert had outgrown into an overcoat for John. Mary had a big red geranium in bloom for Christmas, and a row of Jerusalem cherry trees, full of berries. It was the first year she had ever grown these; Doctor Ed brought her the seeds from Omaha when he went to some medical convention. They reminded Rosicky of plants he had seen in England; and all afternoon, as he stitched, he sat thinking about those two years in London, which his mind usually shrank from even after all this while.

He was a lad of eighteen when he dropped down into London, with no money and no connections except the address of a cousin who was supposed to be working at a confectioner's. When he went to the pastry shop, however, he found that the cousin had gone to America. Anton tramped the streets for several days, sleeping in doorways and on the Embankment, until he was in utter despair. He knew no English, and the sound of the strange language all about him confused him. By chance he met a poor German tailor who had learned his trade in Vienna, and could speak a little Czech. This tailor, Lifschnitz, kept a repair shop in a Cheapside basement, underneath a cobbler. He didn't much need an apprentice, but he was sorry for the boy and took him in for no wages but his keep and what he could pick up. The pickings were supposed to be coppers given you when you took work home to a customer. But most of the customers called for their clothes themselves, and the coppers that came Anton's way were very few. He had, however, a place to sleep. The tailor's family lived upstairs in three rooms; a kitchen, a bedroom, where Lifschnitz and his wife and five children slept, and a living-room. Two corners of this living-room were curtained off for lodgers; in one Rosicky slept on an old horsehair sofa, with a feather quilt to wrap himself in. The other corner was rented to a wretched, dirty boy, who was studying the violin. He actually practised there. Rosicky was dirty, too. There was no way to be anything else. Mrs. Lifschnitz got the water she cooked and washed with from a pump in a brick court, four flights down. There were bugs in the

17

place, and multitudes of fleas, though the poor woman did the best she could. Rosicky knew she often went empty to give another potato or a spoonful of dripping to the two hungry, sad-eyed boys who lodged with her. He used to think he would never get out of there, never get a clean shirt to his back again. What would he do, he wondered, when his clothes actually dropped to pieces and the worn cloth wouldn't hold patches any longer?

It was still early when the old farmer put aside his sewing and his recollections. The sky had been a dark grey all day, with not a gleam of sun, and the light failed at four o'clock. He went to shave and change his shirt while the turkey was roasting. Rudolph and Polly were coming over for supper.

After supper they sat round in the kitchen, and the younger boys were saying how sorry they were it hadn't snowed. Everybody was sorry. They wanted a deep snow that would lie long and keep the wheat warm, and leave the ground soaked when it melted.

"Yes, sir!" Rudolph broke out fiercely; "if we have another dry year like last year, there's going to be hard times in this country."

Rosicky filled his pipe. "You boys don't know what hard times is. You don't owe nobody, you got plenty to eat an' keep warm, an' plenty water to keep clean. When you got them, you can't have it very hard."

Rudolph frowned, opened and shut his big right hand, and dropped it clenched upon his knee. "I've got to have a good deal more than that, Father, or I'll quit this farming gamble. I can always make good wages railroading, or at the packing house, and be sure of my money."

"Maybe so," his father answered dryly.

Mary, who had just come in from the pantry and was wiping her hands on the roller towel, thought Rudy and his father were getting too serious. She brought her darning-basket and sat down in the middle of the group.

"I ain't much afraid of hard times, Rudy," she said heartily. "We've had a plenty, but we've always come through. Your father wouldn't never take nothing very hard, not even hard times. I got a mind to tell you a story on him. Maybe you boys can't hardly remember the year we had that terrible hot wind, that burned everything up on the Fourth of July? All the corn an' the gardens. An' that was in the days when we didn't have alfalfa yet,—I guess it wasn't invented.

"Well, that very day your father was out cultivatin' corn, and I was here in the kitchen makin' plum preserves. We had bushels of plums that year. I noticed it was terrible hot, but it's always hot in the kitchen when you're preservin', and I was too busy with my plums to mind. Anton come in from the field about three o'clock, an' I asked him what was the matter.

" 'Nothin',' he says, 'but it's pretty hot, an' I think I won't work no more today.' He stood round for a few minutes, an' then he says: 'Ain't you near through? I want you should git up a nice supper for us tonight. It's Fourth of July.'

"I told him to git along, that I was right in the middle of preservin', but the plums would taste good on hot biscuit. 'I'm goin' to have fried chicken, too,' he says, and he went off an' killed a couple. You three oldest boys was little fellers, playin' round outside, real hot an' sweaty, an' your father took you to the horse tank down by the windmill an' took off your clothes an' put you in. Them two box-elder trees was little then, but they made shade over the tank. Then he took off all his own clothes, an' got in with you. While he was playin' in the water with you, the Methodist preacher drove into our place to say how all the neighbours was goin' to meet at the schoolhouse that night, to pray for rain. He drove right to the windmill, of course, and there was your father and you three with no clothes on. I was in the kitchen door, an' I had to laugh, for the preacher acted like he ain't never seen a naked man before. He surely was embarrassed, an' your father couldn't git to his clothes; they was all hangin' up on the windmill to let the sweat dry out of 'em. So he laid in the tank where he was, an' put one of you boys on top of him to cover him up a little, an' talked to the preacher.

"When you got through playin' in the water, he put clean clothes on you and a clean shirt on himself, an' by that time I'd begun to get supper. He says: 'It's too hot in here to eat comfortable. Let's have a picnic in the orchard. We'll eat our supper behind the mulberry hedge, under them linden trees.'

"So he carried our supper down, an' a bottle of my wild-grape wine, an' everything tasted good, I can tell you. The wind got cooler as the sun was goin' down, and it turned out pleasant, only I noticed how the leaves was curled up on the linden trees. That made me think, an' I asked your father if that hot wind all day hadn't been terrible hard on the gardens an' the corn.

" 'Corn,' he says, 'there ain't no corn.'

" 'What you talkin' about?' I said. 'Ain't we got forty acres?'

" 'We ain't got an ear,' he says, 'nor nobody else ain't got none. All the corn in this country was cooked by three o'clock today, like you'd roasted it in an oven.'

" 'You mean you won't get no crop at all?' I asked him. I couldn't believe it, after he'd worked so hard.

" 'No crop this year,' he says. 'That's why we're havin' a picnic. We might as well enjoy what we got.'

"An' that's how your father behaved, when all the neighbours was so discouraged they couldn't look you in the face. An' we enjoyed ourselves that year, poor as we was, an' our neighbours wasn't a bit better off for bein' miserable. Some of 'em grieved till they got poor digestions and couldn't relish what they did have."

The younger boys said they thought their father had the best of it. But Rudolph was thinking that, all the same, the neighbours had managed to get ahead more, in the fifteen years since that time. There must be something wrong about his father's way of doing things. He wished he knew what was going on in the back of Polly's mind. He knew she liked his father, but he knew, too, that she was afraid of something. When his mother sent over coffee-cake or prune tarts or a loaf of fresh bread, Polly seemed to regard them with a certain suspicion. When she observed to him that his brothers had nice manners, her tone implied that it was remarkable they should have. With his mother she was stiff and on her guard. Mary's hearty frankness and gusts of good humour irritated her. Polly was afraid of being unusual or conspicuous in any way, of being "ordinary," as she said!

When Mary had finished her story, Rosicky lay aside his pipe.

"You boys like me to tell you about some of dem hard times I been through in London?" Warmly encouraged, he sat rubbing his forehead along the deep creases. It was bothersome to tell a long story in English (he nearly always talked to the boys in Czech), but he wanted Polly to hear this one.

"Well, you know about dat tailor shop I worked in in London? I had one Christmas dere I ain't never forgot. Times was awful bad before Christmas; de boss ain't got much work, an' have it awful hard to pay his rent. It ain't so much fun, bein' poor in a big city like London, I'll say! All de windows is full of good t'ings to eat, an' all de pushcarts in de streets is full, an' you smell 'em all de time, an' you ain't got no money,— not a damn bit. I didn't mind de cold so much, though I didn't have no overcoat, chust a short jacket I'd outgrowed so it wouldn't meet on me, an' my hands was chapped raw. But I always had a good appetite, like you all know, an' de sight of dem pork pies in de windows was awful fur me!

"Day before Christmas was terrible foggy dat year, an' dat fog gits into your bones and makes you all damp like. Mrs. Lifschnitz didn't give us nuthin' but a little bread an' drippin' for supper, because she was savin' to try for to give us a good dinner on Christmas Day. After supper de boss say I can go an' enjoy myself, so I went into de streets to listen to de Christmas singers. Dey sing old songs an' make very nice music, an' I run round after dem a good ways, till I got awful hungry. I t'ink maybe if I go home, I can sleep till morning an' forget my belly.

"I went into my corner real quiet, and roll up in my fedder quilt. But I ain't got my head down, till I smell somet'ing good. Seem like it git stronger an' stronger, an' I can't git to sleep noway. I can't understand dat smell. Dere was a gas light in a hall across de court, dat always shine in at my window a little. I got up an' look round. I got a little wooden box in my corner fur a stool, 'cause I ain't got no chair. I picks up dat box, and under it dere is a roast goose on a platter! I can't believe my eyes. I carry it to de window where de light comes in, an' touch it and smell it to find out, an' den I taste it to be sure. I say, I will eat chust one little bite of dat goose, so I can go to sleep, and tomorrow I won't eat none at all. But I tell you, boys, when I stop, one half of dat goose was gone!"

The narrator bowed his head, and the boys shouted. But little Josephine slipped behind his chair and kissed him on the neck beneath his ear.

"Poor little Papa, I don't want him to be hungry!"

"Da's long ago, child. I ain't never been hungry since I had your mudder to cook fur me."

"Go on and tell us the rest, please," said Polly.

"Well, when I come to realize what I done, of course, I felt terrible. I felt better in de stomach, but very bad in de heart. I set on my bed wid dat platter on my knees, an' it all come to me; how hard dat poor woman save to buy dat goose, and how she get some neighbour to cook it dat got more fire, an' how she put it in my corner to keep it away from dem hungry children. Dey was a old carpet hung up to shut my corner off, an' de children wasn't allowed to go in dere. An' I know she put it in my corner because she trust me more'n she did de violin boy. I can't stand it to face her after I spoil de Christmas. So I put on my shoes and go out into de city. I tell myself I better throw myself in de river; but I guess I ain't dat kind of a boy.

"It was after twelve o'clock, an' terrible cold, an' I start out to walk about London all night. I walk along de river awhile, but dey was lots of drunks all along; men, and women too. I chust move along to keep away from de police. I git onto de Strand, an' den over to New Oxford Street, where dere was a big German restaurant on de ground floor, wid big windows all fixed up fine, an' I could see de people havin' parties inside. While I was lookin' in, two men and two ladies come out, laughin' and talkin' and feelin' happy about all dey been eatin' an' drinkin', and dey was speakin' Czech,—not like de Austrians, but like de home folks talk it.

"I guess I went crazy, an' I done what I ain't never done before nor since. I went right up to dem gay people an' begun to beg dem: 'Fellow-countrymen, for God's sake give me money enough to buy a goose!'

"Dey laugh, of course, but de ladies speak awful kind to me, an' dey take me back into de restaurant and give me hot coffee and cakes, an' make me tell all about how I happened to come to London, an' what I was doin' dere. Dey take my name and where I work down on paper, an' both of dem ladies give me ten shillings.

"De big market at Covent Garden ain't very far away, an' by dat time it was open. I go dere an' buy a big goose an' some pork pies, an' potatoes and onions, an' cakes an' oranges fur de children,—all I could carry! When I git home, everybody is still asleep. I pile all I bought on de kitchen table, an' goin in an' lay down on my bed, an' I ain't waken up till I hear dat woman scream when she come out into her kitchen. My goodness, but she was surprise! She laugh an' cry at de same time, an' hug me and waken all de children. She ain't stop fur no breakfast; she git de Christmas dinner ready dat morning, and we all sit down an' eat all we can hold. I ain't never seen dat violin boy have all he can hold before.

"Two three days after dat, de two men come to hunt me up, an' dey ask my boss, and he give me a good report an' tell dem I was a steady boy all right. One of dem Bohemians was very smart an' run a Bohemian newspaper in New York, an' de odder was a rich man, in de importing business, an' dey been travelling togedder. Dey told me how t'ings was easier in New York, an' offered to pay my passage when dey was goin' home soon on a boat. My boss say to me: 'You go. You ain't got no chance here, an' I like to see you git ahead, fur you always been a good boy to my woman, and fur dat fine Christmas dinner you give us all.' An' da's how I got to New York."

That night when Rudolph and Polly, arm in arm, were running home across the fields with the bitter wind at their backs, his heart leaped for joy when she said she thought they might have his family come over for supper on New Year's Eve. "Let's get up a nice supper, and not let your mother help at all; make her be company for once."

"That would be lovely of you, Polly," he said humbly. He was a very simple, modest boy, and he, too, felt vaguely that Polly and her sisters were more experienced and worldly than his people.

# VI

The winter turned out badly for farmers. It was bitterly cold, and after the first light snows before Christmas there was no snow at all,—and no rain. March was as bitter as February. On those days when the wind fairly punished the country, Rosicky sat by his window. In the fall he and the boys had put in a big wheat planting, and now the seed had frozen in the ground. All that land would have to be ploughed up and planted over again, planted in corn. It had happened before, but he was younger then, and he never worried about what had to be. He was sure of himself and of Mary; he knew they could bear what they had to bear, that they would always pull through somehow. But he was not so sure about the young ones, and he felt troubled because Rudolph and Polly were having such a hard start.

Sitting beside his flowering window while the panes rattled and the wind blew in under the door, Rosicky gave himself to reflection as he had not done since those Sundays in the loft of the furniture-factory in New York, long ago. Then he was trying to find what he wanted in life for himself; now he was trying to find what he wanted for his boys, and why it was he so hungered to feel sure they would be here, working this very land, after he was gone.

They would have to work hard on the farm, and probably they would never do much more than make a living. But if he could think of them as staying here on the land, he wouldn't have to fear any great unkindness for them. Hardships, certainly; it was a hardship to have the wheat freeze in the ground when seed was so high; and to have to sell your stock because you had no feed. But there would be other years when everything came along right, and you caught up. And what you had was your own. You didn't have to choose between bosses and strikers, and go wrong either way. You didn't have to do with dishonest and cruel people.

They were the only things in his experience he had found terrifying and horrible; the look in the eyes of a dishonest and crafty man, of a scheming and rapacious woman.

In the country, if you had a mean neighbour, you could keep off his land and make him keep off yours. But in the city, all the foulness and misery and brutality of your neighbours was part of your life. The worst things he had come upon in his journey through the world were human,— depraved and poisonous specimens of man. To this day he could recall certain terrible faces in the London streets. There were mean people everywhere, to be sure, even in their own country town here. But they weren't tempered, hardened, sharpened, like the treacherous people in cities who live by grinding or cheating or poisoning their fellow-men. He had helped to bury two of his fellow-workmen in the tailoring trade, and he was distrustful of the organized industries that see one out of the world in big cities. Here, if you were sick, you had Doctor Ed to look after you; and if you died, fat Mr. Haycock, the kindest man in the world, buried you.

It seemed to Rosicky that for good, honest boys like his, the worst they could do on the farm was better than the best they would be likely to do in the city. If he'd had a mean boy, now, one who was crooked and sharp and tried to put anything over on his brothers, the town would be the place for him. But he had no such boy. As for Rudolph, the discontented one, he would give the shirt off his back to anyone who touched his heart. What Rosicky really hoped for his boys was that they could get through the world without ever knowing much about the cruelty of human beings. "Their mother and me ain't prepared them for that," he sometimes said to himself.

These thoughts brought him back to a grateful consideration of his own case. What an escape he had had, to be sure! He, too, in his time, had had to take money for repair work from the hand of a hungry child who let it go so wistfully; because it was money due his boss. And now, in all these years, he had never had to take a cent from anyone in bitter need,—never had to look at the face of a woman become like a wolf's from struggle and famine. When he thought of these things, Rosicky would put on his cap and jacket and slip down to the barn and give his work-horses a little extra oats, letting them eat it out of his hand in their slobbery fashion. It was his way of expressing what he felt, and made him chuckle with pleasure.

The spring came warm, with blue skies,—but dry, dry as a bone. The boys began ploughing up the wheat-fields to plant them over in corn. Rosicky would stand at the fence corner and watch them, and the earth was so dry it blew up in clouds of brown dust that hid the horses and the sulky plough and the driver. It was a bad outlook.

The big alfalfa-field that lay between the home place and Rudolph's came up green, but Rosicky was worried because during that open windy winter a great many Russian thistle plants had blown in there and lodged. He kept asking the boys to rake them out; he was afraid their seed would root and "take the alfalfa." Rudolph said that was nonsense. The boys were working so hard planting corn, their father felt he couldn't insist about the thistles, but he set great store by that big alfalfa field. It was a feed you could depend on,—and there was some deeper reason, vague, but strong. The peculiar green of that clover woke early memories in old Rosicky, went back to something in his childhood in the old world. When he was a little boy, he had played in fields of that strong blue-green colour.

One morning, when Rudolph had gone to town in the car, leaving a work-team idle in his barn, Rosicky went over to his son's place, put the horses to the buggy-rake, and set about quietly raking up those thistles. He behaved with guilty caution, and rather enjoyed stealing a march on Doctor Ed, who was just then taking his first vacation in seven years of practice and was attending a clinic in Chicago. Rosicky got the thistles raked up, but did not stop to burn them. That would take some time, and his breath was pretty short, so he thought he had better get the horses back to the barn.

He got them into the barn and to their stalls, but the pain had come on so sharp in his chest that he didn't try to take the harness off. He started for the house, bending lower with every step. The cramp in his chest was shutting him up like a jack-knife. When he reached the windmill, he swayed and caught at the ladder. He saw Polly coming down the hill, running with the swiftness of a slim greyhound. In a flash she had her shoulder under his armpit.

"Lean on me, Father, hard! Don't be afraid. We can get to the house all right."

Somehow they did, though Rosicky became blind with pain; he could keep on his legs, but he couldn't steer his course. The next thing he was conscious of was lying on Polly's bed, and Polly bending over him wringing out bath towels in hot water and putting them on his chest. She stopped only to throw coal into the stove, and she kept the tea-kettle and the black pot going. She put these hot applications on him for nearly an hour, she told him afterwards, and all that time he was drawn up stiff and blue, with the sweat pouring off him.

As the pain gradually loosed its grip, the stiffness went out of his jaws, the black circles round his eyes disappeared, and a little of his natural colour came back. When his daughter-in-law buttoned his shirt over his chest at last, he sighed.

"Da's fine, de way I feel now, Polly. It was a awful bad spell, an' I was so sorry it all come on you like it did."

Polly was flushed and excited. "Is the pain really gone? Can I leave you long enough to telephone over to your place?"

Rosicky's eyelids fluttered. "Don't telephone, Polly. It ain't no use to scare my wife. It's nice and quiet here, an' if I ain't too much trouble to you, just let me lay still till I feel like myself. I ain't got no pain now. It's nice here."

Polly bent over him and wiped the moisture from his face. "Oh, I'm so glad it's over!" she broke out impulsively. "It just broke my heart to see you suffer so, Father."

Rosicky motioned her to sit down on the chair where the tea-kettle had been, and looked up at her with that lively affectionate gleam in his eyes. "You was awful good to me, I won't never forgit dat. I hate it to be sick on you like dis. Down at de barn I say to myself, dat young girl ain't had much experience in sickness, I don't want to scare her, an' maybe she's got a baby comin' or somet'ing."

Polly took his hand. He was looking at her so intently and affectionately and confidingly; his eyes seemed to caress her face, to regard it with pleasure. She frowned with her funny streaks of eyebrows, and then smiled back at him.

"I guess maybe there is something of that kind going to happen. But I haven't told anyone yet, not my mother or Rudolph. You'll be the first to know."

His hand pressed hers. She noticed that it was warm again. The twinkle in his yellow-brown eyes seemed to come nearer.

"I like mighty well to see dat little child, Polly," was all he said. Then he closed his eyes and lay half-smiling. But Polly sat still, thinking hard. She had a sudden feeling that nobody in the world, not her mother, not Rudolph, or anyone, really loved her as much as old Rosicky did. It perplexed her. She sat frowning and trying to puzzle it out. It was as if Rosicky had a special gift for loving people, something that was like an ear for music or an eye for colour. It was quiet, unobtrusive; it was merely there. You saw it in his eyes,—perhaps that was why they were merry. You felt it in his hands, too. After he dropped off to sleep, she sat holding his warm, broad, flexible brown hand. She had never seen another in the least like it. She wondered if it wasn't a kind of gypsy hand, it was so alive and quick and light in its communications,—very strange in a farmer. Nearly all the farmers she knew had huge lumps of fists, like mauls, or they were knotty and bony and uncomfortable-looking, with stiff fingers. But Rosicky's was like quicksilver, flexible, muscular, about the colour of a pale cigar, with deep, deep creases across the palm. It wasn't nervous, it wasn't a stupid lump; it was a warm brown human hand, with some cleverness in it, a great deal of generosity, and something else which Polly could only call "gypsy-like,"—something nimble and lively and sure, in the way that animals are.

Polly remembered that hour long afterwards; it had been like an awakening to her. It seemed to her that she had never learned so much about life from anything as from old Rosicky's hand. It brought her to herself; it communicated some direct and untranslatable message.

When she heard Rudolph coming in the car, she ran out to meet him.

"Oh, Rudy, your father's been awful sick! He raked up those thistles he's been worrying about, and afterwards he could hardly get to the house. He suffered so I was afraid he was going to die."

Rudolph jumped to the ground. "Where is he now?"

"On the bed. He's asleep. I was terribly scared, because, you know, I'm so fond of your father." She slipped her arm through his and they went into the house. That afternoon they took Rosicky home and put him to bed, though he protested that he was quite well again.

The next morning he got up and dressed and sat down to breakfast with his family. He told Mary that his coffee tasted better than usual to him, and he warned the boys not to bear any tales to Doctor Ed when he got home. After breakfast he sat down by his window to do some patching and asked Mary to thread several needles for him before she went to feed her chickens,—her eyes were better than his, and her hands steadier. He lit his pipe and took up John's overalls. Mary had been watching him anxiously all morning, and as she went out of the door with her bucket of scraps, she saw that he was smiling. He was thinking, indeed, about Polly, and how he might never have known what a tender heart she had if he hadn't got sick over there. Girls nowadays didn't wear their heart on their sleeve. But now he knew Polly would make a fine woman after the foolishness wore off. Either a woman had that sweetness at her heart or she hadn't. You couldn't always tell by the look of them; but if they had, everything came out right in the end.

After he had taken a few stitches, the cramp began in his chest, like yesterday. He put his pipe cautiously down on the window-sill and bent over to ease the pull. No use,—he had better try to get to his bed if he could. He rose and groped his way across the familiar floor, which was rising and falling like the deck of a ship. At the door he fell. When Mary came in, she found him lying there, and the moment she touched him she knew that he was gone.

Doctor Ed was away when Rosicky died, and for the first few weeks after he got home he was hard driven. Every day he said to himself that he must get out to see that family that had lost their father. One soft, warm moonlight night in early summer he started for the farm. His mind was on other things, and not until his road ran by the graveyard did he realize that Rosicky wasn't over there on the hill where the red lamplight shone, but here, in the moonlight. He stopped his car, shut off the engine, and sat there for a while.

A sudden hush had fallen on his soul. Everything here seemed strangely moving and significant, though signifying what, he did not know. Close by the wire fence stood Rosicky's mowing-machine, where one of the boys had been cutting hay that afternoon; his own work-horses had been going up and down there. The new-cut hay perfumed all the night air. The moonlight silvered the long, billowy grass that grew over the graves and hid the fence; the few little evergreens stood out black in it, like shadows in a pool. The sky was very blue and soft, the stars rather faint because the moon was full.

For the first time it struck Doctor Ed that this was really a beautiful graveyard. He thought of city cemeteries; acres of shrubbery and heavy stone, so arranged and lonely and unlike anything in the living world. Cities of the dead, indeed; cities of the forgotten, of the "put away." But this was open and free, this little square of long grass which the wind for ever stirred. Nothing but the sky overhead, and the many-coloured fields running on until they met that sky. The horses worked here in summer; the neighbours passed on their way to town; and over yonder, in the cornfield, Rosicky's own cattle would be eating fodder as winter came on. Nothing could be more undeathlike than this place; nothing could be more right for a man who had helped to do the work of great cities and had always longed for the open country and had got to it at last. Rosicky's life seemed to him complete and beautiful.

# Snow in Summer

## HELEN HULL

*A housewife married to a somewhat dull dentist sud-denly wins a $10,000 novel contest! She is flown to New York for gay parties and publicity but returns home to her family a wiser but by no means sadder woman. Here is a very amusing and well-written tale that the whole family will enjoy.*

HAZEL ran down the stairs to the basement, caught her heel on a step, flung out her hand against the white-washed cement wall, and just didn't fall. She stared at her outstretched smarting hand, and shook it gingerly. Nothing sprained, thank Heaven! Her tongue lapped at the reddening scratches and she crossed more cautiously to snap off the racket of the washing machine. At the final subsiding rumble she gave a sigh of relief. There was always the chance that the whirling rhythm confined in that sleek, white-shining drum might someday get the better of her, explode, fill the whole basement with its froth and din. She wouldn't have told George about the animosity between her and that machine, but she knew that someday she would fail to make something fast, and it would electrocute her or drown her in suds, or flail her to bits. George had given it to her for a Christmas present, two years ago. She could see him now, explaining how it worked, a clear flush like a boy's standing out on his cheekbones. She had demurred a little. Think how much it cost! Why, that would pay the laundry for weeks and weeks!

"But this will last for years, Hazel! Years! I can keep it in order. Don't you like it?"

He would have laughed at her if she had explained how it terrified her. She took a deep breath of the quiet in the basement, and watched the motes dance in the morning sun-shaft through the low window. Her tongue took a last dart along her abraded palm, and she flexed her slim fingers. It would have been too awful if she had wrenched something! Her mind picked up the game with time it played so constantly these days. She'd be back in half an hour. Another hour to rinse and hang out the clothes, ten minutes to brush up the living room, she had the salad ready. Well, say ten o'clock. If no one telephoned, she might have two hours—but she must be careful. A kind of warning, the narrow escapes she'd been having. Just because she rushed so.

She held herself to a sedate pace up the stairs, a propitiatory offering to this household *poltergeist*. After eight, the Dutch clock over the yellow breakfast table said, and Lorna hadn't touched her breakfast. From the living room came voices, George's, exasperated, "But if you'd just watch, you'd see how I do it. See, this spring—" and John, "Gee, Dad, I'm late now. I tried to put that spring back. Where's Mother, anyway?"

Hazel was there instantly, her eyes round with dismay under the crisp fringe of lashes. Had John upset that typewriter again? George was hunched over the table, elbows, square shoulders absorbed, the tuneless hum with which he always worked (like a little dynamo, thought Hazel), breaking into a satisfied, "There it is. Now don't throw it on the floor if you can help it."

"I never did," said John. "Ole second-handed thing." He peered over his father's shoulder as George rattled the shift bar triumphantly.

"Will it run?" asked Hazel. "I warned you to be gentle with it!"

"Oh, sure." John croaked a little, being casual, and reached for his schoolbag. "It's time we got a move on."

George turned, brushing at the square tips of his fingers. "Lucky John spoke of it if you want to use it. Thought you sent the bills all out." He came briskly across the room, a sturdy, compact figure, blond and well-scrubbed, his blue eyes alert and sanguine.

"Yes," said Hazel, vaguely, while she made automatic inspection of her son. He looked—well, grubby and stringy—beside his father. Growing so fast this last year or so. His face had a thin, surprised look. Hazel slid two fingers into a sagging pocket of his coat and drew out a limp, smudged rag which she dangled, her fine nose crinkling.

"Aw, gee, I thought I had a clean one." John squirmed past her and started up the stairs, three steps at a stride.

"Tell Lorna to come along this instant," Hazel called after him. "I'm getting the car now."

"I don't see what she does all this time." George opened the front door. "The postman's late, too, and this is the day my dental journal comes. He's not even in sight."

Hazel pulled a blue felt hat down over her soft hair, called, "Lorna!

30

You must drink your milk!" and ran out to the dining room. The keys should be there on the buffet, in the silver cup, behind the candlesticks ... in the corner of the top drawer. Where had she left them? Oh, not in the car again!

"Looking for something?"

(Oh, darn! Now he would know—) Her glance darted sidewise at him, caught the round bright expectancy in his eyes. "You've got them! Oh, you—" she thrust out her hand. "Please!"

"And where were they?" He spun the chain in a flash of metal on a taunting finger. "Lucky for you I happened—Ouch!" He jumped back, as Hazel, lunging for them, stubbed against his polished toe. "The time you'd save if you had a little system!"

"Meet you at the front door," called Hazel, hurrying out through the kitchen. Fall chrysanthemums and marigolds marched in rows of bright disks along the straight gravelled drive to the small garage, and in the next yard, beyond the row of barberries, Polish Annie was hanging out sheets. Well, Mrs. Marks could afford a washer-woman; she had no children. Hazel swung back the doors, edged along the fenders of the small sedan, and slid under the wheel, wriggling to free her knees from the pull of her blue piqué frock. She fitted in the key, made a few in-determinate movements of her hands, her face serious in concentration. Brake, gears, clutch. "It's valuable practice," George insisted. "I won't get the car out any more. You know how to drive, only you won't relax and let it be automatic." At least she hadn't driven into the back of the garage for days! Her toe pressed the starter button, and holding her breath she emerged in a bucking and erratic course which landed her, after a final parabola, in front of the house. George was probably right, but if only she could start off head first perhaps she wouldn't mind so much. Like that nightmare in which she went leaping backward through all the streets of the town, unable to stop because she'd forgotten the word. She laid a finger on the horn, but before she pressed it the front door opened and George stepped out on the tapestry bricks of the entrance. For a moment he stood there, hands lifted to fit on his new gray hat. For a moment Hazel looked at him, clear of the mists, the manifold subtleties of her intimacy with him, her emotion toward him. He might have been a stranger, seen for the first time in one of those intuitive flashes when she could see almost the stranger's image of himself, the way he hoped the world saw him. Confident, not exactly jaunty, but full of a kind of well-being which was a matter of equilibrium, inner and outer.

He really likes his life, she thought. Teeth are terribly important, they're fascinating, a dentist is practically the mainstay of the world, he likes the town, he likes this house, having a family. He's really as happy as anyone I ever saw. As he called into the house, "Come along, you two! Mother's waiting!" Hazel shivered, and her tight fingers swung the wheel a trifle. When he found out what she was doing, he would think it very funny. Now with driving, he enjoyed teaching her, he didn't really mind that she was stupid about learning. It would be dreadful if ever she did anything to shake this content of his. Not that he was smug; he worked too hard.

The three of them, George, John, and Lorna, were rushing at the car, and Hazel, tipping forward the seat beside hers, forgot the moment of strange inspection.

"Did you get any breakfast?" She saw, in the fresh curls at the back of Lorna's fair head, the cause for her delay. That rose sweater was growing too snug over small young breasts; Lorna liked the color and refused to wear anything else.

"She's banting, Mother." John plumped in beside his sister. "I hear her jiggling the bathroom scales every time I want to get in."

"If I was as skinny as you, I wouldn't say anything," began Lorna.

"All nonsense," said George, dropping the front seat and pulling shut the door with a sharp bang. "Eat what you want and work hard and you'll be the way you're meant to be."

"My goodness!" Lorna's voice came shrilly over the clash as Hazel, sliding forward, poked the gear lever toward reverse. "Just because I don't enjoy guzzling!"

Hazel could feel the restrained patience with which George held himself until she fumbled into third gear and popped down the street. It would be almost better if he spoke out, except that when he just thought she could pretend she didn't know it. Now she was reasonably safe until she had to start up again after she dropped the children at school.

"Guzzle? Who guzzles? We, they, it est guzzledator."

Poor John and his Latin! Hazel laughed, partly a crumb of nervousness, partly amusement, and George, turning a moment from his alert vicarious driving, said, "You remember I like my girl as she is! None of your anemic slats for me!"

Of course Lorna did take after his people. Hazel drove along her thoughts drifting, melting one into the next, just at the edge of awareness, hazily beyond the focus of her attention on this hazardous business of driving. Lorna was a trifle on the solid side, but she had George's coloring, fair skin and hair. She wasn't exactly pretty, but later, when her character had firmed out—This corner was a bad one; Hazel peered left, right, and met George's blue glance as he peered first right then left. She pushed down her toe and leaped across the intersection. Just last summer, while she was in camp, Lorna had jumped out of child-hood into—well, not maturity, but some of its superficial concerns. As if something had stepped too hard on the gas. Life ought to have a good driver, going along smoothly— She swerved, sucking in her breath, as a brown and woolly dog trotted across the road. George seized the wheel as she bumped over the curb, and swung the car back into the road. A long blue car rolled past, the chauffeur grinning. Mr. Mac-Andrews, on his way to the factory. Her knees had that untied feel-ing!

"You missed that one, Mother," said John. "Better luck next time!"

"It's those impulsive movements," said George, "that keep women from driving as well as men."

"Would you run down a dog?" cried Hazel.

"I never have. But if I had to choose between hitting one and wrecking the family——"

Hazel found herself biting hard on her upper lip. She pushed it out and ran the tip of her tongue over it. That was why she had that little fringe of chapped skin always after she had to drive. The shadows under the tall maples along the street were full of dogs! Why had she ever thought it would be nice to live out at the edge of town, in the new residence section? Three, two blocks more; she turned up a side street to avoid the few business blocks, and came through the small park to the high school, rocking the car as she pushed valiantly with both feet on clutch and brake. George got out, and the children clambered after him; John's books caught on the hinge of the seat, and as he stooped to free the strap he winked solemnly at Hazel. She watched a moment after George sat again beside her. Lorna had called out, a group of girls had turned, and she went toward them, her dark skirt tight with the quick movement of sturdy legs, the sunlight brilliant on her hair. John dawdled behind her, banging his strapped-books against his thigh. Then Hazel peered sidewise under her lashes at her husband, and for a fleeting instant saw, in an unfamiliar contraction of muscles between his brows a kind of puzzled wonder. But all he said was, "John ought to try out for one of the teams. He's spindling. Needs filling out." Then the wonder dis-

33

appeared, and he was comfortable again, knowing what to do. "Well, time to be off."

There was again a moment of suspended attention, of withheld comment while Hazel got under way, fairly smoothly this time. Then George said, in the uninflected, almost talking-to-himself tone of one who has no doubt of his listener's response, "I think I'm booked every hour today. That means night work again. Mrs. Wills's upper, and there'll be two sets of X-rays."

(Monday night. If I get the children off to their rooms early, I'll have sat two more hours.) Hastily, as George's silence nudged at her, "It seems forever since you've had a free evening."

"I really need a laboratory assistant, a mechanic." His hand darted toward the emergency brake. "Look out! That truck——"

With a squawk of the horn Hazel dodged around the red bulk as it swung out from the curb. "I saw it," she said. Well, she had, just as George spoke. "You'd never find one to suit you," she added, incautiously. These few blocks of morning business traffic took her mind off her words.

"I'm not unnecessarily particular," said George, calmly. "I didn't want another fender crumpled. And as for my work, it just has to be right. Take an inlay. It fits or it doesn't. And bridge-work——"

"I just meant—" Hazel was a trifle breathless, slowing behind the huge gray bus from the city, and then swinging past it as the one traffic light of the town, on the bank corner, showed green—"that you do everything so well yourself—" There, she drew up at the curb without grazing the tires. Sunlight glinted on the brass sign beside the entrance to offices above the bank. Dr. George Curtis. On the whole she'd done pretty well this morning. "You're a kind of genius, everything you touch, now aren't you, darling?"

"Well, I shouldn't go that far." George smiled. "Pulling my leg, eh? Just because I like things right. Anyway, I couldn't afford an assistant. Not till the X-ray machine is paid for, and the kids are educated, and the Building and Loan is settled. The more I make, the harder I work."

"But look at the reputation you're getting." Hazel was serious now, pride luminous in her eyes. "Even Doctor Brown sending you cases, asking you to consult with him—You're really educating the town."

George nodded, his mouth firm at the corners. He didn't need her encouragement exactly; he had no doubts about himself. But he rather liked a salvo of trumpets before he rode away into his busy day. "Yes,

I think all that new equipment is justifying itself. If only John wasn't so clumsy! Lots he could do to help me, a boy his age. I wouldn't dare trust him in the door. Take that typewriter this morning. Why, any boy could have fixed that. Sometimes I suspect he's putting it on, too lazy to try."

"Oh, no! I know just how he feels! Things like—like cars and type-writers are just malicious, the way they go wrong. John isn't lazy. He just knows you can fix it, whatever it is, just as I do."

"But John's a boy! He makes me uncomfortable he's so stupid."

"You don't really think he's stupid." Hazel laid her hand over George's, her finger-tips pressed, sensitive and light, against his knuckles. "He hasn't got your hands, but you wait!"

"You'd think I'd nothing to do but sit here and chin!" George gathered himself up alertly, brushed her cheek in a kiss which was less a caress than an absent-minded symbol of affection established past inquiry, and let himself briskly out of the car. "Blow twice when you come this noon, then I won't waste time waiting for you." He wheeled; his erect head and straight sturdy back vanished in the hallway.

At least he no longer waited to inspect her departure. Hazel smiled, remembering the day he had run after her for a block to tell her to re-lease the brake. She could drive home now in her own way, and leave the car in front of the house, safe for her noon pilgrimage.

As she drove at a snail-easy pace out the wide street, she thought, it would be like a fairy tale, so much so that it can't happen. I'm just a silly fool, having a dream. That's why I don't dare speak of it. George would try not to laugh, but he'd get that rosy, amused look. Ten thou-sand dollars. Think what I could do! The mortgage, the X-ray machine, college.

It had all started with the typewriter. If George hadn't brought that home! She let herself into the quiet house, and stood at the door of the living room, looking at the thing, the round white disks of the keys dancing under her intent stare. He'd picked it up cheap, second hand, and set it in order. Better business to have his bills typed. Could she learn to run it? She had learned, after a fashion, holding herself to the attempt in spite of clatter and extraordinary results until she no longer wasted George's excellent stationery. If other people do it, then you can, she told herself. She had been telling herself that about a great many things, ever since her marriage. Such as keeping the house in order. She threw aside her hat, and moved quickly about the living room, gathering

35

sheets of the Sunday paper, plumping cushions on the divan, brushing kernels of popped corn into the ash of the fireplace, straightening lamp shades, magazines. It was queer about marriage. You expected it to be— well, a prolongation of a state of feeling. There was that about it, of course. But what you didn't expect was that you had, suddenly, to become an expert at all sorts of things you'd never dreamed of doing.

Until she had married George, she had never done anything, in the sense of tackling the great variety of material items out of which life seemed to be composed. Her mother had spoiled her, of course, but like George her mother had been so competent that she forestalled activity from less skillful competitors. And they had been so proud of her, her mother and father, for her graceful accomplishments in school. The darlings, she thought, as she hurried into the kitchen for a dust cloth. If they knew what I'm trying, they'd be sure— She felt that queer jerk deep in her consciousness, like the sensation of being dropped too quickly in a swift elevator, with which she came upon the fact of their being dead. It had happened so suddenly, and had interrupted the pattern of her life with George so little that for long busy stretches she almost forgot.

If her father had not gone to that training camp on the Lakes the dreadful winter of the flu epidemic, he would still be alive. And she might never have known George. There had been too few doctors, and her father had worked night and day trying to save the boys. When, finally, he had almost died himself with pneumonia, Hazel and her mother had gone to Chicago, and waited until they could bring him home. Hazel, seventeen, had met George, had thought him an archangel, Michael himself, his bright hair and fair skin brilliant in his uniform of petty officer making him a thing of life in a scene of appalling death. Her father had said, "We need a good modern dentist in Lounsberry. If you ever get out of this, and want to locate, think us over."

Her father had come home with a heart never the same, and so, in a way which faced life and not death, had Hazel. When, a year later, her father said that a fellow named Curtis had turned up, sort of prospecting for a dentist's office, Hazel knew she had just been waiting. And later—she could see her father's face now, as he had talked with her, waxy, wrinkles down the long cheeks, around the deep eyes like a bit of used paraffin paper—"But, good Lord, Hazel! I thought you'd want someone different—someone you'd meet at college—" she had said, "He is different. I don't want to go to college."

"And I'm responsible for getting him here!"

36

"You've always got me what I wanted!"

"I'd like to, as long as I can." Something had happened to his face, like a hand giving the paraffin paper another crumple.

He had died before Lorna was born, and her mother, rather like a clock there is no one to wind, had quietly run down a few years later.

Then for years Hazel had gone about her new business of housewife and mother, thinking, when she at rare intervals looked at herself, that the slim, dreaming girl who had written poetry, who had delivered the class valedictory, who—but what did it matter? She was gone, perhaps her bones were still the same, but her very flesh was different.

An hour later the clothes-horse in the backyard oscillated gently with its burden, the planes of linen and garments making in the sunlight a design of labor done. Hazel came into the living room with two square black hatboxes which she set one on each side of the straight chair. She seated herself between them, and for a moment relaxed, spine soft, suds-crinkled finger-tips pressed against cheekbones. But she couldn't be tired, not until this job was done. A month ago she had dropped into a bog of consternation: she had been mad to start such a thing, she was too ignorant, too ill-equipped, she had better throw hatboxes and all into the fire. That had been just after the children had returned from their summer at camp, and George had come back from his fishing trip. Perhaps she had worked too many hours while she was alone. At any rate, after a few days she had swung herself into the double rhythm of taking care of the family and stealing time for herself, a half hour, an hour, whenever she was alone. Second wind, her father would have called it. "People don't begin to use themselves, there's an inner reservoir they don't tap. I see it often enough in a crisis. I tell you, Hazel, some of the old boys that did so much, generals, geniuses, what-not, they'd learn how to dip in, how to work up second wind."

Hazel wasn't sure just what her father had meant, but she knew she had to finish this task if she wanted to be at ease with her self-esteem, and the very compulsion seemed to produce the necessary energy. She pushed back her shoulders, and her face lost its soft, relaxed aimlessness. The upper lip looking long and Irish under the fine nose, pulled down, its curve straightening, and the eyebrows, even, fine accents of the structure of wide brow and eye sockets, drew together. She whisked off the lids of the two hatboxes, picked out of that on the left an exercise book with a mottled cover, and from that on the right, sheets of white paper. She propped the copybook against a pile of George's *National Geo-*

*graphics,* and slid the paper under the roller of the machine.

It had really started with the typewriter, she thought, again. Until George had brought it home, she had just scribbled in her copybooks; she would buy them for a nickel at the drug store which kept school supplies, and no one ever wondered what she did with them. She couldn't remember just when she had started that. After the children were both old enough to go to school, and she was efficient enough so that she no longer lost the frantic race between the length of a day and the tasks she must finish,—or was it when George began to go back to his office after dinner? At first he had had time during the day, poor boy, because not many people noticed his shiny new sign. She could remember well enough the first day he had been busy every hour. "Wasn't I right, Hazel? Even if I offended Mrs. Betts, insisting that she had to pay when she forgot her appointment, you see it made them think I was busy and couldn't be fooled with. Now you see!" What she saw, among other things, was that now she had long evening hours on her hands. She couldn't leave the children, and there wasn't much to do if she had left them, as she didn't care for bridge, and the moving picture theatre was open only on Saturday. George said, "We can get a maid pretty soon, if you want one, although with all this modern equipment—" Then, before they reached even the point of discussing a maid, along came the depression, so that people couldn't pay their bills, even when they could no longer put off a visit to George, and George worked harder than ever.

She had tried reading. But she knew most of the books in the small library, and she found nerves twitching so that her feet jumped, as they had when a little girl she had sat beside her mother through a long sermon. Reading for hours and hours would be all right when she was an old woman, but now it was too like watching someone else run and dance and live when inside her something turned and twisted and pressed to break into its own movement.

When the children were little she had told them stories, about her own childhood, about her father, about his people. Lorna never listened long, but John loved them, and gradually Hazel had woven a long serial which went on night after night, held rigorously by the boy to fidelity in every statement. "No, Mother! You said he had his possessions tied in a hand-kerchief on a stick, not in a bag at all!"

She had always liked her father's yarns about his people. Restless footed, he had called them, coming from Ireland and southern England to this country, settling in the east, and then the restless footed moving on, west again. Perhaps, after all, it had all started with the unused copybook she had found the first summer the children were in camp, and the sharpened pencil. Put the two together, and there was Hazel, starting to set down the story she had spun so many nights for her son. When she had filled one book, a nickel bought another. Her handwriting was amusingly uncertain, a product of the period when the public schools swung from Spencerian script to round and horizontal letters; Hazel had made a queer combination of the two. But at the end of an evening with the copybook, slipped into a table drawer as she heard George at the door, she had a half-guilty, warm-cheeked contentment.

When she had started the first copybook she had no clear notion of what she meant to do, and telling George seemed too like confessing a private vice, trotting out a fragment of day-dream. When she had filled two books she hid them in a hatbox on her closet shelf, under a winter hat. She was finding writing like wine, and tippling on words she set down many things she had never known she felt. It was unlikely that George would have curiosity enough to read all the scribbled pages, but she ran no risk. And she didn't want him to point out with patient good humor that she was wasting hours of time. Then last spring, at the final meeting of the Ladies' Literary Society, a lecturer from the University had given her the final push into what seemed at moments a life of crime. Certainly it took as much scheming and equivocation as a clandestine love affair. She typed CHAPTER SIXTEEN at the top of the sheet, and, a little ridge of concentration between her brows, began vigorously to peck. "The country is looking for new voices," the lecturer had said: "The middle west must grow more articulate. There may be someone among you ready with the next great novel." Then as proof of the country's eagerness he had cited awards, fellowships, prize contests. "Here's a new publishing house, just being launched. Does it look for established authors already with repute? No. It offers ten thousand dollars for the best first novel from a writer who has never published a thing."

A good many of the club ladies had gathered around the lecturer to ask questions. After all, they had paid him twenty-five dollars just to come over from Ann Arbor, and he had talked only an hour. "But don't you think, Professor Elson, when so many things in the world are unpleasant, that our writers should give us what is pure and sweet?" Hazel, being part of the refreshment committee, was passing cakes. If she could get him alone for one second, could ask him one question! No hope. Miss

Emma, one of the two Buckley girls, who wrote poems for the Lounsberry *Weekly Record*, was holding her cup of tea dangerously near his crisply buttoned coat and bubbling at him through her very new teeth. Hazel offered cakes to them, with a protective glance at Miss Emma. (George had been funny, about the way her transformation had slipped while she was biting on plaster for the upper plate.) But the young lecturer wasn't laughing at her; he was concerned with escape, he had an engagement, he had appreciated the audience very much indeed, very receptive, and he had edged past the barrier of silk bosoms and teacups disappearing just as the ladies' quartette started the Spring Song.

She couldn't have asked him without someone overhearing, anyway. But after two days in which she dodged and twisted only to find the same idea in the middle of her thoughts every time she opened her mind's eye, she wrote to Professor Elson. A friend of hers was writing a book, would he please send her the name of the new publishers he'd spoken about. When he didn't answer, she wrote a second time. She was sorry to trouble him, but would he please? Then she watched for the postman, and luckily reached the door first the day the envelope addressed in her own hand came back to her, with a printed announcement, and an apology scrawled in the margin: sorry, my secretary overlooked your request.

October first. Ten more days. She tapped more briskly, and the paper slid crooked as she reached the bottom of the page. She managed to finish the line, if slightly on the bias, and pulled out the sheet. Page 292. She wasn't sure how many pages a book should have. Some of Dickens seemed very long, and she'd looked at "Anthony Adverse" with dismay. Well, a man might find time to write as many pages as that; she couldn't. "Pere Goriot" was much shorter, and her father had liked that. She was a little troubled because the typewriter lacked quotation marks and authors seemed to use them. On one page she tried inserting them by hand, but the pen marks looked unprofessional. Lucky for her the machine had capital letters and periods. She adjusted the next sheet. Yes, the typewriter really was responsible. She had been struggling with the exercises George had brought home, until she was sick of the sly gray fox and the aid of the party, and she had suddenly thought it would be more fun to copy a piece out of one of her copybooks. That had done it. Almost like seeing one's self in print to have the transformation from intimate careless scribbling into the uniform impersonality of printed letters in straight rows. (Or almost straight; a few hops and glides of letters.)

For the first time she had thought of her own words as standing out apart from her, making a shape for someone else to see. The idea that she might make a book had started right then, although she had waited for the circular from Professor Elson before she admitted it.

John alone had suspected anything. "What on earth do you pound that ole typewriter so much for?" he asked. "I woke up last night and you were just a-going at it!"

"Just practicing." Hazel thought: I can't tell John, because I'd be so mortified then if I didn't get the prize. I should have taken up painting. That doesn't make a noise.

She had time for another page before starting luncheon. Only part of this last copybook left. Do not insert name of author on script. Script was this thickening pile of sheets. Write title of book and name and address on separate sheet, and enclose in sealed envelope. She had already done that. "Your Hand Upon the Gate," by Hazel Browning Curtis. She had thought of naming the book "Restless Feet," but decided it sounded too much like horses. Her concentrated haste had brushed color over the narrow bridge of her nose and under her eyes when at quarter before twelve she tied the covers on the two hatboxes and carried them upstairs to the closet shelf.

Five minutes behind schedule, having turned the gas low under her lunch dishes, and set the table, she ran out to the car. She could drive fairly fast with no passengers aboard. High school was already dismissed; she kept a quick eye out for her two, among the drifting groups, girls with sunlight on their curled heads—(I'm positively the only girl in my class who hasn't had a permanent, Mother!)—boys dawdling behind the girls in noisy pairs or trios . . . scuffling, shrieking out jokes which the girls pretended not to hear. They act just as we used to, thought Hazel, in spite of all the talk. Playing up to each other before they know why— There's John! Straddling a hydrant at the corner. He propelled himself with a minimum of effort into the car. "Here we are again," he said.

"Have you seen Lorna?"

"She went on over town."

"I'm not very late, am I?" Hazel let the clutch pedal jump up, the car bucked gaily down the street.

"I haven't waited more'n an hour or two." John had a solemn drawl.

"Yes, you!" Hazel laughed. "Have a good morning?"

"Lousy."

"John!"

"Pardon muh. Stinko, then. Honest, I bet I'll flunk that Latin. No sense to it."

"Nonsense. You never flunked anything yet. Don't say that to your father!"

"He'll know soon enough. Then I'll be more popular than I am now."

Hazel stared straight ahead, her mouth firm. She'd have to talk to George; he had been riding John too much about—oh, springs out of typewriters and such! "If you were more popular," she said, lightly, "you'd—" she jammed down the brake as the traffic light jumped red at her, and a car following cracked against the bumper. She peered guiltily over her shoulder, but the grimy face of the truck driver behind seemed unperturbed. Too much to handle car and domestic nuances together! As she drove across the street she saw Lorna, standing in the triangular recessed entrance of the drug store, her face lifted in gay absorption to that of a strange young man whose red head bent toward her, shooting up from broad shoulders on which stretched a grayish sweat shirt with extraordinary inked designs. Hazel poked the nose of the car toward the curb, and peered at John. Something startling about the pose of the two figures, obliviousness, challenge. John was staring gloomily at his father's sign, as if he hadn't seen Lorna. "Who's the boy?" asked Hazel. It couldn't offend John's code to tell her that.

"What boy?" John overdid his inspection of the neighborhood. "Oh, him! He's new this year. Daniels his name is. He plays football."

Lorna had given a little start, spying the car, and after a moment of concentrated animation, quick words too low to reach Hazel, strolled out to the curb, her creamy blandness implying that she had been waiting tedious hours. So this is the next one, thought Hazel. Just a day or so ago she'd asked Lorna where Tommy Burke kept himself, and Lorna had said, "That dope! My goodness, how should I know?" This boy looked—well, older. John got out, muttering he'd like a back door to the car so he wouldn't have to move around all the time, and Hazel punched the horn button twice. Unnecessarily, because as she blew George appeared at the doorway, hat under his elbow, and beside him a young woman. Hazel was thinking: Lorna's only sixteen, but she looks older. Something about that red-head I don't like. Just the way Lorna looked at him. Lorna tossed her head as she climbed into the car, and her smile at Hazel was bright with defiance. Don't worry, darling, I won't say a word; I know better than that! Why didn't George come along, and who was the woman, anyway? Hazel leaned forward; the edge of the door cut her view. "You'll have to wait," drawled John, "till Dad finishes his lecture." A hint of laughter crinkled at the corners of Hazel's eyes, but she kept her mouth sober. It was true, George did have his serious, now-I-will-tell-you-all manner, one forefinger beating against the palm of an outstretched hand. His hat slid down as his finger grew emphatic, and he stooped for it, brushed it off without losing a word. The woman was very smart, like a red-winged blackbird in tailored suit and scarlet purse to match the long quill on her small hat. Even her hair lay in a black and shining swirl, like feathers, and she had certainly repainted her mouth if she'd been having anything done to the teeth that gleamed as she laughed. "I'll think it over." She waved her purse, and strolled away, her dark, indifferent eyes not even grazing the car or Hazel's half curious face. It is time for fall clothes, thought Hazel. But George hadn't sent a glance after that smart figure. A suit does things for you, her thoughts jumped along. But she must have at least a dead tooth! She wondered if George's habit of monologue had grown a little, perhaps because his listener so often had a mouth too full of cotton and rubber dams to answer back! But John mustn't laugh at his father. Just because George was so much in earnest——

He sat beside her, the clean whiff of antiseptic soap filling the car as he banged shut the door. "I'm glad to sit down," he said.

Hazel backed gingerly out from the curb and drove down the block of stores. At the corner where the large sign LOUNSBERRY HOUSE announced progress in neon letters, she turned, just as the woman in the black suit started across the street. The woman moved ahead with an arrogant indifference to small town traffic, and Hazel stalled the engine. "I wish people would look where they're going!" she said, as she trod on the starter.

"It is a good idea," said George.

(Only he means me, thought Hazel.)

"I wonder if she's staying at the hotel." George craned his neck.

Hazel couldn't say "Who is she"; suddenly she felt too cross to say anything. But Lorna asked. "Is she a new patient, Father?"

(Even her voice sounds excited, thought Hazel. She's trying to start something else, so I won't ask about her new boy friend.)

"She may be," George was saying. "She's making a canvas for a dental supply company, she's a representative of the concern, but we got to talking about her own teeth. She's practically agreed to come back for some X-rays. She's a very intelligent woman."

"Be kinda hard on her," said John, reflectively, "if she had to have a tooth pulled every time she got an order."

"She said," continued George, "that she seldom saw an office, except in the largest cities, so well equipped as mine."

"My goodness," said Lorna, "I shouldn't think she'd like to go all around like that!"

"I don't know." George stopped eying the street ahead for a moment to turn his head toward his daughter. "Not that I'd like you to go on the road. But she has her own car, and she seems to like it."

She does, does she, thought Hazel, with unexpected wryness. Well, I hope she doesn't sell George something terribly expensive. Like that new washbasin with footpedals, so he didn't have to touch the faucets after he'd washed his hands. Oh, *dear!* I mustn't be so edgy. Nothing's happened. Lorna's had beaux before, and George—as she rounded a corner into their own street she let her elbow rest against his arm, and her tension relaxed. She even smiled a little, remembering George, years ago. "A dentist is about as safe as a man can be. Any woman knows she hasn't got a throb of sex appeal left when she gets her mouth wide open and a drill going in it." Even a swanky saleswoman was a dead tooth to George. Typing always made her nervous, this double life was getting her down. If she weren't so near the end— When she brought the car successfully to a stop in front of the white house, she had pushed herself into her usual busy and quiet acceptance of the three of them as her family home for lunch, all separate undercurrents submerged.

On Friday afternoon, the last day of September, Hazel was hunting for a piece of paper large enough to fold around a box. It would be a joke, she thought, if after all these months of work she couldn't send off her book because she couldn't wrap it properly! She rummaged through the pile on top of the broom closet, and off it slid, grazing her nose. Odds and ends; the only thing in the pile large enough was a brown paper bag from the grocer's, rumpled but intact. Hazel smoothed it out on the table. Something fatally appropriate, a tag of domesticity. She might better save the money the postage would cost. Her fingers were listless with dejection as she lifted the tattered lid of the box— (the paper on which she had copied the book had come in the box, and she might have been more careful of it if she had known she would use it as casket). Yes, casket. That was just the way she felt about it! She'd expected elation and triumph; if she didn't hurry she wouldn't have the courage to send the thing away! There lay the sealed envelope, her name inside, "Your Hand Upon the Gate" somewhat aslant on the outside. She tied a piece of twine about the box, and slid it into the paper bag. With a little folding over along the sides, at the end, she could make it serve. Ship by express or first class mail said the directions.

She stared at the window, where fall drizzle and fog pressed flat and gray, seeming in its monotone to be without depth, drabness painted on the glass. If she went to the Lounsberry post office, Mrs. Pickett or Sam would come to the window. "What's in it, Hazel?" The Pickett back yard had touched the back yard of the Browning place when Hazel was a girl. People had complained that Mrs. Pickett was worse than a daily gossip column, but after Sam came back from the war his amputated foot carried him right through civil service and change in administration. Hazel couldn't hand under the lifted grill such a parcel as this, with the inscription: Prize Novel Contest, Horn and Westerby, Publishers. She could hear Mrs. Pickett. Like the time she had told George about the money order for the new office chair for Christmas! That would be a way for George to hear what his wife had been doing! "I'm not a bit surprised," Mrs. Pickett would say. "Hazel always had her nose in a book when she was a little girl." Brr! Her very skin felt too tight, chill-shrunken, at the inevitable calamity.

If she had time to go into the city—But she had to send the thing today or never at all, and even if she had time—already the clock pointed to half-past three—she couldn't conceal a trip to town. "But whatever did you go in for? You didn't say you were going!" Hazel decided that a life of crime presented unique difficulties. She might drive to the next village. The postmaster there didn't know her, and if she took a back road out of Lounsberry—"You have to be careful," George had said that noon. "These damp leaves falling are almost the worst hazard." She saw herself in a ditch, she heard George or Lorna or John explaining, in sombre, tragic tones, "We don't understand what she was doing, she never went to Roseville," and hastily, before her imagination could bog her into immobility, she buttoned on a raincoat and pulled a hat well down on her troubled head.

She reached Roseville without a skid, parked the car in front of a chain grocery, the one note of color in the drenched, deserted street, and the box bulging under the raincoat, to keep it dry, she darted from the car into the one story building, the sign almost lost in the dinginess of the window. The postmistress was fat and suspicious. "What's in it?" she said, as Hazel had feared. "Typewriting," said Hazel. "I—I'd like to register it." The postmistress turned it round and round. Did she smell a bomb, or hear it ticking? "You oughta seal it, then."

After a despairing ten minutes Hazel had found glue at the shoe-repair and fruit shop on the corner, had stuck down the ends of the grocery bag, and talking too much, she couldn't seem to stop, about weather, roads, the automobile plant between Roseville and Lounsberry, at last had the stamps affixed, and the thin strip with the registry number in her fingers. "The mail goes out today, of course," she said, finally.

"Gone," said the postmistress.

"Oh!" Hazel crumpled the receipt in her palm. "But this has to go today!"

"Postmarked the thirtieth," said the postmistress. She reached for the surrendered box, as if to sniff out the reason for such urgency, and Hazel, backing toward the door, murmured something.

As she drove toward Lounsberry, the windshield wiper keeping a rhythmic half circle of clearness, she tried to remember what she *had* said. She thought: of course Roseville people know George. Lots of them come over. Maybe the postmistress herself— Then she remembered the woman's mouth, with the white china display, and drove more swiftly along the rain-dark road. That postmistress didn't know George. But what did people do when they had something like—well, like a murder, say, to hide?

She came in to Lounsberry by the upper road, past the schoolhouse, down into the business block. Too late to pick up the children, too early for George. She'd stop for oranges, and if anyone asked her, that was where she had been. As she passed the bank corner she glanced up toward the windows of George's office. The neatly shirred pongee curtains she had made caught streaks of red from the traffic light, bars against the amber glow behind them. Well, she thought, I've wasted a dollar and sixty-seven cents. And how many hours! And now it's all over, but anyhow, George needn't know.

The judges appointed by Horn and Westerby, Publishers, were having their committee meeting. As the date for release of the prize announcement was January fifteenth, and this was January thirteenth, they knew severally, and in various irking ways, that they must, today, commit

46

themselves. They met in Mr. Horn's new office, thirty-two stories above Fifth Avenue, and Mr. Horn himself had dropped in for a few minutes. "I don't intend to offer suggestions," he said. "I just want to repeat that this isn't a Nobel Prize you're awarding. We want a book to sell. We've got the organization, we've got a staggering sales campaign—did I tell you we're planning to ship by motor truck and trailer, with loud speakers?—all we need is a book." He was a dapper little man, with an exaggeration of grimace and gesture which kept his hair rumpled and cut premature wrinkles in his thin face. He whirled now and darted from the room as if the loud speaker had summoned him.

The members of the committee looked at each other. "Nice little pep talk," murmured Carlton, a plumpish, bald book-columnist on a daily paper. He was irritated at his presence at the committee meeting anyway. He had no recollection of making Horn any promise to serve as judge, but Horn had cited place and date, a cocktail party a year ago, when the staidest firm in town showed what they could do for a novelist. Either the Scotch had made him incautious, or he hadn't believed Horn would find anyone with funds to back him. He'd told Horn he never read novels any more. Too ephemeral. He didn't tell Horn he found it easier to establish himself by expressing violent opinions on books no one else was likely to read. But Horn had promised real publicity for the judges. He was a good salesman; that was why he'd hooked Westerby as partner. "The advertising agent turned into the custodian of our literature," Carlton added.

Letitia Thomaston blinked her myopic and large brown eyes in Carlton's direction, and the lavender orchid which she had bought for herself that noon trembled on her silver fox scarf. Carlton had never spoken of *one* of her books, although for several days after each of her latest serials appeared in covers she looked at his column. She didn't read it, she just glanced at the title he had so captiously selected. When Alf Horn had spoken to her about being a judge, he had said, "Carlton's one of them. You might get chummy with him. He could do a lot for you." Not that she needed much done, but what she always said was, when thousands of people just run to get the next issue of my serial, it seems strange that no reviewer can understand my message. Carlton's face, well outside her radius of clear vision, was an amber egg. He looks just like a changeling, she said to herself; a disagreeable baby. "I need you on that committee, Letty," Horn had urged her, "to balance Carlton. You know what the public likes. He's too—" Now had Alf called him

AUTHORS' GOLD

erotic or exotic? Not that there was much difference. And as Alf had promised, there weren't many manuscripts left to read by the time the office had combed out the hopeless.

"It is a great rethoponthibility," said Letitia Thomaston. "Bestowing such a large thum on an unknown writer when we don't know who it is and our own names are attached to the award!" She spoke in accelerated tempo and the listener was not sure whether she really lisped or just slid over some of the consonants. "Personally I think it was a mithtake to limit the prize to new writers. Everybody who can write is in print already, and a great many of them ought not to be."

"I know what the mistake was," said Carlton, gloomily. "I should have written a novel instead of being a judge. I could use the ten grand."

"I always meant to write one," said Mrs. Rudolph Arner, the third judge. "But I never have had time."

For an instant Letitia and Carlton stared at her, united fleetingly by hostility toward an amateur. Mrs. Arner, sleek, plump, well clothed in a dark frock so simple and extreme that Letitia had felt a doubt of her own velvet, had a way of appearing on committees, a pleasant little moon illumined by her husband's reputation as essayist and editorial writer. She entertained frequently and well, and she seldom interfered much with committee decisions. She was a little troubled at present, because her second cousin's daughter had submitted a manuscript for this contest, and Mrs. Arner thought in glancing at papers, she had recognized it. She had said, firmly, "You must not give me an inkling, otherwise I can not be on the committee." Her second cousin Minna had cried, "You know what it would mean to us!" Mrs. Arner did know, among other things, that such an award would mean Rudolph could stop sending a monthly check to Minna. But she knew, too, the untemporizing scorn Rudolph would feel for any shade of nepotism, and that knowledge of Rudolph buttressed a certain crack of practicality in her own honor. The trouble right now was that she thought she knew, without intending to know, without pre-knowledge, which manuscript had come from Minna's girl. Should she lean backwards in an attempt to escape suspicion from Rudolph, and vote it down? Especially when she wasn't sure?

"But then, if we had all written books, we couldn't give each other the money, now could we?" Her secret dilemma heightened the slight accent of her husky, rich speech.

48

"We might as well get down to business." Carlton's implication was that the women had been talking for hours. "Shall we vote at once, or do you (grudgingly) prefer discussion?"

"What's the use of being a committee if you can't talk?" Mrs. Arner jumped her chair forward until she could reach the pile of manuscripts on the glass-topped table. "I can't remember them by name, anyway. Names seem to have nothing to do with what's in a book nowadays." If she got them to talking she could see whether that one had a chance. She couldn't help it if they chose it; even Rudolph couldn't blame her for that. Only five had survived the earlier meetings.

Carlton twirled his wrist until he could see the face of his watch. "I've got to get out of here before night," he said. "Let's vote."

"Before we vote—" Miss Thomaston's orchid was choreatic—"I must go on record. There is one book there I think we should discard. If by any chance it has two votes I should be compelled to resign from the committee. I could not allow my name to be associated with such— such—" She had wound herself into such tight sibilance she had to stop.

"You mean my choice, I suppose," Carlton's face had no expression, except for a widening of nostrils. "'Alley Cat.' The only book in the lot with any guts."

"That's just it! That's all it's got! No, Mr. Carlton, your jaded palate may relish that rank taste, but my finger has rested for years on the pulse of the reading public. I know how their heart beats!"

"Oh God!" Carlton's lips made the words without a sound, and Mrs. Arner wriggled on her chair. Something stimulating about real argument, especially when she could see each side so clearly! Carlton said, aloud, "Since you have been so frank, may I explain that your choice offends me even more? Obsolete and immoral saccharinity. Resigning wouldn't be enough! I'd have to commit suicide!"

"Then those two cancel each other," said Mrs. Arner. "I don't believe either would fit a loud speaker."

They voted on the three remaining, three times, and each time each book had one vote. Mrs. Arner did not vote for the book she thought Minna's daughter had submitted, and she couldn't decide from the printing on the slips which of the other two had chosen it. Carlton looked as if at any moment his boredom would become complete paralysis, and Letitia Thomaston wore a glaze of indignity.

"I'm tired of this," said Carlton. "Let's draw lots. They're all tepid.

Horn will blow hard and get his money back. What difference does it make?"

"It makes a difference to me. I am not part of a lottery, I am a judge. My first choice is thtill 'Ordeal By Love.'" (And mine is "Alley Cat," muttered Carlton.) "But since I have no co-operation, and since it is almost five o'clock—" she blinked hostile eyelids toward Carlton, and then turned toward Mrs. Arner bending forward to pull some focus around the woman's face. "I should think *we* might agree—"

"I'm not a bit dogmatic," said Mrs. Arner, hopefully. "I don't really know which to pick, and so I voted for 'Aspic and Honey.'"

"At least it begins with an A," said Carlton. Mrs. Arner smiled at him. He didn't bother her at all; Rudolph could be much more sarcastic.

"But I'm willing to change." Mrs. Arner took a long breath. Not even Rudolph could impute partiality to her now. She didn't really know it was Ethel May's book; she only knew that Ethel May had a modern way of writing, without ordinary aids to the reader such as punctuation and capitals, and the pages of this book had the same queer nakedness. "I'll vote for the one about the hand on the gate, if you will."

"And this," said Carlton, as he agreed, "is the way democracy works." When he opened the door, Horn leaped up from a chair, with the capped and spurred air of one whose horse paws and prances to be off. "Yes," said Carlton, "it is the unanimous decision of the committee. And if you ever catch me again!"

"Oh goodness, don't tell me it's meat pie night again!" Lorna gave a wriggle intended for a shudder as Hazel slid the casserole onto the mat in front of George.

"We have to finish the roast." Hazel spoke indistinctly, nibbling at the tip of a finger she had just burned.

"What's wrong with meat pie?" asked George, bisecting the brown crust neatly. "Especially your mother's."

"They're so—so common." Lorna leaned her forehead against her hand, but at her mother's glance she thought better of that elbow on the table and sat upright again, while John muttered, "Just a little taste of pheasant, please."

(Nothing suits her, thought Hazel, when she comes out of her trance far enough to see us at all!) George, knife poised for a transverse cut, looked at his daughter. "You'd do well to learn how to make a pie like this," he said, tranquilly. "Your husband will appreciate it some day."

"He looks like a hearty eater, too," said John, very low. Hazel shook her head at him, and Lorna decided not to hear him.

"I can remember—" George served with a dexterous turn of the wrist—"when your mother's pies weren't like this."

"Why bring that up?" asked Hazel, her finger still smarting.

"Oh, well!" Lorna disposed of the argument. "Cooking's old fashioned. You buy things in cans and boxes. Just listen to the radio!"

A sharp buzz of the front doorbell caught George with his mouth just opening for a homily upon the home, the hearth, the kitchen.

"That's probably for me—" but although Lorna pushed back her chair and flung aside her napkin, John beat her in a dash for the hall.

Hazel saw George glance at his daughter, his blue eyes candidly alarmed, saw him seal back a protest. He's worried, too, she thought, about that Daniels boy coming so often, although he won't say a word.

Lorna expected him; she poised at the edge of her chair, every nerve waving toward the front door, to catch his voice. They all heard John's "H'ryuh, Bo," and, "How long you been working there?" and then the door shut. John strolled back, exasperatingly slow, thumb and finger pinched at the corner of a yellow envelope.

"'Satelegram," he said. Lorna slumped. A telegram was adult disaster, and did not touch her suspense.

"Let's have it!" George reached for it. "Now who on earth——"

"It says Hazel Browning Curtis," said John, parting with it reluctantly.

Well, I don't know anyone who'd be dead, thought Hazel, and she opened it. It roared at her, each printed word, the room rocked up at a queer arc, and faintly she heard George, impatient, "Who is it? What does it say?"

"It says—" her lips were stiff, "it says I got it."

John stood behind her chair and read it aloud. "Delighted to offer you congratulations your book unanimous selection of judges for award send photo wire biographical details immediately representative will fly west to arrange trip to New York presentation of check publication being rushed."

"That's a queer mistake," said George. "John, you better call up the office at once and tell them. There may be some other message for us."

Hazel's heart, buffeted by consternation and amazement, began to beat swiftly; the blood burned in her ears, her temples. "I don't think it can be a mistake," she said. "It says my name."

"But what—" George stared at her. ("What have you been up to that I don't know about," flickered in his eyes, a premonitory doubt of stability as if the earth's crust heaved slightly.) "Here, let's see it."

Hazel waved the sheet toward him, and pressed her fingers against her temples, trying to push back the flush of guilt, of shock. If only the news had come when she was alone! Giving her a minute to get used to it.

"Horn and Westerby," said George. "Never heard of them. Whose trip to New York? What book? If you know what it's about——"

"Yes, I know." Hazel took a long breath, to inflate the feeble squeak in which her voice had come out. "I must have got the prize. I didn't expect to."

"What prize?" asked George, and Lorna said, "Did you win a trip to New York? Why, *Moth*-er!"

"I won more than that." Hazel thought: I'll say it, and see if it's true. "I won the prize. Ten thousand dollars."

George's eyes were round and light blue, just the color of his broad-cloth shirt, the pupils contracted to dots. John loped around the table to lean over his father's shoulder and stare at the yellow paper. "Ten thousand bucks! Oh boy oh boy oh boy!" he chanted.

"It doesn't say ten thousand," said George, slowly.

"That's the only prize there was." Hazel gave herself a little shake. There, she wouldn't cry. She'd been afraid she might. The paroxysm in her chest was quieting. "I thought I wouldn't say anything—I didn't really expect to get it."

"I don't understand yet what you did." George's expression of doubt thickened.

"I wrote a book. A novel." Hazel's color had subsided, her eyes were bright under the fringe of lashes, her pallor, the uncertainty of her mouth had entreaty. They all looked as if she'd suddenly stood on her head in the middle of the table! "You aren't any more surprised than I am," she said, and as her eyes met those of her husband's she caught a flash of the clairvoyance which lived at times between them. You shouldn't ever be so sure you know everything about me! She smiled at him.

"You mean these people—" he laid a finger on the telegram, "whoever they are——"

"They're publishers," said Hazel.

"Are going to give you ten thousand dollars for something you wrote out of your head?"

"Of course," said Hazel, "there's a good deal of work getting it out of your head." She had, suddenly, a new feeling, a tardy response to the stimulus of an unfamiliar drug. Her book had been selected. Unanimously. She, Hazel Browning Curtis, had written it! "Let me see that telegram!"

"I don't see when you found time."

"That's why you pecked away on that ole typewriter!" John dropped into his chair, his face screwed in dark concentration on this phenomenon in his own house. "Ten thousand bucks! Why, you're rich, Mother!"

"I haven't got a photograph, except that one with the children years ago. I couldn't wire biographical details. What would I say? I think you might congratulate me! You haven't one of you——"

They did then, George adding stiffly, "If we'd known anything about it—have to get over the shock." Lorna thought it was like something in the movies, exactly! And wouldn't people's eyes stick out! George said he wouldn't say anything about it until they saw the check. Hazel did not notice until late that evening, when she cleared away the dishes, that he had scarcely touched his dinner. He had said, "Well, we ought to celebrate. But I promised two inlays for tomorrow. Even if I've got a rich wife, I suppose I must go on working." Hazel went to the door with him. "You know," he said, slowly, "I knew you had something on your mind. I felt it. Only I thought for a while it was another baby. You were absent-minded, that way."

"Well, aren't you at least glad that wasn't it?"

"I don't know." George held his muffler in place with his chin as he jerked into his overcoat. "I'd understand that. But ten thous— Why, my best year I didn't clear— And never saying a word—"

Hazel's hand wavered upward. She wanted to poke a finger into the buttonhole of his lapel, to explain that her silence had been a lack of confidence not in him, but in herself. "I never expected to win the prize," she began.

"I'm surprised you confided that in us!" George drew himself stubbornly away from her finger. "Mere accident, perhaps, the telegram coming as it did."

"I hadn't made any plans." Hazel shivered as the raw January wind pushed around George's stiff figure into the warmth of the hall. It was too bad of George not to be whole-heartedly pleased— "How could I when I never expected—you're just surprised because you didn't think I was smart enough to do it!" She didn't know where her sudden anger

53

leaped from, the words curling like a wave over the blond rock of her husband's face.

"I didn't say that." He shrugged, and thrust his hands into pockets. "You needn't get mad just because I'm surprised. Only how—" his breath puffed out a great white feather in the frosty air, "however can I tell what else you're up to? But you're cooling off the whole house. Shut the door." And he strode with finality out of the range of light toward the car.

Hazel shut the door, hand braced against a desire to slam it. She ought to be high with excitement, delight, and instead George had done this to her. That was why she hadn't told him: she had known just how he would take it. She broke the thin string of accusations, seeing his face just before he had swung down the walk. Oh, poor George! The delicate, assured balance of their lives knocked suddenly out of kilter! A balance of expectancy, habit, knowledge. And she had been resentful, instead of wise. She'd heard that success was bad for people; was she already proof of that? She heard Lorna at the telephone, in the muffled effect of lips sealed against the receiver. As she walked past her daughter, the murmur ceased, and the blue eyes rolled up at her ingenuously. John sat at the dining room table, one hand rustling in a large cracker box, the yellow telegram propped against his tumbler.

"Are you still hungry, Johnny?" Hazel glanced at the table. He'd had the rest of the gingerbread, and all the milk. But she hadn't noticed much about what he ate.

"I guess not." John munched. "Just thought I'd eat a cracker. Say, Mother, are you sure it's ten thousand dollars? It just says award."

Hazel opened a drawer of the buffet, and from under the imitation leather box for knives and forks took out a folded paper. "You can read it," she said, and John frowned as he smoothed out creases and read the announcement.

"Maybe they won't pay it," he said, darkly. "Lots of those prize things are fakes. I knew a fellow and he drew the number for a car, but they gave it to someone in the firm. He never saw it!"

"Oh, but this is different!" Hazel's fingers closed over the telegram, and she read it slowly. "Books aren't like drawing numbers for cars! Why, a professor gave me that notice. He'd know if it was a fake! And here's my name and address——"

"John's just being smart, Mother!" Lorna was at the door, dark beret pulled toward one ear, coat over her arm. "Don't let him fozzle you."

"Just because I have brains enough to raise a question!" began John, but Hazel interrupted.

"Are you going out, Lorna? Tonight?"

"Why, I told you, Mother! We're meeting at Agnes' house to talk over the Senior play. I explained this afternoon. You must have forgotten, with all the excitement and everything." Lorna was forbearing, kind.

"Didn't you meet last Friday?" asked Hazel.

"Of course *one* meeting can't decide *everything* about a thing like that!"

"Not when you think who's there," said John in falsetto.

"You know—" Hazel hesitated. Lorna was so intrenched in righteousness, and her forbearance was so egg-shellish— After all, if George didn't want his daughter going out during the week, he might see to it himself! "That coat really isn't warm enough for tonight," she finished.

"I can't wear that other old thing!" Lorna tugged the coat over her shoulders, buttoned it with an air of drama. "Honestly, I'd rather freeze to death! *Mother!*" her face changed from its slightly reserved hostility into glowing supplication. "Oh, Mother! I just thought—with all that money— Oh, could I have a fur coat? Could I?"

Hazel looked down at the yellow paper, and again, slowly, there expanded within her a bright bubble. Somehow, among them, they had almost obliterated the extraordinary fact that she, Hazel Browning Curtis, had won the prize!

"We'll see," she said, deliberately. "After I know more about this."

Lorna's hands, pulling the belt through the buckle, stopped, and her eyes stopped too, round, and almost thoughtful. "Would you rather I didn't go tonight? I—if there's anything——"

"Any little thing like a fur coat?" queried John, reaching for another cracker.

"Don't be late," said Hazel. Her hands, automatically, began to pile together dishes from the table. The silver clattered.

"Of course I said I'd be there," Lorna waited.

"Of course." Hazel pushed open the door into the kitchen, and blinked her lashes. It would be ironic if after all her care in handling Lorna, her tender noninterference, her attempts to erect invisible safeguards just to keep the child from blundering too early into what she thought was love, bribery should now prove effective. Lorna would stay home, if Hazel wished, with a fur coat in the offing! Money was a weapon Hazel had never had a chance to try. It might be stronger than words or wisdom. A reminiscent flush of embarrassment showed in Hazel's face as she poked her head through the shoulder loops of an apron. That night last week when she had tried to talk with Lorna! She'd been strictly contemporary, using bold and simple words about what a strong instinct sex was, and how it might blot out all the other interests that were important for her development, and that would be all right if she belonged to a primitive tribe, but she had to think about earning her living, getting a proper education— Hazel had been proud of her little speech, and at the end Lorna had looked at her pityingly and said, "Of course, Mother, we belong to entirely different generations!"

She hadn't even been surprised that her mother had written a book! I suppose—Hazel turned the faucet and held a finger in the stream of water, testing the temperature—I was as self-absorbed as she is, at her age. Maybe I hid it better. I don't know. Lorna's like George, you know just where they are. George had been surprised. She clattered the dishpan into the sink. That water wasn't hot. Never was, unless the furnace was roaring. Why—she stood motionless, and the water purled over the edges of the pan. She could install a new heating plant, if she wanted to. That oil burner, automatic, that the agent had been so persistent about last summer. She could do anything she liked! Almost. Of course, at this very moment, whether she liked or not, she had to do dishes in lukewarm water. Was that a way to celebrate?

There should be someone to tell, someone who would say, "Marvelous! Wonderful!" Her mind clicked off a line of people, neighbors along the street, women in the church, in the literary society, girls grown older who had been her best friends when she was a girl. Queer, the way marriage altered your intimacies, absorbed whatever it was that ran out searching for friends. Turned you into a small principality with guards along the border. Well, it would come out in the paper, and then they'd all know. As George said, better wait until she had the check.

In the quiet kitchen, above the soft note of the water, the ticking of the porcelain clock grew louder. A queer, hard tone, the beat of metal under porcelain, like a premonitory whir which might someday shiver the china into fragments. Hazel listened, her upper lip caught between her teeth, her eyes bright and rebellious. She didn't like that clock. It had run her life for her too long, measuring her inefficiency against its methodical progress. Time you had those dishes done, it said right now! Hazel looked at the stacked plates. She didn't like them, either. George's mother had sent the set, not as a wedding present, just as an extra. "We don't need them, now the family is so small," she had written. "It will save you buying any."

Heavy, old-fashioned ware, with a design in yellowish-green which crawled and twined around the borders. George had been delighted. "Makes me feel at home," he had said. One of the hired girls who helped out a few weeks after the birth of Lorna or John had broken one plate. That was all. Hazel stared at them, the design began to swim around the plate, the clock had the vibratory tone of breaking china. Suddenly Hazel seized the pile, thumbs on top, fingers spread, held it well away from her body, and with a little push to help out gravity, dropped it.

John poked the door open and looked in, his face solemn. Hazel with her toe spun off the top plate, sole survivor among the shards.

"Migosh," said John, "another revolution in China!"

"I can buy some more," said Hazel.

The telephone burst into a prolonged and unnatural clangor.

"Gleeps!" said John. "They gone crazy, too?" He vanished, the ringing ceased, and in a moment John was at the door again, his thin face twitching, as if his air of nonchalance had grown too tight for his skin. "New York calling for Hazel B. Curtis," he paged her in his deepest tone, holding the door ajar.

New York calling, or Mars would like to speak to you. Hazel slid past John, sat down at the telephone stand, and after an instant blew a somewhat winded "Hello," toward the mouthpiece.

"Is that you, Mrs. Curtis? Someone in New York *says* he wants to talk to you." That was Flora Robb, Jessie's oldest girl. Hazel had heard she was night operator. "At least they have your address."

"Yes," said Hazel firmly. Flora needn't sound so incredulous! Well, George's caution about saying nothing would do no good now, with Flora on the line.

"Here's your party."

The brisk, staccato voice was, as Hazel said later, just as clear as if he'd been right in the room. Yes, she was Hazel Curtis, yes, she'd written the book, yes, she'd had the telegram, yes, she was delighted. Something both stimulating and breathtaking in the rapid pelting of words. A little information for a news story to be released at once. Had she ever written before? What did she do? Oh, fine! Two children, husband was what? A remote voice interloped, words about three minutes, and the staccato bristled. How did you happen to write a book? (John had crept near, head bent as if he listened to New York.) Hazel floated above the earth, herself the golden bubble, even the intent and repressed astonishment in John's face a remote thing, caution quite gone. How had she happened to write—those lonely evenings, with George at the office— Any message, how you feel at winning the prize? What will you do with it? And now, Mrs. Curtis, we want you to drop in for a few days. We're rushing the book through the press, need you for publicity hints. No, we've decided it's much better for you to come to New York, meet all of us, sign contracts, of course you can manage, matter of paramount importance. Wire me, I'll meet you. What's that? Can't afford— Nonsense, you're rich. I'll mail you a check for expenses. Work up radio and movie ends when you come. Congratulations.

The hall door opened as the voice ceased, and Hazel swung dizzily around on the stool, finger-tips tingling. George, both hands embracing a pyramid of green paper, kicked the door shut behind him. The kick jarred his hat forward, and he peered from under the brim with raffish suspicion. "I thought you weren't going to tell anyone yet."

"I wasn't." Hazel giggled. George did look comical! "He was telling me." (This must be like being drunk, she thought. It's a grand feeling!) "But he's going to put it in all the papers!"

"Was that the very guy that's handing you ten thousand bucks?" drawled John.

"How'd he get here so soon?" George pushed his chin over the crackling paper.

"New York calling, Dad. I bet Florabelle got an earful that time."

"I hope what I said was all right. Goodness, I can't remember what I did say! But how could I go to New York?" Whirling away from them, across a continent— "I could hire someone to come in— Oh, it's too— too——"

"Utter," said John. "Just too utter! That's the word."

George set down his parcel on the console-table, propping it against the wall. "I'll have to put up the car," he said.

"Lemme, Dad." John angled past him a whoop floating back as he slapped the door shut. George took off his coat, folded his muffler into a pocket, and opened the door of the hall closet, his movements deliberate and prolonged.

"I wish you could come to New York with me," said Hazel. "I'm not used to going places by myself."

"It sounds as if you would be," said George into the closet.

"Would you rather I just stayed here?"

"Of course not." George turned, and smiled, just a quirk of the corners of his mouth. "I mean of course I would." He shoved the green bundle along the table. "I bought you that. They didn't have much to choose from. Maybe you won't want it—if you're going away."

Hazel pulled off the metal clips, folded away the noisy paper, the red azalea danced.

"Of course I want it!"

"He had some roses, but I thought this would last longer." George cleared his throat. "You—you didn't think I wasn't pleased, did you? I mean I just never thought of your writing a book, and then to have it turn out that it was my wife——"

He's trying so hard, thought Hazel, looking up from the red blossoms. She could see only the shadows cast by his quick and secret thoughts, in a shifting of tautness about his mouth, about his grave blue eyes. Not the thoughts. Never the thoughts themselves. Suddenly she stepped close to him, her hands slid between his arms and rigid body, clasped tight against his hard back. "Darling!" she said. His arms strained around her, urgent, and they kissed, the wryness of shock or fear or strangeness gone as their blood remembered all their knowledge of each other.

"You know—" Hazel sniffed, liking the faint clean odor, the cool firmness of his cheek— "I'd rather give it back than have it make any differance. It couldn't, now could it?"

"I hope not, old lady." George's embrace relaxed. "Not if you keep your head. You couldn't give back ten thousand. That's a lot of money."

Hazel withdrew slowly. Too bad, the way saying things changed your feeling— "Goodness!" she spoke briskly. "I haven't even finished the dishes! You put the plant on the living room table. I'll be through in a little while."

She slipped through the door into the kitchen, and stooped to gather up the fragments of china. She didn't, suddenly, want George to see that mess. As the pieces clinked softly into the waste basket, she thought, and the back of her neck prickled, almost with fear, that perhaps it was a bad omen, this first gesture of hers. You'll always have to pick up the pieces, if you smash things, she told herself. But what a silly way to feel. As if good fortune was too much for her!

Hazel left for New York late in March, after three changes of the date. The first time John had the flu. He had pretended that he felt perfectly well, but at the very moment when Hazel kissed him good-bye, she caught the unmistakable faint whiff of fever about him. Stripping off her gloves, she took his temperature, ignoring the awful faces he made. (Never worry about your children, her father had told her. Find out right away.) When she read the thermometer she asked George please to send a wire that she couldn't come. John hadn't been very sick, but only, she was sure, because she popped him into bed that minute. The second time the housekeeper left just as Hazel meant to go. George had something to do with it, although Hazel couldn't ask him what. "All I ask is a woman competent enough to take charge of things," he said. "I can't give up all my business, unimportant as it may seem to you, to look out for the children." The news stories had done that to George. Mr. Horn had played up the, "Wife seeks solace for lonely hours in writing. Beside the cradles of her sleeping children she composes great book. Domesticity palls upon this remarkable woman." The first time George read that he had been too outraged to listen to Hazel. By the tenth time Hazel had ceased any attempt to explain the difference between what she had meant and what the stories said. It was too bad they'd called George a struggling young dentist. Hazel couldn't honestly blame him for being angry, but she blamed him for not believing her when she protested that she hadn't told reporters such things. George did drive her into the city for her train this third time when she made an actual getaway; a formal George who made comments on the state of affairs in Michigan as indicated by objects of the landscape. He left her at the stairs which led up to her track, and his kiss had the effect of chastisement. "When you come back," he said, "I hope I'll recognize you."

Hazel brushed away tears which burned her lids, and suddenly parting, blade-sharp, cut through the layers of awkward hostility, of self-reproducing misunderstandings, and she was in his arms. "Don't let anything happen to you while I'm gone! Oh, George, darling! I don't want to go."

"You're the one things will happen to. We'll be all right." But he kissed her again, and this time he loved her and reassured her.

"Nothing that will make any difference between us, will it? Say it won't. I couldn't bear it!" Never had she loved him more, the firm clip of his arms, the little wave of his chin as he tossed off too much emotion, the everything that was George.

"When you get this all over and settle down again—" A porter jostled them, climbing past with luggage, but the moment was gone, anyway.

"I don't want to settle down." Hazel folded her hands under her collar, pushing the soft beaver against her chin, and stared at George, her eyes startled. "I didn't mean that. I mean—but you know!" Challenge rang like a silver disk struck softly, clear under the hubbub of the station noises. We can't go back as we were, exactly, she was saying. But we do still love each other.

"You mustn't miss your train." George retreated into practical matters. "Send me a wire in the morning."

She couldn't sleep. There was, she thought, something appalling about a train trip. Surrendering yourself, giving up your freedom. You kept an illusion that you were free to make choices: you could eat dinner or go to bed early, but all the time you were being propelled through space, your destination fixed. Wasn't it a good deal like life, except that on the train you had at least chosen your destination? Who bought the ticket for life? Weren't you propelled along as inevitably, with as much illusion of freedom, through time instead of across miles of country? When she had started to write a book she hadn't said please give me a ticket away from George, and yet look! She wouldn't have thought George would take it as he had. But she couldn't be sorry she had done it! As the train rolled eastward George was diminished by more than space, and the next day, vague and brilliant, seemed to come to meet her minute by minute, just as she rolled toward it mile after mile.

After the first flurry of news stories, people in Lounsberry had acted almost as if nothing had happened. Except George. The Ladies Literary Society had thought it would be nice to have Hazel tell them about the book, but they had their meetings all arranged, and of course they hadn't read the book yet. Was it laid in the town, and had she put them in it? Insurance agents, numerous and persistent as English sparrows, had rung the telephone and doorbell, automobile salesmen, young men representing investment companies. It seemed silly to hide in one's own house, but Hazel tried that, instructing the new housekeeper to say that she was out. The woman complained that she couldn't do a lick of work for arguing at the door, and George came home one evening, stiff and cold with indignation. Two of his patients had cancelled appointments, one for herself, one for her little girl whose teeth George was straightening. Mrs. Wills and Mrs. Parsons. "They're insulted because you wouldn't see them when they called. Must you ruin my business, too?" Hazel had written notes to them, trying to soothe them, and Mrs. Parsons did bring back her child, as the brace had to be adjusted. Mrs. Wills said that some people couldn't stand good luck.

After that Hazel answered the bells herself, when she wasn't trying to

decide which letters should have answers. Advertising letters, begging letters—(the world was suddenly crammed with worthy institutions for sea-
men, blind men, orphans, Lithuanian cripples, indigent actresses, and
worn out horses, all of which institutions would totter unless she re-
mitted . . .) letters from women in Oklahoma, Alaska, Texas, and the
Bronx who had written novels they wished to send her, letters from men
in prison, in a lumber camp, on farms, in the haberdashery business who
had plots for novels they would share with her, one dreadful note on
brown paper threatening the children unless she mailed a thousand dollars to X B, General Delivery. George had taken that up with the police,
and they had watched for a while to see if anyone claimed the envelope
thus addressed. But as the officer said, "A real gangster wouldn't bother
with chicken feed like that. Just some nut."

Weeks ago the crest of the flood had dropped, almost as suddenly as it
had risen, and the postman no longer made his joke about needing an
extra mailbag just for Hazel. She wondered whether someone in some
other town had unwittingly made himself such a target. Even Mr. Horn
ceased to wire or telephone so often. He was rushing the book through,
proofreading it in the office to save time; he consulted her about various
matters of which she knew nothing, and Hazel caught the wind stirred
by his rush even over the telephone.

She tried to fit the solid Pullman pillow between shoulder and cheek,
tried to wriggle into comfort under the tight blanket. Here in the dark
cubicle, with unexplained shafts of brilliant light striking at intervals
under the drawn shade, she could admit that she had liked it. Not everything, of course. Like being transposed into a different key. Hazel, with
variations. I wouldn't tell George that, she said. But I like it. And New
York should be more exciting still, because that would concern the book
itself, not just the prize. People would read her book. She hoped the
dresses she had bought would be all right. As the clerk had said, black
lace was always good. George couldn't have stood it if she'd bought that
red dress with no back at all, although she had looked at herself for a long
time before she let it slide down to the waiting hands of the saleswoman.
She hoped her speech would be all right, too. She hoped she wouldn't be
frightened. She hoped John and his father would get along while she was
gone. Better, perhaps, than these past weeks while she was there, with
George so edgy, and John so quick to catch moods.

And Lorna—Hazel frowned, a concentrated and baffled tenderness ex-
panding through her body at the thought of her daughter. She must have

quarreled with the Daniels boy. Queer, Hazel had worried about their
intimacy, and yet when she saw the boy downtown with that red-headed
Gwendolyn Baratsky, who had more reputation of the wrong kind than
any other girl in town, she was furious. John ceased to tease Lorna, an
ominous sign. Hazel tried unobtrusively to assure Lorna of support or
sympathy or whatever she most needed. (At her age a heart, even broken,
should heal quickly, like your bones.) But Lorna went about with a surface hard and prickly, resisting intrusion. She shut herself into her own
room, and said she supposed they wanted her to do some studying, didn't
they? She carried her secret, whatever it was, in a sort of fourth dimension, where no one could touch it. When Hazel said, "Don't you want
to go to the movies?" or "Why don't you and Tommy go to the Club
dance tomorrow?" Lorna had looked at her, and for an instant her fair,
round, unchanged face had seemed a mask over lean torment. "When
I want to go places, you and Father say I'm going too much, and when I
want to stay home you won't let me alone." I just have to stand by,
thought Hazel, waiting for contact. I'll get something for her in New
York, a new dress.

The next morning she was the first passenger to appear as a finished
and civilized product, being driven by anxiety lest the train arrive at
Grand Central and she find herself ejected, like one of those dreams in
which you walk down a street with your clothes over your arm! The
porter found her a seat forward, beyond all the bulging green curtains,
and she looked out at the great river running down in the sunlight as fast
as the train, at patches of dingy snow, at gulls on old sunken piers, her
fingers tense over her new brown purse.

"Take a taxi to the hotel," Horn had written. "I'll engage rooms for
you there, and drop in early." It was strange to get off the train and know
that not one of the people at the gate waited for her. Always George or
the children waited for her, with that grand moment of recognition ex-
ploding like a Roman candle between them. Unless, indeed, George and
the children were with her on the train. But the red-cap rushed her to a
cab, and the cab rushed her in spurts to the hotel. New York wasn't
unlike the other cities she knew, except perhaps that the chasms of the
narrow streets were deeper, cut sharper angles, and the blue sky was
buttressed incredibly far above by towers extraordinary and varied. Her
name, the name of Alfred Horn meant nothing to the hotel clerk, and
Hazel searched in her bag for the letter. Surely he had said this hotel!

"Will you please register, Madam?" Why, he had known, all the time! The bell boy whisked her to the elevator, the swift ascent reminded Hazel she had had no breakfast, their feet were silent on the deep nap past polished doors, and then the bell boy lingered, having indicated ice water, radio, phone. "Yes, it's a nice room," said Hazel, and then the persistence of his shrewd, pimpled face reminded her, and she opened her purse again. How much should you give him—she'd given the porter more than George said, because he seemed to expect it . . . oh, dear! . . . She found a quarter, and then a dime, and sighed as he withdrew with no excess of gratitude. Outside the windows lay New York, superimposed silhouettes, with shadow-accents, city haze dimming the sky color. Hazel gazed at the mulberry and blue of rug and hangings, the reddish cast of modern maple, she wondered how they made the pleats of the valance, and decided to unpack her dresses.

As she unlocked the case, the door trembled under a tattoo. Hazel opened it, and was swept back into the room by the influx of several men, Mr. Horn himself, a photographer, a reporter. Mr. Horn all but embraced her, holding both her hands. "Hazel Browning Curtis, at last! Well, well, this is wonderful! Just a minute for some pictures." The next hour was a blur of holding her head this way and that while silver bulbs exploded in silent dazzles, of answering questions, no she didn't know how she liked New York yet, no, she hadn't started another book, (keep George out of it, she warned herself; don't mention George!) Mr. Horn seems very young, she thought. He'll wear himself out, he's too intense. Then the photographer disappeared, the reporter folded up his sheets, and Mr. Horn said, "Now we'll go over to the office. I've made a luncheon engagement for you, good chance, Mrs. Canterbury's literary luncheons. One of her speakers fell down, and she'll tuck you in. She has a crowd of females, soaks 'em plenty, tells them about books, dames lap it up, don't have to read, see? They don't buy books, but Canterbury gets good notices."

"But I couldn't think up a speech——"

"You don't have to say anything. Get up and give 'em a look. Come along."

"But do I look all right?" cried Hazel, desperate to brace herself against the rush. Mr. Horn was worse than the train, the way he propelled her inevitably ahead.

"Why, yes," Mr. Horn looked at her, the crease deep between his bright, dark eyes. "Little brown wren from the middle west. Yes, you're fine. We'll play up that aspect. Homebody."

*Wren,* in her new coat that even Lorna had said did things for her! But Mr. Horn wouldn't hear her if she told him what she thought of his wren. And when he stopped at the florist shop in the lobby, and bought a spray of gardenias tied with silver ribbon for her, she decided to say nothing about his bird lore.

The offices of Horn and Westerby seemed a trifle bare. Perhaps she had expected something more like a library, instead of this series of cubbyholes in and out of which moved men and young women, each with an air of being in a great hurry to reach some other spot before it was forever too late. Hazel sat beside Mr. Horn's flat desk, trying politely not to read any of the fascinating letters which littered the top, and meeting in such rapid succession that she never sorted them out the sales manager, the advertising man, the business manager, the publicity head, and what else. The telephone rang often, and Mr. Horn, hooking the mechanism between chin and shoulder, talked into it and over it at the same time. Finally he said, "Well, that's about the line-up. Reviews ought to begin Sunday. If we get a good break—Is there anything else you'd like to ask?"

"Could I see it? The book, I mean?"

"Good God, haven't you seen it?" Horn pressed the buzzer. *"Didn't* we ship you some?" A thin dark girl in horn-rimmed glasses looked in; her glance at Hazel said plainly, what is a mere author doing here? "Bingham, get me a copy of 'The Hand,' willya?"

"If I can find one. We sent out all we had around."

"Well, find one. And order a bunch sent up here. Mrs. Curtis ought to sign a few."

Then for a few minutes he was intensely silent, looking over papers, and Hazel wondered whether only a homebody would ask to see her book. The Bingham girl came back, and Hazel had it in her own hands, her own book, "Your Hand Upon the Gate" in zig-zags above white palings on a red ground, a gold band sealing it, announcing the ten thousand dollar prize award. She was afraid she might cry, her throat hurt, but Mr. Horn said, "Take it along. Canterbury may not have a copy. Hold it up when you get up to talk. Pretty neat job, we think here at the office."

So Hazel held it through the luncheon, although she found it hard to keep her knees stiff enough to support bag and book. Mrs. Canterbury had swept up to her in peach lace, a gold cap on assisted-gold hair, her animation as applied as her lipstick. So sweet of Mrs. Curtis to consent to come, she hadn't read the book, but she would say all she could, and

Mrs. Curtis could speak just a few words to the ladies. A remarkable group, highly intelligent. Then she swept away to project herself around a plumpish man with white hair and a pink face, evidently her favorite guest. Hazel was seated well down the long table, between two women from the suburbs who talked across her, and across the table to the women opposite. If they knew I had a book, thought Hazel, they might talk to me. But as she swallowed tomato bisque, thick and not too hot, the dismal emptiness, partly physical, began to ease away.

The woman across stared at her, the wired bow on her turban quivering. "Aren't you one of the speakers?" she asked. "I didn't catch the name."

"Curtis," said Hazel.

Never heard of it, signalled the woman's well-pruned eyebrows. "We hoped to hear Stark Young today," she said. "Mrs. Canterbury is very good usually about taking up only the books you have to know about. My life is too full for reading, but I think when someone gives you a good digest it is really better than if you read the book yourself, because she can pick out just the salient points, don't you agree with me?"

Fortunately she did not wait for Hazel's answer, but turned her wired bow toward the woman on her left, and the two confided in undertones, while Hazel jabbed at her chicken à la king. For the first time in her life she felt the apologetic uneasiness of a performer. Because she had written a book she ceased to be one of the ladies lunching, and became a questionable part of the entertainment for which they paid. Getting up to speak would be exposing herself to all their arrows. But Mr. Horn said it would be good for the book. Her left hand spread over the smooth surface of the book, pressed it hard against her flesh. She had to stay.

The ladies adjourned to a reception room where gold chairs stood in rows before a low platform. Mrs. Canterbury strolled back and forth on the platform, fitting the gestures of her jewelled hands less to her words than to her intended emotional effects, while she offered her digests of the books on her program. She was gay, very feminine, she made little jokes, she referred at times to the quality of her audience, she pattered briskly through the story, and at crucial points of deaths or lovers' meetings she quoted lines with elocutionary histrionics. She really works hard for her money, thought Hazel. Wouldn't the Lounsberry Literary Society love her! Hazel wound her ankles tightly together and clasped book and purse. What would she say when she had to stand on that platform? She tried to remember lines from the speech she had written for the dinner.

They wouldn't do; she couldn't thank these women for giving her the prize!

Mrs. Canterbury swayed at the platform edge, hands extended gracefully.

"And now, Ladies, we have a little special treat. We hoped for Stark Young, but fate intervened, fate in the form of a teeny little flu germ. So we have a new writer. I can't tell you about her book, as I haven't read it, as I didn't know until this morning we would have the pleasure of hearing her. But since it has won a prize of ten thousand dollars I am sure we will all want to read it if only to see why it should be given so much money. I present Hazel Browning Curtis, who will tell us the story of—what is the title?" And to Hazel, in an undertone, as the latter rose, she said, "The ladies are getting a little restless. Don't talk too long."

Hazel didn't. As she collapsed in the taxi on the way to her own hotel, her face burning, her heart still racing, she was sure only that she hadn't talked too long. She scrambled through her mind, trying to hear echoes of what she had said. A spurt of anger had lifted her clear of the symptoms of stage fright, and she rather thought she had said that perhaps someone there would read the book out of curiosity, as Mrs. Canterbury had suggested, and as she'd written the story she wouldn't bother to tell it over, there was the book, and she'd held it out, flaunting its gold band, and she didn't know how to make a speech, this was her first, and so she'd stop. Had she said thank you or not? Her mouth quirked at the corners. "My goodness, she got my dander up, as George would say. Now, see here!" She sat forward in the cab, her pulses calming. "Can't go 'round losing your temper. But acting as if she were doing me a favor, when I thought I was the one——"

She decided that if she moved fast she could bathe and dress before Mr. Horn called for her. Quarter to five, he had said. A cocktail party. She supposed she couldn't wear the black lace. She'd have to come back again to dress for dinner. She wished she had bought that red one, just to dispose of the wren idea. She was in the tub, having scrubbed it thoroughly with her wash-cloth (how did she know who had last used it!) when the 'phone rang. She popped out, seized a bath towel, and left a trail of damp prints across the mulberry rug. Mr. Horn calling. Was she ready?

"I thought you said quarter to five!"

"I got wind of another tea. For an English author, but we'll drop in. Bound to meet some people there."

"I'm taking a bath," said Hazel.

"Bring it right along! How soon can you make it?"

"Five minutes."

She did, too. Being a mother was good training in speed at one's toilet. The gardenias had brown smudges on the outer petals, but Hazel re-pinned them to her coat. She powdered her nose, and wondered whether she might buy a lipstick, just to use in New York. George always liked her own color better, but of course he had such close-ups of mouths.

At midnight Hazel closed the door of her hotel room, brushed back her hair with a slow, heavy hand, and sank down on the bed. Someone had turned down the blankets. Nice. If ever she could stir again! She did not feel tired, so much as extinguished. Blotted out, scattered, lost. As if, presenting herself again and again to all these strange men and women, hostile or indifferent or bland or self-absorbed, none of them coming out to look for her, some of them cagey, suspicious (don't think you'll get me to write you a good review by smiling at me!) she came at last to non-existence, annihilation. The teas were easier than the dinner, although just as annihilating, for when Horn convoyed someone up to meet her—most of the names she didn't understand—the someone murmured, "Ah, Horn's prize!" or "How do you like New York?" and then hailed an acquaintance or strolled off toward the bar. One darkish man seemed friendly, and asked whether she was at work on a second book. Just as they had begun a real talk, Horn dragged her away. "Has he got you signed up yet?" Mr. Horn's cocktails had accelerated his ordinary tempo. "Biggest pirate in town, steals authors under their publisher's nose." At the second party, which a literary agent, a friend of Horn's, was giving for him and his author, Hazel thought she met again some of the guests from the first. But she wasn't sure. Her face had stiffened, her mouth felt dry from too many smiles, but she found corners of tables and windowsills where she could set down the cocktails presented to her whenever anyone observed her without one.

At the dinner, however, she had to sit at the speakers' table, and try to talk. On one side sat Mr. Carlton, a member of the committee which had chosen her book, and Hazel, although partially extinguished, had thought, he at least must have read it. But when she said she was glad to meet him because he had liked her book well enough to select it, he stared at her gloomily, the light strong on his bald forehead, and said, "Don't thank me. Now I suppose you'll write another. Or perhaps—" a spark through his gloom, "you're one of these one-book authors."

"I don't know," said Hazel. "I haven't thought of another one yet."

Then, slyly—she couldn't help it, he looked so cross—"Would you mind if I did?" (After all, someone had to write books if a critic kept his job!)

"Mind? Oh, no. Not at all." (Nothing in his life!) "You know, I've been considering a project. I think authors should be licensed before they can practice. Like doctors, or lawyers." The tip of his thin nose twitched, and he stroked his chin thoughtfully. That idea would do for a column. "Board of examiners, penalties for illegal practice—why hasn't it been done long before?" He turned to the woman at his left, and Hazel heard him repeating his proposition with sardonic elaboration. Mr. Horn explained later, in a rapid two-minute survey of the evening before he handed Hazel into her taxi; "That's just Carlton's line, being rude to authors. Likes to bully 'em. What he said about your book wasn't bad. Some quotable phrases. Couldn't very well pan it when he helped pick it. Never heard him enthusiastic about anything except a treatise on the family life of the three-toed sloth. On the whole the evening was a great success. You made a nice little speech."

"I didn't know it was going to be broadcast. I was frightened." That awful disk, set up between her and all the staring eyes! If she'd known, she could have told John to tune in.

"One of my last minute breaks. One of the things I do best, getting breaks that way. Get a good rest. I'll give you a ring in the morning."

Hazel pushed back her coat and let it lie in a mound around her. She hadn't thought of needing a real evening wrap. In Lounsberry everyone just wore a winter coat because it was so cold at night, but here even the new beaver collar looked—well all right! wren-like—among velvets and ermine, even if the ermine was rabbit. Not that it made any difference. "If I'd been a Hottentot princess in beads maybe someone would have seen me. I'm not sure." But in her handbag was the envelope, heavy cream, with her name, and inside it an engraved slip. Not the real check. "I'll give you that tomorrow," Horn had said. "Have to figure out the deductions I've advanced." And on the table beside the bed lay the book.

Hazel reached for it, the black lace falling away from her arm. Her dress had been all right, she thought, although not striking— She turned the volume slowly, and slid the gold band carefully off. Then she opened it. She looked at the first page, and the printed words spoke to her in her own voice. Reading them was like life flowing back into her, it was like writing them again, and yet different, almost creation in reverse. She turned the page and read the next, wondering how she had happened to say just that, and yet feeling the words drop softly, rightly, as if she held within her the archetype from which they had been made, and each word fitted into its own place.

A long time later Hazel closed the book. She didn't know, really whether it was good or not, not being able to tell how much was there in words to reach other people and how much was in her own feeling. But she had written it, and for the first time she had read her own book. It's not like having a child, she thought, with sudden scorn for that old comparison. A child is separate from you right away, and a book— She laid the volume on the table. It's more like ectoplasm, it seems to be separate, there it is, and here I am, but it's really me, all the copies everywhere. She wondered, in alarm, what she had been up to, scattering herself in pieces all over the earth! But she did like that last scene, where the restless footed one of the third generation came home at last, and the woman he loved welcomed him, her hand upon the gate. She'd always liked the poem.

Her foot had gone to sleep, and she hobbled across to the dresser, unclasping the string of pearls (George's present last Christmas: he'd said he wished he could give her real ones, but these were pretty good). She poked them, still warm, into a double circle, and stamped on her prickling foot. She must get to bed, or she'd look dreadful tomorrow. She did now, with smudges under her eyes and a mazed whiteness on her face. Presently, her purse safe under her pillow and the table lamp drawn so close she couldn't miss it in the dark, she lay small and flat in the strange room, and looked out at the amber haze which filled the sky, a haze which was not steady but fluctuated to the rhythm of flashing signs and beacons.

Mr. Horn telephoned the next morning. He was rushed, number of things just came up, but he'd made an appointment for her with Grawn, an agent, to talk over movie possibilities. Just run over and have a chat. "Don't commit yourself to anything. See what he says. I'll take care of any actual offers. Then drop in here at the office. A few advance reviews have come in. Um, fair. Fair."

Hazel waited for a long time in an outer office, with engrossed and oblivious people rushing past her until she suffocated under the dull cloak of invisibility. She peered at herself in a small mirror. She'd bought a lipstick that morning and tried it; now she wasn't sure it helped. At last a bored young woman escorted her down corridors and into Mr. Grawn's office. He sat with a dingy window at his back, a little man with a large head gray-crested, and a slow, deep voice.

"Ah, yes, Mrs. Browning. Horn suggested I see you. Just what have you in mind?"

"Nothing," said Hazel, trying to arrange herself easily on the hard chair. "Mr. Horn told me to come."

"Ah, yes, let's see, your book is going well, is it?" His small, white hands moved slowly among papers, found a memorandum. " 'Your Hand Upon the Gate.' I don't believe that title would sell. Ah, yes. Prize book, Horn says he's launching big publicity campaign. Frankly, Mrs.—" he glanced at the memorandum— "Browning Curtis, it would be well to wait. If the book is a smash hit, we can work up good bids for it. Otherwise, I may say the motion picture business is incalculable. No one can prophesy. Why, I could tell you—" And then for what seemed hours to Hazel, blinking her eyes against the light, seeing Mr. Grawn's stiff gray crest prismatic, he did tell her, stories of books he had sold, of books he had not sold, of fabulous prices, of extraordinary rivalries, until he ended, accusingly, "If it had been serialized, that would help. You could, of course, run out to Hollywood? If the book is a hit, I often place authors. Say five hundred a week, to begin with? It's valuable experience for a time. You mustn't stay too long, though, or you lose your public. Nice of you to drop in."

Hazel, dropping down in the elevator, wasn't sure whether she would find herself in Hollywood when she walked out upon the street. It was still New York, and she asked a traffice policeman how to reach the offices of Horn and Westerby, if she walked. If she went under her own power, she might step out of the Alice-in-Wonderland daze. Five hundred a week. How could she go to Hollywood? Anyway, who had asked her to go? Three blocks over, five up. But walking in New York was not like walking in Lounsberry. Her usual firm, smooth stride, which could shake nonsense out of her mind, turning into dodgings and delays. It's not really walking, she thought, it's wriggling through.

Again she waited, although not so long, in the triangular little reception room at Horn and Westerby's, watching the telephone girl shift plugs and say "Who's calling? Just a moment, please, Who's calling? Just—" Mr. Horn burst into the room, seized her hand, ushered her swiftly along the corridor. Had she seen Grawn? Of course, it was just a wedge. An opening attack. Oh, Grawn never read anything! You bet he'd grab it if it showed signs of going over big. Now she must look at the lay-out for the ads. He whisked smooth sample sheets past her, rattling off names, the *Times*, the *Tribune*, some of the trade journals, these little ones for

71

daily papers. Hazel's color deepened. All those about her book! "Of course, Mrs. Curtis, a publisher can do only so much. He can launch a book, and we're doing a big job on the launching. After that, it's up to the book. Word of mouth is what does it. If people like it—get to talking about it— If you have any suggestions, any original publicity— I'm sorry to say some of the reviews aren't as whole-hearted as they might be. Trouble with a prize novel, reviewers like to say why in the name of God was this book chosen! Don't mind them. I suppose you'd like to look them over? This one's the best. Good selling review. Tells the story, see, catches interest, calls it good wholesome book of familiar type. Carlton comes out and says he preferred 'Alley Cat.' That was runner-up, going to put it out next week. Here, look 'em over." He pushed toward her a pile of clippings and blue-penciled sheets. "Remember, a panning's better than no attention. May start talk. Yes, Bingham?"

The secretary's spectacles glinted at Hazel. "You here again?" they suggested. Aloud she said, "Mr. Smith says he has an appointment with you."

"So he has." Horn jumped up. "I'll leave you here, Mrs. Curtis. Amuse yourself."

When, an hour or so later, he came back, Hazel was sitting straight and still beside the desk, on which she had ranged the papers, her eyes dark with bewilderment under the thick lashes, petals of vivid color on her cheekbones. Mr. Horn's tentative glance investigated her mood.

"Mr. Horn," she asked, "did you by any chance read my book?"

"Why, yes, certainly. Of course." He flung himself into his chair, lighted a cigarette. "You smoke? No."

"What did you think of it?"

"Damned good book, of course. Now don't let some of those cracks disturb you. I never knew an author yet who could take criticism. Have to take it. Part of the game."

"Are you sure these are all about my book?" Hazel pointed at the clippings. "I thought maybe they mixed up the titles."

Horn jackknifed into a sudden laugh. "Say, that's rich!" he shouted. "That's a good one on reviews!"

"I wasn't sure. They blame me for so many different things I thought there might be a mixup." She shivered, as if she had been driven confused and stumbling down a long gauntlet where men cracked whips of phrases as she fled. No book ignoring the social and economic problems of the present deserves consideration. Style is spontaneous and fresh, but plot is hackneyed. Style is labored with affectations of modernity, although the plot has originality. Another family cycle; surely the time has come when we might be spared this banal repetition. Refreshing to find an authentic picture of the American scene, although the characters unfortunately are mere wooden types. The characters have a three-dimensional vitality; it is a pity that the action is nothing but moralizing, a projection of Miss Curtis' ideas of good and evil. The book has promise; the prize will give it undue attention, and no doubt destroy the author's future growth. Carlton's column had been the worst, perhaps because she had met him, and could hear him saying the words as she read. "There was another entry, virile, salty, full-bodied, with the tenacious hold on life hinted in the title, 'Alley Cat.' Not a pretty little book to win a prize. But Horn and Westerby, having presented the circulating library readers with a chocolate marshmallow, may put themselves on the publishing mat with a real book. Watch for it."

"Anyway—" Hazel thrust out her chin, her upper lip drew down long and Irish, her color deepened—"I did get the prize! Even if it made them mad. That's the way they sound, just mad!"

"Sure," said Horn, "they're all frustrated novelists. Don't let 'em worry you. Now, what have you got on for this afternoon?"

You couldn't say nothing to a question like that. Hazel shook her head.

"I have to run out of town. Terribly sorry."

(Golf, thought Hazel. Or fishing. She knew that masculine air of inevitable, foredoomed preoccupation.)

"I thought you might like to shop, look around a little. The office is closed Saturday, of course. But Monday is a full day. In the morning I want you to see a pair of the cleverest radio agents in town. Fleeman and Flower. Chance to do a program for them. One of their biggest clients is looking for something new. In the afternoon you're to autograph books at one of the department stores. I've got the girls here all lined up to drop in at intervals, get a book, get it autographed, suggest there's a big demand, see? We can use 'em later. Why don't you look around for a place to settle here in town? You might as well stick around."

"But I've got a family," said Hazel.

"Bring 'em along. Good thing for a writer to be here on the ground. Get to know the right people."

"My husband wouldn't leave his business." Hazel braced her heels on the floor. If she didn't watch out, Horn's dynamo would have whirled her forever away from Lounsberry and the three there. She would be a star sucked out of her proper constellation by his velocity, and go spinning alone in the dry unreality of his orbit.

"He's a dentist, isn't he? Hm. Might be openings here. I wouldn't know. Out of my line. You aren't planning to leave him, then? Not that divorce or separation is much use as publicity. Too common. But more than one woman when she pulls off a big thing of her own finds it makes a difference."

Hazel set her teeth into her lower lip. It wouldn't do to tell her publisher that he was impertinent. Anyway, his inquiry had a terrible impersonality, quite as if she were a horse he had entered for a race, and he looked at her teeth, ran a hand over her hocks.

"Let's see." He flung out his wrist, read his watch. "Why don't you run down to Atlantic for the week-end? I can telephone for a reservation. Now, why isn't that an idea?"

"No." Hazel got to her feet quickly, before he shipped her off. "You needn't have me on your mind. I'd much rather stay here. Only I'd like some of my money."

Mr. Horn's face changed; he became almost husbandly. "Certainly. Now, you've had five hundred. I suppose if I give you the rest, you'll spend it before you leave town!" He waggled a finger at her.

"I'd like a thousand now," said Hazel with dignity. She hadn't meant to ask for so much, but he drove her to it.

After further persiflage Mr. Horn arranged to deposit it for her, and wrote out a card of identification. "Not a bad little publicity stunt, prize author goes shopping. See if I can't get one of the sob sisters to do a story. I'll be seeing you Monday, then. Have a good time, and don't buy Brooklyn Bridge!"

Hazel went back to her hotel, and as she ate luncheon she wrote on a slip of paper the names George, Lorna, and John, with dotted lines after each. A dress for Lorna. A watch for John, a good wrist watch, something like Mr. Horn's. For George—he'd like something for the office. She found the telephone directories in a long corridor of booths, and studied the Red Book until she had several addresses. The desk clerk, being urged, indicated which one was not too far from the hotel, and presently Hazel had convinced a supercilious young woman in an outer office that she was in earnest about buying a piece of dental equipment, and followed a tall, thin salesman into the show rooms. She wanted something quite expensive. No, she wasn't a dentist, her husband was. No, not in town, in Lounsberry. That was in Michigan. (Still there, solid and familiar, in spite of these strange days!) He had a good office chair. And an X-ray. In the next room she stopped, entranced, as if George stood beside her, and all his delight in perfect mechanism flowed into her. "These are the newest units, chromium and a new treatment of steel." Marvelous shining robots, with hinged and crooked elbows, dazzling metal threads through intricate wheels. The salesman swung the arms, turned a button and the drills sang and water gurgled. "You can spend as much as you like, depending upon the accessories." She was one with George again as she signed the check and arranged for the shipping. Just as quickly as possible. Freight was too slow. Express. She wished it might go by air-mail!

Lorna's dress was easy, and John's watch, and when at the end of the day Hazel returned to the hotel she was thoroughly happy. She could even stand being called a chocolate marshmallow! She bought an evening paper, and rode up to her room. For a time she sat at the window, watching the geometric silhouette of the city flatten against the sky, the sharp forms merging into dimness, light-pierced. Then she spread the paper open on her knees. At the third page she stopped, the sheet crackling in her fingers. "Prize-winning Housewife Visits City." It stared up at her, shadowless, blanched by the flashlight, startled, a picture with her name beneath it. Hazel read through the article, a half column. Then she re-read it, her face white as anger closed a tight hand over her heart, her breathing. At least, she thought, George would never see it. Nobody at home would see it. "Modest, pleasant little middle-aged housewife comes to city to claim prize. From hamlet nestling in hills of distant Michigan—" I suppose they think we have Indians and buffaloes—"Slight air of distracted anxiety, as she thinks of babies she has left for this momentous trip." Hazel folded the paper, picture inside, and thrust it into the wastebasket. "Somewhat dazed by the city, by the whole adventure, she finds herself figure in fairy tale." I never said that! "She thought it would be nice to write a book, and here she is! We can see housewives all over the land hearing of her good luck, neglecting pots and pans to dash off best sellers."

"I'm not middle-aged! I'm not modest. I—I certainly don't feel pleasant!" Hazel confronted her reflection in the mirror, and color ran up her soft throat into her face. She wondered who wrote the article. One of those smart, hard young things at the dinner last night. "It's dreadful, having to know how I seem to strangers, who don't know me, don't care—". She looked about the room, her anger changing subtly into desperation. Suppose she had to stay here always, with such articles, or such book reviews all she had! She would cease to exist, that was all. She wouldn't be herself any longer, because no one would know what she was. She moved swiftly to the telephone on a stand; she couldn't even stop to sit down.

"I want an out-of-town number," she said, her voice urgent. "In Michigan. Lounsberry. Two eight six three. No, I'll speak to anyone there."

"What's your room number?" and then, "I will con-nect you with long distance."

Listening, Hazel heard the quick calling of exchanges across the country, Buffalo, Cleveland, Detroit, each transporting her nearer home, strides on seven-league boots across the land.

"Here's your number!" and then John's voice, his blessed telephone voice, affecting boredom, the quality thinned a trifle. Tears in her eyes, in her throat. "It's Mother, John!"

"Why, hello!" His drawl quickened. "How are you? Say, you sounded swell on the radio. Dad saw in the paper about the broadcast, and we all sat up."

"You did! Are you all right, John?"

"Sure. How's ole New York?"

"Oh, it's fine. Is Father there?"

"No. He went in town to a meeting."

(He hadn't said anything about a meeting—)

"And Lorna went off as soon as she ate her dinner."

"Where did she go?"

"I dunno. Ketch me asking that gal anything."

"Poor Johnny, all alone!"

"Well, I got my hat on, all set for the movies. Some of the fellows are going."

"Don't be too late, will you, dear. It's not long since you were sick." Hazel closed her eyes, her fingers tight over the instrument, straining for each inflection of his voice. She could see him, thin shoulders hunched as he bent toward the telephone there in the hall.

"Say, when you coming home?"

"Very soon. Next week."

"Not till then?"

"I have to do some things Monday. I have to see some radio men, John! Maybe they'll give me a job. And perhaps I'll be in the movies." She laughed, and the excitement she had not felt suddenly prickled through her veins as she offered it to John. "But I'll tell you all about it soon. Good-night, Johnny. Tell Father and Lorna I'm sorry they weren't home."

She held the receiver hard against her ear until the click which followed his "So long" broke the thread between them. She felt better. Like having her foot go to sleep, the way these two days had made her feel, and John's voice sent blood racing so that her own self woke up. She wouldn't let them get her down again.

Monday evening Mr. Horn escorted Hazel to the Wolverine, although he protested her departure. "To be sure, there weren't many customers at the bookstore, but you can't rush things. If you'd stay a few weeks——"

*Many,* thought Hazel. Two, besides the girls from the office who had pretended to be customers, and she'd sat on that chair for three hours. "If you really need me, I could come back. But I don't want to stay now." She had been stern with herself on Saturday and Sunday, buying a little guide book and booting herself over town to see what a visitor to New York should see, but she wasn't going to put in any more days paying solitary visits to fishes at the Aquarium or marbles at the Museum. She was going home.

Mr. Horn advised the porter about the placing of her bags. On the seat beside her he piled a large box of candy, all red cellophane and bows, a smaller glossy florist's box, and several magazines. Then he lolled against the arm of the seat, knee up, ears pricked for the "All Aboard," which would release him. "I hope you've had a good time," he said. " 'Sbeen a pleasure to meet you. You try a few scripts for Fleeman and Flower, and I'll see if I can get a contract out of them. Of course they felt, too, that you ought to stay here, be on hand for conferences."

"I couldn't do what they want," said Hazel, and for a moment Mr. Fleeman's face swam out from the green plush of the opposite seat, coming too close to hers as it had in the morning interview, black velvet hair, deeply lined white skin, sharp beak. "Something like Amos and Andy, only not colored, with a touch of Eddie Cantor, a few old songs thrown in (people like hymns), a real heart interest, and perhaps room for a touch of amateur hour."

"They don't know what they want," said Horn, briskly, "except they know what's pulled the best the last year or so. All those radio guys are crazy, but if you give 'em something good they'll pay real money for it. You try."

77

Hazel had her face set toward home. Although the train had not yet moved, she had already surrendered herself to the journey, and Horn's words danced like the final faint notes of a fantasia terminating with the wind instruments.

"Don't worry about your book," he was saying. "We're backing it with all we've got. Well, happy landing!" He pumped her hand, and was gone.

Hazel arranged her coat and hat neatly on the opposite seat. She untied the metallic cord and peered into the florist's box. More gardenias. She'd give them to Lorna, if they lasted until morning. She opened one of the magazines, turning the thick, smooth pages of advertisements until she reached an illustration. Posed against a pillar, a stairway winding below her to nothing at all, urns and palms behind her, incredibly tall and slender and arching backward, one arm above her head, so that the satin sheath of gown caught highlights on every curve she owned, stood a girl, her eyelids inscrutable not with the weight of ages of sin, like Mona Lisa, but with well applied eyeshadow. Hazel stared at the photograph. Now that, she thought, is the way you're supposed to look. What it really is is just a picture a man took of a girl in a dress that wasn't even her own, a girl from some small town who had that kind of figure. Like that girl Lorna knew who got a job modeling. The train was moving now, and Hazel leaned back, hands folded on the magazine, her face close to the window. If she could put her finger on it, she'd know something about New York that was like that photograph. The New York she'd seen, at least. For here, outside the window as the train climbed above street level and pried its way between dingy, close-pressing apartment buildings, was another city, washing flying on a fire-escape, a woman leaning with elbows on a dirty cushion, and then as the train gathered speed, too quick a winding past of interiors for Hazel to see anything but lights which marked rooms where people lived. She sighed. The whole fantasia of the past days, with its abrupt rhythm, its dissonances, was growing very faint. Later she might decide what it all meant. But if she'd known what happened when you wrote a book—no, not when you wrote it; when you had it published, when you took a prize! She could see dark water now, and great advertising signs flooded with light, and dimly on the window the shape of her own face. She thrust out her chin, and worried a little at her lip. She'd do it again.

Horn walked jauntily through the station. It was late, but Millbeau, the salesman for the eastern territory, had agreed to wait for him. Like to run over the order sheets with him, tell him about the campaign for "Alley Cat." "The Hand" wasn't going to do much here in the East. Carlton had crabbed it, but he'd have to howl for the "Cat," he'd committed himself. Out in the sticks the "Hand" might move better. Women like Hazel ought to go for it, prize band on it and all. But he'd cut the advertising, at least till reorders started. Jeese, was he glad to be rid of that woman! He paused a moment at the curb, snapping his fingers, eyeing a girl that passed, her tight dark dress catching the good line from thigh to knee. Not that she wasn't a good sort, nice eyes, if she knew how to use 'em. But personally he didn't fall for that flower of the field type. Didn't get on with 'em. Something appalling about that kind of naïveté. Probably never see her again. Didn't think she had another book in her. If he didn't get his money (Westerby's!) back on her, he would on "Alley Cat." First book sweet and pure, second strictly modern and soiled, good beginning for the firm. Then he had at least another half dozen manuscripts he could spread over the summer and fall, if nothing better came in. Just as he'd thought, the prize had been good bait, giving them a quick choice for their list, even if Westerby'd been skeptical about the sales value of a prize. "Make it a million, someone'd hear you. Ten grand? Bah!" And Horn had snapped, "What you think this is, a relief project?" That had tickled Westerby. He knew how to handle him! Then Horn darted across the street, swinging his arms in excess motion, jostling the crowd as he hurried, his nostrils wide, his face shifting in quick grimaces, all the superficial aspects of the city, the brilliance of the shop windows, the concentrated drive of the crowds, the rhythm of traffic the stimuli which nourished him.

Hazel had not wired that she was coming home. The children would be in school, and George would not like to leave his office. She took the bus out from the city, watching with content the familiar, flat country wheel past, fields winter-brown, farm dooryards muddy, the only hint of spring some quality in the sunlight, as if the angle at which it struck meant a stirring in the earth. The bus stop in Lounsberry was just across from George's office. She wanted to see him so much that she felt in every muscle the climbing of his stairs, the pushing open of the door. And then she'd find someone waiting in his office, thumbing over a magazine, and George, white-coated, bending over a patient in the chair. Their meeting must be more than that! No interference. No static! But how to get home? She could telephone the Murphy boy. If he were home, he'd come for her. As she turned toward the grocery store, Bill Pakaloupus, the owner's son, came out, arms full of bags and baskets, the morning orders.

"Morning, Mis' Curtis." He bobbed his head. "Just going out to your place. You going away?" He saw her luggage.

"No, I've been," said Hazel. She glanced at the Pakaloupus car, a battered sedan converted into a truck on week-days by removing the rear seat. "Could you give me a lift, Bill? I don't want to bother Dr. Curtis."

"Sure. Climb right in."

Hazel did, her eyes bright with amusement. Famous author comes home.

"I seen a woman at your house Sattiday," said Bill, as he clattered around the corner. "I thought mebbe you was sick."

"No. I've been to New York."

"Yeuh? Was you down on Washington Street? The old man lived there when he first come across. Guess you're glad to be back, ain'tcha?"

Hazel hung on to the rattly door-frame as they swooped up the street.

"Can't waste time." Bill grinned, his teeth white in his swarthy face. Then when he swung into the driveway at the Curtis house and stopped, with all the groceries bouncing, he refused Hazel's money. "Ain't you one of our good customers? 'Sa real treat to have company." He carried her suitcase to the front door, and disappeared around the house with a basket.

The front door was locked, and Hazel waited. Bill backed out of the yard, waving to her, and presently the housekeeper opened the door. "Why, Mrs. Curtis!" Her high, firm bosom pumped reproachful breath through her words. "I didn't know you were coming home today!" She was larger than Hazel, with an effect of polish on the planes of her wide, hard face.

"No, I didn't send word," said Hazel, managing to enter her own house. "Everything all right?"

"The Doctor said he wouldn't be home for lunch, and the children said they'd get something at the drug store because it was too far to walk and so I never planned a thing for this noon because all I ever take is a cup of tea."

"I'll call up my husband," said Hazel. "I guess you can find something."

She waited until Lizzie's broad and still reproachful rear had vanished into the kitchen. Then she called George. Yes, this was Hazel. No, she wasn't calling from New York, she was home! And George said, "For heck's sake, why didn't you let us know?"

"I knew you'd be busy this morning." Hazel swallowed a thistle before she went on. "You've got the car, haven't you? Can't you pick up John and Lorna, and come home for lunch?"

"Of course I want to see you! But I didn't know you'd be here. I made arrangements—if I can get hold of the party, I'll let you know. But it's pretty awkward." And then, almost caustically, "Have you had a grand time?"

"Oh, yes. Wonderful. Don't bother about lunch." Hazel held the instrument at a distance, hating it. "I'll see you tonight."

"It's not that lunch is a bother, Hazel. Please be reasonable. How could I know when you were coming? You told John you didn't know—" After a moment's pause he went on, and now his voice had lost its self-vindicating tone, had grown crisply professional. A patient must have come into the office. "The party I have the appointment with isn't in town yet, but if I can get hold of them, I'll explain. But it's a piece of business. Quite important."

"Well," said Hazel, "if I have to have a tooth pulled, would you have time to see me?"

"What's that? Is that tooth I filled bothering you again?"

She laughed. "No. *That's* not bothering me. See you later."

Ridiculous to feel such disappointment. She knew how George disliked suddenness or change. He planned his day, and he wanted it to go by schedule. He planned his life—and what a jolt she'd given him! Her mouth was soft and contemplative, and the pencil in her fingers drew a row of little birds with cocky tails and stiff legs, a row that marched across the cover of the telephone directory. Suppose he never accepted the jolt. She bent her head a trifle, evoking the quality of his voice. Clear, fresh, each syllable, each word distinct; it's a blond voice, thought Hazel. No shadows. But strong, like sunlight. She had heard it all these years, and never thought before how precisely George it was. Things have got to be all right, she told herself, ignoring the way a shred of apprehension clung to her mood, for all she brushed away her disappointment.

She considered telephoning to the school. But John and Lorna would not have time for the long walk home, and perhaps they, like George, had made dates for their sandwiches at the drug store counter. She'd been gone only—she counted off the days on her fingers—five days, and when she came back, she found the pattern so changed it didn't include her at all! What would happen if she went to Hollywood? But women did do things like that, lots of them. She heard Lizzie stomping about overhead, her feet expressing annoyance that Hazel had taken advantage of her, arriving unheralded before the roomwork was done. Better wait till she's through, thought Hazel. The living room was in stiff order, the small rugs each in the wrong place. Hazel moved about quietly, changing the rugs, pulling chairs out from the wall, until the room was hers again. She glanced over the mail piled on a corner of the table, advertisements, circulars, letters from three clipping bureaus enclosing several of the reviews she had already endured. Then she carried her bag to her own room and unpacked, alert for signs of what George had been doing these five days. He must have worn his new gray suit today. The blue one needed pressing; she'd call the tailor. Then she saw, on the lower shelf of the night stand between the twin beds, her book! Her heart gave a thud, and she couldn't move. An end of the gold prize band showed; George had marked his place with it. Where had he got it? And what, dear God, what did he think about it? Imagine him lying there, turning page after page in his slow, deliberate way, George, who never read anything except the paper and his dental journals! He might have said something, when she telephoned.

Her hands trembled as she hung away the black lace dress, the new silk dressing gown. She took off the brown silk, and buttoned herself into a clean linen frock. She peered into the bathroom cabinet. Those cold tablets had been moved. Now which of them— Still seeking news, she went into John's room. The brown rep curtains hung in straight folds, the brown and yellow cover was spread smooth on the bed, a few books stood between the bronze lion bookends she had given him Christmas. His neckties were a stringy jumble in the top drawer. She sat down on the bed, crossing her ankles, and her heel struck something hard. Her hand, groping, touched smooth leather, and she was on her feet, drawing out a suitcase. John's, bought for camp last summer. She sank to the floor beside it, her knees weak, and pushed at the catch. John's suitcase, packed! Pajamas, shirts, sweater, little balls of socks, the case with brushes, the cup he'd won in the Junior tennis match. She closed the lid, snapped the lock, and pushed the case out of sight beneath the bed. Then she got to her feet, brushing out wrinkles in the blue linen. Whatever he'd planned, he must come home first. But where, this time of year— Had George said, done something? Once, when John was just a little fellow, he'd run away. But all boys do that—Hazel could see him, riding home with the milkman, dirty and tired, but proud because the man let him hold the reins. Was he in school, after all? If he'd packed the suitcase, he meant to take it. She wanted to run through the streets to the school, to be sure he was there, safe. But he'd never forgive her. She would have to wait. Perhaps it was some school trip, some legitimate plan she had not heard about. Oh, John!

She went quickly to the door of Lorna's room, her eyes dark, her lip caught between her teeth. Rose and blue, ruffled and feminine orderliness, surely she would find no clue to disaster, no vague threat here. She looked at the small painted desk, her hand lifting, fingers curved, importunate. The drawers there might have notes from that boy. That was different, prying. Fair enough to look for clues, when she had such hunger. But no prying. She opened the closet door, and the dresses swayed on their hangers, neat blue pasteboard containers for shoes, for stockings, sat in decorous rows, and a whiff of sachet blew out. Hazel closed the door and went away. Her daughter's room kept secrets as well as did her daughter. But she's like George, thought Hazel. She has his passion for fitness, for orderliness. If she has it about her own life——

Lizzie served tea, toast, and an egg, with an air of that being more than one might expect, especially as she'd been trying to finish the ironing. She'd ordered the things for dinner before she knew Mis' Curtis was coming, and she hoped it would suit. Hazel wandered into the living room. She supposed she'd better keep the woman for a while, at least. "Although I might feel less an interloper in my own house if I had the dinner to get."

She tried to take a nap, but when she lay down the clatter of the Pullman trucks over the ties began again in her head. The minister's wife telephoned. Would Mrs. Curtis meet with the Ladies' Aid on Friday, and give a little talk about her trip to New York? They would charge ten cents admission for the tea and sandwiches. "I knew you were back," she added, "because I saw you with the grocer boy." (You would! thought Hazel.) Yes, she could come Friday, unless something came up to prevent.

"You aren't going to Hollywood right away, are you? I said I'd never believe Mrs. Curtis would leave her family to mingle with the kind of people we hear of out there, even if we do try to be charitable, where there's so much smoke——"

"Who said I was going?"

"It was in the paper, how you were considering an offer."

Mr. Horn must have put it in! And George must have seen it! "I'm

83

not going immediately," said Hazel. "Nothing's settled. I won't go before Friday, anyway." She could see the face of the woman, spare, dun, with a look of bitter exhaustion in the sagging folds about mouth and chin, like that of a swimmer spent from the effort to keep above the surface of gentility. Not since the depression had the church made up the full amount of the Reverend Mr. Morrison's small salary. She must almost hate Hazel for her sudden fortune! "I'll see you then," Hazel finished, "I'm sure I can make it."

This would account for George's tone on the telephone. He saw her alighting for a moment, en route to California. "We'll play it up," Horn had said. "That's the way to create a demand, make those fellows think someone else is hot on your track." She went uneasily upstairs, thinking that if she had alighted she had found a threat of quicksands where the earth had always been firm and stable. She'd change her dress. Not one of the new ones. The blue silk with the lace collar that George always liked. She dressed slowly, watching the hands of the small clock crawl. The children couldn't possibly come before four, and they might be later.

It was five when John came. Hazel sat in the living room, the evening paper unread on her lap, her cold hands folded over it. She heard a car stop, heard John's, "So long. Thanks for the lift." She went quickly into the hall, the secret and ignored dread of the long afternoon peeling away like a dry husk. He pushed open the door and looked at her, silent, but she saw a great gulp move in his thin throat. "Hello," he said, "when'd you blow in?"

"Oh, this morning." She had to kiss him, had to run her fingers, feather-light, over his stiff young head, although she held tight to the passion of tenderness which cried in every nerve-end for release. "How are you, Johnny? Come tell me what you've been doing. Did you miss me?" She slipped a hand under his arm, pulled him into the living room, down on the divan beside her.

John let his strapped bundle of books plunk to the floor, and dangled his hands between his knees. "I noticed you weren't around," he drawled. "You don't seem much different."

"You haven't changed much yourself." Hazel laughed. She thought, that line his head makes, rising from his neck, that sweet boy line— But his color isn't good, too white.

"Say, did they really give you the money?"

"Yes, they really did. I brought you something. It's there on the table, the small box."

John looked at her, his mouth moving around words, and then, without speaking, he crossed to the table, his coat hitched up in funny wrinkles. He came back with the box, and opened it slowly. The flat gold rectangle lay in his palm, and he twitched at the leather strap. "Gee, it's a pippin! It's a good one, too. But you know—" his face twitched, "Dad'll probably say I oughtn't to have it."

"What nonsense, John! Father isn't like that." Hazel pushed back his cuff, and buckled the watch about his thin wrist. "There!"

"You don't know." John held out his hand, shook down the sleeve to see how much of watch remained in view. "You don't know—" and suddenly his face had despair, complete because without perspective, his parted lips dry, his forehead creased. "He's fed up with me. He said so." He gulped. "He'll tell you about it, don't worry. First I meant to clear out, get the hell away. Only then you called up, and I didn't like to run out on you. An' I was talking with a fellow down by the freight yard, and he says times ain't what they used to be and you can't bum your way any more because if you haven't got a job then you have to go on relief or in a camp, and I couldn't because they'd look up my family. So I thought I'd wait and talk it over with you."

Hazel sat very still. He seemed balanced so precariously on a thin taut wire of confidence that a clumsy move from her would knock him headlong beyond her reach, into what pit of foolhardiness or danger? "Would you mind," she asked, "telling me what happened? I'm glad you waited. I should have felt let down if I'd come home—" She couldn't go on. That suitcase!

"The car got smashed." John hunched forward, knees pressing his hands together. "I was just driving along, and this fellow comes around the corner too fast and skids into me. It was sleety, see? Honest, I didn't do a thing wrong, but the fenders were crumpled and the running board stove up, and Dad said I oughtn't to be out loose."

"He'd be upset, John, but he didn't mean——"

"You didn't hear him!" John's fingers dug into his hair. "I can't help it if a mug skids into me! I can't help it if I haven't got a license yet. I just took the car to go down town, I wasn't going on any joy ride the way he said."

"You weren't hurt," said Hazel, softly.

"I wish I had been."

"Oh, hush! The car can be repaired, and your father was just worried——"

"He stays mad—" a glint of humor touched John's mouth, "because he has to walk and that reminds him all the time."

"Anyone may have an accident." Hazel spoke briskly. "Now you unpack your suitcase and hang around with us a little longer. I sort of like having you here."

John straightened his shoulders, and rolled his eyes at her, round and surprised. "You knew—" he began, when outside another car stopped. "See here," he said, "when you go to Hollywood——"

"Sh!" said Hazel. "They're coming." And close to his ear she added, "You stick around, and if ever I should go, I'll take you along."

Then George and Lorna were in the hall, Lorna with little shrieks of welcome, George with a restrained and somewhat questioning heartiness.

Lorna loved her dress, white chiffon, soft and swirling. She held it up and posed before the hall mirror, and Hazel thought, she looks happier, less subdued, something has happened to her, too. "And this is for you." Hazel handed George the catalogue of dental supplies, open at the smooth cut of the marvelous dentists' unit, all black and shining chromium. "Only I couldn't bring it. It's coming soon, by express." George looked.

"You mean you ordered it for me?"

"Yes, sir." Hazel stood close to him, her finger on the page. "That very one! Don't you like it?"

"Yes, yes. It's just what I've needed."

"If it isn't exactly the one you want, we could send a wire—" Hazel pushed herself against that skim of reservation over his acceptance. "What isn't right, George? I wanted it to be perfect."

"It's quite all right. This is one of the best supply houses. I am afraid you were pretty extravagant."

Hazel shook her head. She knew that almost uttered *but,* that withholding of the kind of delight he should have. Better let it alone, rang a small warning. She couldn't, she had to dash on, no matter what! "You might as well tell me," she said. "It's really not a trifle, and we might still change it——"

"Trifle! Of course not. There's nothing to tell. I was just wishing you might have consulted me——"

(Dear Heavens, was his pride hurt again?) "But George, darling, you don't consult about presents!"

"You see, I practically gave an order for just such a unit this very noon. That shows I really want it!" He was defensive, prodded into explanation. "I meant to buy it on time, of course. But it would have been nice if you could have placed the order here. I've taken a good deal of her time."

"At luncheon?" asked Hazel, and down the street like a picture on a banner unfurling in a gust of angry wind marched the figure of that saleswoman, that red-winged blackbird person, arrogant and smart. You had luncheon with her, you wouldn't come home, said Hazel's sealed, dark look. And why not, after all you've been up to, answered George's steady, unrepentant gaze. This, thought Hazel, can't go on now, with the children listening. It must wait. Her stiff smile at George was a rain ticket. That was one thing about having children. You had to postpone settling difficulties, and sometimes after such postponement you couldn't find them again. Either they had evaporated, or you had mislaid them and they waited to trip you in some dark corner of your life.

"Dinner should be ready," she said. "I'm famished. Last night, on the train, I was too tired to eat, and Lizzie wouldn't give me much lunch. She, like the rest of you, hadn't expected me. Wash your faces, my lambs, and let's sit down."

With the soup, Hazel began an account of her trip to New York. As she talked, she listened, thinking, Mr. Horn should hear me! He'd give me a job as publicity liar right away. She had moved in a glitter, in a dazzle, rushing from triumph to triumph, meeting famous men and women, being toasted in cocktails, dined and wined and fêted, sought after by radio (they said my voice was excellent!), by motion pictures, pursued by rival publishers (Well, Mr. Horn said she was!), Lorna leaned forward, elbows on table, chin propped on crossed hands, her blue eyes wide, her lips parted. John listened more soberly, frowning, glancing at his father. And George ate methodically, with an air of one who has often heard such recitals, but as Hazel mounted with animation from one glory to another, his color changed, until instead of his usual clear flush on cheekbones, his face was pale except for a curious dull red along the line of jaw. She couldn't stop. She was saying, see, you never guessed how wonderful I am, you don't believe it now, this is the kind of life I could have, and you are indifferent, cruel, you take saleswomen in black suits and red feathers to lunch!

"Do they just have parties all the time? Honestly, Mother, I don't see how you can bear it to come back to Lounsberry!" Lorna sighed.

"They implored me to stay." Hazel was reckless. She'd decked that little brown wren of Mr. Horn's out with bird of paradise feathers until she almost believed the bird had worn them! "They said you had to be on the ground to catch the early worms. (Confound that bird.) I mean to meet the right people, work up radio programs, everything."

"You had to come home sometime," said John, "unless you stayed forever. Don't they know you've got folks? Parties all the time would be sickening, if you ask me."

"Oh, I'd love it!" said Lorna, and George did not look up from his plate.

After dinner Lorna wished to try on the new frock. Hazel watched George settle himself with the evening paper. "You don't have to go back to the office?" she asked, brightly, from the doorway.

"How can I, with no car? Or didn't John tell you about his latest piece of brilliance?"

John bolted up the stairs as if his father's words yapped at his heels.

"Oh, yes. Well, I'm glad something keeps you home. I mean you drive yourself just too hard."

George shifted his paper. "That was why you wrote your book, wasn't it? Those lonely evenings while the struggling dentist struggled."

Hazel drew a quick breath, and mounted the stairs, her feet clipping each step sharply. If he was going back to the very beginning, if those first silly interviews still rankled— For the first time, with a galvanic shock as if the thought had physical existence, Hazel said to herself, "Perhaps we are finished. I've destroyed his contentment, his notion of our marriage, of me, his sufficiency. He feels belittled." She paused at the top of the stairs, one hand clinging to the rail, and everything about her, the light, the walls, the sounds of the house receded. She was alone in a dark void, her blood had curdled in that keen pain under her heart, and no stimuli could touch her. She mustn't faint, that would be absurd. Somewhere she found her will, she stirred her curdled blood, she drew light and sound and the shape of walls and floor back into her consciousness.

"See, Mother, how do you fasten this?" Lorna was calling her, and Hazel went quickly into her room. She would finish with this, she would say good-night to Lorna and to John, and then, and then! Eagerness beat up in her, as if the very chemistry of her body had changed. She wanted to confront George, to have this out. She was through with sidewise fencing, with gentle subterfuge, with postponements.

She fastened the girdle, catching the sweet warmth of her daughter's round, soft body. Lorna pirouetted, the toes of her gold strapped dancing sandals shining. "It's adorable, Mother! Put on your new black dress and let's pretend it's a party. We could show Father."

"Not tonight." Hazel adjusted the puffed caps at the shoulders. "It is sweet, and it fits very well."

"It's only a paper moon, it's on-ly a painted sky—" sang Lorna, taking dance steps. "Did all the people have on lovely dresses at the parties? Didn't they think you looked simply swell in yours?"

Hazel sat down on the bed. Her exhibition mood had vanished, and said said, drily, "No one spoke of it." She sat there, her brow crinkling, while Lorna swept down stairs to show her father. Just what had happened to Lorna? Suddenly she had it, tangible as if it lay between her clasped fingers. Why, Lorna was actually thinking about her, Hazel! Little, first attempts— She had moved a step out of the childish prison of her self. Hazel watchèd the girl draw the soft clinging folds carefully over her head, watched her move about the room, thinking how sweet she is, that milk and honey white and gold, just that bra' and panties— "However do you keep warm enough?" she said.

"Oh, I couldn't breathe if I had to wear more clothes!" Lorna hung away the dress, tied the cord of a blue bathrobe firmly around her waist, and sat down beside Hazel. "You know—" she studied her pink toes, and then rushed on. "The girls think it's wonderful, to have a mother that can do what you do. They asked me everything about you. And Miss Chalmers, in English class, said we should be very proud, and maybe I might inherit some of your ability. I don't think I'll get married for years and years." She sighed. "I'm not really very smart, yet, but maybe—if I worked—I could do something, and go to New York and get my picture taken and everything." She hugged her round knees and brooded.

It hasn't been a total loss, then, thought Hazel. She relaxed, quiescent, receptive, waiting. At long, long intervals, and always after the girl had come out at the end of some experience, some stiff ascent in her development, she had a moment when she wished to talk. Just a few phrases, a seal the child placed on something she was done with.

"It isn't always being in love, is it, when you go all soft and squidgy inside being kissed, even if you think it is? Anyway, some boys just work too fast. Only when he got another girl right off, just because I wouldn't— But it's all right now. I see my future much more clearly."

"That's good, darling," said Hazel, quietly. She must keep her horror out of her voice. That dreadful boy!

"Good-night!" cried Lorna. "Look how late it is, and me with scads of homework." Confessional was over, she would have no more of it.

She jumped to her feet, tugging at the cord about her waist. "I'll just say it was so exciting having you come home that I forgot about work!"

Hazel gave her a quick hug. "Good girl," she said, and Lorna pretended to be absorbed in the book she had opened. John's door was ajar, and Hazel laid one hand against her throat, as she saw what the boy was doing. The trophy cup sat on the dresser, and John was stowing away in a drawer the contents of his suitcase. She stepped past silently, and went down the stairs.

George stood at a window of the living room, hands hooked together behind his back. He did not hear her, and Hazel looked at him, gray suit snug over truculent square shoulders, smooth light head well up, heels together. Her glance hurried about the familiar room, and all the furniture, the rugs, the lamps, chosen over so many years, lived with, looked back at her bleakly, meaning gone from them. George hadn't even turned on the radio! She walked in, selecting a strip of bare wood beyond the rug, and George said, not moving, "I thought you must have gone to bed."

"No," said Hazel. "I haven't."

"I thought you probably were pretty tired after all you've been doing."

"No, I'm not."

He turned then, reluctantly, as if he heard in her voice the restrained violence of her intention to get at him, as if he preferred more silence, more dodging, more sly undercuts.

"I just want to say this. I don't mean to stand in your way at all. You can go on to Hollywood or New York or wherever you want to. As Lorna said, Lounsberry isn't much to come back to. I can't compete with your offers. Lorna can go to college next fall. And John—a good stiff school somewhere would be good for him. He needs some sense pounded into him. We'll close the house. I'd rather live at the hotel. And later——"

Hazel sat down. "Yes," she prompted. "Later?"

"Later we could arrange for a divorce. A nice, quiet one, that wouldn't upset the children. You could stop off at Reno, say, on your way to Hollywood."

"You've got everything planned without even asking me——"

"Ask you? What was there to ask you? When you've shown in every move you've made what you really want! When all our life meant was that you were so bored you had to say so publicly! From the minute that telegram came about the prize you were different. You haven't known I existed. You haven't thought or cared about anything except what was

90

happening to you, what was being said about you." George spoke with a quiet, unmodulated fluency which meant that all these words, worn round and smooth from constant turning in his mind, rolled out with no effort. He could not know they were amazing, because to him they were rote-familiar. "I've always known you didn't really care about my work, you never listened when I tried to explain it, it was only the way I made a living for us, and now that you can make so much more money you don't have to pretend. I waited till you'd been to New York. I don't know quite what I hoped for. But now I see it's no use. All these grand things—I won't stand in your way. You wouldn't say this to me, because you'd think, mistakenly, 'Poor George! I mustn't hurt him.' But I believe in extracting dead teeth. I can't stand things as they are. It's upsetting my work." His blue eyes had a sudden wintry gleam. "Do you know what I did yesterday? I mixed up two sets of X-rays, and I pulled out the wrong tooth. That is, it was the right tooth in the wrong mouth. The plate showed a shadow, but it wasn't Mrs. MacAndrew's shadow." He broke off with an impatient gesture, his hand implying, but you don't care about that!

Hazel sat back in her chair, her hands limp, her heart beating so heavily she felt it in her wrists. Dear Lord, it was like reading another terrible interview, or review of her book, this trying to see what George saw of her! The self she thought she was had shrunk into a dried pea, rattling in shells provided by other people! She didn't care about dentistry. George had told her that before. But who else could, the way George did? Was it true, that she was selfish, indifferent, absorbed? That grand picture she'd built up, of herself in New York! She'd come rushing home, and now George was pitching her out, making her over into a hard, demanding creature— Perhaps——

"George Curtis," she said, fiercely, "are you getting rid of me for another woman? Are you—that woman you took to lunch? That saleswoman? Are you in love with her?"

"No," said George. "Not yet. We have things in common."

"Oh!" cried Hazel. She flung out her arms, her eyes brilliant under the heavy lashes. "George, you idiot! I won't be extracted. I'm not a dead tooth! You—" was it laughter that sprang from the tight coil of feeling?—"you've mixed your X-ray pictures all up. Oh, don't you know I've thought about you every second? I've been so wretched because you didn't like it—I've been terrified! I had to make you think I had a grand time, didn't I? I didn't even feel real until I got home—and then you wouldn't come— Oh, I won't let you be so stupid that you don't know what I want first!"

"You mean you'd give up your Hollywoods and everything?"

"I didn't mean that. We could leave that till it came up. But I mean if we tried, I'd get used to being somebody, not a big somebody, and you'd get used to it, and it wouldn't make any more difference than—than your filling a tooth!"

"You don't think I mind that all this happened to you?"

Hazel looked up at his strained face, the light gleaming on his forehead, on his neatly brushed fair hair.

"I had a feeling you were a different woman, not the girl I married. But I——"

Hazel slid to her feet, clasped her hands behind his head, and kissed him. "There!" she murmured, against his lips. "Same girl."

Later they sat together on the divan, hands linked, Hazel's head on his shoulder. She thought: he did mind, terribly, just what we neither of us ever will know. But I've got him back. Dear Lord, help me look interested in dentistry or machinery or anything else he wants to talk about! I do love him so much.

George said, clearing his throat, "I bought a copy of your book. Twofifty. They had quite a pile of them in Hudson's."

Hazel held her breath. She wanted to sit away from him, to watch his face, but she kept her head down against the solid shoulder.

"It's a good story. I don't see how you thought it all up. It wasn't exactly like your father's folks, although I recognized some of it. I was glad you ended it that way."

Hazel relaxed again. "I tell you," she said, dreamily, "when I write the next one, you can read it as I go along. You could make suggestions."

# Night Bus

## SAMUEL HOPKINS ADAMS

*Night Bus, a swift-moving story of our life and times, looks deeply, romantically and humorously into human hearts. The characters are endearing, the manner of telling deft and entertaining, and like* It Happened One Night *(the motion picture made from this story), it will captivate any one who enjoys gay adventure and romance.*

THROUGH THE resonant cave of the terminal, a perfunctory voice boomed out something about Jacksonville, points north, and New York. The crowd at the rail seethed. At the rear, Mr. Peter Warne hoisted the battered weight of his carryall, resolutely declining a porter's aid. Too bad he hadn't come earlier; he'd have drawn a better seat. Asperities of travel, however, meant little to his seasoned endurance.

Moreover, he was inwardly fortified by what the advertisement vaunted as "The Best Fifteen-cent Dinner in Miami; Wholesome, Clean and Plentiful." The sign had not exaggerated. Mr. Warne, who was an expert, knew. Appetite sated, ticket paid for, a safe if small surplus in a secure pocket; on the whole, he was content with life.

Behind him stood and, if the truth must be told, shoved a restive girl. Like him she carried her own luggage, a dressing case, small and costly. Like him she had paid for her ticket to New York. Her surplus, however, was a fat roll of high-caste bills. Her dinner at the ornate Seafoam Club had cost somebody not less than ten dollars. But care sat upon her somber brow, and her expression was a warning to all and sundry to keep their distance. She was far from being content with life.

All chairs had been filled when Peter Warne threaded the aisle, having previously tossed his burden into an overhead bracket. Only the rear bench, stretching the full width of the car, offered any space. Three passengers had already settled into it; there was accommodation for two more, but the space was piled full of baled newspapers.

"Hi!" said the late arrival cheerfully to the uniformed driver, who stood below on the pavement looking bored. "I'd like one of these seats."

The driver turned a vacant gaze upon him and turned away again.

"Have this stuff moved, won't you?" requested the passenger, with unimpaired good humor.

The official offered a fair and impartial view of a gray-clad back.

Mr. Warne reflected. "If you want a thing well done, do it yourself," he decided. Still amiable, he opened the window and tossed out four bundles in brisk succession.

Upon this, the occupant of the uniform evinced interest. "Hey! What d'you think you're doin'?" He approached, only to stagger back under the impact of another bale which bounded from his shoulder. With a grunt of rage, he ran around to the rear door, yanked it open and pushed his way in, his face red and threatening.

Having, meantime, disposed of the remainder of the papers, Mr. Warne turned, thrust his hand into his rear pocket, and waited. The driver also waited, lowering but uncertain. Out popped the hand, grasping nothing more deadly than a notebook.

"Well, come ahead," said its owner.

"Come ahead with what?"

"You were figuring to bust me in the jaw, weren't you?"

"Yes; and maybe I *am* goin' to bust you in the jor."

"Good!" He made an entry in the book. "I need the money."

The other goggled. "What money?"

"Well, say ten thousand dollars damages. Brutal and unprovoked assault upon helpless passenger. It ought to be worth that. Eh?"

The official wavered, torn between caution and vindictiveness. A supercilious young voice in the aisle behind Peter Warne said: "Do you mind moving aside?"

Peter Warne moved. The girl glided into the corner he had so laboriously cleared for himself. Peter raised his cap.

"Take my seat, madam," he invited, with empressement. She bestowed upon him a faintly speculative glance, indicating that he was of a species unknown to her, and turned to the window. He sat down in the sole remaining place.

The bus started.

Adjustment to the motion of ten tons on wheels is largely a matter of technique and experience. Toughened traveler as he was, Peter Warne sat upright, swaying from the hips as if on well-oiled hinges. Not so the girl at his side. She undertook to relax into her corner with a view to forgetting her troubles in sleep. This was a major error. She was shuttled back and forth between the wall and her neighbor until her exasperation reached the point of protest.

"Tell that man to drive slower," she directed Peter.

"It may surprise you, but I doubt if he'd do it for me."

"Oh, of course! You're afraid of him. I could see that." Leaning wearily away, she said something not so completely under her breath but that Peter caught the purport of it.

"I suspect," he observed unctuously and with intent to annoy, "that you are out of tune with the Infinite."

Unwitherable though his blithe spirit was, it felt the scorch of her glare. Only too obviously he was, at that moment, the focal point for a hatred which included the whole universe. Something must have seriously upset a disposition which, he judged, was hardly inured to accepting gracefully the contrarieties of a maladjusted world.

She looked like that. Her eyes were dark and wide beneath brows that indicated an imperious temper. The long, bold sweep of the cheek was deeply tanned and ended in a chin which obviously expected to have its own way. But the mouth was broad, soft and generous. Peter wondered what it would look like when, as, and if it smiled. He didn't think it likely that he would find out.

Beyond Fort Lauderdale the bus was resuming speed when the feminine driver of a sports roadster, disdaining the formality of a signal, took a quick turn and ran the heavier vehicle off the road. There was a bump, a light crash, a squealing of brakes, and the bus lurched to a stop with a tire ripped loose. After a profane inspection, the driver announced a fifteen-minute wait.

They were opposite that sign manual of Florida's departed boom days, a pair of stone pillars leading into a sidewalked wilderness and flanked by two highly ornamental lamp-posts without glass or wiring. The girl got out for a breath of air, set her dressing case at her feet and leaned against one of the monuments to perishable optimism. As she disembarked, her neighbor, in a spirit of unappreciated helpfulness, had advised her to walk up and down; it would save her from cramps later on.

Just for that she wouldn't do it. He was too officious, that young man. Anyway, the fewer human associations she suffered, the better she would like it. She had a hate on the whole race. Especially men. With a total lack of interest, she observed the parade of her fellow wayfarers up and down the road, before shutting them out from her bored vision.

A shout startled her. The interfering stranger on the opposite side of the road had bounded into the air as if treacherously stabbed from behind, and was now racing toward her like a bull at full charge. At the same time she was aware of a shadow moving away from her elbow and dissolving into the darkness beyond the gates. Close to her, the sprinter swerved, heading down the deserted avenue. Beyond him she heard a crash of brush. His foot faught in a projecting root and he went headlong, rising to limp forward a few yards and give it up with a ruefully shaken head.

"Lost him," he said, coming opposite her.

"I don't know why that should interest me." She hoped that she sounded as disagreeable as she felt. And she did.

"All right," he replied shortly, and made as if to go on, but changed his mind. "He got your bag," he explained.

"Oh!" she ejaculated, realizing that that important equipment was indeed missing. "Who?" she added feebly.

"I don't know his name and address. The thin-faced bird who sat in front of you."

"Why didn't you catch him?" she wailed. "What'll I do now?"

"Did it have much in it?"

"All my things."

"Your money and ticket?"

"Not my ticket; I've got that."

"You can wire for money from Jacksonville, you know."

"Thank you. I can get to New York all right," she returned, with deceptive calm, making a rapid calculation based on the six or eight dollars which she figured (by a considerable overestimate) were still left her.

"Shall I report your loss at the next stop?"

"Please don't." She was unnecessarily vehement. One might almost suppose the suggestion had alarmed her.

Joining the others, she climbed aboard. The departed robber had left a chair vacant next the window. One bit of luck, anyway; now she could get away from that rear seat and her friendly neighbor. She transferred herself, only to regret the change bitterly before ten miles had been covered. For she now had the chair above the curve of the wheel, which is the least comfortable of bus seats. In that rigorously enforced distortion of the body she found her feet asleep, her legs cramped. Oh, for the lesser torments of the place she had so rashly abandoned!

Twisting her stiffening neck, she looked back. The seat was still vacant. The chatty young man seemed asleep.

Lapsing into the corner, she prepared for a night of heroism. The bus fled fast through the dark and wind. Exigencies of travel she had known before; once she had actually slept in the lower berth of a section, all the drawing-rooms and compartments being sold out. But that was less cramped than her present seat. Just the same, she would have stood worse rather than stay at home after what had happened!

If only she had brought something to read. She surveyed her fellow passengers, draped in widely diverse postures. Then the miracle began to work within her. She grew drowsy. It was not so much sleep as the reflex anaesthetic of exhaustion. Consciousness passed from her.

Sun rays struck through the window upon her blinking lids. White villas slid by. A milk cart rattled past. Stiff and dazed, she felt as if her legs had been chilled into paralysis, but all the upper part of her was swathed in mysterious warmth. What were those brown, woolly folds?

The tanned, quick-fingered hands explored, lifted a sleeve which flopped loose, discovered a neatly darned spot; another; a third. It had seen hard service, that garment which wrapped her. She thought, with vague pleasure of the senses, that it had taken on a sturdy personality of its own connected with tobacco and wood smoke and strong soap; the brisk, faintly troubling smell of clean masculinity. She liked it, that sweater.

From it, her heavy eyes moved to her neighbor who was still asleep. By no stretch of charity could he be called an ornament to the human species. His physiognomy was blunt, rough and smudgy with bristles; his hair reddish and uncompromisingly straight.

Nevertheless, a guarded approval might be granted to the setting of the eyes under a freckled forehead, and the trend of the mouth suggested strong, even teeth within. Nose and chin betokened a careless good humor. As for the capable hands, there was no blinking the stains upon them.

His clothing was rough and baggy, but neat enough except for a gaping rent along one trouser leg which he had come by in chasing her thief. For the first time in her life, she wished that she knew how to sew. This surprised her when she came to consider it later.

For the moment she only smiled. It was a pity that Peter Warne could not have waked up at the brief, warm interval before her lips drooped back to weariness.

Nearly an hour later, he roused himself at the entrance to Jacksonville where a change of lines was due, and his first look rested upon a wan and haggard face.

"Breakfast!" said he, with energy and anticipation.

The face brightened. "The Windsor is a good place," stated its owner.

"I wouldn't doubt it for a minute. So is Hungry Joe's."

"Do you expect me to eat at some horrid beanery?"

"Beans have their virtue. But oatmeal and coffee give you the most for your money."

"Oh, money! I'd forgotten about money."

"If you want to change your mind and wire for it——"

"I don't. I want to eat."

"With me?"

She speculated as to whether this might be an invitation; decided that it probably wasn't. "If the place is clean."

"It's cleaner than either of us at the present moment of speaking," he grinned.

Thus recalled to considerations of femininity, she said: "I'll bet I look simply *terrible!*"

"Well, I wouldn't go as far as that," was the cautious reply.

"Anyhow, there's one thing I've got to have right away."

"What's that?"

"If you must know, it's a bath."

"Nothing doing. Bus leaves in fifty minutes."

"We can tell the driver to wait."

"Certainly, we can tell him. But there's just a possibility that he might not do it."

This was lost upon her. "Of course he'll do it. People always wait for me," she added with sweet self-confidence. "If they didn't, I'd never get anywhere."

"This is a hard-boiled line," he explained patiently. "The man would lose his job if he held the bus, like as not."

She yawned. "He could get another, couldn't he?"

"Oh, of course! Just like that. You haven't happened to hear of a thing called unemployment, have you?"

"Oh, that's just socialistic talk. There are plenty of jobs for people who really want to work."

"Yes? Where did you get that line of wisdom?"

She was bored and showed it in her intonation. "Why, everybody knows that. Bill was saying the other day that most of these people are idle because they're just waiting for the dole or something."

"Who's Bill?"

"My oldest brother."

"Oh! And I suppose Bill works?"

"We-ell; he plays polo. Almost every day."

Mr. Warne made a noise like a trained seal.

"What did you say?"

"I said, 'Here's the eatery.' Or words to that effect."

The place was speckless. Having a healthy young appetite, the girl disdained to follow the meager example of her escort, and ordered high, wide and handsome. Directing that his fifteen-cent selection be held for five minutes, Peter excused himself with a view to cleaning up. He returned to find his companion gone.

"At the Windsor, having my bath," a scrawl across the bill of fare enlightened him. "Back in half an hour."

That, he figured after consultation of his watch, would leave her just four minutes and twenty seconds to consume an extensive breakfast and get around the corner to the terminal, assuming that she lived up to her note, which struck him as, at the least, doubtful. Well, let the little fool get out of it as best she could. Why bother?

Peter ate slowly, while reading the paper provided free for patrons. At the end of twenty-five minutes, he was craning his neck out of the window. A slight figure turned the corner. Relief was in the voice which bade the waiter rush the order. The figure approached—and passed. Wrong girl. Peter cursed.

Time began to race. Less than five minutes to go now. Half of that was the minimum allowance for getting to the starting place. Peter bore his grip to the door, ready for a flying take-off, in case she appeared. In case she didn't . . . People always waited for her, did they? Well, he'd be damned if he would! In one short minute he would be leaving. Thirty seconds; twenty; fifteen; five. Sister Ann, do you see anything moving? *Malbrouck s'en va-t'en guerre.* No dust along the road? We're off!

Such was the intention. But something interfered; an intangible something connected with the remembrance of soft contours on a young, sleeping face, of wondering eyes slowly opened. Peter dashed his valise upon the floor, kicked it, cast himself into a chair and sulked. His disposition was distinctly tainted when the truant made triumphal entrance. She was freshened and groomed and radiant, a festal apparition. Uprose then Mr. Warne, uncertain where to begin. She forestalled him.

"Why, how nice you look!" By virtue of his five minutes, the freedom of the washroom, and a pocket kit, he had contrived to shave, brush up, and make the best of a countenance which, if by strict standards unbeautiful, did not wholly lack points. "How much time have I for breakfast?"

"Plenty," barked Peter.

"Swell! I'm starving. I *did* hurry."

"Did you?" he inquired, between his teeth.

"Of course I did. Didn't you just say I had plenty of time?"

"You certainly have. All day."

She set down her coffee cup. "Why, I thought our bus——"

"Our bus is on its way to New York. The next one leaves at eight tonight."

"I do think you might have telephoned them to wait," she protested. A thought struck her impressionable mind. "Why, you missed it, too!"

"So I did. Isn't that extraordinary!"

"Because you were waiting for me?"

"Something of the sort."

"It was awfully nice of you. But why?"

"Because the poor damfool just didn't have the heart to leave a helpless little hick like you alone," he explained.

"I believe you're sore at me."

"Oh, not in the least! Only at myself for getting involved in such a mix-up."

"Nobody asked you to miss the old bus," she stated warmly. "Why did you?"

"Because you remind me of my long-lost angel mother, of course. Don't you ever go to the movies? Now, do you still want to go to New York?"

"We-ell; I've got my ticket. I suppose that's still good."

"Up to ten days. At this rate, it'll take us all of that to get there. The thing is to figure out what to do now."

"Let's go to the races," said she.

"On what?" he inquired.

"I've got some money left."

"How much?"

She examined her purse. "Why, there's only a little over four dollars," she revealed in disappointed accents.

"How far d'you think that'll take you?"

"I could bet it on the first race. Maybe I'd win."

"Maybe you'd lose, too."

"I thought you had that kind of disposition the minute I set eyes on you," she complained. "Pessimist!"

"Economist," he corrected.

"Just as bad. Anyway, we've got a whole day to kill. What's your dashing idea of the best way to do it?"

"A park bench."

"What do you do on a park bench?"

"Sit."

"It sounds dumb."

"It's cheap."

"I hate cheap things, but just to prove I'm reasonable I'll try it for a while."

He led her a block or so to the area of palms and flowers facing the Windsor where they found a bench vacant and sat down. Peter slouched restfully. His companion fidgeted.

"Maybe the band will play by and by," said he encouragingly.

"Wouldn't that be nah-ice!" murmured the girl, and Peter wondered whether a hard slap would break her beyond repair.

"How old are you, anyway?" he demanded. "Fifteen?"

"I'm twenty-one, if you want to know."

"And I suppose it cost your family a bunch of money to bring you to your present fine flower of accomplished womanhood."

"You shouldn't try to be poetic. It doesn't, somehow, go with your face."

"Never mind my face. If I take you to the station and buy you a ticket to Miami—day coach, of course," he interpolated, "will you go back, like a sensible girl?"

"No, I won't. Think how silly I'd look, sneaking back after having——"

"You'll look sillier trying to get to New York at your present rate of expenditure," he warned, as she failed to complete her objection.

"If you can put up the price of a ticket to Miami," said she, with a luminous thought, "you might better lend me the money. I'll pay you back—twice over."

"Tha-anks."

"Meaning you won't?"

"Your powers of interpretation are positively uncanny."

"I might have known you wouldn't." She turned upon him an offended back.

"My name," he said to the back, "is Peter Warne."

A shrug indicated her total indifference to this bit of information. Then she rose and walked away.

He called after her: "I'll be here at six-thirty. Try not to keep me waiting *more* than half an hour."

Just for that—thought the girl—I'll be an hour late.

But she was not. It annoyed her to find how a day could drag in a town where she knew nobody. She went to a movie. She lunched. She went to another movie. She took a walk. Still, it was not yet six o'clock.

At six-thirty-one she started for the park. At six-thirty-four she was at the spot, or what she had believed to be the spot, but which she decided couldn't be, since no Peter Warne was visible. Several other benches were in sight of the vacant band stand. She made the rounds of all. None was occupied by the object of her search. Returning to the first one, she sat down in some perturbation. Perhaps something had happened to Peter Warne. Nothing short of an accident could explain his absence.

There she sat for what seemed like the better part of an hour, until an ugly suspicion seeped into her humiliated mind that she had been left in the lurch. And by a man. A clock struck seven. She rose uncertainly.

"Oh!" she said, in a long exhalation.

Peter Warne was strolling around the corner of the stand.

"Where have you been?" she demanded, like an outraged empress.

He remained unstricken. "You were late," he observed.

"I wasn't. What if I was. Only a minute."

"Nearer five."

"How do you know? You must have been watching. You were here all the time. And you let me think you'd gone away. Oh! Oh! *Oh!*"

"You're pretty casual about keeping other people waiting, you know."

"That's different." She spoke with a profound conviction of privilege.

"I'm not going to argue that with you. Have you any money left?"

"A dollar and four cents," she announced, after counting and recounting.

Coolly he took her purse, transferred the coins to his pocket, and handed it back. "Confiscated for the common necessity," he stated, and she refrained from protest. "Come along."

She fell into step with him. "Could I please have something to eat?"

"Such is the idea. We'll try Hungry Joe's again."

This time he did the ordering for both of them; soup, hash, thick, pulpy griddle cakes and coffee. Total, sixty-five cents. Fortified by this unfamiliar but filling diet, she decided to give Mr. Peter Warne a more fitting sense of their relative status. Some degree of respect was what her soul demanded to bolster her tottering self-confidence. She had heard that a married woman was in a better position to assert herself than a girl. On that basis she would impress Peter.

"You've been treating me like a child," she complained. "You may as well understand right now that I'm not. I'm a married woman. I'm Mrs. Corcoran Andrews." She had selected this name because Corcoran, who was her third or fourth cousin, had been pestering her to marry him for a year. So he wouldn't mind. The effect was immediate.

"Huh?" jerked out the recipient of the information. "I thought Corker Andrews married a pink chorine."

"They're divorced. Do you *know* Corker?"

"Sure I know Corker."

"You're not a *friend* of his?" The implication of her surprise was unflattering.

"I didn't say that." He grinned. "The fact is, I blacked his boots once for three months."

"What did you do that for?"

"What does a man black boots for? Because I had to. So you're Cor— Mr. Andrews' wife." His regard rested upon her small, strong, deeply browned left hand. She hastily pulled it away.

"My ring's in the bag that was stolen."

"Of course," he remarked. (What did he mean by that?) "Time to be moving."

They emerged into a droning pour of rain. "Can't you get a taxi?" she asked.

"We walk," was the uncompromising reply, as he tucked his hand beneath her arm. They caught the bus with little to spare, and again drew the rear seat.

Outside someone was saying: "Since Thursday. Yep; a hundred miles up the road. There'll be bridges out."

Feeling sleepy and indifferent, she paid no heed. She lapsed into a doze which, beginning bumpily against the wall, subsided into the unrealized comfort of his shoulder.

Water splashing on the floor boards awakened her; it was followed by the whir of the wheels, spinning in reverse.

"Got out by the skin of our teeth," said Peter Warne's lips close to her ear.

"What is it?"

"Some creek or other on the rampage. We'll not make Charleston this night."

He went forward, returning with dreary news. "We're going to stay in the nearest village. It looks like a night in the bus for us."

"Oh, no! I can't stand this bus any longer. I want to go to bed," she wailed.

He fetched out his small notebook and fell to figuring. "It'll be close reckoning," he said, scowling at the estimate. "But if you feel that way about it——" To the driver he shouted: "Let us off at Dake's place."

"What's that?"

"Tourist camp."

"Aren't they awful places? They look it."

"The Dake's chain are clean and decent enough for anybody," he answered in a tone so decisive that she followed him meekly out into the night.

Leading her to a sort of waiting room, he vanished into an office, where she could hear his voice in colloquy with an unseen man. The latter emerged with a flash light and indicated that they were to follow. Her escort said to her, quick and low: "What's your name?"

"I told you," she returned, astonished. "I'm Mrs. Cor——"

"Your first name."

"Oh. Elspeth. Why? What's the matter?" She regarded him curiously.

"I had to register as Mr. and Mrs.," he explained nervously. "It's usual for a husband to know his wife's first name."

She asked coldly: "What is the idea?"

"Do you mind," he urged, "talking it over after we get inside?"

Their guide opened the door of a snug cabin, lighted a light and gave Elspeth a shock by saying: "Good night, Mrs. Warne. Good night, Mr. Warne. I hope you find everything comfortable."

Elspeth looked around upon the bare but neat night's lodging: two bunks separated by a scant yard of space, a chair, four clothes hooks, a shelf with a mirror above it. Peter sat down his carryall and sat at the head of a bunk.

"Now," said he, "you're free to come or go."

"Go where?" she asked blankly.

"Nowhere, I hope. But it's up to you. You're a lot safer here with me," he added, "than you would be by yourself."

"But why did you have to register that way? To save appearances?"

"To save two dollars," was his grim correction, "which is more to the point. That's the price of a cabin."

"But *you're* not going to stay *here.*"

"Now, let me explain this to you in words of one syllable. We've got darn little money at best. The family purse simply won't stand separate establishments. Get that into your head. And I'm not spending the night outside in this storm!"

"But I—I don't know anything about you."

"All right. Take a look." He held the lamp up in front of what developed into a wholly trustworthy grin.

"I'm looking." Her eyes were wide, exploring, steady, and—there was no doubt about it in his mind—innocent.

"Well; do I look like the villain of the third act?"

"No; you don't." She began to giggle. "You look like a plumber. A nice, honest, intelligent, high-principled plumber."

"The washroom," he stated in the manner of a guidebook, "will be found at the end of this row of shacks."

While she was gone, he extracted a utility kit from his bag, tacked two nails to the end walls, fastened a cord to them and hung a spare blanket, curtain-wise, upon it.

"The walls of Jericho," was his explanation, as she came in. "Solid porphyry and marble. Proof against any assault."

"Grand! What's this?" She recoiled a little from a gaudy splotch ornamenting the foot of her bed.

"Pajamas. My spare set. Hope you can sleep in them."

"I could sleep," she averred with conviction, "in a strait-jacket." She had an impulse of irrepressible mischief. "About those walls of Jericho, Peter. You haven't got a trumpet in that big valise of yours, have you?"

"Not even a mouth organ."

"I was just going to tell you not to blow it before eight o'clock."

"Oh, shut up and go to sleep."

So they both went to sleep.

Something light and small, falling upon her blanket, woke Elspeth.

"Wha' za'?" she murmured sleepily.

"Little present for you," answered Peter.

"Oh-h-h-h-h-h!" It was a rapturous yawn. "I never slept so hard in my *whole* life. What time is it?"

"Eight o'clock, and all's well before the walls of Jericho."

She ripped the small package open, disclosing a toothbrush. "What a snappy present! Where did it come from?"

"Village drug store. I'm just back."

"How nice of you! But can we afford it?" she asked austerely.

"Certainly not. It's a wild extravagance. But I'm afraid to cut you off from all luxuries too suddenly. Now, can you get bathed and dressed in twenty minutes?"

"Don't be silly! I'm not even up yet."

"One—two—three—four——"

"What's the count about?"

"On the stroke of ten I'm going to break down the wall, drag you out and dress you myself if neces——"

"Why, you big bum! I believe you wou——"

"——five—six—seven——"

"Wait a *minute!*"

"——eight—ni-i-i-i——"

A blanket-wrapped figure dashed past him and down to the showers. After a record bath she sprinted back to find him squatted above a tiny double grill which he had evidently extracted from that wonder-box of a valise.

"What we waste on luxuries we save on necessities," he pointed out. "Two eggs, one nickel. Two rolls, three cents. Tea from the Warne storehouse. Accelerate yourself, my child."

Odors, wafted from the cookery to her appreciative nostrils, stimulated her to speed. Her reward was a nod of approbation from her companion and the best egg that had ever caressed her palate.

"Now you wash up the dishes while I pack. The bus is due in ten minutes."

"But they're greasy," she shuddered.

"That's the point. Get 'em clean. Give 'em a good scraping first."

He vanished within. Well, she would try. Setting her teeth, she scraped and scrubbed and wiped and, at the end, invited his inspection, confident of praise. When, with a pitying glance, he silently did over two plates and a cup before stacking and packing them, she was justifiably hurt. "There's no suiting some people," she reflected aloud and bitterly.

Flood news from the northward, they learned on boarding the bus, compelled a re-routing far inland. Schedules were abandoned. If they made Charleston by nightfall they'd do pretty well, the driver said. Elspeth, refreshed by her long sleep, didn't much care. Peter would bring them through, she felt . . .

Yellow against the murk of the night sky shone the lights of Charleston. While Peter was at the terminal office making inquiries, Elspeth, on the platform, heard her name pronounced in astonishment. From a group of the company chauffeurs a figure was coming toward her.

"Andy Brinkerhoff! What are you doing in that uniform?"

"Working. Hello, Elspie! How's things?"

"Working? For the bus company?"

"Right," he chirped. "This being the only job in sight and the family having gone bust, I grabbed it. What-ho!"

"How awful!"

"Oh, I dunno. I'd rather be the driver than a passenger. What brought you so low, Elspie?"

"Sh! I've beat it from home."

"Gee! Alone?"

"Yes. That is—yes. Oh, Andy! I never dreamed how awful this kind of travel could be."

"Why don't you quit it, then?"

"No money."

The lad's cherubic face became serious. "I'll raise some dough from the bunch. You could catch the night plane back."

For a moment she wavered. In the distance she sighted Peter Warne scanning the place. There was a kind of expectant brightness on his face. She couldn't quite picture him going on alone in the bus with that look still there. She flattered herself that she had something to do with its presence.

"I'll stick," she decided to herself, but aloud: "Andy, did you ever hear of a man named Peter Warne?"

"Warne? No. What about him?"

"Nothing. What's a telegram to Miami cost?"

"How much of a telegram?"

"Oh, I don't know. Give me a dollar." And then she wrote out a message:

MR. CORCORAN D. ANDREWS, BAYSIDE PLACE, MIAMI BEACH, FLA.
  Who what and why is Peter Warne Stop Important I should know Stop On my way somewhere and hope to get there some

time Stop This is strictly confidential so say nothing to nobody
Stop Having a helluvaruff time and liking it Stop Wire Bessie
Smith, Western Union, Raleigh, N. C. Eʟ

"Oh, here you are," said Peter, barely giving her time to smuggle the
paper into Brinkerhoff's hand. "We're going on. Think you can stand
it?"

"I s'pose I've got to," replied Elspeth.

Incertitude had discouraged about half the passengers. Consequently,
the pair secured a window chair apiece. At the moment of starting there
entered a spindly young male all aglow with self-satisfaction which glossed
him over from his cocky green hat to his vivid spats.

By the essential law of his being it was inevitable that, after a survey of
the interior, he should drop easily into a seat affording an advantageous
view of the snappy-looking girl who seemed to be traveling alone. He
exhumed a magazine from his grip and leaned across.

"Pardon *me*. But would you care to look at this?"

Elspeth wouldn't but she looked at Mr. Horace Shapley with attention
which he mistook for interest. He transferred himself with suitable pre-
liminaries to the vacant chair at her side and fell into confidential dis-
course.

His line, so Elspeth learned, was typewriter supplies and he hailed from
Paterson, New Jersey. Business was punk but if you knew how to make
yourself solid with the girl behind the machine (and that was his specialty, believe *him*), you could make expenses and a little bit on the side.

Elspeth glanced across at Peter to see how he regarded this development.
Peter was asleep. All right, then; if he wanted to leave her unprotected
against the advances of casual strangers! Unfamiliar with this particular
species, she was mildly curious about its hopeful antics.

She smiled politely, asked a question or two, and Mr. Shapley proceeded
to unfold romantic adventures and tales of life among the typewriters.
The incidents exhibited a similarity of climax: "And did *she* fall for me!
Hot momma!"

"It must be a fascinating business," commented his listener.

"And how! I'll bet," said Mr. Shapley, with arch insinuation, "you
could be a naughty little girl yourself, if nobody was lookin'." He offered
her a cigaret. She took it with a nod and tossed it across the aisle, catching
the somnolent Peter neatly in the neck. He woke up.

"Hi!"

"Come over here, Peter." He staggered up. "I want you to know" (with a slight emphasis on the word) "Mr. Shapley."

"Pleezetomeetcha," mumbled that gentleman in self-refuting accents.

"He thinks," pursued Elspeth, "that I'm probably a naughty little girl. Am I?"

"You can't prove it by me," said Peter.

"Say, what's the idea?" protested the puzzled Mr. Shapley.

"I don't like him; he nestles," stated Elspeth.

"Aw, now, sister! I was just nicin' you along and——"

"Nicing me along!" Elspeth repeated the phrase with icy disfavor. "Peter; what are you going to do about this?"

Peter ruminated. "Change seats with you," he said brightly.

"Oh!" She choked as she rose. As she stepped across her neighbor to gain the aisle, he gave a yelp and glared savagely, though it was presumably an accident that her sharp, high heel had landed upon the most susceptible angle of his shin. After a moment's consideration, Peter followed her to her new position.

So entered discord into that peaceful community. Mr. Shapley sulked in his chair. Elspeth gloomed in hers. Discomfort invaded Peter's amiable soul. He perceived that he had fallen short in some manner.

"What did you expect me to do about that bird?" he queried.

"Nothing."

"Well, that's what I did."

"I should say you did. If it had been me, I'd have punched his nose."

"And got into a fight. I never could see any sense in fighting unless you have to," he argued. "What happens? You both get arrested. If I got arrested and fined here, how do we eat? If they jug me, what becomes of you? Be sensible."

"Oh, you're sensible enough for both of us." It was plain, however, to the recipient of this encomium, that it was not intended as a compliment. "Never mind. What are we stopping for?"

The halt was occasioned by evil reports of the road ahead, and the chauffeur's unwillingness to risk it in darkness.

"I'll do a look-see," said Peter, and came back, pleased, to announce that there was a cheap camp around the turn. Without formality, the improvised Warne family settled in for the night.

Silence had fallen upon the little community when an appealing voice floated across the wall to their seventy-five-cent Jericho. "Peter. Pe-*ter!*"

"Mmpff."

"You're not a very inquisitive person, Peter. You haven't asked me a single question about myself."

"I did. I asked you your name."

"Because you had to. In self-protection."

"Do you want me to think up some more questions?"

She sniffed. "You might show a *little* human interest. You know, I don't like you much, Peter. But I could talk to you, if you'd let me, as freely as if you were—well, I don't know how to put it."

"Another species of animal."

"No-o-o-o. You mustn't belittle yourself," said she kindly.

"I wasn't. And I didn't say an inferior species."

It took her a moment to figure this out, and then she thought she must have got it wrong. For how could his meaning possibly be that her species was the inferior? . . . Better pass that and come to her story. She began with emphasis:

"If there's one thing I can't stand, it's unfairness."

"I thought so."

"You thought *what?*"

"Somebody's been interfering with your having your own sweet way, and so you walked out on the show. What was the nature of this infringement upon the rights of American womanhood?"

"Who's making this stump speech; you or me?" she retorted. "It was about King Westley, if you want to know."

"The headline aviator?"

"Yes. He and I have been playing around together."

"How does friend husband like that?"

"Huh? Oh! Why, he's away, you see. Cruising. I'm staying with Dad."

"Then he's the one to object?"

"Yes. Dad doesn't understand me."

"Likely enough. Go ahead."

"I'll bet you're going to be dumb about this, too. Anyway, it was all right till King got the idea of finding the lost scientific expedition in South America. Venezuela, or somewhere. You know."

"Professor Schatze's? South of the Orinoco. I've read about it."

"King wants to fly down there and locate them."

" 'S all right by me. But where does he figure he'll land?"

"Why, on the prairie or the pampas."

"Pampas, my glass eye! There isn't any pampas within a thousand miles of the Orinoco."

"What do you know about it?"

"I was there myself, five years ago."

"You were! What doing?"

"Oh, just snooping around."

"Maybe it wasn't the same kind of country we were going to."

"*We?*" She could hear a rustle and judged that he was sitting upright. She had him interested at last.

"Of course. I was going with him. Why, if we'd found the expedition I'd be another Amelia Earhart."

Again the cot opposite creaked. Its occupant had relaxed. "I guess your family needn't have lost any sleep."

"Why not?" she challenged.

"Because it's all a bluff," he returned. "Westley never took a chance in his life outside of newspaper headlines."

"I think you're positively septic. The family worried, all right. They tried to keep me from seeing him. So he took to nosing down across our place and dropping notes in the swimming pool, and my father had him arrested and grounded for reckless flying. Did you ever hear anything like that?"

"Not so bad," approved Peter.

"Oh-h-h-h! I might know you'd side against me. I suppose you'd have had me sit there and let Dad get away with it."

"Mmmmm. I can't exactly see you doing it. But why take a bus?"

"All the cars were locked up. I had to sneak out. I knew they'd watch the airports and the railroad stations, but they wouldn't think of the bus. Now you've got the whole story, do you blame me?"

"Yes."

"I do think you're unbearable. You'd probably expect me to go back."

"Certainly."

"Maybe you'd like to send me back."

"You wouldn't go. I did try, you know."

"Not alive, I wouldn't! Of *course* you wouldn't think of doing anything so improper as helping me any more."

"Sure, I will," was the cheerful response. "If you've got your mind set on getting to New York, I'll do my best to deliver you there intact. And may God have mercy on your family's soul! By the way, I suppose you left some word at home so they won't worry too much."

"I did not! I hope they worry themselves into convulsions."

"You don't seem to care much about your family," he remarked.

"Oh, Dad isn't so bad. But he always wants to boss everything. I—I expect I didn't think about his worrying. D'you think he will—much?" The query terminated in a perceptible quaver.

"Hm. I wonder if you're really such a hard-boiled little egg as you make out to be. Could you manage with a bag of pecans for dinner tomorrow?"

"Ouch! Do I have to?"

"To wire your father would come to about the price of two dinners."

"Wire him? And have him waiting in New York for me when we get there? If you do, I'll jump through the bus window and you'll never see me again."

"I see. Westley is meeting you. You don't want any interference. Is that it?"

"I left him a note," she admitted.

"Uh-huh. Now that you've got everything movable off your mind, what about a little sleep?"

"I'm for it."

Silence settled down upon the Warne ménage.

Sunup brought Peter out of his bunk. From beyond the gently undulant blanket he could hear the rhythm of soft breathing. Stealthily he dressed. As he opened the door, a gust of wind twitched down the swaying screen. The girl half turned in her sleep. She smiled. Peter stood, bound in enchantment.

In something like panic he bade himself listen to sense and reason. That's a spoiled child, Peter. Bad medicine. Willful, self-centered—and sweet. (How had that slipped in?) Impractical, too. Heaven pity the bird that takes her on! Too big a job for you, Peter, my lad, even if you could get the contract. So don't go fooling with ideas, you poor boob.

Breakfast necessities took him far afield before he acquired at a bargainer's price what he needed. Elspeth had already fished the cooking kit out of the bag and made ready in the shelter of the shack. Not a word did she say about the fallen blanket. This made Peter self-conscious. They breakfasted in some restraint.

A wild sky threatened renewal of the storm. Below the hill a shallow torrent supplanted the road for a space. Nevertheless, the bus was going on. Elspeth washed the dishes—clean, this time.

"You get out and stretch your legs while I pack," advised Peter.

As she stepped from the shack, the facile Mr. Shapley confronted her.

"The cream off the milk to you, sister," said he, with a smile which indicated that he was not one to bear a grudge. "I just want to square my-self with you. If I'd known you was a married lady——"

"I'm not," returned Elspeth absently.

Mr. Shapley's eyes shifted from her to the shack. Peter's voice was raised within: "Where are your pajamas, Elspeth?"

"Airing out. I forgot 'em." She plucked them from a bush and tossed them in at the door.

"*Oh*-oh!" lilted Mr. Shapley, with the tonality of cynical and amused enlightenment. He went away cocking his hat.

Warning from the bus horn brought out Peter with his bag. They took their seats and were off.

The bus' busy morning was spent mainly in dodging stray watercourses. They made Cheraw toward the middle of the afternoon. There Peter bought two pounds of pecans; a worthy nut and one which satisfies with-out cloying. They were to be held in reserve, in case. In case of what? Elspeth wished to be informed. Peter shook his head and said, darkly, that you never could tell.

North of Cheraw, the habits of the bus became definitely amphibian. The main route was flowing in a northeasterly direction, and every side road was a contributory stream. A forested rise of land in the distance held out hope of better things, but when they reached it they found cars parked all over the place, waiting for a road-gang to strengthen a doubtful bridge across the swollen river.

"Let's have a look at this neck of the woods," Peter suggested to Elspeth.

To determine their geographical circumstances was not difficult. Rising waters had cut off from the rest of the world a ridge, thinly oval in shape, of approximately a mile in length, and hardly a quarter of a mile across. On this were herded thirty or forty travelers, including the bus passengers.

There was no settlement of any sort within reach; only a ramshackle farmhouse surrounded by a discouraged garden. Peter, however, nego-tiated successfully for a small box of potatoes, remarking to his companion that there was likely to be a rise in commodity prices before the show was over.

A sound of hammering and clinking, interspersed with rugged pro-fanity, led them to a side path. There they found a well-equipped house-keeping van, the engine of which was undergoing an operation by its owner while his motherly wife sat on the steps watching.

"Cussin' never done you any good with that machine, Abner," said she. "It ain't like a mule."

"It is like a mule. Only meaner." Abner sighted Peter. "Young man, know anything about this kind of critter?"

"Ran one once," answered Peter. He took off his coat, rolled up his sleeves, and set to prodding and poking in a professional manner. Presently the engine lifted up its voice and roared.

Elspeth, perched on a log, reflected that Peter seemed to be a useful sort of person to other people. Why hadn't he done better for himself in life? Maybe that was the reason. This was a new thought and gave her something to mull over while he worked. From the van she borrowed a basin of water, a bar of soap and a towel, and was standing by when he finished the job.

"What do I owe you, young man?" called Abner Braithe, from the van.

"Noth—*uh!*" Elspeth's well-directed elbow had reached its goal in time.

"Don't be an idiot!" she adjured him.

A conference took place.

"You see," said Peter at its close, "my—uh—wife doesn't sleep well outdoors. If you had an extra cot, now——"

"Why, we can fix that," put in Mrs. Braithe. "We haven't got any cot, but if you can sleep in a three-quarter bed——"

"We can't," said both hastily.

"We're used to twin beds," explained Elspeth.

"My wife's quite nervous," put in Peter, "and—and I snore."

"You don't," contradicted Elspeth indignantly, and got a dirty look from him.

It was finally arranged that, as payment for Peter's services, the Braithes were to divide the night into two watches; up to and after one A. M., Elspeth occupying the van bed for the second spell while Peter roosted in the bus. This being settled, the young pair withdrew to cook a three-course dinner over a fire coaxed by Peter from wet brush and a newspaper; first course, thin potato soup; second course, boiled potatoes with salt; dessert, five pecans each.

"We've been Mr. and Mrs. for pretty near three days now, Peter," remarked the girl suddenly, "and I don't know the first darn thing about you."

"What d'you want to know?"

"What have you got in the line of information?"

"Not much that's exciting."

"That's too bad. I hoped you were an escaped con or something, traveling incog."

"Nothing so romantic. Just a poor but virtuous specimen of the half-employed."

"Who employs you?"

"I do. I'm a rotten employer."

"Doing what? Besides blacking boots."

"Oh, I've had nothing as steady as that since. If you want to know, I've been making some experiments in the line of vegetable chemistry; pine tar, to be exact. I'm hoping to find some sucker with money to take it up and subsidize me and my process. That's what I'm going to New York to see about. Meantime," he grinned, "I'm traveling light."

"What'll the job be worth if you do get it?"

"Seven or eight thousand a year to start with," said he, with pride.

"Is *that* all?" She was scornful.

"Well, I'll be—— Look here, Elspeth, I said per year."

"I heard you. My brother Bill says he can't get along on *ten* thousand. And," she added thoughtfully, "he's single."

"So am I."

"You didn't tell me that before. Not that it matters, of course. Except that your wife might misunderstand if she knew we'd been sl—traveling together."

"I haven't any wife, I tell you."

"All right; all *right!* Don't bark at me about it. It isn't my fault."

"Anything else?" he inquired with careful politeness.

"I think it's going to rain some more."

They transferred themselves to the bus and sat there until one o'clock, when he escorted her to the Braithe van. He returned to join his fellow passengers, leaving her with a sensation of lostness and desertion.

Several small streams, drunk and disorderly on spring's strong liquor, broke out of bounds in the night, came brawling down the hills and carried all before them, including the bridge whereby the marooned cars had hoped to escape.

"I don't care," said Elspeth, when the morning's news was broken to her. She was feeling gayly reckless.

"I do," returned Peter soberly.

"Oh, you're worrying about money again. What's the use of money where there's nothing to buy? We're out of the world, Peter. I like it, for a change. What's that exciting smell?"

"Fish." He pointed with pride to his fire, over which steamed a pot.

Dishing up a generous portion he handed it to her on a plate. "Guaranteed fresh this morning. How do you like it?"

She tasted it. "It—it hasn't much personality. What kind of fish is it?"

"They call it mudfish, I believe. It was flopping around in a slough and I nailed it with a stick. I thought there'd be enough for dinner, too," said he, crestfallen by her lack of appreciation.

"Plenty," she agreed. "Peter, could I have four potatoes? Raw ones."

"What for?"

"I'm going marketing."

"Barter and exchange, eh? Look out that these tourists don't gyp you."

"Ma feyther's name is Alexander Bruce MacGregor Andrews," she informed him in a rich Scottish accent. "Tak' that to heart, laddie."

"I get it. You'll do."

Quenching his fire, he walked to the van. A semicircle of men and women had grouped about the door. Circulating among them, Abner Braithe was taking up a collection. Yet, it was not Sunday. The explanation was supplied when the shrewd Yankee addressed his audience.

"The morning program will begin right away. Any of you folks whose money I've missed, please raise the right hand. Other news and musical ee-vents will be on the air at five-thirty this P. M. and eight tonight. A nickel admission each, or a dime for the three performances."

Having no nickel to waste on frivolities, Peter moved on. Elspeth, triumphant, rejoined him with her booty.

Item: a small parcel of salt.

Item: a small parcel of pepper.

Item: a half pound of lard.

Item: two strips of fat bacon.

Item: six lumps of sugar.

"What d'ye ken about that?" she demanded. "Am I no the canny Scawtswumman?"

"You're a darn bonny one," returned Peter, admiring the flushed cheeks and brilliant eyes.

"Is this the first time you've noticed that?" she inquired impudently.

"It hadn't struck in before," he confessed.

"And now it has? Hold the thought. It can't hurt you." (He felt by no means so sure about that.) "Now Mr. Shapley"—her eyes shifted to the road up which that gentleman was approaching—"got it right away. I wonder what's his trouble."

Gratification, not trouble, signalized his expression as he sighted them.

His bow to Elspeth was gravely ceremonious. He then looked at her companion.

"Could I have a minute's conversation apart with you?"

"Don't mind me," said Elspeth, and the two men withdrew a few paces.

"I don't want to butt into your and the lady's private affairs," began Mr. Shapley, "but this is business. I want to know if that lady is your wife."

"She is. Not that it's any concern of yours."

"She said this morning that she wasn't married."

"She hasn't got used to the idea yet," returned Peter, with great presence of mind. "She's only been that way a few days. Honeymoon trip."

"That's as may be," retorted the other. "Even if it's true, it wouldn't put a crimp in the reward."

"What this?" demanded Peter, eying him in surprise. "Reward? For what?"

"Come off. You heard the raddio this morning, didn'cha?"

"No."

"Well, is that lady the daughter of Mr. A. B. M. Andrews, the yachtin' millionaire, or ain't she? 'Cause I know she is."

"Oh! You know that, do you! What of it?"

"Ten grand of it. That's what of it," rejoined Mr. Shapley. "For information leadin' to the dis——"

"Keep your voice down."

"Yeah. I'll keep my voice down till the time comes to let it loose. Then I'll collect on that ten thou'. They think she's kidnaped."

"What makes you so sure of your identification?"

"Full description over the air. When the specifications came across on the raddio I spotted the garments. Used to be in ladies' wear," he explained.

"If you so much as mention this to Mi—to Mrs. Warne, I'll——" began Peter.

"Don't get rough, now, brother," deprecated the reward-hunter. "I ain't lookin' for trouble. And I'm not sayin' anything to the little lady, just so long as you and me understand each other."

"What do you want me to understand?"

"That there's no use your tryin' to slip me after we get out of this place. Of course, you can make it hard or easy for me. So, if you want to play in with me and be nice, anyway—I'm ready to talk about a little cut for you ... No? Well, suit yourself, pal. See you in the mornin'."

He chuckled himself away. Peter, weighing the situation, discovered in himself a violent distaste at the thought of Mr. Horace Shapley collecting Elspeth's family's money for the delivering up of Elspeth. In fact, it afflicted him with mingled nausea and desire for manslaughter. Out of this unpromising combination emerged an idea. If he, Peter, could reach a wire before the pestilent Shapley, he could get in his information first and block the reward.

Should he tell Elspeth about the radio? Better not, he concluded.

It was characteristic of her and a big credit mark in his estimate of her, that she put no questions as to the interview with Shapley. She did not like that person; therefore, practically speaking, he did not exist. But the mudfish did. With a captivating furrow of doubt between her eyes, she laid the problem before her partner: could it be trusted to remain edible overnight?

"Never mind the fish. Can you swim?"

She looked out across the brown turbulence of the river, more than two hundred yards now to the northern bank. "Not across that."

"But you're used to water?"

"Oh, yes!"

"I've located an old boat in the slough where I killed the fish. I think I can patch her up enough to make it."

"Okay by me; I wouldn't care to settle here permanently. When do we start?"

"Be ready about ten."

"In the dark?"

"We-ell, I don't exactly want the public in on this. They might try to stop us. You know how people are."

"Come clean, Peter. We're running away from something. Is it that Shapley worm?"

"Yes. He thinks he's got something on me." This explanation, which he had been at some pains to devise, he hoped would satisfy her. But she followed it to a conclusion which he had not foreseen.

"Is it because he knows we're not married?"

"He doesn't know ex——"

"I told him we weren't. Before I thought how it would look."

"I told him we were."

"Did he believe you?"

"Probably not."

"Then he thinks you're abducting me. Isn't that priceless!"

"Oh, absolutely. What isn't so funny is that there are laws in some states about people—er—traveling as man and wife if they're not married."

She stared at him, wide-eyed. "But so long as—— Oh, Peter! I'd *hate* it if I got you into any trouble."

"All we have to do is slip Shapley. Nobody else is on." He sincerely hoped that was true.

The intervening time he occupied in patching up the boat as best he might. He had studied the course of various flotsam and thought that he discerned a definite set of the current toward the northern bank which was their goal. With bailing they ought to be able to keep the old tub afloat.

Through the curtain of the rushing clouds the moon was contriving to diffuse a dim light when they set out. The opposite bank was visible only as a faint, occasional blur. Smooth with treachery, the stream at their feet sped from darkness into darkness.

Peter thrust an oar into Elspeth's hand, the only one he had been able to find, to be used as a steering paddle. For himself he had fashioned a pole from a sapling. The carryall he disposed aft of amidships. Bending over Elspeth as she took the stern seat, he put a hand on her shoulder.

"You're not afraid?"

"No." Just the same, she would have liked to be within reach of that firm grasp through what might be coming.

"Stout fella! All set? Shove!"

The river snatched at the boat, took it into its secret keeping—and held it strangely motionless. But the faintly visible shore slipped backward and away and was presently visible no more. Peter, a long way distant from her in the dimness, was active with his pole, fending to this side and that. It was her job to keep them on the course with her oar. She concentrated upon it.

The boat was leaking profusely now. "Shall I bail?" she called.

"Yes. But keep your oar by you."

They came abreast of an island. As they neared the lower end, an uprooted swamp maple was snatched outward in the movement of the river. Busy with her pan, Elspeth did not notice it until a mass of leafy branches heaved upward from the surface, hovered, descended, and she was struggling in the grasp of a hundred tentacles.

"*Peter!*" she shrieked.

They had her, those wet, clogging arms. They were dragging her out into the void, fight them as she would in her terror and desperation. Now another force was aiding her; Peter, his powerful arms tearing, thrusting, fending against this ponderous invasion. The boat careened. The water poured inboard. Then, miraculously, they were released as the tree side-slipped, turning again, freeing their craft. Elspeth fell back, bruised and battered.

"Are you all right?"

"Yes. It t-t-tried to drag me overboard!"

"I know." His voice, too, was unsteadied by that horror.

"Don't go away. Hold me. Just for a minute."

The skiff, slowly revolving like a ceremonious dancer in the perform-ance of a solo waltz, proceeded on its unguided course. The girl sighed.

"Where's my oar?" It was gone.

"It doesn't matter now. There's the shore. We're being carried in."

They scraped and checked as Peter clutched at a small sapling, growing at the edge of a swampy forest. From trunk to trunk he guided the course until there was a solid bump.

"Land ho!" he shouted, and helped his shipmate out upon the bank.

"What do we do now?"

"Walk until we find a road and a roost."

Valise on shoulder, he set out across the miry fields, Elspeth plodding on behind. It was hard going. Her breath labored painfully after the first half-mile, and she was agonizingly sleepy.

Now Peter's arm was around her; he was murmuring some encourag-ing foolishness to her who was beyond courage, fear, hope, or any other emotion except the brutish lust for rest . . . Peter's voice, angry and harsh, insisting that she throw more of her weight on him and *keep* moving. How silly! She hadn't any weight. She was a bird on a bough. She was a butterfly, swaying on a blossom. She was nothing . . .

Broad daylight, spearing through a paneless window, played upon her lids, waking her. Where was the shawl of Jericho? In its place were boards, a raw wall. Beneath her was fragrant hay. She was actually alive and rested. She looked about her.

"Why, it's a barn!" she exclaimed. She got up and went to the door. Outside stood Peter.

"How do you like the quarters?" he greeted her. "Room"—he pointed to the barn—"and bath." He indicated a huge horse trough fed by a trickle of clear water. "I've just had mine."

She regarded him with stupefaction. "And now you're *shaving*. Where's the party?"

"Party?"

"Well, if not, why the elaborate toilet?"

"Did you ever travel on the thumb?"

She looked her incomprehension. He performed a digital gesture which enlightened her.

"The first rule of thumb," explained Peter, "is to look as neat and decent as you can. It inspires confidence in the passing motorist's breast!"

"Is that the way we're going to travel?"

"If we're lucky."

"Without eating?" she said wistfully.

"Tluck-tluck!" interposed a young chicken from a near-by hedge, the most ill-timed observation of its brief life.

A handy stick, flung deftly, checked its retreat. Peter pounced. "Breakfast!" he exulted.

"Where do we go now?" inquired his companion, half an hour later, greatly restored.

"The main highways," set forth Peter, thinking of the radio alarum and the state police, "are not for us. Verdant lanes and bosky glens are more in our line. We'll take what traffic we can."

Hitch-hiking on sandy side roads in the South means slow progress. Peter finally decided that they must risk better-traveled roads, but select their transportation cautiously. It was selected for them. They had not footed it a mile beside Route 1, when a touring car, battered but serviceable, pulled up and a ruddy face emitted welcome words.

"Well, well, well! Boys *and* girls! Bound north?"

"Yes." It was a duet, perfect in accord.

"Meet Thad Banker, the good old fatty. Throw in the old trunk."

"What's the arrangement?" queried Peter, cautious financier that he was.

"Free wheeling," burbled the fat man. "You furnish the gas and I furnish the spark." They climbed in with the valise. "Any special place?" asked the obliging chauffeur.

"Do we go through Raleigh?" asked the girl, and upon receiving an affirmative, added to Peter: "There may be a wire there for me."

Which reminded that gentleman that he had something to attend to. At the next town he got a telegraph blank and a stamped envelope. After some cogitation, he produced this composition, addressed to Mr. A. B. M. Andrews, Miami Beach, Fla.

Daughter taking trip for health and recreation. Advise abandonment of efforts to trace which can have no good result and may cause delay. Sends love and says not to worry. Undersigned guarantees safe arrival in New York in a few days. Pay no reward to any other claimant as this is positively first authentic information.

PETER WARNE

To this he pinned a dollar bill and mailed it for transmission to Western Union, New Orleans, Louisiana, by way of giving the pursuit, in case one was instituted, a pleasant place to start from. Five cents more of his thin fortune went for a newspaper. Reports from the southward were worth the money; there was no let-up in the flood. Competition from Mr. Shapley would be delayed at least another day.

Mr. Thad Banker was a card. He kept himself in roars of laughter with his witty sallies. Peter, in the rear seat, fell peacefully asleep. Elspeth had to act as audience for the conversational driver.

At Raleigh she found the expected telegram from Corcoran, which she read and thrust into her purse for future use. Shortly after, a traffic light held them up and the policeman on the corner exhibited an interest in the girl on the front seat quite disturbing to Peter.

The traffic guardian was sauntering toward them when the green flashed on. "Step on it," urged Peter.

Mr. Banker obliged. A whistle shrilled.

"Keep going!" snapped Peter.

Mr. Banker still obliged, slipping into a maze of side streets. It did not occur to Peter that their driver's distaste for police interference was instinctive. Also successful, it began to appear; when a motor cop swung around unexpectedly and headed them to the curb. The license was inspected and found in order.

"Who's the lady?" the officer began.

"My niece," said Mr. Banker, with instant candor.

"Is that right, ma'am?"

"Yes. Of course it is." (Peter breathed again.)

"And this man behind?"

"Search me."

"He thumbed us and Uncle Thad stopped for him." (Peter's admiration became almost more than he could bear.)

"Have you got a traveling bag with you, ma'am?" (So the radio must have laid weight on the traveling bag, now probably in some Florida swamp.)

"No. Just my purse."

The cop consulted a notebook. "The dress looks like it," he muttered. "And the description sort of fits. Got anything on you to prove who you are, ma'am?"

"No; I'm afraid—— Yes; of course I have." She drew out the yellow envelope. "Is that enough?"

"Miss Bessie Smith," he read. "I reckon that settles it. Keep to your right for Greensboro at Morrisville."

"Greensboro, my foot! Us for points east," announced the fat man, wiping his brow as the motorcycle chugged away. "Phe-e-e-ew! What's it all about? Been lootin' a bank, you two?"

"Eloping," said Peter. "Keep it under your shirt."

"Gotcha." He eyed the carryall. "All your stuff in there?"

"Yes."

"How about a breath of pure, country air? I'm not so strong for all this public attention."

They kept to side roads until long after dark, bringing up before a restaurant in Tarboro. There the supposed elopers consulted and announced that they didn't care for dinner. "Oh, on me!" cried Mr. Banker. "Mustn't go hungry on your honeymoon."

He ordered profusely. While the steak was cooking, he remarked, he'd just have a look at the car; there was a rattle in the engine that he didn't like. As soon as he had gone, Elspeth said:

"Wonder what the idea is. I never heard a sweeter-running engine for an old car. What's more, he's got two sets of license cards. I saw the other one when that inquiring cop——"

But Peter was halfway to the door, after slamming some money on the table and snapping out directions for her to wait, no matter how long he took. Outside, she heard a shout and the rush of a speeding engine. A car without lights sped up the street.

With nothing else to do, Elspeth settled down to leisurely eating . . .

At nine-thirty, the waiter announced the closing hour as ten, sharp. Beginning to be terrified for Peter and miserable for herself, she ordered more coffee. The bill and tip left her a dollar and fifteen cents.

At nine-fifty, the wreckage of Peter entered the door. Elspeth arose and made a rush upon him, but recoiled.

"Peter! You've been fighting."

"Couldn't help it."

"You've got a black eye."

"That isn't all I've got," he told her.

"No; it isn't. What an *awful*-looking ear!"

"*That* isn't all I've got, either." His grin was bloody, but unbowed.

"Then it must be internal injuries."

"Wrong. It's a car."

"Whose car?"

"Ours now, I expect. I had to come home in something."

"Where's the fat man?"

The grin widened. "Don't know exactly. Neither does he, I reckon. That big-hearted Samaritan, my child, is a road-pirate. He picks people up, plants 'em, and beats it with their luggage. Probably does a little holdup business on the side."

"Tell me what happened, Peter. Go on and eat first."

Between relishing mouthfuls, he unfolded his narrative. "You didn't put me wise a bit too quick. He was moving when I got out but I landed aboard with a flying tackle. Didn't dare grab him for fear we'd crash. He was stepping on it and telling me that when he got me far enough away he was going to beat me up and tie me to a tree. That was an idea! So when he pulled up on some forsaken wood road in a swamp, I beat him up and tied him to a tree."

"Why, Peter! He's twice as big as you."

"I can't help that. It wasn't any time for half measures. It took me an hour to find my way. But here we are."

"I'm glad," said she with a new note in her voice.

"Jumping Jehoshaphat! Is *that* all we've got left?" Aghast, he stared at the sum she put in his hands. "And it's too cold to sleep out tonight. It's an open car, anyhow. Oh, well; our transportation's going to be cheap from now on. What price one more good night's rest? Torney's Haven for Tourists is three miles up the highway. Let's get going."

Torney's provided a cabin for only a dollar. Before turning in, Peter returned to the car, parked a few rods away against a fence, to make a thorough inspection. His companion was in bed on his return.

"I've changed the plates to another set that I found under the seat. Indiana, to match the other set of licenses. It'll be safer in case our friend decides to report the loss, after he gets loose from his tree. There's a nice robe, too. We've come into property. And by the way, Elspeth; you're Mrs. Thaddeus Banker till further notice."

Elspeth pouted. "I'd rather be Mrs. Peter Warne. I'm getting used to that."

"We've got to live up to our new responsibilities." Seated on his cot, he had taken off his shoes, when he started hastily to resume them.

"Where are you going?" she asked plaintively. "Looking for more trouble?"

"Walls of Jericho. I forgot. I'll get the robe out of the car."

"Oh, darn the robe! Why bother? It's pouring, too. Let it go. I don't mind if you don't." All in a perfectly matter-of-fact tone. She added: "You can undress outside. I'm going to sleep."

As soon as he withdrew she got out Corcoran's reply to "Miss Bessie Smith," and read it over again before tearing it into fragments. It ran as follows:

> What's all this about P. W.? Watch out for that bird. Dangerous corner, blind road, and all that sorta thing. At any given moment he might be running a pirate fleet or landing on the throne of the Kingdom of Boopadoopia. Ask him about the bet I stuck him on in college, and then keep your guard up. I'm off for a week on the Keys so you can't get me again until then. Better come back home and be a nice little girl or papa spank. And how!
>
> CORK

The scraps she thrust beneath her pillow and was asleep almost at once. But Peter lay, wakeful, crushing down thoughts that made him furious with himself. At last peace came, and dreams . . . One of them so poignant, so incredibly dear, that he fought bitterly against its turning to reality.

Yet reality it was; the sense of warmth and softness close upon him; the progress of creeping fingers across his breast, of seeking lips against his throat. His arms drew her down. His mouth found the lips that, for a dizzying moment, clung to his, then trembled aside to whisper:

"No, Peter. I didn't mean—— Listen!"

Outside sounded a light clinking.

"Somebody's stealing the car!"

Elspeth's form, in the lurid pajamas, slid away from Peter like a ghost. He followed to the window. Silent as a shadow the dim bulk of the Banker automobile moved deliberately along under a power not its own. Two other shadows loomed in its rear, propelling it by hand.

"Shall I scream?" whispered the girl.

He put a hand on her mouth. "Wait."

Another of his luminous ideas had fired the brain of Peter Warne. In his rôle of Thad Banker, he would let the robbers get away, then report the theft to the police and, allowing for reasonable luck, get back his property (né Mr. Banker's) with the full blessing of the authorities.

"I'm going to let 'em get away with it," he murmured. "As soon as they really start, I'll telephone the road patrol."

The dwindling shadow trundled out on the pike, where the engine struck up its song and the car sped southward. Simultaneously Peter made a rush for the camp office. It was all right, he reported, on getting back. He'd been able to get the police at once.

"But suppose they don't catch 'em."

"That'll be just too bad," admitted Peter. He yawned.

"You're sleepy again. You're always sleepy."

"What do you expect at three o'clock in the morning?"

"I'm wide awake," complained Elspeth.

Something had changed within her, made uncertain and uneasy, since she had aroused Peter and found herself for one incendiary moment in his arms. She didn't blame him; he was only half awake at the time. But she had lost confidence in him. Or could it be herself in whom she had lost confidence? In any case, the thought of sharing the same room with him the rest of that night had become too formidable.

"Please go outside again, Peter. I'm going to get dressed. I'm restless."

"Oh, my gosh!" he sighed. "Can't you count some sheep or something?"

"No; I can't." A brilliant idea struck her. "How d'you expect me to sleep when they may be back with the car any minute?"

"And then again, they may not be back till mornng."

But Elspeth had a heritage of the immovable Scottish obstinacy. In a voice all prickly little italics she announced that she was *going to get up*. And she was going to walk off her nervousness. It needn't make any difference to Peter. He could go back to bed.

"And let you wander around alone in this blackness? You might not come back."

"What else could I do?"

The forlorn lack of alternative for her struck into his heart. Absolute dependence upon a man of a strange breed in circumstances wholly new. What a situation for a girl like her! And how gallantly, on the whole, she was taking it! How sensible it would be for him to go back to that telephone; call up her father (reverse charges, of course) and tell him the whole thing. *And* get himself thoroughly hated for it.

No; he couldn't throw Elspeth down. Not even for her own good. Carry on. There was nothing else for it, especially now that luck was favoring them. The car, if they got it back, was their safest obtainable method of travel. Her dress was the weak spot and would be more of a danger point after Horace Shapley contributed his evidence to the hunt. Couldn't something be done about that? . . . The dress appeared in the doorway, and Peter went in to array himself for the vigil.

The two state police found the pair waiting at the gate. Apologetically they explained that the thieves had got away into the swamp. Nothing could have suited Peter better, since there would now be no question of his being held as complaining witness. To satisfy the authorities of his ownership was easy. They took his address (fictitious), wished him and his wife good luck, and were off.

"Now we can go back to bed," said Peter.

"Oh, dear! Can't we start on?"

"At this hour? Why, I suppose we could, but——"

"Let's, then." In the turmoil of her spirit she wanted to be quit forever of Torney's Haven for Tourists and its atmosphere of unexpected emotions and disconcerting impulses. Maybe something of this had trickled into Peter's mind, too, for presently he said:

"Don't you know it's dangerous to wake a sound sleeper too suddenly?"

"So I've heard."

"You can't tell what might happen. I mean, a man isn't quite responsible, you know, before he comes quite awake."

So he was apologizing. Very proper.

"Let's forget it."

"Yes," he agreed quietly. "I'll have quite a little to forget."

"So will I," she thought, startled at the realization.

They packed, and chugged out, one cylinder missing. "I hope the old junkheap holds together till we reach New York," remarked Peter.

"Are we going all the way in this?"

"Unless you can think of a cheaper way."

"But it isn't ours. It's the fat man's."

"I doubt it. Looks to me as if it had been stolen and gypped up with new paint and fake numbers. However, we'll leave it somewhere in Jersey if we get that far, and write to both license numbers to come and get it. How does that set on an empty conscience?"

"Never mind my conscience. That isn't the worst emptiness I'm suffering from. What's in the house for breakfast? It's nearly sunup."

"Potatoes. Pecans." He investigated their scanty store and looked up. "There are only three spuds left."

"Is that all?"

Something careless in her reply made him scan her face sharply. "There ought to be five. There are two missing. You had charge of the larder. Well?"

"I took 'em. You see——"

"Without saying a word about it to me? You must have pinched them out when we were on the island and cooked them for yourself while I was working on the boat," he figured somberly. Part of this was true, but not all of it. The rest she was saving to confound him with. "Do you, by any chance, still think that this is a picnic?"

Now she *wouldn't* tell him! She was indignant and hurt. He'd be sorry! When he came to her with a potato now, she would haughtily decline it—if her rueful stomach didn't get the better of her wrathful fortitude.

In resentment more convincing than her own, he built the wayside fire, boiled the water and inserted one lone potato; the smallest at that. He counted out five pecans, added two more, and handed the lot to her. He then got out his pocketknife, opened it, and prodded the bubbling tuber. Judging it soft enough, he neatly speared it out upon a plate. Elspeth pretended a total lack of interest. She hoped she'd have the resolution to decline her half with hauteur. She didn't get the chance.

Peter split the potato, sprinkled on salt, and ate it all.

With difficulty, Elspeth suppressed a roar of rage. That was the kind of man he was, then! Selfish, greedy, mean, tyrannical, unfair, smug, bad-tempered, uncouth—her stock ran thin. How idiotically she had overestimated him! Rough but noble; that had been her formula for his character. And now look at him, pigging down the last delicious fragments while she was to be content with a handful of nuts. Nuts! She rose in regal resentment, flung her seven pecans into the fire, and stalked back to the car.

Somewhere in the vicinity of Emporia, eighty miles north of their breakfast, he spoke. "No good in sulking, you know."

"I'm *not* sulking." Which closed that opening.

Nevertheless, Elspeth was relieved. An oppressive feeling that maybe his anger would prove more lasting than her own had tainted her satisfaction in being the injured party. One solicitude, too, he exhibited. He kept tucking her up in the robe.

This would have been less reassuring had she understood its genesis. He was afraid that her costume might be recognized. He even thought of suggesting that she might effect a trade in some secondhand store. In her present state of childish petulance, however, he judged it useless to suggest this. Some other way must be found.

Some money was still left to them. Elspeth saw her companion shaking his head over it when their gas gave out, happily near a filling station. His worried expression weakened her anger, but she couldn't bring herself to admit she was sorry. Not yet.

"There's a cheap camp seventy miles from here," said he. "But if we sleep there we can't have much of a dinner."

"Potatoes," said the recalcitrant Elspeth. She'd teach him!

They dined at a roadside stand which, in ordinary conditions, she would have considered loathsome. Every odor of it now brought prickly sensations to her palate.

The night presented a problem troubling to her mind. No shared but unpartitioned cabin for her! Last night's experience had been too revelatory. What made things difficult was that she had told him she needed no more walls of Jericho to insure peaceful sleep. Now if she asked him to put up the curtain, what would he think?

Pursuant to his policy of avoiding large cities and the possible interest of traffic cops, Peter had planned their route westward again, giving Richmond a wide berth. They flashed without stop through towns with hospitable restaurants only to pull up at a roadside stand of austere menu, near Sweet Briar.

Never had Elspeth seen the important sum of twenty-five cents laid out so economically as by Peter's method. Baked beans with thick, fat, glorious gollops of pork; a half-loaf of bread, and bitter coffee. To say that her hunger was appeased would be overstatement. But a sense of returned well-being comforted her. She even felt that she could face the morning's potato, if any, with courage. Meantime, there remained the arrangements for the night.

Peter handled that decisively, upon their arrival at the camp. Their cabin was dreary, chill, and stoveless. When he brought in the robe from the car, she hoped for it over her bunk. Not at all; out came his little tool kit; up went the separating cord, and over it was firmly pinned the warm fabric.

With a regrettable though feminine want of logic, Elspeth nursed a grievance; he needn't have been at such pains to raise that wall again without a request from the person most interested. She went to sleep crossly but promptly.

In the morning the robe was tucked snugly about her. How long had that been there? She looked around and made a startling discovery. Her clothes were gone. So was Peter. Also, when she looked out, the car. The wild idea occurred to her that he had stolen her outfit and run away, *à la* Thad Banker. One thing was certain: to rise and wander forth clad in those grotesque pajamas was out of the question. Turning over, she fell asleep again.

Some inner sensation of his nearness awoke her, or perhaps it was, less occultly, his footsteps outside, approaching, pausing. She craned upward to bring her vision level with the window. Peter was standing with his side face toward her, a plump bundle beneath his arm. Her clothes, probably, which he had taken out to clean. How nice of him!

He set down his burden and took off his belt. With a knife he slit the stitches in the leather, carefully prying something from between the strips. It was a tight-folded bill.

So he had been holding out on her! Keeping her on gnat's diet. Letting her go hungry while he gorged himself on boiled potato and salt, and gloated over his reserve fund. Beast! This knowledge, too, she would hold back for his ultimate discomfiture. It was a composed and languid voice which responded to his knock on the door.

"Hello! How are you feeling, Elspeth?"

"Very well, thank you. Where have you been?"

"Act two, scene one of matrimonial crisis," chuckled Peter. "Hubby returns early in morning. Wife demands explanation. Husband is ready with it: 'You'd be surprised.'" There was a distinct trace of nervousness in his bearing.

"Well, surprise me," returned Elspeth, with hardly concealed hostility. "Where are my clothes?"

"That's the point. They're—uh—I—er—well, the fact is, I pawned 'em. In Charlottesville."

"You—pawned—my—clothes! Where's the money?" If that was the bill in the belt, she proposed to know it.

"I spent most of it. On other clothes. You said your feet hurt you."

"When we were walking. We don't have to walk any more."

"How do you know? We aren't out of the woods yet. And you don't need such a fancy rig, traveling with me. And we do need the little bit extra I picked up on the trade."

Stern and uncompromising was the glare which she directed upon his bundle. "Let me see."

Her immediate reaction to the dingy, shoddy, nondescript outfit he disclosed was an involuntary yip of distress.

"Don't you like 'em?" he asked.

"They're terrible! They're ghastly!"

"The woman said they were serviceable. Put 'em on. I'll wait outside."

It would have taken a sturdier optimism than Peter's to maintain a sun-kissed countenance in the face of the transformation which he presently witnessed. Hardly could he recognize her in that horrid misfit which she was pinning here, adjusting there.

"Hand me the mirror, please."

"Perhaps you'd better not——"

"Will you be so good as to do as I ask?"

"Oh, all *right!*"

She took one long, comprehensive survey and burst into tears.

"Don't, Elspeth," he protested, appalled. "What's the difference? There's no one to see you."

"There's me," she gulped. "And there's you."

"I don't mind." As if he were bearing up courageously under an affliction.

"I'm a *sight,*" she wailed. "I'm hideous! Go and get my things back."

"It can't be done."

"I won't go out in these frightful things. I won't. I won't. I *won't!*"

"Who's going to pay the rent if you stay?"

Obtaining no reply to this pertinent inquiry, he sighed and went out. Down the breeze, there presently drifted to Elspeth's nostrils the tang of wood smoke. Her face appeared in the window.

"About those missing potatoes," said she. (How mean she was going to make him feel in a minute!) "Are you interested in knowing what became of them?"

"It doesn't matter. They're gone."

"They're gone where they'll do the most good," she returned with slow impressiveness. "I gave them away."

"Without consulting me?"

"Do I have to consult you about everything I do?"

"We-ell, some people might figure that I had an interest in those potatoes."

"Well, I gave them to a poor old woman who needed them. She was hungry."

"Umph! Feeling sure, I suppose, that your generosity would cost you nothing, as I'd share the remainder with you. Error Number One."

"Peter, I wouldn't have thought anyone could be so des-des-despisable!"

This left him unmoved. "Who was the starving beneficiary? I'll bet it was that old creature with the black bonnet and gold teeth in the bus."

"How did you know?"

"She's the sort you would help. In case you'd like to know, that old hoarder had her bag half full of almond chocolates. I saw her buy 'em at Charleston."

"Hoarder, yourself!" Enraged at the failure of her bombshell, she fell back on her last ammunition. "What did you take out of your belt this morning?"

"Oh, you saw that, did you? Watchful little angel!"

"I'm not! I just happened to see it. A bill. A big one, I'll bet. You had it all the time. And you've starved me and bullied me and made me walk miles and sleep in barns, while you could just as well have——"

"Hired a special train. On ten dollars."

"Ten dollars is a lot of money." (Ideas change.)

"Now, I'll tell you about that ten dollars," said he with cold precision. "It's my backlog. It's the last resort. It's the untouchable. It's the dead line of absolute necessity."

"You needn't touch it on my account." (Just like a nasty-tempered little brat, she told herself.) "Of course, starvation isn't absolute necessity."

"Can you do simple arithmetic?"

"Yes, I'm not quite an idiot, even if you do think so, Peter."

"Try this one, then. We've got something over five hundred miles to go. Gas will average us seventeen cents. This old mudcart of Banker's won't do better than twelve miles on a gallon. Now, can any bright little girl in this class tell me how much over that leaves us to eat, sleep and live on, not counting oil, ferry charge and incidentals?"

"I can't. And I don't want to," retorted Elspeth, very dispirited. A long, dull silence enclosed them like a globe. She shattered it. "Peter!"

"What?"

"D'you know why I hate you?"

"I'll bite," said he wearily. "Why?"

"Because, darn you! you're always right and I'm always wrong. Peter! Peter, dear! A potato, Peter. Please, Peter; one potato. Just one. The littlest. I know I don't deserve it, but——"

"Oh, what's the *use!*" vociferated Peter, throwing up both hands in abject and glad surrender. And that quarrel drifted on the smoke of their fire down to the limbo of things become insignificant, yet never quite to be forgotten.

Two young people, haggard, gaunt, shabby, bluish with the chill of an April storm, drove their battered car aboard the Fort Lee ferry as the boat pulled out. They were sharing a bag of peanuts with the conscientious exactitude of penury: one to you; one to me. Quarter of the way across, both were asleep. At the halfway distance the whistle blared and they woke up.

"We're nearly there," observed the girl without any special enthusiasm.

"Yes," said the man with still less.

A hiatus of some length. "Why didn't you tell me about blacking Corker's boots?"

"What about it?"

"It was on a bet, wasn't it?"

"Yes. In college. I picked the wrong team. If I'd won, the Corker would have typed my theses for the term. What put you on?"

"A telegram from Cork."

"Oh! The one to Bessie Smith that saved our lives in Raleigh?"

She nodded. "Anyway, I knew all the time you weren't a valet," she asserted.

He cocked a mild, derisive eye at her. "You're not building up any rosy picture of me as a perfect gentleman, are you?"

"No-o. I don't know what you are."

"Don't let it worry you. Go back to sleep."

"You're always telling me to go to sleep," she muttered discontentedly. She rubbed her nose on his shoulder. "Peter."

He sighed and kissed her.

"You needn't be so solemn about it."

"I'm not feeling exactly sprightly."

"Because we're almost home? But we'll be seeing each other soon."

"I thought that headliner of the air was waiting to fly you somewhere."

"Who? Oh-h-h-h, King." She began to laugh. "Isn't that funny! I'd absolutely forgotten about King. He doesn't matter. When am I going to see you?" As he made no reply, she became vaguely alarmed. "You're not going right back?"

"No. I've got that possible contract to look after. Down in Jersey."

"But you'll be in town again. And I'll see you then."

"No."

"Peter! Why not?"

"Self-preservation," he proclaimed oracularly, "is the first law of nature."

"You don't want to see me again?"

"Put it any way you like," came the broad-minded permission, "just so the main point gets across."

"But I think that's absolutely lousy!" Another point occurred to her. "There's no reason why you shouldn't if it's because—well, that business about my being married was a good deal exaggerated. If that makes any difference."

"It does. It makes it worse."

"Oh! . . . You don't seem surprised, though."

"Me? I should say not! I've known from the first that was all bunk."

"Have you, Smarty? How?"

"You tried to put it over that you'd been wearing a wedding ring. But there was no band of white on the tan of your finger."

"Deteckative! I haven't had a bit of luck trying to fool you about anything, have I, Peter? Not even putting across the superior-goddess idea. And now you're the one that's being snooty."

"I'm not. I'm being sensible. See here, Elspeth. It may or may not have been called to your attention that you're a not wholly unattractive young person—and that I myself am not yet beyond the age of——"

"Consent," broke in the irrepressible Elspeth.

"——damfoolishness," substituted Peter, with severity. "So," he concluded, with an effect of logic, "we may as well call it a day."

"Not to mention several nights." She turned the brilliance of mirthful eyes upon him. "Wouldn't it be funny if you fell in love with me, Peter?"

"Funny for the spectators. Painful for the bear."

"Then don't do it, Bear!" Another idea occurred to her. "How much money have you got left?"

"Forty-odd cents."

"Now that you're in New York you can get more, of course."

"Yes? Where?"

"At the bank, I suppose. Where does one get money?"

"That's what I've always wanted to know," he grinned.

"I can get all I want tomorrow. I'll lend you a hundred dollars. Or more if you want it."

"No; thank you."

"But I borrowed yours!" she cried. "At least, you paid for me."

"That's different."

"I don't see how." Of course she did see, and inwardly approved. "But—but I owe you money!" she cried. "I'd forgotten all about that. You'll let me pay that back, of course."

If she expected him to deprecate politely the idea she was swiftly undeceived. "The sooner, the better," said Peter cheerfully.

"I'll bet you've got it all set down in that precious notebook of yours."

"Every cent." He tore out a leaf which he handed to her.

"Where can I send it?"

He gave an address on a street whose name she had never before heard; Darrow, or Barrow, or some such matter.

In the splendor of the great circular court off Park Avenue, the bedraggled automobile looked impudently out of place. The doorkeeper almost choked with amazement as the luxurious Miss Elspeth Andrews, clad in such garments as had never before affronted those august portals, jumped out, absently responding to his greeting.

"I think your father is expecting you, miss," said he.

"Oh, Lord!" exclaimed Elspeth. "Now, what brought him here?"

Peter could have told her, but didn't. He was looking straight through the windshield. She was looking at him with slightly lifted brows.

"Good-by, Elspeth," said he huskily.

"Good-by, Peter. You've been awfully mean to me. I've loved it!"

Why, thought Peter as he went on his way, did she have to use that particular word in that special tone at that unhappy moment?

Between Alexander Bruce MacGregor Andrews and his daughter, Elspeth, there existed a lively and irritable affection of precarious status, based upon a fundamental similarity of character and a prevalent lack of mutual understanding. That she should have willfully run away from home and got herself and him on the front pages of the papers, seemed to him an outrage of the first order.

"But it was your smearing the thing all over the air that got us into the papers," pointed out Elspeth, which didn't help much as a contribution to the *entente cordiale*. Both sulked for forty-eight hours.

Meantime, there arrived by special delivery a decidedly humid shoebox addressed in an uncompromisingly straight-up-and-down hand—just exactly the kind one would expect, thought the girl, knowing whose it was at first sight—full of the freshest, most odorous bunch of arbutus she had ever beheld. Something about it unmistakably defined it as having been picked by the sender.

Elspeth searched minutely for a note; there was none. She carried the box to her room and threw three clusters of orchids and a spray of gardenias into the scrapbasket. After that she went to a five-and-ten-cent store, made a purchase at the toy counter, had it boxed, and herself mailed it to the address given her by Peter Warne. The shipment did not include the money she owed him. That detail had escaped her mind.

"Scotty, dear." She greeted her father in the style of their companionable moods. "Do let's be sensible."

Mr. Andrews grunted suspiciously. "Suppose you begin."

"I'm going to. Drink your cocktail first." She settled down on the arm of his chair.

"Now what devilment are you up to?" demanded the apprehensive parent.

"Not a thing. I've decided to tell you about my trip."

Having her narrative all duly mapped out, she ran through it smoothly enough, hoping that he would not notice a few cleverly glossed passages. Disapproval in the paternal expression presently yielded to amused astonishment.

"Nervy kid!" he chuckled. "I'll bet it did you good."

"It didn't do me any harm. And I certainly found out a few things I'd never known before."

"Broadening effect of travel. Who did you say this young man was that looked after you?"

"I'm coming to that. The question is, what are you going to do for him?"

"What does he want?"

"I don't know that he exactly wants anything. But he's terribly poor, Scotty. Why, just think! He had to reckon up each time how much he could afford to spend on a meal!"

"Yes? I'm told there are quite a few people in this country in the same fix," observed Mr. Andrews dryly. "How much'll I make out the check for?"

"That's the trouble. I don't believe he'd take it. He's one of those indebe-goshdarn-pendent birds. Wouldn't listen to my lending him some money."

"Humph! That probably means he's fallen for your fair young charms. Be funny if he hadn't."

"I'll tell you what would be funnier."

"What'd be funnier?"

"If I'd fallen for him," was the brazen response.

"Poof! You're always imagining you're in love with the newest hero in sight. Remember that young Danish diplo——"

"Yes; I do. What of it? I always get over it, don't I? And I'll get over this. You'd think he was terrible, Dad. He's sure rough. You ought to have seen Little Daughter being bossed around by him and taking it."

"Is that so?" said her father, spacing his words sardonically. "Bossed you, did he? He and who else?"

"Oh, Peter doesn't need any help."

The grin was wiped off the Andrews face. "Who?"

"Peter. That's his name. Peter Warne."

"*What?*"

"Gracious! Don't yell so. Do you know him?"

"I haven't that pleasure as yet. Just let me make sure about this." He went into the adjoining room, whence he emerged with a sheaf of papers. "Peter Warne. So he's poor, is he?"

"Desperately."

"Well, he won't be, after tomorrow."

"Oh, Scotty! How do you know? Is he going to get some money? I'm so glad!"

"Some money is correct. Ten thousand dollars, to be exact."

"From his tar-pine or something process? How did *you* know about it?"

"From me. I don't know anything about——"

"From you?" Her lips parted; her eyes were wide and alarmed. "What for?"

"Information leading to the discovery and return of Elspeth, daughter of——"

"The reward? For me? Peter? I don't believe it. Peter wouldn't do such a thing. Take money for——"

"He has done it. Put in his claim for the reward. Do you want to see the proof?"

"I wouldn't believe it anyway."

Alexander Andrews studied her defiant face with a concern that became graver. This looked serious. Selecting a letter and a telegram from his dossier, he put them into her reluctant hand. At sight of the writing her heart sank. It was unmistakably that of the address on the box of arbutus. The note cited the writer's telegram of the fourteenth ("That's the day after we got off the island," thought Elspeth. "He was selling me out then.") and asked for an appointment.

"He's coming to my office at ten-thirty Thursday morning."

"Are you going to give him the money?"

"It looks as if I'd have to."

"He certainly worked hard enough for it," she said bitterly. "And I expect he needs it."

"I might be able to work a compromise," mused the canny Scot. "Though I'm afraid he's got the material for a bothersome lawsuit. If any of the other claimants"—he indicated the sheaf of letters and telegrams— "had a decent case, we could set off one against the other. The most insistent is a person named Shapley."

"Don't let him have it," said the girl hastily. "I'd rather Peter should get it, though I'd never have believed—— Sold down the river!" She forced a laugh. "I brought a price, anyway."

"I've a good mind to give him a fight for it. It would mean more publicity, though."

"Oh, no!" breathed Elspeth.

"Enough's enough, eh? Though it couldn't be worse than what we've had."

"It could. Much worse. If you're going to see Pe—Mr. Warne, I'd better tell you something, Father. I've been traveling as Mrs. Peter Warne."

*"Elspeth!"*

"It isn't what you think. Purely economy—with the accent on the 'pure.' But it wouldn't look pretty in print. Oh, damn!" Her voice broke treacherously. "I thought Peter was so straight."

Her father walked up and down the room several times. He then went over and put his arm around his daughter's shoulders. "It's all right, dawtie. We'll get you out of it. And we'll find a way to keep this fellow's mouth shut. I'm having a detectaphone set up in my office, and if he makes one slip we'll have him by the short hairs for blackmail."

"Peter doesn't make slips," returned his daughter. "It's his specialty not to. Oh, well, let's go into dinner, Scotty."

Resolutely, she put the arbutus out of her room when she went up to bed that night. But the spicy odor from far springtime woodlands clung about the place like a plea for the absent.

Stern logic of the morning to which she sorrowfully awoke filled in the case against Peter. Nevertheless and notwithstanding, "I don't believe it," said Elspeth's sore heart. "And I won't believe it until—until——"

Until Peter had his chance. But would she see Peter again?

Severe as were the fittings of Mr. Alexander Bruce MacGregor Andrews' spacious office, they were less so than the glare which apprised Peter Warne, upon his entry, that this spare, square man did not like him and probably never would. That was all right with Peter. He was prepared not to like Mr. Andrews, either. On this propitious basis the two confronted each other.

After a formidable silence which the younger man bore without visible evidence of discomposure, his host barked:

"Sit down."

"Thank you," said Peter. He sat down.

"You have come about the money, I assume."

"Yes."

"Kindly reduce your claim to writing."

"You'll find it there." He handed over a sheet of paper. "Itemized."

"What's this?" Mr. Andrews' surprised eye ran over it.

"Traveling expenses. Elsp—your daughter's."

The father gave the column of figures his analytical attention. "Boat, twenty dollars," he read. "You didn't take my daughter to Cuba, did you?"

"I had to steal a boat to get through the flood. The owner ought to be reimbursed. If you think that's not a fair charge, I'll assume half of it. Everything else is split."

"Hmph! My daughter's share of food, lodging and gasoline, excluding the—er—alleged boat, seems to figure up to eighteen dollars and fifty-six cents. Where did you lodge?"

"Wherever we could."

With the paper before him Mr. Andrews began to hammer his desk. "You have the temerity, the impudence, the effrontery, the—the—anyway, you come here to hold me up for ten thousand dollars and on top of that you try to spring a doctored expense account on me!"

"Doctored!" echoed Peter. "Maybe you think you could do it for less?"

Taken aback, Mr. Andrews ceased his operations on the desk. "We'll pass that for the main point," he grunted. "Upon what do you base your claim for the ten thousand dollars?"

"Nothing," was the placid reply. "I made no claim."

"Your telegram. Your letter——"

"You couldn't have read them. I simply warned you against paying anybody else's claim. You had others, I suppose."

"Others! A couple of hundred!"

"One signed Horace Shapley?"

"I believe so."

"I don't like him," observed Peter, and explained.

"Then your idea," interposed Mr. Andrews, "was to get in first merely to block off this other person. Is that it?"

"Yes."

"And you aren't claiming any part of the reward?"

"No."

"You're crazy," declared the other. "Or maybe I am. What *do* you want?"

Peter gently indicated the expense account. Mr. Andrews went over it again.

"You mean to tell me that you kept my daughter for five days and more on a total of eighteen dollars and fifty-six cents?"

"There are the figures."

Mr. Andrews leaned forward. "Did she kick much?"

Peter's grin was a bit rueful. "There were times when——"

"You'd have liked to sock her. I know. Why didn't you present your bill to her?"

"I did. I reckon she just forgot it."

"She would! . . . Have a cigar." As the young fellow lighted up, his entertainer was writing and entering a check.

"As a matter of correct business, I ought to have Elspeth's O. K. on this bill. However, I'll pass it, including the boat. Receipt here, please." The amount was $1,038.56.

Shaking his head, Peter pushed the check across the desk. "Thank you, but I can't take this, Mr. Andrews."

"Bosh! Elspeth told me you were broke."

"I am . . . No; I'm not, either. I forgot. I've just made a deal on a new process of mine. Anyway, I couldn't take that—that bonus."

"That's funny. If you're no longer broke, I should think you'd be above bringing me a trifling expense account for—er—entertaining my daughter."

"It's a matter of principle," returned Peter firmly.

Mr. Andrews rose and smote his caller on the shoulder. "I begin to see how you made that little spitfire of mine toe the mark. More than I've been able to do for the past ten years. Eighteen dollars and fifty-six cents, huh?" He sank back in his chair and laughed. "See here, my boy; I like you. I like your style. Will you take that money as a present from me?"

"Sorry, sir, but I'd rather not."

The older man stared him down. "Because I'm Elspeth's father, eh? You're in love with her, I suppose."

Peter grew painfully red. "God forbid!" he muttered.

"What do you mean, God forbid?" shouted the magnate. "Better men than you have been in love with her."

"All right, Mr. Andrews," said Peter in desperation. "Then I am, too, I have been from the first. Now, you tell me—you're her father—what's the sense of it with a girl like Elspeth? I'm going back to Florida with a contract for eight thousand a year, to complete my process."

"That's more than I was making at your age."

"It's more than I expect to be making at yours," said Peter with candor. "But how far would that go with her? Look me over, sir. Even if I had a chance with Elspeth, would you advise a fellow like me to try to marry her?"

"No, I wouldn't!" roared the father. "You're too darn good for her."

"Don't talk like a fool," snapped Peter.

"Just for that," reflected Mr. Andrews as his caller withdrew, jamming a substituted check into his pocket, "I'll bet you'll have little enough to say about it when the time comes."

He sent for Elspeth and left her alone with the detectaphone. What that unpoetic cylinder spouted forth rang in her heart like the music of the spheres with the morning and evening stars in the solo parts. So *that* was how Peter felt about it.

Memory obligingly supplied the number on Darrow or Farrow or Barrow or whatever strange street it was. The taxi man whom she hailed earned her admiration by knowing all about it.

Peter said: "Come in," in a spiritless manner. With a totally different vocal effect he added: "What are *you* doing *here?*" and tacked onto that "You oughtn't to be here at all."

"Why not?" Elspeth sat down.

He muttered something wherein the word "proper" seemed to carry the emphasis, and in which the term "landlady" occurred.

"Proper!" jeered his visitor. "You talk to me about propriety after we've been traveling together and sharing the same room for nearly a week!"

"But this is New York," he pointed out.

"And you're packing up to leave it. When?"

"Tonight."

"Without the ten thousand dollars reward?"

"How did you know about that? Your fath——"

"I've just come from his office. You might better have taken the check."

"Don't want it."

"That's silly. What," she inquired reasonably, "have you got to get married on?"

"Eight thousand a ye—— I'm not going to get married," he interrupted himself with needless force.

"Not after compromising a young and innocent——"

"I haven't compromised anyone." Sulkily and doggedly.

"Peter! I suppose registering me as your wife all over the map isn't compromising. Did you ever hear of the Mann Act?"

"B-b-b-but——"

"Yes; I know all about that 'but.' It's a great big, important 'but,' but there's another bigger 'but' to be considered. We know what happened and didn't happen on our trip, *but* nobody else would ever believe it in this world. I certainly wouldn't."

"Nor I," he agreed. "Unless," he qualified hastily, "the girl was you."

"Or the man was you."

They laughed with dubious heartiness. When they had done laughing, there seemed to be nothing to follow, logically. Elspeth got up slowly.

"Where are you going?" demanded Peter, in a panic.

"If you don't like me any more"—she put the slightest possible stress on the verb, leaving him to amend it if he chose—"I'm sorry I came."

To this rueful observation, Peter offered no response.

"You did like me once, you know. You as much as admitted it."

Peter swore.

"Did you or did you not tell my father that you would never get over it?"

"It?"

"Well—me."

"Your father," said Peter wrathfully, "is a human sieve."

"No; he isn't. There was a detectaphone listening in on everything you said. I got it all from that."

"In that case," said the now desperate and reckless Peter, "I may as well get it off my chest." And he repeated what he had earlier said about his feelings, with a fervor that wiped the mischief from Elspeth's face.

"Oh-h-h-h!" she murmured, a little dazed. "That's the way you feel."

"No, it isn't. It isn't half of it."

"Where do we go from here?" thought the girl. The atmosphere of sprightly combat and adventure had changed. She was not breathing quite so easily. Her uncertain look fell upon an object at the top of the half-packed carryall. "Oh!" she exclaimed. "You got my present."

"Yes; I got it."

"I hoped you liked it." Politely.

"Not particularly."

Her eyes widened. "Why not?"

"Well, I may be oversensitive where you're concerned, but I don't care so much about being called a tinhorn sport, because—well, I don't know, but I suppose it's because I let you pay back the money for our trip. What do I know about the way girls look at those things, anyway!" he concluded morosely.

One girl was looking at him with a mixture of contempt, amusement, pity, and something stronger than any of these. "Oh, you boob!" she breathed. "That isn't a tin horn. That's a trumpet."

"A *trumpet?*"

"The kind What's-his-name blew before the walls of Jericho, if you have to have a diagram. Oh, *Pee*-ter; you're such a dodo!" sighed Elspeth. "What am I ever going to do about you? Would you like to kiss me, Peter?"

"Yes," said Peter. And he did.

"This means," he informed her presently, and dubiously, "our having to live in a Florida swamp——"

"On eighteen dollars and fifty-six cents?"

"On eight thousand a year. That isn't much more, to you. You'll hate it."

"I'll love it. D'you know where I'd like to land on our wedding trip, Peter?"

"Yes. Dake's Two-dollar Cabins; Clean; Comfortable; Reasonable."

"*And* respectable. You're too clever, Peter, darling."

"Because that's exactly what I'd like. Social note: Mr. and Mrs. Peter Warne are stopping in Jaw-jaw on their return trip South."

"Let's go," said Elspeth joyously.

Mrs. Dake, in the wing off the tourist-camp office, yawned herself awake of an early May morning and addressed her husband. "That's a funny couple in Number Seven, Tim. Do you reckon they're respectable?"

"I should worry. They registered all right, didn't they?"

"Uh-huh. Wouldn't take any other cabin but Seven. And wanted an extra blanket. This hot night."

"Well, we could spare it."

"That isn't the only queer thing about 'em. After you was asleep, I looked out and there was the young fellah mopin' around. By and by he went in, and right soon somebody blew a horn. Just as plain as you ever heard. What do you know about that, Tim?"

Mr. Dake yawned. "What they do after they're registered and paid up is their business, not our'n."

Which is the proper and practical attitude for the management of a well-conducted tourist camp.

# Monsieur Beaucaire

## BOOTH TARKINGTON

*A dashing Frenchman loves a beautiful English-woman in the days of swordplay and gay pageantry. Neither Booth Tarkington nor Monsieur Beaucaire need any introduction. The story is included here because it is so thoroughly delightful and possesses that quality of charm and excitement which is the very essence of this anthology.*

THE YOUNG FRENCHMAN did very well what he had planned to do. His guess that the Duke would cheat proved good. As the unshod half-dozen figures that had been standing noiselessly in the entryway stole softly into the shadows of the chamber, he leaned across the table and smilingly plucked a card out of the big Englishman's sleeve.

"Merci, M. le Duc!" he laughed, rising and stepping back from the table.

The Englishman cried out, "It means the dirty work of silencing you with my bare hands!" and came at him.

"Do not move," said M. Beaucaire, so sharply that the other paused. "Observe behind you."

The Englishman turned, and saw what trap he had blundered into; then stood transfixed, impotent, alternately scarlet with rage and white with the vital shame of discovery. M. Beaucaire remarked, indicating the silent figures by a polite wave of the hand, "Is it not a compliment to monsieur that I procure six large men to subdue him? They are quite devote' to me, and monsieur is alone. Could it be that he did not wish even his lackeys to know he play with the yo'ng Frenchman who Meestaire Nash does not like in the pomp-room? Monsieur is unfortunate to have come on foot and alone to my apartment."

The Duke's mouth foamed over with chaotic revilement. His captor smiled brightly, and made a slight gesture, as one who brushes aside a boisterous insect. With the same motion he quelled to stony quiet a resentful impetus of his servants toward the Englishman.

"It's murder, is it, you carrion!" finished the Duke.

M. Beaucaire lifted his shoulders in a mock shiver. "What words! No, no, no! No killing! A such word to a such host! No, no, not mur-r-der; only disgrace!" He laughed a clear, light laugh with a rising inflection, seeming to launch himself upon an adventurous quest for sympathy.

"You little devilish scullion!" spat out the Duke.

"Tut, tut! But I forget. Monsieur has pursue' his studies of deportment amongs' his fellow-countrymen."

"Do you dream a soul in Bath will take your word that I—that I——"

"That M. le Duc de Winterset had a card up his sleeve?"

"You pitiful stroller, you stableboy, born in a stable——"

"Is it not an honor to be born where monsieur must have been bred?"

"You scurvy foot-boy, you greasy barber, you cutthroat groom——"

"Overwhelm'!" The young man bowed with imperturbable elation. "M. le Duc appoint' me to all the office' of his househol'."

"You mustachioed fool, there are not five people of quality in Bath will speak to you——"

"No, monsieur, not on the parade; but how many come to play with me here? Because I will play always, night or day, for what one will, for any long, and al—ways fair, monsieur."

"You outrageous varlet! Every one knows you came to England as the French Ambassador's barber. What man of fashion will listen to you? Who will believe you?"

"All people, monsieur. Do you think I have not calculate', that I shall make a failure of my little enterprise?"

"Bah!"

"Will monsieur not reseat himself?" M. Beaucaire made a low bow. "So. We must not be too tire' for Lady Malbourne's rout. Ha, ha! And you, Jean, Victor, and you others, retire; go in the hallway. Attend at the entrance, François. So; now we shall talk. Monsieur, I wish you to think very cool. Then listen; I will be briefly. It is that I am well known to be all, entire' hones'. Gamblist? Ah, yes; true and mos' profitable; but fair, al—ways fair; every one say that. Is it not so? Think of it. And—is there never a w'isper come to M. le Duc that not all people belief him to play al—ways hones'? Ha, ha! Did it almos' be *said* to him las' year, after when he play' with Milor' Tappin'ford at the chocolate-house——"

"You dirty scandal-monger!" the Duke burst out. "I'll——"

"Monsieur, monsieur!" said the Frenchman. "It is a poor valor to insult a helpless captor. Can he retort upon his own victim? But it is for you to think of what I say. True, I am not reco'nize on the parade; that my frien's who come here do not present me to their ladies; that Meestaire Nash has reboff' me in the pomp-room; still, am I not known for being hones' and fair in my play, and will I *not* be belief', even I, when I lif' my voice and charge you aloud with what is already w'isper'? Think of it! You are a noble, and there will be some hang-dogs who might not fall away from you. Only such would be lef' to you. Do you want it tol'? And you can keep out of France, monsieur? I have lef' his service, but I have still the ear of M. de Mirepoix, and he know' I never lie. Not a gentleman will play you when you come to Paris."

The Englishman's white lip showed a row of scarlet dots upon it. "How much do you want?" he said.

The room rang with the gay laughter of Beaucaire. "I hol' your note' for seven-hunder' pound'. You can have them, monsieur. Why does a such great man come to play M. Beaucaire? Because no one else willin' to play M. le Duc—he cannot pay. Ha, ha! So he come' to good Monsieur Beaucaire. Money, ha, ha! What I want with money?"

His Grace of Winterset's features were set awry to a sinister pattern. He sat glaring at his companion in a snarling silence.

"Money? Pouf!" snapped the little gambler. "No, no, no! It is that M. le Duc, impoverish', somewhat in a bad odor as he is, yet command the *entrée* any-where—onless I— Ha, ha! Eh, monsieur?"

"Ha! You dare think to force *me*——"

M. Beaucaire twirled the tip of his slender mustache around the end of his white forefinger. Then he said: "Monsieur and me goin' to Lady Malbourne's ball to-night—M. le Duc and me!"

The Englishman roared, "Curse your impudence!"

"Sit quiet. Oh, yes, that's all; we goin' together."

"No!"

"Certain. I make all my little plan'. 'Tis all arrange'." He paused, and then said gravely, "You goin' present me to Lady Mary Carlisle."

The other laughed in utter scorn. "Lady Mary Carlisle, of all women alive, would be the first to prefer the devil to a man of no birth, barber."

" 'Tis all arrange'; have no fear; nobody question monsieur's guest. You goin' take me to-night——"

"No!"

"Yes. And after—then *I* have the *entrée*. Is it much I ask? This one little favor, and I never w'isper, never breathe that—it is to say, I am always forever silent of monsieur's misfortune."

"*You* have the *entrée!*" sneered the other. "Go to a lackey's rout and dance with the kitchen maids. If I would, I could not present you to Bath society. I should have cartels from the fathers, brothers, and lovers of every wench and madam in the place, even I. You would be thrust from Lady Malbourne's door five minutes after you entered it."

"No, no, no!"

"Half the gentlemen in Bath have been here to play. They would know you, wouldn't they, fool? You've had thousands out of Bantison, Rakell, Guilford, and Townbrake. They would have you lashed by the grooms as your ugly deserts are. *You* to speak to Lady Mary Carlisle! 'Od's blood! You! Also, dolt, she would know you if you escaped the others. She stood within a yard of you when Nash expelled you the pump-room."

M. Beaucaire flushed slightly. "You think I did not see?" he asked.

"Do you dream that because Winterset introduces a low fellow he will be tolerated—that Bath will receive a barber?"

"I have the distinction to call monsieur's attention," replied the young man gayly, "I have renounce' that profession."

"Fool!"

"I am now a man of honor!"

"Faugh!"

"A man of the parts," continued the young Frenchman, "and of deportment; is it not so? Have you seen me of a fluster, or gross ever, or, what shall I say—*bourgeois*? Shall you be shame' for your guest' manner? No, no! And my appearance, is it of the people? Clearly, no. Do I not compare in taste of apparel with your yo'ng Englishman? Ha, ha! To be hope'. Ha, ha! So I am goin' talk with Lady Mary Carlisle."

"Bah!" The Duke made a savage burlesque. "'Lady Mary Carlisle, may I assume the honor of presenting the barber of the Marquis de Mirepoix?' So, is it?"

"No, monsieur," smiled the young man. "Quite not so. You shall have nothing to worry you, nothing in the worl'. I am goin' to assassinate my poor mustachio—also remove this horrible black peruke, and emerge in my own hair. Behol'!" He swept the heavy curled, mass from his head as he spoke, and his hair, coiled under the great wig, fell to his shoulders, and sparkled yellow in the candle-light. He tossed his head to shake the hair back from his cheeks. "When it is dress', I am transform'; nobody can know me; you shall observe. See how little I ask of you, how very little bit. No one shall reco'nize 'M. Beaucaire' or 'Victor.' Ha, ha! 'Tis all arrange'; you have nothing to fear."

"Curse you," said the Duke, "do you think I'm going to be saddled with you wherever I go as long as you choose?"

"A mistake. No. All I requi—— All I beg—is this one evening. 'Tis all shall be necessary. *After,* I shall not need monsieur."

"Take heed to yourself—after!" vouchsafed the Englishman between his teeth.

"Conquered!" cried M. Beaucaire, and clapped his hands gleefully. "Conquered for the night! Aha, it is riz'nable! I shall meet what you send—after. One cannot hope too much of your patience. It is but natural you should attemp' a little avengement for the rascal trap I was such a wicked fellow as to set for you. I shall meet some strange frien's of yours after to-night; not so? I must try to be not too much frighten'." He looked at the Duke curiously. "You want to know why I create this tragedy, why I am so unkind as to entrap monsieur?"

His Grace of Winterset replied with a chill glance; a pulse in the noble-man's cheek beat less relentlessly; his eye raged not so bitterly; the steady purple of his own color was returning; his voice was less hoarse; he was regaining his habit. " 'Tis ever the manner of the vulgar," he observed, "to wish to be seen with people of fashion."

"Oh, no, no, no!" The Frenchman laughed. " 'Tis not that. Am I not already one of these 'men of fashion'? I lack only the reputation of birth. Monsieur is goin' supply that. Ha, ha! I shall be noble from to-night. 'Victor,' the artis', is condemn' to death; his throat shall be cut with his own razor. 'M. Beaucaire'——" Here the young man sprang to his feet, caught up the black wig, clapped into it a dice-box from the table, and hurled it violently through the open door. " 'M. Beaucaire' shall be choke' with his own dice-box. Who is the Phoenix to remain? What advantage have I not over other men of rank who are merely born to it? I may choose my own. No! Choose for me, monsieur. Shall I be chevalier, comte, vicomte, marquis, what? None. Out of compliment to monsieur can I wish to be anything he is not? No, no! I shall be M. le Duc, M. le Duc de—de Chateaurien. Ha, ha! You see? You are my *confrère.*"

M. Beaucaire trod a dainty step or two, waving his hand politely to the Duke, as though in invitation to join the celebration of his rank. The Englishman watched, his eye still and harsh, already gathering in craftiness. Beaucaire stopped suddenly. "But how I forget my age! I am twenty-three," he said, with a sigh. "I rejoice too much to be of the quality. It has been too great for me, and I had always belief' myself free of such ambition. I thought it was enough to behol' the opera without wishing to sing; but no, England have teach' me I have those vulgar desire'. Monsieur, I am goin' tell you a secret; the ladies of your country are very diff'runt than ours. One may adore the demoiselle, one must worship the lady of England. Our ladies have the—it is the beauty of youth; yours remain comely at thirty. Ours are flowers, yours are stars! See, I betray myself, I am so poor a patriot. And there is one among these stars—ah, yes, there is one—the poor Frenchman has observe' from his humble distance; even there he could bask in the glowing!" M. Beaucaire turned to the window, and looked out into the dark. He did not see the lights of the town. When he turned again, he had half forgotten his prisoner; other pictures were before him.

"Ah, what radiance!" he cried. "Those people up over the sky, they want to show they wish the earth to be happy, so they smile, and make this lady. Gold-haired, an angel of heaven, and yet a Diana of the chase! I see her fly by me on her great horse one day; she touch' his mane with her fingers. I buy that clipping from the groom. I have it here with my dear brother's picture. Ah, *you!* Oh, yes, you laugh! What do you know! 'Twas all I could get. But I have heard of the endeavor of M. le Duc to recoup his fortunes. This alliance shall fail. It is not the way—that heritage shall be safe' from him! It is you and me, monsieur! You can laugh! The war is open', and by *me!* There is one great step taken: until to-night there was nothing for you to ruin, to-morrow you have got a noble of France—your own *protégé*—to besiege and sack. And you are to lose, because you think such ruin easy, and because you understand nothing— far less—of divinity. How could you know? You have not the fiber; the heart of a lady is a blank to you; you know nothing of the vibration. There are some words that were made only to tell of Lady Mary, for her alone—*bellissima*, divine, *glorieuse!* Ah, how I have watch' her! It is sad to me when I see her surround' by your yo'ng captains, your nobles, your rattles, your beaux—ha, ha!—and I mus' hol' far aloof. It is sad for me— but oh, jus' to watch her and to wonder! Strange it is, but I have almos' cry out with rapture at a look I have see' her give another man, so beautiful it was, so tender, so dazzling of the eyes and so mirthful of the lips. Ah, divine coquetry! A look for another, *ah-i-me!* for many others; and even to you, one day, a rose, while I—I, monsieur, could not even be so blessed as to be the groun' beneath her little shoe! But *to-night*, monsieur—ha, ha!—*to-night*, monsieur, you and me, two princes, M. le Duc de Winterset and M. le Duc de Chateaurien—ha, ha! you see?—we are goin' arm-in-arm to that ball, and *I* am goin' have one of those looks, *I*! And a rose! *I*! It is time. But ten minute', monsieur. I make my apology to keep you waitin' so long while I go in the nex' room and execute my poor mustachio—that will be my only murder for jus' this one evening—and inves' myself in white satin. Ha, ha! I shall be very gran', monsieur. François, send Louis to me; Victor, to order two chairs for monsieur and me; we are goin' out in the worl' to-night!"

# II

The chairmen swarmed in the street at Lady Malbourne's door, where the joyous vulgar fought with muddled footmen and tipsy link-boys for places of vantage whence to catch a glimpse of quality and of raiment at its utmost. Dawn was in the east, and the guests were departing. Singly or in pairs, glittering in finery, they came mincing down the steps, the ghost of the night's smirk fading to jadedness as they sought the dark recesses of their chairs. From within sounded the twang of fiddles still swinging manfully at it, and the windows were bright with the light of many candles. When the door was flung open to call the chair of Lady Mary Carlisle, there was an eager pressure of the throng to see.

A small, fair gentleman in white satin came out upon the steps, turned and bowed before a lady who appeared in the doorway, a lady whose royal loveliness was given to view for a moment in that glowing frame. The crowd sent up a hearty English cheer for the Beauty of Bath.

The gentleman smiled upon them delightedly. "What enchanting people!" he cried. "Why did I not know, so I might have shout' with them?" The lady noticed the people not at all; whereat, being pleased, the people cheered again. The gentleman offered her his hand; she made a slow courtesy; placed the tips of her fingers upon his own. "I am honored, M. de Chateaurien," she said.

"No, no!" he cried earnestly. "Behol' a poor Frenchman whom emperors should envy." Then reverently and with the pride of his gallant office vibrant in every line of his light figure, invested in white satin and very grand, as he had prophesied, M. le Duc de Chateaurien handed Lady Mary Carlisle down the steps, an achievement which had figured in the ambitions of seven other gentlemen during the evening.

"Am I to be lef' in such onhappiness?" he said in a low voice. "That rose I have beg' for so long——"

"Never!" said Lady Mary.

"Ah, I do not deserve it, I know so well! But——"

"Never!"

"It is the greatness of my onworthiness that alone can claim your charity; let your kin' heart give this little red rose, this great alms, to the poor beggar."

"Never!"

She was seated in the chair. "Ah, give the rose," he whispered. Her beauty shone dazzlingly on him out of the dimness.

"Never!" she flashed defiantly as she was closed in. "Never!"

"Ah!"

"Never!"

The rose fell at his feet.

"A rose lasts till morning," said a voice behind him.

Turning, M. de Chateaurien looked beamingly upon the face of the Duke of Winterset.

"'Tis already the daylight," he replied, pointing to the east. "Monsieur, was it not enough honor for you to han' out madame, the aunt of Lady Mary? Lady Rellerton retain' much trace of beauty. 'Tis strange you did not appear more happy."

"The rose is of an unlucky color, I think," observed the Duke.

"The color of a blush, my brother."

"Unlucky, I still maintain," said the other calmly.

"The color of the veins of a Frenchman. Ha, ha!" cried the young man. "What price would be too high? A rose is a rose! A good-night, my brother, a good-night. I wish you dreams of roses, red roses, only beautiful red, red roses!"

"Stay! Did you see the look she gave these street folk when they shouted for her? And how are you higher than they, when she knows? As high as yonder horse-boy!"

"Red roses, my brother, only roses. I wish you dreams of red, red roses!"

# III

It was well agreed by the fashion of Bath that M. le Duc de Chateaurien was a person of sensibility and *haut ton;* that his retinue and equipage surpassed in elegance; that his person was exquisite, his manner engaging. In the company of gentlemen his ease was slightly tinged with graciousness (his single equal in Bath being his Grace of Winterset); but it was remarked that when he bowed over a lady's hand, his air bespoke only a gay and tender reverence.

He was the idol of the dowagers within a week after his appearance; matrons warmed to him; young belles looked sweetly on him, while the gentlemen were won to admiration or envy. He was of prodigious wealth: old Mr. Bicksit, who dared not, for his fame's sake, fail to have seen all things, had visited Chateaurien under the present Duke's father, and descanted to the curious upon its grandeurs. The young noble had one fault, he was so poor a gambler. He cared nothing for the hazards of a die or the turn of a card. Gayly admitting that he had been born with no spirit of adventure in him, he was sure, he declared, that he failed of much happiness by his lack of taste in such matters.

But he was not long wanting the occasion to prove his taste in the matter of handling a weapon. A certain led-captain, Rohrer by name, notorious, amongst other things, for bearing a dexterous and bloodthirsty blade, came to Bath post-haste, one night, and jostled heartily against him in the pump-room on the following morning. M. de Chateaurien bowed, and turned aside without offense, continuing a conversation with some gentlemen near by. Captain Rohrer jostled against him a second time. M. de Chateaurien looked him in the eye, and apologized pleasantly for being so much in the way. Thereupon Rohrer procured an introduction to him, and made some observations derogatory to the valor and virtue of the French.

There was current a curious piece of gossip of the French court: a prince of the blood royal, grandson of the late Regent and second in the line of succession to the throne of France, had rebelled against the authority of Louis XV, who had commanded him to marry the Princess Henriette, cousin to both of them. The princess was reported to be openly devoted to the cousin who refused to accept her hand at the bidding of the king; and, as rumor ran, the prince's caprice elected in preference the discipline of Vincennes, to which retirement the furious king had consigned him. The story was the staple gossip of all polite Europe; and Captain Rohrer, having in his mind a purpose to make use of it in leading up to a statement that should be general to the damage of all Frenchwomen, and which a Frenchman might not pass over as he might a jog of the elbow, repeated it with garbled truths to make a scandal of a story which bore none on a plain relation.

He did not reach his deduction. M. de Chateaurien, breaking into his narrative, addressed him very quietly. "Monsieur," he said, "none but swine deny the nobleness of that good and gentle lady, Mademoiselle la Princesse de Bourbon-Conti. Every Frenchman know' that her cousin is a bad rebel and ingrate, who had only honor and rispec' for her, but was so wilful he could not let even the king say, 'You shall marry here, you shall marry there.' My frien's," the young man turned to the others, "may I ask you to close roun' in a circle for one moment? It is clearly shown that the Duke of Orleans is a scurvy fellow, but not——" he wheeled about and touched Captain Rohrer on the brow with the back of his gloved hand—"but not so scurvy as thou, thou swine of the gutter!"

Two hours later, with perfect ease, he ran Captain Rohrer through the left shoulder—after which he sent a basket of red roses to the Duke of Winterset. In a few days he had another captain to fight. This was a ruffling buck who had the astounding indiscretion to proclaim M. de Chateaurien an impostor. There was no Chateaurien, he swore. The Frenchman laughed in his face, and, at twilight of the same day, pinked him carefully through the right shoulder. It was not that he could not put aside the insult to himself, he declared to Mr. Molyneux, his second, and the few witnesses, as he handed his wet sword to his lackey—one of his station could not be insulted by a doubt of that station—but he fought in in the quarrel of his friend Winterset. This rascal had asserted that M. le Duc had introduced an impostor. Could he overlook the insult to a friend, one to whom he owed his kind reception in Bath? Then, bending over his fallen adversary, he whispered: "Naughty man, tell your master find some better quarrel for the nex' he sen' agains' me."

The conduct of M. de Chateaurien was pronounced admirable.

There was no surprise when the young foreigner fell naturally into the long train of followers of the beautiful Lady Mary Carlisle, nor was there great astonishment that he should obtain marked favor in her eyes, shown so plainly that my Lord Townbrake, Sir Hugh Guilford, and the rich

Squire Bantison, all of whom had followed her through three seasons, swore with rage, and his Grace of Winterset stalked from her aunt's house with black brows.

Meeting the Duke there on the evening after his second encounter, de Chateaurien smiled upon him brilliantly. "It was badly done; *oh,* so badly!" he whispered. "Can you afford to have me strip' of my mask by any but yourself? You, who introduce' me? They will say there is some bad scandal that I could force you to be my god-father. You mus' get the courage yourself."

"I told you a rose had a short life," was the answer.

"Oh, those roses! 'Tis the very greates' rizzon to gather each day a fresh one." He took a red bud from his breast for an instant, and touched it to his lips.

"M. de Chateaurien!" It was Lady Mary's voice; she stood at a table where a vacant place had been left beside her. "M. de Chateaurien, we have been waiting very long for you."

The Duke saw the look she did not know she gave the Frenchman, and he lost countenance for a moment.

"We approach a climax, eh, monsieur?" said M. de Chateaurien.

# IV

There fell a clear September night, when the moon was radiant over town and country, over cobbled streets and winding roads. From the fields the mists rose slowly, and the air was mild and fragrant, while distances were white and full of mystery. All of Bath that pretended to fashion or condition was present that evening at a *fête* at the house of a country gentleman of the neighborhood. When the stately junket was concluded, it was the pleasure of M. de Chateaurien to form one of the escort of Lady Mary's carriage for the return. As they took the road, Sir Hugh Guilford and Mr. Bantison, engaging in indistinct but vigorous remonstrance with Mr. Molyneux over some matter, fell fifty or more paces behind, where they continued to ride, keeping up their argument. Half a dozen other gallants rode in advance, muttering among themselves, or attended laxly upon Lady Mary's aunt on the other side of the coach, while the happy Frenchman was permitted to ride close to that adorable window which framed the fairest face in England.

He sang for her a little French song, a song of the *voyageur* who dreamed of home. The lady, listening, looking up at the bright moon, felt a warm drop upon her cheek, and he saw the tears sparkling upon her lashes.

"Mademoiselle," he whispered then, "I, too, have been a wanderer, but my dreams were not of France; no, I do not dream of that home, of that dear country. It is of a dearer country, a dream country—a country of gold and snow," he cried softly, looking at her white brow and the fair, lightly powdered hair above it. "Gold and snow, and the blue sky of a lady's eyes!"

"I had thought the ladies of France were dark, sir."

"Cruel! It is that she will not understan'! Have I speak of the ladies of France? No, no, no! It is of the faires' country; yes, 'tis a province of heaven, mademoiselle. Do I not renounce my allegiance to France? Oh, yes! I am subjec'—no, content to be slave—in the lan' of the blue sky, the gold, and the snow."

"A very pretty figure," answered Lady Mary, her eyes downcast. "But does it not hint a notable experience in the making of such speeches?"

"Tormentress! No. It prove' only the inspiration it is to know you."

"We English ladies hear plenty of the like, sir; and we even grow brilliant enough to detect the assurance that lies beneath the courtesies of our own gallants."

"*Merci!* I should believe so!" ejaculated M. de Chateaurien; but he smothered the words upon his lips.

Her eyes were not lifted. She went on: "We come, in time, to believe that true feeling comes faltering forth, not glibly; that smoothness betokens the adept in the art, sir, rather than your true—your true——" She was herself faltering; more, blushing deeply, and halting to a full stop in terror of a word. There was a silence.

"Your—true—lover," he said huskily. When he had said that word both trembled. She turned half away into the darkness of the coach.

"I know what make' you to doubt me," he said, faltering himself, though it was not his art that prompted him. "They have tol' you the French do nothing al—ways but make love, is it not so? Yes, you think *I* am like that. You think I am like that now!"

She made no sign.

"I suppose," he sighed, "I am unriz'nable; I would have the snow not so col'—for jus' me."

She did not answer.

"Turn to me," he said.

The fragrance of the fields came to them, and from the distance the faint, clear note of a hunting-horn.

"Turn to me."

The lovely head was bent very low. Her little gloved hand lay upon the narrow window ledge. He laid his own gently upon it. The two hands were shaking like twin leaves in the breeze. Hers was not drawn away. After a pause, neither knew how long, he felt the warm fingers turn and clasp themselves tremulously about his own. At last she looked up bravely and met his eyes. The horn was wound again—nearer.

"All the cold was gone from the snows—long ago," she said.

"My beautiful!" he whispered; it was all he could say. "My beautiful!" But she clutched his arm, startled.

"*'Ware the road!*" A wild halloo sounded ahead. The horn wound loudly. "*'Ware the road!*" There sprang up out of the night a flying thunder of hoof-beats. The gentlemen riding idly in front of the coach scattered to the hedge-sides; and, with drawn swords flashing in the moon, a party of horsemen charged down the highway, their cries blasting the night.

"Barber! Kill the barber!" they screamed. "Barber! Kill the barber!"

Beaucaire had but time to draw his sword when they were upon him. "*À moi!*" his voice rang out clearly as he rose in his stirrups. "*À moi,* François, Louis, Berquin! *À moi,* François!"

The cavaliers came straight at him. He parried the thrust of the first, but the shock of collision hurled his horse against the side of the coach.

"Sacred swine!" he cried bitterly. "To endanger a lady, to make this brawl in a lady's presence! Drive on!" he shouted.

"No!" cried Lady Mary.

The Frenchman's assailants were masked, but they were not highway-men. "Barber! Barber!" they shouted hoarsely, and closed in on him in a circle.

"See how he use his steel!" laughed M. Beaucaire, as his point passed through a tawdry waistcoat. For a moment he cut through the ring and cleared a space about him, and Lady Mary saw his face shining in the moonlight. "*Canaille!*" he hissed, as his horse sank beneath him; and, though guarding his head from the rain of blows from above, he managed to drag headlong from his saddle the man who had hamstrung the poor brute. The fellow came suddenly to the ground, and lay there.

"Is it not a compliment," said a heavy voice, "to bring six large men to subdue monsieur?"

"Oh, you are there, my frien'! In the rear—a little in the rear, I think. Ha, ha!"

The Frenchman's play with his weapon was a revelation of skill, the more extraordinary as he held in his hand only a light dress sword. But the ring closed about him, and his keen defense could not avail him for more than a few moments. Lady Mary's outriders, the gallants of her escort, rode up close to the coach and encircled it, not interfering.

"Sir Hugh Guilford!" cried Lady Mary wildly, "if you will not help him, give me your sword!" She would have leaped to the ground, but Sir Hugh held the door.

"Sit quiet, madam," he said to her; then, to the man on the box, "Drive on."

"If he does, I'll kill him!" she said fiercely. "Ah, what cowards! Will you see the Duke murdered?"

"The Duke!" laughed Guilford. "They will not kill him, unless—be easy, dear madam, 'twill be explained. Gad's life!" he muttered to Molyneux, " 'Twere time the varlet had his lashing! D'ye hear her?"

"Barber or no barber," answered Molyneux, "I wish I had warned him. He fights as few gentlemen could. Ah—ah! Look at that! 'Tis a shame!"

On foot, his hat gone, his white coat sadly rent and gashed, flecked, too, with red, M. Beaucaire, wary, alert, brilliant, seemed to transform himself into a dozen fencing-masters; and, though his skill appeared to lie in delicacy and quickness, his play being continually with the point, sheer strength failed to beat him down. The young man was laughing like a child.

"Believe me," said Molyneux, "he's no barber! No, and never was!"

For a moment there was even a chance that M. Beaucaire might have the best of it. Two of his adversaries were prostrate, more than one were groaning, and the indomitable Frenchman had actually almost beat off the ruffians, when, by a trick, he was overcome. One of them, dismounting, ran in suddenly from behind and seized his blade in a thick leather gauntlet. Before Beaucaire could disengage the weapon, two others threw themselves from their horses and hurled him to the earth. *"À moi! À moi, Françoise!"* he cried as he went down, his sword in fragments, but his voice unbroken and clear.

"Shame!" muttered one or two of the gentlemen about the coach.

" 'Twas dastardly to take him so," said Molyneux. "Whatever his deservings, I'm nigh of a mind to offer him a rescue in the Duke's face."

"Truss him up, lads," said the heavy voice. "Clear the way in front of the coach. There sit those whom we avenge upon a presumptuous lackey. Now, Whiffen, you have a fair audience, lay on and baste him."

Two men began to drag M. Beaucaire toward a great oak by the road-side. Another took from his saddle a heavy whip with three thongs.

"*À moi, Françoise!*"

There was borne on the breeze an answer—"*Monseigneur! Monseigneur!*" The cry grew louder suddenly. The clatter of hoofs urged to an anguish of speed sounded on the night. M. Beaucaire's servants had lagged sorely behind, but they made up for it now. Almost before the noise of their own steeds they came riding down the moonlit aisle between the mists. Chosen men, these servants of Beaucaire, and like a thunderbolt they fell upon the astounded cavaliers.

"Chateaurien! Chateaurien!" they shouted, and smote so swiftly that, through lack of time, they showed no proper judgment, discriminating nothing between non-combatants and their master's foes. They charged first into the group about M. Beaucaire, and broke and routed it utterly. Two of them leaped to the young man's side, while the other four, swerving, scarce losing the momentum of their onset, bore on upon the gentlemen near the coach, who went down beneath the fierceness of the onslaught, cursing manfully.

"Our just deserts," said Mr. Molyneaux, his mouth full of dust and philosophy.

Sir Hugh Guilford's horse fell with him, being literally ridden over, and the baronet's leg was pinned under the saddle. In less than ten minutes from the first attack on M. Beaucaire, the attacking party had fled in disorder, and the patrician non-combatants, choking with expletives, consumed with wrath, were prisoners, disarmed by the Frenchman's lackeys.

Guilford's discomfiture had freed the doors of the coach; so it was that when M. Beaucaire, struggling to rise, assisted by his servants, threw out one hand to balance himself, he found it seized between two small, cold palms, and he looked into two warm, dilating eyes, that were doubly beautiful because of the fright and rage that found room in them, too.

M. le Duc Chateaurien sprang to his feet without the aid of his lackeys, and bowed low before Lady Mary.

"I make ten thousan' apology to be the cause of a such *mêlée* in your presence," he said; and then, turning to Françoise, he spoke in French: "Ah, thou scoundrel! A little, and it had been too late."

Françoise knelt in the dust before him. "Pardon!" he said. "Monseigneur commanded us to follow far in the rear, to remain unobserved. The wind malignantly blew against monseigneur's voice."

"See what it might have cost, my children," said his master, pointing to the ropes with which they would have bound him and to the whip lying beside them. A shudder passed over the lackey's frame; the utter horror in his face echoed in the eyes of his fellows.

"Oh, monseigneur!" François sprang back, and tossed his arms to heaven.

"But it did not happen," said M. Beaucaire.

"It could not!" exclaimed François.

"No. And you did very well, my children——" the young man smiled benevolently—"very well. And now," he continued, turning to Lady Mary and speaking in English, "let me be asking of our gallants yonder what make' them to be in cabal with highwaymen. One should come to a polite understanding with them, you think? Not so?"

He bowed, offering his hand to conduct her to the coach, where Molyneux and his companions, having drawn Sir Hugh from under his horse, were engaged in reviving and reassuring Lady Rellerton, who had fainted. But Lady Mary stayed Beaucaire with a gesture, and the two stood where they were.

"Monseigneur!" she said, with a note of raillery in her voice, but raillery so tender that he started with happiness. His movement brought him a hot spasm of pain, and he clapped his hand to a red stain on his waistcoat.

"You are hurt!"

"It is nothing," smiled M. Beaucaire. Then, that she might not see the stain spreading, he held his handkerchief over the spot. "I am a little—but jus' a trifling—bruise'; 'tis all."

"You shall ride in the coach," she whispered. "Will you be pleased, M. de Chateaurien?"

"Ah, my beautiful!" She seemed to wave before him like a shining mist. "I wish that ride might las' for al—ways! Can you say that, mademoiselle?"

"Monseigneur," she cried in a passion of admiration, "I would what you would have be, should be. What do you not deserve? You are the bravest man in the world!"

"Ha, ha! I am jus' a poor Frenchman."

"Would that a few Englishmen had shown themselves as 'poor' tonight. The vile cowards, not to help you!" With that, suddenly possessed by her anger, she swept away from him to the coach.

Sir Hugh, groaning loudly, was being assisted into the vehicle.

"My little poltroons," she said, "what are you doing with your fellow-craven, Sir Hugh Guilford, there?"

"Madam," replied Molyneux humbly, "Sir Hugh's leg is broken. Lady Rellerton graciously permits him to be taken in."

"*I* do not permit it! M. de Chateaurien rides with us."

"But——"

"Sir! Leave the wretch to groan by the roadside," she cried fiercely, "which plight I would were that of all of you! But there will be a pretty story for the gossips to-morrow! And I could almost find pity for you when I think of the wits when you return to town. Fine gentlemen you; hardy bravoes, by heaven! to leave one man to meet a troop of horse single-handed, while you huddle in shelter until you are overthrown and disarmed by servants! Oh, the wits! Heaven save you from the wits!"

"Madam."

"Address me no more! M. de Chateaurien, Lady Rellerton and I will greatly esteem the honor of your company. Will you come?"

She stepped quickly into the coach, and was gathering her skirts to make room for the Frenchman, when a heavy voice spoke from the shadows of the tree by the wayside.

"Lady Mary Carlisle will, no doubt, listen to a word of counsel on this point."

The Duke of Winterset rode out into the moonlight, composedly untieing a mask from about his head. He had not shared the flight of his followers, but had retired into the shade of the oak, whence he now made his presence known with the utmost coolness.

"Gracious heavens, 'tis Winterset!" exclaimed Lady Rellerton.

"Turned highwayman and cutthroat," cried Lady Mary.

"No, no," laughed M. Beaucaire, somewhat unsteadily, as he stood, swaying a little, with one hand on the coach-door, the other pressed hard on his side, "he only oversee'; he is jus' a little bashful, sometime'. He is a great man, but he don' want *all* the glory!"

"Barber," replied the Duke, "I must tell you that I gladly descend to bandy words with you; your monstrous impudence is a claim to rank I cannot ignore. But a lackey who has himself followed by six other lackeys——"

"Ha, ha! Has not M. le Duc been busy all this evening to justify me? And I think mine mus' be the bes' six. Ha, ha! You think?"

"M. de Chateaurien," said Lady Mary, "we are waiting for you."

"Pardon," he replied. "He has something to say; maybe it is bes' if you hear it now."

"I wish to hear nothing from him—ever!"

"My faith, madam," cried the Duke, "this saucy fellow has paid you the last insult! He is so sure of you he does not fear you will believe the truth. When all is told, if you do not agree he deserved the lashing we planned to——"

"I'll hear no more!"

"You will bitterly repent it, madam. For your own sake I entreat——"

"And I also," broke in M. Beaucaire. "Permit me, mademoiselle; let him speak."

"Then let him be brief," said Lady Mary, "for I am earnest to be quit of him. His explanation of an attack on my friend and on my carriage should be made to my brother."

"Alas that he was not here," said the Duke, "to aid me! Madam, was your carriage threatened? I have endeavored only to expunge a debt I owed to Bath and to avenge an insult offered to yourself through——"

"Sir, sir, my patience will bear little more!"

"A thousan' apology," said M. Beaucaire. "You will listen, I only beg, Lady Mary?"

She made an angry gesture of assent.

"Madam, I will be brief as I may. Two months ago there came to Bath a French gambler calling himself Beaucaire, a desperate fellow with the cards or dice, and all the men of fashion went to play at his lodging, where he won considerable sums. He was small, wore a black wig and mustachio. He had the insolence to show himself everywhere until the Master of Ceremonies rebuffed him in the pump-room, as you know, and after that he forebore his visits to the rooms. Mr. Nash explained (and was confirmed, madam, by indubitable information) that this Beaucaire was a man of unspeakable, vile, low birth, being, in fact, no other than a lackey of the French king's ambassador, Victor by name, de Mirepoix's barber. Although his condition was known, the hideous impudence of the fellow did not desert him, and he remained in Bath, where none would speak to him."

"Is your farrago nigh done, sir?"

"A few moments, madam. One evening, three weeks gone, I observed a very elegant equipage draw up to my door, and the Duke of Chateaurien was announced. The young man's manners were worthy—according to the French acceptance—and 'twere idle to deny him the most monstrous assurance. He declared himself a noble traveling for pleasure. He had taken lodgings in Bath for a season, he said, and called at once to pay his respects to me. His tone was so candid—in truth, I am the simplest of men, very easily gulled—and his stroke so bold, that I did not for one moment suspect him; and, to my poignant regret—though in the humblest spirit I have shown myself eager to atone—that very evening I had the shame of presenting him to yourself."

"The shame, sir!"

"Have patience, pray, madam. Ay, the shame! You know what figure he hath cut in Bath since that evening. All ran merrily with him until several days ago Captain Badger denounced him as an imposter, vowing that Chateaurien was nothing."

"Pardon," interrupted M. Beaucaire. " 'Castle Nowhere' would have been so much better. Why did you not make him say it that way, monsieur?"

Lady Mary started; she was looking at the Duke, and her face was white. He continued: "Poor Captain Badger was stabbed that same day——"

"Most befitting poor Captain Badger," muttered Molyneux.

"—And his adversary had the marvelous insolence to declare that he fought in *my* quarrel! This afternoon the wounded man sent for me, and imparted a very horrifying intelligence. He had discovered a lackey whom he had seen waiting upon Beaucaire in attendance at the door of this Chateaurien's lodgings. Beaucaire had disappeared the day before Chateaurien's arrival. Captain Badger looked closely at Chateaurien at their next meeting, and identified him with the missing Beaucaire beyond the faintest doubt. Overcome with indignation, he immediately proclaimed the imposter. Out of regard for me, he did not charge him with being Beaucaire; the poor soul was unwilling to put upon me the humiliation of having introduced a barber; but the secret weighed upon him till he sent for me and put everything in my hands. I accepted the odium; thinking only of atonement. I went to Sir John Wimpledon's *fête*. I took poor Sir Hugh, there, and these other gentlemen aside, and told them my news. We narrowly observed this man, and were shocked at our simplicity in not having discovered him before. These are men of honor and cool judgment, madam. Mr. Molyneaux had acted for him in the affair of Captain Badger, and was strongly prejudiced in his favor; but Mr. Molyneux, Sir Hugh, Mr. Bantison, every one of them, in short, recognized him. In spite of his smooth face and his light hair, the adventurer

Beaucaire was writ upon him amazing plain. Look at him, madam, if he will dare the inspection. You saw this Beaucaire well, the day of his expulsion from the rooms. Is not this he?"

M. Beaucaire stepped close to her. Her pale face twitched.

"Look!" he said.

"Oh, oh!" she whispered with a dry throat, and fell back in the carriage.

"Is it so?" cried the Duke.

"I do not know—I—cannot tell."

"One moment more. I begged these gentlemen to allow me to wipe out the insult I had unhappily offered to Bath, but particularly to you. They agreed not to forestall me or to interfere. I left Sir John Wimpledon's early, and arranged to give the sorry rascal a lashing under your own eyes, a satisfaction due the lady into whose presence he had dared to force himself."

" '*Noblesse oblige*'?" said M. Beaucaire in a tone of gentle inquiry.

"And now, madam," said the Duke, "I will detain you not one second longer. I plead the good purpose of my intentions, begging you to believe that the desire to avenge a hateful outrage, next to the wish to serve you, forms the dearest motive in the heart of Winterset."

"Bravo!" cried Beaucaire softly.

Lady Mary leaned toward him, a thriving terror in her eyes. "It is false?" she faltered.

"Monsieur should not have been born so high. He could have made little book'."

"You mean it is false?" she cried breathlessly.

" 'Od's blood, is she not convinced?" broke out Mr. Bantison. "Fellow, were you not the ambassador's barber?"

"It is all false?" she whispered.

"The mos' fine art, mademoiselle. How long you think it take M. de Winterset to learn that speech after he write it out? It is a mix of what is true and the mos' chaste art. Monsieur has become a man of letters. Perhaps he may enjoy that more than the wars. Ha, ha!"

Mr. Bantison burst into a roar of laughter. "Do French gentlemen fight lackeys? Ho, ho, ho! A pretty country! We English do as was done to-night, have our servants beat them."

"And attend ourselves," added M. Beaucaire, looking at the Duke, "somewhat in the background? But, pardon," he mocked, "that remind' me. François, return to Mr. Bantison and these gentlemen their weapons."

"Will you answer a question?" said Molyneux mildly.

"Oh, with pleasure, monsieur."

"Were you ever a barber?"

"No, monsieur," laughed the young man.

"Pah!" exclaimed Bantison. "Let me question him. Now, fellow, a confession may save you from jail. Do you deny you are Beaucaire?"

"Deny to a such judge?"

"Ha!" said Bantison. "What more do you want, Molyneux? Fellow, do you deny that you came to London in the ambassador's suite?"

"No, I do not deny."

"He admits it! Didn't you come as his barber?"

"Yes, my frien', as his barber."

Lady Mary cried out faintly, and, shuddering, put both hands over her eyes.

"I'm sorry," said Molyneux. "You fight like a gentleman."

"I thank you, monsieur."

"You called yourself Beaucaire?"

"Yes, monsieur." He was swaying to and fro; his servants ran to support him.

"I wish—" continued Molyneux, hesitating. "Evil take me!—but I'm sorry you're hurt."

"Assist Sir Hugh into my carriage," said Lady Mary.

"Farewell, mademoiselle!" M. Beaucaire's voice was very faint. His eyes were fixed upon her face. She did not look toward him.

They were propping Sir Hugh on the cushions. The Duke rode up close to Beaucaire, but Françoise seized his bridle fiercely, and forced the horse back on its haunches.

"The man's servants worship him," said Molyneux.

"Curse your insolence!" exclaimed the Duke. "How much am I to bear from this varlet and his varlets? Beaucaire, if you have not left Bath by to-morrow noon, you will be clapped into jail, and the lashing you escaped to-night shall be given you thrice tenfold!"

"I shall be—in the—Assembly—Room' at nine—o'clock, one week—from—to-night," answered the young man, smiling jauntily, though his lips were colorless. The words cost him nearly all his breath and strength. "You mus' keep—in the—backgroun', monsieur. Ha, ha!"

The door of the coach closed with a slam.

"Mademoiselle—fare—well!"

"Drive on!" said Lady Mary.

M. Beaucaire followed the carriage with his eyes. As the noise of the wheels and the hoof-beats of the accompanying cavalcade grew fainter in the distance, the handkerchief he had held against his side dropped into the white dust, a heavy red splotch.

"Only—roses," he gasped, and fell back in the arms of his servants.

# V

Beau Nash stood at the door of the rooms, smiling blandly upon a dainty throng in the pink of its finery and gay furbelows. The great exquisite bent his body constantly in a series of consummately adjusted bows: before a great dowager, seeming to sweep the floor in august deference; somewhat stately to the young bucks; greeting the wits with gracious friendliness and a twinkle of raillery; inclining with fatherly gallantry before the beauties; the degree of his inclination measured the altitude of the recipient as accurately as a nicely calculated sand-glass measures the hours.

The King of Bath was happy, for wit, beauty, fashion—to speak more concretely: nobles, belles, gamesters, beaux, statesmen, and poets—made fairyland (or opera bouffe, at least) in his dominions; play ran higher and higher, and Mr. Nash's coffers filled up with gold. To crown his pleasure, a prince of the French blood, the young Comte de Beaujolais, just arrived from Paris, had reached Bath at noon in state, accompanied by the Marquis de Mirepoix, the ambassador of Louis XV. The Beau dearly prized the society of the lofty, and the present visit was an honor to Bath: hence to the Master of Ceremonies. What was better, there would be some profitable hours with the cards and dice. So it was that Mr. Nash smiled never more benignly than on that bright evening. The rooms rang with the silvery voices of women and delightful laughter, while the fiddles went merrily, their melodies chiming sweetly with the joyance of his mood.

The skill and brazen effrontery of the ambassador's scoundrelly servant in passing himself off for a man of condition formed the point of departure for every conversation. It was discovered that there were but three persons present who had not suspected him from the first; and, by a singular paradox, the most astute of all proved to be old Mr. Bicksit, the traveler, once a visitor at Chateaurien; for he, according to report, had by a coup of diplomacy entrapped the impostor into an admission that there was no such place. However, like poor Captain Badger, the worthy old man had held his peace out of regard for the Duke of Winterset. This nobleman, heretofore secretly disliked, suspected of irregular devices at play, and never admired, had won admiration and popularity by his remorse for the mistake, and by the modesty of his attitude in endeavoring to atone for it, without presuming upon the privilege of his rank to laugh at the indignation of society; an action the more praiseworthy because his exposure of the impostor entailed the disclosure of his own culpability in having stood the villain's sponsor. To-night, the happy gentleman, with Lady Mary Carlisle upon his arm, went grandly about the rooms, sowing and reaping a harvest of smiles. 'Twas said work would be begun at once to rebuild the Duke's country seat, while several ruined men might be paid out of prison. People gazing on the beauty and the stately but modest hero by her side, said they would make a noble pair. She had long been distinguished by his attentions, and he had come brilliantly out of the episode of the Frenchman, who had been his only real rival. Wherever they went, there arose a buzz of pleasing gossip and adulation.

Mr. Nash, seeing them near him, came forward with greetings. A word on the side passed between the nobleman and the exquisite.

"I had news of the rascal to-night," whispered Nash. "He lay at a farm till yesterday, when he disappeared; his ruffians, too."

"You have arranged?" asked the Duke.

"Fourteen bailiffs are watching without. He could not come within gunshot. If they clap eyes on him, they will hustle him to jail, and his cutthroats shall not avail him a hair's weight. The impertinent swore he'd be here by nine, did he?"

"He said so; and 'tis a rash dog, sir."

"It is just nine now."

"Send out to see if they have taken him."

"Gladly." The Beau beckoned an attendant, and whispered in his ear.

Many of the crowd had edged up to the two gentlemen with apparent carelessness, to overhear their conversation. Those who did overhear repeated it in covert asides, and this circulating undertone, confirming a vague rumor that Beaucaire would attempt the entrance that night, lent a pleasurable color of excitement to the evening. The French prince, the ambassador, and their suites were announced. Polite as the assembly was, it was also curious, and there occurred a mannerly rush to see the newcomers. Lady Mary, already pale, grew whiter as the throng closed round her; she looked up pathetically at the Duke, who lost no time in extricating her from the pressure.

"Wait here," he said; "I will fetch you a glass of negus," and disappeared. He had not thought to bring a chair, and she, looking about with an increasing faintness and finding none, saw that she was standing by the door of a small side-room. The crowd swerved back for the passage of the legate of France, and pressed upon her. She opened the door, and went in.

The room was empty save for two gentlemen, who were quietly playing cards at a table. They looked up as she entered. They were M. Beaucaire and Mr. Molyneux.

She uttered a quick cry and leaned against the wall, her hand to her breast. Beaucaire, though white and weak, had brought her a chair before Molyneux could stir.

"Mademoiselle——"

"Do not touch me!" she said, with such frozen abhorrence in her voice that he stopped short. "Mr. Molyneux, you seek strange company!"

"Madam," replied Molyneux, bowing deeply, as much to Beaucaire as to herself, "I am honored by the presence of both of you."

"Oh, are you mad!" she exclaimed, contemptuously.

"This gentleman has exalted me with his confidence, madam," he replied.

"Will you add your ruin to the scandal of this fellow's presence here? How he obtained entrance——"

"Pardon, mademoiselle," interrupted Beaucaire. "Did I not say I should come? M. Molyneux was so obliging as to answer for me to the fourteen frien's of M. de Winterset and *Meestaire* Nash."

"Do you not know," she turned vehemently upon Molyneux, "that he will be removed the moment I leave this room? Do you wish to be dragged out with him? For your sake, sir, because I have always thought you a man of heart, I give you a chance to save yourself from disgrace— and—your companion from jail. Let him slip out by some retired way, and you may give me your arm and we will enter the next room as if nothing had happened. Come, sir——"

"Mademoiselle——"

"Mr. Molyneux, I desire to hear nothing from your companion. Had I not seen you at cards with him I should have supposed him in attendance as your lackey. Do you desire to take advantage of my offer, sir?"

"Mademoiselle, I could not tell you, on that night——"

"You may inform your high-born friend, Mr. Molyneux, that I heard everything he had to say; that my pride once had the pleasure of listening to his high-born confession!"

"Ah, it is gentle to taunt one with his birth, mademoiselle? Ah, no! There is a man in my country who say strange things of that—that a man is not his father, but *himself.*"

"You may inform your friend, Mr. Molyneux, that he had a chance to defend himself against accusation; that he said all——"

"That I did say all I could have strength to say. Mademoiselle, you did did not see—as it was right—that I had been stung by a big wasp. It was nothing, a scratch; but, mademoiselle, the sky went round and the moon dance' on the earth. I could not wish that big wasp to see he had stung me; so I mus' only say what I can have strength for, and stan' straight till he is gone. Beside', there are other rizzons. Ah, you mus' belief! My Molyneux I sen' for, and tell him all, because he show courtesy to the yo'ng Frenchman, and I can trus' him. I trus' you, mademoiselle—long ago—and would have tol' you ev'rything, excep' jus' because—well, for the romance, the fon! You belief? It is so clearly so; you do belief, mademoiselle?"

She did not even look at him. M. Beaucaire lifted his hand appealingly toward her. "Can there be no faith in—in—" he said timidly, and paused. She was silent, a statue, my Lady Disdain.

"If you had not belief' me to be an impostor; if I had never said I was Chateaurien; if I had been jus' that Monsieur Beaucaire of the story they tol' you, but never with the *heart* of a lackey, an hones' man, a *man,* the man you know, *himself,* could you—would you——" He was trying to speak firmly; yet, as he gazed upon her splendid beauty, he choked slightly, and fumbled in the lace at his throat with unsteady fingers.— "Would you—have let me ride by your side in the autumn moonlight?" Her glance passed by him as it might have passed by a footman or a piece of furniture. He was dressed magnificently, a multitude of orders glittering on his breast. Her eye took no knowledge of him.

"Mademoiselle—I have the honor to ask you: if you had known this Beaucaire was hones', though of peasant birth, would you——"

Involuntarily, controlled as her icy presence was, she shuddered. There was a moment of silence.

"Mr. Molyneux," said Lady Mary, "in spite of your discourtesy in allowing a servant to address me, I offer you a last chance to leave this room undisgraced. Will you give me your arm?"

"Pardon me, madam," said Mr. Molyneux.

Beaucaire dropped into a chair with his head bent low and his arm outstretched on the table; his eyes filled slowly in spite of himself, and two tears rolled down the young man's cheeks.

"An' live men are jus'—*names!*" said M. Beaucaire.

# VI

In the outer room, Winterset, unable to find Lady Mary, and supposing her to have joined Lady Rellerton, disposed of his negus, then approached the two visitors to pay his respects to the young prince, whom he discovered to be a stripling of seventeen, arrogant-looking, but pretty as a girl. Standing beside the Marquis de Mirepoix—a man of quiet bearing—he was surrounded by a group of the great, among whom Mr. Nash naturally counted himself. The Beau was felicitating himself that the foreigners had not arrived a week earlier, in which case he and Bath would have been detected in a piece of gross ignorance concerning the French nobility—making much of de Mirepoix's ex-barber.

" 'Tis a lucky thing that fellow was got out of the way," he ejaculated, under cover.

"Thank me for it," rejoined Winterset.

An attendant begged Mr. Nash's notice. The head bailiff sent word that Beaucaire had long since entered the building by a side door. It was supposed Mr. Nash had known of it, and the Frenchman was not arrested, as Mr. Molyneux was in his company, and said he would be answerable for him. Consternation was so plain on the Beau's trained face that the Duke leaned toward him anxiously.

"The villain's in, and Molyneux hath gone mad!"

Mr. Bantison, who had been fiercely elbowing his way toward them, joined heads with them. "You may well say he is in," he exclaimed, "and if you want to know where, why, in yonder card-room. I saw him through the half-open door."

"What's to be done?" asked the Beau.

"Send the bailiffs——"

"Fie, fie! A file of bailiffs? The scandal!"

"Then listen to me," said the Duke. "I'll select half-a-dozen gentlemen, explain the matter, and we'll put him in the center of us and take him out to the bailiffs. 'Twill appear nothing. Do you remain here and keep the attention of Beaujolais and de Mirepoix. Come, Bantison, fetch Townbrake and Harry Rakell yonder; I'll bring the others."

Three minutes later, his Grace of Winterset flung wide the card-room door, and, after his friends had entered, closed it.

"Ah!" remarked M. Beaucaire quietly. "Six more large men."

The Duke, seeing Lady Mary, started; but the angry signs of her interview had not left her face, and reassured him. He offered his hand to conduct her to the door. "May I have the honor?"

"If this is to be known, 'twill be better if I leave after; I should be observed if I went now."

"As you will, madam," he answered, not displeased. "And now, you impudent villain," he began, turning to M. Beaucaire, but to fall back astounded. "'Od's blood, the dog hath murdered and robbed some royal prince!" he forgot Lady Mary's presence in his excitement. "Lay hands on him!" he shouted. "Tear those orders from him!"

Molyneux threw himself between. "One word!" he cried. "One word before you offer an outrage you will repent all your lives!"

"Or let M. de Winterset come alone," laughed M. Beaucaire.

"Do you expect me to fight a cutthroat barber, and with bare hands?"

"I think one does not expec' monsieur to fight anybody. Would *I* fight you, you think? That was why I had my servants, that evening we play. I would gladly fight almos' any one in the worl'; but I did not wish to soil my hand with a——"

"Stuff his lying mouth with his orders!" shouted the Duke.

But Molyneux still held the gentlemen back. "One moment," he cried.

"M. de Winterset," said Beaucaire, "of what are you afraid? You calculate well. Beaucaire might have been belief'—an impostor that you yourself expose'? Never! But I was not goin' reveal that secret. You have not absolve me of my promise."

"Tell what you like," answered the Duke. "Tell all the wild lies you have time for. You have five minutes to make up your mind to go quietly."

"Now you absolve me, then? Ha, ha! Oh, yes! Mademoiselle," he bowed to Lady Mary, "I have the honor to reques' you leave the room. You shall miss no details if these frien's of yours kill me, on the honor of a French gentleman."

"A French what?" laughed Bantison.

"Do you dare keep up the pretense?" cried Lord Townbrake. "Know, you villain barber, that your master, the Marquis de Mirepoix, is in the next room."

Molyneux heaved a great sigh of relief. "Shall I——" He turned to M. Beaucaire.

The young man laughed, and said: "Tell him come here at once."

"Impudent to the last!" cried Bantison, as Molyneux hurried from the room.

"Now you goin' to see M. Beaucaire's master," said Beaucaire to Lady Mary. " 'Tis true what I say, the other night. I cross from France in his suite; my passport say as his barber. Then to pass the *ennui* of exile, I come to Bath and play for what one will. It kill the time. But when the people hear I have been a servant they come only secretly; and there is one of them—he has absolve' me of a promise not to speak—of him I learn something he cannot wish to be tol'. I make some trouble to learn this thing. Why I should do this? Well—that is my own rizzon. So I make this man help me in a masque, the unmasking it was, for, as there is no one to know me, I throw off my black wig and become myself—and so I am 'Chateaurien,' Castle Nowhere. Then this man I use', this Winterset, he——"

"I have great need to deny these accusations?" said the Duke.

"Nay," said Lady Mary wearily.

"Shall I tell you why I mus' be 'Victor' and 'Beaucaire' and 'Chateaurien,' and not myself?"

"To escape from the bailiffs for debts for razors and soap," gibed Lord Townbrake.

"No, monsieur. In France I have got a cousin who is a man with a very bad temper at some time', and he will never enjoy his relatives to do what he does not wish——"

He was interrupted by a loud commotion from without. The door was flung open, and the young Count of Beaujolais bounded in and threw his arms about the neck of M. Beaucaire.

"Philippe!" he cried. "My brother, I have come to take you back with me."

M. de Mirepoix followed him, bowing as a courtier, in deference; but M. Beaucaire took both his hands heartily. Molyneux came after, with Mr. Nash, and closed the door.

"My warmest felicitations," said the Marquis. "There is no longer need for your incognito."

"Thou best of masters!" said Beaucaire, touching him fondly on the shoulder. "I know. Your courier came safely. And so I am forgiven! But I forget." He turned to the lady. She had begun to tremble exceedingly. "Faires' of all the English fair," he said, as the gentlemen bowed low to her deep courtesy, "I beg the honor to presen' to Lady Mary Carlisle, M. le Comte de Beaujolais. M. de Mirepoix has already the honor. Lady Mary has been very kind to me, my frien's; you mus' help me make my acknowledgment. Mademoiselle and gentlemen, will you give me that favor to detain you one instan'?"

"Henri," he turned to the young Beaujolais, "I wish you had shared my masque—I have been so gay!" The surface of his tone was merry, but there was an undercurrent, weary-sad, to speak of what was the mood, not the manner. He made the effect of addressing every one present, but he looked steadily at Lady Mary. Her eyes were fixed upon him, with a silent and frightened fascination, and she trembled more and more. "I am a great actor, Henri. These gentlemen are yet scarce convince' I am not a lackey! And I mus' tell you that I was jus' now to be expelled for having been a barber!"

"Oh, no!" the ambassador cried out. "He would not be content with me; he would wander over a strange country."

"Ha, ha, my Mirepoix! And what is better, one evening I am oblige' to fight some frien's of M. de Winterset there, and some ladies and cavaliers look on, and they still think me a servant. Oh, I am a great actor! 'Tis true there is not a peasant in France who would not have then known one 'born'; but they are wonderful, this English people, holding by an idea once it is in their heads—a mos' worthy quality. But my good Molyneux here, he had speak to me with courtesy, jus' because I am a man an' jus' because he is al—ways kind. (I have learn' that his great-grandfather was a Frenchman.) So I sen' to him and tell him ev'rything, and he gain admittance for me here to-night to await my frien's.

"I was speaking to messieurs about my cousin, who will meddle in the affair' of his relative'. Well, that gentleman, he make a marriage for me with a good and accomplish' lady, very noble and very beautiful—and amiable." (The young count at his elbow started slightly at this, but immediately appeared to wrap himself in a mantle of solemn thought.) "Unfortunately, when my cousin arrange' so, I was a dolt, a little blockhead; I swear to marry for myself and when I please, or never if I like. That lady is all things charming and gentle, and, in truth, she is—very much attach' to me—why should I not say it? I am so proud of it. She is very faithful and forgiving and sweet; she would be the same, I think, if I—were even—a lackey. But I? I was a dolt, a little unsensible brute; I did not value such thing' then; I was too yo'ng, las' June. So I say to my cousin, 'No, I make my own choosing!' 'Little fool,' he answer, 'she is the one for you. Am I not wiser than you?' And he was very angry, and, as he has influence in France, word come' that he will get me put in Vincennes, so I mus' run away quick till his anger is gone. My good frien' Mirepoix is jus' leaving for London; he take' many risk' for my sake; his hairdresser die before he start', so I travel as that poor barber. But my cousin is a man to be afraid of when he is angry, even in England, and I mus' not get my Mirepoix in trouble. I mus' not be discover' till my cousin is ready to laugh about it all and make it a joke. And there may be spies; so I change my name again, and come to Bath to amuse my retreat with a little gaming—I am al—ways fond of that. But three day' ago M. de Marquis send me a courier to say that my brother, who know where I had run away, is come from France to say that my cousin is appease'; he need me for his little theatre, the play cannot go on. I do not need to espouse mademoiselle. All shall be forgiven if I return, and my brother and M. de Mirepoix will meet me in Bath to felicitate.

"There is one more thing to say, that is all. I have said I learn' a secret, and use it to make a man introduce me if I will not tell. He has absolve' me of that promise. My frien's, I had not the wish to ruin that man. I was not receive'; *Meestaire* Nash had reboff me; I had no other way excep' to use this fellow. So I say, 'Take me to Lady Malbourne's ball as "Chateaurien."' I threw off my wig, and shave, and behol', I am M. le Duc de Castle Nowhere. Ha, ha! You see?"

The young man's manner suddenly changed. He became haughty, menacing. He stretched out his arm, and pointed at Winterset. "Now I am no 'Beaucaire,' messieurs. I am a French gentleman. The man who introduce' me at the price of his honor, and then betray' me to redeem it, is that coward, that cardcheat there!"

Winterset made a horrible effort to laugh. The gentlemen who surrounded him fell away as from pestilence. "A French gentleman!" he sneered savagely, and yet fearfully. "I don't know who you are. Hide behind as many toys and ribbons as you like; I'll know the name of the man who dares bring such a charge!"

"Sir!" cried de Mirepoix sharply, advancing a step towards him; but he checked himself at once. He made a low bow of state, first to the young Frenchman, then to Lady Mary and the company. "Permit me, Lady Mary and gentlemen," he said, "to assume the honor of presenting you to His Highness, Prince Louis-Philippe de Valois, Duke of Orleans, Duke of Chartres, Duke of Nemours, Duke of Montpensier, First Prince of the Blood Royal, First Peer of France, Lieutenant-General of French Infantry, Governor of Dauphiné, Knight of the Golden Fleece, Grand Master of the Order of Notre Dame, of Mount Carmel, and of St. Lazarus in Jerusalem; and cousin to His most Christian Majesty, Louis the Fifteenth, King of France."

"Those are a few of my brother's names," whispered Henri of Beaujolais to Molyneux. "Old Mirepoix has the long breath, but it take' a strong man two day' to say all of them. I can suppose this Winterset know' now who bring the charge!"

"Castle Nowhere!" gasped Beau Nash, falling back upon the burly prop of Mr. Bantison's shoulder.

"The Duke of Orleans will receive a message from me within the hour!" said Winterset, as he made his way to the door. His face was black with rage and shame.

"I tol' you that I would not soil my hand with you," answered the young man. "If you send a message no gentleman will bring it. Whoever shall bear it will receive a little beating from Françoise."

He stepped to Lady Mary's side. Her head was bent low, her face averted. She seemed to breathe with difficulty, and leaned heavily upon a chair. "Monseigneur," she faltered in a half whisper, "can you—forgive me? It is a bitter—mistake—I have made. Forgive."

"Forgive?" he answered, and his voice was as broken as hers; but he went on, more firmly: "It is—nothing—less than nothing. There is—only jus' one—in the—whole world who would not have treat' me the way that you treat' me. It is to her that I am goin' to make reparation. You know something, Henri? I am not goin' back only because the king forgive' me. I am goin' to *please* him; I am goin' to espouse mademoiselle, our cousin. My frien's, I ask your felicitations."

"And the king does not compel him!" exclaimed young Henri.

"Henri, you want to fight me?" cried his brother sharply. "Don' you think the King of France is a wiser man than me?"

He offered his hand to Lady Mary.

"Mademoiselle is fatigue'. Will she honor me?"

He walked with her to the door, her hand fluttering faintly in his. From somewhere about the garments of one of them a little cloud of faded rose-leaves fell, and lay strewn on the floor behind them. He opened the door, and the lights shone on a multitude of eager faces turned toward it. There was a great hum of voices, and over all, the fiddles wove a wandering air, a sweet French song of the *voyageur*.

He bowed very low, as, with fixed and glistening eyes, Lady Mary Carlisle, the Beauty of Bath, passed slowly by him and went out of the room.

# Death of a Country Doctor

## MARY MEDEARIS

*This vibrant story of a doctor's loveable family was
later made by Mary Medearis into the best-selling
novel,* Big Doc's Girl, *now in its fourteenth edition.
This is a story you will never forget, by a writer you
will want to remember.*

### Winter

I WAS FIFTEEN the winter that my father died.

Little Doc, my brother one year younger, stood at the foot of the stairs
that evening, one hand leaning against the banister post. He had come
from upstairs. The living room where we sat, we three sisters, was peaceful and full of busy thoughts. Night had crept into the room. The firelight and the lamp on the desk made the only light. Melie Kate studied
at the desk, her nine-year-old head bent over arithmetic problems. Ruth,
seven, sat cross-legged in front of the fire. Her head leaned against my
knees as she read her lesson aloud for the third time.

Suddenly I became aware that Little Doc was still standing at the staircase. A pounding flame roared through me, and I turned to him with an
effort. His tall figure stood silent. He nodded only once: a world crashed
to bits. My eyes followed him, unable to pull away, as he walked across
the floor and into the dining room. The door closed softly and my
thoughts were left behind.

My thoughts! I must find the answer now to the question that had lain
dormant until Death had brought it to life. What do the four of us do
now? Where do we go? Futile now to hold for Mother's return in time.
"Four more months," the letters from the sanitarium always said. "Maybe six months. Maybe a year. You must make other plans." Yes, I must
think now.

How does one begin thinking again when seemingly the very essence
of one's life has suddenly been dissolved? For six long months—summer

*Reprinted from* Story. *Copyright, 1941, by Story Magazine, Inc.*

and autumn—the warp in the woof of my daily living had been the thread of Father's life; that life being consumed so mercilessly by a strange brain disease. Even in sleep, the conscious mind had slept while the subconscious kept guard for the slightest stir in the next room. The very heartbeat of the day had been Father. Father waiting so childishly patient for the smallest pause in the day's chores. "Read now." Shakespeare, Cervantes, "Arabian Nights," "Pickwick Papers." "Read Shelley tonight, Mary. 'Adonais.'" That horrible line— "—and cold hopes swarm like worms within our living clay." "Father, don't make me read that again. It has the feeling of putty—lifeless, encasing putty."

Those hours of reading were finished. Death, with a touch of his blasting finger had erased all pages of books. I sat unmoving; a clear, cold feeling surrounded me. I looked down from a high ground; aware of no thoughts, only sensory touches to my being. The dry crackling of the flames. The drone of Ruthie's voice. The weight of her head against my knees. The soft markings of Katie's pencil with the chewed eraser. A rain crow mourning in the woods. The shouting stillness of the Presence upstairs. The dirge of the dialing phone in the other room.

Two thoughts entered slowly and heavily. Melie Kate and Ruth. One can live with Aunt Melicent, the other with Uncle Eldon. Uncle Eldon, with his quick intellect, must understand that Ruthie's stolid ways of thinking take patient thoughtfulness. Aunt Melicent mustn't guide Melie Kate's musical fingers too much; her shyness is like a sensitive plant. Little Doc and I can decide later where we can go. "Six more months," the letter always said. "Maybe a year. You must make other plans."

Melie Kate yawned and stretched like a cat. Ruth's voice paused in midsentence as she turned a page. "Ruthie—" My voice was cracked and dry. "Ruthie—sit here by me. The light's bad there."

Early in the dawn of the next morning the wagons began arriving. The first one creaked beneath my bedroom window in the last shadows of the night. It stopped in the road outside. Hushed voices blended with the crunch of footsteps on the frozen ground and the leathery clink of the horses' harness. Farmers taking produce to the town curb markets, I thought. They often stopped to water their horses from the trough that Father had built in the corner by the oak tree.

The stars were still out when the second wagon groaned into the yard. Footsteps stamped on the crusted ground and up the steps of the front porch. A door opened and the footsteps muffled into the house.

Strange! I walked to my bedroom door and to the top of the stairs. A cadence of whispering voices came from below. Busy voices. A head came around the corner of the staircase and seeing me, the rest of the body followed. Fat old Fräulein from across the road. "Ah, Miss Mary, the dust that you've let lay in this house! It can't be here when the Doctor gets back. Tell me where the cloths be."

"In the closet under the stairs," I answered. "Who else is there?"

"Come down for yourself if you can't be sleeping. They're people from back country."

People from back country! Ten and twenty miles back country! Four hours' ride in their creaky wagons—and here they were in the dawn. What manner of grapevine had sent the news of the death of their Doctor so quickly?

I knocked on Little Doc's door. No answer. He must be downstairs with Fräulein and the hushed voices. I hadn't undressed; back to my room for shoes and a sweater and I was downstairs too. I stood by the banister, the same place that Little Doc had stood the evening before. Fräulein had found the dust cloths; she was in every corner at once, dust flying from the whirling cloth in her hands. Little Doc stood by a great bearded man at the front door. A man from the back country. His heavy mackintosh dripped with snow and his boots were wrinkled and smelling of oil.

"I heerd about Big Doc," he said, his enormous hands twisting his stained hat. "We brung turnips." I held out my hand. He crossed to me in two great strides.

"I'll get you a spade," Little Doc said. "You can bury them in the back yard if you've time." They went through the door toward the kitchen, Little Doc's tall lankiness coming only to the huge Pole's shoulder.

Two women sat by the fireplace. "I'm Hank Farris' wife," one said. I remembered. Hank Farris worked on the railroad. "Hank blowed the whistle three times when the train come by tonight, and we knowed Big Doc was dead. Berta and me thought you'd be needing someone to do the cookin'."

"It's kind of you. There's no bread."

"We brung bread," Berta said. "Eggs, too."

By ten o'clock that morning the yard was full of wagons and battered trucks from back country. People from the town hadn't arrived yet. It was too early.

The sun shone gloriously and warm. Horses stamped and whinnied in the woods where they were tied. Indoors, the atmosphere was charged with the bustle of busy people. A warm odor of fresh bread came from the kitchen. Fräulein darned socks in the dining room. "I found these in the basket on the sewing machine," she said reprovingly, a finger through a hole in the toe. "Little Doc's, too."

A young Polish girl with old-woman eyes pushed a plump infant toward me. "This is Mary Kate Ruth." Mary Kate Ruth, named for the three daughters of the country doctor, who had taken the young mother into his house one midnight when a hospital couldn't be reached in time. The baby had been delivered on the long table in the living room. "Not one cry from that mother," Father told us afterward. "She looked at me with those suffering eyes and said, 'Don't worry, Big Doc—we won't wake your babies.' " Those anguished fingernails had left deep scratches on the varnish of the table.

I turned away and stood in the doorway to the living room. Around the fireplace were the men from the back country. Their pipes were lit. "See this thumb? Thar's where the buzz saw went clean through it. Big Doc stuck it back on and danged if they didn't grow smack together again." The thumb reached down with a forefinger and struck a match on the brick fireplace. A haze of smoke spiraled toward the ceiling.

"It's mighty funny," said a gaunt man with a black beard. "I always thought if Doc ever died it'd be of pneumonia. He never buttoned that overcoat of his'n. Never wore no gloves neither. Wife'd say, 'Git in here, Doc, and stick them hands in this hot water.' Doc'd laugh and say, 'Now, tush, Miz Arrington, you know I cain't breathe when my hands got gloves on 'em. They can't feel,' he'd say. 'Might as well be dead hands.' "

Jake Granther propped a booted foot on an andiron. "When Doc gouged a bullet out'n that laig he larned me a poem." He spat thoughtfully into the fire. "Mighty educated man, Big Doc was. Poem went, 'Tobaccy is a dirty weed. I like it. It makes you thin, It makes you lean, It takes the hair plumb off your bean, It's the worst damned stuff I've ever seen. I like it.' "

Fräulein brushed past me toward the men at the fireplace. "Up, Jake. Big Doc's coming home." Jake's foot came off the andiron and he looked toward the window. A long black car was driving into the yard. The men rose and turned toward the door. The man with the scarred thumb knocked his pipe against the mantelpiece.

A song soared upward. A song in my heart. No song of grief, a song of love. Love for a roaring train that ploughed through the night, trumpeting to the countryside that Big Doc, with his rough kind hands wouldn't be knocking at their doors any longer. Love for an inarticulate Pole, whose sympathy lay in turnips buried in the frost of the back yard. Love for Fräulein's hands that brushed away the dust, for long scratches on a table; for bread and eggs in the kitchen. Where was the problem that had weighted down my heart? There was no problem. Big Doc had released us. Released the four of us to find our life together. The four of us were one.

Melie Kate stood in the doorway with me. Ruth touched my sleeve. "Aunt Melicent's car is coming up," she said, close to me. "Sister—wherever you're going, I'm going too." The words of the eternal Ruth. I couldn't see her; a fog was between us. I could only hear Little Doc's voice in the distance, speaking the words for me. "Yes, Ruthie. No one's going anywhere. We're staying here."

## Spring

It was the last Sunday in May. There was a cool smell of hawthorn in the air; and spring grass, and new mint leaves by the back porch steps. The sun was molten, pouring through the open windows of the living room into oblong blocks of yellow warmth. I sat on the floor in the block by the bookcase, looking through Mother's scrapbook. Funny! You'd never think Mother was sentimental. There was an old recital program, dated from a year when she was Molly Hendricks, and up on one corner was her handwriting, "Dr. Robert Anderson sat across to the left. I think Smike's hands must have looked like his."

A door slammed upstairs. Little Doc called "Sister!" but I didn't answer. He tore down the stairs, pausing at the landing to clear the last five steps in a leap that jarred the whole house. He yelled out the side window. "Sister! Hey, Sister!"

Without looking up, I said, "I'll laugh the day you fall from the top to the bottom."

"You've got a long wait then, Sourface," he answered pleasantly. "Get up and find Melie Kate and Ruth. We're going on a picnic."

"Who said so?"

"Mother did."

I looked up at that. We hadn't been on a picnic since Father had died, and Mother had been home for four spring Sundays with not a word for a picnic before. Then I remembered. Ruth's eighth birthday! It was two days past, yes, but a picnic on a birthday Sunday was tradition. I closed the scrapbook and scrambled to my feet. "All right, I'll find them. You get the basket."

The two little sisters were making a hospital among the roots of the big oak tree in the far corner of the yard. "Come on in, Katie and Ruth. We're going on a picnic." Melie Kate's eyes shone. She was on her feet in an instant, but Ruth kept stolidly carving steps out of a tiny clay hillock.

"Come on, Ruthie."

"In a minute."

We waited impatiently. "Hurry, Ruthie!"

"I can't hurry. There's been a wreck and I've got to get these steps finished before the ambulance gets here."

"It's the door to the operating room," Melie Kate explained.

"Well, we're going on in," I said. "You'll get left." Melie Kate took my hand and we ran across the yard. "It's a hash picnic," I called back from the porch.

The picnic basket was on the kitchen table, and Little Doc pulled the lid over the top as Melie Kate and I came through the door from the dining room. "I've already put in my part," he said. "I'm going to the attic and get the water jars."

"Wait for me," I called after him. "Here, Katie. Quick! You wait in the dining room until I put my hash in the basket. You can fix yours while I'm helping Little Doc." I pushed her into the dining room and closed the door. Then I hurried toward the back porch for the box of marshmallows behind the flour bin in the pantry. Mother stood at the back porch table, turning to glower and brandish the carving knife as I opened the door.

"Here, young lady! Scoot! No looking in on a hash picnic." I closed the door quickly.

"Oh, dear!" There was a jar of pickled watermelon rind on the top of the cabinet, so I dropped that in the basket and covered the top again. "All right, Melie Kate." She opened the door so quickly that I suspected an eye at the keyhole. I glared sternly, but her face was candid and inquiring. "Children who peek get thrown in the creek," I sang as I raced up the stairs after Little Doc.

But something had happened to Little Doc. He wasn't laughing any more. His face was expressionless, and he stood far off behind his eyes and mouth. He spoke shortly, "You don't need to help."

"But I always help you—" He had the two jars in his arms and started downstairs.

"Aren't you driving?" he asked over his shoulder.

"Yes. Mother doesn't feel well enough yet."

"You'd better get the car out then and let me do this."

"It's in the driveway," I answered in a small voice, but I knew that wasn't right. Little Doc didn't want me to help him. "Guess maybe I'd better see if Ruthie's come in though."

Ruthie had come in, so I took the car keys out of the wooden shoe on the mantelpiece and sat in the car to wait. It gave me time to think about that stony look on Little Doc's face. I had time to think about it all the while that we drove through the town and out the Conway Pike toward our old picnic grounds. I didn't even argue when Melie Kate suggested the two poplars by Cricket Creek. I was remembering the times that I had run against that look of Little Doc's during the past few months. We would be having such fun together, the two of us, and then suddenly without a breath of warning, he would back off. Far off, behind an impenetrable wall. Oh, Little Doc, what's happening? You never shut doors on me before!

We reached Cricket Creek, and Little Doc rolled two big stones in front of the back wheels to keep the car from rolling away. Father had started that. One day he had squinted at the two front headlights and said, "That critter's got a wicked eye. I don't trust just brakes to hold it."

Mother and I spread the tablecloth under the two big poplars, and Melie Kate and Ruth scampered off for stones to weight the corners down. Little Doc pulled out the back car seat for Mother to sit on.

"I love hash picnics," Mother said. "Remember what happened the first one we ever had?"

They would never let me forget it! I had told each of the others that I hoped someone would think to put in tuna fish sandwiches because I liked them so much—and everyone had put in tuna fish sandwiches. Thirty-four tuna fish sandwiches, and one pickle that Mother had remembered.

Little Doc grinned at me and I grinned back. Why, nothing was wrong! It must have been my imagination—that tone in his voice before.

Someone had to see if the car was ready! I called happily, "Hey, Katie. A stone here."

"It's coming," Mother said dryly.

It was coming, clenched in both of Melie Kate's arms. She ran in a

183

beeline for me, Ruth close at her heels, a stick in her hands and fury on her face. "I saw it first," Ruth yelled. "I saw that rock first." I held out my hands for the stone, and Little Doc took the stick from Ruthie's stubborn hands. "We'll use this to roast marshmallows," he said. "Go back and get three more."

"No. Wait!" Mother sat on the car seat. "Let's open the basket. We can get the roasting sticks later."

We sat around the tablecloth in tense excitement. Mother was maddeningly slow in taking the lid off. She pulled out a brown paper sack, peered deliberately inside.

"That's not fair, Mother. What's in it?" Solemnly she turned it upside down. "Knives!" We all groaned. "And glasses."

"ONE glass."

"That's Ruthie's," I said gayly. "Lazy thing. Serve her right if everyone had to eat just what they brought."

Mother unwrapped sandwiches. "Look! Cornbread and onion sandwiches. That's Little Doc's."

Melie Kate pealed with merriment. "He's got jelly on the cornbread, too. That's terrible."

"Oh, I don't know. I like it. Anyway, look at yours." We always recognized Katie's sandwiches; the bread was ragged on the edges where she pulled the crusts off.

"How did Melie Kate get in my family of crust eaters?" Mother asked. "She'll make sissies out of all of us."

"What's Sister's hash?"

"Marshmallows."

Little Doc smirked. "Always marshmallows."

"No, it isn't!" A blank silence from all four.

"No marshmallows?"

"Nope!" I was smug. "I won't be taken for granted any more."

"Doesn't really matter," Little Doc said. "You always ate all of them anyway."

Mother finished emptying the basket of her apples, and the stalk of bananas and thick ham sandwiches. "This is the last of the ham," she remarked. A shadow brushed out gaiety. Jess Arrington from the back country had brought us that hog the day that Big Doc died.

I reached for one of the sandwiches with the ragged edges. Suddenly a sharp whack and a surprised howl of pain from Melie Kate. The stick was in Ruth's hands. "It was my stone," she explained.

"All right, Ruth! That's enough!" Mother picked up two of the ham sandwiches and a banana and put them in Ruthie's hands. "Go behind that hickory tree to eat your lunch."

Ruth scuffed forlornly toward the tree. None of us said a word. In a moment she had turned and flounced back to the table. She picked up the glass, turned on her heel, and marched primly behind the tree.

Little Doc looked at Mother. "We'll have to forgive her. She's the only one who brought a glass."

Melie Kate sighed decisively. "Yes. Guess we will."

"No, we won't!" Mother was firm. "She sits right there until we've finished. We can drink out of the fruit jar lids."

"They leak," Melie Kate said hopefully, but Mother handed the jar of watermelon preserves across to Little Doc. "See if you can open this with your scout knife. I can't budge it."

It wasn't long until the last sandwich was finished, and the last apple rolled surreptitiously to Ruth, who still sat behind the hickory tree. I sat waiting for Little Doc to suggest that we go down the road to find a persimmon tree to shake down. Always after a picnic, Little Doc and I went on foraging journeys together. Once we had found an Indian burial mound. Once we had caught eighty-two crawfish in the shallow creek. That was the day that Father and Melie Kate and Ruth had come marching down upon us, blowing shrilly on three willow whistles and ordering immediate release of the eighty-two prisoners of war. Under their stern eyes we had been forced to empty the rusty cans of their scratching, clawing captives, and watch them scuttle away under pebbles and black roots. Then Father had turned and started off with his long swinging stride. "Follow in my footsteps, men," he called back, and Ruth looked at the distance between his seven-league footprints. "But Father, you don't make many." That humorously gentle expression as he looked at her. Then an abrupt blow on his whistle and they were piping through the trees again.

Little Doc got to his feet at last, and I rose with him. "Guess I'll go down to the creek and skip stones," he said, not looking at anyone. "Come on, Melie Kate and Ruth. I'll show you how." It was a long second before Melie Kate scrambled to her feet and ran after him.

Ruth's head poked inquiringly from behind her tree. "Go on, Ruthie," Mother said softly, and the two little sisters copied Little Doc's long awkward strides down the path to the creek.

I didn't want to stand there, too big and too clumsy, an empty feeling in my hands, but I couldn't seem to sit down either. Mother stood with me. "There might be cattails up the creek, Sister. We can clear this up later." I followed her through the trees and up the side of the creek. We gathered great armloads of white haw-apple blossoms and long feathery grasses. "Look, Sister—" A wide bare space between the trees was a carpet of tiny blue star flowers. Mother's voice was warm and happy as it always was when we were wandering through the woods.

My heart was miserable. I wanted to ask her something, but what could I ask? "Mother, doesn't Little Doc want me to help him any more?" That wasn't it. Little Doc was my brother; we always worked together. "Mother, I don't believe that Little Doc wants me for his best friend any longer." I couldn't say that out loud. Not even to myself. Little Doc and I had never talked about being friends; our feeling was too deeply wedged in to be poured into an empty shell of words. It had begun far back in Clendenin School, when a third-grade boy had smashed a Valentine box that I had made, and Little Doc, only a second-grader, had kicked him in the shin until it bled. Little Doc had been beaten up, and afterward we had walked the six blocks home together, not saying anything. We couldn't. You can't talk about a feeling like that.

Mother and I lay on our backs beneath a giant maple tree and looked up through the depth of green leaves. The clear feeling of space was comforting. Mother's voice seemed to come from nowhere. "I wish I knew what to say to you, Sister." I lay still; I should have known I wouldn't have to ask. "Do you know what the word jealousy means?"

I shook my head. "Little Doc isn't jealous of me if that's what you're saying."

"No, he's proud of you—"

"And I'm proud of him, Mother." Words wanted to tumble out now. "He's the only boy in school who'll graduate when he's only fifteen. And when Frank picked him to work in his grocery store this summer, I was so proud that I hurt inside." The feeling came back, just remembering it.

Mother said, "Remember the day that he got a bonus from the *Gazette* for having the only hundred per cent paper route in town?" I remembered. Father had said, "A job well done," and Little Doc had sat in his place at the head of the table that night. After supper when we went into the living room, I had sat at the piano and played every piece that I had ever learned. "That was one sort of jealousy," Mother said.

"Oh, no, Mother! No, it wasn't! Little Doc had done his job well and I wanted to show that I was doing mine well too."

"That's what I mean, Sister. Sometimes people don't know when they're jealous, and I don't believe that Little Doc knows right now that he's got a kind of jealousy for you. But he has. He's trying to push you away from him, because you're standing in a place that he wants." I started to speak, but Mother put her hand over my mouth. "Little Doc wants Big Doc's place. You're the eldest, you see, and when the four of you stayed there all these months waiting for me to come home, you had to be the head of the house. You had to be the leader. I know what a load of responsibility fell on you. I've never quite been able to tell you how very proud I've been."

My throat ached at her words, but I couldn't understand her. True, my word had always been the final one, and I had done the speaking for the four of us, but Little Doc and I had always made the decisions together. He had done as much as I.

After a time Mother said, "Maybe, Sister, you could give your place to Little Doc now and take a place with me, would you? If you're going to be a piano teacher in my place someday, it's time you learned to keep lesson books and had a pupil or two of your own to supervise. You can have your place, Little Doc can have his—not too close together—" I felt that she was groping for something. "Anyway, the head of a family should be a man. Little Doc's our man now."

It was good to lie like a part of the warm hard earth, the sun making little golden feathers of light through the dense leaves overhead. I took a deep breath of contentment and relief. "I could die here," I thought happily.

"Sister!" Mother spoke sharply and sat up. "I smell wild plums."

I sniffed the air. "That's only spring."

She walked quickly to the creek. "Come here. Just come here and look." I groaned and rolled over reluctantly. Mother was jubilant. "Can't fool this nose of mine." Down the three-foot bank, nearly hidden by brush, was a thicket of wild plum bushes. "We'll have wild plum and apple jelly until I'm gray-headed. What can we put them in?"

I was excited with her. "There." A lard bucket lay at the foot of the bank. "You start picking and I'll go back for the picnic basket."

I started on a run, past the maple tree, over the carpet of blue star flowers, on through the woods toward the two big poplars. My heart was light and the sun was warm.

Little Doc stood near the poplar trees.

"We found wild plums," I shouted.

He didn't move. Just looked at me, a tight look on his face, his open scout knife in his hands. Then I saw Melie Kate. She lay on the car seat by the picnic basket, her body racking with sobs, a deep gash in the calf of one leg. "A rattlesnake," Little Doc said. "I had to cut it." I looked at him numbly. "That's what Father would have done," he said. "I made a tourniquet and sucked the poison out."

He closed the knife with a snap and picked up one of the empty water jars. "Get some water out of the creek and bathe her head." He looked around. "Ruthie!" She wasn't in sight, but behind the hickory tree was a frightened little voice. "Come here, Ruthie. I want you to go after Mother." He turned to me. "Where is Mother?"

"Up the hill. She can find her if she follows the creek."

The sunshine looked queer, and something in my stomach made me turn and walk blindly toward the creek. I filled the water jar and turned back. The world was stabbed with stars and darkness. Then my forehead was wet, and Little Doc shook me gently. "Sister! Sister!"

"I'm all right—"

"I'm sorry, Sister, but you'll have to go after Mother. Ruth won't know what to say." He helped me to my feet.

"What can I say?"

"Say that Melie Kate is sick and I think we ought to get back right away. Be careful not to scare her. She isn't well herself yet." I dazedly picked up the jar. He took it from me. "I'll get that. You go on."

I turned and walked shakily up the creek bank again. Soon I ran. It was so far.

Mother's face was shiny and perspiring, and the lard bucket was full of wild plums. "Sister. What's happened?"

My eyes almost gave me away. "Nothing much, Mother. Melie Kate's ill and Little Doc says we ought to leave right away." My eyes must have said more. Mother climbed quickly up the bank, and I had time to pick up the bucket of plums before we started back together.

Little Doc had everything ready. Melie Kate was propped up in the back seat of the car, her face tear-stained and pitifully frightened.

Mother got in and held Melie Kate's head in her lap. She looked at the bleeding leg with the two ominous punctures. "We've got to get a doctor," she said quietly. What doctor? Father had always been our doctor. "What doctor, Little Doc?"

"Dr. White," he said. Of course, Doctor White. Father had begun practicing with Dr. White when he had first come to town twenty years before. It couldn't have been anyone else.

My stomach felt queer again. My hands were clammy. "I can't drive," I thought desperately. "I can't drive. I'm shaking all over." I started blindly around the car but Little Doc brushed me aside. "I'll drive."

I looked at him in bewilderment. "You don't know how."

"Yes, I do. Frank's been teaching me in his delivery truck. I've been driving wholesale loads from the warehouse for him." He sat in the driver's seat and I got in gratefully beside him.

"Wait a minute," Mother said, "Ruthie." She held the back door open. Ruthie dumped the big white rock on the floor by Mother's feet, then climbed in the front seat between Little Doc and me.

A relaxed sense of peace stole over me. Everything was all right. Little Doc was driving fast and surely, and Dr. White was waiting at the other end. Everything was all right now.

I turned and looked at Little Doc. His eyes were straight on the road ahead, and his chin was set as firmly as Big Doc's ever was. Mother was right! He had Big Doc's way! I hadn't seen it before. How incongruous and strangely pathetic Little Doc looked to me in that one brief moment. Little Doc and Big Doc: the crooked cowlick and boyish mouth, the set of the chin and the bony, gentle hands.

Ruth leaned over and spoke in my ear. "I just remembered, Sister. Melie Kate did really see that rock first. When I looked at it I was looking sort of sideways. I mean I wasn't looking right straight at it, I think." I squeezed her hand tight.

Then it was evening. The sun had left the living room, and I sat on the floor by the bookcase again, Mother's scrapbook on my knees. Little Doc made a fire of kindling wood in the fireplace, against the evening chill.

Mother came from the kitchen and stood in the doorway. "I've been thinking, Little Doc. Now that you're working at Frank's you'll be needing a door key. You'd better take your Father's. It's upstairs in the top bureau drawer." She went back to the kitchen, and Little Doc propped the poker carefully against the fireplace before he went upstairs.

I turned a page to an old recital program of Mother's pupils. There, third down the list was Elizabeth Walker's name. Elizabeth Walker had grown into Mrs. Thomas now, and her little Elizabeth was old enough to go to school. Maybe she would take piano lessons. Mother had said that I might have a pupil or so of my own this summer. I'll ask tomorrow.

Upstairs a door closed. All at once I realized that I sat tense; listening for something. Waiting for something that I couldn't place.

Little Doc came down the stairs, each step firm and steady, one right after the other. He paused at the landing. I heard the keys jingle as he fixed them in his pocket. He said, "Think I'll go up to Frank's and see when he'll be needing me to work."

He started down the last five steps. A stumble, a thudding crash, then silence. I knew what had happened, but I couldn't move. My eyes couldn't come away from the recital program.

In a moment he got up and walked slowly to the front door. "I won't be gone long. I'll come back and beat you at checkers." I turned a page.

"You just think you will. Don't hurry though. I'm going to look through Mother's lesson books while you're gone." As I spoke, I knew what Mother had groped for. Little Doc in his place. I in mine. Parallel, but a space between.

"Well," Little Doc still stood at the door, "so long—Mary."

I didn't want to say it, but he was making me. "So long, Robert," I said.

## Summer

Big Jake Granther stood at our side door. The dust of the back country was on his faded jeans, and his face was brown from the hot June sun.

"Good morning, Mr. Granther," I said. "It's been a long time since you've knocked at our door. I hope all are well at your house."

"All are well," he answered. "How are your folks?"

"All are well, thank you."

He leaned one bony hand against the door casing. "Could I have words with Miz Doc?"

"She's giving a piano lesson—" Beyond him, and parked by the side of the road, was his wagon loaded high with melons for the curb market. A half-hour wait might mean loss of the early morning customers. "Wait a moment. I'll call her. Please come in."

"No thank'ee. I'll wait here ma'am."

When Mother came in from the living room, I walked back to the kitchen and closed the door. Something in Jake's manner had made me vaguely uneasy. It might have been his odd request to speak with Mother. Those weather-beaten faces at our side door had always meant, "I want Big Doc—tell him Ezzie's baby's a-bornin'." It was the town faces at the front door that asked, "Is your Mother in? I want to see about piano lessons." But then it might have been the unfamiliar look in Jake Granther's eyes when he spoke to me. A keen, straight look.

The kitchen door opened and Mother stood there. "Mary, how old are you?"

"Fifteen. You know."

"Are you old enough to be a teacher?"

"A piano teacher?" My heart was a trip hammer. "You were only fourteen."

"Yes." Her eyes were through me now. She must have seen that little pig-tailed girl of years ago, riding off down the road on the brown horse, Penny, a music roll tied to the saddle horn. "Yes. Well!" She spoke briskly. "The people around Zion Hill have bought an organ for the church and they want someone to show them how to play it. Jake Granther's come for you. He says there are six to take lessons until you have to come in for school again." She hesitated. "It's twenty miles back country."

I knew what she meant. Twenty miles back country, with the rutted roads and uncertain trips to the curb markets, might mean a month before I could get home again. I nodded my head. "I'm already fifteen, Mother."

She closed the door and her footsteps went straight back to the side door. I sat still, afraid to move. This was the moment that I had known would come since the first time I had sat on the fourth step behind the banisters to hear Mother give a piano lesson. A voice at the door had finally come for me! I had thought it would be the front door, though. No matter. It had come. And what a teacher I would be! My pupils would practice faithfully, and I would never let them make a mistake. I would have my own lesson book, and sit on the porch after supper to mark down the day's lessons. I might even ride a horse now, as Mother had done. I would wave from the road as we went by, and the people in the houses would wave back. "That's Big Doc's gal," they would say. "I hear she's most as good as her Ma a-teaching." A little shiver went down my spine.

Mother stood in the kitchen doorway again. "You'll have to do your own packing, Sister. I teach until after two this afternoon, and Jake's coming for you as soon as he's sold out at the curb market." Her eyes were soft and her mouth had a quirk to it. "You may use my big suitcase this time. It's under the quilts in my closet."

The sun was two hours past our chimney when Jake Granther returned for me. He swung Mother's big suitcase in the back of the empty wagon, and pulled me up to the high seat beside him. The family stood in a row to see me off. The two little sisters, Melie Kate and Ruth, were wide-eyed with awe at my close proximity to big Jake Granther with the black beard. Little Doc, home from his job in Frank's grocery store in honor of the occasion, was stolidly expressionless at my leaving him for the first time. He handed me his beanshooter; the old one with the three nicks on the handle for the three boys at school who had tried to take it away from him. "Here. It's good luck."

Mother put a small gray ledger in my lap. My lesson book! A lesson book and a beanshooter! "I know how David felt," I said, and I laughed with excitement. That rocky dirt road ahead was the road to my Glorious Adventure.

But look! Coming down the road was a small figure with a music satchel in its hand. Mother's two o'clock pupil. Goliath! Suddenly the adventure dropped away and hard panic was there from underneath.

"Mother." I gripped her hand tightly. "Mother, I've never taught before. How will I know?"

Mother's other hand pulled my head down to hers. "Don't you worry, Sister. You'll know." Her voice was soft, but her eyes looked as my heart felt. "You'll know," she said again.

Jake Granther flipped the reins and clucked to the horses, and we were bumping down the rutted road. I clutched my lesson book and Little Doc's beanshooter, and looked straight between old Samson's ragged ears. The road ahead was still a rocky white curve. Heat rays made shimmering will-o'-the-wisps.

In my chest was a shriveled lump where a moment before had been a full-bloom balloon of excitement. Suppose I couldn't teach after all? Suppose I couldn't even begin a lesson? Oh, surely I should know that. That fourth step behind the banisters had a worn spot on the varnish from the years that I had sat there, listening to the lessons that Mother had begun and ended. Only now all those lessons seemed to have rolled into one big lesson—no beginning, no ending. Just pieces from one whole.

After a long time I leaned over and asked of Jake Granther's profile, "Am I to live at your house?"

"Your Ma said to. My house is easy walking to the church house, and thar's where you'll be teaching." His elbows leaned on sharp bony knees, and suddenly I had a picture of rows of grizzled Ichabod Cranes, at rows of organs, long grasshopper legs doubled up until their knees bumped the bottom of the keyboard with every pump of the pedal.

I leaned over again. "Will I have any boys to teach?"

Jake thought for a moment. "Jess Arrington's young'un aims to take. He's got a hawg of his own to pay with." He turned then, and his eyes twinkled at me. "I got a girl yore age."

Mother had told me what to say. "I'll teach her then for my board."

"We was aiming fer her to take," he answered. "We got pertaters and peanuts extry."

"Well, my father said you've got another girl. I'll teach her for them." We must have gone a quarter of a mile before he answered that.

"Her name's Dorcas. Her Ma died when she was borned and she ain't right in the haid. She sings funny-like." He jerked impatiently on the reins and squinted at the blinding sun. "If them horses git a-moving we'll git thar 'bout sundown."

The road wound on, and the sun dipped lower. Jake Granther had said right. The wagon topped the rise of Zion Hill as the last red and gold ribbons streaked behind the hickory grove. A great field of cotton stretched on either side of the road, and upon the side of the next hill was a small white house.

Jake pointed a gnarled finger at the fields of curved green rows. "Thet's my ground," he said. "My pa give it to me when I was eleven y'ar old." The clean brown smell of fresh earth was in the air.

"It smells good," I said.

He looked over the new-turned furrows and pulled out his snuffbox. "Hit was a day like this'n the first time I ever plowed thet ground. Pa brung me out to thet fence yonder and hitched up the team and said, 'This field's yourn, Jake, soon's you larn to plow it.' "

He stopped, and I felt that he wanted me to say something. "You must have been proud, Mr. Granther."

He chuckled. "I was skeered. Skeered plumb holler, I can tell you." He chuckled again. "Pa'd planted corn thet spring and them little green shoots was no taller'n my elbow. They kept a-whisperin' as plain like. 'Don't git thet iron tooth too clost my roots,' they said, 'don't you let it git too clost.' "

His face became grave, and his hand still held the unopened snuffbox.

"Sometimes I wisht I could remember the feelin' I got thet morning when Pa walked down thet road and left me thar all by myself. Everybody ought to remember the feelin' they git the first time they start workin' their own ground." He shook his head. "I git thinkin' most back thar sometimes, and then, piff! Hit goes through. Like leanin' on a fence post and it ain't thar. Then I git to thinkin' maybe thar warn't no beginnin'. Maybe I was born in plowin'."

I wanted to say something, but then I saw the other white building that I hadn't seen before.

"That looks like a church," I said. Jake nodded.

"Reckon thar'll be quite a meetin' thar tonight, too. Folks thought you might play the orgin fer 'em."

Something inside me turned sickeningly. Oh, not so soon! Let me wait until tomorrow! Let me wait right here until tomorrow! But the wagon rumbled on, past the church, past the field, and up the road to the house on the hill.

We walked down the hill after supper. Gert, who was my age, and Dorkie, the queer one, were with us this time. It was dark, with white scaly clouds in a still sky. "Mackerel sky," Jake said. "Rain tomorrer." We walked down the road, past the field, and up the path to the whitewashed, one-room church house. A wagon was drawn up by the well.

"Hit's them Bascoms," Gert said disdainfully. "They're allus fust come."

The Bascoms sat in a long row on the second bench from the front. They had lit the four wall lamps, and a dim yellow light filled the square church room. Heavy green curtains had been pulled in front of the pulpit to make the room into a meetinghouse.

Jake strode up the aisle. "Miz Bascom, meet Big Doc's gal." Mrs. Bascom smiled carefully, and Mr. Bascom leaned over the bench to shake my hand in a horny grip. "Pleased to meetcha, Teacher." The four little Bascoms stared as one great solemn eye.

Granny Bascom leaned her hands on her cane and said doubtfully, "She hain't so big."

"Thet's 'cause she don't eat nothin'," Gert explained loudly. "Shoulda seen her at supper. Two biscuits and a spoonin' of grease beans. She won't git no man thet'a way." They all laughed, and Gert smiled archly in her wisdom.

I went up to the organ. It stood shiny and new against the thick green curtains, the lid thrown back waiting for me. I sat on the bench and pressed my fingers down on the cold white keys. There was no sound. The four little Bascoms giggled in whispers. "Teacher fergot to pump it." My feet fumbled for the long flat pedals, and I pumped them with all my might. A great roaring chord swelled out, and echoed back in over-tones from the walls. Another chord, softer this time, to swallow the shakiness in my hands, and then a melody. Any melody. Anything to start thinking in.

In a moment I felt safer; wrapped round in the music from the "looking over" that had already begun. I played carefully; nothing too far away from these people, nothing condescending. Mendelssohn's "Spring Song"; "The Lost Chord." The plantation songs, a hymn or so.

I turned around. "What's your favorite, Granny Bascom?"

Her rheumy eyes were misty. "The Old Rugged Cross. Thank'ee kindly." She hummed it in a quaver as I played it.

"And yours, Mrs. Bascom?"

"The Jericho Road, maybe."

"I don't know that one. Is there music?"

Jephtha, Jess Arrington's young-un, had come in. He propped a hymn book on the scrolled rack in front of me, and held a lamp by my left shoulder to light the pages of notes. I heard Granny Bascom humming again.

"Sing, Jephtha, you and Gert. Let's all sing." Jephtha and Gert started with me, and the four little Bascoms burst out in the middle of the second line.

It was when we reached the last verse that I became conscious of other voices than the Granthers' and the Bascoms' in the singing back of me. I heard a horse neigh in the woods; a wagon creak up to the well. We finished the hymn, and a strange voice called out, "Sweet Hour of Prayer." I was glad that I knew that one without music.

Under the voices was the sound of more wagons in the yard, and coughing motors of rattling trucks. Footsteps clumped up the three plank steps and down the bare boards of the aisle. Long, heavy boot strides, and short lighter steps. Jephtha turned the pages for another hymn and whispers came from the front row.

"How you payin' Teacher?"

"Preserves. I done canned thirty-six quarts. How're you?"

"I got money."

Incredulous whispers swooped down like bees.

"Where'd you git it?"

"I chopped cotton," defiantly. "Pa said I could spend it fer anything. Look! I got blood blisters."

I played quickly; quickly to drown something that seemed to cry out. My fingers wouldn't stop now. The music rolled on; the rhythm grew broader as more voices came in with more footsteps. Jake Granther sang mightily, his heavy boots beating time on the bare planked floor. Dorkie, the queer one, stood against the side of the bench at first, her strange high voice weaving a silver thread in the heavy-woven voices from the benches. Soon her head leaned full against my shoulders, but it was vaguely comfortable to play that way.

The words of the song, "And Isaiah said, 'Ho, all ye that thirsteth, Come ye to the waters—'" These people sang for music as they sang for rain. Jake Granther had said that six had planned to take lessons, but the room was full of children's voices. What would they get? I would ask the minister if I could have a meeting every Tuesday night. A singing meeting. I would take no pay for that. They could call it a Singing Practice, if they wanted to, and sing all their hymns and folk songs. I could teach them songs that I knew. Perhaps the one that my father loved to sing on cold winter evenings. "Jaybird sitting on a crooked limb, I cocked my gun and I shot at him, Said he, 'Young man, don't you do thet agin'', Yip, Yi, Yip ti yi, Eat pa'ched corn and sit by the fire." Yes, they would like that one.

"Play two-hundred-six, Teacher. We got a quartet fer it." The four little Bascoms stood by the side of the organ and opened their mouths like sparrows. "Just like a tree-ee, that's planted by the wa-ters—" they sang.

Dorcas sat on the bench by my right arm now. Her odd-shaped hands were on the keys an octave above mine, and her fingers followed the pattern that mine were making.

"Can you play, Dorkie?"

"She picks 'em out," Jephtha answered by my ear. "I heerd her after preaching last Sunday."

"Will you play this, Dorkie, and let me rest a while?" She didn't look up. I slid down the bench, and she put her hands where mine had been. Not a break in the rhythm. The four voices sang on. Nothing had changed.

A strange, prickling feeling crept over me. Somewhere, sometime, that had all happened before. The room, the music, the twisted hands—it was happening ahead of me. Part of my dream, perhaps.

In a blinding flash I saw it again. It wasn't a dream. I was looking down on it; looking down from between banister posts. It was Mother at the piano, playing on and on, and behind a chair was a cowering little boy with vacant eyes. The room fills with music, and the little boy creeps closer until he stands at Mother's elbow. Suddenly his hands crash down on the keys. "Can you play, Rickie?" That furious pounding.

"This is horses," he shrieks. "Someone hurt them."

Mother reaches down and holds his hands tightly in hers. "It's over now." That deafening silence and the stillness of the small figure. "It's over, Rickie."

"My name's Dorkie."

I looked down. I was standing by the bench, and my hands gripped Dorkie's until the knuckles were white. The room was still. The singing had stopped, and that voice in the silence was mine.

I knew what came next. I turned. "I want to teach you a song that I know. A song that Big Doc used to sing." The rows of faces smiled; brown, weather-beaten faces, small eager faces, old, wrinkled faces. "I want the men on this side of the aisle and the women on the other." There was a scrambling for seats. The four little Bascoms tumbled over each other and shrilled excitedly. Granny Bascom picked up her cane and hobbled across the aisle.

Jake Granther stood in the doorway. His hands were in his pockets, and his eyes watched the crowding people. I wanted him to look at me. I wanted to cry out, "Look, Jake Granther! Look what's happened! I'm teaching! I've always known how to teach. Remember what you said to me this afternoon? You said, 'Everybody ought to remember the feeling they get the first time they start plowing their own ground.' I want to remember this feeling all my life. It began just a moment ago. It began with Dorkie's head on my shoulder. No! No, it was Dorkie's hands on the keys of the organ." Strange, twisted hands—Rickie's hard pounding from a hurt heart—eyes behind the banisters, and another little girl riding down the road on a horse named Penny—it twists far, far back—I can't touch it any longer. "It's too far back, Jake, and I'm too tired to find it now. Later I'll think back—"

Dorkie's eyes were big and black in front of me. I put my hands on the keys again. "Listen, Dorkie. Listen closely. Watch my hands and pick this out. 'Jay bird sitting on a crooked limb, I cocked my gun and I shot at him—' "

# Annie Laurie

## ZONA GALE

*Annie Laurie, a tale of a small midwestern town, is a
tender love story written with dramatic artistry and
beautiful insight. Zona Gale here demonstrates how
richly she deserves her high rank in American literature.*

SHE LEFT the train at something called Morrel's Land-
ing. She looked about on all that there was of it, left her traveling-bag
and her violin case with the curious ticket man, whose only conversation
was "Yep"; and said to the decrepit taxi's robust driver: "Mr. Martin
Lowe—do you know him?"

The taxi driver shouted in a great voice, "Mart Lowe? Two dollars,
though—it's quite a smart piece out."

She looked as if she had the fare, which may have been why he demanded it. Not that in all probability he knew chinchilla, or was intuitive
as to the admirable line of the hat or the bag. But there was about Miss
Lina Bothwell unquestionably a something, or so his demand and his
deference seemed to say. And by the frown on his face and by his far
look he may have been wondering: "Now what would she know about
Mart Lowe or his missus?"

What, she might have retorted, should she know about Morrel's Landing at all—that assemblage of blistered and blighted buildings? It was
a town, she observed, which did not even show outdated and ragged
amusement posters—manifestly there had never been any amusement
posters there. Windows of "stores" stared out blindly, save that here and
there were affixed handbills calling to the Old Fiddlers' Contest to be held
in "Post-Office Hall" that same night.

"I have arrived," Lina thought, "at the height of the season." As the
Old Fiddlers' advertisements persisted, fluttering from every telegraph-
pole, she thought: "I wish I'd let Mr. Jaquith come there too, when he
suggested coming—we'd have gone to hear the old fiddlers . . ."

*Reprinted by permission of Wm. Ll. Breese.*

The road ran out through rough March ruts, thickly covered by snow which had arrived with winter fury, and was clearly thinking of beginning again. Dead trees, dead farmhouses, dead corn husks and stacks— all the sodden sleep of the country in early March. Three miles out, and at the end of a mile of criminal cross-road, the taxi floundered into the most moribund farmyard of all.

"Not here!" said Miss Lina Bothwell, with determination.

"Here," said the taxi man. "Two dollars, Ma'am."

She made him ask, at the unpainted door. Confirmed by the brown man and the thin blue woman who appeared on the threshold as if by one control, the chauffeur took his fee and shattered the dead quiet of the place as he rattled away. The two in the doorway stood staring at Miss Lina Bothwell, her chinchilla, and her admirable hat and bag.

She stepped up to them, none of her misgivings in her face, but instead a gentleness and a hesitancy, but whether of life or of art there was nobody there to determine. She said:

"Mr. Lowe, I am Lina Bothwell—Marian's daughter. I promised her to find you. May I come in?"

The blue woman said, "Good land," but the man, his attention suddenly ingathered and something gigantic coming into his look, said: "Her girl? Little Marian's girl? Lord Almighty." He added: "We were expecting her, but not—you"—a flattery unintended and direct.

She followed them into the kitchen. The kitchen was bright with paint and firelight and blooming plants.

"Throw off your things," the woman said as if by appointment, and then, still as if in the clutch of some routine which no exigency had ever disturbed, turned to the cupboard and took down a teapot and canister. "Stir up the fire, Mart," she said.

And he, though his face still said "Lord Almighty," stooped and stirred and replenished the fire, as if routine were the life of life.

Lina sat down before the hearth. Twilight was coming, and the red glow from the draft of the range was on her brown hair and her smooth face. The black gown was a miracle not lost on the woman, nor were the buckled shoes and the enameled watch. But Martin Lowe seemed to discern nothing save the core of some incredible moment. He faced about from the fire and stared down at her.

"I hadn't seen Marian in thirty years," he said.

If she noticed that first person singular, Lina gave no sign. Mrs. Martin Lowe went on brewing tea.

Martin Lowe almost whispered. "You wrote to me—three months ago. It's all I know—tell me about her."

She averted her eyes and held her voice steady and said: "It was quite sudden. No illness—no warning. She had time to say only one thing—she said, 'Find Mart . . .' and then she looked at me, and she went. But the look I knew—she had often talked with me about you."

Mrs. Lowe spoke out sharply. "I trust," she said, "she lived to regret leaving her home and her folks."

"Leaving Mr. Lowe, yes," said Lina quickly. "But she never regretted leaving the farm and Morrel's Landing. Oh, no—she was glad that she left. Why, her life—you can't imagine how full it was!" She spoke with eager pride. "Travel—audiences—praise—friends—oh, she had everything. How could she regret? But she never forgot."

Martin Lowe clasped his hands loosely between his knees and sat looking down at them.

"I remember the day my father brought her home," he said. "I was man-grown. She was twelve—pretty as a flower. He told us she was to be our sister—and none of us knew anything more than that, except that she wasn't our sister. She"—he drew his breath sharply, and added only— "she lived with us until she was twenty. Then she went with Valentine." His eyes burned on Lina's eyes. "Was—was he good to her?" he demanded tensely.

"No," said Lina, flushing, "he was not. She left my father when I was three—then came all her success with her singing. She said—she's told me how you used to help her—and to play on your violin for her to sing."

Martin Lowe got to his feet and began walking up and down the kitchen, up and down the kitchen. "Yes," he said, "I used to play for her to sing."

"Tea!" said Mrs. Lowe, less like an invitation than an explosion. She pushed her husband toward a chair at the table, but he did not see her. While she and Lina sat down, he kept on with his caged walk about the room.

"Here, in this very room," he said, "winter evenings, summer evenings. I would stand there—she would stand there by the cupboard. The others would sit here—and she'd sing like an angel of God."

"Here's your cup with two lumps in it," said his wife; "best not let it get cold."

Lina stared about the kitchen. This, then, was the very house from which her mother had escaped, had made her way out with that young choir-leader and gone to the city, to life, to music, and to death.

"Have you a picture of her—then?" Lina cried.

With a manner of running from the room, Martin Lowe disappeared beyond an inner door. A breath of cold air came from there, like the air of a yesterday.

Suddenly Mrs. Lowe leaned toward her guest. This woman's face was hard and pointed and terribly alert. She said in a tone of unexpected depth and richness:

"He was always in love with her, you know. I expect you did know. She was no blood relation to any of them. Mart, he idolized her. . . The whole prairie knew that. And your ma was just as crazy about him only—she wanted to get away more'n she wanted him."

Lina stared at her. So that was it! That was why she had been told about "Mart" from the time that she could remember her mother, that mother who, then, had had everything excepting the one thing . . .

He came back with the picture in his hands, and suddenly Lina saw how handsome he had been, the great frame, the deep eyes, the flickering brows, the heavy hair. He was a man of sixty. "Man-grown" when her mother had come there, he had watched her slow ripening to womanhood, had loved her and lost her and had never forgotten, as she had not forgotten.

"Here," he said.

Something vast in Lina opened and closed as she looked on the picture of her mother at twenty—a picture that she had never seen—and whose untroubled beauty was like a wound. Lina lifted her eyes and saw that as the photograph had pierced her, so it was piercing him. She took the picture, held it in her hands, and as she could not speak of it, she said:

"The violin—do you play that now?"

At once he began that caged walking up and down again. "No," he said. "No. No." He said no more, and suddenly his wife laughed.

"He did," she said; "he played evenings till it almost drove me crazy—mournful pieces, nothing else."

She seemed to stop short of telling something more, and Lina said:

"That's what I do—play the violin, as best I can. I'm with some people who are playing tomorrow in Chicago—I left them to come here."

He looked at her sharply. "There's a symphony concert in Chicago tomorrow night," he said. "I read the advertisement. Jaquith plays."

She nodded. "I've a little place in the orchestra."

"My lord," said Martin Lowe, "then you've heard him—Milo Jaquith."

"Yes," she said, and said no more. But something like color or flowing line had come into her voice and into her face.

Martin Lowe spoke as a man speaks of a god: "I read every word I can find about him. Once I thought I'd hear him before I die. But I guess not—I guess not."

She said, "He's wonderful beyond words"—that light and that color still in her voice, and then cried quickly: "But you! Aren't you playing down in Morrel's Landing tonight? The whole town was covered with posters about the Fiddlers' Contest."

He dropped his eyes. "No," he said only. "No."

His wife laughed. "He means that for me," she said harshly. "I gave away his fiddle. I expect I done wrong. But I couldn't stand his mournful tunes every night, and us alone here—never a soul. He hasn't any fiddle now."

Abruptly Lina understood her. Here on this desolate farm, away from living voices and events. . . She looked out at the yard deep and still in the snow, beginning to fall again. Her thought could understand the woman, but with her heart she understood Martin Lowe. And how gallant he was!

He lifted his eyes, and smiled, saying cheerfully: "If it hadn't been for that, I expect I'd been down there, tuning up with the worst of them."

Out of an unwilling pride his wife spoke. "He took a prize last year," she said.

As if to silence her, he began speaking his thoughts, his eyes again on those loosely clasped hands.

"I guess she was right—I did play a lot of wailing music. I always liked that kind most as much as the dance ones. I didn't blame her. But I took a lot of comfort—" He looked over in the corner by the cupboard, as if he could still see someone standing there, for whom he played. "We used to plan," he said, "your—your ma and I . . . We were going to play for the whole world. Well, she did, I guess. And I've never been out of the State. Never across the state-line." He laughed a little. "I thought I might go down to hear them tonight," he said, "but the mare went lame yesterday." He sighed, with the terrible patience of those who have had nothing.

Lina stood up quickly. "I haven't told you what I came for," she said. "I will in a minute—but first: I left my violin down at the station. Let's go down and get it, and you play in the contest tonight."

He looked up, without entertaining the dream for an instant. "I'd like mighty well to tuck a fiddle under my chin again," he said.

"We'll go down," said Lina, but he looked at her incredulously.

"The mare is lame," he said gently. "And we haven't got a telephone—and no neighbor that I'd ask to take anything out such a night."

Lina laughed. "Haven't you ever walked four miles?"

"Me! But you couldn't get down there."

"Try me!" she cried. "I do miles and miles. Couldn't we all walk down to the village, and go to the concert—and I'll catch my train at midnight instead of early in the morning. You'll go, Mrs. Lowe?"

"Me?" said Mrs. Lowe. "I wouldn't cross the road to hear all the fiddles in the country. I'd cross the road and go the other way—excuse me. He can go," she added magnanimously.

"Let's be starting, then," cried Lina.

Still he looked at her unbelievingly. "You wouldn't want me to use your fiddle," he said.

"I'd love to have you use my fiddle," said Lina.

Mrs. Lowe said shrilly: "But you can't go without your suppers!" And when Lina smiled that aside, she cried: "Mart! You must eat something."

And in her tone, Lina thought, leaped all that solicitude for his stomach that she had denied him for his soul. The woman's anxiety touched the girl, and she spoke to her gently—a good creature, who brought some great fleece-lined rubber boots, the pride of her heart, and herself put them over the small buckled shoes.

Mrs. Lowe said, "It's a good thing you wrote you was coming—so he's got on his best suit"—and herself brought his sheepskin coat. He was still saying hesitating, uncertain words as they stepped outside.

As they met the thick harsh rush of the cold Lina's spirit rose to breast it, and she cried: "This is going to be wonderful! Oh I *hope* Mother knows."

He opened the gate for her and shut it sharply on his words: "No more than she's ever known anything about me these thirty years—you can be sure of that." Startled by the bitterness in his voice, she looked up at him. "I don't believe in death and life mixing," he explained grimly.

And because of the mask that had settled over his face, she tried to bring back its feeling, and said: "Tell me about my mother leaving this farm—didn't she say good-by to you?"

The kindness and the sadness came back upon his face like visible light. He said: "I know now that she did—but I didn't know it then. She came to me by that gate, where I was tying up a rose-bush, and she kissed me—anybody passing might have seen her. She said: 'Mart, don't ever think I don't love you!' I guess she'd want me to tell you that. It was that night she went with him. But first we had the evening—playing and singing. She made me play for her—she sung 'Annie Laurie' like an angel of God—I can hear her voice whenever I try. Isn't it wonderful how you can hear the voices of folks that have died—tones and drops and little lifts? I can hear her now . . ."

"Yes," Lina said and thought, "Mixing death and life!"

He went on as if she were not there: "And most always I hear her voice in 'Annie Laurie.' It kind of seems like her song—your ma's and mine. When bedtime came that night, and I was putting away my fiddle, she whispered to me: "If I die, I'll come and sing for you to play. And if you die, you come and play for me.' I didn't laugh at her—I thought too much of her." He stopped, and said shortly, "I guess you know how much I thought of her," and when Lina assented he seemed pleased.

"It was that night she went with him," he ended. "In the morning she was gone without any word. I never saw her any more. I didn't blame her. She wanted to get out and try her wings. She was brave and she went. I was a fool and I stayed." He waved his arm, a gaunt circular motion, at the sweep of the farms and the hills. "She let her music get out of this," he said, "and she gave it to folks. I kept mine in me and it turned to acid."

Lina cried gaily: "But you're going to let it out tonight, remember. I'll wager you'll be the best fiddler there!"

He corrected with bitterness. "Old fiddler," he said, "old fiddler," and added harshly: "Don't you expect anything of me tonight. My wrist and my fingers are too stiff—I ain't played in two months—not since she gave away my fiddle—except as I've pretended I was playing something." He took her arm to guide her over the frozen furrows of the road. "I've walked with your—your ma a thousand times here," he said. "Seems like you ought to be her."

She said softly: "Perhaps I am—a little. She never seems very far, somehow." He said nothing.

Now they gave themselves silently to meeting the wind and snow. When they reached the main road the darkness had come down and the cold, which augured clearing clouds, was increasing; but if it occurred to Lina that now they might find a telephone at one or another of these isolated houses, and summon that hardy taxi driver, this seemed not to enter the thought of her companion, deep in his pioneer psychology of thrift. But so far she was enjoying her adventure, and now she raised her voice above the wind and said:

"I haven't told you what I came to see you about—besides just seeing you, you know, for Mother."

"Wasn't that enough?" he said. "I'm going to live on this—seeing you, that belong to her. You look like her, some," he added. "I think it's your forehead . . ."

It seemed a pity to break that with her news; but if she got her train at midnight, she wouldn't perhaps see him again alone. But the wind was cutting and buffeting them, and this seemed no moment for her news to be given. She glanced up at the dogged figure, facing the storm as he had faced his life, and she thought of the old dreams of this man—of love, of music—coming back to his bleak world, lifting their heads, mounting into his darkness. How much he must have longed to get away. As she looked at him, she could almost see above his head the long arc of his strong desire for flight.

She thought: "Mr. Jaquith should see him," and wished again: "If I had dared to let him drive down here when he wanted to—" and even wished faintly that he were a man and not quite a god.

The two kept on, still in silence, Lina now calculating the time. So impassably bad was the going that they had been able to make but slow progress. And now the cold was so intense she began to be afraid she would have to stop for warmth at a farmhouse. Two cars had overtaken them without offering to halt.

"Cold?" Martin Lowe shouted abruptly, and at the absurdity of the question she shot back, "Warm as toast," and plodded on.

It was at the end of another quarter-mile that she saw the yellow flood of light from a far car come streaming down a side road.

"I think they ought to pick us up," she shouted to the amazed Martin, and darted through the snow. She need not have hurried. A rod from the main road the car snorted, spluttered and stopped dead. Lina kept on, plowed through a great drift, and came breathlessly to that car as a man alighted from the driver's seat and the light flashed on within the car and the rear door came open. Then she laughed out gaily, breathlessly, and cried:

"Please, kind Sir—give us a ride?"

"Miss Bothwell!" the man cried. "My word. Good heavens. Thank God."

"Say some more of them for me," said Lina.

"I've been looking for you since noon," this man shouted. "I was a fool to let you go off alone. I started out in the car right behind your train—"

"Instead of resting for Chicago!" she cried. "I've probably given you pneumonia, and Mr. Lowe too—oh, Mr. Jaquith!" she said, "I don't want him to know who you are—would you mind?"

To this he said merely: "But what are you doing on the king's highway, this mad night?" But now Martin Lowe had come up and with the chauffeur was stamping down the deep drift that had stalled the motor.

Lina cried, "Mr. Lowe—it's a friend of mine. It's Mr. Jack—and his big car. And we're invited to ride, aren't we, Mr. Jack?"

"You are not," said the big fur figure deeply. "You're commanded to ride, by Jove. And now what's it all about?" He brushed the snow from the chinchilla, and housed Lina under fur robes in the car, and when the three men had beaten down the snow, and the two came into the warmth, Martin Lowe said:

"I heard they had them heated and lighted under glass—but I never saw one."

Lina saw the molded and weathered face flushed and shining, and she plunged into her story to the man who hung on her words.

The lights of Morrel's Landing, such as they were, were winking bravely through the storm when the car plowed down the main street. Already it was eight o'clock, and as they passed the hall, up a flight of wooden outside stairs, they caught the sound of violins. And at the sound Martin Lowe's head came up, and he said, "I haven't heard one all winter. Not since haying, when they had a barn-dance. . . Say, but I can't use your fiddle!" he cried to Lina. "Such a scraper as me!"

They had drawn up at the little wooden station to get the violin. But the building lay black and untenanted.

"Shut up tight till the ten-thirty comes through," said Martin Lowe. "I'd ought to have thought of that."

Watching Lina as she directed the driver to find the agent, Mr. Jaquith suddenly said: "I say, don't bother. I've a violin."

She looked at him breathlessly. "Yours?" said Lina, to whom and to the thousands who heard him, his violin was a kind of ark.

Jaquith smiled at Martin Lowe. "Some men I'd let play on it and some men I wouldn't. This is one of the men who can take it. Drive to the

207

building where you see two lighted windows instead of one," he told the chauffeur.

Martin Lowe looked at him with deep eyes. "Say," he said, "I guess the world's got more music in it than I've been thinking it had—everybody with a violin!"

It was Jaquith himself who laid the case in Martin Lowe's hands, who received it as if it had been a child.

The three went up the unsteady outside staircase and stepped into the hall. A room seating not a hundred was filled and lighted by gas which beat down on the little platform, where on wooden chairs were seated six old men. One had now taken his place before the others. His head was bent, his eyes were on the floor, his violin was in place. He waited until the confusion of the entrance had ceased, then waveringly and on a single string, his music began. This man was seventy, his hair scanty and white, his face thin and priestlike, his arms and legs angular and fragile, the hands on his poor instrument were knotted and veined. On that one string, waveringly, there crept about the room a melody which he knew and loved. Back of him sat the five other old men, their violins across their knees. None of them was less than sixty, some of them were far more and every one of them had been true enough to the authentic voice to come here with pride and to do as much as he could.

Her chin buried in her coat, her face partly hidden, Lina thought: "This is going to kill me." She glanced at Jaquith and her heart blossomed like a flower. For in his face as in her feeling there was only the exclud-ing sense of the deep spirit, one ray of which had once touched these old men and still held them captive. Somewhere, in far youth, or in unlived dreams, the love of music had moved them, claimed them. Somehow, from farm and store, they had kept that claim clean and alive. Here in this bleak little "hall" moved the wing of the god, stirring the ash of a divine fire—faint, far, crowded out, but never forsaken or for-gotten.

And the people! When the old man ceased, they shouted and clapped their approval, had him back, as if for them too—above curiosity and boredom—flamed the same signal. And catching sight of Martin, they shouted: "Mart! Get up there with your fiddle, Mart!"

He had opened the case, had lifted the beautiful violin, had flashed an unspeakable look at the man who had lent it to him; and now Martin too went to the platform. To Jaquith, Lina murmured her utter grati-tude and gave him in a word Martin's dour history.

But Jaquith said only: "You feel it so—good Lord, do you feel for the whole world? Does anyone feel the way you feel? Today I've been wretched away from you."

She looked at him and away—and the smoky room was a place of a thousand lights.

Once more a thin strand of tone floated out from a twisted figure on the wooden chair.

"If I could play them as they are," Jaquith whispered. "If I could play them . . ."

And the next player was blind and was guided to his seat and played gaily and quite sweetly from his darkness. Then came an old man, whose wife took the piano and played with him, her anxious face turned toward him, eager for him to do his best.

Then it was Martin Lowe's turn, and when he stood up, so straight and grave, before his neighbors, Lina's eyes brimmed. For a moment he stood quiet—the man who had heard a voice and had failed to follow, but had never forgotten; and then he began to play. But the rich and sonorous tone of the instrument could not cover the triviality and the clumsiness of the thin little melody that he chose. His hands were stiff, he was in terrible embarrassment, Lina ached for him. The next piece was better—but still stiff, still inept. Then he seemed to recover something. He stood quiet, seemed to listen, turned toward Lina. And suddenly she rose, and Jaquith stood beside her, and Martin Lowe looked at them and then he began to play.

"Maxwelton braes are bonnie . . ."

The violin all but spoke the words—an arrangement of his own, an arrangement, Lina divined, which he had made years before for the little girl who stood and sang by the cupboard.

Not from the hearts of those in the little room alone, but from some web of loved tone and word stretched round the world, the soul of the old song surged and flowed into the violin in this man's hands. Was it his hands alone, Lina wondered, or was it the invisible hands of the man whose great instrument he did not know that he held; and the hands of others who had held it and of him who had fashioned it?

"Gie'd me her promise true . . ."

209

And was it the web of music alone—or of love itself poured down the years through the channel of that lyric, that more than any other song in the world spoke the hearts of men in their highest hour?

"And for bonnie Annie Laurie . . ."

The crest of the beauty wavered over the room. Martin's eyes were on hers. And in that moment it came to Lina that it was not the web of music alone, nor the web of its tenderness that spoke here—but the love of one man for one woman, and of one woman, and she dead, for this man. It was their old dream that went crying through the air.

In the utter quiet of the others, he ceased and sat down; then the rude applause burst out, sweeping the room. And over their clapping and cries, Jaquith's voice boomed out:

"Bravo! Bravo! Bravo!"

Suddenly Martin, who was seated, his look on the violin on his knees, lifted his eyes and met those of Jaquith. Martin sprang to his feet and spoke, his voice hoarse and passionate:

"Neighbors—I met a man and he lent me his fiddle. Just now I've seen the name on the plate. The name says Milo Jaquith—it's him! Right here in this hall—*it's him!*"

There were those in the little Morrel's Landing audience to whom the name meant nothing. But the old men who had played that night, they knew. They laid their violins on the floor and got to their feet, clapping and calling; and the audience joined them, and over their clamor came the voice of Martin Lowe:

"Milo Jaquith, come up here and play for us, that never heard good music in our whole lives."

Milo Jaquith emerged from his great fur coat and went down the narrow aisle. When they saw him, the light figure, the beautiful face, the clamor ceased. For there was about him that which marked him as greater than they, greater than any whom they had ever seen. On the platform he grasped the hand of Martin Lowe, then, of all the old men standing there, their faces living at last. Then he made them sit down again, and he played.

A cave of darkness pierced by a ray of splendor—a desert sweet with a giant flower perfuming the miles—an empty heart opening to the life it had never known—all these were in the playing of Milo Jaquith in the little room. If there were those whose lives had not let them even know the great name, there was no one whose being was not kindled by the sovereign beauty of what he gave them.

One by one, when at last they let him cease, the seven old men rose and grasped his hand—Jaquith, in whom God had spoken, and they who had once heard God's voice in a sound far off, and could not forget. It was as if in that room all the beating love of music in all the hearts that have worshipped it and might not follow it, and all the wistful fingers grown stiffened with toil, that once might have drawn down harmony, and all the voices that sang but a few notes in their youth and then were silenced by life—as if all these came into the little hall and for one moment of time spoke in the faces of the people. Spoke clearest of all in the faces of the old fiddlers who stood, bent and peering from misty eyes, when Lina and Jaquith and Martin left the hall.

Sitting in the car that was to take Martin Lowe to his home after the express should have left at midnight, they had his promise to drive to Chicago next day to hear the symphony. Martin was still breathless with his wonder.

"I never thought God cared this much about me," he said more than once. Then he turned to Lina. "I want you to know, and I guess you do know, that your ma was there in the hall tonight—singing with me her song, just like she used to sing it over by the cupboard."

Lina said only: "I know"; and Martin added to himself: "I guess music kind of mixes life and—them that we don't see any more."

When they had told him good-by, and the train had taken them to carry them to their junction, Lina began planning for Martin—and half of her thought was on Martin, but all of it was on the man at her side.

"I want to get him a violin when he comes down tomorrow," she said, "and tickets for him for all the music in Chicago this winter."

To which Jaquith answered: "You know what my following you around like this means."

"I haven't thanked you," she tried to say.

"It means," he went on, as simply as anybody in love, "that I'm going to follow you around all my life, if you'll let me."

She looked at him as Martin had looked from the platform. "You!" she said. "You—whom everybody adores—and I just play a violin in the last row of your orchestra—"

"You're not going to marry me to play to me," he told her. "I can play to myself."

"You wonderful thing," said Lina. "If I hadn't loved you before, I should love you for the way you were to Martin Lowe." Then she looked at Jaquith blankly. "Do you know," she cried, "I forgot to tell him what I went down there to tell him. That my mother's will left him fifty thousand in securities . . ."

Milo Jaquith merely said: "But never mind what you didn't tell him. What else are you going to tell me?"

# His Very Successful Wife

## MARGARET AYER BARNES

*Sylvia Wainroot had to choose between a husband and a career for herself. Her story has a wide and basic appeal, for it is the drama of adjustment in the lives of two people in this complex present day world. His Very Successful Wife is a noteworthy combination of drama, suspense and romance written by a Pulitzer prize-winning author.*

LYING WIDE AWAKE in bed at half past seven in the morning, Sylvia Wainroot told herself reprovingly that she'd lived too long alone with Jimmy, Junior, and old Emma. She was absurdly set in her ways. Old-maidish, really. Fussy about trifles. Jim hadn't complained, but she knew that he'd noticed it. And he'd noticed other things about her that were different.

Well, it was natural that she'd be a little changed. For three anguished years of constant anxiety while Jim was fighting the war in the Pacific, and another long year while he was stationed in Japan, she had had to do without him and had learned self-reliance. A lot of things had happened in the course of those years. She'd grown older, for one thing. She was nearly twenty-five. She'd produced Jimmy, Junior, singlehanded, as it were. She had taken a job which she loved and made good at it. She had rented this flat and hired old Emma. She had organized her life on a basis of loneliness, and if gradually, unconsciously, she had come to feel less lonely, she had waited for Jim with unswerving loyalty. It was only six weeks ago that he had come back to her—the same dear old Jim and just as much in love with her, not wounded, not nerve-racked, not anything abnormal. After all her apprehension it still sometimes seemed incredible. She was blessedly thankful to have him safe at home.

So why, she now wondered in honest perplexity, did those silly trifles seem to get her down?

*Permission to reprint granted by Paul R. Reynolds & Son.*

Take this morning, for instance, and what she called the traffic problem. What if she did have to wait twenty minutes, while Jim monopolized the microscopic bathroom? She ought to relax. She was edgy and irritable, and she had a busy day before her in the office. She wished she could doze off again, but that was impossible. No one could doze, while Jim took his shower. She lay listening impatiently to the splash of falling water and her husband's wayward baritone raised cheerfully in song.

"And the caissons go rolling along!" he was caroling, and from the other bedroom she could now hear Jimmy, Junior, shouting, "Daddee! Daddee!" from the prison of his crib.

She glanced at her wrist watch, frowning a little, and caught the first whiff of early-morning coffee, which meant that the invaluable Emma was up and that breakfast, as usual, would be ready on time. But if Jim didn't hurry, she herself would be late and have to dash off for her nine-o'clock appointment without that second cup which made all the difference. On that thought she jumped up and slipped into her kimono—such a pretty one it was; Jim had brought it from Japan—and called shrilly to her husband, "Jim, aren't you nearly through?"

"In a jiffy!" he shouted, and abruptly stopped singing.

As the splashes of water subsided to a patter, she stood silently contemplating the disorder of the bedroom. Since Jim had come home the flat seemed so much smaller. As a matter of fact, it wasn't so small. A living-room, a dining-room with kitchenette, two bedrooms. Sylvia was employed in a real-estate office and knew all about the New York housing shortage, so she was well aware they were lucky to have it. When she had rented it three years before, she had taken great pains to make it attractive. But the larger of the bedrooms was Jimmy, Junior's nursery—for old Emma slept there, too, and he needed space to play in—and this little room, which had once seemed so adequate, was now much too crowded to keep at all neat. She had furnished it sparsely, because it was so tiny, with gay flowered chintz and nice old mahogany, a bureau, one chair and a narrow little day bed, which stood like a sofa against one of the walls. Now a cot had been added for Jim to sleep on, which spoiled the look of everything and took up all the floor space, and poor Jim had really no place for his clothes. He had said he was used to that, after life in the Army. Jim was always good-natured, but he wasn't very tidy. There were his pajamas lying on the floor. And his neckties on the light bracket and his coat on the chair-back and his trousers suspended from an open bureau drawer.

The feminine daintiness of the bedroom was destroyed—the meticulous order that Sylvia delighted in. But she had something even more important on her mind.

"I'm sure I don't know how long Emma will stand for it," she thought with a sigh, picking up the pajamas.

For Emma of late had seemed somewhat grumpy, and Emma was the rock on which Sylvia's life was built. An elderly Scotchwoman, the soul of integrity, she took care of Jimmy, Junior, and kept the flat in order and cooked the family breakfast and her own and nursery meals. Sometimes she even cooked dinner for Sylvia, and she'd always been willing to wash up after cocktail parties. A treasure like that could not be replaced, and without her, Sylvia feared she could never keep her job. With the problem of service what it was today, she would have to stay home and look after Jimmy, Junior. So the slightest sign of grumpiness was a signal of disaster. Sylvia did not know what on earth she could do about it, and, in a way, she did not blame Emma. Since Jim had come back, there seemed so much more to do. A man in the household made a different sort of work. There had to be more food and much more picking up. And Jim was at home a good part of the day.

For Jim had no job as yet and was looking for one carefully, still on terminal leave and taking his time about it, because he was trying to find one with a future. So far he hadn't, and this had begun to worry him, which was something that Sylvia could well understand. Her own job was so good and promised such advance. Any house would sell now, with a roof and four walls. Prices were rocketing, and with them, commissions. Her salary had very nearly doubled in a year. Sylvia had a theory about working wives. She was certain they understood their husbands' business problems better than the wives who stayed home and were mired in housework. Marriage, she thought, besides everything else it was, could be a business partnership that was vital and stimulating. Jim was twenty-eight years old, with a good education that had turned him out a competent hydraulic engineer. Yet he hadn't her experience in working for a living. For he'd never had a job, unless you counted the summer tutoring he'd done while at college, and his work as an officer in the U. S. Engineers. Naturally he felt he'd lost a lot of time, like all his generation, while fighting the war. He was just about to graduate and was engaged to Sylvia, when the Japs bombed Pearl Harbor.

That seemed to her now a long time ago. When she had met Jim she was eighteen years old and a sophomore at Radcliffe, determined even then to have a career. She didn't know just what, being young and rather visionary. But something important—of that she was sure. Her father and mother had died in her childhood, and the great-aunt who'd brought her up was a strongminded spinster who had always been hipped on the feminist cause. "Hipped" was Sylvia's own word for it when she knew that Jim loved her, and all Aunt Myra's teaching had gone by the boards. When war was declared she'd left college to marry him. This was a blow to all Aunt Myra's hopes for her, and the belligerent old lady had not long survived it.

Sylvia, submerged in young married happiness, moving with Jim to a succession of Army camps and already harassed by their imminent parting, had not had much time to mourn for her then. But though she had laughed at Aunt Myra, she had loved her, and in the last four years she had very often thought of her, aware that at heart she supported her aunt's doctrines. Sexual equality was what they came down to—the right of women to work and be paid for it, to stand on a common economic base with men. Marriage interfered with this—at least people used to think so—so her great-aunt had opposed it. She had been slightly comic, like all old-fashioned feminists—a pioneer champion of causes now won. She had thought of women's rights as in conflict with men's privileges. That might have been true once, but now it seemed ridiculous.

"Sorry, Sylly, darling," said Jim, barging in, with nothing but a bath towel wrapped around his slim loins. "Have I made you late again?"

"Yes, but I can hurry," said Sylvia amiably. Yet she didn't, for a moment. She stood looking at Jim. Sitting down on the cot, he groped under it for his shorts and the socks and the garters he'd tucked into his shoes. A tall, tanned young man, hard-muscled and wiry. His hands were long and lean, with sensitive fingers, his features clear-cut, his eyes candid and blue. Around them little smiling lines were paler than his tan. Conscious of her gaze, he looked up at her and grinned.

"You look swell in that kimono," he said, and she wondered how she'd managed to live without him for those four lonely years. She thanked God she'd kept herself slim and desirable, seeing herself for an instant as he saw her, her slight figure wrapped in the folds of scarlet silk, her soft brown hair falling over her shoulders, her bright eyes reflecting the happiness of loving him.

But when she'd picked up his bath towel from the cot where he'd flung it and walked into the bathroom to find water on the tiles and his shaving brush and razor and wet, messy soap bowl cluttering the washstand beside her neat toilet lotions, she thought again of Emma and frowned in annoyance. She'd have to wipe up everything before she took her shower.

As she did so, she thought of the Army camps they'd lived in and the cramped quarters everywhere they'd been so glad to share. Boarding-houses, tourist cabins, fourth-rate hotels. All that mattered then was that they could be together. She would never forget that last week before he sailed, or the boarding-house bedroom on a San Francisco hill, with the view from its window of the transports in the harbor. Every minute had been precious and yet shot with anguish, because of the uncertainty as to when he'd have to go. Then, when his orders came, there'd been his hurried packing and their drive in a taxi to the crowded wartime docks. Thousands of sailors and soldiers were swarming there, small boats were chugging out to the transports at anchor. Stopped by a sentry at a gate, she had parted with him and thought her heart was breaking as she lost him in the crowd. Back in the boarding-house, their room seemed forlorn, without Jim's things lying about in confusion. She had stood at the window looking down at the harbor, but she didn't even know which transport was his.

She had wakened the next morning to find them all gone, slipped through the Golden Gate in some hour of darkness.

She'd had nothing to do then but go back to New York to live with Jim's family and wait for Jimmy, Junior. Jim's family had been wonderful. She loved them all dearly. They never forgot she had no family of her own. His father and his mother, his sister and kid brother had all made her feel that she really belonged to them. And how they had rejoiced when her son had been born! Kind, loving people—and so understanding. They had even understood, when she was well and strong again, why she'd wanted a job and a home of her own. Jim's mother, perhaps, hadn't *quite* understood, saying, "Sylvia, dear, you know it isn't necessary." And she did know it wasn't. There was plenty of money. Jim's father was a very distinguished physician. But he had backed her up. He admired independence. They both knew her devotion to Jim never wavered—never could waver, Sylvia amended, as, the bathroom quite neat again, she stepped into her shower.

Twenty minutes later, when she entered the dining-room, Jim was eating scrambled eggs and conversing with his son, perched beside him in his high chair with a bowl of oatmeal. Emma's broad back was visible through the kitchenette door.

"Are Jap dogs like our dogs?" Jimmy, Junior, was inquiring, his blue

217

eyes, wide with interest, fixed on his father, his head a sunny aureole of short golden curls.

"Well, not exactly. Some look like little dragons."

"Did you talk Japanese to them?"

"Sure," said Jim. "I had to."

"I wish I had a dog that looked like a dragon."

"You ought to have a puppy."

Jimmy, Junior's eyes sparkled. But Sylvia had glanced toward the kitchenette door. Strange how Emma's spine could express disapproval!

"Good morning, Emma," she said very cordially. "I've just time for coffee." Then, as Emma turned with the pot in her hand, she threw another glance at her to gauge her morning mood.

"Dour," murmured Jim, who was quick to read her thought.

This was patently true.

Sylvia frowned at him, then sunnily smiled. "A cup of your good coffee is just what I need," she said effusively to Emma, who did not reply.

"See?" said Jim brightly.

She frowned at him again. He could not understand that Emma was important and that he must not joke about her. For Emma was no fool.

She had barely sipped her coffee when the telephone rang.

"I'll go," offered Jim, sounding slightly subdued. Then from the living-room he called, "It's for you."

It always was for her, and often it was business. For people who wanted to buy or sell real estate or were desperately trying to find houses or apartments were apt to call agents at home at any hour.

"It's Olive," said Jim, as she joined him at the telephone.

Olive Gaynott was a colleague of Sylvia's at the office, her immediate superior and intimate friend. Sylvia'd seen a lot of her in the last four lonely years, but when Jim had come home he hadn't seemed to take to her. That was why he hadn't chatted with her over the phone. Yet Olive was very attractive to men. "He ought to be civil," thought Sylvia, fretfully.

Then, "Hello, Olive." She listened for a moment. "No!" she broke in again, her voice rising joyfully. "*Have* they? How wonderful— Yes— Of course I can— I'll see you right away. I'm just starting downtown."

She hung up the receiver and turned quickly to Jim. "I'll have to have the car today. I hope you don't need it." Her manner had changed, her voice turned brisk and businesslike. "Olive wants me to take some people out on Long Island. We have a white elephant there—thirty acres, a house with twenty rooms—and these lunatics may buy it. They're rolling in money. He's been making munitions. I talked this place up to them last week in the office, and now they've called up to say that they're interested. It's a great break for me, if I can put the sale through. I'd get a lot of kudos and a whopping commission." She was back in the dining-room by this time, gulping coffee, standing at the table, not bothering to sit down.

"I don't need the car," said Jim. He stood watching her, his clear eyes faintly clouded with a puzzled expression. It was at moments like this, she had noticed, when she was concentrated on some stroke of business, feeling hurried and preoccupied and thoroughly professional, that Jim seemed to realize that somehow she had changed.

"Good-by, Jimmy, angel," she said. "Be a good boy. You must rest after lunch today, Emma, while he's napping."

"I have no time to rest," observed Emma tersely.

Sylvia contemplated her grim profile for an instant, bent over the dishes in the kitchenette sink. Then she slipped her arm compellingly through her husband's, pushing him before her down the hall to their bedroom, turning to face him when she had closed the door.

"You must go out to lunch, Jim," she said. "You will, won't you?" He still had that puzzled look, and Sylvia found it irritating. "Now, Jim, don't be silly. You can lunch with your mother."

"I lunched with her yesterday."

"Well, she always loves to have you." She'd already moved away from him toward the closet door. With hat and coat in hand, she turned to her mirror. "I've no time to discuss it, Jim. You know I'm late this morning. Olive was already down at the office. I'm sorry to dash off, but you'll be going out soon."

"Why will I?" asked Jim.

"Oh, Jim—" She paused, exasperated.

"As a matter of fact, I'll be busy here all morning. I've some letters to write to personnel managers and some blanks to fill out—a lot of correspondence."

"Can't you do that this evening?" She tipped her hat to the right angle.

"Have you forgotten I'm looking for a job?"

Sylvia ignored the slight edge in his voice. "I know, Jim," she said and slipped into her coat. "But you noticed yourself—Emma *is* rather dour. She likes to have Jimmy and the flat to herself. That's really why she stays with me. Because she always has. I'm never underfoot around here in the daytime."

"And am *I* underfoot?" asked Jim, rather ominously.

"Well, darling, aren't you? From Emma's point of view? I mean, it's not the same for her with you writing in the living-room. As a matter of fact, it's today that she cleans it. And lunch *is* a bother."

"Well, for heaven's sake," said Jim. "Is this flat ours or Emma's? You're paying that woman forty dollars a week—"

"Keep your voice down!" said Sylvia, on a sudden note of warning.

But Jim was aroused. "What d'you want me to do? Go out and pound the pavements? Sit on a park bench?"

"Don't stand there shouting rhetorical questions," said Sylvia in a sharp and sibilant whisper. "Do have a little sense, Jim. Emma's simply invaluable. Do you think that I want to stay home and do the housework?"

"You might want to stay home and see something of Jimmy. I like to, anyway. We have a fine time. He's been locked up alone every day with that sourpuss—"

"He loves her," said Sylvia. "She's a wonderful nurse. You don't understand what you're talking about, Jim. You don't see my difficulties. You've been away so long. I had this flat running without any friction, which is something to accomplish, I assure you, in these days, and I want to keep it so."

"But look here—" said Jim.

"I *can't* stop to argue. You've *got* to be reasonable."

Their eyes met for an instant, and then she kissed him hurriedly. The kiss was no more than a peck on his cheek, and she didn't give him time to make the gesture of returning it. Before he could speak she walked out of their bedroom, throwing a quick glance down the hall toward the dining-room, noting thankfully that Jimmy, Junior's prattle in his high chair was all but inaudible over the rush of running water and the light clink of crockery in the kitchenette sink. Emma, washing dishes, could not have overheard them. Nevertheless, Sylvia felt angry and upset. Had Jim meant to imply that she neglected Jimmy, Junior? That was absurd, but it had pricked her vanity. No child could be healthier or happier than Jimmy. What's more, thanks to Emma, he was very well-behaved. And she'd certainly been a success as a homemaker. On her way to the front door, a glance into the nursery, sunny and gay with its animal wallpaper, and another at her cozy, sophisticated little living-room, with fresh flowers on the desk and new books on the table and a fire neatly laid to kindle on the hearth, reassured her as to that and increased her indignation. Aunt Myra, she thought fleetingly, would have been very proud of her. And Olive, who lived in an apartment hotel, always told her admiringly she did not know how Sylvia managed it. Olive had no children, though she had had two husbands, both of whom, unhappily, had proved to be mistakes.

Half an hour later, when she entered her office, twenty minutes late for that nine-o'clock appointment and still feeling annoyed by Jim's lack of appreciation, Olive was already seated at her desk. The two girls shared a room next to Mr. Finnester's office. Mr. Isadore Finnester was head of the firm. A clever, genial man who was making a fortune out of the rise in real-estate values, he was a kindly and generous employer, which was one of the reasons why Sylvia loved her job.

Olive looked up, her glance friendly yet appraising. "You're late," she observed. "Your client is waiting."

"I know," said Sylvia. "But I couldn't help it. Emma's acting up again."

"Why? Because of Jim?"

It didn't sound impertinent, the way Olive said it. Sylvia had confided her domestic complications. Now she said, "It will be simpler when he has a job."

"Much, I should think." So Olive dismissed Jim. For all that she liked men and so many men liked her, she had as low an opinion of husbands as Aunt Myra. She had no intention of marrying again. She sat there at her desk looking crisply executive, older than Sylvia by five or six years, smartly dressed in her spotless white blouse and gray business suit, good-looking, well-groomed, her blonde bob sleekly shining, her mouth ruby-lipsticked, her long nails dark red.

Sylvia, putting her hat in the closet and smoothing her hair before the mirror that hung there, found herself thinking once more of her great-aunt. Olive was the apotheosis of the old lady's dreams. She was the New Woman, independent, successful, commanding a salary many men would have envied. Yet Sylvia knew Aunt Myra would not have approved of her. She would have distrusted her smart sophistication. For Aunt Myra's feminism was dowdy and unworldly. Her idea of the New Woman was a girl with flat heels, a girl without a wave, and certainly without lipstick, and even more certainly without carmine-lacquered fingernails. She could never have brought herself to countenance such frivolities. To her they would have indicated weakness of mind. And she wouldn't have cared for Olive's private life. Not for her divorces, or her men friends, or her cocktails. For little as Aunt Myria had seemed to think of husbands, she had thought even less of divorces and divorced women, and she'd been a faithful member of the Women's Christian Temperance Union. She had envied—on behalf of her sex—men's strength, not their weaknesses. Indeed, one of the doctrines she had impressed upon Sylvia was that women, emancipated, were to reform the world.

"You can see your client in here," observed Olive, as Sylvia, smiling at these private thoughts, emerged from the closet. "I'm going to talk to Finnester about a house in Greenwich. And he wants to see you before you start for Long Island. He thinks that you've actually landed those people, and he's awfully pleased with you. He wants to sell that place, and he'll shave the price a little."

"Maybe he won't have to," said Sylvia spiritedly—thinking, it must be confessed, of her commission. She felt pleasantly elated by Mr. Finnester's praise, efficient again and briskly executive. Already her argument with Jim seemed less important, and, as always when safe in the haven of her office, domestic disturbances seemed very far away.

The client turned out to be a fussy little woman who wanted the impossible—a small midtown apartment. But Sylvia commanded the patience in dealing with her that she sometimes found it impossible to exercise at home. This was her business life, this was what she was good at, and the fussy little woman would be putty in her hands. She offered her a garret in the depths of Greenwich Village and a cellar in the Bronx, which she didn't call a cellar.

"It has a sunken living-room, three feet below the street level. I think if you featured it, it would have amazing charm," she was saying persuasively, when her telephone rang. "Excuse me," she smiled. And then, "Hello," curtly.

"Hello, Sylly." It was Jim's voice. "I've been thinking about you."

"Have you?" She tried not to sound interrupted.

"Yes, I have. About us both. I'm sorry for that row. Of course you have to have things running smoothly here. I thought you might be worried, so I gave you a ring. I'll go out to lunch and I'll put off those letters."

"Oh—well, that's fine," said Sylvia heartily. But a little too briefly and somewhat impersonally.

Jim seemed to notice it. He said, "I guess you're busy."

"Well, yes—I am."

"O.K.," said Jim. "Good-by."

"Oh, dear," thought Sylvia, feeling sorry but helpless. Dear old Jim— that was nice of him. But what could she do? He really shouldn't call her up at the office. Like that—just for nothing. She turned back to her client. But the spell she had cast around that cellar was broken. The fussy little woman had had time to reconsider. She was gathering up her gloves and her bag.

"I think it would be damp," she said, "and my husband has lumbago. And I'm not so crazy about rooms that are sunken. Steps aren't so good for me—not any more. My doctor says it's only a touch of arthritis. But I was thinking of a penthouse, you know, in the East Fifties."

Sylvia politely escorted her to the door. She didn't like the way Jim had said "O.K. Good-by," but neither did she like to lose that silly client. In another two minutes she would have made an appointment to look at that cellar, and it *had* possibilities. Now she'd have to tell Olive that she had muffed the deal. It wasn't important, but muffing was muffing. However, she could now call Jim and explain—

Just then the telephone on her desk rang again.

Olive's voice said in her ear, "Mr. Finnester wants to speak to you as soon as you're free."

"I'll come right in," said Sylvia, feeling just a little harried. Jim would simply have to wait. He shouldn't have called.

Mr. Finnester was seated in the chair behind his desk, with it tipped back a little beneath the weight of his rotundity. His dark eyes were reflective; he was assembling his thoughts. As always, he was smoking an excellent cigar.

Olive was waiting to assist at the conference.

"Come in, Sylvia," said Mr. Finnester, with great affability. His attitude toward her was pleasantly paternal. She was what he thought of as "a great little girl." Clever, too, very capable, with a flair for a sale. He was sure she'd make a hit with that maker of munitions, but she was nice and tactful, and his wife would like her, too.

Sylvia was aware that this was what he thought of her and would not have gainsaid it. She knew she'd been successful. But she took a straight chair with a very modest air.

"You don't need advice, I guess," said Mr. Finnester. He always said that, and then he always gave it to her. Sylvia invariably listened respectfully and then laughed about it later with Olive in their room. Both girls knew they got on better with Mr. Finnester than the men he employed did, and it was because they listened. At the end of twenty minutes their employer was still speaking, emphasizing his points with a wave of the cigar.

"It's just the sort of place that even today, when people will buy anything, is a drug on the market. But he could keep it up. He's got money to burn. His wife seems to want to break into the smart set, and their daughter's all set to be a Long Island glamour girl. Don't forget that the ladies are the ones you have to please. I'm telling you this—"

As if Sylvia didn't know it! She was always quick to estimate the character of her clients.

Then his telephone rang.

"Hello," growled Mr. Finnester, who didn't like interruptions. "Yes, she's here, but she's busy." He clicked back the receiver. Then he paused a moment to relight his cigar. "Now, Sylvia, I'm telling you if you pull this off for us—" The phone rang again. "Hello," growled Mr. Finnester. He listened for a minute, then, sounding aggrieved, "Oh, all right. Put it through. Here, Sylvia. It's for you. Seems it's important."

"For me? Oh, I'm sorry." She stepped quickly to the telephone.

Incredibly, annoyingly, it was Jim's voice again. Excited, too. Exhilarated. "Hey, Sylly," he said. "Guess who's in town! No less than old Masterbrook."

"Old Masterbrook?" she echoed. It didn't mean a thing to her.

"Yes. Masterbrook—why, you know him. Duncan T. Masterbrook, the Big Boy, in person."

"Oh, yes. Of course." He was one of Jim's professors. She remembered, now, meeting him when they were engaged. A pleasant old man, with the wildest gray whiskers. But he was *the* Masterbrook—it was all coming back to her—tops, she recalled, in the hydraulic field.

"He's here for the day," Jim was saying, still excitedly, "and he just called me up. Of course I had written him. It's simply super, darling. He has a job for me in mind. He didn't say what—hadn't time to go into it. Of course he's awfully busy, with a lot of appointments. But he wants us to lunch with him and talk it over then. One o'clock at the club, and you mustn't be late. It's too good to be true, for any job of Masterbrook's is sure to be a knockout, and to have him recommend me—"

Then Sylvia interrupted. "Well, Jim, that's simply wonderful. I'm ever so glad. But you know I can't lunch with you."

"Why not?" asked Jim blankly.

"I'm going to Long Island."

"Oh, *that*—I'd forgotten. . . . Well, can't you put it off?"

"I certainly can't."

"Oh, yes. Of course you can. Masterbrook spoke of you. He remembers you, Sylly."

"Well, that's nice of him, Jim. But—"

"I want him to see you."

"It isn't important."

"Yes, it is. I'm kind of proud of you."

That touched her, but she said, "Just the same, I can't do it."

There was an instant's silence in which she glanced at Mr. Finnester. He was puffing the cigar, his eyes fixed on the ceiling, looking patient and put-upon, yet faintly amused. Olive met her eyes with a quizzical smile.

When Jim spoke again his voice was not exhilarated. "Aren't you interested in this job?"

"Why, of course I am, Jim."

"Not enough to put off a junket to the country."

"It *isn't* a junket. You don't understand."

"Well, no—I guess I don't."

"Oh, Jim, do be sensible. You can tell me all about it when I come home this evening. I'm sorry to miss Masterbrook—"

"You don't sound so damn' sorry."

"Jim, I can't go on talking. I'm in Mr. Finnester's office."

"Well—you won't lunch with us? That's your last word?"

"It has to be, Jim. I can't. But—good luck to you." She hung up the receiver and said apologetically, "That was my husband, Mr. Finnester. You were saying—"

Mr. Finnester's dark eyes relinquished the ceiling. He tipped his chair forward and leaned his elbows on his desk. "I was saying," he said, "that if you pull this off for us, you'll be a damn' good agent, which is what I think you are. You have a fine future, Sylvia, in this business. Now good luck to *you*. Go pick up your clients."

Olive followed Sylvia back to their room.

"Well," she said emphatically, "you have your complications."

"I don't want to talk about it." She wouldn't have Jim criticized.

"Oh, very well." Olive's smile was still quizzical. "Forget it, that's all. Don't let it get you down."

That was easier said, however, than done. Jim's point of view had been utterly unreasonable, but yet she felt conscience-stricken. And the funny thing was that, away from the telephone and no longer constrained to defend her course of conduct, she wanted to have lunch with him and she wanted to meet Masterbrook. They would have had an awfully good time.

But when she'd put on her hat and coat and fresh lipstick and gone out to her car, a snappy little roadster, which had taken a great many clients to the country, she began to feel more cheerful in the brisk November air. It was pleasant, sunny weather, nice for driving out of town, and the sea would look blue from the house and its terraces. So far, so good, she thought, her spirits rising. Weather made a lot of difference in showing a place. As she drove up through the traffic on Park Avenue to the Waldorf, where the maker of munitions and his wife were awaiting her, she thought of Finnester's words: "You have a fine future." This was the largest deal she'd ever tried to put through. The price was very high, but not half what it had cost. She must hold that happy thought. The place was a bargain. The dazzling digits of her commission danced before her.

When the maker of munitions and his florid wife had joined her in the car, she had all but forgotten Jim.

"Are you sure you can fit in? I'm sorry it's so small."

"Oh, yes. We're very comfortable."

Then they plied her with questions.

How large was the swimming-pool? They couldn't remember. And had Sylvia said that there was an old gardener who went with the place and was wonderful with roses? There *was* a special rose garden, hadn't she told them, copied after one that was somewhere in England? Oh— in Hampton Court? How very, very interesting. And how far was the house, exactly, from a yacht club? If they bought it, of course their daughter would sail. Did Sylvia know what class of boats raced there? And as to the interior, she'd said it was furnished, but did she mean adequately and did that include linen? Linen *and* rugs, and what kind of rugs? The munition-maker's wife only cared for "Orientals." Oh—an Aubusson carpet, really, in the drawing-room? Well, that was very nice. The room was Louis Quatorze? And the library was English? Sort of Jacobean? Now, they wanted to be clear about it—there were seven servants' bedrooms and six for the family? Did Sylvia realize that was only three guest-rooms? They expected to do a lot of "entertaining"—

"There's a lovely site," said Sylvia, sweetly suggestive, "where you could build a guest-house, down by the pool. Don't you think that the fun of a place is improving it? And every improvement makes it seem so much your own."

Yes, they agreed, of course that was true, and the wife murmured something about "a Petit Trianon."

Sylvia entered into the spirit of this fantasy, trying to feel like a woman with seven servants and a house with twenty rooms, which she thought was too small. The grumpiness of Emma returning to her mind, she wondered where on earth this florid little woman, so expensively dressed, so expansive in manner, would find the seven servants to fill the seven bedrooms, and pictured her dealing with seven separate grumpinesses. Sylvia thanked heaven fervently that that wasn't *her* problem, as the questions continued and the traffic slipped by them.

After two hours they arrived at the house.

"They were clients in a million," said Sylvia to Olive.

"*With* a million," said Olive.

"Oh, it must be more than that. Of course, it was lucky that they haven't any taste. Those grounds are really lovely, but the house is terrific. The more money people have, the worse houses they build."

"That's very true," said Olive reflectively. "It takes nature to defeat them. Or maybe it's their gardeners. Gardeners always seem to have more taste than architects. Anyway, Sylvia, you're a very clever girl. I never saw Finnester more pleased about anything."

The two girls were sitting in a quiet little cocktail lounge, not far from their office building, at the close of the day.

"Yes, he was pleased," said Sylvia reflectively.

"Wonderful to bring them right back to the office to sign on the dotted line. That was quick work, old dear."

Sylvia smiled. She felt tired, but elated. Finnester had said a lot of nice things to her, and she had that commission safely in the bag. She was pleased with herself and pleased with the world. When Olive had suggested, at the end of their office hours, that they celebrate together over a cocktail, it had seemed the very nicest of all things to do.

She sipped her Martini, savoring its flavor. She and Olive had often dropped in at this cocktail lounge for a drink before dinner, before Jim came home. She hadn't been there since, and now she realized she'd missed it. Nevertheless, she knew she ought to hurry.

"I *should* have gone straight home," she thought somewhat remorsefully, not liking to admit that in all the excitement—the completion of the sale, Mr. Finnester's satisfaction, his generous praise and Olive's congratulations—she hadn't remembered this, or perhaps hadn't wanted to. She'd been thinking of Jim, off and on, of course, all day. But somehow when she had come back to the office—

"What's the matter?" asked Olive. "Are you worried about anything?"

"Of course not," said Sylvia.

Olive looked at her critically. "You ought to be on the crest of the wave. You were, until just now. Have another Martini."

"Oh, no. Two's my limit. I really ought to go."

Olive's calm gaze appraised her for a moment in silence. And then she asked abruptly, "What did Jim say on the telephone this morning?"

Sylvia looked startled, then slightly uncomfortable. "Why, you know. You heard. He wanted me to lunch with him."

"But why did he have to make such a row?"

"It wasn't a row. He just wanted me, that's all. One of his professors had turned up in town; very distinguished. He has a job for Jim. He wanted me to meet him."

"It didn't occur to him you have a job of your own?"

The provoking thing was that of course it really hadn't. "Oh, *that*—" he'd said, when she'd mentioned Long Island. It had really slipped his mind. He had thought it of no importance.

Fortunately Olive didn't wait for an answer. "All men are alike," she said, "when they're married. He thinks your proverbial place is the home. Now, you're just as bright as Jim, and maybe you're brighter. What are you laughing at?"

"You remind me of my great-aunt."

"*Your great-aunt?*" echoed Olive, arching penciled eyebrows, which were plucked to little scimitars over her shrewd eyes. Her blonde bob was gleaming, her lipsticked mouth smiling; her carmine-nailed hand was grasping her cocktail glass. No one could really have looked less like Aunt Myra.

But, "Yes," insisted Sylvia. "She used to talk like that. But, Olive, it's silly. At least in these days. Jim would never seriously stand in my way. He's going to have this job, and that will make it easier to run things at home. We'll both leave the flat every morning after breakfast, and have some more money, which of course will be pleasant, and Emma will calm down again—"

"It sounds like the millennium."

"It will be," said Sylvia. "And now I *must* go."

She was eager to see Jim now, to hear what he would tell her, to tell him, herself, of her successful day.

When she let herself into the flat, with her latchkey, he was sitting on the love seat by the living-room fire. Jimmy, Junior, adorable in diminutive pajamas and his little plaid wrapper and scarlet felt slippers, was climbing all over him, like a very active vine.

"Hi, Mummy! We're roughhousing!" he squealed between giggles.

Jim stood up abruptly, his son under his arm. Over this wriggling burden he kissed her. "You're late, sweet," he said. "Come have a drink and celebrate."

It was then that she noticed the table by the love seat, the whisky and the glasses and the makings for old-fashioneds.

But Jim hadn't been drinking. He'd been waiting for her. Impossible to say, "I've just had two Martinis." Instead, she asked eagerly, "Jim, what about the job?"

"That's what we're celebrating." He dropped Jimmy to the hearth rug.

"Don't keep me in suspense," she laughed, and bent over the child. She kissed the nape of his neck, and he began to wriggle.

Then Emma appeared in the living-room door.

Sylvia glanced at her. Those glances were a habit. "Good evening, Emma," she said, very courteously, thankful to see that the grumpiness had lightened. It always *was* worse, she'd noticed, in the mornings. "Run along now, Jimmy," she said. "It's your bedtime."

"Oh, no! *Please,* no!" cried Jimmy appealingly.

"You know that you never keep Emma waiting." To this pious observation, Sylvia added, "We're going to be in this evening, you know, Emma. Why don't you go out?"

Emma actually smiled as she took Jimmy in custody. But the atmosphere brightened when she went.

"Make mine a weak one," said Sylvia hastily, for Jim had begun to mix the old-fashioneds. "And *what* about the job?"

She knew it must be wonderful, he looked so awfully happy. He handed her her glass and then raised his own.

"Well, here's to Masterbrook," he said. "He's turned the trick for me. And here's to Thunder Dam."

*"Thunder Dam?"* she repeated.

"That's where the job is," said Jim, beaming.

Sylvia stared at him. "The job? But what is it?"

"Why, you've heard of it, haven't you?"

She shook her head blankly.

"Darling, you must have. It's been in all the newspapers—pictures and articles. It's a Government project and still mostly on paper. They're just starting construction. Masterbrook figures it will take about six years. To build it, I mean. After that they'll have to run it. It's handled by a wonderful group of engineers. Masterbrook's been out there, acting as consultant. So when he had my letter—"

"Jim," she interrupted, "where on earth is it?"

"It's out in Oregon."

"*Oregon?*" she echoed.

"Marvelous country, he told me. Virgin pine forests—wild and unspoiled—the most glorious air."

"Jim, don't be silly. You sound like a guidebook. You can't mean you'd actually consider going out there?"

"Why not?" he asked briefly.

"But, Jim—you could get a job in New York."

"I haven't," he said.

"But you *could*," insisted Sylvia. "Or maybe in New Jersey—all those tunnels and things."

"Be sensible," said Jim. "I tell you this is a super-job. It's a wonderful opening for a hydraulic engineer."

It was all so ridiculous, she felt merely impatient. "And what do you think that *I'd* do at Thunder Dam?" The impatience was perceptible in the timbre of her voice.

Before he could answer, the telephone rang.

"I'll go," said Jim. "Hello— It's for you."

She stepped to the desk. "Yes, this is Mrs. Wainroot— Certainly I remember you," professionally cordial. "You came in last week— Yes, it's still on our list. Several other people are considering it now— Well, it's about seven miles from the station, but there are good commuters' trains— Yes, an old farmhouse, smothered in lilac bushes. The most lovely weathered shingles. Such a sleepy little village— No, it hasn't gas, but you could put in electricity— It has a surface well— Oh, I don't think you need worry about that. I don't believe there are any fireplugs, but the village has a fire engine. I wouldn't wait too long. You see, these other people are very much taken with it— Fine! Come in tomorrow."

She replaced the receiver and picked up her old-fashioned, strolling to the fire to stand sipping it in silence. Speech, at the moment, did not seem to her necessary. It was exactly as if she had put on an act to demonstrate just what she *couldn't* do at Thunder Dam. Then she observed that Jim was not impressed.

"Don't you ever get sick of that racket?" he inquired.

Their eyes met for an instant, and his had that puzzled look. "Certainly not," she said crisply. "I love it."

"I suppose you'll really miss it."

The positive future tense struck here ear. She glanced up, alarmed, but before she could speak, "Oh, Sylly," he pleaded, "it was the chance of a lifetime. It never even dawned on me not to accept it."

"You mean—you *have* accepted it? Without consulting me?"

"You weren't around," said Jim, and he said it rather curtly. "It was urgent, you see. They had to have an answer. Masterbrook called them on the telephone from the club. I have to show up there the first of next week."

*"The first of next week?"* It just didn't seem possible. Sylvia weakly sank down on the love seat. Jim picked up her glass to freshen her drink.

"I've told Mother and Dad," he was saying, "and they were wonderful. Of course they're going to miss us. They're going to miss Jimmy."

*"When* did you tell them?" Beyond reason, this angered her.

"As soon as I left Masterbrook. I had to tell someone. Why, Sylly, you don't realize—I was walking on air. I went straight uptown to see Dad at the hospital, and then we went back to the house to talk to Mother. At first she was upset—but you know how Mother is. Before I left, she was planning to come out to visit us and bring the whole family."

"Well," said Sylvia grimly, "you seem to have settled everything."

"There wasn't much to settle. Mother wants you to stay with her while you're closing up here. I don't suppose you and Jimmy can get off with me on Friday. We can't take many things, but fortunately there's a house for us. They've put up quite a village a stone's throw from the dam site. It's one of those experiments in Government housing."

She could see it. Too awful, she was sure. Graceless shacks on a mud bank. Cape Cod cottages or flat-roofed modern boxes. All alike and all staring at the scar on the river bank, at the stark silhouette of chimneys and cranes.

It was then that she noticed Emma standing in the doorway. She had on her hat and coat, and her face was enigmatic.

"I'm going out now," she said. "Jimmy's asleep."

Impossible to tell what she had overheard. But what difference did it make? She would never go with them. Suddenly, absurdly, this seemed the last straw.

"Very well, Emma." The words came mechanically. And then, from force of habit, "Have a good time."

She heard the front door shut. She was very close to crying. Of course, without a job, she wouldn't need Emma. But her certain desertion seemed a cataclysmic symbol of the shambles Jim had made of her entire life.

He was saying, "It's late. We ought to cook dinner."

"I don't want any dinner," said Sylvia childishly.

"Of course you do," said Jim.

Then suddenly she flared out at him. "Go out somewhere and eat. I'll stay here with Jimmy. I don't want to talk about this another minute."

"Why, Sylly—" He seemed thunderstruck.

"I mean it," she said. "What good is there in talking? You haven't once considered me. You didn't give a thought to me. I've been working like a slave since nine o'clock this morning. I come home dead-tired and you hit me when I'm down. You're completely self-centered. You haven't even asked me how my deal came out today. You forgot it—that's all. Or else you didn't care."

"I did—I do care." Then he succumbed to honesty. "I guess I did forget it. I'm very sorry, Sylly. But I've had an awful lot on my mind."

"Well, what about my mind? Or do you think I haven't one? You don't show the slightest interest in my work. But I want to tell you that I sold that place on Long Island. Those people I took out there paid eighty thousand dollars for it. Mr. Finnester's commission will be five per cent. He'll give me a quarter of it, and that's a lot of money."

"Of course it is," said Jim. Then lamely, "That's fine, Sylly."

"You bet it's fine," she said.

"But, Sylly, is it worth it? I mean—you're exhausted. You're just a nervous wreck."

"It's worth just as much as a dam out in Oregon and a life in the wilderness." Her voice was breaking now. She tried to control it. The thought flashed across her mind: "I'm just a little tight." But she couldn't stop talking. "Jim, I'd go crazy there. I love New York. And I'm making so good in the real-estate business. Call it a racket, if you like. But it's booming. And I'm really *damn'* good at it. You could ask Mr. Finnester. Or Olive. She'd tell you."

"Oh—Olive," said Jim. It was his first show of temper.

Sylvia's eyes blazed at him. "And what's wrong with Olive?"

"She's a very hard-boiled egg. Her values are all twisted."

"You can leave Olive out of it," said Sylvia. "She's my friend. She warned me of this. She said that you'd do it."

"Do *what?*" Jim demanded. And now he looked angry.

"Stand in my way." Had Olive really said that? Or had she, herself, merely said that he wouldn't? Sylvia felt confused. But yet strangely truculent. Suddenly the line she must take seemed quite clear. "In any case," she said, "I won't go to Oregon."

Jim stood there looking at her, and he didn't seem familiar. Tight-lipped and stern, with obstinate eyes.

"I am going," he said.

"Then you'll go without me."

"Sylvia, do you mean that?"

She felt a little scared. "He thinks your proverbial place is the home." Olive had said *that*. She remembered her saying it. This was the moment to prove that it wasn't.

"Certainly I mean it," she said. And felt less scared. He never would do it.

But Jim was looking down at her with contempt in his eyes. "If you can talk me over with Olive and let her give you advice and then throw it in my teeth, you—well, you're just not the girl that I thought you were."

The unfairness of that was utterly enraging.

But Jim was going on, his voice coldly judicial. "It's probably better that you *don't* go to Oregon. You've put everything quite plainly. I know how you feel. You've made a life for yourself that you like. I haven't any place in it. I've felt that for some time. I tried not to feel it. But—well, it didn't work. If we're going to bust up, I'd rather bust here. I can make a new start in the West. It will be easier." He turned from her abruptly and walked to the door. On the threshold he added, "Now I'm getting the hell out of here."

He disappeared into the hall, and she wanted to cry out to him. But no—she wouldn't. She had too much pride. She rose from the love seat and stood listening, motionless. In the shock of his attack she'd achieved complete sobriety. She heard his hurried footsteps, as he moved about their room. A bureau drawer opening. A dull thud in the closet. The minutes passed slowly, but there were not many of them before he was approaching again down the hall. He paused at the nursery. Entered it. Then silence. This was a nightmare. But no, it was real. Jim, hat and bag in hand, was standing in the doorway.

She found her voice then. "Where are you going?"

"I'm not sure. I'll let you know. I'll call you up tomorrow. I'll have to come back for the rest of my clothes."

233

For an instant he stood there, looking awkward and embarrassed, his eyes not meeting hers.

And then she said, "Jim—"

His lips twitched defensively. "No, Sylvia. Don't. No use going over it. Before I leave for Oregon we must talk about Jimmy. But we have three days."

Again the sense of nightmare.

"Well, so long," he added, with that odd touch of awkwardness.

As she heard the front door open and close with finality, she was filled with sudden anger at the thought of his injustice. He was stubborn, unfeeling and utterly selfish. He had treated her outrageously and didn't even know it. Suffused with self-pity, she began to cry helplessly. But tears cannot quench the spark of self-reliance. So presently she dried them and pulled herself together.

She had lived four years without him and could do it again.

Sylvia's alarm clock shrilled on her bedside table, rousing her from the heavy sleep into which she had fallen after long hours spent tossing on her bed, facing disaster alone in the dark. On the stage of her thoughts, in the silence of the night, she and Jim had re-enacted their dismal little drama, repeating their lines and going through the motions that had swept them irresistibly to the brink of catastrophe and then over the brink to the climax—the curtain. She had struggled for detachment and partially achieved it. The conflict between them came to seem to her inevitable, and the catastrophic climax its logical end. But Jim, she'd thought bitterly, was the villain of the piece. His self-centered obstinacy had brought about the tragedy. And yet she felt the need for self-justification. He had wanted to tear her life up by the roots. She couldn't stand for that. No woman would. She dwelt on Jim's faults, his selfishness, his ruthlessness, tossing them like fuel on the flame of her anger, the emotion above all others which annihilates sleep.

But she had slept at last, for four blessed hours, and now the alarm clock was prodding her to wakefulness. She was conscious of its trill, then of drowsy emergence from a stupor of fatigue. The bedroom was dark. It was a dreary morning. Beyond her gray windowpanes it seemed to be raining. She clicked on her lamp and blinked in its light. This shone down uncompromisingly on Jim's cot beside her bed—which, empty, unslept in, roused her instantly to full consciousness. How *could* she have forgotten, when even half-awake, that she and Jim had separated,

234

that their marriage had smashed, that she was left alone to pick up the pieces? Alone with Jimmy, Junior. Alone with her job. Well, thank God she had them. A job and a son. Even as she thought all this, it still seemed impossible. But yet it had happened, the evening before. And it was the next morning, it was seven o'clock, and as on other mornings she would have to get up and dress and have her breakfast and hurry down to the office. The scent of Emma's coffee would soon be on the air.

She could do with a good cup of coffee, she thought, astonished to find herself conscious of hunger. Last night she'd had no dinner, couldn't bring herself to cook, had merely drunk a glass of milk and nibbled a cracker before she had dropped exhausted on her bed. What a night it had been—three o'clock before she slept. Now she felt like a wreck and must look like God's wrath.

She had slipped out of bed with her mirror in mind before she remembered that that no longer mattered. She paused, distinctly shocked. Such trifles brought it home to you.

She thought, "I *won't* think about Jim." Not that way, at any rate. Not of how he used to feel about her. And certainly not of how she'd felt about him.

On that tonic resolve, she screwed her hair up on two hairpins, telling herself it was restful and relaxing to feel free to look like a fright if you wanted to, and noticed as she did so that the flat seemed very quiet. Why? Oh, of course—no baritone in the bathroom. Funny, how Jim always sang in his shower. He couldn't keep a tune, but it sounded sort of cheerful. "Watch it!" thought Sylvia. She was turning sentimental. Eternal vigilance, it seemed, was required. She ought to be concentrating on the things that had annoyed her. No waiting this morning for Jim to bathe first, no picking up the clothes he had dropped around their bedroom, no shaving brush and razor and messy soap bowl on the washstand.

The shock of her cold shower was pleasantly invigorating. It seemed to clear her mind and improve her morale. But later, in her bedroom, that unslept-in cot arrested her, suggesting a new field for anxious speculation. Though certainly it was no longer her affair, she couldn't help wondering where Jim had spent the night, and struggled to dismiss the more lurid possibilities. They weren't very likely, she tried to tell herself sensibly. Jim hadn't been reduced to reckless despair. He was something of a Puritan, and he was fastidious. He'd undoubtedly gone to some decorous hotel. Or back to his father's house. That was very probable. "And good heavens," she thought, "what his family must have said about

235

me!" But they'd have to say it sometime. She couldn't worry about that. But yet she did worry. Because it was unfair. And because they'd been so kind to her and had loved her like a daughter. In spite of that, she knew, they would all take Jim's side. And there was Jimmy, Junior. He was the worst of it. They'd talk as if *she* were the one who was leaving him.

"Oh, dear," she thought distractedly, "it's going to be so awful. How can people live through it? And yet so many do. Live through it and like it, so far as you can tell, and pick themselves up and go on to new experiences."

It was just at that moment that the telephone rang.

"*Jim?*" she thought wildly. And then, "No, of course not." It would be some silly client at this unearthly hour. Not yet half-past seven, but clients had no conscience. Dressed in her slip, not bothering about a wrapper, with her hair still skewered up on those two spikes of hairpins, she ran to the living-room to answer the call.

On its threshold she stopped, absolutely dumbfounded. For an instant she distrusted the evidence of her eyes. Then she drew a sharp breath—a gasp it was, really. Jim, under his trench coat, lay asleep on the window seat. The coat of his uniform was hanging on a chair. His shoes were on the floor, his necktie beside them. He was soundly sunk in slumber, his head on a sofa cushion. This much she saw before the phone rang again.

She leaped quickly to silence it before it should awaken him. This somehow seemed essential. "Hello," she murmured cautiously.

A woman's voice answered, politely apologetic. "Oh, dear Mrs. Wainroot, it's frightfully early. I *hope* you weren't asleep. This *is* Mrs. Wainroot?"

Sylvia nodded. A pause. And then she realized that over the telephone of course you must speak. Her "Yes" was a mere breath, and the voice went on briskly:

"I'm just getting off for an eight-o'clock train, and I wanted an appointment for this morning in your office. You don't know me, but last month you sold my aunt's place in Westchester. You got such a good price for it. Now, our house is just half a mile down that road. I don't really want to sell it, but it *is* a seller's market and my husband thinks that we should. It needs a new furnace, and of course we can't get one. But it has a lovely view of the Westchester hills. Do you think, if we sold it, you could find us an apartment? About eight or nine rooms and not too expensive—"

Standing by the desk, her eyes on Jim on the window seat, and shivering in her slip—for a window was open—Sylvia desperately broke in on this monologue. She had hardly heard a word of it, but she could hear her heart. Hear it or feel it, she didn't know which, bouncing about in her chest like a wild thing.

"Come in any time," she whispered conspiratorially. "I can't talk now." Then she hung up the receiver.

And what to do next, she wondered, still stupefied. Tiptoe silently from the room? Yes, that would be best. Let Jim explain later. It would take some explaining. But she paused by the window seat for another breathless glance at him. Could this possibly mean that he had come back to her, that he'd given up Oregon, that he had capitulated? He looked so defenseless, relaxed like that in sleep. And young, very boyish, his hair comically rumpled, his shirt collar open— That tie on the floor! She stooped to pick it up, and then saw that he was stirring, turning his head restlessly as if he felt her presence. She was struck with a sudden sense of panic. He mustn't find her staring at him.

He opened his eyes.

Vague they were at first, still clouded with sleep; then remembrance, recognition, slowly gave them expression. He smiled a little foolishly. "Hello, Sylly," he said.

Abruptly, absurdly, she thought of her hair, and still in that panic, she removed the wire hairpins. It was a mistake, she realized instantly. Damp, clammy elf locks fell about her ears. Considering everything, she felt naked in her slip. "What are you doing here?" she heard herself saying.

On that he sat up, looking tousled, without dignity. No man was at his best in the morning, before he'd shaved. "Well, I was sleeping," he said idiotically.

"So I see," she retorted, for severity seemed obligatory. He hadn't, after all, made any overture of sentiment. "But why are you here?"

He was still half-asleep, but it was all coming back to him. "Well—" Then he paused. His embarrassment was obvious. "*You* ought to know all about the housing shortage."

Sylvia did. "What of it?" she asked shortly.

"I couldn't get into any hotel."

"You couldn't get in?"

"I couldn't get a room. I tried about thirty of them—raced around in a taxi—uptown and downtown—not a bed to be had. And the Y.M.C.A., I found, was full up."

How perfectly ludicrous! Yet how quite to be expected. Why hadn't she thought of it when he walked out into the night? It made a farce of his departure. It burlesqued his heroics. Sylvia, for her life, could not have helped smiling. Worse than that, laughter sparkled in her eyes.

"Why didn't you go to your father's house?" she asked, remembering as she did so those lurid possibilities that she'd tried to dismiss and which now seemed no nonsensical. Jim's thought had been a Y.M.C.A.!

"Father's house? Oh—" Again he looked embarrassed. "Well, I don't know. I just didn't want to."

She knew just as well as if he had told her—though this was another thing that she hadn't thought of—that he had funked facing his family with the news. She could understand that. It was just the way she felt.

"About three o'clock it started to rain—a hell of a downpour," Jim was saying morosely. "Thunder and lightning. Didn't you hear it?"

"I was sound asleep," said Sylvia superbly.

Jim's eyes met hers. "Yes, I suppose you were."

With these words a little curtain of restraint fell between them. Jim broke the slight pause. "So I came back here. There really wasn't anything else I could do. I still had my latchkey. Of course, I feel a fool."

*There really wasn't anything else he could do.* That was why he'd come back. A mere matter of necessity.

"Well, your return *is* slightly anticlimactic." She hoped that her voice sounded careless and carefree. "But now that you're here, you'd better stay for breakfast. I'll be dressed in a moment, and then you can shave."

She saw the implications of that last observation register on his face, which stiffened a little. She had made them deliberately, sustained by her pride. Then she turned from the window seat to walk out of the room, wishing that her exit could be distinguished by more dignity than was possible to achieve in a skimpy rayon slip, with the handicap of the elf locks straggling about her ears.

Fifteen minutes later, dressed for the office, with more care than usual and a liberal use of lipstick—there was nothing like lipstick to keep up your courage—she was seated beside Jimmy in his high chair at the breakfast-table, with Emma presiding over the kitchenette range, when Jim strolled into the dining-room, looking quite himself again.

"Good morning, Emma," he said, most meticulously.

Sylvia didn't care for the irony in his tone. It had occurred to her, as she finished dressing, that it was just as well that he had turned up for breakfast. Explanations with Emma could now be postponed. They would be awkward, and, frankly, she dreaded them.

"I suppose you'll be busy today, dear, in the office," said Jim very blandly, unfolding his napkin.

"Very," said Sylvia, and thought, *"Damn* his irony!"

Jimmy made it worse by saying, "Mummy's always busy."

"Always," agreed Jim. "Mummy's very important."

Sylvia's eyes flashed at him. She said, "Drink your milk, Jimmy." When next she glanced at Jim, he didn't look so brash. In fact, he looked sorry. And a little ashamed.

Jimmy said, "Daddy, what'll *we* do today? Will you take me to the Zoo? You said you would sometime."

Emma came in with Jim's eggs, looking grumpy. There was something portentous about Emma that morning. It would have worried Sylvia, if she hadn't been preoccupied. And of course she never liked any talk about the Zoo. She always thought Jimmy would catch some disease there, referring to measles and scarlet-fever germs as if they were caged with the lions and tigers.

"I want to see a Yellow Dog Dingo," Jimmy was continuing. Jim had read him the "Just So Stories."

"Maybe they don't have one there," said Jim, rather absently.

"Daddy, do they have an Elephant's Child?"

"I wouldn't know," said Jim.

"But couldn't we see?"

"I'm afraid not today."

"Why, Daddy?"

"Well, it's raining."

"They wouldn't keep an Elephant's Child out in the rain. He'd be in the house, Daddy. Couldn't we go?"

Jim shook his head.

"Well, could we go tomorrow?"

"Jimmy, stop teasing," said Sylvia sharply. She felt she couldn't listen to this a moment longer, and she'd found that she wasn't so hungry after all. Standing up, she said abruptly, "I must be on my way."

Jim made no comment, though she waited for an instant. Now she was on her feet, she didn't really want to go. Jim shouldn't have come back. He must know that himself, now. Leaving the room, she blinked tears from her eyes.

But a few minutes later she had herself in hand, when she came out of her bedroom, dressed for the street, and paused to pick up her umbrella in the closet off the hall.

"Good-by, Jimmy dear," she called to her son, who was visible in his high chair through the dining-room door.

"Mummy, don't you think that maybe it'll stop raining?"

"I don't know at all, dear. Be a good boy."

She waited again, to see if Jim would call to her, looking down the hall in the direction of the dining-room, her attitude unconsciously one of strained attention.

"Sylvia."

She wheeled. He was standing in the living-room. Again she was conscious of the beating of her heart.

"May I speak to you for a moment?"

"Why, certainly." She joined him.

"I hope," he said diffidently, "you know I didn't plan this. I mean, to come back and upset things this way. I'm sorry I did it, and it really wasn't necessary. I could have spent the night in a railroad station."

"Don't be absurd." She tried hard to make it casual.

"But now that I'm here, I'd better pack up my clothes. Then I'll see Father—maybe lunch with Mother. Anyway, when you come home I'll be gone. But I'll see you again, for we'll have to plan for Jimmy. I—well, I'm going to miss him. I'll want him sometimes, Sylvia. I hope you'll be generous."

"I'll try to be, Jim." She was moved by compassion. But Jimmy was so little—not yet four years old. How could Jim possibly take care of him, living alone in a shack in a housing project, working all day on that Government dam? Unless, of course, he should marry again. That might easily happen, for the woods out in Oregon—those virgin pine forests Jim had spoken of so lyrically—would doubtless be full of predatory females, waiting to pounce on an unattached man. Funny, to think of Jim marrying again—of Jimmy with a stepmother, like a child in a fairy tale. No, it wasn't funny. It was curiously shocking.

It was then that she heard Emma's step in the hall. Jim heard it, too, and turned away impatiently, pacing the width of the room to the window seat, to stand gazing out at the roofs in the rain.

"Mrs. Wainroot," said Emma, appearing on the threshold, looking even more portentous than she had in the dining-room, "before you go I want to talk to you. I'm leaving next week."

"Why, Emma, what's happened?" gasped Sylvia in consternation. So

240

very much had happened that the question was absurd. But Emma didn't know about it—couldn't have known.

"It's time I made a change," she was saying mysteriously. In spite of the grumpiness, she looked pleased with her bombshell.

"But *why?*"

Emma shrugged. "You know why, Mrs. Wainroot."

"I don't know at all." This was perfectly appalling. On top of everything else! With all she had on her mind! Emma was difficult. Emma could be maddening. But still it was impossible to carry on without her. The flat would collapse around Sylvia's ears. There was Jimmy—and her job— Maids were simply nonexistent. "What's the trouble?" she asked.

Emma merely shrugged again. "I've never been a one," she said, "to complain. Not that things have been the same since Mr. Wainroot came home. It was clearly understood there was only two in the family. But no one could say I haven't done my duty."

"No one *has* said it," Sylvia pointed out, struggling again with that impulse to slap her. She was so clearly enjoying the scene. *"What* are you talking about?" she demanded.

"I've got ears, Mrs. Wainroot," Emma reminded her.

Then Sylvia remembered her standing in that doorway, dressed to go out, the evening before. Jim had been speaking of closing the flat, of moving to Oregon, of the house near the dam site. And he'd said a lot more that she couldn't recall. She had thought at the time that Emma might have overhead him and would be upset, but it had slipped her mind— and no wonder—in their quarrel. And Emma *had* gone out. She hadn't heard the end of it. Now, the thing was to temporize.

"Why, Emma," she said brightly, "you didn't understand. I'm not going away. It's just Mr. Wainroot."

As the words left her lips, she remembered Jim was hearing them. He was still standing behind her near the window seat, looking out at the roofs and the silver fall of rain. In the pause, while Emma stared at her, stubborn but bewildered, what she had said seemed horribly irrevocable. Of course, it was nothing she hadn't said before. But she'd said it to Jim, and that seemed very different. In telling Emma, she was telling the world.

When he spoke, it was with the irony she'd resented at breakfast. "You don't have to worry, Emma. I'm leaving immediately. Then everything here will be just as it used to be."

But in Emma's present mood that wasn't satisfactory. "Oh, no, Mr.

Wainroot. I think I'll make the change."

"Now, Emma," coaxed Sylvia, "you've been very happy with us."

Emma's happiness, it seemed, was not the point at issue, and her next words dismissed it. "Of course you can do as you like, Mrs. Wainroot."

That was a joke, and Sylvia smiled cynically. But the reference of the statement was not at all clear.

Emma elucidated it with a dispassionate detachment that her alacrity to push her advantage belied. "Five dollars more a week is the least I could consider. I could get ten."

It was perfectly true. The sky was the limit, where wages were concerned. Maids were paid what they asked for. That was all there was to it.

"I'll give you five," said Sylvia desperately. Forty-five dollars a week!

Emma considered this, calmly judicial. "Well," she said at last, grudgingly, "I guess that will do. While Mr. Wainroot's out at that dam. But when he comes back—"

"Oh, when I come back," Jim's voice was that of Santa Claus, with an overtone for Sylvia of utter derision which made any suggestion of his return seem ridiculous, "you shall have that ten, Emma. Little enough for having to put up with me."

Even Emma seemed to notice that something was wrong. She looked taken aback for an instant. That was something.

When she'd turned, without thanks, to walk back down the hall, "Well," said Sylvia nervously, "that's that." She felt humiliated.

Jim made no comment, and his silence seemed to indicate that domestic arrangements were no longer his affair.

But Sylvia continued in self-justification, "She's very reliable, and of course she's fine with Jimmy."

"I doubt that," said Jim. "She's so damn' disagreeable."

It was something to have aroused him from his attitude of detachment. But he didn't understand. Why, Emma was a treasure! A comment on the times, perhaps, but none the less true.

"Well, I must go now," she said somewhat abruptly, breaking a pause that was beginning to seem awkward. She should have been off half an hour before.

"I'll give you a ring," said Jim, "sometime tomorrow. But not at the office."

"Fine," said Sylvia calmly. Yet those last words had pricked her. She couldn't help regretting that twice yesterday morning she'd had to cut him off—yes, positively *had* to—when he'd called her at her desk and then later at a conference. A client had been sitting beside her at the desk; the conference had been with her employer, Mr. Finnester. The subject of that conference returned to her mind—her triumph of yesterday, the eighty-thousand-dollar sale. A twenty-room house on thirty Long Island acres. Mr. Finnester had called it a drug on the market. Yet she had sold it. It had been a great achievement. But now its importance seemed rather curiously to dwindle. . . .

She heard Jimmy calling, "Daddee!" as she closed the front door.

From the steps of the apartment house she hailed a cruising taxi, because she was late and because it was raining. But perhaps now she couldn't afford such little luxuries. Emma's strike for a raise had brought money to her mind. It hadn't occurred to her to think of it before, but when marriages smashed of course you had to plan. . . .

So she sat in the taxi, reviewing her resources. There would be a lot of things that she couldn't afford. In the past, she admitted, she'd had her extravagances. She liked pretty clothes and good food and entertainment. She had furnished the flat perhaps a trifle lavishly. She had gone to plays and concerts. She ran her own car. Her salary, good as it was, plus commissions, had never been large enough to meet her expenses. But she had a little income from a trust fund from Aunt Myra, and there'd been her allotment from Jim's Army pay. His father and mother had helped out with presents. Now she didn't even know just what she could count on, because her commissions were a fluctuating revenue. This was a new and disconcerting sensation. It made her watch the taxi meter, as never before.

It made her think of Jimmy, and those thoughts were serious. Jim, she knew very well, would want to help support him. It was right that he should, perhaps, but how could she consent to it? How could she let money be their one remaining bond? Cashing Jim's check every month or every quarter—even if she spent every cent of it on Jimmy—would smack of the degradation of alimony and put her in a class with women she despised.

Of course, there were exceptions. She had remembered Olive. And at this remembrance, Sylvia sighed. Olive must already be down in their office, and Sylvia dreaded meeting her this morning, for Olive's keen eyes were much too perceptive. She would want to be confided in; she would want to give advice; and Sylvia shrank from the thought of such confidences.

Olive was seated at her desk, looking over some house plans. "Why, Sylvia," she said promptly, "what's the matter? You look—"

"Haggard?" Sylvia attempted to achieve the light touch.

"No. But are you ill?"

"Not at all. I didn't sleep well. Sorry I'm late."

"Why didn't you sleep?"

"Oh, I don't know. I just lay awake, thinking. You know how you do."

Olive merely looked at her, with slightly lifted eyebrows, leaning back in her desk chair, calmly appraising. It was perfectly obvious that look inquired "Jim?"

Sylvia evaded it by stepping into the closet to hang up her hat and coat and smooth her hair before the mirror there. She was thinking of Jim's words in their quarrel last night. "If you can talk me over with Olive and let her give you advice and then throw it in my teeth, you—well, you're not the girl that I thought you were." That had been unjust, and it had enraged her. Olive might know too much about their marriage, but most of it she'd guessed and some of that was wrong. At least, it had been wrong. Now Olive was justified. Facing the mirror, she was shocked by her reflection. Circles under her eyes, no color in her cheeks. "Haggard" was the word, she thought. Jim must have noticed it.

Emerging from the closet, she found Olive's eyes waiting for her, with the watchful concentration of a cat at a mouse hole.

"I have a new client," she said very cheerfully. "She rang me up this morning at practically dawn. Have we anyone listed who'd like to buy a house in Westchester? She has one to sell, and she wants an apartment."

"Sylvia," said Olive, "you're really very gallant."

But then, opportunely, Sylvia's telephone rang.

She stepped quickly to her desk. "Hello," she said crisply.

"Hello, Sylvia, darling!"

It was Jim's mother's voice, and its familiar accents instantly threw Sylvia into utter confusion. But he couldn't have told her yet — she wouldn't have said "darling." The voice was going on, still warmly affectionate.

"I *had* to call you up. I hope you're not busy. Isn't it wonderful, dear, about Oregon? I mean, of course, wonderful about Jim's splendid job. We're going to miss you so. *That's* perfectly dreadful. But I wouldn't want Jim to be tied to my apron strings. Sons turn into men, and we have to let them go. You'll realize, Sylvia, when Jimmy grows up. Jim says this is such an amazing opportunity. And he'll make the most of it. We know he'll go far. You know it, too, dear. You've always been so proud of him. Now, tell me—when do you think you'll get off?"

"I—I don't know," said Sylvia faintly. How on earth should she handle this? It seemed the last straw.

"Why, darling," said her mother-in-law, "you sound a little downcast. I suppose you *will* have a great deal to do. But when Jim leaves on Friday, you must come straight to us. We want to take care of you while you're closing the apartment. And it will be a joy to have Jimmy in the house. I suppose you'll lose Emma. But do you really care? It will be so much easier, living in the country, and you'll be at home and the workmen will have wives. The workmen on the dam, I mean. You'll find some nice woman. You mustn't be discouraged. You're not, are you dear?"

"Oh, no. No—I'm not." What else could she say?

"Of course we knew you wouldn't be. You're such a brave girl. My goodness—when I think of how you lived without Jim for those four long years of constant anxiety! You kept us all up, through the entire war. And now you'll be together, dear. That's all that really counts—"

It was too much. She simply couldn't stand it. "I'm afraid I can't talk any longer," she said.

"Oh, dear, I do run on so!" Her mother-in-law laughed. "I know I shouldn't ring you like this in the office. I wanted to call you both up last night, but I knew you'd have so much to talk about together. Can you dine with us this evening?" Then, as Sylvia didn't answer, "Or tomorrow night, dear. Ask Jim which he'd rather."

"I think—not tonight," said Sylvia evasively.

"Well, then after dinner we may come up to see you. Just for an hour, to hear all your plans. Would that be a bother?"

"N-no," said Sylvia weakly.

Her hands were shaking visibly as she hung up the receiver. Of course by this evening Jim would have told them. She could dismiss that visit from her mind. But her mother-in-law's loving, emphatic volubility and her perfect trust had unnerved Sylvia completely.

Olive asked curiously, "Who was that on the telephone?"

"It was Jim's mother. Asking us to dinner."

Olive seemed to wonder why that was so upsetting. "What happened," she asked, "about that job of Jim's?"

"He got it," said Sylvia. "He likes it. It's excellent."

Olive said dryly, "And the millennium dawned?"

Sylvia remembered that yesterday she had said it would. That was before she knew about Oregon. Now she said evasively, "Yes. In a way."

"Perhaps a cloudy sunrise?" Olive suggested.

"Olive," said Sylvia, "it's none of your business." She was instantly ashamed of this sudden burst of temper.

But Olive did not seem to mind the rebuff. Again she merely raised her finely-plucked eyebrows. "If you say so," she agreed. Then, picking up the house plans, she rose from her desk, to add with equanimity, "I have to speak to Finnester. I'll tell him about your client. Maybe he has an apartment up his sleeve. He's still all lit up about your sale yesterday. Don't forget that you're really a very bright girl. Let's try to have lunch together." And then she was gone.

"A bright girl," thought Sylvia. Yes, she was that. Sitting down at her desk, she looked around her office, trying to recapture the magic it had held for her, the blithe exhilaration of business success. She couldn't seem to do it. Perhaps work was the answer. Sighing, she opened the desk's filing drawer. She took out a list of clients and ran her glance over it. Two people—no, three—wanted Westchester houses. There wasn't any doubt she could put through that sale. As for finding an apartment—

"Oh, the hell with it!" thought Sylvia. She rose from the desk to walk over to the window, to stand looking listlessly out at the view. She thought of Jim watching the rain on the roofs, while she was talking to Emma. Now it had stopped, the skyscrapers were visible, the sun was breaking through thin silvery clouds. Jimmy would once more be teasing for the Zoo. Jim would be packing, just as he always packed, tossing his clothes any-which-way into suitcases. When she came home there'd be no trace of him anywhere. . . .

Her telephane rang, and the switchboard girl said pleasantly, "A lady to see you, Mrs. Wainroot."

"Send her in."

It was the new client, straight from the railroad station. A talkative woman, as most of the clients were. It had always amused Sylvia to listen to their chatter. She'd liked sizing people up, peeking into their lives, feeling she was capable of straightening things out for them. This morning it struck her as something of a bore.

"I suppose you might say that it needed some repairs," the caller was saying earnestly. "I told you about the furnace, and it *should* be repainted, and just lately the roof has taken to leaking. Of course it's impossible to buy cedar shingles, and it *costs* so much nowadays to get anything done. So it really does seem as if the time had come to sell it, and besides, I'm not satisfied with the local school. I said to my husband when a child as bright as Junior is called inattentive you can only blame the teacher. We thought that perhaps a progressive play school in the city—"

"Yes, indeed," agreed Sylvia, "the progressives are so wonderful. I feel very sure we can find you an apartment, and there'll be no trouble in selling the house. It sounds charming. We'll ask a top price for it." Her regular sales talk, but her heart was not in it.

Nevertheless, when the client had left her, she remembered a penthouse up on East Eightieth Street that might go on the market and would exactly suit her. There had been some talk of its owner leaving town. But a telephone call disabused her of that dream. "No," a woman's voice said testily, "we're staying right here. That's positively final, so don't call up again."

Why, Sylvia wondered, had she once thought this such fun?

But at least she could talk about her client's problems with Olive at their luncheon in the corner cafeteria. Curious, how she was fighting shy of confidences. Olive, she supposed, was really her best friend. She could be counted on for sympathy and encouragement. But—what had Jim said of her? "Her values are all twisted." It wasn't surprising he'd come to that conclusion. Olive had never appreciated Jim.

"And why do I care if she hasn't?" thought Sylvia. An insoluble question in her present confusion. "It's just," her thoughts continued, "that I feel so black and blue. It hurts when I'm touched. I don't want to talk about it."

But Olive discreetly made no reference to Jim, and their noon hour passed tranquilly in shop talk on real estate, in little office jokes about Mr. Finnester and in Olive's recital of her plans for the evening. An old beau had turned up who was taking her out to dinner. Later, of course, they'd go to some show. Later still, they would make a round of the night-clubs. It sounded gay and carefree, and Sylvia rather envied her. How strange it would seem to go night-clubbing with a beau! A beau who wasn't Jim. She had never done that, in the four years he'd been at the war.

At her desk after luncheon, she tried hard to keep busy, to feel, as she used to, important and executive. Unfortunately it was a rather idle day. Late in the afternoon she had a conference with Mr. Finnester. During their talk she showed so little of her usual enthusiasm that he glanced at her astutely and said she looked tired.

Sylvia met his kind dark eyes. "I guess I am—a little."

"Too much excitement?" He smiled at her pleasantly and brushed cigar ash off his waistcoat.

For an instant she was startled, but then of course she realized that he was referring to yesterday's sale—the eighty thousand dollars. Her big personal triumph. So she assented that it *had* been exciting. But her tone lacked conviction, and Mr. Finnester seemed puzzled. He had always seen Sylvia on the crest of the wave.

Back in her own office, she was once more subjected to Olive's dispassionate, critical gaze. "Honestly, Sylvia, you're simply all in," she said. "You ought to go home. Or maybe you ought not to." She pointed these last words with a slightly mocking smile, and, when Sylvia didn't answer, continued emphatically, "You won't tell me what's happened, but naturally I know. You've had a row with Jim. You should call that man down. You can't go on working without peace at home. Why, Sylvia, it's absurd! Just tell him you won't stand for it. You don't have to take it. You're young and attractive—"

"This is the moment," thought Sylvia, "to tell her." It was a good opening. She could hear herself saying, "Well, Olive, I'm not taking it." But she couldn't. She tried to. And then she said aloud, "I *am* going home. It's nearly five o'clock."

As she walked into the coat closet, Olive sat watching her, curious but, as always, emotionally unmoved. Nothing ever disturbed the blonde gleam of her long bob, or ruffled her expression of sharp sophistication, or troubled the depths of her shrewd gray-green eyes. She looked ever so much older than Sylvia at that moment, and more worldly-wise, and a trifle contemptuous.

But when Sylvia appeared again, dressed for the street, she said very kindly, "Let me know if I can help you."

"Yes, I will, Olive," said Sylvia, "if you can. I'll see you in the morning," she added quite casually.

Then, somewhat precipitately, she hurried from the room.

Out in the street in front of the office building, in the clear bracing dusk of the fine November evening, she thought it would do her good to walk home. The day in the office had been an ordeal. But that was because she had felt so distracted. Jim must have told his family by this time. "When he leaves town," she decided, "I'll tell Olive, and she'll tell Mr. Finnester, and I can settle down." Some day, she knew, she'd look back with detachment on this turmoil of pain and anxiety and bewilderment, and perhaps then her marriage would seem like a dream. Or if not quite a dream, a mere nostalgic memory. Even now she felt better, walking briskly through the crowd—the five-thirty crowd, streaming out of the office

248

buildings. Three years ago, when she'd taken her job, she had thought it thrilling every evening to mingle with it, to be part of the pulsating life of the great city, a wage-earner, a breadwinner, a girl with a career. She had been determined then to succeed. And now she had succeeded. That had its own thrill. Mr. Finnester had said yesterday that she had a fine future. Success was perhaps a lonely satisfaction, but curiously personal and something to depend on. No man could take it from her—not even Jim. She felt calmer in mind when she reached her apartment house, but tired enough as she took out her latchkey to hope she'd find Emma in a good mood. Perhaps if she was she would scramble an egg for Sylvia, though that had never been in their agreement. Emma prepared breakfast and her own meals and Jimmy's. "It was clearly understood"— Emma's own grumpy phrase for it—that Sylvia cooked dinner for herself and for Jim. But just for herself tonight it hardly seemed worth while. . . .

As the front door swung open, she heard Jimmy laughing—laughing as the little boy never laughed with Emma, an appreciative squeal of pure childish glee. What's more, the laughter came from the living-room, where Emma never allowed him to play. Then she heard Jim's voice. It startled her tremendously.

"So the Elephant Child picked up Yellow Dog Dingo in his little gray trunk and tossed him into the river. But it wasn't the great gray-green greasy Limpopo. It was that little brook in the Park."

Sylvia, by this time, was at the living-room door. There sat Jim on the love seat with Jimmy on his lap, basking in the warmth of a crackling fire.

"Hi, Mummy!" shrieked Jimmy. "Daddy's telling a Just So Story. He's making it up. It's not in the book. Oh Mummy, we've been to the Zoo! It was wunnerful! There was an Elephant's Child an' a Yellow Dog Dingo an' Old Man Kangaroo an' a 'normous Rhinoceros an' a Camel-With-His-Hump an' a Leopard With His Spots! Just like the book, Mummy! All of them were there!"

Jim had put the child down and was rising to his feet. He looked somewhat conscience-stricken and very much abashed. "You see, it cleared up," he said, in apology. "Jimmy wanted to go so much—"

"Oh, Mummy, we had lunch there! We had choklit ice cream an' cream-chicken an' popcorn—"

Sylvia was staring at Jim in astonishment. After a moment, "Where's Emma?" she asked.

"I told her," said Jim, "she could have the day off." He looked a little proud of this stroke of diplomacy. But then his glance wavered from hers, and he added, "I was only waiting for her to come back. I thought she'd be here before you were, you see, Sylvia. And then I was going—"

She brushed this aside. "Have you seen your father?"

"No, I haven't." He looked crestfallen.

"Or your mother?"

"No." A pause. Then he added dejectedly, "Sylvia, I'm sorry. I haven't even packed. You see, Jimmy was here and I wanted to talk to him— I wanted the day with him—"

"Oh, I see," she said wearily. It all still had to be done. She had thought it would be over.

"Sylvia," said Jim, "I can pack very quickly."

Jimmy had been listening without understanding. But this he understood. "Oh, Daddy, don't pack! *Please* finish the story!"

Sylvia looked from one to the other. The compassion she'd felt for Jim that morning swept over her. This day with his son seemed infinitely pathetic. Jimmy's childish eagerness tore at her heart. "Maybe you'd better," she said at last, uncertainly.

"I'll hurry," said Jim, and turned toward the door.

"No," she called him back. "I meant finish the story."

Jimmy seized his hand to tug him back to the love seat.

"Wait a minute, Jimmy," said Jim. He stood looking at her. She couldn't quite fathom the meaning of his gaze. It was puzzled, it was tentative, it seemed to ask a question. Sylvia herself was thinking very fast. She knew what she could do for them both, and she'd do it. She really should have thought of doing it before.

So when Jim asked gravely, "Just what do you mean?" she was ready with her answer and could give it to him quickly.

"I mean I'll pack, myself. Just an overnight bag. You can stay here with Jimmy and I'll go to Olive. If you're leaving on Friday that will give you two days—two days and two nights—"

But Jim's face had changed. At the mention of Olive it had hardened perceptibly. The tentative look in his eyes had disappeared. It was as if somehow she'd answered his question.

"Oh, Olive—" he said with deliberate scorn. "Yes, she'd love to take you in."

This was all very queer. "Don't you want to stay here, Jim?" she asked.

"Of course," he said, "I want to."

He said it so savagely her eyes widened in surprise. She made a little move in the direction of the door. Then she had another thought and looked at him doubtfully. "I think Emma *might* be willing to cook you some supper."

"I'll have supper with Jimmy if I cook it myself," said Jim very shortly.

Sylvia got herself out of the room. It was the work of five minutes to pack her overnight bag, and Emma returned to the flat while she was doing so. From her bedroom she heard Jim saying calmly in the hall, "Mrs. Wainroot's going out. I'm eating with Jimmy in the dining-room tonight."

"Well, Mr. Wainroot," said Emma disapprovingly, "there's chops in the icebox, but who's going to get 'em ready?"

"You are," said Jim.

Sylvia trembled for her answer. But after a moment of dumfounded silence, she only flounced angrily off down the hall. She'd cook the chops, but she'd slam them on the table. Sylvia knew all of Emma's little ways. Bag in hand, she left the bedroom, and then she heard Jim's voice again. He was continuing the story by the fire.

"So Old Man Kangaroo hopped after the Rhinoceros. But of course the Rhinoceros couldn't hop at all." Then he saw her in the doorway and rose to his feet.

"Where you going?" asked Jimmy.

"Out," she said vaguely.

Jim very politely took her bag from her hand. "I'll see you to a cab," he said.

But that was all he did say. They descended in the elevator in uncomfortable silence, and out on the sidewalk Jim whistled for the cab. When Sylvia was seated in it and he'd handed her the bag, "We still have to talk about Jimmy," he reminded her.

"Yes," she said. "I'll get in touch with you."

Then he closed the cab door.

"Well, lady," said the taxi driver, "where am I taking you?"

Sylvia turned quickly away from the back window, from which she'd been watching Jim re-enter the apartment house. The taxi was in motion. It had nearly reached the corner. She hastily gave the driver Olive's address.

It wasn't until then that she suddenly remembered what Olive had told her of her plans for the evening—the old beau, the show and the round of the night clubs. She'd have gone out by this time—it was seven o'clock— and she wouldn't be home till the early morning hours. This was very annoying, for Olive had no maid—just a girl who came in every morning to do the housework. There wasn't any way to get into her flat. Well, Sylvia reflected, she'd have dinner somewhere. Maybe put in the time until midnight at the movies. After that she'd simply have to wait for Olive at her door. The old beau would bring her home, and that would be embarrassing—to be found like a waif, with her bag, in the hall.

Sylvia directed the taxi driver to take her to a tearoom on a side street in the neighborhood, where she had occasionally dined in the past. It was anything but gay—in fact, rather dreary—but its prices were moderate, and she knew they'd have an egg dish and a salad and hot coffee. She felt too exhausted to want anything more.

That brief meal, however, was quickly consumed, and after two cigarettes the evening was before her. She borrowed a newspaper from the girl at the cashier's desk and glanced over the movie ads with a feeling of distaste. She felt far too restless for that sort of entertainment. She'd only sit worrying alone in the dark. She thought of telling Olive—as she'd have to—that night. Much as she dreaded it, she'd be glad to get it over. In the meantime, she had such a sense of wasting time. There was so much to do—at least, so much to talk about—before Jim went away, but they weren't getting at it. She'd feel much more tranquil when everything was settled. She thought of Jim's solitary evening in the flat. She wondered how late he'd let Jimmy sit up, and if Emma would be cross about it. . . .

Then abruptly she remembered. It was the measure of her confusion of mind that up to that moment she had totally forgotten what her mother-in-law had said to her over the telephone when she had called her that morning in her office. "Well, then, after dinner we may come up to see you. Just for an hour, to hear all your plans." She'd dismissed it from her mind, for she'd thought Jim would tell them. He had said that he would. But of course, now he hadn't. Her mother-in-law's voice seemed to echo in her ears, eager, affectionate, completely unsuspecting. "To hear all your plans." Oh, she couldn't let it happen! It would be too great a shock to them—finding her gone and Jim there alone. Her voluble mother-in-law might go all to pieces.

So Sylvia picked up her purse and her gloves and reached under the table for her overnight bag. She must telephone Jim to call them up and head them off, make some excuse— But that wasn't practical. Jim wouldn't be convincing, inventing excuses. Nice men weren't good liars, whereas the nicest women— Then it occurred to her that she needn't trouble Jim. She could call her mother-in-law herself from the tearoom and never let her know that she wasn't at home. She could say she had a headache, or that Jim was very tired, or that he had to go out to a business appointment. That last would be best. It sounded more believable.

In a matter of minutes she was standing at the telephone in a dark little booth behind the cashier's desk. She was saying to Jim's mother, "He was terribly sorry, but he had to dash out right after early supper. You see, he had said he'd meet this engineer who's just come back from Oregon. He works on the dam. He was going to give Jim some pointers on his job."

"Of course," said Jim's mother, as always sympathetic, "I can see that would be valuable. But we'll come up, anyway. He may not keep Jim long, and we want to see you, too, dear."

This was what happened, thought Sylvia, when you lied. At least, it *could* happen to the very best of liars and had happened to her, and she had to make the best of it. But she hadn't a split second in which to formulate a plan. As she spoke, indeed, the plan seemed to formulate itself, her words spilling out to meet the emergency.

"Oh, no, you mustn't trouble. Jim said he'd be late. I tell you what I'll do. Emma's here to stay with Jimmy. I—I'll come to see *you*."

"Why, that would be lovely, dear."

"I'll be there in a few minutes."

She still only half-realized to what she had committed herself. The worst had been averted, but what an evening was before her! "I wonder," she thought, as she hung up the receiver, "if I'll have the nerve to tell them. They ought to be told. It wouldn't be any harder for me than for Jim. Perhaps not as hard, because they don't love me so."

But they loved her enough to bring tears to her eyes, and she had not, unfortunately, arrived at a decision as to just what she *would* do when, fifteen minutes later, her taxi drew up at her father-in-law's door.

The street was a quiet one, lined with brownstone houses, and Jim's father's house did not differ from its neighbors, except for the polished brass plate on its door, which read *Dr. James Wainroot* in old-fashioned script lettering.

The Wainroots had lived in it for nearly thirty years. Their three children had been born there and once "filled it to bursting," as Mrs. Wainroot said with a nostalgic smile. Now that Jim was married, and Betty, his sister, was a student at Vassar, and Bill, his kid brother, had gone off to boarding-school, it seemed rather large for herself and her husband. Yet the house still preserved an air of family life, a sense of the past and a promise for the future. Pictures of Jim and Betty and Bill, taken at all ages, could be seen in every room. Pictures of Sylvia, too, as a bride, or taken with Jim in his uniform on their honeymoon, or holding Jimmy, Junior, as a baby, in her arms. Pictures of Jimmy in all stages of development, sleeping and creeping and toddling and walking. Too many pictures, perhaps, to please a decorator, yet they seemed to belong with the somewhat shabby furniture and the long rows of books and the old-fashioned etchings and the warm, faded colors of the rugs and upholstery that had seen family service for so many years. Dr. Wainroot never wanted to have anything changed. And though Mrs. Wainroot laughed at this, she herself was no innovator. "I like it as it is," she said, "because it seems home."

Sylvia was aware of the charm of the house, different as it was from her own smart apartment, and knew it had a quality that could not be imitated, but was acquired only through the passage of time. "Lived-in," she called it. Its serenity was contagious. But tonight she was feeling far from serene.

The door was opened promptly, in answer to her ring, by Netty, a gray-haired family factotum, who had once been Jim's nurse and now served as waitress.

"Why, Mrs. Jim," she said, "you look like you're traveling. Here—let me have that bag. The family's at dinner. Just finishing, though. Where's Mr. Jim? Is he parking the car?"

"No, he didn't come tonight," said Sylvia uncertainly, feeling self-conscious because of that bag.

"Sylvia?" called her mother-in-law. "We're still in the dining-room."

Sylvia walked slowly down the length of the hall, past the straight flight of stairs and the wide door to the living-room, through which she saw tall bookcases and a fire on the hearth and her mother-in-law's rocker and her father-in-law's Morris chair and Jimmy's last picture, taken with Jim, which stood on a table by an overflowing darning basket. Then she was at the dining-room door.

Dr. and Mrs. Wainroot were seated at the table, drinking their coffee in the soft shine of candlelight and looking not old—indeed, not even elderly—but yet indescribably Darby-and-Joan. Dr. Wainroot was tall and lean and loosely built—a man in his late fifties, with dark hair slightly silvered and arrestingly keen and kindly dark eyes. His habitual expression was attentive, yet impersonal, a physician's guarded mask, conveying sympathy with detachment. His wife was five years younger, inclined of late to plumpness, with fair graying hair, round blue eyes and a dimple that made you aware she'd been a pretty girl. Sweet, regular features topped off her double chin. If not exactly youthful, her manner was vivacious. The most elderly thing about them was a subtle sense of intimacy, conveyed without words, which was conjugal and parental. It was, in brief, the Darby-and-Joan touch.

Mrs. Wainroot said at once, "Sit down, dear. Have some coffee. Netty," she added, "bring a cup for Mrs. Jim."

Dr. Wainroot had risen to pull a chair up to the table. But he confined his greeting to a very friendly smile.

"Clear, dear? One lump?" continued Mrs. Wainroot. "That will be all, Netty. You needn't wait." A little silver coffee set stood at her elbow, and as she poured the coffee she went on talking volubly. "It was sweet of you, Sylvia, to make time for us tonight. You must be so busy, packing for Jim. Remember we're expecting you tomorrow night for dinner. I'll have duck and applesauce. Jim loves it so. And now you must tell me if there's anything he needs—I mean, to take with him—and I'll get it to-morrow. How soon will you be able to give up your job? I suppose you can't walk out on Mr. Finnester without notice. Or is he the nice kind, who would understand? You've so much to do that's really more important. . . ."

Mrs. Wainroot rattled on, without pausing for answers. Her manner of speaking suggested an actress—some veteran comedienne beloved by her public—reciting a speech she had learned in a play. Jim and his father always laughed at her loquacity. But tonight Dr. Wainroot merely very vaguely smiled. He sat back in his chair behind a screen of cigarette smoke, with his eyes fixed on Sylvia, who grew more and more uncomfortable. Miserably preoccupied with what seemed her guilty secret, she felt that each word that her mother-in-law uttered was making it more difficult to explain what had occurred.

It was when Mrs. Wainroot abruptly inquired, "When do you think you and Jimmy will leave, dear?" that she recognized an opening that might not come again. Not to tell seemed by this time deliberate deception. A little pause lengthened while she pulled herself together.

Then, "There's something," she faltered, "that I—I must say to you. . . ."

Dr. Wainroot interrupted as if he hadn't heard. "Oregon," he said, "is a beautiful State. I once went there on a camping trip, many years ago. And I understand that a lot of it's still wild. I'd like to see it again."

"Well, you will, dear. We must go out to visit them before very long."

With these words Mrs. Wainroot had risen from her chair.

Sylvia followed her into the hall. She had missed her opportunity, but she'd tell them in the living-room. She'd tell them as soon as they were settled round the fire.

Then Dr. Wainroot spoke. "I can run you home, Sylvia. My car's out in front."

"Why, James," said Mrs. Wainroot, "it's very early yet."

"But I have to go back to the hospital," said Dr. Wainroot, "and I don't like Sylvia to go home alone. I guess I'm a gentleman of the old school. I think girls should be protected on the city streets at night." Smiling very humorously, he was holding her coat for her.

"Oh, dear, yes," said his wife, for this was one of her anxieties. "All these terrible holdups. Only last week— Did you see it in the paper, dear?" She kissed Sylvia affectionately.

It seemed a little odd to hurry her off so, yet Sylvia was thankful things had taken this turn. The blow for Jim's mother could now be postponed. She could talk with his father alone in the car. It was then that she remembered her bag by the door. If her mother-in-law saw it. . . . But the bag wasn't there. She glanced around the hall. Dr. Wainroot was holding it, under the overcoat that lay on his arm.

"Come, Sylvia," he said, as he opened the front door.

As soon as she was seated in the doctor's coupé, she lost that sense of respite she'd had. It wouldn't take ten minutes to drive to her apartment.

So, as the first red traffic light stopped them, she forced herself to say, "I've something to tell you. It will be a shock to you. I'm not going to Oregon."

"Why not?" asked Dr. Wainroot.

She threw a quick glance at him. He was watching the light, and his face looked just as usual—what she could see of it in the dark of the coupé. She was finding his question somewhat difficult to answer. Ridiculous to say, "I don't want to leave my job." Yet that was the reason. And it had seemed adequate.

"Jim and I," she said, "have quarreled."

He accepted that calmly. "Suppose we take a little turn through the Park." Not waiting for an answer, he set the car in motion, slipping past the changing light, turning west down a side street.

Sylvia had been braced for something very like a scene, and she couldn't understand his composure. Perhaps the word "quarreled" had sounded too trivial. She said, "It was serious."

"What happened?" he asked.

That was painful to remember, but she forced herself to do it. Their harsh, angry words seemed to sound in her ears. The mere memory of those words was emotionally disturbing. She said, "He took that job without ever consulting me. I came home from the office, tired out, and he told me. I'd had a hard day, I'd made a big commission, I'd sold a place on Long Island for eighty thousand dollars. But he didn't think that had any importance. He's never had the slightest respect for my work. It never crossed his mind that I wouldn't want to give it up and go out to live in a shack in the wilderness."

"He asked a lot of you," her father-in-law said mildly.

As he spoke, he was turning in the entrance to the Park. The winding road ahead of them, dark and deserted, looked almost like a country road at that hour of the night. Yet the sense of their surroundings dispelled that illusion. The sound of the traffic on Fifth Avenue was audible. The leafless trees were outlined against a luminous city sky. A rampart of skyscrapers with twinkling lighted windows defined the farther distance above the bare treetops. It was one of Sylvia's favorite views of New York.

"Out there in the Pacific," continued Dr. Wainroot, "I guess he didn't realize that you were taking root here and learning to love it and growing up and changing. When he came back, you'd made your own life. You had your own interests and your job and your son. You aren't the same girl that he married five years ago."

Sylvia had often had this same thought, but now, from Dr. Wainroot, she couldn't accept it. "I think I am," she said, a trifle indignantly.

He shook his head. "You were nineteen years old then and a sophomore at college. Jim was a kid, too—not quite twenty-three. That's the trouble with war marriages. That's why they're so risky. The boy and the girl have to grow up apart. Sometimes they change, along very different lines."

"We haven't changed so much," said Sylvia stubbornly. "Jim seems just the same."

"Oh, he does?" said Dr. Wainroot.

"It's just—" She paused helplessly.

"Just what?"

"That he's so *obstinate!* You know he could find a job in New York."

"Perhaps," said Dr. Wainroot. "But not as good as this one. This job is exceptional."

"Well, my job is, too."

"When a wife's job conflicts with her husband's, something breaks."

"Not necessarily," said Sylvia emphatically.

In the light of a street lamp she saw Dr. Wainroot smile. "Which side of this problem are you arguing, my dear?"

"I'm not arguing at all," said Sylvia inaccurately. It was true she felt very confused in her mind. "But it's unfair to blame me," she said.

"I'm not blaming you."

"You're not saying everything you have in your mind."

He rewarded that insight with another friendly smile. "No. We seldom do. But I will if you want me to. Jim's a brilliant boy. You agree to that, don't you?"

"Y-yes," she said faintly. And then, with more spirit, "You don't think that I'm as important as he is."

"Oh, yes, I do. Perhaps more important. But I don't think that your work is as important as his. With any sort of luck he should have a fine career."

"What about my career?"

Dr. Wainroot did not hesitate. "Hydraulic engineering is a positive profession. It develops the natural resources of this country. Building dams is more constructive than selling city real estate. And when you've made a sale, what have you?"

"I have a commission."

Dr. Wainroot laughed at that. "You don't think that's so very important. Not in itself, my dear Sylvia. I know you. You think it's important because it shows what you can do. You do it very well. I'm not denying it. But you've a bigger job on your hands than selling real estate—as a matter of fact, than building any dams. I think it's the biggest job in the world. You're bringing up a child."

"I haven't neglected him."

"No, of course you haven't. But he ought to have two parents. He ought to grow up in a united home. You ought to live in one, and so, God knows, ought Jim. There's a lot to say, Sylvia, for old-fashioned holy wedlock. A continuous relationship of love and of loyalty, shared interests, understanding, forbearance—and fun. You and Jim are young now. You're very self-reliant. But you won't always be so. And there's all the life to come. It will turn out to be what you've made of it, Sylvia, with Jim or without him—"

"Please stop," said Sylvia.

"Was I making a speech?" asked Dr. Wainroot, pleasantly.

"It wasn't that," said Sylvia. She said it rather shakily. She was thinking miserably, "Of course, he doesn't know. He doesn't understand, because I haven't told him, that our marriage has smashed, that it's too late to talk like that, that even if it's true I can't do anything about it. And now I'll have to tell him—"

Dr. Wainroot broke the pause. "I think Jim's at fault. He was very hotheaded to walk out on you last night."

She looked up at him quickly, tremendously startled. "How did you know he did?"

For an instant her father-in-law seemed disconcerted. "You should be a lawyer, my dear, not a 'realtor.' As a matter of fact, Jim talked with me tonight. Over the telephone, when you had left the flat."

"So you *knew?*" she fairly gasped.

"Yes."

"Did Jim's mother?"

"No, I didn't tell her. I hoped we'd never have to."

"So *that's* why you hurried me out of the house, and why you weren't shocked, and why—" She broke off suddenly. Something vastly more important had flashed into her mind. "What did Jim say?"

"He said just about what you did."

The smile in his voice encouraged her to ask breathlessly. "But *how* did he say it?"

"How?"

She felt foolish. "I mean, did you think—did he seem at all—sorry?"

"What do *you* think?"

She thought it for a moment in silence. "You'd better take me home," she said at last tremulously.

"Sylvia," said her father-in-law, "you're absolutely right."

But she wasn't sure enough of that not to feel shaken when, twenty minutes later, she stood at her front door. Dr. Wainroot had left her on the steps of the apartment-house, firmly refusing to go with her any farther. Now, in her panic, she needed his support. For suppose that Jim wasn't—well, sorry any longer? He'd had two long hours in which to think things over. Or hadn't been as sorry as his father had thought he was.

Nervously she inserted her key in the door. Nervously she opened it and slipped into the hall. And there was Jim, sitting by the living-room fire. Just sitting there, not reading, gazing at the crumbling logs, so deep in his thoughts that he hadn't heard the door. But he saw her at once as she stood on the threshold and stared as if he couldn't at first believe his eyes. Then he sprang to his feet.

She said, "I've seen your father."

He didn't ask how or where she had seen him, but oddly, apprehensively, "Did—did he tell you?"

"Tell me?" she echoed. "Tell me what?"

That confused him. "Why—that I'll give up the job at the dam."

*"Give it up?"*

"If you'll come back. If you'll try to forgive me."

"You told your father that?"

"Yes. I called him up this evening. We went into everything. I asked him to talk to you. I thought, if you'd seen him—*why are you laughing?*"

"Oh, Jim," she gasped hysterically, "he's such an old fraud!"

"Who is?"

"Your father. Such a *dear* fraud. Such a clever one!"

"Are you crazy?"

"No, I'm not. I've never been saner. Oh, Jim, will you *really* give up the job?"

"Yes. Of course I will."

"And stay in New York?"

"Yes."

"Oh—*dear* Jim!"

Then he had her in his arms.

"Sylvia, my sweet—my dear—*Now* what's the matter?"

She was laughing again. "Do you think I'd let you do it? Do you think that I'm going to spoil your career? Oh, Jim—I've been so awful! So horrid—so selfish! But I'll make it up to you out at that damn' dam!"

"Sylvia—my God!—do you know what you're saying?"

"Of course I do, darling. We're going to Oregon. I'll live in a shack with you and Jimmy and like it."

He stood gazing down at her with his heart in his eyes. "I don't know what I've done—or can do—to deserve you."

She began to cry at that, filled with tender humility. "That's just the way I feel."

"Oh, there's something *you* can do." He was grinning irrepressibly. "Let me be the one," he begged, "to fire Emma."

Her tears turned to laughter again in his arms.

# The Revolt of Mother

## MARY E. WILKINS

*What happened when a patient farmwife discovered
her husband was planning to build a new barn rather
than a much-needed farmhouse is ably told by Mary
E. Wilkins with understanding, freshness and charm.
The short story of New England life and character is
Mary E. Wilkins' special field and in it she stands
supreme.*

"FATHER!"

"What is it?"

"What are them men diggin' over there in the field for?"

There was a sudden dropping and enlarging of the lower part of the
old man's face, as if some heavy weight had settled therein; he shut his
mouth tight, and went on harnessing the great bay mare. He hustled the
collar on to her neck with a jerk.

"Father!"

The old man slapped the saddle upon the mare's back.

"Look here, father, I want to know what them men are diggin' over
in the field for, an' I'm goin' to know."

"I wish you'd go into the house, mother, an' 'tend to your own affairs,"
the old man said then. He ran his words together, and his speech was
almost as inarticulate as a growl.

But the woman understood; it was her most native tongue. "I ain't goin'
into the house till you tell me what them men are doin' over there in the
field," said she.

Then she stood waiting. She was a small woman, short and straight-
waisted like a child in her brown cotton gown. Her forehead was mild
and benevolent between the smooth curves of gray hair; there were meek
downward lines about her nose and mouth; but her eyes, fixed upon the
old man, looked as if the meekness had been the result of her own will,
never of the will of another.

They were in the barn, standing before the wide open doors. The spring air, full of the smell of growing grass and unseen blossoms, came in their faces. The deep yard in front was littered with farm wagons and piles of wood; on the edges, close to the fence and the house, the grass was a vivid green, and there were some dandelions.

The old man glanced doggedly at his wife as he tightened the last buckles on the harness. She looked as immovable to him as one of the rocks in his pasture-land, bound to the earth with generations of blackberry vines. He slapped the reins over the horse, and started forth from the barn.

*"Father!"* said she.

The old man pulled up. "What is it?"

"I want to know what them men are diggin' over there in that field for."

"They're diggin' a cellar, I s'pose, if you've got to know."

"A cellar for what?"

"A barn."

"A barn? You ain't goin' to build a barn over there where we was goin' to have a house, father?"

The old man said not another word. He hurried the horse into the farm wagon, and clattered out of the yard, jouncing as sturdily on his seat as a boy.

The woman stood a moment looking after him, then she went out of the barn across a corner of the yard to the house. The house, standing at right angles with the great barn and a long reach of sheds and outbuildings, was infinitesimal compared with them. It was scarcely as commodious for people as the little boxes under the barn eaves were for doves.

A pretty girl's face, pink and delicate as a flower, was looking out of one of the house windows. She was watching three men who were digging over in the field which bounded the yard near the road line. She turned quietly when the woman entered.

"What are they digging for, mother?" said she. "Did he tell you?"

"They're diggin' for—a cellar for a new barn."

"Oh, mother, he ain't going to build another barn?"

"That's what he says."

A boy stood before the kitchen glass combing his hair. He combed slowly and painstakingly, arranging his brown hair in a smooth hillock over his forehead. He did not seem to pay any attention to the conversation.

"Sammy, did you know father was going to build a new barn?" asked the girl.

The boy combed assiduously.

"Sammy!"

He turned, and showed a face like his father's under his smooth crest of hair. "Yes, I s'pose I did," he said, reluctantly.

"How long have you known it?" asked his mother.

" 'Bout three months, I guess."

"Why didn't you tell of it?"

"Didn't think 'twould do no good."

"I don't see what father wants another barn for," said the girl, in her sweet, slow voice. She turned again to the window, and stared out at the digging men in the field. Her tender, sweet face was full of a gentle distress. Her forehead was as bald and innocent as a baby's, with the light hair strained back from it in a row of curl-papers. She was quite large, but her soft curves did not look as if they covered muscles.

Her mother looked sternly at the boy. "Is he goin' to buy more cows?" said she.

The boy did not reply; he was tying his shoes.

"Sammy, I want you to tell me if he's goin' to buy more cows."

"I s'pose he is."

"How many?"

"Four, I guess."

His mother said nothing more. She went into the pantry, and there was a clatter of dishes. The boy got his cap from a nail behind the door, took an old arithmetic from the shelf and started for school. He was lightly built, but clumsy. He went out of the yard with a curious spring in the hips, that made his loose home-made jacket tilt up in the rear.

The girl went to the sink, and began to wash the dishes that were piled up there. Her mother came promptly out of the pantry, and shoved her aside. "You wipe 'em," said she; "I'll wash. There's a good many this mornin'."

The mother plunged her hands vigorously into the water, the girl wiped the plates slowly and dreamily. "Mother," said she, "don't you think it's too bad father's going to build that new barn, much as we need a decent house to live in?"

Her mother scrubbed a dish fiercely. "You ain't found out yet we're women-folks, Nanny Penn," said she. "You ain't seen enough of men-folks yet to. One of these days you'll find it out, an' then you'll know that we know only what men-folks think we do, so far as any use of it goes, an' how we'd ought to reckon men-folks in with Providence, an' not complain of what they do any more than we do of the weather."

"I don't care; I don't believe George is anything like that, anyhow," said Nanny. Her delicate face flushed pink, her lips pouted softly, as if she were going to cry.

"You wait an' see. I guess George Eastman ain't no better than other men. You hadn't ought to judge father, though. He can't help it, 'cause he don't look at things jest the way we do. An' we've been pretty comfortable here, after all. The roof don't leak—ain't never but once—that's one thing. Father's kept it shingled right up."

"I do wish we had a parlor."

"I guess it won't hurt George Eastman any to come to see you in a nice clean kitchen. I guess a good many girls don't have as good a place as this. Nobody's ever heard me complain."

"I ain't complained either, mother."

"Well, I don't think you'd better, a good father an' a good home as you've got. S'pose your father made you go out an' work for your livin'? Lots of girls have to that ain't no stronger an' better able to than you be."

Sarah Penn washed the frying-pan with a conclusive air. She scrubbed the outside of it as faithfully as the inside. She was a masterly keeper of her box of a house. Her one living-room never seemed to have in it any of the dust which the friction of life with inanimate matter produces. She swept, and there seemed to be no dirt to go before the broom; she cleaned, and one could see no difference. She was like an artist so perfect that he has apparently no art. To-day she got out a mixing bowl and a board, and rolled some pies, and there was no more flour upon her than upon her daughter who was doing finer work. Nanny was to be married in the fall, and she was sewing on some white cambric and embroidery. She sewed industriously while her mother cooked, her soft milk-white hands and wrists showed whiter than her delicate work.

"We must have the stove moved out in the shed before long," said Mrs. Penn. "Talk about not havin' things, it's been a real blessin' to be able to put a stove up in that shed in hot weather. Father did one good thing when he fixed that stove-pipe out there."

Sarah Penn's face as she rolled pies had that expression of meek vigor which might have characterized one of the New Testament saints. She was making mince-pies. Her husband, Adoniram Penn, liked them better than any other kind. She baked twice a week. Adoniram often liked a piece of pie between meals. She hurried this morning. It had been later than usual when she began, and she wanted to have a pie baked for dinner. However deep a resentment she might be forced to hold against her husband, she would never fail in sedulous attention to his wants.

Nobility of character manifests itself at loop-holes when it is not provided with large doors. Sarah Penn's showed itself to-day in flaky dishes of pastry. So she made the pies faithfully, while across the table she could see, when she glanced up from her work, the sight that rankled in her patient and steadfast soul—the digging of the cellar of the new barn in the place where Adoniram forty years ago had promised her their new house should stand.

The pies were done for dinner. Adoniram and Sammy were home a few minutes after twelve o'clock. The dinner was eaten with serious haste. There was never much conversation at the table in the Penn family. Adoniram asked a blessing, and they ate promptly, then rose up and went about their work.

Sammy went back to school, taking soft sly lopes out of the yard like a rabbit. He wanted a game of marbles before school, and feared his father would give him some chores to do. Adoniram hastened to the door and called after him, but he was out of sight.

"I don't see what you let him go for, mother," said he. "I wanted him to help me unload that wood."

Adoniram went to work out in the yard unloading wood from the wagon. Sarah put away the dinner dishes, while Nanny took down her curl-papers and changed her dress. She was going down to the store to buy some more embroidery and thread.

When Nanny was gone, Mrs. Penn went to the door. "Father!" she called.

"Well, what is it!"

"I want to see you jest a minute, father."

"I can't leave this wood nohow. I've got to git it unloaded an' go for a load of gravel afore two o'clock. Sammy had ought to helped me. You hadn't ought to let him go to school so early."

"I want to see you jest a minute."

"I tell ye I can't, nohow, mother."

"Father, you come here." Sarah Penn stood in the door like a queen; she held her head as if it bore a crown; there was that patience which makes authority royal in her voice. Adoniram went.

Mrs. Penn led the way into the kitchen, and pointed to a chair. "Sit down, father," said she; "I've got somethin' I want to say to you."

He sat down heavily; his face was quite stolid, but he looked at her with restive eyes. "Well, what is it, mother?"

"I want to know what you're buildin' that new barn for, father?"

"I ain't got nothin' to say about it."

"It can't be you think you need another barn?"

"I tell ye I ain't got nothin' to say about it, mother; an' I ain't goin' to say nothin'."

"Be you goin' to buy more cows?"

Adoniram did not reply; he shut his mouth tight.

"I know you be, as well as I want to. Now, father, look here"—Sarah Penn had not sat down; she stood before her husband in the humble fashion of a Scripture woman—"I'm goin' to talk real plain to you; I never have sence I married you, but I'm goin' to now. I ain't never complained, an' I ain't goin' to complain now, but I'm goin' to talk plain. You see this room here, father; you look at it well. You see there ain't no carpet on the floor, an' you see the paper is all dirty, an' droppin' off the walls. We ain't had no new paper on it for ten year, an' then I put it on myself, an' it didn't cost but ninepence a roll. You see this room, father; it's all the one I've had to work in an' eat in an' sit in sence we was married. There ain't another woman in the whole town whose husband ain't got half the means you have but what's got better. It's all the room Nanny's got to have her company in; an' there ain't one of her mates but what's got better, an' their fathers not so able as hers is. It's all the room she'll have to be married in. What would you have thought, father, if we had had our weddin' in a room no better than this? I was married in my mother's parlor, with a carpet on the floor, an' stuffed furniture, an' a mahogany card-table. An' this is all the room my daughter will have to be married in. Look here, father!"

Sarah Penn went across the room as though it were a tragic stage. She flung open a door and disclosed a tiny bedroom, only large enough for a bed and bureau, with a path between. "There, father," said she—"there's all the room I've had to sleep in forty year. All my children were born there—the two that died, an' the two that's livin'. I was sick with a fever there."

She stepped to another door and opened it. It led into the small, ill-lighted pantry. "Here," said she, "is all the buttery I've got—every place I've got for my dishes, to set away my victuals in, an' to keep my milk-

266

pans in. Father, I've been takin' care of the milk of six cows in this place, an' now you're goin' to build a new barn, an' keep more cows, an' give me more to do in it."

She threw open another door. A narrow crooked flight of stairs wound upward from it. "There, father," said she, "I want you to look at the stairs that go up to them two unfinished chambers that are all the places our son an' daughter have had to sleep in all their lives. There ain't a prettier girl in town nor a more lady-like one than Nanny, an' that's the place she has to sleep in. It ain't so good as your horse's stall; it ain't so warm an' tight."

Sarah Penn went back and stood before her husband. "Now, father," said she, "I want to know if you think you're doin' right an' accordin' to what you profess. Here, when we was married, forty year ago, you promised me faithful that we should have a new house built in that lot over in the field before the year was out. You said you had money enough, an' you wouldn't ask me to live in no such place as this. It is forty year now, an' you've been makin' more money, an' I've been savin' of it for you ever since, an' you ain't built no house yet. You've built sheds an' cowhouses an' one new barn, an' now you're goin' to build another. Father, I want to know if you think it's right. You're lodgin' your dumb beasts better than you are your own flesh an' blood. I want to know if you think it's right."

"I ain't got nothin' to say."

"You can't say nothin' without ownin' it ain't right, father. An' there's another thing—I ain't complained; I've got along forty year, an' I s'pose I should forty more, if it wa'n't for that—if we don't have another house. Nanny she can't live with us after she's married. She'll have to go somewheres else to live away from us, an' it don't seem as if I could have it so, noways, father. She wa'n't ever strong. She's got considerable color, but there wa'n't never any backbone to her. I've always took the heft of everything off her, an' she ain't fit to keep house an' do everything herself. She'll be all worn out inside of a year. Think of her doin' all the washin' an' ironin' an' bakin' with them soft white hands an' arms, an' sweepin'! I can't have it so, noways, father."

Mrs. Penn's face was burning; her mild eyes gleamed. She had pleaded her little cause like a Webster; she had ranged from severity to pathos; but her opponent employed that obstinate silence which makes eloquence futile with mocking echoes. Adoniram rose clumsily.

"Father, ain't you got nothin' to say?" said Mrs. Penn.

"I've got to go off after that load of gravel. I can't stan' here talkin' all day."

"Father, won't you think it over, an' have a house built there instead of a barn?"

"I ain't got nothin' to say."

Adoniram shuffled out. Mrs. Penn went into her bed-room. When she came out, her eyes were red. She had a roll of unbleached cotton cloth. She spread it out on the kitchen table, and began cutting out some shirts for her husband. The men over in the field had a team to help them this afternoon; she could hear their halloos. She had a scanty pattern for the shirts; she had to plan and piece the sleeves.

Nanny came home with her embroidery, and sat down with her needle-work. She had taken down her curl-papers, and there was a soft roll of fair hair like an aureole over her forehead; her face was as delicately fine and clear as porcelain. Suddenly she looked up, and the tender red flamed all over her face and neck. "Mother," said she.

"What say?"

"I've been thinking—I don't see how we're goin' to have any—wedding in this room. I'd be ashamed to have his folks come if we didn't have anybody else."

"Mebbe we can have some new paper before then; I can put it on. I guess you won't have no call to be ashamed of your belongin's."

"We might have the wedding in the new barn," said Nanny, with gentle pettishness. "Why, mother, what makes you look so?"

Mrs. Penn had started, and was staring at her with a curious expression. She turned again to her work, and spread out a pattern carefully on the cloth. "Nothin'," said she.

Presently Adoniram clattered out of the yard in his two-wheeled dump cart, standing as proudly upright as a Roman charioteer. Mrs. Penn opened the door and stood there a minute looking out; the halloos of the men sounded louder.

It seemed to her all through the spring months that she heard nothing but the halloos and the noises of saws and hammers. The new barn grew fast. It was a fine edifice for this little village. Men came on pleasant Sundays, in their meeting suits and clean shirt bosoms, and stood around it admiringly. Mrs. Penn did not speak of it, and Adoniram did not mention it to her, although sometimes, upon a return from inspecting it, he bore himself with injured dignity.

"It's a strange thing how your mother feels about the new barn," he said, confidentially, to Sammy one day.

Sammy only grunted after an odd fashion for a boy; he had learned it from his father.

The barn was all completed ready for use by the third week in July. Adoniram had planned to move his stock in on Wednesday; on Tuesday he received a letter, which changed his plans. He came in with it early in the morning. "Sammy's been to the post-office," said he, "an' I've got a letter from Hiram." Hiram was Mrs. Penn's brother, who lived in Vermont.

"Well," said Mrs. Penn, "what does he say about the folks?"

"I guess they're all right. He says he thinks if I come up country right off there's a chance to buy jest the kind of a horse I want." He stared reflectively out of the window at the new barn.

Mrs. Penn was making pies. She went on clapping the rolling-pin into the crust, although she was very pale, and her heart beat loudly.

"I dun' know but what I'd better go," said Adoniram. "I hate to go off jest now, right in the midst of hayin', but the ten-acre lot's cut, an' I guess Rufus an' the others can git along without me three or four days. I can't get a horse round here to suit me, nohow, an' I've got to have another for all that wood-haulin' in the fall. I told Hiram to watch out, an' if he got wind of a good horse to let me know. I guess I'd better go."

"I'll get out your clean shirt an' collar," said Mrs. Penn calmly.

She laid out Adoniram's Sunday suit and his clean clothes on the bed in the little bedroom. She got his shaving-water and razor ready. At last she buttoned on his collar and fastened his black cravat.

Adoniram never wore his collar and cravat except on extra occasions. He held his head high, with a rasped dignity. When he was all ready, with his coat and hat brushed, and a lunch of pie and cheese in a paper bag, he hesitated on the threshold of the door. He looked at his wife, and his manner was defiantly apologetic. "*If* them cows come today, Sammy can drive 'em into the new barn," said he; "an' when they bring the hay up, they can pitch it in there."

"Well," replied Mrs. Penn.

Adoniram set his shaven face ahead and started. When he had cleared the door-step, he turned and looked back with a kind of nervous solemnity. "I shall be back by Saturday if nothin' happens," said he.

"Do be careful, father," returned his wife.

She stood in the door with Nanny at her elbow and watched him out of sight. Her eyes had a strange, doubtful expression in them; her peaceful forehead was contracted. She went in, and about her baking again. Nanny sat sewing. Her wedding-day was drawing nearer, and she was getting pale and thin with her steady sewing. Her mother kept glancing at her.

"Have you got that pain in your side this mornin'?" she asked.

"A little."

Mrs. Penn's face, as she worked, changed, her perplexed forehead smoothed, her eyes were steady, her lips firmly set. She formed a maxim for herself, although incoherently with her unlettered thoughts. "Unsolicited opportunities are the guideposts of the Lord to the new roads of life," she repeated in effect, and she made up her mind to her course of action.

"S'posin' I *had* wrote to Hiram," she muttered once, when she was in the pantry—"s'posin' I had wrote, an' father's goin' wa'n't none of my doin'. It looks like a providence." Her voice rang out quite loud at the last.

"What you talkin' about, mother?" called Nanny.

"Nothin'."

Mrs. Penn hurried her baking; at eleven o'clock it was all done. The load of hay from the west field came slowly down the cart track, and drew up at the new barn. Mrs. Penn ran out. "Stop!" she screamed— "stop!"

The men stopped and looked; Sammy upreared from the top of the load, and stared at his mother.

"Stop!" she cried out again. "Don't you put the hay in that barn; put it in the old one."

"Why, he said to put it in here," returned one of the haymakers, wonderingly. He was a young man, a neighbor's son, whom Adoniram hired by the year to help on the farm.

"Don't you put the hay in the new barn; there's room enough in the old, ain't there?" said Mrs. Penn.

"Room enough," returned the hired man, in his thick, rustic tones. "Didn't need the new barn, nohow, far as room's concerned. Well, I s'pose he changed his mind." He took hold of the horses' bridles.

Mrs. Penn went back to the house. Soon the kitchen windows were darkened, and a fragrance like warm honey came into the room.

Nanny laid down her work. "I thought father wanted them to put the hay into the new barn?" she said, wonderingly.

"It's all right," replied her mother.

Sammy slid down from the load of hay, and came in to see if dinner was ready.

"I ain't goin' to get a regular dinner to-day, as long as father's gone," said his mother. "I've let the fire go out. You can have some bread an' milk an' pie. I thought we could get along." She set out some bowls of milk, some bread, and a pie on the kitchen table. "You'd better eat your dinner now," said she. "You might jest as well get through with it. I want you to help me afterward."

Nanny and Sammy stared at each other. There was something strange in their mother's manner. Mrs. Penn did not eat anything herself. She went into the pantry, and they heard her moving dishes while they ate. Presently she came out with a pile of plates. She got the clothes-basket out of the shed, and packed them in it. Nanny and Sammy watched. She brought out cups and saucers, and put them in with the plates.

"What you goin' to do, mother?" inquired Nanny, in a timid voice. A sense of something unusual made her tremble, as if it were a ghost. Sammy rolled his eyes over his pie.

"You'll see what I'm goin' to do," replied Mrs. Penn. "If you're through, Nanny, I want you to go up-stairs an' pack up your things; an' I want you, Sammy, to help me take down the bed in the bedroom."

"Oh, mother, what for?" gasped Nanny.

"You'll see."

During the next few hours a feat was performed by this simple, pious New England mother which was equal in its way to Wolfe's storming of the Heights of Abraham. It took no more genius and audacity of bravery for Wolfe to cheer his wondering soldiers up those steep precipices, under the sleeping eyes of the enemy, than for Sarah Penn, at the head of her children, to move all their little household goods into the new barn while her husband was away.

Nanny and Sammy followed their mother's instructions without a murmur; indeed, they were overawed. There is a certain uncanny and superhuman quality about all such purely original undertakings as their mother's was to them. Nanny went back and forth with her light loads, and Sammy tugged with sober energy.

At five o'clock in the afternoon, the little house in which the Penns had lived for forty years had emptied itself into the new barn.

Every builder builds somewhat for unknown purposes, and is in a measure a prophet. The architect of Adoniram Penn's barn, while he designed it for the comfort of four-footed animals, had planned better than he knew for the comfort of humans. Sarah Penn saw at a glance its possibilities. Those great box-stalls, with quilts hung before them, would make better bed-rooms than the one she had occupied for forty years, and there was a tight carriage-room. The harness-room, with its chimney and shelves, would make a kitchen of her dreams. The great middle space would make a parlor, by-and-by, fit for a palace. Up-stairs there was as much room as down. With partitions and windows, what a house would there be! Sarah looked at the row of stanchions before the alloted space for cows, and reflected that she would have her front entry there.

At six o'clock the stove was up in the harness-room, the kettle was boiling, and the table set for tea. It looked almost as homelike as the abandoned house across the yard had ever done. The young hired man milked, and Sarah directed him calmly to bring the milk to the new barn. He came gaping, dropping little blots of foam from the brimming pails on the grass. Before the next morning he had spread the story of Adoniram Penn's wife moving into the new barn all over the little village. Men assembled in the store and talked it over, women with shawls over their heads scuttled into each other's houses before their work was done. Any deviation from the ordinary course of life in this quiet town was enough to stop all progress in it. Everybody paused to look at the staid, independent figure on the side track. There was a difference of opinion with regard to her. Some held her to be insane; some, of a lawless and rebellious spirit.

Friday the minister went to see her. It was in the forenoon, and she was at the barn door shelling peas for dinner. She looked up and returned his salutation with dignity, then she went on with her work. She did not invite him in. The saintly expression of her face remained fixed, but there was an angry flush over it.

The minister stood awkwardly before her, and talked. She handled the peas as if they were bullets. At last she looked up, and her eyes showed the spirit that her meek front had covered for a lifetime.

"There ain't no use talkin', Mr. Hersey," said she. "I've thought it all over an' over, an' I believe I'm doin' what's right. I've made it the subject of prayer, an' it's betwixt me an' the Lord an' Adoniram. There ain't no call for nobody else to worry about it."

"Well, of course, if you have brought it to the Lord in prayer, and feel satisfied that you are doing right, Mrs. Penn," said the minister, helplessly. His thin gray-bearded face was pathetic. He was a sickly man; his youthful confidence had cooled; he had to scourge himself up to some of his pastoral duties as relentlessly as a Catholic ascetic, and then he was prostrated by the smart.

"I think it's right jest as much as I think it was right for our forefathers to come over from the old country 'cause they didn't have what belonged to 'em," said Mrs. Penn. She arose. The barn threshold might have been Plymouth Rock from her bearing. "I don't doubt you mean well, Mr. Hersey," said she, "but there are things people hadn't ought to interfere with. I've been a member of the church for over forty year. I've got my own mind an' my own feet, an' I'm goin' to think my own thoughts an' go my own ways, an' nobody but the Lord is goin' to dictate to me unless I've a mind to have him. Won't you come in an' set down? How is Mis' Hersey?"

"She is well, I thank you," replied the minister. He added some more perplexed apologetic remarks; then he retreated.

He could expound the intricacies of every character study in the Scriptures, he was competent to grasp the Pilgrim Fathers and all historical innovators, but Sarah Penn was beyond him. He could deal with primal cases, but parallel ones worsted him. But, after all, although it was aside from his province, he wondered more how Adoniram Penn would deal with his wife than how the Lord would. Everybody shared the wonder. When Adoniram's four new cows arrived, Sarah ordered three to be put in the old barn, the other in the house shed where the cooking-stove had stood. That added to the excitement. It was whispered that all four cows were domiciled in the house.

Towards sunset on Saturday, when Adoniram was expected home, there was a knot of men in the road near the new barn. The hired man had milked, but he still hung around the premises. Sarah Penn had supper all ready. There were brown-bread and baked beans and a custard pie; it was the supper that Adoniram loved on a Saturday night. She had on a clean calico, and she bore herself imperturbably. Nanny and Sammy kept close at her heels. Their eyes were large, and Nanny was full of nervous tremors. Still there was to them more pleasant excitement than anything else. An inborn confidence in their mother over their father asserted itself.

Sammy looked out of the harness-room window. "There he is," he announced, in an awed whisper. He and Nanny peeped around the casing. Mrs. Penn kept on about her work. The children watched Adoniram leave the new horse standing in the drive while he went to the house door. It was fastened. Then he went around to the shed. That door was seldom locked, even when the family was away. The thought how her father would be confronted by the cow flashed upon Nanny. There was a hysterical sob in her throat. Adoniram emerged from the shed and stood looking about in a dazed fashion. His lips moved; he was saying something, but they could not hear what it was. The hired man was peeping around a corner of the old barn, but nobody saw him.

Adoniram took the new horse by the bridle and led him across the yard to the new barn. Nanny and Sammy slunk close to their mother. The barn doors rolled back, and there stood Adoniram, with the long wild face of the great Canadian farm horse looking over his shoulder.

Nanny kept behind her mother, but Sammy stepped suddenly forward, and stood in front of her.

Adoniram stared at the group. "What on airth you all down here for?" said he. "What's the matter over to the house?"

"We've come here to live, father," said Sammy. His shrill voice quavered out bravely.

"What"—Adoniram sniffed—"what is it smells like cookin'?" said he. He stepped forward and looked in the open door of the harness-room. Then he turned to his wife. His old bristling face was pale and frightened. "What on airth does this mean, mother?" he gasped.

"You come in here, father," said Sarah. She led the way into the harness-room and shut the door. "Now, father," said she, "you needn't be scared. I ain't crazy. There ain't nothin' to be upset over. But we've come here to live, an' we're goin' to live here. We've got jest as good a right here as new horses an' cows. The house wa'n't fit for us to live in any longer, an' I made up my mind I wa'n't goin' to stay there. I've done my duty by you forty year, an' I'm goin' to do it now; but I'm goin' to live here. You've got to put in some windows and partitions; an' you'll have to buy some furniture."

"Why, mother!" the old man gasped.

"You'd better take your coat off an' get washed—there's the washbasin—an' then we'll have supper."

"Why, mother!"

Sammy went past the window, leading the new horse to the old barn. The old man saw him, and shook his head speechlessly. He tried to take off his coat, but his arms seemed to lack the power. His wife helped him. She poured some water into the tin basin, and put in a piece of soap. She got the comb and brush, and smoothed his thin gray hair after he had washed. Then she put the beans, hot bread, and tea on the table. Sammy came in, and the family drew up. Adoniram sat looking dazedly at his plate, and they waited.

"Ain't you goin' to ask a blessin', father?" said Sarah.

And the old man bent his head and mumbled.

All through the meal he stopped eating at intervals, and stared furtively at his wife; but he ate well. The home food tasted good to him, and his old frame was too sturdily healthy to be affected by his mind. But after supper he went out, and sat down on the step of the smaller door at the right of the barn, through which he had meant his Jerseys to pass in stately file, but which Sarah designed for her front house door, and he leaned his head on his hands.

After the supper dishes were cleared away and the milk-pans washed, Sarah went out to him. The twilight was deepening. There was a clear green glow in the sky. Before them stretched the smooth level of field; in the distance was a cluster of haystacks like the huts of a village; the air was very cool and calm and sweet. The landscape might have been an ideal one of peace.

Sarah bent over and touched her husband on one of his thin, sinewy shoulders. "Father!"

The old man's shoulders heaved: he was weeping.

"Why, don't do so, father," said Sarah.

"I'll—put up the—partitions, an'—everything you—want, mother."

Sarah put her apron up to her face; she was overcome by her own triumph.

Adoniram was like a fortress whose walls had no active resistance, and went down the instant the right besieging tools were used. "Why, mother," he said, hoarsely, "I hadn't no idee you was so set on't as all this comes to."

# My Lady of the Indian Purdah

## ELIZABETH COOPER

*The following story is of a great love, of a woman's sacrifice because of that love, of a nation's gain because of that sacrifice. The romantic voice of India speaks in these pages. Elizabeth Cooper's beautiful romance is somewhat reminiscent of Donn Byrne's Messer Marco Polo.*

THE GREAT CANNON from the palace wall boomed a message so that all the world might know the tidings.

The men, sitting before their doorways, watching their naked babies playing in the sands, stopped their talk to listen. The women, dressed in their gay reds and yellows, their bare brown arms with bracelets as their only covering, stopped in the act of lifting water-jar to hip or shoulder. Their kohl-blackened eyes turned towards the palace from which came the sound that caused all within the royal city to stop their toil and listen.

*One*—they counted. Then, *two*—loudly the cannon spoke its message. After a moment, *three*—they murmured.

Every one was silent, waiting for the next sound, but nothing came from the palace walls, and the little cloud of smoke floated away in the evening air.

The men again placed pipes to lips. "Only a girl," they said. The women picked up water-jars and drew together in little groups. "Only a woman-child," they whispered, and in low voices discussed the birth of the first-born of their Overlord.

# II

In the women's quarters of the palace which overlooked the city, there brooded an air of hushed expectancy. Whether the women were in their own apartments or in the shaded archways of the courtyards, or idling in the baths or gardens, when the first gun boomed forth, they stopped their chatter and not a sound was there to break the silence. Like the women at the well they counted—*one*—then *two*—then *three*.

A rustle ran through all the palace. "A woman-child," they also whispered, then settled back to their tasks, some to their broidering, others to the weaving of the marigolds with which they decked their gods, others to their gossip or to the decoration of their pretty faces.

The Queen had given birth to a woman-child. It was not worth their envy.

# III

Within the room set aside for the bringing of new life into the palace world, my Princess lay surrounded by her women, her great black, wondering eyes wide with pain, her tiny fingers feebly fluttering in my hands. Her eyes looked longingly towards the door, and I, who knew her every thought, bent to her lovingly. All within the room knew that the hours were numbered for the little Queen who lay there and no wish must be denied her.

"Nanda!" she whispered. "Nanda!"

I turned to a waiting-woman and, after a moment, the Maharajah came to the archway. The fluttering hands left mine and reached towards the boy who swiftly knelt before her. He caught the hands in his and held them close as he looked into the eyes that his keen eyes of love could see would soon be closed to him. A smile came to the lips of the girl-wife, and she released one hand and groped for his face.

"Nanda," she whispered, "where art thou? It is day, yet I cannot see thee clearly."

He touched the tiny fingers with his lips and after a moment she said:

"Put thy hand upon my head, my lord; it gives me rest."

"Natara, Natara!" the Rajah cried. "Thou art my breath, my life, my water in the sand! Thou must not leave me!"

Her voice was like a softened sob, yet a smile was in her eyes as she said:

"My Nanda, if I had passed the Land of Shadows, thy voice would call me back."

She lay so still that only the faint flutterings of her breath told that she yet lived. Again she opened wide her midnight eyes and said:

"My loved one, do not sorrow. I have had my great desire. The gods have granted me the thing for which I longed, and I have lived. Thy voice has comforted me, thine arms have been my joy, and when dreams have come I turned and touched thy hand and stilled my fright. And now—now—I have given thee a child."

The Rajah brushed the damp curls from off her forehead and waited for the faltering voice to speak again. At last she said, so softly he could scarcely hear her:

"Dear Lord, I will take my rest in safety. I shall wait for thee, because I am my beloved's through all eternity."

She was quiet for a moment and then she tried to smile.

"Perhaps the gods take me to themselves for the sin of worshiping thee instead of them. Thy voice of love was sweeter in my ears than prayers."

The Rajah pressed her to him in an agony of sorrow. She pushed the turban from his forehead so that she could look more clearly into his eyes, and said:

"Nanda," and in her eyes was the look of other worlds, "Nanda, thou shalt for a time become heavy with sorrow, but afterwards thou wilt live in the memory of our love and that memory will become sweeter with the passing years."

"My beloved," the Rajah whispered, "I will not be far from thy door, my head will forever rest upon thy threshold."

She raised her heavy, saddened eyes.

"I would see our child, my lord, I would see it in thy arms."

The child was brought and laid within the Rajah's arms. The mother touched the tiny face with finger-tips.

"Take my baby, my Natara," she said. "Another Natara for thee to love and guard. She is my gift of love to thee."

He answered:

"She will be the breath of my breath, the heart of my heart. Thou needst not fear for her."

The mother was quiet, caressing the tiny face, fondling the dark head that nestled within the curves of the father's arms. All the magic mystery of motherhood was in the dark eyes.

"She is but a woman-child, a flower drifting on the flood of the river."

Then she looked into the Rajah's eyes, and her own were eager, pleading.

"Nanda," she said, "our child of love is born a Princess, to be used as a pawn in the game of life. Promise me," and she turned to me, "promise me, you two who love me, promise me she will have love. Not power, nor rank, nor wealth, but let her know the love that we have known—for love is life in all its fulness. It will open for her the doors of everlasting happiness. Without it she will drink deep of the bowl of sorrow. O Nanda,—Amina,—promise. Bring my baby love and love alone."

The Rajah bent towards the Queen and said with voice that trembled in its earnestness:

"My Heart of Rose, I promise thee. Love is her birthright, and she shall have it." He straightened his bent form and stood upright. "I am the King, Natara. Nanda, the King, and I promise thee."

She looked for a long moment into his eyes, and then she turned to me.

"Take my baby, Amina. Thou hast passed all thy life within a palace, thou understandest. Guard her—keep her—" Then the soft voice faltered and only the great black eyes spoke to me.

I bent close to her so that she alone could hear.

"She shall be closer to me than the vein within my neck, she will be my child, mine own. No harm shall come to her."

A smile of contentment came to the young Queen's face. She lay quietly for a moment, then she raised her eyes, that looked like some blurred tapestry, to those of the Rajah, who was kneeling by her side, and whispered:

"Touch thy lips unto mine eyes, my lord, and bring me sleep."

Soon she slept as a tired child sleeps when one sways the cradle.

# IV

Thus did my Princess come to me. It was the dawning of my real day when I held the baby within my arms. A breath of motherhood came to me and changed my world.

# V

At first, when the sun was taken from the Rajah's sky, he was inconsolable. He was like a land whose harvest had been reaped. With night in his soul, he shut the gates of the world and lived alone with his sorrow. But the fetters of youth are strong, and the boy became a man. Love does not die when the loved one dies; it simply finds a new mode of expression, and Nanda covered the world with the shadow of his love. He devoted himself to the affairs of his kingdom until he was known throughout all India as "Nanda the Just, the Kind," and the Prince who loved his people. All heads bowed to him in respect and love.

The red rose of passion bloomed no more for him. He did not choose another Queen. He sent for the son of his brother and made him heir to the throne, as a woman could not reign within the kingdom.

Although Natara could never be the queen of his kingdom, she was queen of the Rajah's heart. Her mother's apartments were given her. Guards were placed at the archways and ever bowing women, whose hands were joined in perpetual salute, served her with noiseless steps. She held her own small court, where only children of noble blood were bidden to entertain the Princess.

It was the Rajah's pleasure to see her dressed in the most beautiful fabrics that came from the Imperial looms. Her saris were of the rarest silks, with embroideries of gold and silver. She was decked with pearls and gems of untold value. All India was searched for jewels with which to enhance her beauty. The Rajah would have taken the half moon's silver for a covering for her feet if that were possible.

As she grew older, poets sang of the ivory of her face with its touch of rose at cheek and lip. She was likened to the lily, and her grace to the fresh reed bending over the rivulet. In their songs they said that seeing her was like breathing the warm, sweet breath of spring, and that her passionate, dreaming, wistful eyes were dark and deep as mysterious skies. If court poets could be believed, all the beauty of Indian womanhood was to be found within one small body. And it was true. My Princess had a beauty that caught your breath when she passed by.

Yet with all the flattery, Natara remained as simple as a child, loving the beautiful silks and satins, taking joy in the great strings of pearls and emeralds and rubies that were placed before her; but it was the joy of a child with a new toy. They were all a part of her beautiful life, the same as the birds and the flowers, the lotus-ponds and the lace-like screens that shut her from the world outside. She did not know that women sold their souls for the baubles with which she played so carelessly.

# VI

Natara spent happy years, passing from childhood to young womanhood by the side of her father. Nothing that affected her or that he thought could give her pleasure was too slight for his Royal notice. He would leave his Hall of Audience to go to her, to play with her, to walk with her in the gardens or to tell her stories in the moonlight.

Her days were uneventful, but I tried to fill them with little duties that made them pass quickly. In the morning we rose, and after the ceremonial cleansing we did pooja before the household altar. Then, after the morning meal, we joined the women in the courtyards or in some chosen apartment, where we looked at silks or jewels or perfumes sent behind the screens by the merchants of the city. These were brought to us by clever women, who not only sold their silks and perfumes, but gave as added gifts a whole shopful of gossip. Through them we learned of the events occurring in the city, the marriages and births, the quarrels and intrigues of the women in other palaces. It was all brought to us and emptied into our laps, and the idling women listened eagerly to the news of the world outside our walls.

But not alone through these clever gossip-mongers were we informed of the actions of our friends, as relatives or acquaintances were constantly visiting the women of the palace and giving them the scandals of the day. Although there was no Queen nor reigning favorite, the palace was filled with women who had come to live under the protection of the great King. There were relations to the utmost degree, aunts, cousins and cousins' cousins, many of them widows, who, on their bereavement, had returned to the home roof-tree, instead of remaining with the families of their late husbands. All of these noble women had hosts of servants and poor relations; consequently the purdah hummed like a hive of busy bees upon a sunny day.

In the afternoons Natara passed long hours idling in the perfumed waters of the bath, where the young girls of the Court had battles royal with roses as their weapons, or where they lay on marble couches and allowed their slaves to make their fair skins still fairer with scented oils and powders.

At times they dressed in wondrous costumes and enacted the old-time plays, or listened to the musicians or watched the dancers that were kept for the amusement of the women. In the evenings from behind the marble screens they listened to the singers or watched the jugglers, or heard the long discourses of the pundits who came from far and near to entertain the Rajah.

The Rajah, as the Princess grew older, believed that Saraswati, the Goddess of Knowledge, should be enthroned within our rooms. Gurus were brought from the sacred college and from them Natara learned Sanscrit, the language used by many who came to the palace and which she must master if she would profit by their discourses. French and English were added to her studies, in order, as the Rajah said, that she might understand the Western mind through what they had given the world in literature. The great King and the Princess read together or listened to the court reader, who was chosen for his musical voice, and she learned that books can charm into pure gold the leaden hours.

The Rajah believed it the privilege of the great to foster piety and learning; consequently he kept a staff of pundits whose lives were made free from anxiety so that they might heap up knowledge and pore over ancient texts. Many students dwelt in the palace, and any one, whatever his belief, who was famous for his learning, was invited to rest within the walls.

Many a bare-footed preacher, wearing the yellow robe of Buddha and appealing for alms in his sacred name, was given lodging for a few days because of some chance remark that he let fall before listening ears, with the hope that he might have some new truth or the old truth in a new garment, to which the King would be pleased to listen.

Wandering monks from all castes and all creeds were lodged within the guest rooms. The King would ask these holy men, "What have you seen elsewhere?" and he listened attentively to the tales of their journeys as they wandered from State to State. He ended by saying, "What have you noted here?" and often some innovation or search was started that came from the suggestion of a world-weary old man, that unkind tongues would call a traveling beggar.

Teachers came from the far north, from the college by the Sacred River to teach Natara the eternal truths of the Vedas, the folk-lore of the Puranas, and the legends contained within the Upanishads. She learned the doctrine of Maya, the illusion of all things. A blind Moslem came to chant the Koran in order that she could understand the meaning of the call of the Muezzin, "There is no God but God, and Mohammed is His Prophet."

Against my wishes knowledge of the religion of the Western world was brought to her. With it I had no quarrel except that I could not feel that God had favored the Western race by sending them the *only* Prophet. He may have been a great Prophet, but I cannot admit that he stands alone in the history of the world as the only messenger of God. We have seen two, Rama and Krishna. They have come back to lay hold on the hearts of men, for the protection of the good, for the destruction of the evil, and they will return again and again as the world has need of them.

But I respect the Western religion. A person has a right to hold his own belief if he does not try to force it upon another. I may admire the medicine that cures another of his ills, but I should not be forced to drink of it because it has been of benefit to him.

There are as many Gods as worshipers. Each of us has his own God, but it is the one God in the many forms we have created, one Spirit manifesting itself in many forms. Names of God are but names, after all. Why should not God have an infinity of titles? It does not make him less the one God. I may call my God Shiva and single out certain aspects of importance to me. You may call him Vishnu and emphasize other aspects, but it is really the same God that we worship, who possesses all the virtues that we adore.

Religion is a simple thing, after all. It is the wise men, the priests, who hurt religion, which is only an instinct of the heart to worship something stronger than itself. These wise men try to read something into it which, instead of simplifying it, makes it more elaborate and difficult to understand.

Let the world have its temples, its mosques, its churches. When one leaves their doors, one takes something from the holy place one has not brought to it. Something is found there, comfort, hope, or at least a sense of duty done or a God pleased. The true religion lies in service, not in floating incense nor in wreathing the God with flowers nor the sprinkling of Ganges water on a Sacred Bull. A glass of cold water is just as sweet whether given in the name of Vishnu or the Christ upon the Cross, if given with the hand of love.

But I have wandered far from the women's courtyard and the life of my young Princess. I will return to it.

All of her hours were not given to study nor to the poring over of old manuscripts. The thing she loved best, and which would cause all of the women to come hurrying from their apartments, was the wandering poet-singer who was asked to chant his songs.

In the courtyard of the King's apartments, the marble floors would be covered with rare rugs; soft cushions and low divans would be placed near tables loaded with fruits and wines; perfumed smoke would rise from hidden braziers, and quiet servants would pass among the guests to light a pipe or fill a glass.

The women in the shadows behind the purdah would kneel in the silence and hear words falling like water, drop by drop, as the singer chanted the Mahabharata, where mighty warriors, beautiful women and great saints moved to and fro across the scene in glittering confusion.

These tales were never tiresome. We loved the heroes and the gods, and from the first ringing words of the *Gita,* "Yield not to unmanliness, O Son of Pritha. Ill doth it become thee. Shake off this weakness and arise, O Terror of Foes," until Krishna bursts forth on the sight of the worshipers as the Universal Form, in whom all that exists is One—we sat entranced.

We heard often the story of Rama and Sita, or they chanted the beautiful poems of Kalidasa, those mystical songs whose rhythm moves the world.

Each day had its record of pleasure, of pain and of work done.

So passed the girlhood of my Natara.

# VII

One day when Natara was nearing womanhood, her father came to our apartment, and, after watching Natara for a time, he turned to me and said:

"Amina, she is now nearly a woman grown."

He called Natara to him and, turning back her head with his hand, he looked long into her eyes.

"Little one, thou art more and more like thy mother. Thine eyes—they draw the heart from out my body."

He was silent for a time, then rising he took her by the hand and said: "Come with me, Natara; I have a gift for thee."

Motioning for me to follow, he led us through the Audience Hall, then through his own apartment to a garden. In the wall of the garden was a small door of sandalwood inlaid with ivory. My heart stood still as I saw the Rajah place a key within the lock. I knew that that door had been closed, even to me who loved her, since the passing of the Queen.

As the door slowly swung open, he stepped back for us to enter. Natara stopped within the gateway and gave a cry of delight, then held out her hands to the vision of beauty before her. Even I, who knew that dream garden, could not repress a cry as I saw it again in all its magic loveliness.

"Father, Father, what is it?" Natara half whispered, as if the beauty before her was an unsubstantial dream that might be shattered if she spoke too loudly.

The Rajah was silent, self-absorbed, and did not answer. His face was white, for a moment his lips quivered, then he brushed his hands across his eyes, as if to brush away some vision unseen by us.

"It was our Palace of Love, our beautiful Garden of Dreams."

# VIII

How can I describe that garden made by a great King who had all the riches of the world at his command, for the woman he loved!

Leading from the gate was a long, straight piece of water held within low marble walls, in the center of which rose fountains at equal distance, sending their spray high into the air. Along each side of the water was a walk of white marble on which was sculptured flowers, bordered with ebony and silver. On the outside of the walk were beds of brilliant flowers, gorgeous blossoms that glowed in the sunshine. Behind was a row of trees in bloom and over the mass of scarlet and gold, green-turbaned heads of palms could be seen standing like sentinels to guard this beauty.

The avenue ended at a marble palace, placed on the borders of a lake whose waters glistened and glimmered in the dying sunlight. It was like a dainty jewel-box with its fluted columns, its fairy-like balconies, its gleaming terraces and its delicately carved walls of purest white marble. The garden which surrounded it on the three sides was aglow with color, roses and climbing jasmine and red hibiscus among the dark trees. Near the farther wall we saw the dance of the sunbeams upon the white flower of the almond-trees.

We walked slowly down the pathway and at the entrance of the palace were met by the two old servants whom my mistress had brought from her father's home. They knelt and touched our feet with their foreheads, tears streaming down their faces in their joy that the palace of their beloved mistress would echo again to voices other than those of servitors.

The King spoke not a word. We wandered from room to room. It was like a knife-thrust in my heart to see again the place where we had spent so many hours of happiness.

Each room seemed more perfect than the other, if that were possible. They were all doorless and opened one into the other or led to terraces or balconies through carved arched openings.

There was a central courtyard where slender silver rods supported the rose-silk awnings which shaded the flower-filled court. A fountain in the center sent its spray of perfumed water into the air. The panels and the walls opening on this court were transparent, and the marble was so delicately chiseled that they resembled fragile pieces of lace.

Each room was different. In one the walls were of roses, each flower and leaf so perfectly carved, it seemed as if one could pluck them from their setting. In another, rose-colored lotus flowers wandered over the moss-green walls, as if recently brought from the lotus ponds outside. In other rooms the panels were filled with flowers, the leaves and blossoms of which were formed of gold and and lapis lazuli and agate and porphyry, and there were glints of emeralds and rubies, and diamonds were set as dewdrops upon the opening buds. But it was so fine, so rare, so deftly wrought, that the purity of the snow-white rooms was in no wise marred.

Before the bedroom was a screen of chiseled ivory. The Rajah hesitated a moment, then throwing back his head as if he would meet his sorrow bravely, we entered. The room resembled a casket made of lace, and there came from it a perfume like some breath of tenderness, to welcome us. The entire nest was of transparent chiseled marble behind which hung curtains of rose-colored silk, through which gleamed softly shaded lights. It seemed as if there were a presence in the room, as if all of the love of the world had been centered here.

We passed to the dressing-room where the tables were filled with the articles of the toilet, articles of gold inset with precious jewels. The Rajah touched them with caressing fingers, and murmured to himself, "I gave them to her, these things that touched her body. It is the little things we give the loved one, great gifts are for every one."

From the dressing-room we entered the bath, where the water flowed over black marble traced with silver, giving the appearance of ripples in the sunlight.

We passed to the terrace that led to the lakeside. At the bottom of a flight of steps a boat, shaped like a great basket of flowers, was anchored. At the back of the boat was a raised dais on which was a divan piled with cushions of silk and gold embroideries, and over the dais was stretched an awning of red and gold, supported by slender golden rods.

From the terrace a flight of steps led to the roof of the palace. There had been placed rugs and divans, small tables with fruits and sweetened drinks, and at each corner incense arose from silver braziers.

We went to the balustrade facing the garden and looked at the beauty spread before us, at the rose gardens, the lotus pond, the tiny pavilion at the water's edge, at everything that love and fabulous wealth could lavish upon the setting of a loved one.

"Father," said Natara, "why have you never brought me here before?"

He sighed.

"I have never been here myself in all these years. When the roses have gone and the garden has withered, who wishes to return? I felt I could never see it again. A wealth of dreams and hopes and love are all contained within this casket. The very stones speak to me of the past, and the dust is fragrant with its memories."

After a few moments of silence, he said:

"Natara, I give this, my jewel palace, to you, as a hiding place from the wind, a covering from the tempest. You may need it in times to come. It is thine, and perhaps it will live again in thee."

Leaning his arms upon the balustrade, he looked over the garden.

"Love and happiness and joy and laughter were always standing at the gate of this enchanted garden. I was stifled in ceremony and lost in a sea of obligations in that great palace there, but here I left all worldly care behind. When I unlocked the door, with silent steps she came to me. I placed my heart within the dimple of her chin. I kissed her neck where clinking jewels tried to hide its beauty. I forgot the world, we were alone, we two—

"O Natara, all memories, all desires fade away like the flowers from the mogra-tree, but the memory of love remains. My bird of a thousand songs is silent, but her song still sings in my living heart and I listen for its music through the stillness of the night. It sounds—it is there, always, forever, an undercurrent I can always hear, like the muffled voice of the wind among the listening palm-trees."

For a time he did not speak, then he continued in a low voice:

"Still she comes to me. I can hear the chime of her jeweled anklets, feel the soft touch of her rose-leaf hands, and see her loving face which haunts my dreams like rain at night."

He was silent. Then, forming a seat of cushions for Natara upon the rug, he threw himself upon the divan, one arm laid lightly across her shoulder as she sat below him.

"Natara," he said, "I have never spoken to thee of thy mother. I could not speak of her, but now—I will open my heart to thee. I will tell thee of that love which is the seed of all happiness."

Natara caressed his hand softly. It seemed to me that an overwhelming sense of tenderness and union took place between them as they sat there bathed in the mystic radiance of the dying light.

He spoke softly, a far-away look in his brooding eyes.

"I found that perfect face, that perfect love, the fulfilment of the dreams that come to men when they are young. I can see her standing here swaying like a lotus in a soft current. Her voice was as sweet as the song of the bulbul singing upon the mango-tree; her smile was the flower in the fields; her laugh, the rustle of the wind in the palm-trees. When she raised her face it was like a blossoming flower, her lips the opening bud of the first rose. I took the gold from the hills, the pearls from the sea, to cover her, yet she was not to me, because of them, more precious. We do not love a woman because of beauty nor grace, nor because of tinkling anklets. We love her because she sings a song we alone can understand. Our hearts had sung it countless times before, and we had responded as the lute string responds to the hand of the player. When we hear the call we follow it from land to land, from heart to heart and on and on throughout the eternal ages. We had been lovers throughout the past, we will be lovers for all the future. It is written."

Then he spoke more softly, as if speaking to some one we could not see.

"My Natara! As soon as I opened my eyes to thee, I closed them to all the world outside. I swept out the chambers of my heart and made it ready to be the dwelling-place of thee, my beloved."

He was silent, then he said in a tone I had never heard before:

"She was the sun of all my thoughts. When she came into a room she lit up the darkness with her sunshine. Fortune put a goblet of joy into my hands and I drank deep quaffs, and then, as if jealous of my happiness, it was snatched away. It taught me that love is but a messenger sent before the feet of sorrow."

He bent his head and we left him to his memories.

After a time he spoke again:

"Then—then—night came to me shrouded and silent. I lived within the darkened chamber of my soul. I said at first, 'The gods have broken me with their anger and multiplied my sorrows without use.' I said again in my bitterness, 'There will be no music in the world for me. I will grow gray behind some curtained window.'

"I passed my days and nights in dreams, dreams that took me back to the jeweled kingdom of the past. But at last I knew that even though the flower fades and dies, he who has possessed the flower must not mourn for it forever. In my infinite loneliness I learned my lesson. I learned that life is made for service, not for brooding in the silence over memories of the past. I learned that there are two voices ever calling us, one to count the sea's buried dead, the other to find its treasured pearls. I felt that there were no pearls for me, but I would look for them, and—I found my people.

"I know now that I am but an arrow sent into space to guide them for a time. I tried to leave behind me the shadowed valley and climb the mountains on which the sun might still be shining. But—" he repeated softly:

"The way to Thee lies over grief and pain,
The soul gropes on, the darkness doth remain."

He threw himself back upon the divan, his arms crossed beneath his head, seemingly intent upon the sunset, which, like a miser, was hiding its gold. He said so softly we could scarcely hear him:

"How fearful a thing is the longing for a person! How long the creeping days to one who waits! Oh, when I speak of her I feel once more the clasp of her arms, the kiss of her lips, her eyes of tenderness, the depth of her love."

He rose abruptly from the couch and, stretching out his arms, said:

"I am like a bird who has lost his wings and can no longer mount the skies."

He walked up and down the carpet, then he went to Natara and, raising her, he said:

"But it is of your life I would speak, of you I must think."

He brought her to the divan and drew her down beside him, his arm around her waist.

"My dreams for you are that you see life through a haze of happy days. I would set the wine of your life in a golden goblet. I would carry your lamp through the stormy night. I have given the love that I had for my dear one to thee, and I would that I could pluck the world like a fruit from the sky to place in your rosy palm. I have promised that he who comes searching for thee as wife, shall have only one gift with which he can buy your heart—love. I want you to know this love of which I have spoken to you. Thy lover's voice is the music that will cause the world to sing for you, and when you wear the wedding bracelet it will be for you the symbol of the love that lives through all eternity.

"Being loved—that is a glorious thing. But it is not the most glorious. Loving—that is it—pouring out your soul in love and devotion to the one you love. Ah, Natara, the Prince of your Dreams will come to you and fill your life with the desires of your heart. Take nothing less."

After a time he rose and with his arm around Natara they walked to the balustrade overlooking the valley. They watched the scene for a time, then we left the terraced roof and passed through the rooms below, where the soft white witchery of moonlight filtered through the lace-like panels, throwing fairy-like shadows upon the marble floors.

Over it all was a subtle sadness, a regret weighted with faint perfume, as of an old blue china bowl in which had been gathered rose leaves, long since faded.

# IX

When Natara was a woman grown, her father died. The whole country mourned him, as every one, from the great feudal lord to the lowliest pariah, felt that he had lost a friend. It could have been fitly written upon his tomb, "He sleeps in Peace, for he has made tranquil the hearts of men."

As for Natara and myself, the sun was darkened in our sky. In the palace of the new Rajah, a different song was chanted. There was a vast ocean between the life that was now lived within the palace walls and what it had been before Achmed came to the throne. It was impossible to find peace within that humming city which was rapidly filling with women whose fears and hopes depended upon the momentary whim of the King.

A great change had come as soon as the influence of the old Rajah was removed. New faces were constantly added to the harem, new favorites would arise and sway the women's world for a time, to be soon supplanted by another favorite. Women were brought from the North, the South, the East and the West. They brought their women and their slaves, their gods and their superstitions. I have heard it said that there are thirty-three million gods in India. I quite believe the tale, and I am sure they all found a resting-place beneath the palace roof.

Each woman had her signs and her omens by which she was guided in sickness and health. Each woman had her philtres and her formulas for compounding medicines or brewing magic potions that would charm a recreant lover or make ill a hated rival.

If the Rajah had drunk all of the love potions that ambitious women brewed for him, he would soon have been called to rest in the bosom of Brahma. If he had worn all of the amulets and charms that fair hands made for him, he would not have found a place on his Royal Person on which to put the state jewels. If the gods had answered all the prayers that were sent to them by anxious hearts, they would have had no time to listen to the cries of the rest of India.

These women who used religion as a means of furthering their little hopes and ambitions, who tried to enter into a partnership with their gods, offering them incense and garlands in exchange for aid in their jealous intrigues and palace plots, were constantly bowing before their altars, wreathing their gods with marigolds or burning odorous woods or incense. The women's quarters reeked with the heavy smell of fading flowers and musk. The old keeper of the harem was in desperation. Yet she encouraged the women in their worship. As she said to me, "When they are weaving garlands to deck their gods they are not brewing poisons to feed their rivals."

I found that under the new order a palace full of idle, jealous women can stir up more trouble than a province in rebellion. And I also learned another thing, which I was obliged to impress upon Natara, who, with a young girl's impulsiveness, was often in trouble: "Wisdom is made up of ten parts, nine of which are silence and the tenth is brevity." I had the Court writer make a scroll which I hung beside her bed: "Words, like the tusks of an elephant, once out, cannot be put into the mouth again."

I was tired of the palace. I was tired of the jangling, wrangling, jealous women. I saw more clearly day by day that it was no place for a young girl. I did not care to have her days passed with these idle, pleasure-loving dolls, whose dainty henna-tinted hands had never fulfilled a useful service, whose lives were dominated solely by the emotions of jealousy, passion, greed and what they called love. It was the one word heard continuously—love—love—love. The courts resounded with it, yet I knew it was not love of which they spoke, but that which takes the place of love within all palace walls.

I decided to take Natara to the White Palace. When I told His Highness, much to my astonishment, he refused to give the permission. I could not understand him. But he would not explain why he wished Natara to live in her present apartments. Of course, his word was law, and I could do nothing.

I pondered over the problem many nights, and at last came to the conclusion that he was intending to take the palace for some favorite, and if Natara was installed within it with all her women, he could not easily dispossess her.

But the gods were on my side. There came a climax. The Rajah in his wild extravagance needed funds, and in his eagerness to refill his gold-box went too far, even for a Rajah.

The outer apartments of the palace were filled with women, relatives of the Royal House, many of them widows, and all, because of their blood claims, drew an allowance from the Imperial treasury.

The Rajah decided that he would take their allowance, and, what was worse in their eyes, their jewels. He argued that widows must clothe themselves only in white, eat but one meal a day, attend no festivities, consequently need no jewels, so why should so many precious rupees that were now needed so urgently by his Royal self, be expended for their support, and tied up in useless jewelry. These women were only a burden to the state, which he interpreted as meaning Achmed the Rajah.

The women might not have rebelled at the loss of their allowance in money, knowing that they were certain of support, but any woman will fight for her jewels, whether she wear them or not.

They were in a seething state of rebellion. All they needed was a leader. They found one.

A favorite cousin of the late Rajah was a woman from the hills who was not only beautiful but clever, and the Rajah had given her many jewels and presents, including an estate near her father's home. She felt that the confiscation of the jewels and the personal fortunes of the women was aimed at her, as the new Rajah had long cast his greedy eye upon her possessions. She was frightened and spent long nights in planning a way of escape to her estate, where she knew she could call upon her father for protection. But she was not allowed to leave the palace, as a watch was kept upon all her movements. At last she conceived a plan, and for a purdah woman it was a desperate plan, and could only have been conceived in desperation.

The Rajah's tomb had been erected at the end of the vast palace gardens, outside the wall. The city temple was near it and across the street was the great Mohammedan mosque. It faced the main thoroughfare of the city, connecting the business section with the two big places of worship.

At mid-day, when all of the men of the city were going to their worship, or kneeling in silent prayer, two hundred women from the Imperial palace rushed from a breach they had made in the palace wall, and threw themselves around the tomb of the Rajah.

There was consternation in both temple and mosque. No man might look upon the face of a woman of the palace. Men intent upon worship gave one frightened, hurried glance at the wailing women and fled, many so hurried in their flight that they left their shoes and prayer-mats.

The whole city buzzed with the news. It was an unheard-of thing. Every one was shocked to the depths of his being by this amazing act on the part of the palace women. The Rajah sent his Court Chamberlain, his Minister of State, and even the general of his troops to command the women to return to their apartments. They refused, unless he would promise not to take their jewels. The Rajah's pride was aroused. He would not make the promise—the women remained. All day and all night and all of the second day they stayed beside the tomb, and not a man in the city dared visit mosque or temple. It practically stopped the business of the city, as the main street could not be used, and no one dared to come to the bazaars to trade. The merchants closed their shops, waiting for the storm to pass.

The Rajah was desperate. At last he sent for me and I found him pacing up and down his apartment like a tiger chained. He threatened to turn his Northern Pathans upon the women and force them to return to the palace; but I told him that would only make more trouble. Those barbarians from the North would like only too well to have our soft dark-eyed women in their power, but it would rouse sympathy in the people of the city and might lead to a general uprising.

Then I saw my opportunity. I, too, would bargain. I showed him that the whole country was laughing at him, that the bazaars rang with the story of the trouble in the harem of the Rajah who was too weak to control his women-folk, and I agreed that if he would give me his promise, before his Minister of State, that Natara and I with her court could go to the White Palace and make it permanently her home, I would get the women to come in. At first he refused—but finally he gave me the promise, and I had it tied by every way I knew, as I did not wholly trust his Royal word unwitnessed.

I sent a messenger to the women, and told them that I would see that they had justice, and I also dropped a few hints regarding the Pathans waiting outside the city. The women had confidence in me, and perhaps they were hungry and martyrdom was no longer a novelty, so they came back to their courtyards. I sent the Rajah away on a three days' hunting trip, and after many tears and much talk, the matter was adjusted, not to every one's satisfaction, but I made them see that they could not take up a permanent abode upon the Rajah's tomb, and it were better to keep part of the fish than to give it all to the whale.

When it came to Sita, the woman who had planned and incited the others to their rash act, she could not be found. While the excitement was at its height, when all eyes were directed to the temple courtyard, she, with her women and many carts, had slipped by an outer gate, and by the time she was missed she was safely within her father's land. I laughed to myself, and in my heart was secretly glad. The jewels would be as well with her as adorning the pretty body of a Lucknow dancing girl.

I sent cart-load after cart-load of wailing women to a palace in the country, and when the Rajah returned all was peace again.

# X

I took my little one and her women to the White Palace. I locked the gate and kept the key. No one could enter without my permission.

My Princess should have the chance to grow in purity, to live amongst the flowers, the birds, a chance to keep her mind clean as a burnished mirror.

# XI

Life within the enclosing walls of the quiet garden moved to a different rhythm than that of the Court. Instead of living in a world of hateful thoughts and violent emotions, we were in a world of beauty, of charm, a charm as intangible and subtle as a perfume.

We were happy in our garden. We were in the heart of a wonderful silence, yet we knew that life was about us everywhere, although its tones were hushed to a shadowy monotone. We knew that each day would bring the same sweet peace, and from it would pour forth sunshine and song of birds and the golden wine of a new day.

We watched the outside world from the balustrade of the roof. From sunrise to sunset we saw the life of the people move on, and the hum of labor and the chink of tools rose up as if in some vast monastery accompanied by the chanting of prayers in the near-by temples. Religion is entwined with the every-day toil of the people of India, who are a spiritual people, and they invoke their gods before starting the work of a new day.

We watched the potter sensing his wheel, or the school-boy his ink and brush, as if asking these humble creatures to give of their best. Women on their way to and from the river would stop before a bo-tree or a tulsi-plant to salute it, joining their hands and bowing their heads in prayer. In the early morning we saw housewives kneeling upon their doorsteps busied with the ceremony of the Salutation of the Threshold, drawing a pattern upon the pavement in lines of powdered rice, with flowers arranged at regular intervals within it. This delicate handiwork would remain for only a few hours, but it marked the fact that cleansing and worship had been performed.

In the heat of the day we passed the hours in the courtyard, which was a great well of coolness and shadow where the soft white witchery of the sun filtered through the latticed screens.

When the rain came we listened to its falling as it swept across the lake, like the patter of tiny feet upon a roadway. The birds with their draggled wings became silent on the tamarind-trees and the only noise was the water running in rills through the narrow grooves with the sound of laughing women.

At night, when purple shadows filled the air, we went to the boat and lay there in the quiet, hearing the chatter of sleepy birds as they cuddled into their resting-places to wait for the dawn to lift the leaves from about their heads. We listened to the wind's song through the treetops as though some harp had caught a strayed breeze from an unknown world and brought its message to us. At last even the nests of the birds became silent and the murmur of the palm-trees was stilled and only the soft hush of the darkness was around us. Vast and deep the night seemed to enfold us, until the moon came slowly up the sky as if he were a watchman with his lantern passing by. At times the lone cry of a night bird came to us, or the sad call of a flute from some lover passing to the village, who left the trace of his song across the hush of the night.

The scent of sandal and flowers was woven with the sleepy incense of the night, and we were lulled to a dreamy peace until the fairies of sleep would come sailing by in their elfin boats and tell us it was time to leave the splendor of the dark blue night, lighted by large soft stars that throb and gleam with an unearthly brilliance, and seek our rest.

Those days, passed within the courtyard or upon the housetop, surrounded by women who loved her, were happy days for Natara. Laughter was as natural to her as the song to the bird, and her whole being sang like a stream amongst the pebbles.

She did not feel her isolation, nor that she was barred from the world outside. We women of the East are like tall white lilies, set in the dimness beside some altar, screened from the very glances of the faithful at their prayers. The purdah, in whose shadow we sit, is not a prison, but a shrine. Bereft of its concealment, we would be frightened, feel dishonored.

Natara did not crave the life of the world outside our walls, but she wanted love. The song of the birds, the perfume of the flowers, the murmur of the quiet waters and the peace of moonlit nights, only brought to the surface what was slumbering underneath, the cry for human love—a woman's birthright. She began to talk shyly, as young girls will, of the Prince who would one day come for her, and I could see that she was dreaming dreams and having visions of her own.

When we first came to the palace I had installed upon the throne in our little temple, Saraswati, the Goddess of Knowledge. Each day I saw Natara go to the gardens and gather the sweetest smelling flowers and the white mango-blossoms before going to the temple. I followed her there one day and found that Saraswati was dethroned and in her place was Madan, the God of Love. She was strewing the floor with fresh mangopetals, and on Madan's neck and tiny wrists were wreaths of jasmine.

Natara did not see me as I stood quietly in the shadow of the archway, and after her offering of the fragrant flowers, she knelt before the god, and murmured softly:

"If I were only a flower, to be made into a garland for thy neck, but I have woven my heart with the flowers, and you will send me my lover, the Prince of my Dreams."

# XII

We, in the peace and quiet of our enclosing walls, heard little gossip of the palace, as I did not encourage visitors from its women's quarters. Yet, news did creep in, and I knew that the Rajah's Court was spoken of as the most extravagant, the most luxurious, the most corrupt, in all India. His Highness seemed possessed with the wild desire to spend in reckless prodigality, to scatter rupees broadcast, to give jewels to favorites, to entertain more royally than any prince since the time of the Great Moguls. He gave durbar after durbar. He invited the neighboring rulers to visit him, and they came with their nobles and trains of attendants until our streets were filled with strange faces and noise and clamor resounded from every side.

Dancing girls were brought from the South, from Calcutta and from Bombay, at fabulous prices, and we, even in our garden, were never free from the distant sounds of music and revelry. Hunting parties were organized, and the men, with their army of servants, their elephants, their trained leopards and their dogs, would go away for days.

The women of the Court shared in the excitement, and from behind the screens watched the dancing girls, or viewed from their balconies the battles between animals in the great arena without the walls. The women reveled in the changing scenes, although their interest was mingled with jealousy as they saw their Lord throw a necklace over the rounded throat of some beauty who had pleased him with her dancing. They had no need for worry, as the infatuation could only be for a time. These dancing girls were for the most part owned by temples, and no amount of money would tempt the greedy priests to part with their most lucrative possessions.

Although the head of the harem forbade it, the dancers were brought secretly into the women's apartments, where their jewels were appraised, their saris valued, their dancing practised before an appreciative audience, who treated these pretty little false-faced women as amusing toys.

These clever entertainers who, like the broken cowrie, had been to many markets, and gained a knowledge of the world in which they plied their trade, did not hesitate to use all of their arts to charm the sheltered women of the palace. They told them stories which it were better they did not hear and shrieks of laughter would resound throughout the corridors. But when the servant, who had been stationed to watch for old Helima, silently held up her hand, there was a scurrying of dancers' feet, and when the Mistress of the Harem entered with frown to ask the cause of merriment, all would be peace and she was greeted with quiet voices and child-like eyes, as they chatted of the price of silks in Madras.

# XIII

The city was thrown into great excitement when it was known that Naranabad, the most powerful Maharajah in India, was to visit our Court. Our Rajah was delighted at the honor, and decided to excel himself in prodigality of entertainment. He would show the world that there was one Prince in India who understood the manner in which a Royal guest should be entertained.

Word was sent to all the provinces commanding the zemindars to present themselves at the capital, bringing with them elephants, camels, horses and men-at-arms. They were ordered to array themselves in their finest apparel, to bring their jewels from their treasure-chests. They must add to the magnificence of the Court. Nothing was to be spared to make of this great durbar an occasion to be spoken of in after years with bated breath.

Hundreds of tents were erected outside the palace grounds. They were hung with silks and rare embroideries, with rugs and tiger-skins upon the floors. A palace within the gardens was given the visitor and his suite, and within it no luxury known to our world was forgotten.

From our roof we watched the arrival of the nobles. They came by the tens with their attendants, and were assigned to their tents, in front of which were placed lances with pennants flying from their points. From each tent-top a great banner with coat-of-arms proclaimed to the world the name and rank of the noble sheltered therein.

It made a scene of color never to be forgotten. The brilliant sunshine, the gaily striped tents with their pennants swaying in the breeze, the passing elephants with their broidered housings, their howdahs of gold and silver lacquer flashing in the sunlight, camels, the horses with their daring riders, all made a scene of splendor that was dazzling to the eyes.

At last the great Prince came. He was conducted to the palace, and then the world seemed turned to madness. Entertainment followed entertainment. The place was filled with music, the harp-strings jingled and the drums beat night and day.

The mad revel was to culminate in a durbar held in the great courtyard of the palace, the evening before our guest was to say farewell. Natara and I were commanded to join the court women, where from behind lace-like marble walls we could see all that was passing in the court below, ourselves unseen.

At last the night arrived. We women took our places on the hidden balcony that ran around the four sides of the courtyard. Natara and I were seated directly opposite the two thrones from which the Rajahs were to view the pageant.

The trumpets sounded. Our Rajah, arrayed in all his jewels, a great diamond gleaming in the aigret of his turban like a wicked eye, came into the courtyard with his nobles dressed in their official robes. He seated himself, and they formed three great semicircles around their King. The English Resident and his attachés came, saluted, and were given places near the throne. As one of the staff of the Resident bowed before the Rajah, I heard a low sigh from Natara. I turned to her; she was looking with eyes of interest at a young man who stood before the King. He was tall and fair, with deep-blue eyes, and he stood at his ease as if it were a thing of every-day occurrence to stand before a Maharajah as his guest.

When all were within their places assigned to them, there was a vast volume of sound as the trumpets announced the entrance of Naranabad with his men. Our King rose and stepping down the five steps leading to the throne, conducted Naranabad to the seat beside him. As they stood side by side before the thrones, they were a striking pair. Our Rajah was a few years younger, more graceful, standing in his shining robes and glittering jewels. But Naranabad, although his evil face bore marks of dissipation, bore himself with kingly pride.

As I looked down upon them, so proud in all their glory, I thought:

"You have all the rank and power and riches of the world within your hands; but in the end you will mount the pyre the same as your pipe-bearers, and your bodies will not make a greater ash."

When all was quiet the durbar commenced.

Flaming torches were placed at equal distances round the courtyard. The great doors were thrown open and to the sound of marching music, elephants, two by two, came in and dividing at the entrance went to places near the walls, where they stood around its three sides facing the throne. They were covered with velvet hangings that swept the ground. Their howdahs shone like gold, and from their ears swung hoops of gold and silver, inset with sparkling glass or semi-precious jewels, which sparkled as they waved their fan-like ears. Their faces and trunks were painted gorgeous colors, and their anklets jingled as they moved their great unwieldy feet.

The trumpets sounded. Another band of elephants came in and separating at the entrance went to their places a little in front and between their standing brothers, but they, at word of command, knelt down. The camels came, their ugliness hidden by rich draperies, and they formed a standing row before the elephants, then others came and knelt as did the elephants.

Again the trumpets sounded. A band of horsemen, arrayed in warrior dress of olden days, dashed into the arena and swinging to left and right took their places before the kneeling camels. Soldiers clothed in glittering armor took their stand before the horsemen, their shields on arm, their lances held on guard before them.

Within this living square the games took place. Men tilted from their horses' backs; they fought with swords, with lances, played all the games of war known to our world in days gone by. The victors came and bowed low before the Rajah and received reward.

When tiring of the fiercer combats, the Rajah waved his hand and jugglers entered. Clever men did mysterious things that made us hold our breath with awe. But when they had exhausted their skill, rugs were placed upon the ground and musicians entered and seated themselves at left and right. Servants placed wreaths of fragrant flowers upon the necks of the guests, and fruit and wine were offered. That was the signal that the gentler part of the entertainment was to begin.

The musicians chanted songs of battle and songs of love until all were thrilled with a wanton madness that caused the eyes to glisten and the faces flush.

At last the dancers entered. Women with bodies lithe as serpents swayed back and forth upon the carpet. With noiseless steps, except for the tinkle of their anklets, they told with subtle gesture the story of their loves, their hates and passions as it is known in the dancers' world.

We watched them languidly, as all were waiting for the entrance of the great dancer who had come from the South. She was the most famous dancer in all India, and her name was known from Madras to Peshwar.

At last the other dancers finished and arranged themselves before the musicians. The music stilled to a murmur, then it burst forth in one loud cry of joy. Standing in the great open doorway, with the black night behind her, stood a thing of gold and glitter that caused all eyes to stare, and a murmured long-drawn word that sounded like a sigh came from every throat. From the jewels in her head-dress, the gems in her ears, the necklaces on her beautiful throat, the naked arms circled from wrist to shoulder with glittering bracelets, to the bangles on anklets and the rings on henna-stained toes, she was a thing of witchery, made to drive men mad.

She came forward and bowed low before the throne, then commenced her dance. Behind her, singers intoned the melody to the accompaniment of throbbing drums and flutes.

At first the dance was slow and graceful as the waving of trees in a light breeze. She approached, she retired, she begged and then she flaunted. She returned again and again with head thrown back and with half-opened lips that showed her pearly teeth, she begged the men before her to follow, she lured them with arms and breasts and languorous eyes. She reproached, she laughed, and her laughter was like music. She mocked with sparkling eyes and tried to leave her conquest, but love was strong; she returned, conquered by her own passion, and stretching out her arms imploringly she offered all in one final whirl of madness when she seemed a glittering flame that whirled and whirled until she dropped, like some fallen star, upon the mat.

When all was over we seemed to waken as if from some rare dream. The Rajahs left the courtyard, which was a sign that all might take their leave.

I, with the other women, rose and for a moment looked down into the buzzing courtyard, where the guests were standing in small groups chatting with their friends. I watched them for a time, then turned to find Natara. I spoke to her; she did not answer. She was staring into the courtyard, and I looked to see what had so enthralled her that she did not hear my voice. She was looking at the young Englishman who stood a little apart from the rest. He was a figure to be noticed, his fair face appearing fairer among the crowd of swarthy men.

Suddenly he looked upwards. Natara moved back with a little gasp, and drew her veil across her face. I looked at her in wonder, and with a little anger in my voice said:

"He cannot see you, Natara; why do you shrink?"

A flush rose to her face, but she said nothing, and we joined the other women for the feast within the Queen's apartments.

# XIV

We returned to our garden and soon forgot the days of excitement, but they were to be recalled with a heavy hand.

Naranabad had been gone about a month, when one day the Rajah sent word that he would honor us with a visit. This did not please me at all, but no place, not even the most secluded purdah, could be refused the King; consequently I prepared for his call with the best grace I could summon.

As soon as he entered he asked for Natara. When she came, he stood back and looked at her critically, appraisingly, as he would look at a slave girl brought for his inspection. Natara flushed; I was indignant, and went to the side of Natara. There was something in the air I did not like. I resented the Rajah's attitude.

Finally he said:

"Natara, I have great news for you. Naranabad has asked for you in marriage."

In his excitement he commenced to pace up and down the room and did not see the sudden pallor that came over my face or the flush that rose to the cheeks of Natara. A weakness overcame me and I sat down hastily upon a cushion. The Rajah did not notice my breach of etiquette, and continued talking excitedly, which gave me time to overcome my faintness, and soon I rose again.

"It is wonderful—marvelous— It will unite the two most powerful states in India. Naranabad and Achmed—why, if we join hands in any affair, not even England herself would dare oppose us."

Natara did not answer. He stopped pacing up and down and looked at her curiously.

"What is it, Natara?" he asked. "Do you realize what this means to you? It is fate that works for you—the gods are on your side. I used to reproach your father each time a proposal came for you and he refused.

And now think of what this means to us. It is a great future for you. It is a lucky thing for me that you were kept waiting, although you are eighteen now, an unheard-of age for a girl to be unmarried."

"Wait for Naranabad!" I could not refrain from saying bitterly. "Yes, that is a wonderful future—Naranabad."

He turned swiftly.

"What is the matter with Naranabad?" he asked, glaring at me. "She will be the Maharanee of the most powerful Prince in India."

"What is it to be a Maharanee," I asked, "if your kingdom is divided amongst hundreds, if every pretty face that shows itself is allowed to sway, even for a time, your kingdom? I suppose Natara will share her honors with that dancing girl from the South. Gossip says that you gave her to Naranabad as a parting gift. You seem to be prodigal in your gifts, Your Highness—the most expensive dancing girl in the kingdom—and the Princess Royal."

The Rajah flushed, started to say something, then thought better of the impulse and said simply:

"But she will be Queen. What does it count if for a day or a week or a month a lesser light shines in the heavens? She will always remain the Sun."

"That is not what Natara wants," I replied. "A woman's heart cannot be satisfied with power alone. That does not satisfy the craving for love, and it is love that I will have for Natara."

The Rajah shrugged his shoulders.

"Love," he said. "She will have love. Naranabad will be devoted to her."

"Naranabad!" I said with scorn. "What does he know of love! You cannot produce honey from the thorn, nor do roses grow on willow-branches. The word means no more to him than it does to yonder pea-cock on the wall. He will deck her with jewels, yes. But she already has jewels more precious than any he can give her. She will live in a royal palace, but she has here a palace of dreams; he could never build one of greater beauty. She shall not go to him."

The Rajah was quiet for a moment, then came and stood before me, his face twitching as he tried to control his anger. Finally he said, and there was that in his voice that made final his words:

"You are planting trees in a barren soil, Amina, when you try to change me in this matter. It is more than even in my wildest dreams I had ever hoped for, that one of our house would be the Maharanee of Naranabad."

"Yes, think of it," I said with aloes in my voice. I was not frightened. I am of royal blood myself and I have passed all of my life within a palace and have no fear of kings. "Think of having to be satisfied with a man like Naranabad. His love—bah! A false gem that passes from hand to hand. You are selling her for a golden pot out of which *you* may drink. What value to her his worthless rubbish of rank and wealth! Why—the potter's wife sleeps more happily than would a queen within *his* palace."

Then I felt all of the passion that was within me rise at the thought, and I said, "I would rather see her go to the funeral pyre than to Naranabad!"

The Rajah became white with fury. His eyes flashed and two red spots showed in the white of his cheeks. He said in a voice that quivered with anger:

"Understand me, Amina. This is settled. There will be no more discussion. Natara will become the Maharanee of Naranabad. I will see that this marriage is hastened. I hope you understand."

Turning, he strode from the room.

# XV

I was lost in a Sea of Sorrow. Natara should not go to Naranabad, to the most corrupt Court, ruled by the most corrupt monarch in India. Her father had not trained her for this, to be in the women's quarters of a man like Naranabad, even as his Queen. All of the ideals, the purity, we had tried to instil within her heart, would be there only an added burden. If she was compelled to accept the life that would be given her there, she would have nothing for which to live except power, jewels, dress, and to be satisfied with the empty flattery of obsequious slaves—knowing herself to be a greater slave.

I must find a way to save her. There must be a path leading to the Light.

# XVI

I passed the night with sleepless eyes, wondering what path was open to me; what door I could unlock. There was no one to whom I could appeal, to whom I could go for advice. Every woman in India would think Natara most fortunate, would give their all to exchange places with her.

At last I had an inspiration. There was *one* woman on whom I could call, who would understand. I rose in haste and sent for her.

Mara Iyengar, the daughter of one of the great land-holders in our state, had been betrothed in childhood to a small princeling of a neighboring province. When the time came for the marriage to take place, she disappeared. She had gone to England with her English governess, and her name was mentioned in whispers. The parents were blamed for giving her a foreign teacher, and allowing her to imbibe ideas that did not fit her for the life of an Indian lady. Her father bitterly reproached himself, and her name was never mentioned within her home. She had disgraced her clan, and she was considered an outcast, a pariah.

The disgrace had no effect upon the good spirits of Mara Iyengar. After finishing her education she returned to our city and became the head of a hospital for women. My Princess, the Queen, liked her, and when she learned that Mara was skilled in her profession, she persuaded the Rajah to appoint her as Court physician to the women of the palace.

She retained the place under the new Rajah, and came in and out of the palace freely. She was loved and respected by all, the Rajah especially liking the free, outspoken woman, who treated him as a boy, and often a bad boy. She stood in no awe of His Royal Highness. Perhaps that was the secret of her power, surfeited as he was with flattery and tired of fawning satellites.

It seemed endless hours before I saw Mara crossing the courtyard. But, as I looked into her smiling face, I felt that part of my troubles were to be placed on stronger shoulders than mine. She had evidently come from the palace and the Rajah had heard that she was in my apartments. She was no sooner seated than His Highness was announced.

I had no opportunity of speaking of the matter that was lying so heavily on my heart, and Mara gave no indication before the Rajah that I had sent for her. He came in and stood before her.

"Ah, the Rose still blooms, I see," he said with mock seriousness.

"Through your august favor I still continue to live," she replied with equal seriousness. "Through your blessing my present and future happiness is secure, O Most Mighty One," and she bowed nearly to the floor in seeming humility.

The Rajah laughed and threw himself down upon a divan. "Where have you been for so long?" he said. "Kings, women and climbing plants love those who are near them. You should stay near me, Mara."

"So?" she said. "From henceforth the shadow of your foot shall be my abode. By the way, I left some medicine for one of your numerous and divers progeny, and her mother threw it out of the window and called in a priest, who made some pellets of paper on which were prayers, and the baby swallowed them instead of my medicine. Now I am sorry to tell you that prayers on paper, no matter how beautifully written, will not cure the effects of a not overripe melon."

The Rajah did not look as if the subject interested him overmuch, and said, "Now that is your affair and the mother's. What child was it?"

Mara was quiet for a moment, regarding the Rajah as he lay on the divan, looking very handsome in his lazy, graceful attitude.

"Your Highness," she said finally, "I have often wanted to ask you. How many children have you?"

The King looked at her reproachfully.

"What a question to ask me, Mara! How should I know?" he said languidly.

Mara looked at him in astonishment.

"Well, of all things! Whom should I ask if not you?" she inquired.

"Ask my Minister of Finance. He attends to all such small matters as keeping account of the children. He has to—he pays their bills."

"Is that the duty of a Minister of Finance?" Mara asked laughingly.

"No, not all," the Rajah replied. "It is his business to increase the funds—mine to increase the wants."

"You work night and day to fulfil the duties of your position, do you not, my lord?" she inquired sarcastically.

"I do my best, my little best," he replied mournfully, shaking his head. "But I am weak—and—"

"Thy modesty resembles the lightning in the heavens," she said. "Now flashing and now passing away."

They both laughed and the Rajah made himself more comfortable on the divan.

"Send for my pipe man, Amina," he said. "I will stay awhile. I haven't seen Mara for a long time, and I want a talk with her."

He motioned Mara to a pile of cushions near the divan, and she sat down facing the King, her elbow resting lightly upon the divan. She was the only woman in all his state, with the exception perhaps of the reigning favorite, who would dare to seat herself in so unceremonious a manner. That was her charm to him. She was not a woman to the Rajah; just a clever, quick-witted companion, who did not fear him, nor did she wish to curry favor. She talked as frankly to him as if he were simply the boy companion with whom she had played in childhood's days.

The pipe was brought and when it was lighted to his satisfaction, he smoked for a time in silence. Then he said, as if he had been pondering the subject:

"Do you like the English, Mara?"

"Yes," she replied. "I like them in some ways; in others I do not. They are cold, or at least appear to be cold. They suppress their feelings, restrain emotions, cultivate an appearance of chilliness that does not make for friendship. To me they lop from the tree of life the branches that add beauty and not utility. They are colorless, but—they treat their women well, Your Highness. They have but one wife."

I looked up at this remark. The English have but one wife.

"I know that they bring but one wife to India with them," he said. "But do they really have but one wife? Do they love but one woman? Are they true to her, to one woman?"

Mara laughed. "Well, it has been known in the history of England that her sons have wandered from their own firesides, but they generally wander back again. They really have but one wife at a time."

The Rajah looked up at the ceiling.

"I always wondered why I so thoroughly hate the English. Now I know. They set such a bad example to the world."

He was silent for a moment, then he said:

"If the English left India to-morrow—"

Mara interrupted him.

"If they did," she said sharply, "the next day you and your Northern Pathans would be in the saddle and in three months there would not be a rupee nor a virgin in India."

The King laughed.

"What unkind words from the lips of a friend. You do not realize, Mara, that I am getting old. Neither women nor rupees interest me any more. All that I desire is that in some holy place I may end my days."

Mara turned to me and said solemnly:

"With Kings, with horned beasts and with a river, a man may never enter into understanding."

The Rajah laughed, and was quiet for a time; then he said suddenly:

"I have great news for thee, my friend. Natara is betrothed."

Mara glanced at me quickly and, I am sure, noted the pain in my eyes.

"Betrothed?" she asked. "To whom?"

"Naranabad," he replied.

"Naranabad!" she said with a gasp. "Not Naranabad!"

The Rajah looked at her from beneath his half-shut eyes.

"Yes, Naranabad. It is a great honor. I was sure you would be delighted."

Mara said nothing.

"Aren't you delighted?" he insisted.

Mara repeated in a low, shocked voice:

"Naranabad!"

"Why not Naranabad?" he persisted.

"You know why she should not be given to Naranabad," she replied.

"I do not see the force of your argument, if you are going to make one," the Rajah said. "Naranabad is great and rich and powerful—"

"Folly!" said Mara disdainfully. "He is too old, in the first place; his palace is full of women already."

"But she would be the Maharanee."

"What of that! An empty title. She would be shut up in his dreary old palace, where the windows are so high she could only catch a glimpse of the sky. I have seen his women's quarters. And—why, she is a child,— he is older than Your Highness."

The King flushed.

"I am not ready for the pyre yet, Mara. I am still alive, wonderful though it may appear to you."

"But," said Mara, "you know as well as I that as dark leans to dark, youth leans to youth. And he is the most dissolute Prince in India; his court is a byword for—"

The Rajah interrupted her.

"He is not so bad. He gets credit for many things he never does. You know a Prince is always in the glare of the sunlight—even I—"

Mara laughed.

"You can't make the tail of a dog straight by oiling it," she said tartly. "Look at his evil face—it shows the life he has led."

"He is a very handsome man," said the Rajah. "Next to me—"

"Yes," sarcastically. "You both of you took a portion of the most excellent part of the moon to form your faces. If proof is desired, look at the spots left in the moon."

The Rajah laughed, and settled himself back on the cushions.

"Oh, Mara,—" he commenced, but she interrupted him with a little tone of anger in her voice.

"I can't understand Your Highness. Why should you give Natara to this man? You do not need him in any way. You do not need his money, nor his power, nor anything that is his. Why sacrifice Natara?"

The Rajah flushed and an angry glint came to his eyes.

"Why call it sacrifice? She will be the Queen of the richest and most powerful Prince of India, and Naranabad and I together—we can go far."

"Riches!" Mara replied with scorn. "If you burden the wings of a bird with gold, it can no longer fly in the sky. What does she care for his riches or his power? What—"

The Rajah interrupted her.

"We will not discuss the subject, Mara. Keep your energy; it may be useful. Kicks only raise dust, not crops, from the earth."

He was quiet for a time, looking at her intently, as if studying her with some problem in his mind. Finally he said:

"Mara, I have use for thy restless energy. Come and manage my palace, the women's quarters. I am tired of their bickerings and their quarrels, and Helima is getting old. If you can keep peace in my household, half of my kingdom shall be yours."

He was silent, then he said, half to himself:

"Mohammed said, 'I love not them that sit.' I think he meant all womenkind. Women—" and he threw his arms above his head as if in despair, "I am tired of women!"

Mara laughed.

"On any question regarding women you certainly should be a supreme authority. I have never seen so many women's faces within four walls as there are in your palace."

The Rajah laughed.

"You must admit, Mara, that they are pretty faces. I have shown good taste, if a little faulty judgment."

"Yes," said Mara. "But are you trying to rival Krishna with his sixteen thousand wives? You are no god, you know, my lord."

He waved his hand lightly.

"You are talking nonsense! There are not so many when you come to count them."

"Have you counted them?" she asked.

"No—" he admitted with a laugh. "Why expend my energy uselessly? There are so many other things to do. Take over my women, Mara, and I will go on a pilgrimage, and when I come back I may find a little peace."

"You know I do not believe in pilgrimages, especially for Kings," Mara said, with displeasure in her voice. "You only enrich the temple and the priests. No real prayers ascend from your heart. Why do you think that if you leave off your silks and satins and your jewels for a month, it will wash away the sins of the rest of the year? The gods don't need your lakh of rupees that you scatter to the priests. Unless your heart is clean from lust and pride and avarice, they will be deaf to all your prayers. What is it the poet sings? It fits your case exactly.

> " 'If still, O sinful man, with ash
> Thou dost besmear thy face,
> Or bathest oft, that thus thy soul
> May cast away thy load,
> Thou knowest naught of God, nor of
> Regeneration's face.
> Your mantras, what are they? The Veds
> Are burdened with their weight.' "

The Rajah rose upon the couch and, leaning on his elbow, looked down at the flushed face. I was surprised that there was no anger in his eyes. He said:

"Mara, what eloquence! I will make you court reciter, but—if you don't want me to go on a pilgrimage, I won't go. If you don't want me to pray, I won't pray. It does not make any great difference to the gods, I presume."

"No," she answered tartly. "And if the doctor gives you medicine, it doesn't matter to the doctor whether you take it or not, but it does to you."

"Well—what *do* you approve of my doing? I will be as clay in thy hands—"

Mara started to speak, but the Rajah put up a hand.

"One thing at a time. Let us settle the matter of the palace. I think, if I remember rightly, I made you a present. A harem, complete, full to overflowing, furnished with all that is necessary for a modern up-to-date harem. There is many a man in India who would be grateful for that little present," and he chuckled quietly. "Are you coming to keep peace in my household?"

Mara did not laugh, but said seriously:

"Do you remember the old proverb, Your Highness? 'Many straws united may bind an elephant.' We do not want you bound."

The Rajah regarded her reproachfully.

"Are you comparing my women, my incomparable women, to straws? I am ashamed of you! If they knew it, where would your medicine go when the messenger brings it?"

Then he said with mock seriousness:

"The prophet Mohammed, blessed be his name, said that one of the surest marks of gentleness is tenderness to the weak. Judging of his vast experience, he was speaking of the female sex—and I am only trying to live up to his precepts, by being tender to them all, at least as many of them as I can—"

Mara laughed.

"The prophet also said, 'Verily, my compassion overcometh my wrath.' It is true in my case."

The Rajah looked at Mara for a second, then closed his eyes and lay quietly on the divan. Mara looked at me and then at the man lying before her, and she saw the uselessness of opposing him. She realized it would not benefit Natara to raise again the question of her marriage. She would only make him angry. She leaned over him, and touching his eyes said with low voice:

"Ah, he sleeps. The world is left in darkness."

As he did not answer, she flicked an imaginary speck from his brow.

"Thy face is pure, Your Highness—though it be not washed."

The Rajah sat up and laughed.

"You have learned well the precept, Mara. The gods love them that swallow down their anger."

Mara made a naughty face at him and muttered a foreign word, not of prayer, beneath her breath. The Rajah heard it, and with a show of indignation and shocked dignity rose, although like myself, he could hardly keep a laugh from his lips, as the little oath did sound most ludicrous coming from Mara's pretty mouth.

"Should the virtuous remain near the wicked," said he with mock solemnity, "the effects of the deeds of the wicked will fall upon the virtuous. The sea was put in chains on account of its vicinity to the wicked Ravenu. I will take my departure before I am contaminated."

Mara laughed and threw him a rose.

The Rajah caught it and placed it in his turban. Mara swept him an elaborate curtsy, and he, with a gay laugh and a wave of his hand, strode down the corridor.

# XVII

The moment the Rajah was gone, the expression on the face of Mara changed. She came to me and said in a low voice:

"Is it true, Amina, is it true?"

"Yes," I replied, and my face must have mirrored the bitterness in my heart, "it is true."

Mara sat down.

"To Naranabad, of all men. To *Naranabad*," she repeated as if she could not believe her own words.

I turned to her and stretched out my hands.

"What can I do, Mara! What can I do!"

Mara said nothing, but looked steadily in front of her, seemingly rendered speechless by this unforseen blow.

She said finally in a low tone:

"Naranabad! Why, his very touch would be a pollution!"

"Mara," I cried, and she must have felt the cry of my soul. "Mara, I cannot have her go to Naranabad. I do not know which way to turn. In the stillness of my heart, in the quiet of the night, I have thought and planned and thought again, trying to find the way, but I cannot. I am drowned in an ocean of unhappiness. If she goes to him, she will be like a caged wild bird who has no songs behind the bars."

I rose and walked up and down the room and said in a low voice from which I tried to keep the passion-ring, because in these rooms without doors one can never tell what step may pause outside the archway:

"Mara, you will never know what this means to me. I have been waiting, dreaming of the love that will come to Natara, the love that came to her mother and made of her bud of happiness a flower. Whether I have been in the temple or the balcony, in the palace or the garden, I have been dreaming of the time when Natara should find the love of which her father spoke, love and joy and contentment in the arms of her Prince.

"We promised her mother that love only should be her heritage, that she should not wed for power nor rank nor riches. And I have taught her that love exists, that it will come to her, that it waits for her at the gates of her enchanted garden."

I was silent a moment, pacing up and down the room. I could not sit down, I could not still the movement of my hands that seemed to be beating helplessly against a prison wall.

"You do not know Natara, Mara. She has spent her days in dreams here in this beautiful palace. She has lived a life of beauty. Like the blessed Buddha, nothing but the beautiful has come to her. She has believed that her Prince would come, a Prince like those in the fairy tales, and I have encouraged her. I should not have allowed her to have visions. I should not have allowed her to have the dreams of all young girls. I should have remembered that she is a Princess," I said with bitterness.

"Mara, I have lived all my life within a royal palace, and I have looked about me with eyes of knowledge. I should have known that the love for which I have dreamed for Natara is not to be found within its walls. Look at our palace here, the most beautiful, the most luxurious in all India. It is thought to be the fulfillment of woman's highest desire to be brought to its women's courtyards. They come, young lives, glad with the gladness of youth, and for a time their days are rosy and gold like a glow in the sky before sunrise, but they end in the gray and wan twilight of a hopeless day.

"Look at Sarrojini, the Maharanee. When she came to us she was youth and joy and love itself. She was like a dancing girl floating to the sound of the lute in her happiness. It only lasted for a short time, until a new face peered from behind the purdah. She poured out her love before the Rajah as water is poured in the sand at noonday, and with as little use.

"At last she understood, and only grief remained in her heart. Oh, men are cruel in their lust and pride," I cried passionately. "They do not know that it is only in love that woman's heart hath life. They say, 'I will buy you with money, I will buy you with jewels, I will buy you with a kingdom,' and they do not understand that we would rather have the jewels that tremble on the meadow plant, if gathered by one we love, than all the gems in royal caskets."

I stopped my pacing up and down the room and stood before Mara.

"Mara, I cannot believe that Natara's dreams will not come true, that her visions of love and joy will glide into memory. Pain and longing and unhappiness will come in their stead, pain that she will pray the gods to still, but 'twill only sleep and will wake again and again and become the pain of old. She will sing, yes. Because she is of a brave race, but the song will rise from the lips, not from the heart.

"Mara—Mara—is there no help? I have gone to the gods—there are no gods; they are nothing but lifeless images. They do not hear my sorrow, because I have cried aloud to them and they do not answer. Mara, is there no way?" and I held out my hands to her in supplication.

Mara sat in brooding silence, then she spoke, and I did not need the sound of her voice to tell me that she saw no light.

"No, Amina," she said in a low voice. "I see no help. As well try to reform the curlings of a smoke-wreath as to change a man like the Rajah when he has once made up his mind. Natara cannot, as I did, fly to foreign lands. Natara is a Royal Princess, and she would be returned. No official, either Indian or English, would care to risk a native ruler's anger for the sake of a woman. England herself could not help Natara. She could not find a place in which to hide. I see no way."

I sat down upon the cushions and buried my face in my hands. Mara looked at me for long moments, then she rose and said gently, touching my shoulder with kindly hands:

"I must leave thee, Amina. I will try to think of something, but—but—I cannot give thee hope."

She watched me silently, then she said:

"Go to thy room, Amina, and rest. Thine eyes are heavy for sleep. Let me think, give me the burden—there may be a way, but as yet I cannot see it."

And touching my bowed head lightly with her lips, she left me.

# XVIII

I do not know how long I sat where Mara left me. It seemed I could not move; my body was heavy with the burden of my heart. But at last I rose. I could not go to my chamber. I went to the garden. My feet were weighted as I walked slowly down the path. The birds sang to me; I did not hear their voices. Natara's favorite peacock came to me and spread his jeweled tail, asking for admiration, which he considered his right; but I did not notice him.

I mounted the stair leading to the roof and took my favorite place beside the balustrade. I leaned my arms on the low wall and gazed over the countryside, at the villages in the distance looking like flocks of birds hovering under the great leaves of the palm-trees. But my eyes saw not, my ears heard not the sounds of life that came faintly to me.

As I sat brooding, the sound of a galloping horse came faintly to me, and at the same time I heard the tinkle of anklets, as Natara came to the roof beside me.

A rider turned into the path close beneath the wall. This small roadway connected the two main roads leading from the town, but was never used except by the bare feet of the passing villagers.

As the horse and rider came below me, the pace slackened and the rider looked up. I saw it was the young Englishman whom I had noticed at the durbar. I heard a sound and, turning, saw Natara move back quickly from the balustrade, a rose flush mounting her face, creeping from bare rounded throat and losing itself in her hair. I watched her in astonishment. When the young man had passed, she crept to the balustrade, and watched him intently as he rode slowly on. He looked back as his horse joined the road leading to the country, and it seemed to me that he waved his hand, but I could not be sure.

Natara wandered aimlessly around the roof, humming a little song, now arranging a cushion, now taking a dying leaf from a rose, but coming back again and again to the balustrade, where she cast quick glances from lowered lids to the road up which the rider had passed.

I pondered her actions for a moment, but gave it little thought, as my heart was so burdened with sorrow that small things which would have at other times interested me, drifted idly by with scant notice.

# XIX

The next day I waited in my apartments for Mara. She came, but brought no comfort to me. She said:

"There is nothing can be done, Amina. Natara must obey the head of the house."

I said nothing. There was nothing to say. I realized that my dear one was the Princess of a Royal House, and being so was nothing but a thing to be used in forwarding the interest of that house.

I called Natara and we three mounted to the roof. As usual, my women brought us cushions and placed fruits and sweetened drinks near by. We seated ourselves near the balustrade where we could look over the country. Mara sat quietly smoking cigarettes, a habit she had learned in foreign lands, and my heart was too heavy for the gossip with which we usually passed the time while on the housetop. Natara was also quiet and did not fill our ears with her girlish chatter, but sat quietly weaving a garland of flowers to be used in the evening worship.

At last we heard the sound of galloping hoofs, and, as on the evening before, the young Englishman slackened his pace as he passed beneath the wall. Natara leaned a tiny bit over the balustrade, then moved back quickly. Mara raised herself from the cushions and peered down upon the rider.

"Ah, it is Neil Thornton," she said.

"Who is he?" I asked.

"He is a young attaché in the English service, attached at present to the Residency here. An awfully nice boy. I wonder where he is going?"

She watched him as he turned into the main road, then she said, "Oh, I see. This is a short-cut to the road leading to the polo-field."

As he left the pathway he turned and distinctly waved his hand. Mara watched him in amazement, then turned wondering eyes to me. She saw that I was as much nonplused as she. Then she turned and looked intently at Natara. The hot blood mounted to Natara's brow.

Mara regarded the blushing face before her. She stood up and looked at the retreating figure on horseback. She turned and looked again at Natara, then she slowly sat down. She lighted another cigarette and did not speak for many moments. Finally she called Natara.

"Natara, come here," she said.

Natara came and stood before her. Mara asked softly:

"Have you seen him pass before?"

"Yes, he passed yesterday," answered Natara.

"Only yesterday?" asked Mara.

"No—the day before," answered Natara softly.

"And—?" said Mara with a question in her voice.

"And the day before," answered Natara with a blush.

"Has he seen you?" asked Mara.

Natara hesitated. "Yes, I think so," she said quietly.

Mara did not speak again, but lay back on her cushions smoking one cigarette after another, watching the smoke-wreaths as they curled and passed into the evening air. At last she rose and left without mentioning the subject again.

# XX

The next day it was the same. In the afternoon Mara came and we all three went to the roof. We sat there talking quietly of many things, the events occurring in the city and the gossip of the court, until the galloping horse was heard. I did not move, but looked in the direction of the sound. Mara rose and peered down at the rider. She watched him until at the bend of the path he turned and waved his hand. Then she, much to my surprise and consternation, waved hers in return.

Nothing that Mara did would cause me much surprise, as she was no longer an Indian woman in anything except appearances. She could not be judged by our standards. She had imbibed the ideas of freedom from women of the West, and her code and mine were oceans apart. Consequently I said nothing, but I am afraid my face reflected too well my thoughts, because Mara looked at me and laughed.

"You are shocked, Amina. Shocked to the center of your being, are you not?"

"I must confess," I said, "it is not the usual thing for a woman to wave to a stranger from our palace roof."

"No," said Mara, coolly. "I want him to think it was Natara who waved."

"What!" I exclaimed. I could say nothing more.

"Yes," she repeated. "I want him to think it was Natara who waved."

I could only look at Mara with wonder in my eyes. Then I asked, "Why?"

Mara moved her cushions over beside me; then, turning to Natara, said:

"Natara, take your women and go down for a time. I want to talk with Amina and do not wish listening ears near by."

Natara laughed.

"You think you will have secrets from me? No, Amina will tell me as soon as you are gone. I like secrets, too."

Laughing, she went down the stairway, followed by the three or four women who were at all times in attendance upon her. When we heard them in the courtyard, Mara turned to me.

"Amina, I have a plan, a wild plan it seems when I try to put it into words. But it came to me last night when I was lying awake trying to think of some way to help you. You remember that I said, being an *Indian* woman, there was no escape for Natara. She could not go to a foreign land, as she would be sent back. But if she were *not* an Indian woman, if she were married to a man of another race, she would take the nationality of her husband, and even a Maharajah could not take her from her husband."

I looked at her inquiringly, not clearly understanding nor following where she was trying to lead me. Then she said, a little impatiently:

"That boy who passed here is English, the only son of a great house in England. We will marry him to Natara, then she will be free."

I flung her hands from my shoulder and rose.

"What!" I cried. "Marry an Englishman!" and the scorn I felt for the race was echoed in my voice.

Mara drew me down beside her.

"Don't get excited, Amina," she said soothingly, "until you hear all I have to say. Why should she not marry an Englishman? He is of blood as good as hers, she would not be losing caste except here in India, and I hope that when once she leaves these shores she will never return to them. She would have an opportunity of living a life of freedom of which you could not even dream. She would have her chance for happiness, Amina, and it is her *only* chance."

I was quiet. I could not think clearly. Natara marry an Englishman! I knew little of the English. I had never cared to see the women who from time to time came to the Court to be received by the Maharanee. Many of our women watched them from behind the screens, and when again in their own apartments, made unkind remarks regarding their appearance. The long faces of the foreign women, their great noses, their untidy hair, their little, colorless eyes, and their ugly, ungraceful gowns, all were discussed with much laughter as we women clustered around those who had assisted at the audience. We screamed with glee as one of our pretty girls dressed herself as nearly as possible to look like the ugly wife of the Resident, and mimicked her walk and her high, falsetto voice.

Stories came to us of the home life of the English, of the manner in which they lived in our land. Many things were brought to our ears, gossip, unkind gossip, which plainly showed that English men do not guard carefully their womenfolk. Yet what could one expect from a people where the wives and daughters are allowed to mingle freely, with unveiled faces, with men? Where they receive men in their homes while their husbands are absent. It seemed to us, sheltered and guarded lovingly within the purdah, that every canon of decency and respectability was broken by these, our conquerors from over the seas.

But as I sat there I was not thinking of the morals of the women of England. It was of the men I was thinking. I remembered that Mara had told the Rajah that an Englishman had but *one* wife. That must mean that they loved but one woman with a love that endured, or they would certainly choose another wife. One does not live all one's life with a woman for whom there is no love in the heart.

I thought, if Natara could be the *only* wife of a man! If she could know that he would love and cherish her all her days, even when her face was lined and her hair was white. If she could live, knowing that each day did not bring nearer the knowledge that soon another and a younger woman would supplant her in her husband's heart. If she could give all of her love without fear, without the certain knowledge that it was wasted. If she could feel that no one else shared in the love of her Prince, and that she need not fear hourly that a new face might be added to those within her kingdom and her day of royalty be over. I sighed. I knew these dreams were impossible within a palace, but—and I heard Mara say again:

"Her *only* chance for happiness."

Finally I said:

"But he, Mara. What about him. I do not want Natara to marry a man who does not want her. It is love I am seeking for her, not simply freedom."

Mara sank back on her cushions with a low laugh, and began puffing again at her interminable cigarette. She saw that I would at least listen to her plan.

"Amina, do you not realize how beautiful Natara is? Seeing her each day, you have grown accustomed to her, but she is the most beautiful thing I have ever seen upon this earth. No man could see her and not love her. Our boy there is young, impressionable, is filled with the poetry of the East. He is looking for romance to peer from behind each enclosing wall, is waiting for a hand to beckon him. We will let it be the hand of Natara.

"We will let him find here a love such as he has never dreamed, luxury of which he has never read even in his most extravagant books of fairy tales, and such a girl as his wildest imagination could not conceive. We will woo him with flowers, with perfume, with music and with jewels, with all of the luxury of an Eastern court. We will transport him to Mohammed's paradise, and it will mean only Natara to him."

I listened to her and my breath came quickly.

"Yes, he will love her," I said. "She is made for love as perfume is made for the rose."

Mara was impatient with me.

"Love her? We will send him mad with love."

I was quiet for a moment, thinking; then I said:

"But, Mara, Englishmen do not marry Indian women, nor do Indian women of the better class marry with the English. It is breaking the code of both nations."

Mara studied her cigarette for a time, then she looked at me with a little frown between her eyes.

"Yes, I know that. I realize it fully. I have not figured it out—I know it is not done. It seems impossible—it is a mad idea, but I am at my wit's end."

We were both silent. Finally I said:

"It cannot be done, Mara. You know that the few English women who have braved the opinion of their countrymen and married men of our race, when they come to India they are not received either by their own people or by us. They must live in a world by themselves. And as for the women who give themselves to an Englishman—no one of our class would think of such a thing. A woman who does it is looked upon as lower than a pariah."

"Yes, you are right, Amina. I understand thoroughly, and—and—but Natara is a Princess Royal."

321

"Even marriage with a Princess Royal would be considered a disgrace in English eyes," I said bitterly. "You say this boy is in the Indian Civil Service, his father was in it before him, his grandfather. He has inherited the feelings, the prejudices of all English in regard to the subject people they govern. Even a Princess is a 'native' in his eyes, I am sure. He would not *consider* marriage."

"You are right, Amina, he would not consider marriage with what he calls a 'native' woman. But—as I said, we will drive him mad with love. Give me time and I will give that boy a glimpse of heaven, and he will dare anything to keep it."

"But what would he do, where would he go? He could not remain in India. He could not remain in the Service."

"No, he could not remain in the Service, but why should he? I want him to take Natara to England and never return to this country. In England it would only be remembered that Natara was a Royal Princess—she is rich, fabulously rich in English eyes—they would have the whole world open before them, with the exception of India, and perhaps in time they could return here for a visit, as conditions are changing. But—it is the only thing I see for Natara unless she goes to Naranabad, and we should risk anything to save her from that fate."

"But Achmed—Naranabad—what will they do?"

"I don't know, Amina. I am frank with you. I haven't figured it out as yet. I must have time to make my plans more complete. I hope they will not discover it until Natara is on her way to England. Until she is the wife of an Englishman. This betrothal to Naranabad is not known as yet; Naranabad would not want it known, it would make him the laughing stock of his world. Achmed would have to submit as gracefully as he could, as he would not want to quarrel with the English. He is in enough trouble with them now on his own account. He realizes that he is a little shaky upon his throne, and would not care to start a quarrel. He might feel that it would be a bond, to have the Royal Princess marry the only son of a great house in England. Especially as that house has influence in Indian affairs. He might, after the marriage was really made, feel that he could use it to his own advantage—and he needs all the influence he can get now with the powers that be."

She was quiet, and I left her alone to her thoughts. I went to the courtyard below and busied myself for a while, then returned to the roof. Mara looked at me.

"Amina, this boy must not know who Natara is, he must not see anything except the romance, the love, the beauty. He must not think. The thought of marriage will not enter his mind; it would revolt him, with his training and his Englishman's instincts. But we must make him so mad with love that he will throw all training, all traditions to the winds to possess the woman he loves. We can only plan the one thing now, gain his love and trust to the future that will in some way see the fulfilment of our plans. I will think, think, Amina—a way will be found."

She left me and I sat there long into the night, dreaming new dreams for my loved one, seeing new visions, wondering, fearing, hoping.

# XXI

I can offer no excuse for what we did. For the purdah woman, a woman who had the blood of generations of purdah women in her veins, I was breaking every law and principle of my caste. We are taught that we must live behind the lattice. That no man, with the exception of father or brother, must look upon our face until our marriage night, when the husband's hand may raise the veil. We may not woo nor be wooed until after the marriage vows are taken, and whether love comes to us or not, those vows are final. Any woman of my caste in India would sooner mount the funeral pyre than do what Mara and I were planning to do.

Yet—perhaps there is an excuse for me. I had passed my life in the women's quarters of an Eastern court, where all thought, all action, centered around the one theme—love. Where women passed their lives in beautifying themselves, going to any lengths to enhance their charms that they might hold the love of their lord. We are given love stories to feed the youthful imagination, we listen to women who prattle of only one thing—love.

Yet I had seen only one real love, that of the Rajah for my beloved Princess. The passion that the present Rajah exhibited for first one favorite and then another was not love, and I saw the unhappiness, the jealousy and sorrow that it brought. I saw women break their vials of love before his feet like a fragrance. I saw new faces brought to the palace filled with triumph at their victory, never fearing nor caring for the looks of hatred that glared at them from black eyes. They thought their reign would endure forever. Then I saw the look of happiness give way to looks of wonder, then of pain. The pain gave place to anger, jealousy, and in many cases to acts of madness, when, instead of love philters, white hands brewed poisons which were slyly given to hated rivals. We have had tragedies within our courtyards, sudden deaths, and then the swift retribution when the offending one was taken to a dreary place outside the city, there to pass her days in loneliness and exile.

I had watched it all these many years, and I had long ago decided that if my hands were not made powerless, Natara should be guarded from that life of jealousy and dread.

She should find love, not what that word means within a palace courtyard.

# XXII

We gave no inkling of our secret to Natara. We kept her from the housetop, much to her displeasure.

It was all so simple; afternoons spent upon the roof waiting for the galloping rider. A look over the balustrade, dark eyes that gazed into blue ones, a smile, a wave of the hand, an almond-blossom thrown into the path before the rider, or a flower shyly touched to lips, then dropped into eager, uplifted hands. It was not Natara's hand that dropped the flower, nor her black eyes into which those blue eyes gazed so ardently. But eyes when partially veiled and viewed from a distance are all the same, and those of Mara were just as black and perhaps more seductive than would have been those of the frightened Natara.

A few days passed with nothing but the exchange of glances, then Mara said to me:

"Amina, send away the women whom you cannot trust. Keep the slaves and the musicians, but no one in whom you have not the most implicit confidence. See that you alone have the key to the door that opens to the palace."

I said: "I alone have that key, except the one kept by the Rajah. He has the right to enter at will. I cannot forbid his entrance. He is our King and no door within his realm can be closed to him."

Gradually I found cause to send one woman to her home for a visit, others to friends in distant towns, until there were none within our palace except the women who were mine completely, who would obey me either through love or fear. They were my property, my chattels, the same as the peacock upon the wall, and my will was law to them.

Finally when all was arranged according to Mara's wishes, a note was dropped along with an almond-blossom, the flower of love. It told the eager boy to come to the western gate at sunset of the next day.

# XXIII

Mara came to me early the next afternoon and we spent with Natara long hours in the perfumed waters of the bath. Dexterous hands rubbed her soft body with crushed flowers until she exhaled the faint, sweet odor of jasmine from her very fingertips. The soles of her feet were tinted with the red paste of the Ashoka petals and jeweled sandals were placed upon them. A sari of rose gauze was wrapped around her body, one end draped over her midnight hair, leaving her right arm and shoulder bare except for the pearls with which we partially covered them. Pearls were placed about her throat and we stood back to see the effect of our handiwork. She looked like the bud of a rose. She had a beauty that caught your breath as you gazed upon it.

Natara was not surprised nor especially interested on the fateful after-noon, as we supervised her adornment. Women of the purdah spend end-less hours in the baths each day, and in choosing special gowns and jew-els. It is a thing of which they never tire—the adornment of their pretty persons.

When all was finished, when Natara's appearance suited even the exact-ing taste of Mara, she said to Natara:

"Go pick me some blossoms from the tree by the western gate. I wish to take them to a friend in the city, who, unlike you, does not have the flowers to make a wreath for her gods."

Natara left us and slowly wandered down the pathway. Her favorite peacocks came to her and she caressed them. They followed her, watching with seeming interest as she reached up to pick the rich clusters of bloom.

Mara and I did not speak for a time. I, because my heart was beating so loudly in my breast that I feared it might be heard. For a moment I wished to recall my dear one going so innocently towards that fateful gate which would open for her into an unknown world, a world of love and romance. Would that gate bring happiness or sorrow?

Mara read my face and, coming closer to me, said softly:

"What a beautiful thing is youth! See her there before that gate through which she has never passed, not knowing that through it, all is coming to her, that love and life wait at the gates of her garden—this beautiful garden of dreams."

It was the hour of sunset. Over the chain of hills the red sun went down. It flooded the garden with deep rose, while the sky merged into gold and purple and lastly into a sea of light mingled with fire.

We who watched, waited in breathless silence as a knock was heard on the door. The great gate was swung slowly inward by the gatekeeper. We saw the boy's face as it was framed in the shadow. No word was spoken. It seemed as if the noises of the dying day were stilled to greet his coming. The fragrance of unseen flowers came to him, and standing under a tree covered with glorious, flame-colored blossoms, two peacocks with great fan-like spreading trains beside her, was a figure, lissom, willowy, only half concealed by the flowing gauze that enveloped it.

A startled face, colorless yet suggesting a glow behind it, with great, passionate, dreaming, wistful eyes, shadowed by the gauze of the veil, was turned to him. He stopped. It seemed for the moment that the vision was unreal. Then he started forward and stretched his hands towards this being who appeared half woman and half dream.

Natara hesitated for a moment, frightened, wondering, not understanding—then she went to him.

The great gate closed silently behind them.

# XXIV

Love is a divine essence working through and through innumerable lives for its own glory. We love instinctively, and to those two standing there, something new and unknown touched them with its magic wand, and the old-time miracle worked its will once more.

They did not need to speak. Their souls spoke to each other from their inner world.

# XXV

The silence was broken by the faint sound of a bell in the distant temple. It brought the boy to life as, bending down, he took the hands that were holding the flowers and kissed them. The odor of jasmine came from her finger-tips.

Natara's face rivaled the flowers in color, but she did not withdraw her hand, and after a moment, hand in hand like a pair of children, they came up the pathway, that was filled with the scent of blossoms, where even the air seemed to murmur with some hidden joy.

They entered the palace where the women were putting scented oil in the silver lamps which sent forth a penetrating, aromatic odor that breathes of the East.

Natara led the boy to the stairway opening on to the roof. He gave but one glance to the scene spread out before him, then turned to Natara. He drew her to one of the cushions near the balustrade and seated her gently, then remained standing in front of her to watch this glorious thing that had come to him inside the magic gateway.

A boy passed along the path below them. His voice came to them faintly as he sang his even-song. It was as sweet at Krishna's flute calling lovingly across the meadows. It had the music of the hills, the color and scent of the roses, the swaying of the forests, the rippling of the water in its faint, sweet tones which drifted farther and farther away, until lost in the distance.

Women came to the roof and lighted incense in the braziers. They brought fruits and cakes and sweetened drinks and placed them on low tables, but neither of the two sitting there so silently seemed to see or hear them.

They were together, that was enough. The outside world was closed to them. They saw only each other.

The night wind came up, scented with warm tropical perfumes. The day was done and shadows hid under the trees. After a time the soft witchery of the moonlight filtered through the palm-trees, bathing them in its mystic light. The trees whispered together and threw ink-black shadows as they swayed softly in the evening breeze. Dark bodies came and went in the village below, which was half hidden in the dark green jack-fruit trees, the banana and the slender areca palm, among which fire-flies gleamed like watchmen with their tiny lanterns.

A light laugh was heard as a little boy with shaven head and naked brown body ran to a woman who was rubbing a drinking-pot, turning it round and round in her hands. The sound of unseen bells and conchs came from the distant temple.

Neil leaned to Natara, raised her and drew her to him. He bent her head and, looking into her eyes, found what he sought, and then he kissed her. For a moment Natara was motionless, then joy like a mist clouded her eyes, and lifting her face to the eager one bending over her, she returned his kiss.

They stood together, he holding her close to him, so close she could feel the throbbing of his heart; then I came towards them, and told them he must go.

Slowly, hand in hand, they descended the stairway and walked down the path until they came to the gate beside which stood a slave. As the gate swung open, Neil again took Natara in his arms and, looking into her eyes, said, with lips against her lips, "To-morrow?"

And Natara answered softly, "To-morrow."

Natara stood where Neil had left her. Even the murmur of the palm-trees was stilled and only the soft hush of the darkness was around her. She stood there, her lids lowered and motionless, her hands clasped on her bosom, her whole being absorbed in the wonder of this new beautiful thing that had come to her.

# XXVI

Lovers have always come through the evenings of the past. Each night Natara's lover came to her when the fires of sunset were burning low and the Western sky was a golden flame. Love grew among the scented flowers as they wandered hand in hand within the garden. They were like children, they played seek and find among the trees, they called the stately peacocks from their wall and teased them with their offerings. They threw fruit and cakes to the bands of monkeys that went swinging through the trees, but stayed their flight to chatter angrily and greedily snatch the shower of sweets. They made tiny boats of lotus-petals and sent them filled with wishes across the dark blue waters of the lake.

At first Neil seemed not to understand his surroundings: it was all so new and strange to him. But I could see that his soul was filled with the beauty. He would stand for long moments before the flowered scrolls of lace-like marble that were the windows, or he would touch with caressing fingers the marble flowers inset with jewels that formed the arches and panels of the rooms. The life of the palace seemed a dream life, as if when the gate was shut behind him, he entered another world from that in which he passed his days.

He, with Natara, at the Hour of Peace, would follow the women who lighted the scented oil in the silver lamps, and he watched with curiosity the evening worship as they walked around the tulsi-plant and chanted the even-song. One night Natara took him to her own small temple and showed him Madan upon his throne. "It is our god, the God of Love. Surely you will not deny him your worship!"

With a laugh he scattered magnolia-petals upon the head of the god, and after that each night at Time of Peace they silently stole away to strew the little room with flowers.

There before their God of Love he would take her in his arms and whisper words to her and touch her lips with his, until the temple of Madan became for them a Paradise.

# XXVII

They were not always alone nor wandering in the garden. When the purple twilight began to darken the violet hills, and the golden sun was replaced by stars, I sent for them and placed them upon the balcony that overlooked the courtyard. Slaves were there to pass them fruits and sweets, or to move the air with silken, perfumed fans.

From there they watched, themselves unseen, the dancers in the court below. These beautiful slender bodies turned and writhed and threw out their arms in acts of sweet abandon, until at last they fell as if worn out with their own great madness. When dancers withdrew into the shadowed archways, the singers took their places and intoned in soft, low voices, songs of love and sacrifice.

# XXVIII

Evenings when the moon's light was white and brilliant, I sent them to the lake, where the boat awaited them. There, lying lazily upon a divan, they were slowly rowed around the lake by women rowers whose brown bodies, clothed only in garments of flowers, rose and fell with regular movements as they chanted and rowed to the rhythm of their song. Young girls came from the shore and, grasping the ropes of roses that trailed from the boat, swam along its sides, adding their sweet young voices to the rowers' chant. As the boat passed close to the shores, flowers were flung from unseen hands, or pretty, laughing girls, looking like fairies amongst the shadows of the trees, scattered white petals upon their heads.

Stationed around the lake, hidden by the darkness, soft music came to them faintly over the water. A clear voice sang the verse of an old love song, then the refrain was taken up by others:

"I hunger for thee till my whole frame is weak
Oh, give me the food that I hungrily seek...."

... the words swelling out on the evening air then becoming softer as they drifted away from the singers. Then from another part of the lake came another verse:

"The streams of thy love will new life bestow
On the dry thirsty fields where its sweet waters flow."

Those nights upon the lake were dream nights, with music the enchanter. Music that came from over the water, now nearer, now farther, receding, coming, always eluding. Music incredibly mysterious and remote, rising and falling in passionate rhythm, pulsing in sweetness, lingering in tenderness, dominated ever by its own sadness. Eastern music with its minor tones that sang of love in endless measure. Magic music sung by perfect voices with throb of drum and flute and veena. Music that made the pulses beat, the face flush. The night was filled with its melody.

# XXIX

All memories may fade from me like the flowers from the almond-tree, but the memory of the beauty of this love that I watched grow day by day will stay with me until I hear the Watchman call and life is done.

# XXX

One night when the moon had flooded the earth with its silver light, Neil and Natara went to the lake to listen to the music. It came to them softly over the water, the soft thrum of the strings and the distant monotonous beat of the drums, hardly heard above the faint voices of the singers. When the last tones drifted away, Neil drew a deep breath, as if wakening from a dream.

"I am dreaming, Natara! This beautiful thing cannot be true. This is an enchanted garden. It is not real!"

Natara laughed.

"My garden is not enchanted, Neil. There is no magic within its gates, nor in the moonlight, nor in the whiteness of the sun. The magic is within our hearts."

Neil drew her to him.

"Will it last, Natara?" he asked. "Will it last? Will you always love me?"

Natara gave a happy, contented laugh.

"Thou hast sown within my heart the seed of love, which will grow in strength, as trailing creepers grow in length with each new season. Thou hast bound me with a twisted rope and so long as the sun and moon are within the skies, I am thine, thine own, part of thee."

As they strolled down the pathway to the gate, Natara said:

"How I love this pathway! When I came down it in other days I did not see its beauty, but now it leads to my beloved, it leads me to the gate through which comes my happiness."

Neil held her long in his arms; then, as the waiting slave turned impatiently, he kissed her and was gone.

331

Natara stood as the great gate closed, then turned, a happy smile on her lips, the sound of retreating footsteps beating in her heart, feeling still around her her lover's arms.

# XXXI

Natara raised her eyes and there before her stood her cousin, the Maharajah. They looked at each other in silence. At last, after what seemed an eternity to Natara, he spoke, with a sneer upon his lips and black anger in his voice.

"So this is the way you spend your nights within your garden!"

Natara said nothing.

"You have a lover and an Englishman!"

The Rajah could scarcely control his voice, and Natara trembled at the tone of rage and hate. Still she did not speak and the Rajah made a quick stride and stood in front of her.

"Tell me, how long has this been going on? Tell me, I say!"

He grasped her by the arm. Natara did not answer, and after looking at her with eyes of rage for a moment, he turned and strode towards the palace, Natara walking slowly behind him. As they entered, I, who had seen the meeting, came forward. The King stopped and looked at me.

"What do you mean by allowing such a thing to go on!"

"I do not understand, Your Highness," I said.

"You do not understand! You saw what I saw tonight, Natara in the arms of that young Englishman from the Residency."

"What do you want to know?" I asked, trying to gain time to think.

"I want to know how long this disgraceful thing has been going on!" he said, in such a cold, hard voice, that it frightened even me, who am not afraid of any man, even a King.

"I do not see the disgrace," I said, untruthfully.

"You do not," almost shouted the Rajah. "You, an Indian woman, say that? To meet a man unveiled, she, the daughter of a King? To be unveiled the same as a pariah? To be alone with a man, and one of that race I hate? No man has ever seen her face except her father and I since she went behind the purdah. She would be ruined if it were known. There will be no question of marriage for even a Princess if this tale is told. But I ask how long has this been going on?"

332

"Not long. I cannot tell you the exact time," I answered.

"Oh, you can't!" sneered the Rajah. "There are others who can. Asta!" he called to one of the waiting-women.

"You shall not question Asta," I said. "She is nothing but a slave."

"Yes," he said, "but slaves know the truth."

"She will not tell you, nor will you find out from Natara's household," I said.

"Oh, I will not!" came back sharp and quick from the King, with a cruel ring in his voice. "There is a way to make slaves speak."

I stepped in front of him, my eyes flashing.

"Your Highness, you dare not touch our women."

"I will do with your women what I will if they do not answer my question," he said. "We still have whips in the palace and strong arms to wield them."

At his words Natara stepped forward and faced the King, every line of her body tense with anger.

"You dare not touch my women, Achmed, nor dare you send one of your brutes to my palace to torture them! The slaves are mine, to obey me. They shall not suffer for it. Your word is not law within *my* walls."

The Rajah turned to Natara.

"Oh, you have found your voice!" he sneered. "Then you will tell me what I wish if you do not want your women hurt."

Natara looked at the brutal, dark face, at the straight, cruel lips, and for a moment she was silent, her head downcast. Then she raised her head and moved closer to the King who had thrown himself upon a divan.

"Yes, I will tell you what you wish to know," she said in a low voice.

"When did you first see the Englishman?" he asked.

"At the great durbar for Naranabad," she answered.

"But behind the screens?" he said.

"Yes," she answered.

"When again?" curtly.

"Each day as he went past to the polo-grounds."

"How did you see him?"

"I saw him from the palace roof."

"Did he see you?" he asked.

"Not at first," she answered.

"When did he first see you?"

"About two or three weeks ago."

"When did he first come into the garden?"

"About a week ago, I think," she answered.

The Rajah was quiet for a time, then he said:

"Why have you seen this Englishman?"

Natara did not answer at once; then she lifted her head and faced the cruel face opposite her.

"Because I love him," she answered quietly.

The King look at her in amazement. Finally he sneered:

"You love him! Bah! I suppose you think he loves you!"

"Yes, he does," said Natara.

"Love! An Englishman love! What is that old saying? The gods gave the Indian nine-tenths of the passion of the world, the other tenth, like beggars' dole, was flung to men of colder clime. Love! An Englishman!"

Natara spoke softly.

"I know you will not understand. I am speaking of *love*."

"So am I. What can you know of love, shut here behind the palace walls! What do you know—tell me."

"I do not know, except that love dawned in my heart as the sun when he came," she answered in a low voice.

The Rajah shrugged his shoulders.

"Well, I am glad that I came in time. No harm is done. I presume no one need know about it. We will hasten your marriage before Naranabad hears of it, and this little thing will be forgotten."

Natara stepped forward, a frightened look on her face.

"But, Achmed, I cannot marry Naranabad," she said. "I love Neil." She put out her hand and touched the shoulder of the Rajah. "I cannot marry Naranabad."

"You will marry Naranabad. We will commence the preparations at once."

"But I cannot, Achmed, I cannot. I love Neil. I love him," she repeated, as if the repetition of her words must convince the King of the impossibility of her being given to another.

The King laughed, and it made an ugly sound.

"Love—you do not know what love is, I say. You will love Naranabad just the same. In a month you will be his wife, then you can tell him what love is."

Then fear left Natara.

"Love—it is you who do not know its meaning. Within your cruel, dead heart could not be kindled even the tiniest flame of love. You cannot understand. Ah, Achmed," and her voice broke a little, "if you knew

334

what is within our hearts you could not speak so lightly of giving me to another."

The Rajah looked at her face for a time, studying it curiously, then he drawled:

"What is this thing within your hearts? But speak of yourself. Perhaps," and he looked at her with narrowing eyes, "I might—I only say I might—reconsider if you can make me see this love you say you feel—and that I do not understand."

Natara made a quick step towards him and a light came to her eyes. Perhaps he would not be so hard, perhaps when he understood how dearly she and Neil loved each other, he would not send her to Naranabad. She did not realize that it is as impossible to explain love to him who has not felt it, as the glories of the mogra-tree to one who is blind.

As she stood before him, her dark eyes filled with passion, a flush on her cheek, her small body tense with the strain, she made a very pretty picture. The Rajah appreciated it and leaned back on his cushions and watched her through half-closed eyes. No one could tell what was beneath those lids, nor what passed through his mind.

Natara's half-clenched hand went to her breast as she stepped towards the King.

"Shall I tell you, Achmed? Will you understand?"

Then she restrained not her tongue. She spoke in the fulness of her love, for the sake of that love.

"What is love? Ah, Achmed, I love Neil as the lotus loves the water. My life has become a garden. Love has taught me the meanings of the whispers in flowers and sunsets. I know now why there is music in the wind. We have been so happy here in our garden. It has seemed as if even the birds flying amongst the roses devoured their hearts with envy at the sight of our happiness. I have dreamed all my life of the lover who would come to me, and my dreams have come true. I have always dreaded the darkness, but now I know that the shadows of night will bring him to me and I watch for them with eagerness. When I stand at the gateway and listen for his footsteps, my heart beats so wildly that I cannot hear his knock. Ah, Achmed, can I make you understand what it means to love?" and she stretched out her hands towards him. "I am his lute, his veena. He can draw from me what melody it pleases him and none but him can bring it forth."

She stopped. The King watched each emotion as it passed over her beautiful face. He was silent for a moment, then he rose.

"Very pretty, Natara. Very pretty. You can bring all that wonderful love to Naranabad. He is an expert in—love. It will interest him—for a time," and he laughed a hateful laugh.

Natara stepped backward and the color left her face.

"But, Achmed, you said you would not send me to Naranabad."

"I said—what did I say?" sneered the King.

"You said if I would tell you, you would reconsider. That you would not send me to Naranabad if you understood the depths of my love. And I have told you. I have tried to make you understand."

"No, I did not," the Rajah replied curtly. "I said I might reconsider. I wanted to know what a young girl considered love, and it has been most amusing and instructive. But you go to Naranabad as soon as the arrangements can be made."

"Achmed—Achmed—" she cried. "I cannot! You will not do such a thing. You cannot!"

"What other alternative is there?" he asked.

"I—I—do not know—I have not thought—perhaps I—I can marry Neil and go to his country," she answered.

"You would go to that far-off cold country, amongst a people you do not understand?" he asked.

"A prison would be a rose garden if shared with him," she replied softly.

"You will not go with him, remember that," he said harshly.

"I will, Achmed. You may be King, but I am a Princess Royal, the daughter of a King, and you cannot control me."

"I cannot?" he said. "We will see."

At that moment Mara entered the courtyard. She stopped at sight of the expressions on the faces before her, and would have turned and left the court.

The Rajah regarded her as she stood hesitatingly before the archway; then a look of understanding seemed to come over his face. He turned his gaze from her to me, and a sneer curled his lips and a crafty, venomous light came into his eyes.

As she stepped back he called to her. "Stay, Mara."

She stopped.

He beckoned to her. "Come here."

She came and bowed before him.

He watched her for a moment. "So, I see. You are in this. It is some plan of yours. Amina would not dare and Natara hasn't enough brains to do a thing like this. What has been your idea?"

Mara held her head up proudly, a flush on her face.

"I do not understand you, Your Highness. Plan? What plan?"

"Yes, you understand me. How did that Englishman get in this garden if he were not brought in? And why should he be brought in? Amina wouldn't do it. You have done this—and why?"

Mara did not answer.

"You don't intend to tell me, I see. Well—I can't have you whipped, but perhaps I can figure it out for myself."

He sat silently for a time, watching Mara from his half-closed lids. Then he laughed, a nasty laugh that grated on the ears.

"I think I see it. You thought you could save, I presume you would call it, save Natara from Naranabad. But why an Englishman—they don't marry 'natives,'" and he sneered. "Were you thinking of having her run away with this man? Had you rather have her the mistress of an Englishman than Naranabad's Queen?"

Mara stepped towards the Rajah.

"How dare you, Achmed!"

"Did you think he would marry her?"

"Why not?" said Mara. "She is a Princess, he is of good family—why should they not marry?"

He laughed again. "So you *had* planned it! Natara was to marry an Englishman and become an English lady. Great idea! How about my consent?"

Mara did not reply. He waited a moment for an answer.

"I presume my consent was not to be asked."

"No, Achmed, your consent was not to be asked. I knew it would be useless. But, Achmed, why shouldn't Natara marry this boy? Why should she not go to England with him? There she would be an Indian Princess married to an English noble. She has charm, beauty, great wealth—there would not be any stigma attached to the marriage there. Neil could be placed in the Indian foreign office; he need not come back here. They could have a happy, wonderful life there together. Why not give her this chance for happiness? You know as well as I that her life as Naranabad's Queen would be only a mockery. Be big, Achmed; be kind. Let her go."

Achmed gave her a long look, a menacing look, then he said in a low voice: "Never! Next month Natara goes to Naranabad."

Natara stepped forward.

"I will *not!*" she said. "I will not go to him."

The King turned to her.

"Listen to me, Natara. You say you love this Englishman. If all this rubbish you have told me is true, then you will not care to ruin him. You know—or Mara knows, and I want her to hear all I have to say—you know the English do not interfere with our home affairs. It is fatal for an Englishman to even try to look behind our purdahs. Our women must not be molested, and their quarters are sacred even to that vandal race. Hear me, Natara—if you see this boy again, I will see that he is ruined. I will see that he is recalled in disgrace and no power can ever reinstate him. His future, as far as India is concerned, will be a blank. He comes of a family of Civil Service men, a family of diplomats. Their men have held office in India from the time of the English occupation. His grandfather was a viceroy, his father was a governor, and the son is intended to follow in their footsteps. With Naranabad and me against him, nothing can save him. England would not dare go against us. He will be utterly and forever ruined. I will follow him with my vengeance until he is in his grave."

Natara touched the Rajah's arm.

"But, Achmed, why should you ruin him? You would not do this thing. You would not!"

The Rajah flung her hand from his arm.

"I will use every means in my power, and Naranabad will do the same, to see that he is thoroughly disgraced. I will see that the foreign office dare not give him even a clerk's position. I will make of him a crossing-sweeper, so far as anything that touches India is concerned."

Natara stretched out her hands passionately towards the King.

"Achmed, you would not do this thing! You would not hurt me so! Even the hunter spares the bird that has taken refuge in his bosom. You will not be so cruel!"

The Rajah started towards the archway.

"There is nothing more to be said. If you see this boy again, I will do all that I have said and more if it is in my power to do it."

He was nearing the arch when Natara stepped towards him.

"Achmed, never see him again—"

The Rajah stopped. "Understand, never see him again. My guards will stand from now on at the western gate, and no one can enter from the palace unless I wish it."

Natara stepped towards the Rajah, and her voice was low and tense.

"Now, Achmed, you have given me your commands. I will speak and

338

you will listen to me. I will see Neil once more. I will hear from his lips what it means to him, this loss of position that you seem to think so great. I will see him once more."

The Rajah strode towards her and took her by the arm.

"See him? Never! You will never see him again. Do you understand me?"

Natara looked up into his face, and her own was set and white.

"Do you understand *me*, Achmed? I will see him—to-morrow night. I will talk with him—alone. You do not want a scandal at your court. You do not want the Royal Princess to be found lying broken on the pathway beneath her palace wall. You do not want the Resident to inquire too closely into what would cause the death of Princess Natara. You will place no guard at the western gate to-morrow night."

The King looked at the white face. Then after a moment he said:

"Will you promise me that it will be for the last time?"

"Yes," said Natara, "if what you say is true, if marrying me would mean his ruin, if he prizes the position which you seem to think he values so highly, I will promise never to see him again. But I *will* see him once more."

The Rajah was silent for a time, then he turned to me.

"Amina, for the last time your slave will be at the gate, to-morrow night."

He turned and left the court.

When the sound of the Rajah's footsteps died away, Mara rose from where she had fallen on the cushions, and raged up and down the room like a lion chained.

"How dare he, the brute! How dare he!" She turned to me. "How did he come to enter? You said he rarely came to your palace. Why did you not have a guard placed by the palace door? Why did he come?"

"I cannot tell. It may have been simply a fancy of his to see me or to see Natara. Or, there may be spies within our gates. One can never tell. There were some strange dancing girls—"

"But why did you not guard the doorway? You have been careless, Amina."

"I have not been careless," I replied gently. "I cannot guard against the Rajah. He has the right to enter when he wills. No guard could stop him. He has his guards on the other side of the door, what good to place mine on this side? He is the Rajah, remember."

Natara went to Mara and took her by the arm.

339

"Never mind, Mara. It is done. But tell me, Mara, would it ruin Neil if I went to him?"

Mara led Natara to a couch and drew her down beside her. She put her face in her hands and did not speak for long moments. Then she looked up and her face was drawn and tired.

"Yes, Natara. It would ruin Neil if Achmed should make trouble. I always knew that Neil could not come back to India—but—yes, if Naranabad joined with Achmed, Neil's career would be finished. It is true that the English must not look behind our purdahs. They are closed to them, and any one who dares to enter has all the forces of both countries against him."

Natara looked at her, then said quietly:

"But why did you not think of this before, Mara?"

Mara beat her hands together.

"I did, I did—I have thought of it all! But I thought it could be done quietly, that the secret could be kept until you were on your way to England, and that Achmed, for his own sake, would not interfere after it was done. I had not finished my plans—it all has happened so suddenly—I thought—oh, if once I could have gotten you to England—"

She rose and paced up and down the room.

Natara watched her for a time, then said:

"But would it mean so much to Neil to lose his position?"

"It is not so much the position, dear, but the disgrace. I presume it would break his father's heart. As the Rajah said, Neil comes of a long line of English rulers here in India. He is the last of his line, the last of his race. It is true, Natara, it would be ruin for Neil if two of the most powerful rulers in India demanded his recall. The English Government would not dare go against two men like Naranabad and Achmed. They are the strongest rulers in India and—and—they have the right on their side. But—I will not give up—there will be a way found—he hasn't beaten me yet, Natara—"

Mara again began walking up and down, smoking one cigarette after another.

"I will find a way. You shall not go to Naranabad. Wait, Natara, I will find a way yet."

Natara rose from the couch.

"Mara, I will see Neil to-morrow night, then I will find the way."

Mara turned to Natara.

"Natara, do not tell Neil. He will not give you up. We must have no scandal until we finally decide what we can do. He must not know—just give me a little time to think, to plan—"

"No," Natara said quietly. "He will not know, but I must hear from him the truth. I must know if my love would ruin him." She was silent for a few moments, walking slowly up and down the room. She stopped in front of Mara, and stretched her hands towards her imploringly.

"Help me, Mara. I do not understand. I would leave both worlds to follow him. What are rank and position where there is love? Neil will not give me up."

"No, Natara, Neil will not give you up—he will not have to. We will find a way. Oh, I was so sure that we could get you to England before it would be discovered. I would go with you myself—I was so sure that Achmed would not dare do anything—where have I made the mistake—but we will carry it out, Natara, we will *not* give up."

Mara turned to Natara.

"To-morrow night when you see him, say nothing. He is a hot-headed, passionate boy; he would act rashly and spoil all of our plans, of the new plans that I must make, that I *will* make." Mara looked at her closely. "You have not told him? You have obeyed us in this? He does not know who you are?"

"No; he thinks me one of the ladies of the Court. He has asked few questions. He has only loved me."

"You will tell him nothing, Natara. We must protect him, we must think of him now—I have only thought of you."

"I love him, Mara," Natara said softly. "You need not fear for him."

She sat quietly for a few moments, then, withdrawing herself from Mara's encircling arm, rose and left the courtyard.

Mara sat in brooding silence after Natara left, smoking one cigarette after another, her eyes dark and somber, her mouth a straight hard line. At last she rose and said:

"Amina, I am beaten to-night, but—I will not be beaten. I must think it over—I must have time. We will find a way—we *will*."

Then she left by the palace door.

# XXXII

I followed Natara to her rooms. She sent her women away and we were alone. I could say nothing—I could do nothing. She did not seem to feel my presence. She threw herself upon her bed, her arms above her head, her eyes staring at the silken hangings above her. She was a child no longer, but a woman facing the great problem of her life, and, as all must do, facing it alone. I could not help her even with my great love.

# XXXIII

The next day when the shadows began creeping over the marble traceries, Natara sent for her women. They did not know the sorrow that was tearing through her heart as she allowed herself to be bathed and perfumed and dressed in her most beautiful sari.

Pearls were twined about her throat, her arms and in her hair, and when she stood ready to meet her lover, she seemed a dream.

She came to me with a little caressing gesture and drew my face against hers, lightly brushing my cheek with her lips. I looked at her who was more to me than life. She was not the laughing girl who had gone down the pathway each evening, but a sad, sorrow-crowned woman who stood before me. Her pallid face was emotionless, her whole body tense, her being absorbed in this terrible thing that had come to her.

She went slowly down the pathway to the gate. She stood silently listening for his footsteps through the stillness, until at last the knock was heard, and the gatekeeper swung the great gate inward.

Neil entered in his boyish, eager way, and took Natara in his arms. She lay there quietly for a moment, then they came slowly up the path, Neil with his arm around Natara, her hand pressing his hand so that she might feel its warmth where it lightly touched her waist. They stopped to play a few moments with the peacock that fluttered to them, then mounted the stairway to the roof, Neil's favorite place.

The servants had arranged the cushions as usual near the corner of the balustrade. Neil threw himself down and drew Natara beside him.

342

"What do you think, Natara! I have to go to Bombay next week! The Resident is sending some very private messages to the Governor and he has chosen me to go for him. I'm awfully flattered that he chose me instead of Captain Young, but—I hate to go. I will be away a week, and maybe longer. I hate to leave you, Natara, but—well, I am rather proud that I have been chosen, because the work is really very important. It shows that I am getting on."

Natara was silent and Neil looked at her curiously.

"Aren't you sorry, Natara? Why don't you say something?"

Natara was still silent, and Neil threw himself full-length on the silken cushions and laid his head in Natara's lap. Natara's fingers touched softly Neil's face and hair; then after a time she said:

"Neil, tell me about your work. About your people."

"What about them?" he asked.

"About your grandfather. He was Viceroy in India at one time, was he not?"

"Yes," said Neil, with the reluctance of an Englishman to talk of himself or his family.

"And your father?" inquired Natara.

"Oh, he was Governor of Madras for a time," he answered.

"All of your people have been Indian officials, have they not?"

"Yes," said Neil.

"Tell me about it, Neil. Tell me about them."

Neil moved uncomfortably and drew to his lips the hand that was touching his hair. Then he answered:

"Well, there is nothing much to tell. We have all been here in India sort of from father to son. It is an understood thing that the men of our race will come out in India."

"And you—" she asked softly.

"Oh," and Neil laughed lightly, "I suffer the usual fate. I walk in father's footsteps. There is nothing else for me, and—and—it is a great thing, Natara, to be an official in India. We can do a lot of good, you know, we who have sort of inherited India and know her customs and traditions. We understand her people much better than the man who is new on the job."

"You—you—like your work, Neil? You would not give up your career?"

Neil laughed again.

"Like it, Natara? I love it! I wouldn't be anything else for the world!

343

Anyway, I couldn't. India is in our blood and we wouldn't be good for anything else. I couldn't imagine a future out of India. I feel that her people are my people, her land my land. It is part of me. Why—I don't even want to go home on leave. And as for living there, well—I just couldn't do it."

"If—if—you went home to live, what would you do in England?" asked Natara.

Neil was quiet for a moment, as if studying the problem placed before him. Then he said:

"I haven't the faintest idea. I'm good for nothing else but this life. I have been trained for it, educated for it. The only thing I have been taught regarding my future is India. And it is a great future, Natara, and—and—I'm awfully ambitious, and—I want to make good. I don't want to fall down, well—for the family's sake, if for nothing else. They expect a lot from me—and I'm going to make good."

"They are proud of you?" asked Natara in a low voice.

Neil laughed an embarrassed laugh.

"All parents are proud of their sons," he said. "And I'm the only son, the last of the line, and they want me to go out in a blaze of glory. The Governor, well—he's a nice old Governor, and the Mater, she's like all mothers, thinks I'm the only boy in the world, and that there is no place too big for me if I only try for it. I'm sure she's got the cushions all planned for the Viceroy's chair I am to sit in one of these days."

"If you did not succeed, it would hurt them?"

"It would kill them, I think," he answered quickly. "But there is no chance that I won't succeed. I have everything in my favor and I'm going to get to the top. I wouldn't disappoint them for the world."

Natara was quiet for a time, then she said:

"Neil, won't it hurt you if it is ever known that you love an Indian woman?"

A quick frown came over the boyish face. Natara did not know the long hours Neil had studied and worried over this problem. He knew India and he knew he was doing the forbidden thing. He knew that he should not have entered the garden. He had entered it lightly at first, expecting only a little romantic adventure. He had shut his eyes to the code of his class that he knew he was breaking. He was blinded by his great love. Whenever the thought thrust itself upon him that he was practically committing a crime in English eyes, especially the eyes of officialdom, he put it away. His case was different. Natara was different;

344

she was not an ordinary woman. And—he would not think of the future. He would just be happy, live in the present. This garden, this girl, this love, was beautiful. He would live in its present beauty. He would not think.

He did not answer for a time, and Natara studied his face anxiously. At last he said:

"Well—it is rather unusual—and perhaps—well, I might have a little trouble if it were known—but—well, let's not talk about it. We're happy now, let's not think of disagreeable things. Where's the music? Let's just be happy to-night."

"I told them not to sing to-night, not for a time. Do you want them?"

"Yes; have them far away so that we can just hear them. I like the music, it goes with the night and the palm-trees and you, Natara, the most beautiful sweetheart in the world."

Natara spoke to one of the women crouching by the balustrade. She left, and soon from the distance could be heard the liquid murmur of music rising and falling through the darkness of the night.

They listened to the music in silence. Neil brought Natara's face to his own, caressing her eyes, her lips, her soft neck. He buried his face in the shadows of her hair.

"You are the most beautiful thing, Natara. But—" and he held her face in his hands. "You have asked me a lot of questions about myself and my family. Now tell me, Natara, about yourself."

Natara said:

"There is nothing to tell, Neil, except what I have told you. I am one of the ladies of the Court of the Princess. I am her namesake, and—and—I have her palace for a time."

"Yes, you are of good blood, one can see that," he said.

"I am of good family," she answered. "My people are Court people—that is all there is to tell."

Neil laughed. "I don't care who you are, Natara. I love you; I'd love you the same if you were a pariah."

Natara bent over him.

"Would you, Neil?" she asked eagerly. "Would you?"

"Certainly, I would. Even if your father was the chief of the Thugs and your mother was a crossing-sweeper. I couldn't help it *now*. I love you, and I don't care a hang about your people."

"But, Neil, would you be willing to lose your position, your career for me?"

A frown came to Neil's face, and he hesitated.

345

"I'd hate to lose my position, I'd hate to disappoint my people, the old man would be heartbroken, and Mother—but I won't lose *you*, Natara. They wouldn't count if it came to losing you. You're just all to me. I'd give up everything and go to Sussex and raise pigs and calves or whatever they raise in Sussex rather than lose you. Oh, Natara!" and he drew her face to him and looked into her eyes. "There's nothing else in the world but just *you*."

They were quiet for a time. Then he said, as if shaking off something that troubled him:

"Let's not think of careers nor the future nor anything but that we are together, and that this is the most beautiful world. Let's just love each other."

At last, at a sign from me, one of the women gave a soft clap of her hands and Natara knew that it was time Neil should go. She started at the slight sound, then she clasped Neil to her as if she would not let him leave her. She bent over him, half covering him with her rose-wrapped body.

"I cannot let thee go, I cannot!" she said in a low tone.

Neil looked at the distant slave resentfully.

"What does she mean by saying that I must go? I have just come!" he complained.

Natara laughed a little sadly.

"You say that each night, Neil."

She looked into his face, as if to impress her memory with each line.

"Do you love me, Neil? Say it again. Say, 'I love you, Natara, I love you.'"

Neil held her close to him.

"How can I tell you, Natara? I can only say I love you—love you—love you."

Natara touched his face with her hands, caressed his eyes, traced the curve of his mouth with her finger-tips, and she said, as if to herself:

"Thy voice will always sound in my heart like the muffled sigh of the wind in the palm-trees. I shall feel forever the prison of thy dear arms."

She held his face in her two hands and looked long into his eyes, her voice so low and tragic that Neil was involuntarily silenced.

"Look at me, Neil. Remember me. Remember my face, my hair, my hands, my voice. Do not forget me. I shall be near you always. On the straying moonbeams I shall lie upon your bosom when you sleep. I shall be the ripples of the water when you bathe. I shall be the music unheard by others that throbs in your heart all day. When you are alone I shall sit by your side and whisper, and when you are in crowded chambers I will fence you about with aloofness."

Neil looked down at her curiously.

"Of course you will be with me always, dear one. Nothing can ever separate us. I am yours and you are mine."

Natara lay in his arms quietly, then she cried, with all the sorrow that was tearing through her heart, in her voice:

"Take me with you, Neil. Take me with you!"

She drew him to her fiercely.

"Take me with you, Neil. I cannot let you go."

Neil spoke to her lovingly, as he would to an impatient child.

"Some day, Natara. We'll plan it all out—some day—"

Natara drew herself slowly from his arms.

"Yes, I understand, Neil. You must go now. Amina is impatient."

Neil reluctantly rose and they went down the stairway. As they came before the little temple, Natara hesitated for a moment, then said:

"Shall we lay the blossoms before Madan?" Then under her breath so Neil did not hear, "For the last time?"

Neil laughed and they entered the temple. From the heaped mass of fragrance before the god they took the white, waxy petals and formed a chain for Madan's neck, bracelets for his tiny arms, and anklets. Natara strewed the floor with the loosened petals. But there was no laughter in her voice, no play, as she urged Neil to bow before the tiny god.

"Just once, Neil. See, I touch his foot with my head. Just once."

"No," laughed Neil. "I will give him all the flowers he wants, but I won't bow to him. You do the worship for the family, Natara."

Natara knelt for a moment in silence before her god, then they went from the palace down the pathway.

# XXXIV

The next night when the setting sun was touching the distant hills with gold, eager, boyish steps came down the roadway and stopped at the usual place. He put out his hand to knock upon the gate—but there was no gate. Neil looked in amazement. The light whistle died upon his lips. There was nothing before him but a great blank wall.

347

He looked along the wall. Had he made a mistake? It could not be. There was no place in the world that he knew so well as this road leading to the western gate.

But there was no gate.

He stepped back and looked up at the wall. There it was, a long, blank wall built of great stones, that looked as if it had been there for centuries. There was no opening, no sign that a gate had ever existed in its unbroken length.

Neil paced slowly back and forth. Then he encircled the place. He walked to the end of the wall, came back and went to the corner, turned and followed to the next corner, then paced down the third side of the enclosure.

There was no gate, nothing but great stones faced him. He could not understand it. He did not know that slaves had worked the entire night through, filling the gateway and that now there was no entrance to the garden by the lake except through the small door that led into the palace of the Rajah. The work had been well done. There was nothing to show that one part of the wall was not as old as the rest. It all had the same appearance, one stone was the same as another.

It seemed hours to Neil that he stood in front of that frowning mass of masonry. Then he thought of the roof. He went hurriedly to a place on the road where he could see the roof. It was deserted. There were no forms to be seen above the balustrade.

In a daze, at last he turned away.

Day after day a haggard, frantic boy came down the roadway searching for the western gate. There was no sight nor sound from within the guarding wall. Nothing to show the heartbreak and sorrow that was within, as preparations were being hurried for the marriage of the Princess Royal.

Neil heard of the marriage, of the great durbar that was to be given, but it meant nothing to him. This other Natara, the Princess, did not interest him. Where was *his* Natara? He could ask no one, he could tell his trouble to no one. Had the past week been a dream?

He could not work, he could not eat, he could not sleep. He passed from a healthy, happy boy into a man with tragedy in his eyes.

The Resident noticed his changed appearance, and, in the kindness of his heart, decided that a change was necessary. He was told that he should go to Bombay at once. There was nothing to do but obey.

The night before he left, watching slaves saw a figure in the moonlight, slowly pacing back and forth before what had once been a gate that led to a garden.

An enchanted garden of Dreams.

# XXXV

I have told the story of my Princess. I have lived again those days and nights passed in the palace by the lake. Now when I am carried to the courtyard in the quiet of the evening, when even the birds have become silent, when the flowers are flinging their sweetness on the evening air and the palms whisper and throw fan-like shadows across the marble, I return again to that past.

Vast and deep the night enfolds me and I drift away in dreams. I see the scroll of the past unrolled before me. I think of those first days when my Royal Mistress came as Queen to Naranabad. The world realized after a time that a great Queen ruled in India, ruled two kingdoms, that of her husband and that of Achmed.

Naranabad and Achmed lived for pleasure. More and more their days and nights were given up to the pursuit of pleasure. More and more without their knowledge the reins of their government were drawn into two kind hands that drove the chariots of State, and they were driven wisely and well. All India knew that from behind the purdah of Naranabad came justice, tempered always with mercy.

Her days were full. There was no Court in the Eastern world that was so magnificent. There were no audiences granted to the women of both Oriental and Western lands that rivaled those of Natara, the Queen of Naranabad. But only I saw her through the long nights when she cried aloud in her sorrow, listening for a footstep through the darkness.

Natara, the girl, would have been content to sit still and drift in dreams back to the Kingdom of the Past, but I knew that dreams alone would never place within her hands the shell of forgetfulness. Yet she did not want to forget. When I would say to her, "Forget, Natara; it is your only path to happiness, to peace," she would cry:

"Forget? Never! If all the kingdoms of the world were offered me in exchange for my memories, I would laugh their gifts to scorn. I want remembrance, but I want it without pain."

I, who had been the cause of the sorrow of my Princess, tried to find another pathway to the door of happiness. She must not yield to the current of despair, she must re-set the water-wheel of life. Natara must leave her girlhood. She must be a queen.

I gave her the example of her father's sorrow and how he filled his saddened days with work. I showed her her people, those simple, ignorant, helpless people, whose lives from their dawn to their setting are passed in little mud-baked villages. We searched for the child checked in its growth, the woman in her suffering—looked where the poor were pushed to the wall, the friendless forgotten—where the fallen were left to die and where the weak were oppressed by the strong, and there she sent her messengers.

From the women's quarters of a palace she sent laughter where before there were tears. I wanted her to cover the world with the shadow of her love. I wanted her to dream great dreams, to have great visions of what could be done in her kingdom for the good, the happiness, of her subjects. We learned that though great the thing a man dreams, it is not so great as are those dreams, and one might as well try to dip out the ocean with a shell as to stop entirely the sorrow caused by man's oppression of his fellow-man. Yet I console myself with the thought that a man's wishes should be the measure of him, not by what he achieves should he be judged, but by what he desires to achieve. In the striving to make those dreams come true is found the only royal road to happiness.

I, in my blindness, thought that love should be the birthright of my Princess, but the gods have touched mine eyes and I see more clearly. She was not to be given to a selfish love, sweet though it was, but love was given her to open a window of her heart. Only a man who has been hungry can be stung into sympathy with the hunger of others, a man who has known the grinding, crushing agony of poverty, can understand its pain. It is the same with sorrow. Only he who has felt the tearing of his own heart-strings, can touch with understanding, kindly hands the quivering nerves of him who is in despair.

When her bowl of happiness was taken from her lips she thought that her day was ended; but life was made richer for countless thousands because of the love that was lost.

Natara loved, she suffered, she lost, but in the end she gained. Life is made up of experiences, not definitions. She lived, through others, perhaps, not through an active happiness of her own; for the torch of joy did not burn brightly in her own hands except to light men's lamps in shadowed homes and their rays shone across her darkened windows.

# XXXVI

Yet,—after all, when everything is ended, nothing is worth a wish save love. Love is life in all its fulness. Whether it brings joy or sorrow as its gift, its coming should be welcomed with open hands. It is the very flower of life, and the perfume of its presence will shed fragrance over the gray days long after the rose has faded.

Above the noise of the world, love's voice will linger in the heart, a never-ceasing song, calling softly, like the murmur of an Eastern river flowing gently to the sea.

## Epilogue

Once in after years, when snow had powdered the locks of Neil, he was sent to Naranabad to exact punishment for an uprising against the English power. The people of the North had in their madness, urged on by England's enemies, risen and burned and killed and looted, and England's answer had been swift and just.

When order was once more restored, she sent as messenger to demand indemnity and lives for the lives taken, her great Ambassador, Neil Thornton. England's terms were hard, and punishment would fall upon the innocent as well as the guilty.

Naranabad became panic-stricken, and, as usual, turned to his Queen for help in his time of trouble. It was she who must ask for mercy for his people.

The Ambassador was summoned to the palace, and from behind a marble screen he heard a voice that for a moment caused the years to fall away and seemed to still the very beating of his heart. But it was only for a moment, and he was again the Ambassador demanding justice in the name of his King.

After he had stated the terms, there was silence. Then that voice which had haunted him all these years, said softly:

"I have been told, Your Excellency, that you passed your early years in India. Have you no remembrance that will cause you to soften your heart to the cries of its people?"

For a moment Neil could not speak as he listened to that low, passionate voice, and he half rose from his chair, his hands grasping its arms until the carved wood cut into his flesh.

"Who are you?" he said in a low, tense voice. "Who are you?"

"I am the Maharanee of Naranabad. But you do not answer my question," the low voice said. "I will ask it again. Has India's nights, with its thousand powers of scent and stars and gloom, no message for you? Will it not take you back to those swift, sweet years when you were young—those golden years with its starlight silence and dreams? Are there no times at twilight too heavy for memory? Have you no divine remembrance of some lost heaven?

"When from some near-by village you hear the throbbing of a drum, the wistful wailing of a flute, now near, now softly distant, does not its plaintive wistfulness speak to your heart? Can you not see the palm-trees erect and slim against a golden sky, and hear as twilight closes the muezzin's mournful chant from the slim minarets half hidden amongst the flowering trees?"

There was silence for a moment, then the low voice continued:

"Do you never, in that cold, bleak homeland of yours, go to the window and instead of seeing the rain and the gray sky, see the sun setting red and gold over the hills, the village clustering at the foot of the neem-trees, hear the temple bells call the women to their worship?

"They say you are as cold as the Tirah's snows. Perhaps you have learned the secret bitterness of things, a sorrow that lies hidden from the world has touched your heart. If thy song has remained unsung, the rose ungathered, should it harden the heart? Has romance never come to you in all its jeweled state? Have you had no lovely dream that once was living truth? Have the breezes that stir among the tamarind-trees, that rustle through the jasmine-flowers, no message for you? Is there no scent that you fear? Does not the magnolia-bloom speak to you from its waxy depth?"

Again there was silence, then:

"Have your blue eyes that conquer no remembrance of darker eyes that dream—eyes lit up by love—of scented, shady closes, where you kissed lips beneath the roses?

"Will you not let that which has been hidden in your heart as its desire speak for India? Will you not let the memory of those passionate days spent in this magic land call to you now when she pleads for her people?"

The face of the Ambassador was as white as the marble screen before which he sat. He could not speak, only stare at the delicate filigree, trying to pierce its secret. At last he said, in a voice, hoarse, drowned with emotion:

"Who are you—I demand to know—who are you?"

There was a rustle, as if some one rose from a seat, and the low tones answered, from a distance:

"I am the voice of India—asking for mercy."

# The Counsel Assigned

## MARY RAYMOND SHIPMAN ANDREWS

*The counsel assigned to defend the young man on trial in that small courtroom was the Great American. Here is yet another short story about the prairie lawyer named Abraham Lincoln, but it takes its place as an admirably written and enjoyable chapter in the book of American idealism.*

A VERY OLD MAN told the story. Some twenty years ago, on a night in March, he walked down the bright hallway of a hotel in Bermuda, a splendid old fellow, straight and tall; an old man of a haughty, high-bridged Roman nose, of hawklike, brilliant eyes, of a thick thatch of white hair; a distinguished person, a personage, to the least observing; not unconscious possibly, as he stalked serenely toward the office, of the eyes that followed. An American stood close as the older man lighted his cigar at the office lamp; a red book was in his hand.

"That's a pretty color," the old fellow said in the assured tone of one who had always found his smallest remarks worth while.

The American handed it to him. As he turned over the leaves he commented with the same free certainty of words, and then the two fell to talking. Cigars in hand they strolled out on the veranda hanging over the blue waters of the bay, which rolled up unceasing music. There was a dance; a band played in the ballroom; girls in light dresses and officers in the scarlet jackets or the blue and gold of the British army and navy poured past.

The old man gazed at them vaguely and smiled as one might at a field of wind-blown daisies, and talked on. He told of events, travels, adventures—experiences which had made up an important and interesting life—a life spent partly, it appeared, in the United States, partly in Canada, where he was now a member of the Dominion Parliament. His enthusiasm, it developed, was for his profession, the law. The hesitating, deep

355

voice lost its weakness, the dark eyes flashed youthfully, as he spoke of great lawyers, of legal *esprit de corps.*

"It's nonsense"—the big, thin, scholarly fist banged the chair arm—"this theory that the law tends to make men sordid. I'm not denying that there are bad lawyers. The Lord has given into each man's hand the ultimate shaping of his career; whatever the work, he can grasp it by its bigness or its pettiness, according to his nature. Doctors look after men's bodies and parsons after their souls; there's an opinion that lawyers are created to keep an eye on the purses. But it seems to me"—the bright old eyes gazed off into the scented darkness of the southern night—"it seems to me otherwise. It seems to me that the right lawyer, with his mind trained into a clean, flexible instrument, as it should be, has his specialty in both fields. I am a very old man; I have seen many fine deeds done on the earth, and I can say that I have not known either heroic physicians or saintly ministers of God go beyond what I've known of men of my own calling. In fact——"

The bright end of the cigar burned a red hole in the velvet darkness, the old man's Roman profile cut against the lighted window, and he was silent. He went on in his slow, authoritative voice:

"In fact, I may say that the finest deed I've known was the performance of a lawyer acting in his professional capacity."

With that he told this story:

The chairman of the county committee stopped at the open door of the office. The nominee for Congress was deep in a letter, and, unpretentious as were the ways of the man, one considered his convenience; one did not interrupt. The chairman halted and, waiting, regarded at leisure the face frowning over the paper. A vision came to him, in a flash, of mountain cliffs he had seen—rocky, impregnable, unchangeable; seamed with lines of outer weather and inner torment; lonely and grim, yet lovely with gentle things that grow and bloom. This man's face was like that; it stood for stern uprightness; it shifted and changed as easily as the shadows change across ferns and young birches on a crag; deep within were mines of priceless things. Not so definitely, but yet so shaped, the simile came to the chairman; he had an admiration for his Congressional candidate.

The candidate folded the letter and put it in his pocket; he swung about in his office chair. "Sorry to keep you waiting, Tom. I was trying to figure out how a man can be in two places at once."

"If you get it, let me know," the other threw back. "We've a use for that trick right now. You're wanted to make another speech Friday night."

The big man in the chair crossed his long legs and looked at his manager meditatively. "I didn't get it quite figured," he said slowly. "That's my trouble. I can't make the speech here Friday."

"Can't make—your speech! You don't mean that. You're joking. Oh I see—of course you're joking."

The man in the chair shook his head. "Not a bit of it." He got up and began to stride about the room with long, lounging steps. The chairman, excited at the mere suggestion of failure in the much-advertised speech, flung remonstrances after him.

"Cartright is doing too well—he's giving deuced good talk, and he's at it every minute; he might beat us yet you know; it won't do to waste a chance—election's too near. Cartright's swearing that you're an atheist and an aristocrat—you've got to knock that out."

The large figure stopped short, and a queer smile twisted the big mouth and shone in the keen, visionary eyes. "An atheist and an aristocrat!" he repeated. "The Lord help me!"

Then he sat down and for ten minutes talked a vivid flood of words. At the end of ten minutes the listener had no doubts as to the nominee's interest in the fight, or his power to win it. The harsh, deep voice stopped; there was a pause which held, from some undercurrent of feeling, a dramatic quality.

"We'll win!" he cried. "We'll win, and without the Friday speech. I can't tell you why, Tom, and I'd rather not be asked, but I can't make that speech here Friday." The candidate had concluded—and it was concluded.

Travelling in those days was not a luxurious business. There were few railways; one drove or rode, or one walked. The candidate was poor, almost as day laborers are poor now. Friday morning at daybreak his tall figure stepped through the silent streets of the western city before the earliest risers were about. He swung along the roads, through woodland and open country, moving rapidly and with the tireless ease of strong, accustomed muscles. He went through villages. Once a woman busy with her cows gave him a cup of warm milk. Once he sat down on a log and ate food from a package wrapped in paper, which he took from his pocket. Except for those times he did not stop, and nine o'clock found him on the outskirts of a straggling town, twenty miles from his starting-point.

The court-house was a wooden building with a cupola, with a front veranda of Doric pillars. The door stood wide to the summer morning. Court was already in session. The place was crowded, for there was to be a murder trial to-day. The Congressional candidate, unnoticed, stepped inside and sat by the door in the last row of seats.

It was a crude interior of white walls, of unpainted woodwork, of pine floors and wooden benches. The Franklin stove which heated it in winter stood there yet, its open mouth showing dead ashes of the last March fire; its yards of stovepipe ran a zigzag overhead. The newcomer glanced about at this stage-setting as if familiar with the type. A larceny case was being tried. The man listened closely and seemed to study lawyers and Judge; he was interested in the comments of the people near him. The case being ended, another was called. A man was to be tried this time for assault; the stranger in the back seat missed no word. This case, too, came to a close. The District Attorney rose and moved the trial of John Wilson for murder.

There was a stir through the courtroom, and people turned on the hard benches and faced toward the front door, the one entrance. In the doorway appeared the Sheriff leading a childish figure, a boy of fifteen dressed in poor, home-made clothes, with a conspicuous bright head of golden hair. He was pale, desperately frightened; his eyes gazed on the floor. Through the packed crowd the Sheriff brought this shrinking, halting creature till he stood before the Judge inside the bar. The Judge, a young man, faced the criminal, and there was a pause. It seemed to the stranger, watching from his seat by the door, that the Judge was steadying himself against a pitiful sight.

At length: "Have you counsel?" the Judge demanded.

A shudder shook the slim shoulders; there was no other answer.

The Judge repeated the question, in no unkind manner. "Have you a lawyer?" he asked.

The lad's lips moved a minute before one heard anything; then he brought out, "I dunno—what that is."

"A lawyer is a man to see that you get your rights. Have you a lawyer?"

The lad shook his unkempt yellow head. "No. I dunno—anybody. I hain't got—money—to pay."

"Do you wish the court to assign you counsel?" He was unconscious that the familiar technical terms were an unknown tongue to the lad gasping before him. With that, through the stillness came a sound of a boot that scraped the floor. The man in the back seat rose, slouched forward, stood before the Judge.

"May it please your Honor," he said, "I am a lawyer. I should be glad to act as counsel for the defence."

The Judge looked at him a moment; there was something uncommon in this loose-hung figure towering inches above six feet; there was power. The Judge looked at him. "What is your name?" he asked.

The man answered quietly: "Abraham Lincoln."

A few men here and there glanced at the big lawyer again; this was the person who was running for Congress. That was all. A tall, gaunt man, in common clothes gave his name. Frontier farmers and backwoodsmen in homespun jeans, some of them with buckskin breeches, most in their shirt-sleeves, women in calico and sunbonnets, sat about and listened. Nobody saw more. Nobody dreamed that the name spoken and heard was to fill one of the great places in history.

The Judge, who had lived in large towns and learned to classify humanity a bit, alone placed the lawyer as outside the endless procession of the average. Moreover, he had heard of him. "I know your name, Mr. Lincoln; I shall be glad to assign you to defend the prisoner," he answered.

The jury was drawn. Man after man, giving his name, and, being questioned by the District Attorney, came under the scrutiny of the deep eyes under the overhanging brows—eyes keen, dreamy, sad, humorous; man after man, those eyes of Lincoln's sought out the character of each. But he challenged no one. The District Attorney examined each. The lawyer for the defence examined none; he accepted them all. The hard-faced audience began to glance at him impatiently. The feeling was against the prisoner, yet they wished to see some fight made for him; they wanted a play of swords. There was no excitement in looking at a giant who sat still in his chair.

The District Attorney opened the case for the People. He told with few words the story of the murder. The prisoner had worked on the farm of one Amos Berry in the autumn before, in 1845. On this farm was an Irishman, Shaughnessy by name. He amused himself by worrying the boy, and the boy came to hate him. He kept out of his way, yet the older man continued to worry him. On the 28th of October the boy was to drive a wagon of hay to the next farm. At the gate of the barn-yard he met Shaughnessy with Berry and two other men. The boy asked Berry to open the gate, and Berry was about to do it when Shaughnessy spoke. The boy was lazy he said—let him get down and open the gate himself. Berry hesitated, laughing at Shaughnessy, and the Irishman caught the pitchfork which the lad held and pricked him with it and ordered him to get down. The lad sprang forward, and, snatching back the pitchfork, flew at the Irishman and ran one of the prongs into his skull. The man died in an hour. The boy had been thrown into jail and had lain there nine months awaiting trial. This was the story.

By now it was the dinner hour—twelve o'clock. The court adjourned and the Judge and the lawyers went across the street to the tavern, a two-story house with long verandas; the audience scattered to be fed, many dining on the grass from lunches brought with them, for a murder trial is a gala day in the backwoods, and people make long journeys to see the show.

One lawyer was missing at the tavern. The Judge and the attorneys wondered where he was, for though this was not the eighth circuit, where Abraham Lincoln practised, yet his name was known here. Lawyers of the eighth circuit had talked about his gift of story telling; these men wanted to hear him tell stories. But the big man had disappeared and nobody had been interested enough to notice as he passed down the shady street with a very little, faded woman in shabby clothes; a woman who had sat in a dark corner of the courtroom crying silently, who had stolen forward and spoken a timid word to Lincoln. With her he turned into one of the poorest houses of the town and had dinner with her and her cousin, the carpenter, and his family.

"That's the prisoner's mother," a woman whispered when, an hour later, court opened again, and the defendant's lawyer came up the steps with the forlorn little woman and seated her very carefully before he went forward to his place.

The District Attorney, in his shirt sleeves, in a chair tipped against the wall, called and examined witnesses. Proof was made of the location; the place was described; eye-witnesses testified to the details of the crime. There appeared to be no possible doubt of the criminal's guilt.

The lad sat huddled, colorless from his months in jail, sunk now in an apathy—a murderer at fifteen. Men on the jury who had hardy, honest boys of their own at home frowned at him, and more than one, it may be, considered that a monster of this sort would be well removed. Back in her dark corner the shabby woman sat quiet.

The sultry afternoon wore on. Outside the open windows a puff of wind moved branches of trees now and then, but hardly a breath came inside; it was hot, wearisome, but yet the crowd stayed. These were people who had no theatres; it was a play to listen to the District Attorney drawing from one witness after another the record of humiliation and rage, culminating in murder. It was excitement to watch the yellow-haired child on trial for his life; it was an added thrill for those who knew the significance of her presence, to turn and stare at the thin woman cowering in her seat, shaking with that continual repressed crying. All this was too good to lose, so the crowd stayed. Ignorant people are probably not wilfully cruel; probably they like to watch suffering as a small boy watches the animal he tortures—from curiosity, without a sense of its reality. The poor are notoriously kind to each other, yet it is the poor, the masses, who throng the murder trials and executions.

The afternoon wore on. The District Attorney's nasal voice rose and fell examining witnesses. But the big lawyer sitting there did not satisfy people. He did not cross-examine one witness, he did not make one objection even to statements very damaging to his client. He scrutinized the Judge and the jury. One might have said that he was studying the character of each man; till at length the afternoon had worn to an end, and the District Attorney had examined the last witness and had risen and said: "The People rest." That side of the case was finished, and court adjourned for supper, to reopen at 7:30 in the evening.

Before the hour the audience had gathered. It was commonly said that the boy was doomed; no lawyer, even a "smart" man, could get him off after such testimony, and the current opinion was that the big hulking fellow could not be a good lawyer or he would have put a spoke in the wheel for his client before this. The sentiment ran in favor of condemnation; to have killed a man at fifteen showed depravity which was best put out of the way. Stern, narrow—the hard-living men and women of the backwoods set their thin lips into this sentence; yet down inside each one beat a heart capable of generous warmth if only the way to it were found, if a finger with a sure touch might be laid on the sealed gentleness.

Court opened. Not a seat was empty. The small woman in her worn calico dress sat forward this time, close to the bar. A few feet separated her from her son. The lawyers took their places. The Sheriff had brought in the criminal. The Judge entered. And then Abraham Lincoln stalked slowly up through the silent benches, and paused as he came to the prisoner. He laid a big hand on the thin shoulder, and the lad started nervously. Lincoln bent from his great height.

"Don't you be scared, sonny," he said quietly, but yet everyone heard every word. "I'm going to pull you out of this hole. Try to be plucky for your mother's sake."

And the boy lifted his blue, young eyes for the first time and glanced over to the shabby woman, and she met his look with a difficult smile, and he tried to smile back. The audience saw the effort of each for the other; the Judge saw it; and the jury—and Lincoln's keen eyes, watching ever under the heavy brows, caught a spasm of pity in more than one face. He took off his coat and folded it on the back of his chair and stood in his shirt sleeves. He stood, a man of the people in look and manner; a comfortable sense pervaded the spectators that what he was going to say they were going to understand. The room was still.

"Gentlemen of the Jury," began Abraham Lincoln, standing in his shirt sleeves before the court, "I am going to try this case in a manner not customary in courts. I am not going to venture to cross the tracks of the gentleman who has tried it for the prosecution. I shall not call witnesses; the little prisoner over there is all the witness I want. I shall not argue; I shall beseech you to make the argument for yourselves. All I'm going to do is to tell you a story and show you how it connects with this case, and then leave the case in your hands."

There was a stir through the courtroom. The voice, rasping, unpleasant at first, went on:

"You, Jim Beck—you, Jack Armstrong——"

People jumped; these were the names of neighbors and friends which this stranger used. His huge knotted forefinger singled out two in the jury.

"You two can remember—yes, and you as well, Luke Green—fifteen years back, in 1831, when a long, lank fellow in God-forsaken clothes came into this country from Indiana. His appearance, I dare to say, was so striking that those who saw him haven't forgotten him. He was dressed in blue homespun jeans. His feet were in rawhide boots, and the breeches were stuffed into the tops of them most of the time. He had a soft hat which had started life as black, but had sunburned till it was a combine of colors. Gentlemen of the Jury, I think some of you will remember those clothes and that young man. His name was Abraham Lincoln."

The gaunt speaker paused and pushed up his sleeves a bit, and the jurymen saw the hairy wrists and the muscles of hand and forearm. Yes, they remembered the young giant who had been champion in everything that meant physical strength. They sat tense.

"The better part of a man's life consists of his friendships," the strong voice went on, and the eyes softened as if looking back over a long road travelled. "There are good friends to be found in these parts; that young fellow in blue jeans had a few. It is about a family who befriended him that I am going to tell you. The boy Abraham Lincoln left his father, who was, as all know, a man in the humblest walk of life, and at twenty-two he undertook to shift for himself. There were pretty pinching times along then, and Abraham could not always get work. One fall afternoon, when he had been walking miles on a journey westward to look for a chance, it grew late, and he realized suddenly that unless he should run across a house he would have to sleep out. With that he heard an axe ring and came upon a cabin. It was a poor cabin even as settlers' cabins go. There was cloth over the windows instead of glass; there was only one room, and a little window above which told of a loft. Abraham strode on to the cabin hopefully. The owner, a strong fellow with yellow hair, came up, axe in hand, and of him the young man asked shelter." Again the voice paused and a smile flashed which told of a pleasant memory.

"Gentlemen of the Jury, no king ever met a fellow-monarch with a finer welcome. Everything he had, the wood-chopper told Abraham, was his. The man brought the tired boy inside. The door was only five feet high and the young fellow had to stoop some to get in. Two children of five or six were playing, and a little woman was singing the baby to sleep by the fire. The visitor climbed up a ladder to the loft after supper.

"He crawled down next morning, and when he had done a few chores to help, he bethought himself to take advice from the wood-chopper. He asked if there were jobs to be got. The man said yes; if he could chop and split rails there was enough to do. Now Abraham had had an axe put into his hands at eight years, and had dropped it since only long enough to eat meals. 'I can do that,' he said.

" 'Do you like to work?' the woodsman asked.

"Abraham had to tell him that he wasn't a hand to pitch into work like killing snakes, but yet—well, the outcome of it was that he stayed and proved that he could do a man's job."

A whispered word ran from one to another on the benches—they began to remember now the youngster who could outlift, outwork and out-wrestle any man in the county. The big lawyer saw, and a gleam of gratification flashed; he was proud always of his physical strength. He went on:

"For five weeks Abraham lived in the cabin. The family character became as familiar to him as his own. He chopped with the father, did housework with the mother, and tended Sonny, the baby, many a time. To this day the man has a clear memory of that golden-haired baby laughing as the big lad rolled him about the uneven floor. He came to know the stock, root and branch, and can vouch for it.

"When he went away they refused to take money. No part of his life has ever been more light-hearted or happier. Does anybody here think that any sacrifice which Abraham Lincoln could make in after life would be too great to show his gratitude to those people?"

He shot the question at the jury, at the Judge, and, turning, brought the crowded court-room into its range. A dramatic silence answered. The tiny woman's dim eyes stared at him, dilated. The boy's bright, sunken head had lifted a little and his thin fingers had caught at a chair at arm's length, and clutched it. The lawyer picked up his coat from where he had laid it, and, while every eye in the court-room watched him, he fumbled in a pocket, unhurried, and brought out a bit of letter-paper. Holding it, he spoke again:

"The young man who had come under so large a weight of obligation prospered in later life. By hard work, by good fortune, by the blessing of God, he made for himself a certain place in the community. As much as might be, he has—I have—kept in touch with those old friends, yet in the stress of a very busy life I have not of late years heard from them. Till last Monday morning this"—he held up the letter—"this came to me in Springfield. It is a letter from the mother who sat by the fire in that humble cabin and gave a greeting to the wandering, obscure youth which Abraham Lincoln, please God, will not forget—not in this world, not when the hand of death has set his soul free of another. The woodsman died years ago, the two older children followed him. The mother who sang to her baby that afternoon"—he swept about and his long arm and knotted finger pointed, as he towered above the court-room, to the meek, small woman shrinking on the front seat—"the mother is there."

The arm dropped; his luminous eyes shone on the boy criminal's drooping golden head; in the court-room there was no one who did not hear each low syllable of the sentence which followed.

"The baby is the prisoner at the bar."

In the hot crowded place one caught a gasp from back by the door; one heard a woman's dress rustle, and a man clear his throat—and that was all.

There was silence, and the counsel for the defence let it alone to do his work. From the figure which loomed above the rude company virtue went out and worked a magic. The silence which stretched from the falling of Lincoln's voice; which he let stretch on—and on; which he held to its insistent witchcraft when every soul in the court-room began to feel it as personally harassing; this long silence shaped the minds before him as words could not. Lincoln held the throng facing their own thoughts, facing the story he had told, till all over the room men and women were shuffling, sighing, distressed with the push and the ferment of that silence.

At the crucial moment the frayed ends of the nerves of the audience were gathered up as the driver of a four-in-hand gathers up the reins of his fractious horses. The voice of the defendant's lawyer sounded over the throng.

"Many times, as I have lain wakeful in the night," he spoke as if reflecting aloud, "many times I have remembered those weeks of unfailing kindness from those poor people, and have prayed God to give me a chance to show my gratefulness. When the letter came last Monday calling for help, I knew that God had answered. An answer to prayer comes sometimes with a demand for sacrifice. It was so. The culminating moment of years of ambition for me was to have been to-night. I was to have made to-night a speech which bore, it is likely, success or failure in a contest. I lay that ambition, that failure, if the event so prove it, gladly on the altar of this boy's safety. It is for you"—his strong glance swept the jury—"to give him that safety. Gentlemen of the Jury, I said when I began that I should try this case in a manner not customary. I said I had no argument to set before you. I believe, as you are all men with human hearts, as some of you are fathers with little fellows of your own at home— I believe that you need no argument. I have told the story; you know the stock of which the lad comes; you know that at an age when his hands should have held school-books or fishing-rod, they held—because he was working for his mother—the man's tool which was his undoing; you know how the child was goaded by a grown man till in desperation he used that tool at hand. You know these things as well as I do. All I ask is that you deal with the little fellow as you would have other men deal in such a case with those little fellows at home. I trust his life to that test. Gentlemen of the Jury, I rest my case."

And Abraham Lincoln sat down.

A little later, when the time came, the jury filed out and crossed to a room in the hotel opposite. The boy stayed. Some of the lawyers went to the hotel bar-room, some stood about on the ground under the trees; but many stayed in the court-room, and all were waiting, watching for a sound from the men shut up across the way. Then, half an hour had passed, and there was a bustle, and people who had gone out crowded back. The worn small woman in the front row clasped her thin hands tight together.

The jury filed in and sat down on the shaky benches, and answered as their names were called, and rose and stood.

"Gentlemen of the Jury," the clerk's voice spoke monotonously, "have you agreed upon a verdict?"

"We have," the foreman answered firmly, woodenly, and men and women thrilled at the conventional two syllables. They meant life or death, those two syllables.

"What is your verdict, guilty or not guilty?"

For a second, perhaps, no one breathed in all that packed mass. The small woman glared palely at the foreman; every eye watched him. Did he hesitate? Only the boy, sitting with his golden head down, seemed not to listen.

"Not guilty," said the foreman.

With that there was pandemonium. Men shouted, stamped, waved, tossed up their hats; women sobbed; one or two screamed with wild joy. Abraham Lincoln saw the slim body of the prisoner fall forward; with two strides he had caught him up in his great arms, and, lifting him like a baby, passed him across the bar into the arms, into the lap, of the woman who caught him, rocked him, kissed him. They all saw that, and with an instinctive, unthinking sympathy the whole room surged toward her; but Lincoln stood guard and pushed off the crowd.

"The boy's fainted," he said loudly. "Give him air." And then, with a smile that beamed over each one of them there, "She's got her baby—it's all right, friends. But somebody bring a drink of water for Sonny."

The American, holding a cigar that had gone out, was silent. The old man spoke again, as if vindicating himself, as if answering objections from the other.

"Of course such a thing could not happen to-day," he said. "It could not have happened then in eastern courts. Only a Lincoln could have carried it off anywhere, it may be. But he knew his audience and the jury, and his genius measured the character of the Judge. It happened. It is a fact."

The American drew a long breath. "I have not doubted you, sir," he said. "I could not speak because—because your story touched me. Lincoln is our hero. It goes deep to hear of a thing like that." He hesitated and glanced curiously at the old man. "May I ask how you came by the story? You told it with a touch of—intimacy—almost as if you had been there. Is it possible that you were in that court-room?"

The bright, dark eyes of the very old man flashed hawklike as he turned his aquiline, keen face toward the questioner; he smiled with an odd expression, only partly as if at the stalwart, up-to-date American before him, more as if smiling back half a century to faces long ago dust.

"I was the Judge," he said.

# Bid the Tapers Twinkle

## BESS STREETER ALDRICH

*Just a simple, unaffected and endearing story of mother love is this tale for those of us who cannot resist Christmas trees, wide-eyed children and carols on a snowy night. Read* Bid the Tapers Twinkle *and, like old Sara Atkin, you will hold Christmas in your heart.*

THE ATKIN HOUSE sat well back in a tree-filled yard on a busy corner of town, its wide frame porch running around two sides, thirty feet of it facing Churchill Avenue, thirty feet facing Seventh Street, its long brick walk sloping across the lot to an iron gateway in the exact corner, as though with impartial deference to both streets.

The arrangement might almost have been symbolic of the character of old Mrs. Atkin, who had lived there for many years, so impartially gracious to her well-to-do Churchill Avenue callers and her hired help from Seventh Street.

Old Sara Atkin had known the town longer than anyone now living in it. Indeed, she had arrived as a bride only a few weeks after the first timbers were laid for the sawmill which became the nucleus of a village. She had seen a store go up near the sawmill, a single pine room with a porch across the front, onto which a man threw a sack of mail from the back of a pony twice a week. She had seen the first house built—a queer little box of a cottonwood house; had seen another follow, and others; then a one-roomed school-house and a stout frame church with a thick spire like a work-worn hand pointing a clumsy finger to the blue sky. She had seen whips of cottonwood trees set out at the edge of the grassy streets, had watched them grow to giants, live out their lives and fall to the ground under the axes of the third generation. She had seen a shining roadway of steel laid through the village and the first iron horse snort its way into the sunset. All these things and many others had old Sara Atkin seen.

John Atkin had gone back to Ohio for her and brought her by wagon and ferry to his bachelor sod house on land he had purchased from the railroad company for two dollars an acre. She had been nineteen then, her cheeks as pink as the wild roses that sprang up in the prairie grass, her eyes as blue as the wild gentians that grew near them.

A few years later they had moved into a new three-room house with a lean-to and turned the soddie over to the stock. John Atkin had possessed the knack of making money where some of his neighbors had not. He had started a general store and a sorghum mill, had shipped in coal and lumber, had prospered to such an extent in a short time that they were able to build the present residence, a castle of a house for the raw prairie town—so unusual, with its parlor and back parlor and its two fireplaces, that people had driven for miles in their top buggies or buckboards to see its capacious framework and the mottled marble of its mantels.

When it was completed, new furniture had come for it too—walnut bedsteads and center tables and a tall hall rack with a beveled-glass mirror. But the house which had once been such a source of pride to the whole community was merely a fussy and rather shabby old place now, with its furniture outmoded. John Atkin had been dead for many years, and Sara, whose cheeks had once been like wild roses, was a great-grandmother.

In the passing years the town had taken on an unbelievable size, and even a bit of sophistication, with its fine homes and university, its business blocks and country clubs. It had grown noisily around Sara Atkin; the tide of traffic now banged and clanged on the paved corner that had once been rutty and grass-grown.

But even though a filling station had gone up across the alley on the Seventh Street side and rather high-priced apartments on the Churchill Avenue side, old Sara would not leave, but stayed on in the fussy house with the walnut hall rack and the marble mantels.

She lived there all alone, too, except for the daily presence of one Jennie Williams, who came ploddingly down Seventh Street each day to work. Once, in Jennie's high-school days, Sara had taken her on temporarily until she could find someone else to help. But Jennie had grown fat and forty waiting for Mrs. Atkin to find another girl.

This morning she came puffingly through the kitchen door in time to see Sara Atkin turning the page of the drug-store calendar on the kitchen wall and pinning back the flapping leaf so that the word "December" stood out boldly.

Old Sara greeted Jennie with a subtle, "Do you know what date this is, Jennie?"

She asked the same darkly mysterious question every year, and, as always, Jennie feigned surprise: "Don't tell me it's December a'ready, Mis' Atkin?"

Yes, it was December; old Sara Atkin's own special month—the one for which she lived, the one toward which all the other months led like steps to some shining Taj Mahal. It was the month in which all the children came home.

"It's true, Jennie. Time again to bid the tapers twinkle fair. Did I ever tell you how our family came to use that expression, Jennie?"

Jennie had heard the explanation every year for a quarter of a century, but she obligingly assumed ignorance.

"How's that, Mis' Atkin?" As a stooge Jennie Williams could not have been surpassed.

Sara Atkin's white old face took on a glow. "Well, it was years ago. My goodness, I don't know how many—maybe forty-one or two; I could figure it out if I took time. But our Dickie was just a little chap—that's Mr. Richard Atkin, you know, my lawyer son—and he was going to speak his first piece in the new schoolhouse on Christmas Eve. The piece he was to give begun:

> "We hang up garlands everywhere
> And bid the tapers twinkle fair.

"When you stop to think about it, Jennie, that's a hard line for anybody to say, let alone a little codger with his first piece. I can just see him—he had on a little brown suit I'd made him and was so round and roly-poly, and he stood up so bravely in front of all of those folks and began so cute:

> "'We hang up garlands everywhere
> And bid the twapers tinkle tair.'

"He knew something was wrong—everyone was grinning—and he stopped and tried again, but this time he got it:

> "'And bid the taters pinkle tair.'

"Everyone laughed out loud and he said, 'I mean:

> "'And tid the bapers finkle fair.'"

369

Sara Atkin laughed at the little memory so dear to her old heart, and Jennie politely followed suit with as extensive a show of hilarity as one could muster after hearing the anecdote for twenty-five years.

"Richard never heard the last of it. And after that whenever Christmas was coming we'd always say it was time to bid the tapers twinkle fair. I guess all big families have jokes that way, Jennie."

"I guess yours more than most folks, Mis' Atkin. My, I never knew anybody to make such a hullabaloo over Christmas as you Atkinses do."

It was just faintly possible that a bit of acidity had crept into Jennie's voice. The coming month was not going to be exactly a period of inertia for fat, slow Jennie. But to old Sara it was merely an invitation to indulge in a line of reminiscences, so that it was almost a half hour before Jennie needed to start working.

Jennie Williams was right. The Atkins made much of Christmas festivities.

There are those to whom Christmas means little or nothing; those whose liking for it is more or less superficial; those who worship it with a love that cannot be told. Sara Atkin had always been one of these last. Christmas to her meant the climax of the year, the day for which one lived. It meant vast preparation, the coming together of the clan. She had never been able to understand women to whom it was merely half interesting, sometimes even a cause for complaint. From the first Christmas in the sod house with a makeshift tree for the baby to the previous year with twenty-one coming, she had sunk herself in loving preparation for the day. No matter what experiences had preceded it—drought, blizzards, crop failures, financial losses, illness—she had approached The Day with a warmth of gladness, an uplift of the spirit which no other season could bring forth.

In those old pioneer days she had neighbors who possessed no initiative by which to make Christmas gifts out of their meager supplies. She herself had known that it took only love and energy to make them.

There had been two sons and two daughters born to her. They were middle-aged now, but by some strange magic she had transmitted to them this vital love for the Christmastime, so that they, too, held the same intense ardor for the day. In the years that were gone sons and grandsons had wrangled with wives that they must go to Grandma Atkin's for Christmas. As for the daughters and granddaughters, they had made it clear from the times of their engagements that it was not even a subject for debate whether they should attend the family reunion.

So now the annual preparations began. Life took on a rose-colored hue for old Sara and a dark blue one for Jennie. Rugs came out to be beaten and curtains down to be washed. Permanent beds were made immaculate and temporary ones installed. A dozen cookbooks were consulted and the tree ordered. Jennie in her obesity and obstinacy was urged gently to try to make more effective motions. Once in her happiness old Sara said chucklingly:

"Jennie, Doctor Pitkin was wrong. Life begins at eighty."

To which Jennie made acrid reply, "Good land, don't tell me you've took up with a new doctor at your age, Mis' Atkin."

Eva, dropping in from a bridge afternoon, found her mother on the couch at the close of a day's preparations, a pan of strung pop corn at her side. The daughter was perturbed, scolded a little.

"Mother, what is there about you that makes you attack Christmas this hard way? You'll make yourself sick. Why don't we all got to the University Club? We can get a private room if we get in our bid right away."

"What—a club? On Christmas? Not while I have a roof over my head."

"But you do so many unnecessary things. No one strings pop corn any more for a tree. That was in the days when there weren't so many decorations."

"There's no law against it," said old Sara. "Or is there," she twinkled, "since the NRA?"

In a few days Eva dropped in again. She had something on her mind, was hesitant in getting it out, averted her eyes a bit when she told it. "Mother, I hope I'm not going to disappoint you too much, but Fred and I think our family will have to go to Josephine's for Christmas. She's the farthest away . . . and can't come . . . and would like to have us . . . and . . ." Her voice trailed off apologetically.

Old Sara was sorry. But, "You do what's best," she said cheerily. She must not be selfish. It was not always possible for all of them to be with her, so she would not let it disturb her.

She told Jennie about it next morning. "There will be five less than we thought, Jennie. My daughter, Mrs. Fleming, and Professor Fleming and their daughter's family won't be here."

Jennie was not thrown into a state which one might term broken-hearted, interpreting the guests' attendance as she did in terms of food and dishes.

The next evening Sara Atkin had a long-distance call from Arnold. He visited with his mother with alarming lack of toll economy—in fact, it was some little time before he led up to the news that they were not coming. He and Mame and the boys were going to Marian's. Marian's baby was only nine months old and Marian thought it better for them all to come there.

When she assured him it was all right old Sara tried her best to keep a quaver out of her voice. In her disappointment she did not sleep well. In the morning she broke the news to Jennie with some slight manipulating of the truth, in as much as she told her there was a faint possibility that not all of Arnold's family might get there.

When the letter from Helen arrived next day she had almost a premonition, so that her eyes went immediately down the page to the distressing statement. They were not coming. They couldn't afford it this year, Helen said—not after the drought. It hurt Sara worse than the others. It wasn't a reason. It was an excuse. That wasn't true about not affording it. It had been a bad year of drought, but Carl had his corn loan. If she had died they could have afforded to come to the funeral. And she could not bring herself to tell Jennie they, too, were not coming. She had too much pride to let Jennie know that Helen and Carl, who had no children to provide for or educate, thought they were too poor to come home for Christmas.

She had scarcely laid the letter and her glasses aside when the phone rang. It was Mr. Schleuter, telling her that the turkeys were in. "I'll save you two as always, Mis' Atkin?"

"Yes," said old Sara. Two turkeys for no one but herself and Richard and Clarice and Jimmie, who was sixteen. But she would not admit that the Atkin reunion was to be composed of four people.

Before breakfast the next morning the night letter came in:

SORRY CAN'T COME MOTHER STOP JIMMIE HAS HARD COLD CAUGHT IT PLAYING BASKETBALL STOP HOPE MESSAGE DOESN'T FRIGHTEN YOU STOP THOUGHT LET YOU KNOW RIGHT AWAY STOP SENDING PACKAGES STOP WILL BE THINKING OF YOU ALL DAY CHRISTMAS                                        RICHARD

Old Sara got up and shut the door between herself and the kitchen, for fear that Jennie would come in and see her before she had gained control of herself. Twenty-one of them. And no one was coming. It was unbelievable. She sat stunned, the telegram still in her hand. She tried to reason with herself, but she seemed to have no reasoning powers; tried to comfort herself, but the heart had gone out of her. All her life she had held to a philosophy of helpfulness, but she knew now she was seeing herself as she really was. A great many people who had no relatives for Christmas gatherings made it a point to ask in those who were lonely. They went out into the highways and hedges and brought them in. The Bible said to do so. Old Sara didn't want to. Tears filled her old eyes. She didn't want lonely people from the highways and hedges. She wanted her own folks. She wanted all the Atkins.

Jennie was at work in the kitchen now. She seemed slower than ever this morning, trudging about heavily in her flatheeled slippers. Sara did not care, did not hurry her, gave her no extra duties.

The morning half over, the phone rang, and it was Mr. Schleuter again. "Ve got de trees dis mornin', Mis' Atkin. Fine nice vons. I tell you first so you can get your choice same as always. Can you come over?"

Jennie was listening, craning her head to hear. Something made old Sara do it. "Yes, I'll come over."

Mr. Schleuter led her mysteriously through the store to the back. "I like you to get the pick. Folks all comin', I suppose? I never saw such relations as you got to have dose goot Christmases. Like when I'm a boy in Germany. Most folks now, it ain't so much to dem any more."

He sent the tree right over by a boy. Sara and Jennie had the big pail ready with the wet gravel in it. The boy told them Mr. Schleuter said he was to stay and put it up. They placed it in the front parlor by the mottled marble fireplace, its slender green tip reaching nearly to the ceiling. Jennie got down the boxes of ornaments and tinsels and placed them invitingly on the mantel. Old Sara started to decorate. She draped and festooned and stood back mechanically to get the effect, her old eyes not seeing anything but her children, her ears not hearing anything but silence louder than ever noise had been.

For the next two days she went on mechanically with preparations. Before Christmas Eve she would rouse herself and ask in some people—the food and decorations must not be wasted. She would probably have Grandma Bremmer and her old-maid daughters. They would be glad to get the home cooking, but Christmas had never meant very much to them. It was just another day at the hotel. Not a vital thing. Not a warm, living experience. Not a fundamental necessity, as it was to the Atkins.

In the meantime her pride would not allow her to tell Jennie or the merchants or the occasional caller who dropped in. "Our family reunion is to be cut down quite a bit this year," she would say casually. "Some of them aren't coming."

Some? Not one was coming.

In the late afternoon before Christmas Eve snowflakes began falling, as lazily as though fat Jennie were scattering them. The house was immaculate, everything prepared.

"Shall I put all the table leaves in, Mis' Atkin?" Jennie was asking.

"No," said old Sara. "You needn't stay to set the table at all. The—the ones that get here will be in time to help."

"Well, good night then, Mis' Atkin, and Merry Christmas."

"Good night, Jennie—and Merry Christmas."

Jennie was gone and the house was quiet. The snowflakes were falling faster. The house was shining from front to back. Beds were ready. The tree was sparkling with colored lights, packages from all the children under its tinseled branches. The cupboards were filled with good food. So far as preparations were concerned, everything was ready for the family reunion. And no one but herself knew that there was to be no reunion.

Later in the evening she would call up the Bremmers. But in the meantime she would lie down in the back parlor and rest. Strange how very tired she felt, when there had been so little confusion. She pulled a shawl about her and lay down on the old leather couch.

Through the archway she could see the tree, shining in all its bravery, as though trying to be gay and gallant. Then she nodded and it looked far away and small. She dozed, awakened, dozed again. The tiny tree out there now had tufts of cotton from a quilt on it, bits of tinfoil from a package of tea, homemade candles of mutton tallow. It was a queer little cottonwood tree trying to look like an evergreen—a tree such as she had in the pioneer days.

She could not have told the exact moment in which she began to hear them, could not have named the precise time in which she first saw them vaguely through the shadows. But somewhere on the borderland of her consciousness she suddenly realized they were out there under the crude little tree. Arnold was examining a homemade sled, his face alight with boyish eagerness. Eva and Helen were excitedly taking the brown paper wrappings from rag dolls. Dickie was on the floor spinning a top made from empty spools. Every little face was clear, every little figure plain. For a long time she watched them playing under the makeshift tree, a warm glow of happiness suffusing her whole being. Some vague previous hurt she had experienced was healed. Everything was all right. The children were here.

Then she roused, swept her hand over her eyes in the perplexity of her bewilderment, felt herself grow cold and numb with the disappointment of it. The children were not here. When you grew old you must face the fact that you could have them only in dreams.

It was almost dusk outside now, with the falling of the early December twilight. Christmas Eve was descending—the magic hour before the coming of the Child. It was the enchanted time in which all children should seek their homes—the family time. So under the spell of the magic moment was she that when the bell rang and she realized it was not the children, she thought at first that she would not pay any attention to the noisy summons. It would be some kind friend or neighbor whose very kindness would unnerve her. But the habit of years was strong. When one's bell rang, one went to the door.

So she rose, brushed back a straying lock, pulled her wool shawl about her shoulders and went into the hallway, holding her head gallantly.

"Merry Christmas, mother. . . . Merry Christmas, grandma." It came from countless throats, lustily, joyfully.

"Bid the tapers twinkle fair, mother."

"He means bid the taters finkle tair, grandma." Laughter rose noisily.

She could not believe it. Her brain was addled. The vision of the children under the tree had been bright, also. This was another illusion.

But if the figures on the porch were wraiths from some hinterland they were very substantial ones. If they were apparitions they were then phantoms which wore fur coats and tweeds and knitted sport suits, shadows whose frosty breath came forth in a most unghostly fashion in the cold air of the December twilight.

They were bursting through the doorway now, bringing mingled odors of frost, holly, faint perfumes, food, mistletoe, evergreens; stamping snow from shoes, carrying packages to the chins—Eva and Fred, Arnold and Mame, Dick and Clarice, Helen and Carl, Josephine and her family, Marian with her husband and baby, Richard's Jimmie, and Arnold's boys. They noisily filled the old hall, oozed out into the dining room, backed up the stairway, fell over the tall old walnut hatrack. They did not once cease their loud and merry talking.

"Aren't we the rabble?"

"Did you ever know there were so many Atkins?"

"We look like a Cecil B. DeMille mob scene."

375

"Mussolini should be here to give us a silver loving cup or something."

They surged around old Sara Atkin, who had her hand on her throat to stop the tumultuous beating of its pulse.

"But I don't understand. Why did—why did you say you weren't coming?" she was asking feebly of those nearest to her.

Several feminine voices answered simultaneously—Eva and Helen and Dick's wife. "To save you working your fingers to the bone, mother. The way you always slave—it's just ridiculous."

"We decided that the only way to keep you from it was just to say we weren't any of us coming, and then walk in the last minute and bring all the things."

"Carl and I couldn't think of an excuse." It was Helen. "So we laid it to the poor old drought. And we'd a perfectly dreadful time—writing and phoning around to get it planned, what everyone should do. I brought the turkey all ready for the oven. . . . Carl, where's the turkey? Get it from the car."

"Fred and I have the tree outside and——" Eva broke off to say, "Why, mother, you've a tree?"

Clarice said, "Oh, look, folks, her packages are under it. And she thought she was going to open them all by herself. Why, that makes me feel teary."

Old Sara Atkin sat down heavily in a hall chair. There were twenty-one of them—some of them flesh of her flesh. They had done this for her own good, they thought. Twenty-one of them—and not one had understood how much less painful it is to be tired in your body than to be weary in your mind, how much less distressing it is to have an ache in your bones than to have a hurt in your heart.

There was the oyster supper, gay and noisy. There were stockings hung up and additional Christmas wreaths. There was Christmas music from a radio and from a phonograph and from the more-or-less unmusical throats of a dozen Atkins. There were Christmas stories and Christmas jokes. There were wide-eyed children put to bed and a session of grown people around the tree. There were early-morning lights on Christmas morning and a great crowd of Atkins piling out in the cold of their bedrooms and calling raucous Merry Christmases to one another. There was a hasty unwanted breakfast with many pert remarks about hurrying up. There was the great family circle about the fireplace and the tree with Arnold Atkin, Jr., calling out the names on the gifts, accompanied by a run of funny flippancies. There were snow banks of tissue paper and entanglements of string. There was the turkey dinner. And through it all, after the manner of the Atkin clan, there was constant talk and laughter.

The noise beat against the contented mind of Sara Atkin all day, like the wash of breakers against the sturdy shore.

All of this transpired until the late Christmas afternoon, when the entire crowd went up to Eva's new home near the campus.

"Don't you feel like coming, too, mother?"

"No, I'm a little tired and I'll just rest a while before you come back."

They were gone. The house was appallingly quiet after the din of the passing day. There was no sound but the padpadding of Jennie Williams in the kitchen. Old Sara lay down on the couch in the back parlor. Through the archway she could see a portion of the disheveled front room, over which a cyclone apparently had swept. The tree with its lights still shining gayly stood in the midst of the débris. In her bodily weariness she nodded, dozed, awakened, dozed. Suddenly the tree blurred, then grew enormous, the green of its branches became other trees, a vast number of them springing from the shadows. They massed together in a huge cedar forest, some candle laden and some electric lighted, but all gallant with Christmas cheer. Under the branches were countless children and grown people. And then suddenly she almost laughed aloud, to see that they were all her own. There were a dozen Arnolds, a dozen Helens—all her boys and girls at all their ages playing under all the trees which had ever been trimmed for them. It was as though in one short moment she had seen together the entire Christmases of the sixty years.

She roused and smiled at the memory of having seen such a wondrous sight. "Well, I suppose there'll not be many more for me," she thought, "but I've passed on the tapers. They all love it as I do. They won't forget to light the tapers after—after I'm gone." Then she sat up and threw off her shawl with vehement gesture. "Fiddlesticks! Imagine me talking that way about dying—as if I were an old woman. I'm only eighty-one. I'm good for a dozen more Christmases. My body isn't feeble—at least—only at times. As for my mind—my mind's just as clear as a bell."

She rose and went out to the dining room. Jennie Williams was trudging about putting away the last of the best dishes. Some of the women had helped her, but there were a dozen things she had been obliged to finish herself. She was tired and cross with the unnecessary work and the undue commotion. Her feet hurt her. She liked the peaceful, slow days better.

"Well, Jennie, it's all over," old Sara said happily. "We had a good time, same as always. We've had a grand day to bid the tapers twinkle fair. Jennie, did I ever tell you how we Atkins happened to start using that expression?"

Jennie jerked her heavy body about and opened her mouth to answer determinedly, for she felt her provocation was great. But she stopped suddenly at the sight of old Sara Atkin standing in the doorway. For old Sara's sweet white face glowed with an inner light, and the illumination from the tree behind her gave the appearance of a halo around her head. Suddenly Jennie Williams had a strange thought about her. It was that she looked like the pictures of Mary the Mother.

"No," said Jennie kindly. "I don't believe you **ever** have. How *did* you?"

# Mother

## KATHLEEN NORRIS

*Here is the story that the whole country has taken to
its heart. Beautifully and poignantly written, it catches
the spirit of home life and motherhood in a small
American town.* Mother *overnight became a fabulous
best-seller and established Kathleen Norris as one of
America's most beloved writers.*

ARCHERTON, A BLUR of flying trees and houses, bright
in the late sunlight; Pottsville with children wading and shouting under
the bridge; Hunt's Crossing; then the next would be Weston—and home.

Margaret Paget, beginning to gather wraps and small possessions together, sighed. She sighed partly because her head ached, partly because
she was uncomfortably mussed after seven hours of travel, largely because
she was going home.

This was August; her last trip home had been between Christmas and
the New Year, eight months ago. She had of course sent a box at Easter:
ties for the boys, a lovely silk scarf for Rebecca, books for Dad; and she
had written Mother for her birthday in June, and enclosed an exquisite
bit of lace in the letter, but somehow it had been "impossible," she wrote
them, to come herself. Margaret had paid a great deal for the lace, as a
sort of salve to her conscience—not that Mother would ever wear it!

That was just the trouble with Mother, Margaret thought, reviewing the
situation with impatience. Lace—why, there was lovely lace on some of
Grandma Swann's old things, up attic, and when did Mother ever wear
it? She was so busy and so tired and so tied down that she never cared
what she wore.

And it was *all wrong*. Even at eighteen, a teacher in the Weston high
school, Margaret had protested in her secret heart that the home problem
was all wrong, and now when the doors of the great world had opened to
her, and she had found herself not alone in her ideas, she was *sure* of it.

Mrs. Carr-Boldt had opened the doors of the world to Margaret Paget.

*Reprinted by permission of Doubleday & Company, Copyright, 1911.*

Her eyes had fallen upon the pretty, aristocratic-looking little school-teacher with that acquisitiveness so becoming to the wives of multimillionaires. "There's my secretary, Miss Totter," said Mrs. Carr-Boldt to her daughter's governess. And Miss Totter, who had been timidly hinting her own qualifications for that desirable post, had of course agreed. "If you can get her," said Miss Totter. "Oh, I'll *get* her," said Mrs. Carr-Boldt confidently, and get her she did. New York, Newport, London, Rome, everything followed. Margaret was exceptionally pretty, clever, and adaptable. She became a personage in the great Carr-Boldt establishments, and the inseparable companion of their mistress. She spoke French and German and Italian; she could order dinners, and order gowns, and engage and discharge servants. She was quite at home in the Carr-Boldt set, which happened to be the richest and idlest in the rich and idle city. Margaret had grown to feel uncomfortable in underthings that were not of the sheerest silk; she honestly missed finger bowls and butter-spreaders when she was at her mother's table. She was spoiled, perhaps, but there was no affectation about her.

Of course there were things to criticise in the Carr-Boldt set, she admitted. They were very wasteful, and very selfish, and very uncharitable in their speech. Yes, and they thought the world was made for them, and that great wealth, especially in the form of tips, could, and very properly should, get anything they wanted. And they took home ties very lightly. Wives dined without husbands, and husbands without wives, and the children—it was more often, the child—was "with his grandmother, don't you know; she loves to have him, and we don't see much of him, anyway." This was of course not the Weston idea, and still less Mother's idea, but——

But, after all, it worked out very well, Margaret thought. And this business of a woman marrying, and immediately having a perfect pack of children, well, "it wasn't fair to herself and it wasn't fair to the children!" Margaret had heard that phrase a hundred times, and used it often herself. One child—or two children—that was the dignified, reasonable way to do. . . . It was time these things were regulated like any other expense. . . .

Margaret sometimes dreamed of what her own home would have been had she and her brother Bruce, say, been the only ones. Bruce was twenty-eight now, and Margaret three years younger. Mother would have had no new responsibilities for a whole quarter-century; Dad's income would have answered very comfortably for four. They could have gone on living in the little brick homestead which they had so quickly outgrown—only six rooms in the whole house, but such quaint, charming rooms! An artist and his wife had the brick house now. It was always pointed out as one of the show places of Weston. Mother and Dad had been in no such pretty place since. They had moved a good deal. The Copley portraits of Great-grandfather and Great-grandmother Paget, the few pieces of old silver, the Canton tea set, these would have helped make an effective setting for four. As it was, they were completely wasted. And Bruce could have had his four years of college, without the alternate years of money-earning, and Margaret could have entertained, traveled perhaps with Mother. . . . Margaret invariably ended these musings with an impatient reiteration that of course Mother was an angel, but it was all wrong!

Here was Weston. Weston looking its very ugliest in the level, pitiless rays of the afternoon sun. The town, like most of its inhabitants, was wilted and grimed after the burden and heat of the long summer day. Margaret carried her heavy suitcase slowly up Main Street. Shop windows were spotted and dusty, and shopkeepers, standing idly in their doorways, looked spotted and dusty too. A cloud of flies fought and surged about the closely guarded door of the butcher shop, a delivery cart was at the curb, the discouraged horse switching an ineffectual tail.

As Margaret passed this cart, a tall boy of fourteen came out of the shop with a bang of the wire-netting door, and slid a basket into the back of the cart.

"Teddy!" said Margaret, irritation evident in her voice, in spite of herself.

"Hello, Mark!" said her brother delightedly. "Say, great to see you! Get in on the four-ten?"

"Ted," said Margaret, kissing him, as the Pagets always quite simply kissed each other when they met, "what are you driving Costello's cart for?"

"Like to," said Theodore simply. "Mother doesn't care. Say, you look swell, Mark!"

"What makes you want to drive this horrid cart, Ted?" protested Margaret. "What does Costello pay you?"

"Pay me?" scowled her brother, gathering up the reins. "Oh, come out of it, Marg'ret! He doesn't pay me anything. Don't you make Mother stop me, either, will you?" he ended anxiously.

"Of course I won't!" Margaret said impatiently.

"Giddap, Ruth!" said Theodore; but departing, he pulled the mare up to add cheerfully, "Say, Dad didn't get his raise."

"Did?" said Margaret brightening.

"*Didn't.*" He grinned affectionately upon her as, with a dislocating jerk, the cart started a ricochetting career down the street, with that abandon known only to butchers' carts. Margaret, changing her heavy suitcase to the rested arm, was still vexedly watching it, when two girls, laughing in the open doorway of the express company's office across the street, caught sight of her. One of them, a little vision of pink hat and ruffles, and dark eyes and hair, came running to join her.

Rebecca was sixteen, and of all the handsome Pagets the best to look upon. She was dressed according to her youthful lights; every separate article of her apparel today, from her rowdyish little hat to her openwork hose, represented a battle with Mrs. Paget's preconceived ideas as to propriety in dress, with the honours largely for Rebecca. Rebecca had grown up, in eight months, her sister thought confusedly; she was no longer the adorable, un-self-conscious tomboy who fought and skated and tobogganed with the boys.

"Hello, darling dear!" said Rebecca. "Too bad no one met you! We all thought you were coming on the six. Crazy about your suit! Here's Maudie Pratt. You know Maudie, don't you, Mark?"

Margaret knew Maudie. Rebecca's infatuation for plain, heavy-featured, complacent Miss Pratt was a standing mystery in the Paget family. Margaret smiled, bowed.

"I think we stumbled upon a pretty little secret of yours today, Miss Margaret," said Maudie, with her best company manner, as they walked along. Margaret raised her eyebrows. "Rebel and I," Maudie went on— Rebecca was at the age that seeks a piquant substitute for an unpoetical family name,—"Rebel and I are wondering if we may ask you who Mr. John Tenison is?"

John Tenison! Margaret's heart stood still with a shock almost sickening, then beat furiously. What—how—who on earth had told them anything of John Tenison? Colouring high, she looked sharply at Rebecca.

"Cheer up, angel," said Rebecca, "he's not dead. He sent a telegram today, and Mother opened it——"

"Naturally," said Margaret, concealing an agony of impatience, as Rebecca paused apologetically.

"He's with his aunt, at Dayton, up the road here," continued Rebecca, "and wants you to wire him if he may come down and spend tomorrow here."

Margaret drew a relieved breath. There was time to turn around, at least.

"Who is he, sis?" asked Rebecca.

"Why, he's an awfully clever professor, honey," Margaret answered serenely. "We heard him lecture in Germany last summer, and met him afterward. And since then he's come occasionally to Mrs. Carr-Boldt's. He was there about a month ago, and I said I was coming home this week-end, and we discovered that his old home is near here, at Dayton." She tried to keep out of her voice the thrill that shook at the mere thought of him, of that enchanted week in Berlin, of those wonderful hours—oh, very few! She had in all honesty to admit that they were few!—when he had come to see her. Nothing, obviously, was farther from his thoughts than love for her; she would be very absurd even to dream it. As for her loving him, why, that feeling put her in the ridiculous position of a thousand other girls to whom he was friendly and kind. "But I can't help it—I can't help it—I can't help it!" throbbed her heart, too agitated just now to know whether to be glad or sorry that he wanted to come tomorrow.

"Do you want him to come? Is he old and fussy?" asked Rebecca.

"I don't know," Margaret answered absently. "No, he's only thirty-five or six. How's Mother?" she broke off to ask abruptly.

"Oh, *she's* fine!" Rebecca said, absently in her turn. When Maudie left them at the next corner she said casually:

"Dad didn't get his raise. Isn't that the limit?"

Margaret shrugged wearily. They were in a quiet side street now, lined with shabby, plain old houses well set back under elms and maples. One of these, reached through a weather-peeled gate, and standing beyond bare garden beds and trampled lawns, was the Paget home. A bulging wire netting door made the front entrance undignified. Indoors, the plain square rooms and everything in them shared a look of hard usage. Old-fashioned sofas sagged in the seats, cushions were generally flat and limp, bookcases disgorged odd volumes and magazines upon the floor beside them. The old square piano was half concealed under untidy sheets of music.

A boy of twelve sat on the piano bench now, sullenly sawing at a violoncello. Another boy, of nine, with big teeth missing when he smiled, stood in the bay window, twisting the already limp net curtains into a tight rope. Each boy gave Margaret a kiss that seemed curiously to taste of dust, sunburn, and freckles, before she followed a noise of hissing and voices to the kitchen, to find Mother.

The kitchen, at five o'clock on Saturday afternoon, was in wild confusion, and insufferably hot. Margaret had a distinct impression that not a movable article therein was in place, and not an available inch of tables or chairs unused, before her eyes reached the tall figure of a woman in a gown of chocolate percale, who was frying cutlets at the big littered range. A woman whose thickly massed black hair was very lightly touched with gray, and whose face, beautiful in outline and expression, was dark with heat, and streaked with perspiration. She turned as Margaret entered, and gave a delighted cry.

"Well, there's my girl! Bless her heart! Look out for this spoon, lovey," she added immediately, giving the girl a guarded embrace. Tears of joy stood frankly in her fine gray eyes. She hesitated for a moment.

"I meant to have all of this out of the way, dear," apologized Mrs. Paget, with a gesture that included cakes in the process of frosting, salad vegetables in the process of cooling, soup in the process of getting strained, great loaves of bread that sent a delicious fragrance over all the other odours. "But we didn't look for you until six."

"Oh, no matter!" Margaret said bravely.

"Rebecca tell you Dad didn't get his raise?" called Mrs. Paget in a voice that rose above the various noises of the kitchen. "Blanche!" she protested, "can't that wait?" For the old negress who was her only servant had begun to crack ice with deafening smashes. But Blanche did not hear, so Mrs. Paget continued loudly: "Dad saw Redman himself; he'll tell you about it! Don't stay in the kitchen in that pretty dress, dear! I'm coming right upstairs."

It was very hot upstairs; the bedrooms smelled faintly of matting, the soap in the bathroom was shriveled in its saucer. In Margaret's own old room, the week's washing had been piled high on the bed. She took off her hat and linen coat, brushed her hair back from her face; flinging her head back and shutting her eyes the better to fight tears, as she did so, and began to assort the collars and shirts and put them away. For Dad's bureau—for Bruce's bureau—for the boys' bureau, tablecloths to go downstairs, towels for the shelves in the bathroom. Two little shirtwaists for Rebecca, with little holes torn through them where collar and belt pins belonged.

Her last journey took her to the big, third-story room where the three younger boys slept. The three narrow beds were still unmade, and the western sunlight poured over tumbled blankets and the scattered small possessions that seem to ooze from the pores of little boys. Margaret set her lips distastefully as she brought order out of the chaos. It was *all wrong,* somehow, she thought, gathering handkerchiefs and matches and "Nick Carters" and the oiled paper that had wrapped caramels from under the pillows that would in a few hours harbour a fresh supply.

She went out on the porch in time to put her arms about her father's shabby shoulders when he came in. Mr. Paget, a broad, gray, fine-looking man in the early fifties, was tired, and he told his wife and daughters that he thought he was a very sick man. Margaret's mother met this statement with an anxious solicitude that was very soothing to the sufferer. She made Mark get Daddy his slippers and loose coat, and suggested that Rebecca shake up the dining-room couch before she established him there, in a rampart of pillows. No outsider would have dreamed that Mrs. Paget had dealt with this exact emergency some hundreds of times in the past twenty years.

Mr. Paget, reclining, shut his eyes, remarked that he had had an "awful, awful day," and wondered faintly if it would be too much trouble to have "somebody" make him just a little milk toast for his supper. He smiled at Margaret when she sat down beside him; they had been chums since her babyhood.

"Getting to be an old, old man, Mark!" said he, and Margaret hated herself because she had to quell an impatient impulse to tell him that he was merely hungry and cross before she could say affectionately, *"Don't talk that way, Dad darling!"* She had to listen to a long account of the recent episode of the "raise." Margaret winced every time her father emphasized the difference between his own social position and that of his employer. She had gotten of late years into the way of feeling herself— with her beauty, and her intelligence, and her Mayflower ancestry, and her ready acceptance by the Carr-Blodt set—as quite the equal, if not the superior, of anyone in Weston. Why, a man Dad's age oughtn't to be humbly asking for a raise; he ought to be dictating now. It was just Dad's way of looking at things, and it was *all wrong.*

"Well, I'll tell you one thing!" said Rebecca, who had come in with a brimming soup plate of milk toast. "Joe Redman gave a picnic last month, and he came here with his mother, in the car, to ask me. And I was the scornfullest thing you ever saw, wasn't I, Ted? Not much!"

"Oh, Beck, you oughtn't to mix social and business things that way!" Margaret said helplessly.

"Dinner!" screamed the nine-year-old Robert, breaking into the room at this point, and "Dinner!" said Mrs. Paget, wearily, cheerfully, from the chair into which she had dropped at the head of the table. Mr. Paget, revived by sympathy, milk toast, and Rebecca's attentions, took his place at the foot, and Bruce, oldest of the children, serious, thin-faced, dark, the chair between Margaret and his mother. Like the younger boys, whose almost confluent freckles had been brought into unusual prominence by violently applied soap and water, and whose hair dripped on their collars, he had brushed up for dinner, but his negligée shirt and corduroy trousers were stained and spotted from machine oil. Margaret, comparing him secretly to the men she knew, as daintily groomed as women, in their spotless white, felt a little resentment that Bruce's tired face was so contented, and said to herself again that it was all *wrong!*

Dinner was the same old haphazard meal she knew so well, with Blanche supplying an occasional reproof to the boys, Ted ignoring his vegetables, and ready in an incredibly short time for a second cutlet, and Robert begging for corn syrup immediately after the soup, and spilling it from his bread. Mrs. Paget was flushed, her disappearances kitchenward frequent. She wanted Margaret to tell her all about Mr. Tenison. Margaret laughed and said there was nothing to tell. She said she was going to telegraph him not to come, looking tentatively at her mother the while, lest she resent what might be construed into a reflection upon the home. But Mother agreed cheerfully that perhaps it would be just as well, as Julie (Margaret's married sister) and Harry might come over tomorrow. Margaret had a chance to reflect bitterly that she couldn't ask her friends here; even Mother saw that!

"I am not in a position to have my children squander money on concerts and candy," Margaret heard her father say, loudly and suddenly. She forgot her own grievance. The boys looked resentful and gloomy; Rebecca was flushed, her eyes dropped, her lips trembling with disappointment.

"I had promised to take them to the Elks' concert," Mrs. Paget interpreted hastily, "but now Dad says the Bakers are coming over to play whist." Margaret could not ignore the obvious appeal.

"Let me take them, Dad," she said. "I'll hold Robert by one ear, and Rebecca by another, and if she flirts with Paul or George or Jimmy Barr or Red, I'll——"

"Oh, Jimmy Barr belongs to Louise, now," said Rebecca radiantly. There was a joyous shout of laughter from the light-hearted juniors, and

Rebecca, seeing her artless admission too late, turned scarlet while she laughed. Dinner broke up in confusion, as dinner at home always did, and everyone straggled upstairs to dress.

Margaret reflected, while changing her dress in a room that was insufferably hot because the shades must be down, and the gaslights as high as possible, that another forty-eight hours would see her speeding back to the world of cool, awninged interiors, uniformed maids, the clink of iced glasses, the flash of yacht sails on blue water, and a certain sweetness and patience came with the thought. She lifted Rebecca's starched petticoat from the bed to give Mother a seat, when Mother came rather wearily in to watch them.

"Sweet girl to take them, Mark," said Mother appreciatively. "I was going to ask Brucie. But he's gone to bed, poor fellow; he's worn out to-night."

"He had a letter from Ned Gunther this morning," said Rebecca, cheerfully—powdering the tip of her pretty nose, her eyes almost crossed with concentration, "and I think it made him blue all day."

"Ned Gunther?" said Margaret.

"Chum at college," Rebecca elucidated; "a lot of them are going to Honolulu, just for this month, and of course they wanted Bruce. Mark, does that show?"

Margaret's heart ached for the beloved brother's disappointment. There it was again, all *wrong*. Before she left the house with the rioting youngsters, she ran upstairs where he was lying; his lamp at his elbow, scientific magazines scattered about him, to kiss him good night. He was very sweet, very cheerful, but through the long evening, while Rebecca glowed like a little rose among her friends, and the boys tickled her ear with their hot breath and whispered comments, above the heat and dust and noise of the hall she heard his last words:

"Come back and take your old job, Mark. They're crazy to get you, and I miss you. I'm getting into a rut."

After the concert, they strolled back slowly through the inky summer dark, finding the house hot and close when they came in. Margaret went upstairs, hearing her mother's apologetic, "Oh, Dad, why didn't I give you back your club?" as she passed the dining-room door. She knew Mother hated whist, and wondered rather irritably *why* she played it. The Paget family was slow to settle down. Robert became tearful and whining before he was finally bumped protesting into bed. Theodore and Duncan prolonged their ablutions until the noise of shouting, splashing, and thumping in the bathroom brought Mother to the foot of the stairs. Rebecca was conversational. She lay with her slender arms locked behind her head on the pillow, and talked. Margaret, restless in the hot darkness, wondering whether the maddening little shaft of light from the hall gas was annoying enough to warrant the effort of getting up and extinguishing it, listened and listened.

Rebecca wanted to join the Stage Club, but Mother wouldn't let her unless Bruce did. Rebecca belonged to the Progressive Diners. Did Mark suppose Mother'd think she was crazy if she asked the family *not* to be in evidence when the crowd came to the house for the salad course? And Rebecca wanted to write to Bruce's chum, not regularly, you know, Mark, but just now and then. He was so nice! And Mother didn't like the idea. Margaret was obviously supposed to lend a hand with these interesting tangles.

". . . . and I said, 'Certainly not! I won't unmask at all, if it comes to that!' . . . And imagine that elegant fellow carrying my old books and my skates! So I wrote, and Maudie and I decided. . . . And Mark, if it wasn't a perfectly *gorgeous* box of roses! . . . That old, old dimity, but Mother pressed and freshened it up. . . . Not that I want to marry him, or anyone. . . ."

Margaret wakened from uneasy drowsing with a start. The hall was dark now, the room cooler. Rebecca was asleep. Hands, hands she knew well, were drawing a light covering over her shoulders. She opened her eyes to see her mother.

"I've been wondering if you're disappointed about your friend not coming tomorrow, Mark?" said the tender voice.

"Oh, no-o!" said Margaret hardily. "Mother—why are you up so late?"

"Just going to bed," said the other soothingly. "Blanche forgot to put the oatmeal into the cooker, and I went downstairs again. I'll say my prayers in here."

Margaret went off to sleep again, as she had so many hundred times before, with her mother kneeling beside her. It seemed but a few moments before the blazing Sunday was precipitated upon them, and everybody was late for everything.

The kitchen was filled with the smoke from hot griddles blue in the sunshine, when Margaret went downstairs; and in the dining room the same merciless light fell upon the sticky syrup pitcher, and upon stains on the tablecloth. Cream had been brought in in the bottle, the bread tray was heaped with orange skins, and the rolls piled on the tablecloth. Bruce, who had already been to church with Mother, and was off for a day's sail, was dividing his attention between Robert and his watch. Rebecca, daintily busy with the special cup and plate that were one of her little affectations, was all ready for the day, except as to dress, wearing a thin little kimono over her blue ribbons and starched embroideries. Mother was putting up a little lunch for Bruce. Confusion reigned. The younger boys were urged to hurry, if they wanted to make the "nine." Rebecca was going to wait for the "half-past-ten," because the "kids sang at nine, and it was fierce." Mr. Paget and his sons departed together, and the girls went upstairs for a hot, tiring tussle with beds and dusting before starting for church. They left their mother busy with the cream freezer in the kitchen. It was very hot even then.

But it was still hotter, walking home in the burning midday stillness. A group of young people waited lazily for letters, under the trees outside the post-office door. Otherwise the main street was deserted. A languid little breeze brought the far echoes of pianos and phonographs from this direction and that.

"Who's that on the porch?" said Rebecca suddenly, as they neared home, instantly finding the stranger among her father and the boys. Margaret, glancing up sharply, saw, almost with a sensation of sickness, the big, ungainly figure, the beaming smile, and the great shock of tawny hair that belonged to nobody else in the world but John Tenison. A stony chill settled about her heart as she greeted him. Oh, if only he wasn't able to stay for dinner! she prayed. She half-heartedly alluded to dinner. Too late. Her mother had already asked him, and he was delighted to stay, he told her. Her mother was upstairs now with her sister, Mrs.—Mrs. Archibald. So Julie and Harry had come! Well, there was no help for it. And of course Margaret loved her married sister, four years her junior, and loved the clever, successful, rather talkative young doctor who was Julie's husband, too. Only it was a little hard to have this fresh confusing element introduced on the particular Sunday of all Sundays that the great Dr. Tenison came!

Margaret presently slipped away, and went into the kitchen, which presented a scene if possible a little more confused than that of the day before, and was certainly hotter. Mrs. Paget, flushed and hurried, in a fresh but rather unbecoming purple gingham, was hastily putting up a cold supper for the younger boys, who, having attended to their religious duties, were to take a long afternoon tramp, with a possible interval of fishing. Theodore and Duncan themselves were hanging over these preparations, tasting jam and stealing occasional olives. Blanche, heavily moaning "The Palms" with the insistence of one who wishes to show her entire familiarity with a melody, was at the range.

Roast veal, instead of the smothered chickens her mother had so often cooked so deliciously, a mountain of mashed potato, an enormous heavy salad already mantled with thick mayonnaise—Margaret could have wept over the hopelessly plebeian dinner!

"Mother, can't I get down the finger-bowls," Margaret asked, "and mayn't we have black coffee in the silver pot afterward?"

Mrs. Paget looked absently at her for a dubious second. "I *don't* like to ask Blanche to wash all that extra glass," she said guardedly, adding briskly to Theodore, "No, no, Ted! You can't have all that cake! Half that," and to Blanche herself, "Don't leave that door open when you go in, Blanche; I just drove all the flies out of the dining room." Then she returned to Margaret with a cordial: "Why, certainly! Anyone who *wants* coffee, after tea, can have it!"

"Nobody but us ever serves tea with a dinner!" Margaret muttered, but Mrs. Paget didn't hear her. She sent the boys upstairs to wash their hands, and when they were gone, said, with a suddenly radiant face, to Margaret:

"Julie tell you?"

Margaret understood. Her sister had been married a year now, and for at least half that time Mother had been eager for the bit of news that had evidently come today. The older woman's eyes were full of joy.

"Is Ju glad?" Margaret asked slowly, curiously; "she seems so young— just twenty-two! And they've been so free!"

"Glad!" Mrs. Paget echoed delightedly. "Why, Mark, it's the happiest time in a woman's whole life! Or, I don't know, though," she added thoughtfully, "I don't know but what I was happiest when you were all tiny, tumbling about me, and climbing into my lap. . . ."

"I hope Julie won't run herself all down," Margaret began disapprovingly. Her mother laughed.

"You remind me of Grandma Paget," she said cheerfully. "She lived ten miles away when we were married, but she came in when Bruce was born. She was rather a proud, cold woman herself, but she was very sweet to me. Well, then little Charlie came, fourteen months later, and she took that very seriously. Mother was dead, you know, and she stayed with me again, and worried me half sick telling me that it wasn't fair to Bruce and it wasn't fair to Charlie to divide my time between them that way.

Well, then when my third baby was coming, I didn't dare tell her. Dad kept telling me to, and I *couldn't,* because I knew what a calamity a third would seem to her! Finally, she went to visit Aunt Rebecca out West, and it was the very day she got back that the baby came. She came up-stairs—she'd come right up from the train, and not seen anyone but Dad; and he wasn't very intelligible, I guess—and she sat down and took the baby in her arms, and, says she, looking at me sort of patiently, yet as if she was exasperated too: 'Well, this is a nice way to do, the minute my back's turned! What are you going to call him, Julia?' And I said: 'I'm going to call her Margaret, for my dear husband's mother, and she's going to be beautiful and good and grow up to marry the President!'" Mrs. Paget's merry laugh rang out. "I never shall forget your grandmother's face."

"Just the same," Mrs. Paget added with a sudden deep sigh, "when little Charlie left us, the next year, and Brucie and Dad were both so ill, she and I agreed that you—you were just talking and trying to walk—were the only comfort we had! I could wish my girls no greater happiness than my children have been to me," finished Mother contentedly.

"I know," Margaret began, half-angrily, "but what about the children?" she was going to add. But somehow the arguments she had used so plausibly did not utter themselves easily to Mother, whose children would carry into their own middle age a wholesome dread of her anger. Margaret faltered, and merely scowled.

"I don't like to see that expression on your face, dearie," her mother said, as she might have said it to an eight-year-old child. "Professor Tenison must take us as he finds us! Run and tell them everything is ready, dear."

More ruffled and angry than she had been for many months, Margaret went out to summon the others to dinner. Maudie had joined them on the porch, and had been urged to stay, and was already trying her youth-ful wiles on the professor. "Well, he'll have to leave on the five o'clock!" Margaret reflected, steeled to bitter endurance until that time. For every-thing went wrong, and dinner was one long nightmare. Professor Teni-son's napkin turned out to be a traycloth, and Blanche cheerfully stated from the kitchen door that there wasn't another clean one that *she* could lay hands on. Even Mother's hurried substitution of her own did not much help matters. The room was very hot, the supply of ice insufficient. There seemed an exhausting amount of passing and repassing of plates. Rebecca and Maudie got "the giggles." Dad dwelt on his favourite griev-ance that the "old man isn't needed these days. They're getting all young fellows into the bank. The president himself isn't forty. They put young college men in there who are getting pretty nearly the money that I am, after twenty years. . . ." In any pause, Mrs. Paget could be heard patiently dissuading little Robert from his fixed intention to accompany the older boys on their walk, invited or uninvited.

Finally the ice cream, in a melting condition, and the chocolate cake, very sticky, made their appearance, and, although these were regular Sunday treats, the boys felt called upon to cheer. Julie asked her Mother in an audible undertone if she "ought" to eat cake. Professor Tenison produced an enormous box of chocolates, and Margaret was disgusted with the frantic scramble her brothers made to secure them.

Julie, kissing her sister good-by, as Margaret and the professor started for a walk, was duly congratulated, and was gracious in turn.

"We all think Dr. Tenison's so nice, Mark," said Julie, assuming the matron suddenly, "so unassuming, considering who he *is!* Don't fall in love with him, Mark!"

"No danger," said Margaret, carelessly, pinning on her hat.

Where they walked or what they talked of she did not know. She knew her head ached, that the village looked very commonplace, and the day was very hot, and that it was more painful than sweet to be thus strolling beside the big, loose-jointed figure, and to send an occasional side glance at John Tenison's earnest face, which wore its pleasantest expression now. Well, it would be over at five, and she could go home, and lie down in the dark, and dream of what life might have been if today could have been the leisurely, luxurious, delightful Sunday she knew the professor had expected.

She came out of a reverie to find him glancing humorously from her to his watch.

"The train was five o'clock, was it?" he said. "I've missed it!"

"Missed it!" echoed Margaret blankly. Then as the horrible possibility dawned upon her, "Oh, impossible!"

"Ten minutes past five," said Dr. Tenison blandly.

Poor Margaret, fighting utter discouragement, struggled for an air of hospitality.

"Then you must come back with me for supper," said she.

"Now, perhaps that's an imposition," said the professor, "perhaps you and I could have a bite at a restaurant?"

For one desperate moment Margaret considered the hotel. But she knew the hotel! And Mother would be angry, too. She laughed philosophically, and was suddenly astonished to find herself in quite a stoically cheerful mood. Things couldn't be any worse than they had been at noon. Professor Tenison was thoroughly disenchanted now, and *let* him be. She couldn't help it! It was cooler now, anyway, and perhaps if they walked up by the graveyard, they could manage to get home a little late, and have just a cold bite *tête-à-tête* when the others were done.

"No, no!" she protested smiling, "we'll take that little walk I told you of, and Mother will give us something to eat later."

Accordingly they turned toward the graveyard, and spent the sunset hour over the old graves. It was almost seven o'clock when they opened the home gate. On the side porch were only Rebecca, enchanting in fresh ruffles, Dad and Mother.

"Well, what luck we waited!" said Rebecca, rising. "Supper's all ready."

"Where are the others?" said Margaret, experiencing the first pleasant sensation in twenty-four hours.

"Ju and Harry went home, boys walking, Rob's at George's," said Rebecca briefly. She gave Margaret a shy, charming little side glance as she presently led the way to the dining room.

It was hardly recognizable now, cool and shady, with a little table set for five in the middle of the room, the old candlesticks and silver teapot presiding over blue bowls of berries and the choicest of Mother's preserved fruits. Some one had found time to put crisp parsley about the old Canton platter of cold meats; some one had made a special trip down to Mrs. O'Brien's for the cream that filled the Wedgwood pitcher. Margaret felt tears press suddenly against her eyes.

"Oh, Beck!" she could only stammer when the sisters went to the kitchen for hot water and tea biscuit.

"Mother did it," said Rebecca, returning her hug with fervour, "she called us all down after you left. Then later Paul and I and the others were walking, and we saw that Professor Tenison had missed the five, and I tore home and told Mother you'd be back, and we just *flew!*"

It was all like a pleasant awakening after a troubled dream. Mother was so gracious and charming behind the urn, Rebecca irresistible in her open admiration of the famous professor. Dad, his sweetest self—delightfully reminiscent of his boyhood, and his visit to the White House in Lincoln's day with "my uncle, the judge."

And after tea they sat on the porch, and the stars came out, and presently the moon sent silver shafts through the dark trees. Little Rob came home and climbed into his father's lap.

393

"Sing something, Mark," said Dad then, and Margaret, sitting on the steps, with her head against her mother's knee, found it very simple to begin in the silence one of the old songs he loved:

> Don't you cry, ma honey,
> Don't you weep no more.

Rebecca, sitting on the rail, one slender arm flung above her head about the pillar, joined her own young voice to Margaret's rich one. The others hummed a little. The professor, sitting, watching them, his locked hands hanging between his knees, saw in the moonlight a sudden glitter on the mother's cheek.

Bruce, tired and happy and sunburned, came through the splashed silver-and-black of the street to sit by Margaret, and put his arm about her, and the younger boys came around the corner of the house; before long all their happy voices rose together on "Believe Me," and "Working on the Railroad," and "Seeing Nellie Home," and half a dozen more of the immortal songs that young people have sung for half a century in the summer moonlight.

It was over too soon, and Margaret walked with her guest to the train at ten o'clock.

"Now I know what makes you what you are," said he. "It's having a mother like that! And now, just now, I've discovered what's been puzzling me all day—I've discovered what *she* gets out of it! This morning, thinking of what such a mother's life is, I couldn't see what *repaid* her, do you see? What made up to her for the unending, *unending* effort, and sacrifice, the pouring out and pouring out of love and sympathy and interest. . . ."

He hesitated, but Margaret did not speak.

"You know," continued John Tenison musingly, "in these days, when a woman thinks she is entitled to entirely ignore the question of children, if she feels that way, or at most to bring up one or two, just the one or two that the family income provides for luxuriously and easily, there's something magnificent in a woman like your mother, who, instead of one destiny, starts eight! Responsibility—that's what people are afraid of! But it seems to me there's no responsibility like that of decreeing that young lives simply *shall not be*. There's a higher tribunal than the social tribunal of this world, Miss Paget, after all, and it seems to me that a woman who stands there, as your mother will, with a forest of new lives about her, and a record like hers, will—will find she has a Friend at court!" he ended whimsically.

They were at a lonely corner, and a garden fence offering Margaret a convenient support, she laid her arms suddenly upon the rose vine that covered it, and her face on her arms, and cried as if her heart were broken.

But coming back from the train, half an hour later, she walked between a new heaven and a new earth. The warm stars seemed just over her head; a thousand little friendly odours came from garden beds and recently watered lawns. She moved through the confusion that always attended the settling-down of the Pagets for the night, like one in a dream, and was glad to find herself lying at last in the darkness beside the sleeping Rebecca again. Now, now she could think!

But it was all too wonderful for reasonable thought. Margaret clasped both her hands over her rising heart. He loved her. She could think of the very words he had used in telling her over and over again. She need not wonder and hope and despair ever again: he had *said* it. He loved her, and had loved her from the very first. His father suspected it, and his chum suspected it, and he had thought Margaret suspected it. And beside him in that career that she had followed so wistfully in her dreams, Margaret saw herself, his wife. Young, and clever, and good to look upon— yes, she was free to admit herself all these good things for his sake!—and his *wife*. Mounting as he mounted, always beside him, the one man in the world she had elected to admire and love! "Dr. and Mrs. John Tenison," so it would be written. "Dr. Tenison's wife." "This is Mrs. Tenison," she seemed already to hear the magical sound of it!

How she loved just being alive tonight! How she loved everything and everybody, Mother and Dad, darling little Beck and old Bruce, all the brothers and sisters! She would see Julie tomorrow, and show her how Mrs. Carr-Boldt's married niece had had her baby's wrappers cut. . . . Dear old Ju! Margaret had a sudden tender memory of the days when Theodore and Duncan and Rob were all babies in turn, how Mother would gather the little daily supply of fresh clothes from bureau and chest every morning, and carry the little bathtub into the sunny nursery window and sit there with only a bobbing downy head and reaching pink fingers visible from the great warm bundle of bath apron. . . . Ju would be doing that now.

Well, suppose she and Bruce had been the only ones. Yes, but it wouldn't have been Bruce and Margaret, it would have been Bruce and Charley. . . . Margaret stirred a little uneasily; frowned in the dark. She thought of all the matrons she knew with only two children, of more who had but one, of most who had none at all. It seemed perfectly incredible, it seemed perfectly *impossible* that if Mother had had but the two, she, Margaret—a pronounced and separate entity, traveled, ambitious, and to be the wife of one of the world's great men—might not have been lying here in the summer night, rich in love and youth and beauty and her dreams!

It was all very puzzling. Margaret sighed, and in answer her mother's voice spoke softly from the doorway:

"Awake, dear?"

Margaret locked her young arms tightly about her mother, as the older woman knelt beside her. "Mother—" she stammered, and stopped. Mrs. Paget kissed her.

"Daddy and I thought so," she said simply, and further announcement was not needed between them. "He is very fine, Mark," said Mrs. Paget presently. "I don't know but what I am glad, dear. I lose my girl, but there's no happiness like marriage, Mark."

"But not until June," Margaret whispered shyly. "John—John goes to Germany for a year, in June. And we thought that would be better than interrupting the term, or trying to settle down anywhere before that. And Mother, I'm going to write Mrs. Carr-Boldt—she can get a thousand girls to fill my place!—and I'm going to take the school here for the term. They'll give it to me, I know, for they've only ten days to get some one now. And I want to see something of Bruce, and sort of stand by Beck! We'll talk in the morning. But it's for you, most of all, Mother, I—I've always loved you, but I never realized—" She broke off pitifully, "Ah, MOTHER!"

For her mother's arms had tightened almost convulsively about her, and the face against hers was wet.

"Is Mother there?" said Rebecca drowsily. "You said your prayers on Mark last night. Come over and say them on me tonight, Mother," said she.

# A Friend of Napoleon

## RICHARD CONNELL

*This ingenious tale of the watchman in a Paris wax-
works and a pair of young lovers illustrates ably why
Richard Connell is known as one of America's best
story-tellers. The notable motion picture* Seven Faces
*was made from this story.*

ALL PARIS HELD no happier man than Papa Chibou.
He loved his work—that was why. Other men might say—did say, in
fact—that for no amount of money would they take his job; no, not for
ten thousand francs for a single night. It would turn their hair white and
give them permanent goose flesh, they averred. On such men Papa Chibou
smiled with pity. What stomach had such zestless ones for adventure?
What did they know of romance? Every night of his life Papa Chibou
walked with adventure and held the hand of romance.

Every night he conversed intimately with Napoleon; with Marat and
his fellow revolutionists; with Carpentier and Caesar; with Victor Hugo
and Lloyd George; with Foch and with Bigarre, the Apache murderer
whose unfortunate penchant for making ladies into curry led him to the
guillotine; with Louis XVI and with Madame Lablanche, who poisoned
eleven husbands and was working to make it an even dozen when the
police deterred her; with Marie Antoinette and with sundry early Christian martyrs who lived in sweet resignation in electric-lighted catacombs
under the sidewalk of the Boulevard des Capucines in the very heart of
Paris. They were all his friends and he had a word and a joke for each
of them, as on his nightly rounds he washed their faces and dusted out
their ears, for Papa Chibou was night watchman at the Musée Pratoucy—
"The World in Wax. Admission, one franc. Children and soldiers, half
price. Nervous ladies enter the Chamber of Horrors at their own risk.
One is prayed not to touch the wax figures or to permit dogs to circulate
in the establishment."

He had been at the Musée Pratoucy so long that he looked like a wax figure himself. Visitors not infrequently mistook him for one and poked him with inquisitive fingers or canes. He did not undeceive them; he did not budge. Spartanlike he stood stiff under the pokes; he was rather proud of being taken for a citizen of the world of wax, which was, indeed, a much more real world to him than the world of flesh and blood. He had cheeks like the small red wax pippins used in table decorations, round eyes, slightly poppy, and smooth white hair, like a wig. He was a diminutive man and, with his horseshoe moustache of surprising luxuriance, looked like a gnome going to a fancy-dress ball as a small walrus. Children who saw him flitting about the dim passages that led to the catacombs were sure he was a brownie.

His title "Papa" was a purely honorary one, given him because he had worked some twenty-five years at the museum. He was unwed, and slept at the museum in a niche of a room just off the Roman arena where papier-mâché lions and tigers breakfasted on assorted martyrs. At night, as he dusted off the lions and tigers, he rebuked them sternly for their lack of delicacy.

"Ah," he would say, cuffing the ear of the largest lion, which was earnestly trying to devour a grandfather and an infant simultaneously, "sort of a pig that you are! I am ashamed of you, eater of babies. You will go to hell for this, Monsieur Lion, you may depend upon it. Monsieur Satan will poach you like an egg, I promise you. Ah, you bad one, you species of a camel, you Apache, you profiteer—"

Then Papa Chibou would bend over and very tenderly address the elderly martyr who was lying beneath the lion's paws and exhibiting signs of distress and, say, "Patience, my brave one. It does not take long to be eaten, and then, consider: The good Lord will take you up to heaven, and there, if you wish, you yourself can eat a lion every day. You are a man of holiness, Phillibert. You will be Saint Phillibert, beyond doubt, and then won't you laugh at lions!"

Phillibert was the name Papa Chibou had given to the venerable martyr; he had bestowed names on all of them. Having consoled Phillibert, he would softly dust the fat wax infant whom the lion was in the act of bolting.

"Courage, my poor little Jacob," Papa Chibou would say. "It is not every baby that can be eaten by a lion; and in such a good cause too. Don't cry, little Jacob. And remember: When you get inside Monsieur Lion, kick and kick and kick! That will give him a great sickness of the stomach. Won't that be fun, little Jacob?"

So he went about his work, chatting with them all, for he was fond of them all, even of Bigarre the Apache and the other grisly inmates of the Chamber of Horrors. He did chide the criminals for their regrettable proclivities in the past and warn them that he would tolerate no such conduct in his museum. It was not his museum of course. Its owner was Monsieur Pratoucy, a long-necked, melancholy marabou of a man who sat at the ticket window and took in the francs. But, though the legal title to the place might be vested in Monsieur Pratoucy, at night Papa Chibou was the undisputed monarch of his little wax kingdom. When the last patron had left and the doors were closed Papa Chibou began to pay calls on his subjects; across the silent halls he called greetings to them:

"Ah, Bigarre, you old rascal, how goes the world? And you, Madame Marie Antoinette; did you enjoy a good day? Good evening, Monsieur Caesar; aren't you chilly in that costume of yours. Ah, Monsieur Charlemagne, I trust your health continues to be of the best."

His closest friend of them all was Napoleon. The others he liked; to Napoleon he was devoted. It was a friendship cemented by years, for Napoleon had been in the museum as long as Papa Chibou. Other figures might come and go at the behest of a fickle public, but Napoleon held his place, albeit he had been relegated to a dim corner.

He was not much of a Napoleon. He was smaller even than the original Napoleon, and one of his ears had come in contact with a steam radiator and as a result it was gnarled into a lump the size of a hickory nut; it was a perfect example of that phenomenon of the prize ring, the cauliflower ear. He was supposed to be at St. Helena and he stood on a papier-mâché rock, gazing out wistfully over a nonexistent sea. One hand was thrust into the bosom of his long-tailed coat, the other hung at his side. Skin-tight breeches, once white but white no longer, fitted snugly over his plump bump of waxen abdomen. A Napoleonic hat, frayed by years of conscientious brushing by Papa Chibou, was perched above a pensive waxen brow.

Papa Chibou had been attracted to Napoleon from the first. There was something so forlorn about him. Papa Chibou had been forlorn, too, in his first days at the museum. He had come from Bouloire, in the south of France, to seek his fortune as a grower of asparagus in Paris. He was a simple man of scant schooling and he had fancied that there were asparagus beds along the Paris boulevards. There were none. So necessity and chance brought him to the Museum Pratoucy to earn his bread and wine, and romance and his friendship for Napoleon kept him there.

The first day Papa Chibou worked at the museum Monsieur Pratoucy took him round to tell him about the figures.

"This," said the proprietor, "is Toulon, the strangler. This is Mademoiselle Merle, who shot the Russian duke. This is Charlotte Corday, who stabbed Marat in the bathtub; that gory gentleman is Marat." Then they had come to Napoleon. Monsieur Pratoucy was passing him by.

"And who is this sad-looking gentleman?" asked Papa Chibou.

"Name of a name! Do you not know?"

"But no, monsieur."

"But that is Napoleon himself."

That night, his first in the museum, Papa Chibou went round and said to Napoleon, "Monsieur, I do not know with what crimes you are charged, but I, for one, refuse to think you are guilty of them."

So began their friendship. Thereafter he dusted Napoleon with especial care and made him his confidant. One night in his twenty-fifth year at the museum Papa Chibou said to Napoleon, "You observed those two lovers who were in here to-night, did you not, my good Napoleon? They thought it was too dark in this corner for us to see, didn't they? But we saw him take her hand, whisper to her. Did she blush? You were near enough to see. She is pretty, isn't she, with her bright dark eyes? She is not a French girl; she is an American; one can tell that by the way she doesn't roll her r's. The young man, he is French; and a fine young fellow he is, or I'm no judge. He is so slender and erect, and he has courage, for he wears the war cross; you noticed that, didn't you? He is very much in love, that is sure. This is not the first time I have seen them. They have met here before, and they are wise, for is this not a spot most romantic for the meetings of lovers?"

Papa Chibou flicked a speck of dust from Napoleon's good ear.

"Ah," he exclaimed, "it must be a thing most delicious to be young and in love! Were you ever in love, Napoleon? No? Ah, what a pity! I know, for I, too, have had no luck in love. Ladies prefer the big, strong men, don't they? Well, we must help these two young people, Napoleon. We must see that they have the joy we missed. So do not let them know you are watching them if they come here to-morrow night. I will pretend I do not see."

Each night after the museum had closed, Papa Chibou gossiped with Napoleon about the progress of the love affair between the American girl with the bright dark eyes and the slender, erect young Frenchman.

"All is not going well," Papa Chibou reported one night, shaking his head. "There are obstacles to their happiness. He has little money, for he is just beginning his career. I heard him tell her so to-night. And she has an aunt who has other plans for her. What a pity if fate should part them! But you know how unfair fate can be, don't you, Napoleon? If only we had some money we might be able to help him, but I, myself, have no money, and I suppose you, too, were poor, since you look so sad. But attend; to-morrow is a day most important for them. He has asked her if she will marry him, and she has said that she will tell him to-morrow night at nine in this very place. I heard them arrange it all. If she does not come it will mean no. I think we shall see two very happy ones here to-morrow night, eh, Napoleon?"

The next night, when the last patron had gone and Papa Chibou had locked the outer door, he came to Napoleon, and tears were in his eyes.

"You saw, my friend?" broke out Papa Chibou. "You observed? You saw his face and how pale it grew? You saw his eyes and how they held a thousand agonies? He waited until I had to tell him three times that the museum was closing. I felt like an executioner, I assure you; and he looked up at me as only a man condemned can look. He went out with heavy feet; he was no longer erect. For she did not come, Napoleon; that girl with the bright dark eyes did not come. Our little comedy of love has become a tragedy, monsieur. She has refused him, that poor, that unhappy young man."

On the following night at closing time Papa Chibou came hurrying to Napoleon; he was a-quiver with excitement.

"She was here!" he cried. "Did you see her? She was here and she kept watching and watching; but, of course, he did not come. I could tell from his stricken face last night that he had no hope. At last I dared to speak to her. I said to her, 'Mademoiselle, a thousand pardons for the very great liberty I am taking, but it is my duty to tell you—he was here last night and he waited till closing time. He was all of a paleness, mademoiselle, and he chewed his fingers in his despair. He loves you, mademoiselle; a cow could see that. He is devoted to you; and he is a fine young fellow, you can take an old man's word for it. Do not break his heart, mademoiselle.' She grasped my sleeve. 'You know him, then?' she asked. 'You know where I can find him?' 'Alas, no,' I said. 'I have only seen him here with you.' 'Poor boy!' she kept saying. 'Poor boy! Oh, what shall I do? I am in dire trouble. I love him, monsieur.' 'But you did not come,' I said. 'I could not,' she replied, and she was weeping. 'I live with an aunt; a rich tiger she is, monsieur, and she wants me to marry a count, a fat leering fellow who smells of attar of roses and garlic. My aunt locked me in my room. And now I have lost the one I love, for he will think I have refused him, and he is so proud he will never ask me again.' 'But surely you could let him know?' I suggested. 'But I do not know where he lives,' she said. 'And in a few days my aunt is taking me off to Rome, where the count is, and oh, dear, oh, dear, oh dear——' And she wept on my shoulder, Napoleon, that poor little American girl with the bright dark eyes."

Papa Chibou began to brush the Napoleonic hat.

"I tried to comfort her," he said. "I told her that the young man would surely find her, that he would come back and haunt the spot where they had been happy, but I was telling her what I did not believe. 'He may come to-night,' I said, 'or to-morrow.' She waited until it was time to close the museum. You saw her face as she left; did it not touch you in the heart?"

Papa Chibou was downcast when he approached Napoleon the next night.

"She waited again till closing time," he said, "but he did not come. It made me suffer to see her as the hours went by and her hope ebbed away. At last she had to leave, and at the door she said to me, 'If you see him here again, please give him this.' She handed me this card, Napoleon. See, it says, 'I am at the Villa Rosina, Rome. I love you. Nina.' Ah, the poor, poor young man. We must keep a sharp watch for him, you and I."

Papa Chibou and Napoleon did watch at the Musée Pratoucy night after night. One, two, three, four, five nights they watched for him. A week, a month, more months passed, and he did not come. There came instead one day news of so terrible a nature that it left Papa Chibou ill and trembling. The Musée Pratoucy was going to have to close its doors.

"It is no use," said Monsieur Pratoucy, when he dealt this blow to Papa Chibou. "I cannot go on. Already I owe much, and my creditors are clamoring. People will no longer pay a franc to see a few old dummies when they can see an army of red Indians, Arabs, brigands and dukes in the moving pictures. Monday the Musée Pratoucy closes its doors for ever."

"But, Monsieur Pratoucy," exclaimed Papa Chibou, aghast, "what about the people here? What will become of Marie Antoinette, and the martyrs, and Napoleon?"

"Oh," said the proprietor, "I'll be able to realize a little on them, perhaps. On Tuesday they will be sold at auction. Someone may buy them to melt up."

"To melt up, monsieur?" Papa Chibou faltered.

"But certainly. What else are they good for?"

"But surely monsieur will want to keep them; a few of them anyhow?"

"Keep them? Aunt of the devil, but that is a droll idea! Why should anyone want to keep shabby old wax dummies?"

"I thought," murmured Papa Chibou, "that you might keep just one—Napoleon, for example—as a remembrance——"

"Uncle of Satan, but you have odd notions! To keep a souvenir of one's bankruptcy!"

Papa Chibou went away to his little hole in the wall. He sat on his cot and fingered his moustache for an hour; the news had left him dizzy, had made a cold vacuum under his belt buckle. From under his cot, at last, he took a wooden box, unlocked three separate locks, and extracted a sock. From the sock he took his fortune, his hoard of big copper ten-centime pieces, tips he had saved for years. He counted them over five times most carefully; but no matter how he counted them he could not make the total come to more than two hundred and twenty-one francs.

That night he did not tell Napoleon the news. He did not tell of any them. Indeed he acted even more cheerful than usual as he went from one figure to another. He complimented Madame Lablanche, the lady of the poisoned spouses, on how well she was looking. He even had a kindly word to say to the lion that was eating the two martyrs.

"After all, Monsieur Lion," he said, "I suppose it is as proper for you to eat martyrs as it is for me to eat bananas. Probably bananas do not enjoy being eaten any more than martyrs do. In the past I have said harsh things to you, Monsieur Lion; I am sorry I said them, now. After all, it is hardly your fault that you eat people. You were born with an appetite for martyrs, just as I was born poor." And he gently tweaked the lion's papier-mâché ear.

When he came to Napoleon, Papa Chibou brushed him with unusual care and thoroughness. With a moistened cloth he polished the imperial nose, and he took pains to be gentle with the cauliflower ear. He told Napoleon the latest joke he had heard at the cabmen's café where he ate his breakfast of onion soup, and, as the joke was mildly improper, nudged Napoleon in the ribs, and winked at him.

"We are men of the world, eh, old friend?" said Papa Chibou. "We are philosophers, is that not so?" Then he added, "We take what life sends us, and sometimes it sends hardnesses."

403

He wanted to talk more with Napoleon, but somehow he couldn't; abruptly, in the midst of a joke, Papa Chibou broke off and hurried down into the depths of the Chamber of Horrors and stood there for a very long time staring at an unfortunate native of Siam being trodden on by an elephant.

It was not until the morning of the auction sale that Papa Chibou told Napoleon. Then, while the crowd was gathering, he slipped up to Napoleon in his corner and laid his hand on Napoleon's arm.

"One of the hardnesses of life has come to us, old friend," he said. "They are going to try to take you away. But, courage! Papa Chibou does not desert his friends. Listen!" And Papa Chibou patted his pocket, which gave forth a jingling sound.

The bidding began. Close to the auctioneer's desk stood a man, a wizened, rodent-eyed man with a diamond ring and dirty fingers. Papa Chibou's heart went down like an express elevator when he saw him, for he knew that the rodent-eyed man was Mogen, the junk king of Paris. The auctioneer in a voice slightly encumbered by adenoids, began to sell the various items in a hurried, perfunctory manner.

"Item 3 is Julius Caesar, toga and sandals thrown in. How much am I offered? One hundred and fifty francs? Dirt cheap for a Roman emperor, that is. Who'll make it two hundred? Thank you, Monsieur Mogen. The noblest Roman of them all is going at two hundred francs. Are you all through at two hundred? Going, going, gone! Julius Caesar is sold to Monsieur Mogen."

Papa Chibou patted Caesar's back sympathetically.

"You are worth more, my good Julius," he said in a whisper. "Goodbye."

He was encouraged. If a comparatively new Caesar brought only two hundred, surely an old Napoleon would bring no more.

The sale progressed rapidly. Monsieur Mogen bought the entire Chamber of Horrors. He bought Marie Antoinette, and the martyrs and the lions. Papa Chibou, standing near Napoleon, withstood the strain of waiting by chewing his moustache.

The sale was very nearly over and Monsieur Mogen had bought every item, when, with a yawn, the auctioneer droned: "Now, ladies and gentlemen, we come to Item 573, a collection of odds and ends, mostly damaged goods, to be sold in one lot. The lot includes one stuffed owl that seems to have moulted a bit; one Spanish shawl, torn; the head of an Apache who has been guillotined, body missing; a small wax camel, no humps; and an old wax figure of Napoleon, with one ear damaged. What am I offered for the lot?"

Papa Chibou's heart stood still. He laid a reassuring hand on Napoleon's shoulder.

"The fool," he whispered in Napoleon's good ear, "to put you in the same class as a camel, no humps, and an owl. But never mind. It is lucky for us, perhaps."

"How much for this assortment?" asked the auctioneer.

"One hundred francs," said Mogen, the junk king.

"One hundred and fifty," said Papa Chibou, trying to be calm. He had never spent so vast a sum all at once in his life.

Mogen fingered the material in Napoleon's coat.

"Two hundred," said the junk king.

"Are you all through at two hundred?" queried the auctioneer.

"Two hundred and twenty-one," called Papa Chibou. His voice was a husky squeak.

Mogen from his rodent eyes glared at Papa Chibou with annoyance and contempt. He raised his dirtiest finger—the one with the diamond ring on it—toward the auctioneer.

"Monsieur Mogen bids two hundred and twenty-five," droned the auctioneer. "Do I hear two hundred and fifty?"

Papa Chibou hated the world. The auctioneer cast a look in his direction.

"Two hundred and twenty-five is bid," he repeated. "Are you all through at two hundred and twenty-five? Going, going—sold to Monsieur Mogen for two hundred and twenty-five francs."

Stunned, Papa Chibou heard Mogen say casually, "I'll send round my carts for this stuff in the morning."

This stuff!

Dully and with an aching breast Papa Chibou went to his room down by the Roman arena. He packed his few clothes into a box. Last of all he slowly took from his cap the brass badge he had worn for so many years; it bore the words "Chief Watchman." He had been proud of that title, even if it was slightly inaccurate; he had been not only the chief but the only watchman. Now he was nothing. It was hours before he summoned up the energy to take his box round to the room he had rented high up under the roof of a tenement in a near-by alley. He knew he should start to look for another job at once, but he could not force himself to do so that day. Instead, he stole back to the deserted museum and sat down on a bench by the side of Napoleon. Silently he sat there all night; but he did not sleep; he was thinking, and the thought that kept pecking at his brain was to him a shocking one. At last, as day began to edge its pale way through the dusty windows of the museum, Papa Chibou stood up with the air of a man who has been through a mental struggle and has made up his mind.

"Napoleon," he said, "we have been friends for a quarter of a century and now we are to be separated because a stranger had four francs more than I had. That may be lawful, my old friend, but it is not justice. You and I, we are not going to be parted."

Paris was not yet awake when Papa Chibou stole with infinite caution into the narrow street beside the museum. Along this street toward the tenement where he had taken a room crept Papa Chibou. Sometimes he had to pause for breath, for in his arms he was carrying Napoleon.

Two policemen came to arrest Papa Chibou that very afternoon. Mogen has missed Napoleon, and he was a shrewd man. There was not the slightest doubt of Papa Chibou's guilt. There stood Napoleon in the corner of his room, gazing pensively out over the housetops. The police bundled the overwhelmed and confused Papa Chibou into the police patrol, and with him, as damning evidence, Napoleon.

In his cell in the city prison Papa Chibou sat with his spirit caved in. To him jails and judges and justice were terrible and mysterious affairs. He wondered if he would be guillotined; perhaps not, since his long life had been one of blameless conduct; but the least he could expect, he reasoned, was a long sentence to hard labour on Devil's Island, and guillotining had certain advantages over that. Perhaps it would be better to be guillotined, he told himself, now that Napoleon was sure to be melted up.

The keeper who brought him his meal of stew was a pessimist of jocular tendencies.

"A pretty pickle," said the keeper; "and at your age, too. You must be a very wicked old man to go about stealing dummies. What will be safe now? One may expect to find the Eiffel Tower missing any morning. Dummy stealing! What a career! We have had a man in here who stole a trolley car, and one who made off with the anchor of a steamship, and even one who pilfered a hippopotamus from a zoo, but never one who stole a dummy—and an old one-eared dummy, at that! It is an affair extraordinary!"

"And what did they do to the gentleman who stole the hippopotamus?" inquired Papa Chibou tremulously.

The keeper scratched his head to indicate thought.

"I think," he said, "that they boiled him alive. Either that or they transported him for life to Morocco; I don't recall exactly."

Papa Chibou's brow grew damp.

"It was a trial most comical, I can assure you," went on the keeper. "The judges were Messieurs Bertouf, Goblin, and Perouse—very amusing fellows, all three of them. They had fun with the prisoner; how I laughed. Judge Bertouf said, in sentencing him, 'We must be severe with you, pilferer of hippopotamuses. We must make of you an example. This business of hippopotamus pilfering is getting all too common in Paris.' They are witty fellows, those judges."

Papa Chibou grew a shade paler.

"The Terrible Trio?" he asked.

"The Terrible Trio," replied the keeper cheerfully.

"Will they be my judges?" asked Papa Chibou.

"Most assuredly," promised the keeper, and strolled away humming happily and rattling his big keys.

Papa Chibou knew then that there was no hope for him. Even into the Musée Pratoucy the reputation of those three judges had penetrated, and it was a sinister reputation indeed. They were three ancient, grim men, who had fairly earned their title, The Terrible Trio, by the severity of their sentences; evildoers blanched at their names, and this was a matter of pride to them.

Shortly the keeper came back; he was grinning.

"You have the devil's own luck, old-timer," he said to Papa Chibou. "First you have to be tried by The Terrible Trio, and then you get assigned to you as lawyer none other than Monsieur Georges Dufayel."

"And this Monsieur Dufayel, is he then not a good lawyer?" questioned Papa Chibou miserably.

The keeper snickered.

"He has not won a case for months," he answered, as if it were the most amusing thing imaginable. "It is really better than a circus to hear him muddling up his clients' affairs in court. His mind is not on the case at all. Heaven knows where it is. When he rises to plead before the judges he has no fire, no passion. He mumbles and stutters. It is a saying about the courts that one is as good as convicted who has the ill luck to draw Monsieur Georges Dufayel as his advocate. Still, if one is too poor to pay for a lawyer, one must take what he can get. That's philosophy, eh, old-timer?"

Papa Chibou groaned.

"Oh, wait till to-morrow," said the keeper gayly. "Then you'll have a real reason to groan."

"But surely I can see this Monsieur Dufayel."

"Oh, what's the use? You stole the dummy, didn't you? It will be there in court to appear against you. How entertaining! Witness for the prosecution: Monsieur Napoleon. You are plainly as guilty as Cain, old-timer, and the judges will boil your cabbage for you very quickly and neatly, I can promise you that. Well, see you to-morrow. Sleep well."

Papa Chibou did not sleep well. He did not sleep at all, in fact, and when they marched him into the enclosure where sat the other nondescript offenders against the law he was shaken and utterly wretched. He was overawed by the great court room and the thick atmosphere of seriousness that hung over it.

He did pluck up enough courage to ask a guard, "Where is my lawyer, Monsieur Dufayel?"

"Oh, he's late, as usual," replied the guard. And then, for he was a waggish fellow, he added, "If you're lucky he won't come at all."

Papa Chibou sank down on the prisoner's bench and raised his eyes to the tribunal opposite. His very marrow was chilled by the sight of The Terrible Trio. The chief judge, Bertouf, was a vast puff of a man, who swelled out of his judicial chair like a poisonous fungus. His black robe was familiar with spilled brandy, and his dirty judicial bib was askew. His face was bibulous and brutal, and he had the wattles of a turkey gobbler. Judge Goblin, on his right, looked to have mummified; he was at least a hundred years old and had wrinkled parchment skin and red-rimmed eyes that glittered like the eyes of a cobra. Judge Perouse was one vast jungle of tangled grizzled whiskers, from the midst of which projected a cockatoo's beak of a nose; he looked at Papa Chibou and licked his lips with a long pink tongue. Papa Chibou all but fainted; he felt no bigger than a pea, and less important; as for his judges, they seemed enormous monsters.

The first case was called, a young swaggering fellow who had stolen an orange from a pushcart.

"Ah, Monsieur Thief," rumbled Judge Bertouf with a scowl, "you are jaunty now. Will you be so jaunty a year from to-day when you are released from prison? I rather think not. Next case."

Papa Chibou's heart pumped with difficulty. A year for an orange—and he had stolen a man! His eyes roved round the room and he saw two guards carrying in something which they stood before the judges. It was Napoleon.

A guard tapped Papa Chibou on the shoulder. "You're next," he said.

"But my lawyer, Monsieur Dufayel—" began Papa Chibou.

"You're in hard luck," said the guard, "for here he comes."

Papa Chibou in a daze found himself in the prisoner's dock. He saw coming toward him a pale young man. Papa Chibou recognized him at once. It was the slender, erect young man of the museum. He was not very erect now; he was listless. He did not recognize Papa Chibou; he barely glanced at him.

"You stole something," said the young lawyer, and his voice was toneless. "The stolen goods were found in your room. I think we might better plead guilty and get it over with."

"Yes, monsieur," said Papa Chibou, for he had let go all his hold on hope. "But attend a moment. I have something—a message for you."

Papa Chibou fumbled through his pockets and at last found the card of the American girl with the bright dark eyes. He handed it to Georges Dufayel.

"She left it with me to give to you," said Papa Chibou. "I was chief watchman at the Musée Pratoucy, you know. She came there night after night, to wait for you."

The young man gripped the sides of the card with both hands; his face, his eyes, everything about him seemed suddenly charged with new life.

"Ten thousand million devils!" he cried. "And I doubted her! I owe you much, monsieur. I owe you everything." He wrung Papa Chibou's hand.

Judge Bertouf gave an impatient judicial grunt.

"We are ready to hear your case, Advocate Dufayel," said the judge, "if you have one."

The court attendants sniggered.

"A little moment, monsieur the judge," said the lawyer. He turned to Papa Chibou. "Quick," he shot out, "tell me about the crime you are charged with. What did you steal?"

"Him," replied Papa Chibou, pointing.

"That dummy of Napoleon?"

Papa Chibou nodded.

"But why?"

Papa Chibou shrugged his shoulders.

"Monsieur could not understand."

"But you must tell me!" said the lawyer urgently. "I must make a plea for you. These savages will be severe enough, in any event; but I may be able to do something. Quick; why did you steal this Napoleon?"

"I was his friend," said Papa Chibou. "The museum failed. They were going to sell Napoleon for junk, Monsieur Dufayel. He was my friend. I could not desert him."

The eyes of the young advocate had caught fire; they were lit with a flash. He brought his fist down on the table.

"Enough!" he cried.

Then he rose in his place and addressed the court. His voice was low, vibrant and passionate; the judges, in spite of themselves, leaned forward to listen to him.

"May it please the honourable judges of this court of France," he began, "my client is guilty. Yes, I repeat in a voice of thunder, for all France to hear, for the enemies of France to hear, for the whole wide world to hear, he is guilty. He did steal this figure of Napoleon, the lawful property of another. I do not deny it. This old man, Jerome Chibou, is guilty, and I for one am proud of his guilt."

Judge Bertouf grunted.

"If your client is guilty, Advocate Dufayel," he said, "that settles it. Despite your pride in his guilt, which is a peculiar notion, I confess, I am going to sentence him to—"

"But wait, your honour!" Dufayel's voice was compelling. "You must, you shall hear me! Before you pass sentence on this old man, let me ask you a question."

"Well?"

"Are you a Frenchman, Judge Bertouf?"

"But certainly."

"And you love France?"

"Monsieur has not the effrontery to suggest otherwise?"

"No. I was sure of it. That is why you will listen to me."

"I listen."

"I repeat then: Jerome Chibou is guilty. In the law's eyes he is a criminal. But in the eyes of France and those who love her his guilt is a glorious guilt; his guilt is more honourable than innocence itself."

The three judges looked at one another blankly; Papa Chibou regarded his lawyer with wide eyes; Georges Dufayel spoke on.

"These are times of turmoil and change in our country, messieurs the judges. Proud traditions which were once the birthright of every French-man have been allowed to decay. Enemies beset us within and without. Youth grows careless of that honour which is the soul of a nation. Youth forgets the priceless heritages of the ages, the great names that once brought glory to France in the past, when Frenchmen were Frenchmen. There are some in France who may have forgotten the respect due a nation's great"—here Advocate Dufayel looked very hard at the judges—"but there are a few patriots left who have not forgotten. And there sits one of them."

"This poor old man has deep within him a glowing devotion to France. You may say that he is a simple, unlettered peasant. You may say that he is a thief. But I say, and true Frenchmen will say with me, that he is a patriot, messieurs the judges. He loves Napoleon. He loves him for what he did for France. He loves him because in Napoleon burned that spirit which has made France great. There was a time, messieurs the judges, when your fathers and mine dared share that love for a great leader. Need I remind you of the career of Napoleon? I know I need not. Need I tell you of his victories? I know I need not."

Nevertheless, Advocate Dufayel did tell them of the career of Napoleon. With a wealth of detail and many gestures he traced the rise of Napoleon; he lingered over his battles; for an hour and ten minutes he spoke eloquently of Napoleon and his part in the history of France.

"You may have forgotten," he concluded, "and others may have forgotten, but this old man sitting here a prisoner—he did not forget. When mercenary scoundrels wanted to throw on the junk heap this effigy of one of France's greatest sons, who was it that saved him? Was it you, messieurs the judges? Was it I? Alas, no. It was a poor old man who loved Napoleon more than he loved himself. Consider, messieurs the judges; they were going to throw on the junk heap Napoleon—France's Napoleon—our Napoleon. Who would save him? Then up rose this man, Jerome Chibou, whom you would brand as a thief, and he cried aloud for France and for the whole world to hear, 'Stop! Desecraters of Napoleon, stop! There still lives one Frenchman who loves the memories of his native land; there is still one patriot left. I, I, Jerome Chibou, will save Napoleon!' And he did save him, messieurs the judges."

Advocate Dufayel mopped his brow, and leveling an accusing finger at The Terrible Trio he said, "You may send Jerome Chibou to jail. But when you do, remember this: You are sending to jail the spirit of France. You may find Jerome Chibou guilty. But when you do, remember this:

You are condemning a man for love of country, for love of France. Wherever true hearts beat in French bosoms, messieurs the judges, there will the crime of Jerome Chibou be understood, and there will the name of Jerome Chibou be honoured. Put him in prison, messieurs the judges. Load his poor feeble old body with chains. And a nation will tear down the prison walls, break his chains, and pay homage to the man who loved Napoleon and France so much that he was willing to sacrifice himself on the altar of patriotism."

Advocate Dufayel sat down; Papa Chibou raised his eyes to the judges' bench. Judge Perouse was ostentatiously blowing his beak of a nose. Judge Goblin, who wore a Sedan ribbon in his buttonhole, was sniffling into his inkwell. And Chief Judge Bertouf was openly blubbering.

"Jerome Chibou, stand up." It was Chief Judge Bertouf who spoke, and his voice was thick with emotion.

Papa Chibou, quaking, stood up. A hand like a hand of pink bananas was thrust down at him.

"Jerome Chibou," said Chief Judge Bertouf, "I find you guilty. Your crime is patriotism in the first degree. I sentence you to freedom. Let me have the honour of shaking the hand of a true Frenchman."

"And I," said Judge Goblin, thrusting out a hand as dry as autumn leaves.

"And I also," said Judge Perouse, reaching out a hairy hand.

"And, furthermore," said Chief Judge Bertouf, "you shall continue to protect the Napoleon you saved. I subscribe a hundred francs to buy him for you."

"And I," said Judge Goblin.

"And I also," said Judge Perouse.

As they left the court room, Advocate Dufayel, Papa Chibou and Napoleon, Papa Chibou turned to his lawyer.

"I can never repay monsieur," he began.

"Nonsense!" said the lawyer.

"And would Monsieur Dufayel mind telling me again the last name of Napoleon?"

"Why, Bonaparte, of course. Surely you knew——"

"Alas, no, Monsieur Dufayel. I am a man the most ignorant. I did not know that my friend had done such great things."

"You didn't? Then what in the name of heaven did you think Napoleon was?"

"A sort of murderer," said Papa Chibou humbly.

Out beyond the walls of Paris in a garden stands the villa of Georges Dufayel, who has become, everyone says, the most eloquent and successful young lawyer in the Paris courts. He lives there with his wife, who has bright dark eyes. To get to his house one must pass a tiny gatehouse, where lives a small old man with a prodigious walrus moustache. Visitors who peer into the gatehouse as they pass sometimes get a shock, for standing in one corner of its only room they see another small man, in uniform and a big hat. He never moves, but stands there by the window all day, one hand in the bosom of his coat, the other at his side, while his eyes look out over the garden. He is waiting for Papa Chibou to come home after his work among the asparagus beds to tell him the jokes and the news of the day.

# *Valedictory*

## MacKINLAY KANTOR

*Children, graduation exercises, memories, and an old man retiring from his labors . . . these are the peaceful and beautiful ingredients of this American Mr. Chips.*

THE PRINCIPAL had told him to reserve the three center rows. As soon as Tyler Morley had turned on the auditorium lights, he began to fasten twine around those seats, thus holding them sacred. They were desks arranged in double rows, two and two.

He thought ribbon would have been better than twine, but the decoration committee had not thought to provide any ribbon. The committee was busy in the domestic-science room, preparing bouquets of flowers which had been brought to the high-school building shortly after supper. The graduating exercises would not begin for an hour. Still, old Ty Morley kept hearing the muffled explosion of big doors on the ground floor, where boys and girls already were arriving.

He barricaded the rear aisles with his little rope of twine, and went to rest his stiff elbows on the window sill. This last moment of May was one of the best evenings May had offered. It wasn't very dark yet; a slice of moon shone clean and bright; and the river timber—a bank of soft maples and cottonwoods stretching along the eastern border of Shelldrake—seemed mysterious with the musk of fresh foliage.

Mr. Morley breathed deeply. He wondered whether the air smelled flowery in Lexington, Nebraska. He had never been to Lexington, but he was going there soon.

The paper had said so, five nights before; it had said so in two different ways and in two different places; and now Mr. Morley brought out his old alligator-hide pocketbook and looked at the clippings again. They were fuzzy from much handling. One item had been cut from a longer article discussing the school-board meeting. The paragraph said that T. A. Morley had tendered his resignation as janitor in the local schools, and that Ed Jensen had been retained to fill the place left vacant by Mr. Morley.

The other item was more important, for it was clipped from the society column, and Mr. Morley had not appeared in the society column since he and his wife entertained the In-His-Name class and the Daughters of the King class of the Baptist Church, in 1911. That was just three weeks before his wife died.

> Friends of T. A. Morley will be interested to hear that he plans soon to leave for Lexington, Nebraska, where he will spend an indefinite time with his daughter, Mrs. R. F. Wackstraw. Mr. Morley paid a personal call to the Clarion office this morning, and stated that he regrets leaving Shelldrake and his many friends here, where he has been employed since 1901 as janitor in the local schools, having also served as constable formerly, and having worked before that for the Western Grain Elevator Company. His many friends and his Comrades of the G. A. R. will be sorry to lose him from our midst. Mr. Morley continues in good health and spirits, although he is well past the seventy mark, but he says he can no longer engage in arduous physical duties. The Clarion wishes him a pleasant journey to Nebraska.

Miss Roache, the Senior adviser, came to the south door of the auditorium, lugging a dripping basket of snowball blooms.

She called, "Ty."

"Yes, ma'am!" said Mr. Morley, and he limped toward her, stuffing the clippings into his wallet.

"Ty, will you please bring up those other baskets? Help Gracey MacIntyre with them. She's so little and they're so big."

"My," he said, and bent down to touch the damp white blooms in the basket, "they're mighty pretty, ain't they?"

"They smell good," said Miss Roache. "Hurry up, Ty. Folks are beginning to come in. We haven't got the stage dressed."

He went down to the domestic-science kitchen, and he found Gracey MacIntyre—a skinny ash-blonde of sixteen—struggling tearfully with baskets of bridal wreath and bleeding hearts. "Half the committee didn't show up," she wailed. "They just let a few of us do the work."

"Well," said Mr. Morley, "don't go plaguing yourself, Gracey. We'll get them up right away. . . . My, that's pretty, ain't it?" He pointed to a long wicker basket filled with yellow iris, and girded at the base with purple crepe paper on which the figures "1922," cut from yellow paper, had been pasted. Purple and gold were the school colors.

416

He thought that he should take "1922" first, because obviously it was to occupy the center of the stage. He bent over and tried to lift it, and suddenly his shoulders felt numb. That wouldn't do. He didn't know what was getting into him; maybe the Decoration Day parade was too strenuous yesterday. That stiffness in his knee didn't seem to let up at all, although he rubbed it with liniment every night.

He remembered how he had gone into No. 4 on the second floor to set a mousetrap, several days previously. Miss Kirkland had been confident that a mouse was in her cupboard. It was late in the afternoon, and cloudy and dark, and the two girls who ran into the room and then out again, didn't see Mr. Morley on his knees in the corner. But one of them said, "Whoo—liniment! I guess Ty's been in here." Probably he smelled of liniment all the time.

The girl who talked about his liniment was Amy Galliver. He remembered the first time he saw Amy; it must have been ten or twelve years before, when she was just a little tyke, starting in Miss Plummer's first grade. That was when he was a janitor of the old South Building.

He was sweeping, he remembered, or getting ready to, and sowing the reddish sweeping compound over the floor. Amy came scooting up the stairs, and she slipped on the sweeping compound and came near breaking her neck. Her face was puffy and red with sudden tears, as he picked her up and brushed off the clinging particles that covered her pink sweater and her long cotton stockings. "Now don't cry, sissy," he had told her. "You won't have no tears left for when you need them! Say," he had said, "I bet I know who you are. I bet you're a Galliver; you've got Galliver written all over your face."

Now he climbed the cold steps of the composition stairway, supporting the heavy basket before him. This wasn't like the stairways in the old South Building. Those were rutty and knotted and dangerous to walk upon. He remembered how he had complained to Amos Apgar, of the school board, about those steps. But Amos said the board was retrenching, and they couldn't afford to do any remodeling at that time. And the next week, Buster Waterfield fell on the stairs and broke his wrist. When Doctor Waterfield got after the school board, they fixed those stairs in a hurry.

Mr. Morley brought up more baskets, and now the girls of the decoration committee—the Junior girls who would not graduate until 1923—were twittering all over the stage.

Two parents had come early. They sat, forlorn but dignified, in the back seats of the reserved section. They were Mr. Isaac Kobitsky and his wife. Mr. Kobitsky dealt in secondhand furniture. But his son Theodore was graduating tonight, and Theodore was a star pupil.

Mr. Morley walked along the back of the auditorium, making certain that all the windows were open.

"Too much draft for you, Mrs. Kobitsky?"

"No," she said. "Is a lovely night. Is beautiful."

Mr. Morley laughed. "I tell you, this is a fine night for graduation. This is one of the finest graduating nights I ever see."

Mr. Kobitsky bowed politely.

"You ought to move up front," said Mr. Morley, "where you can get a real good look at Theodore." The Kobitskys thanked him, but they did not move.

There were many more students trampling through the building now, and when Ty looked from the window again, he heard cars parking in front of the Methodist Church. Beneath the heavy elm branches he saw people coming north on Bank Street. He thought that maybe he'd better go down to the washrooms on the ground floor and see that there were plenty of paper towels. No, it was too late to go in, over on the girls' side; but he'd take a look in the boys' room, just to make sure.

He met Buster Waterfield and Cooky Keane on the first flight of stairs. Buster was getting to resemble his father, though, of course, he didn't have Doctor Waterfield's mustache. But he was a good-looking kid, and Ty stopped a moment to admire the new blue suit that Buster was wearing. "My," he said, "Buster, that's a mighty fine-looking suit."

"Graduation present," said Buster. "Like it?" Proudly, he fingered the sharp-pointed lapels.

"Why," said Ty, "you look like you were dressed up and going some-place!" And perhaps because he was tired at the end of this day, he rested his left hand for a moment on Buster's firm shoulder. "And, Cooky," he said, "you're all togged out too."

Cooky flushed slightly. "Well," he said, "I haven't got a new suit. Got a new tie, that's all."

Mr. Keane had just sold out his Hay, Grain & Feed Company to a man from Mason City, but people said that he had really lost it because of an overdue note.

The janitor laughed, and his right hand lay on Cooky Keane's sleeve. "Far as that goes," he said, "a new suit isn't so downright important, grad-uation or any other time. You just keep on playing that clarinet of yours, and you'll make your mark. You'll have more new suits than you'll know what to do with!"

The Keane boy swallowed. "I'll tell you this, Ty," he whispered. "I did have an offer to play at the Iowa state fair this summer, with Carl King's Band. You know, the big Fort Dodge one."

"What did I tell you?" said Mr. Morley, and journeyed to the wash-room.

He saw smoke when he opened the vestibule door, and the next few steps he took were taken in haste, because for twenty-one years he had lived in dread of fire. But there wasn't any blaze. There were only two freshmen, and one of those was Reverend Lemley's kid, and he was still in short pants.

"I smell smoke in here," said Ty, sniffing until his ragged white mustache moved up and down.

The Lemley kid said, "Aw, go on! You couldn't smell anything through all that brush," and then he shrieked at his own wit and tried to dart away.

But Ty's wrinkled hand tightened on the boy's coat—took him by the scruff of the neck, as it were. "Now you listen to me, Horace Lemley," said Ty. "You give me those cigarettes you've got in your pocket!"

The boy twisted and fought. "Let go me!" he snarled. "I haven't got any cigarettes." But Ty found them, stuffed into a jacket pocket.

"Now you listen here to me," he said. "I'm going to do something about this."

"All the kids smoke," muttered Horace, looking at the floor. His companion in crime shuffled his feet and kept making faces, trying to laugh it off.

"No, they don't," said Ty. "I guess I know who smokes around here and who doesn't. You get to be fifteen or sixteen or seventeen, like Buster or Cooky or somebody, and I wouldn't make no kick. A boy that age doesn't get a chance to smoke enough to hurt him, ordinarily. He just smokes evenings, when he's out with the boys, or something like that. And Buster never touched a cigarette all through football and basketball and track, I'll have you know that! But you're too little. You may be bright, but you ain't more than thirteen. You tell me where you got these cigarettes."

Horace Lemley said, "Found them."

"No you never. Tell me, or I'll tell the Reverend," and so Horace told.

Ty Morley said, "Dinwiddy's Recreation Parlor! Well, Horace, I won't tell your old man. But I bet I give George Dinwiddy an earful tomorrow. He's sold these things to little kids just once too often to suit me. Now you vamoose," and he gave the boy a swat with his hand. They fled; he heard giggles beyond the door, and he shook his head and thought ill of George Dinwiddy.

There were plenty of paper towels. So Ty went to the main entrance to make certain that the doors were hooked open. Folks were coming in now, in a regular procession. Most of the graduation girls had coats wrapped around them to hide the glory of their dresses, though heaven knew it wasn't cold tonight.

Some of them had flowers in their hair, too; and Ty thought about the flowers on the stage again, and he hoped that next year there wouldn't be any drought around graduation time. A drought in late May cut down the supply of garden flowers something terrible. And then, with a shock that left him weak and empty, he realized that he wouldn't be here next time a class got ready to graduate. He'd be away out in Nebraska, with Eunice's folks.

He wondered what kind of graduations they had in Lexington, Nebraska. It wouldn't make much difference, because he wouldn't be janitor any more. He wouldn't know the kids.

And of course he knew these kids—the ones who were graduating upstairs. He had set to work with his broad dustpan and his brown-bristled broom, he had painted the little kindergarten chairs bright red, in the old South Building, before any of these kids was born. He had rung the nine-o'clock gong and the one-fifteen gong and the three-thirty gong, when some of the teachers who helped these young people to graduate were only little children themselves. He guessed that he had talked to each of these kids a million times, and that wasn't counting the occasions when he'd been called in to tell them about the war.

Miss Stark, for instance, would send some youngster traipsing down the basement stairs after Ty Morley, and then he'd mutter and say, "Well, I don't look very good," and then he'd wash his hands and lumber up to No. 2.

Miss Stark would have a big picture of Lincoln on her desk. All those little tads would be sitting there, giggling and squeezing one another because of this break in their routine. Miss Stark would say in a polite voice, "Mr. Morley, we have been learning about Abraham Lincoln today, because it is his birthday, and I was wondering if you had ever seen Abraham Lincoln. . . . Children, Mr. Morley is a member of the Grand Army of the Republic. Those were the men who helped Mr. Lincoln to free all the poor slaves in the South."

She'd say, "How many children have grandfathers or other relatives who helped Mr. Morley and Mr. Lincoln to free the slaves?" and naturally most of the hands in the room would be waving violently. Looking them over, Mr. Morley could recognize the transmitted physical characteristics—infantile and unformed, perhaps, but still ready to be identified—of his friends. That was Bob White's grandson over there by the window, and those were the Neel girls over there—George Neel's granddaughters, those would be—and this little dark girl down in front looked like a Wedding.

So he'd stand there and tell them, "Well, it wasn't slavery, so much as States' rights. You pay attention to what your teacher says, children, and you'll learn a lot of interesting things. She'll tell you all about Abraham Lincoln. Now me, of course I never saw Lincoln. I was a way, way down South—" he drew out the "way, way" extravagantly, so that the children laughed. "I was with the Seventeenth Corpse. The Seventeenth Corpse was part of the Army of the Tennessee, but that's something you'll learn all about some day."

Miss Stark would say, "Questions?" and there'd be a lot of questions. Did Mr. Morley ever see any slaves? Sure, he saw a lot of slaves. Did Mr. Morley shoot any Rebels? "Well," he'd say, jingling with laughter, "I shot at a lot of them, and by jiminy, a lot of them shot at me!"

They would applaud, and he'd go back downstairs shaking his head and chuckling.

It was the same after the superintendent suggested that he and Charley Weidlein change places. The North Building had an extra flight of stairs, and Charley's heart was getting bad, and he couldn't climb stairs very well. So Mr. Morley went over to the old North Building just temporarily, but he stayed there four years. The change was confirmed by the board later on, and he got ten dollars more a month than he'd been getting. He was janitor of the old North Building all the time this class of 1922 went to school there. Upper Fifth, both Six Grades, both Seventh Grades, and Boys' Eighth and Girls' Eighth. Then old Deak Snyder died, and Ty took his place in the high school.

Miss Bidlack used to call him into the Boys' Eighth. "Mr. Morley, the boys are now studying the Civil War. I wondered if you'd tell them a few of your experiences."

He'd stand contentedly beside her desk and say, "Well, I didn't have more than the usual share, I guess. But I was with Sherman on the big advance through the South. I can tell you the dates, if you're interested in dates, and I remember all the places. In the spring of Sixty-four we started over towards North Alabama and Georgia—I mean my brigade. I was in the Fifteenth Iowa Volunteer Infantry. We joined up with McPherson; and our corpse, the Seventeenth, was on the extreme left of his line. We had fighting all the way towards Atlanta. Big Shanty, Kenesaw Mountain, Noonday Creek, Brushy Mountain, Nickajack, and Turner's Ferry. There was constant fighting all the way—skirmish here and skirmish there, and sometimes a regular battle. . . . Nope, I never got hit. They saved me for the fool-killer, I guess!"

The boys would shout and stamp their feet on the floor until the old heating pipes rattled beneath the windows, and Miss Bidlack would say patiently, when the roar had subsided, "How many of Mr. Morley's battles can you name?" And he'd hear them naming his battles as he went away through the cloakroom.

Yes, he knew the boys mighty well. The girls too. Sometimes he thought he liked boys best—maybe that was because he never had any sons of his own. He always liked Rowena Snow; her face looked so peaked and kind of trusting—it made him feel sorry for her.

He first ran into Rowena in the basement of the old South Building, when she was in Miss Dundon's room. Second or Third Grade, that was. A lot of the kids brought their lunch in the winter, when the walking was bad and the weather too cold for them to go home at noon. The kids were supposed to eat together in their home rooms, but Rowena had a trick of sneaking off to an unfinished part of the basement, and she'd hide behind the big timbers and eat her lunch.

Rowena lived with her aunt out on the west end of town, and they were pretty poor; Mr. Morley didn't realize just how poor, until he came upon her unexpectedly, and found the child with her lunch. Old baking-powder biscuits—that was all. Damp and soggy and tasteless. Mr. Morley wouldn't have fed a cat with those things.

He didn't eat any lunch himself that day. But Rowena had two egg sandwiches and two jelly ones, a deviled egg, pickles, a banana and some cupcakes Mr. Morley's wife had baked. On Sunday Mr. Morley wanted to take a walk, and they happened to go past old Miss Snow's property, and they happened to stop in. Miss Snow cried by the quart; actually, there wasn't enough in that house to feed a flea. Miss Snow said she couldn't bear to face the charity people herself, so Mr. Morley went down there and talked with them. The Associated Charity folks saw to it that there was food in Miss Snow's pantry that winter, and then next spring her grown-up nephew came home and got a job in the tile factory, so things were better.

Rowena was smart. She was one of the smartest kids that ever went raring through the Shelldrake schools. She got a hundred all the time, or ninety-eight or ninety-six; she used to show her papers to Mr. Morley, and he'd be delighted. She was valedictorian of her class tonight, and that was a great honor. He knew she'd make a good speech. He'd heard some of the teachers talking, and they said Rowena would get a scholarship to go to Iowa University.

Yes, she was mighty smart. But she wasn't much smarter than Porter Fosselman. Porter was crippled. He used to be one of the most active kids in school, but then they had that big paralysis epidemic when Porter was in the sixth or seventh grade, and his leg was all twisted up after that.

He came fumbling back to school, with blue hollows under his eyes and a queer flame living in them. It was the same blank, hungry flame seen in the eyes of Miss Margy Gillis, as she propelled herself through the streets of Shelldrake in her little chain-driven chair.

Crippled people always had that look in their eyes, it seemed to Mr. Morley. But it didn't hurt their brains. Sometimes it appeared as if they could use their brains better than most people.

Hard on them, though, after they got into high school. The other kids were always having parties and playing games, and in some of the more modern homes they had dancing, although you couldn't dance at a school party. There was that late winter afternoon, a couple of years before, when Ty Morley heard Porter Fosselman crutching his way down to the locker room, and then he heard him sniffling. All the kids were talking about the big Christmas-week party that Joanna Severance was going to give. You couldn't come within a mile of the high school and hear anything but party, party, party. They were going to dance too.

Mr. Morley remembered that he'd seen the Fosselman boy talking to Eleanor Coughlan before the bell rang at noon. Eleanor was a pretty girl, and you couldn't blame any boy for wanting to take her to a party. But, on the other hand, Mr. Morley thought, it was sort of hard on a girl to accept a crippled boy as her escort, especially when she was gay and wanted to dance all the time. If a girl were just a little bit selfish, she'd be apt to tell the crippled boy that she didn't want to go with him.

So Ty Morley blundered out of the boiler room and said, "Hi there,

Porter Fosselman. You know about steam pipes and such; you've learned things like that down at your father's shop, and I heard Mr. Mitchell say you were the best science scholar he had. Well, you come in here and tell me what's wrong with this valve."

So Porter hobbled inside, and at first he was poky and sullen, because he didn't want anybody to see him with his eyes red. But then he got interested in the valve, and he got to explaining about it to Mr. Morley, and Mr. Morley said, "Well, well," and "Now, I never thought of that; maybe there's some kind of a deposit in that elbow, just like you say."

Of course, he wasn't very good at comforting people—not so good as a preacher would have been. He couldn't put his arm around Porter Fosselman and say, "Don't you worry. The thing for you to do is to make yourself so good-natured and good-looking and so clever that you'd please any girl. One thing; you've got a car to drive, and some of the other boys haven't got any car. You could take a girl auto-riding on Sunday afternoon. And if you don't ever act sullen or gloomy, you'll have a real good time when you go to college down at Ames. When girls get a little older and have a little more sense, you'd be surprised how little a man's legs matter."

No, you couldn't talk quite so direct, but you could tell a kind of story. Ty Morley got to telling Porter about a friend of his, who used to be a regular wizard at steam valves and such. He lost his leg in the Civil War— got it shot off at Atlanta when he wasn't much older than—well, just about the age of a high-school boy. That fellow felt downhearted about it, at first; but then he got to studying and perfecting himself, kind of, in the subjects he was interested in, and after a while he had a fine job with the Chicago, Milwaukee & St. Paul.

Mr. Morley couldn't remember the name of the girl that his friend married, but she was one of the prettiest girls in town. She was kind of blond, had big blue eyes, and so on; she got so she was crazy over Mr. Morley's friend, because he was so much smarter and more interesting than a lot of the young bucks around town, and he was certainly on the road to success. Well, they were happily married—they'd been living up in Milwaukee, Wisconsin, for at least forty years. Mr. Morley wasn't sure, but he thought his friend had been made a chief consulting engineer for the C. M. & St. P.

No, you couldn't exactly talk like a parent or a teacher or a minister, because you were just a janitor, and nobody cared much for your advice or encouragement. But there wasn't any law against your making up mild lies of this kind, and there wasn't any rule that said you couldn't pretend there was something the matter with a heating-pipe valve, even though there really wasn't anything the matter with it.

It made Mr. Morley feel warm inside to hear Porter saying, "My gosh, I'm late! Pa will be needing me down at the shop," and to hear him bounding toward the outer door on his rubber-tipped crutches, and to hear him start singing, suddenly, "Toreador, Toreador, don't spit on the floor!"

Mr. Morley was dressed up for the occasion. He had on his suit—that was the way he always spoke of it, because his other clothes were pants and coats and vests that didn't match. But this suit was a good one. He bought it for his wife's funeral, and had worn it only on great occasions since then. He kept his bronze G. A. R. button fastened in the lapel, and recently he had been alarmed to find that the cloth around the buttonhole had mildewed almost all the way through. He had a stiff, clean celluloid collar that was too wide for his neck, and a necktie of gray-and-black stripes. His black shoes were wearing out, but they still looked good when he shined them up. And little loops of gold-and-blue ribbon hung like decorations from the back of each shoe.

Still self-conscious and uncomfortable in his finery, he tiptoed up the stairs, as fewer and fewer people hurried toward the auditorium and as the first strains of the processional smote the air. The processional was Day is Dying in the West. Ty thought that sounded kind of gloomy for a graduation, although the high-school orchestra did play it well. Silently, he closed the doors on the north side of the auditorium, and then he sneaked around the rear to close the doors at the south side.

There was a big crowd; both balconies filled, and a few people standing at the back. The American flag, which hung down in front near the stage, had come loose at one corner and dangled a bit unevenly, and Mr. Morley was chagrined to see it so. He hadn't noticed. He wished that Miss Roache or the principal had told him. He took up his station in a far corner of the room, in the shadow by the dictionary table, and the last members of the graduating class were then mounting the platform steps as the orchestra sawed its way toward a finish.

My, but Rowena Snow looked pretty! She was pale, as always, but it was the pallor of excitement. Her black hair was soft and fluffy, and she had tied it with a blue ribbon. That girl would make her mark, all right, and it was certainly fine that she had won a scholarship. . . . Mr. Morley thought of cold, crushed baking-powder biscuits, and he turned up his nose at the idea.

The class sat in a double semicircle on the stage. The Reverend Mr. Chipperfield arose to pronounce the invocation. Five hundred people bowed their heads, and Mr. Morley bowed with the rest. He stole cautious glances now and then toward the doors, to see that people weren't standing in front of them. That was a fire rule.

The *s* sounds were washing across the silent room, just as they did in chapel. Reverend Chipperfield said: " . . . these young people of Shelldrake who stand tonight on the threshold of their live*s* . . . " and in that moment Ty Morley wished to blow his nose. He thought again of Lexington, Nebraska; suddenly it seemed that he would be a very great distance away from his wife's grave. He hadn't thought of that before.

Every now and then it was difficult for Mr. Morley to see those young people, sitting up on the platform with the superintendent and the principal and the president of the school board. Their faces receded and mingled in a pale mist; even the baskets of flowers seemed confused.

But he could hear well enough, though his glasses were cloudy. He listened to Lester Aiken singing a tenor solo. Yes, Lester had a fine voice—always had had. His voice was rich and mellow, firm with young manhood. And Theodore Kobitsky was the salutatorian, and he was making a splendid speech. He was welcoming all the parents and friends, and saying that the class tried hard, collectively and individually, to live up to the precepts given them by the good example of their elders, and he was saying more things of the same kind.

Theodore had lived up to the precepts given him by Mr. Morley very well indeed. That was when Theodore was in Lower Fifth. Miss Black's room, that used to be—and the bigger boys were always picking on him, and even the ones his own size made life pretty uncomfortable. Because Theodore would fly into a rage, and scream and squawk, and, of course, his tormentors took pleasure in seeing him act that way. It didn't do any good for teachers to lecture or punish the other boys; they just took it out on Theodore, the first chance they got.

It was kind of difficult for a timid boy to fight back. So Mr. Morley showed Theodore a couple of tricks: he had learned those tricks from a railroad detective, long ago, when Mr. Morley served as an officer of the law. A small man could handle a bigger one that way, and thus a small boy could handle a bigger boy.

Theodore only needed a few lessons, and then one day he got his dander up when the boys plagued him, and he threw Buster Waterfield down in the schoolyard gravel so hard that Buster howled. Mr. Morley reckoned that Theodore Kobitsky could hold up his head now, wherever he went. No one had ever picked on him after that.

And the Girls' Glee Club looked beautiful, clustered together up there and singing I Would That My Love. The mist cleared from Mr. Morley's eyes; he watched the girls with pride and satisfaction, and he tried to forget that he might not see any of them again—at least not for a good while. Of course, he'd come back to Shelldrake for a visit, whenever he could afford to, but that wouldn't be very often. He had his pension, but it seemed like he ought to pay board at his daughter's place; it would make him feel more independent. Yes, he supposed that a lot of those girls would be pushing baby carriages when he came back to town.

His vision blurred again. He knew that the vague figure now standing at the front of the platform was Rowena Snow. She didn't have stage fright at all; talked as clearly and bravely as if there weren't five hundred pairs of eyes looking at her. . . . Mr. Morley began to wander mentally once more, through the dark halls of the old South Building. He swept and polished, and he fixed a leaky radiator. There was that window in Miss Dundon's room—it always stuck when she tried to open it. He worked in the North Building, too, and he smelled smoke again—the smoke that bloomed from a basement fire, back in 1915. He heard the tramp, tramp of children's feet shaking the huge stairways and parading out through the open doors; and they squealed and shouted when they got outside, because they thought a fire drill was a lot of fun; they liked to have Mr. Morley ring the fire gong. But it was no false alarm that day.

Slowly, the old man lifted his hands and clasped them together stiffly, and then unclasped them, and saw the pink, drawn scars where the fire had cooked his flesh, long, long ago.

No, of course. That wasn't long—only seven years. That was only four years after his wife died. Let's see, he was seventy-six now. There seemed to be a dream ahead of him, and beyond that dream was the age of eighty, which had always frightened him.

Take Adoniram McCoy—one of the Comrades. He was eighty now, and he seemed much older than Mr. Morley. And Captain Hathaway was eighty-six, and had to stay abed all the time.

So Tyler Morley wanted to interrupt Rowena suddenly. He wanted to say, "Now, Rowena, you better stop that talk. You'd all better go back to

Number One in the old South Building, and we'll start all over again. I guess that would be pleasanter than letting ourselves grow old."

Ty opened his mouth as if he would speak, and he must have made a sound, for two women in seats near by turned to look at him. He edged back into the shadow of the bookcase, and he felt ashamed.

" . . . to the teachers who have counseled us," Rowena was saying, "and to our principal and superintendent. No one of us can forget, for a moment, the debt that he or she owes to parents or relatives who made our education possible. But it has been said that the school is the child's second home, and we feel that the faculty of the Shelldrake schools have loyally encouraged and aided us. Surely each member of the Class of 1922 will wish to return frequently to his or her dear alma mater, and give tribute to those wise friends to whom we owe so much."

Rowena said, "Our hearts are full tonight—full of the hope and ambitions which you, our parents and teachers, have cultivated so generously. But also our hearts are filled with sorrow at this parting. Whether we proceed further in our education in other classrooms, or whether we are immediately to take our places in the workaday world, there cannot but be a feeling of regret that we must leave forever the Shelldrake schools."

It was outlandish even to think it, but Ty Morley had a confused wish that there was some place in all this ritual for mention of the janitor. Oh, that was downright crazy. Rowena might as well mention the window-panes, or the hall doors, or the dictionary, or the bottles in the laboratory.

As far as he was concerned, there had been all too many bottles in the laboratory. He was reminded of them now, when Beatrice Churchill, the class president, came forward to present Miss Roache with a bouquet of roses. Miss Roache was the class adviser, and surely she deserved those roses, because the kids pestered the life out of her with this and that. . . . Bottles in the laboratory, yes. And one day Ty had asked Mr. Mitchell what he meant when he said that that big black flask should never be moved from its place on the shelf.

"That's a life preserver, Ty."

"What?"

"Yes! It should always be handy, in case of trouble with acid. It counteracts the effects of the acid, you see."

It was three years later, and nearly five o'clock in the afternoon, and some girls were in the laboratory, making up work they had missed during the grippe epidemic, when there came that smash of breaking glass and that shuddering scream.

428

It seemed to Mr. Morley now, as he thought of it, that he was much spryer on his feet in those days. Yes, he was much spryer. . . . Beatrice had a few little marks on her neck, but they weren't disfiguring marks, and her face had healed perfectly. It had been awful smart of Mr. Mitchell to tell him about that remedy.

Well, maybe they didn't have either bases or acids in Lexington, and if they had, it would be no concern of his. And now the world was breaking up around him, and diplomas were being presented.

There was the crisp, clean rustle of heavy paper; the Class of 1922 marched rapidly out of Mr. Morley's life. They were moving into the world, and some of them would do fine things, no doubt. No one could be happy forever, but at that moment, Mr. Morley hoped that God might show special consideration to the forty-four boys and girls on the platform.

Reverend Chipperfield was pronouncing the benediction. . . . Oh, yes, that was the school song. The audience knew it, too, and stood there singing it. And maybe the orchestra had played, in between the prayer and the song, or somebody had sung a solo. . . . Mr. Morley had lost track of events.

> *We're the loyal and bold, Shelldrake High,*
> *We're the Purple-and-Gold, Shelldrake High. . . .*
> *Amid the broad green plains that nourish our land,*
> *For honest effort and for learning we stand. . . .*

After everyone had left the auditorium, after the flowers had been carried away, and when the principal had locked his office and gone, Mr. Morley went around turning off lights and closing windows.

He heard steps in the lower hall, and went down hastily to make sure that no loiterer had stayed behind. But it was only Ed Jensen, Mr. Morley's successor.

"Just on my way home," said Ed. "Thought I'd stop in and help you lock up."

"I never swept the auditorium," said Ty apologetically. "Seemed as if I was too blame tired tonight."

Ed Jensen said, "Pshaw, I never expected you to! I'll be on the job bright and early tomorrow. Mr. Cole told me to start in the morning. It's June first, tomorrow. Got to get started with the summer cleaning and painting."

"That's right," said Ty. "Well, Ed, I guess I might as well give you my keys and let you lock up, so's you'll feel at home."

When he reached the corner of the schoolyard, he looked back, and the whole building was dark. Ed had just switched off the last lights, and Mr. Morley could hear the jangling of Ed's keys.

He was an old fool. If Letty were alive now—of course, she had been dead eleven years—but if she were alive now, she would be sitting there on the little screen porch when he got home, and she'd say, "Ty, you're an old fool. You've got no cause to go sniveling around this way. I declare, I think you must have been actually crying, your eyes are so red!"

Of course, his eyes must be red, because they felt damp and harsh and sharp, and the starlight didn't seem to soothe them, nor the smell of flowers in everybody's yards. He heard his footsteps echoing under the dusky arch of trees, all the way out to the 1700 block on West Division Street.

He would go to bed right away, because he was so no-account. Sometimes it was hard to go right to bed when you got home at night, if you were baching it the way Mr. Morley had been doing for eleven years. Sometimes you sat up and read the Yeoman Shield until there were no more cars traveling abroad, not even on Division Street.

Whether you lived alone or not, it was unusual for you to lock your doors in Shelldrake. . . . Mr. Morley moved across the tiny porch, feeling his way through lonely darkness and moving carefully around the sharp rockers of his little chair. His hand found the white knob of the door. He wanted to say to the door, or say to somebody, "Of course, they're just kids! They don't realize how a fellow might feel. It isn't their fault they were busy graduating, and the other folks were busy watching them; you oughtn't to expect them to pay much attention. Ed Jensen is a good man. He'll take care of things."

Standing a moment in the enclosed darkness, he became aware that the living room was not the same. There was something wrong. He could hear the mantel clock and the buzzing of a few insects outside. But now another spirit seemed to dwell there, close beside him. That wasn't as it should have been; Mr. Morley was baching it. It was hard to have Decoration Day and Graduation Day so close together—you got all stirred up, kind of. You began to imagine things.

He lighted the lamp, and he breathed more easily in the comfort of its yellowness. He set the painted china shade carefully upon its brackets, and then his hands ceased to move.

There was something on the table right beside the lamp—something that had not been there at suppertime. It was a package—a little parcel in white tissue paper. Maybe somebody had brought it there after supper.

Maybe it was a mistake. Maybe they had got the wrong house. Maybe—

He held it in his hand. He knew—and yet dared not believe or recognize—what spirit it was, living there beside him. The spirit talked with a confident voice—a stalwart voice, however small. Mr. Morley's hands shook violently, but somehow he got the wrappings loose, and then he had the box open.

The dial was pure and glistening, but the neat numerals buzzed and trembled when he looked at them. He turned the watch in his hands. It was a long while before he could read the inscription:

To Tyler Morley. From His Friends. Class of 1922. S. H. S.
"Blessed be the Ty."

He knew that he must say something aloud, even though there were only the empty room and the happy little watch to hear him. He mumbled hoarsely, "Why, why—why, they must have put in fifty cents apiece!" He sat down in Letty's old rocker.

The watch ran on. It spoke busily, as if assuring Mr. Morley that the spirit of his children would stay close beside him, no matter whether he went to Lexington, Nebraska, or a great deal farther away.

# God and My Father

## CLARENCE DAY

*Few characters in present day writing have been so
beloved as this author's volatile Father and entrancing
Mother. Clarence Day, with his priceless humor,
knocks at the door of our hearts in this famous episode
of Father's baptism.*

IN MY BOYHOOD, I never had a doubt that the beliefs
they taught me were true. The difficulty was to live up to them, and to
love God. Most of the time I was too busy to think of such things: but
then a problem of conduct would face me, or a duty I had forgotten, or
my own private feelings at night after saying my prayers, and at such
times religion would confront me like a Sphinx in the landscape. I would
stand before it like a hypnotized bird before some great ageless serpent,
unable to think of or feel any way of escape.

I believed in the Bible. Creation, to me, meant a Creator. And since
there was some one so great and powerful that He had created us all, I
felt I had better learn His wishes. They were supposed to be good. I
wanted to live in harmony with Him—no battle of wills. Yet I also
wished greatly to get away and live as I liked.

If I could have been sure that the Creator was my ally or friend, that
would have been a great comfort, in those days. It would have not only
saved me from worry, it would have set me free to go about my business
with confidence, both in Him and myself. Or if I could have surrendered
myself to His rather bleak guidance, that again might have been a relief
to me. But—I couldn't do it. I didn't quite trust Him or love Him enough
to do that.

I thought of God as a strangely emotional being. He was powerful; He
was forgiving yet obdurate, full of wrath and affection. Both His wrath

and affection were fitful, they came and they went, and I couldn't count on either to continue: although they both always did. In short God was much such a being as my father himself.

What was the relation between them, I wondered—these two puzzling dieties?

# I *My Father's Religion*

My father's ideas of religion seemed straightforward and simple. He had noticed when he was a boy that there were buildings called churches; he had accepted them as a natural part of the surroundings in which he had been born. He would never have invented such things himself. Nevertheless they were here. As he grew up he regarded them as unquestioningly as he did banks. They were substantial old structures, they were respectable, decent, and venerable. They were frequented by the right sort of people. Well, that was enough.

On the other hand he never allowed churches—or banks—to dictate to him. He gave each the respect that was due to it from his point of view; but he also expected from each of them the respect he felt due to him.

As to creeds, he knew nothing about them, and cared nothing either; yet he seemed to know which sects he belonged with. It had to be a sect with the minimum of nonsense about it; no total immersion, no exhorters, no holy confession. He would have been a Unitarian, naturally, if he'd lived in Boston. Since he was a respectable New Yorker, he belonged in the Episcopal Church.

As to living a spiritual life, he never tackled that problem. Some men who accept spiritual beliefs try to live up to them daily: other men, who reject such beliefs, try sometimes to smash them. My father would have disagreed with both kinds entirely. He took a more distant attitude. It disgusted him when atheists attacked religion: he thought they were vulgar. But he also objected to have religion make demands upon him—he felt that religion too was vulgar, when it tried to stir up men's feelings. It had its own proper field of activity, and it was all right there, of course; but there was one place religion should let alone, and that was a man's soul. He especially loathed any talk of walking hand in hand with his Saviour. And if he had ever found the Holy Ghost trying to soften his heart, he would have regarded Its behavior as distinctly uncalled for; even ungentlemanly.

The only religious leader or prophet I can think of who might have suited my father was Confucius—though even Confucius would have struck him as addled. Confucius was an advocate of peace, and of finding the path; and he enjoined the Golden Rule on his followers long before Christ. My father would not have been his follower in any of these. Finding "the path"? Not even Confucius could have made him see what that meant. He was too busy for that, too hot-tempered for peace, and the Golden Rule he regarded as claptrap; how could things work both ways? Whatever he did unto others he was sure was all right, but that didn't mean that he would have allowed them to do the same things to him. He saw other men as disorderly troops, and himself as a general; and the Golden Rule was plainly too mushy to apply in such circumstances. He disciplined himself quite as firmly as he tried to discipline others, but it wasn't necessarily by any means the same kind of discipline. There was one saying of Confucius', however, with which he would have agreed: "Respect spiritual beings—if there are any—but keep aloof from them." My father would have regarded that principle as thoroughly sound.

When Confucious was asked about the rule to return good for evil, he said: "What then will you return for good? No: return good for good; for evil, return justice." If my father had been asked to return good for evil he would have been even more pithy—his response would have consisted of a hearty and full-throated "Bah!"

If he had been let alone, he would have brought up his sons in this spirit. But my mother's feelings and teachings were different, and this complicated things for us. Like my father, she had accepted religion without any doubtings, but she had accepted more of it. She was far more devout. And she loved best the kind of faith that comforted her and sweetened her thoughts. My father didn't object to this at all—it was all right enough—for a woman: but it led to her giving us instructions that battled with his.

They both insisted strongly, for example, on our going to church, but they didn't agree in their reasons. It was the right thing to do, Father said. "But why do we have to go, Father?" "Because I wish to bring you up properly. Men who neglect going to church are a lazy, disreputable lot." A few might be good fellows, he would admit, but they were the exceptions. As a rule, non-churchgoers were not solid, respectable citizens. All respectable citizens owed it to themselves to attend.

My mother put it differently to us. She said we owed it to God. Church to her was a place where you worshiped, and learned to be good. My father never dreamed of attending for any such reason. In his moral instructions to us he never once mentioned God. What he dwelt on was integrity. My mother once wrote in my plush-covered autograph album, "Fear God and keep His commandments;" but the motto that Father had written on the preceding page, over his bolder signature, was: "Do your duty and fear no one." And nobody could tell him his duty—he knew it without that, it seemed. It wasn't written down in any book, certainly not in the Bible, but it was a perfectly definite and indisputable thing nevertheless. It was a code, a tradition. It was to be upright and fearless and honorable, and to brush your clothes properly; and in general always to do the right thing in every department of life. The right thing to do for religion was to go to some good church on Sundays.

When Father went to church and sat in his pew, he felt he was doing enough. Any further spiritual work ought to be done by the clergy.

When hymns were sung he sometimes joined in mechanically, for the mere sake of singing; but usually he stood as silent as an eagle among canaries and doves, leaving others to abase themselves in sentiments that he didn't share. The hymns inculcated meekness and submission, and dependence on God; but Father was quick to resent an injury, and he had no meekness in him.

> "Jesus, lover of my soul,
>   Let me to thy bosom fly,
> While the nearer waters roll,
>   While the tempest still is nigh."

How could Father sing that? He had no desire to fly to that bosom.

> "Hide me, O my Saviour, hide,
>   Till the storm of life be past;
> Safe into the haven guide,
>   Oh receive my soul at last . . .
> All my trust on thee is stayed;
>   All my help from thee I bring;
> Cover my defenseless head
>   With the shadow of thy wing."

But Father's head was far from defenseless, and he would have scorned to hide, or ask shelter. As he stood there, looking critically about him, high-spirited, resolute, I could imagine him marching with that same independence through space—a tiny speck masterfully dealing with death and infinity.

When our rector talked of imitating the saints, it seemed drivel to Father. What! imitate persons who gave their whole lives to religion, and took only a perfunctory interest in the affairs of this world? Father regarded himself as a more all-round man than the saints. They had neglected nine-tenths of their duties from his point of view—they had no business connections, no families, they hadn't even paid taxes. In a word, saints were freaks. If a freak spent an abnormal amount of time being religious, what of it?

The clergy were a kind of freaks also. A queer lot. Father liked Bishop Greer and a few others, but he hadn't much respect for the rest of them. He thought of most clergymen as any busy man of action thinks of philosophers, or of those scholars who discuss the fourth dimension, which is beyond human knowing. He regarded the self-alleged intimacy of our rector with that fourth dimension most sceptically. He himself neither was nor wished to be intimate with a thing of that sort. But this didn't mean that he doubted the existence of God. On the contrary, God and Father had somehow contrived to achieve a serene and harmonious relation that the clergy themselves might have envied.

How did Father think God felt towards my mother? Why, about the the way he did. God probably knew she had faults, but He saw she was lovely and good; and—in spite of some mistaken ideas that she had about money—He doubtless looked on her most affectionately. Father didn't expect God to regard *him* affectionately—they stood up man to man—but naturally God loved my mother, as everyone must. At the gate of Heaven, if there was any misunderstanding about his own ticket, Father counted on Mother to get him in. That was her affair.

This idea runs far back, or down, into old human thoughts. "The unbelieving husband is sanctified by the wife." (First Corinthians, vii, 14.) Medical missionaries report that today, in some primitive tribes, a healthy woman will propose to swallow medicine in behalf of her sick husband. This plan seems to her husband quite reasonable. It seemed so—in religion—to Father.

As to his mental picture of God, I suppose that Father was vague, but in a general way he seemed to envisage a God in his own image. A God who had small use for emotionalism and who prized strength and dignity. A God who probably found the clergy as hard to bear as did Father himself. In short Father and God, as I said, usually saw eye to eye. They seldom met, or even sought a meeting, their spheres were so different; but they had perfect confidence in each other—at least at most moments. The only exceptions were when God seemed to be neglecting his job—Father's confidence in Him was then withdrawn, instantly. But I'll come to this later.

As to the nature of God's sphere, namely Heaven, compared to Father's, the earth, Heaven wasn't nearly so solid and substantial. Father had all the best of it. Life here on earth was trying, but it shouldn't be—it was all right intrinsically—he felt it was only people's damned carelessness that upset things so much. Heaven on the other hand had a more serious and fundamental defect: the whole place was thin and peculiar. It didn't inspire much confidence. Father saw glumly that the time would come when he'd have to go there, but he didn't at all relish the prospect. He clung to his own battered realm.

Yet its faults and stupidities weighed on his spirit at times: all the chuckle-headed talk and rascality in business and politics. He was always getting indignant about them, and demanding that they be stamped out; and when he saw them continually spreading everywhere, it was maddening. Nature too, though in general sound and wholesome, had a treacherous streak. He hated and resented decay, and failing powers. He hated to see little children or animals suffer. His own aches and pains were an outrage; he faced them with anger. And aside from these treacheries, there was a spirit of rebellion in things. He would come in from a walk over his fields—which to me had seemed pleasant—oppressed by the balky disposition both of his fields and his farmer. He would get up from an inspection of his account books with the same irritation: there were always some bonds in his box that hadn't behaved as they should. And twice a day, regularly, he would have a collision, or bout, with the newspaper: it was hard to see why God had made so many damned fools and democrats.

I would try to persuade him sometimes—in my argumentative years—that it would be better for him to accept the world as it was and adapt himself to it, since he could scarcely expect to make the planet over, and change the whole earth single-handed. Father listened to this talk with suspicion, as to an *advocatus diaboli*. If he ever was tempted to give in, it was only in his weak moments; a minute later he was again on the warpath, like a materialistic Don Quixote.

There was one kind of depression that afflicted Mother which Father was free from: he never once had any moments of feeling "unworthy". This was a puzzle to Mother, and it made her look at Father with a mixture of awe and annoyance. Other people went to church to be made better, she told him. Why didn't he? He replied in astonishment that he had no need to be better—he was all right as he was. Mother couldn't get over his taking this stand, but she never could get him to see what the matter was with it. It wasn't at all easy for Father to see that he had any faults; and if he did, it didn't even occur to him to ask God to forgive them. He forgave them himself. In his moments of prayer, when he and and God tried to commune with each other, it wasn't his own shortcomings that were brought on the carpet, but God's.

He expected a good deal of God, apparently. Not that he wanted God's help, of course; or far less His guidance. No, but it seemed that God—like the rest of us—spoiled Father's plans. He, Father, was always trying to bring this or that good thing to pass, only to find that there were obstacles in the way. These of course roused his wrath. He would call God's attention to such things. They should not have been there. He didn't actually accuse God of gross inefficiency, but when he prayed his tone was loud and angry, like that of a dissatisfied guest in a carelessly managed hotel.

I never saw Father kneel in supplication on such occasions. On the contrary he usually talked with God lying in bed. My room was just above Father's, and he could easily be heard through the floor. On those rare nights when he failed to sleep well, the sound of damns would float up—at first deep and tragic and low, then more loud and exasperated. Fragments of thoughts and strong feelings came next, or meditations on current bothers. At the peak of these, God would be summoned. I would hear him call "Oh God?" over and over, with a rising inflection, as though he were demanding that God should present himself instantly, and sit in the fat green chair in the corner, and be duly admonished. Then when Father seemed to feel that God was listening, he would begin to expostulate. He would moan in a discouraged but strong voice: "Oh God, it's too much. Amen . . . I say it's too damned much . . . No, no, I can't stand it. Amen." After a pause, if he didn't feel better, he would seem to suspect that God might be trying to sneak back to Heaven without doing anything, and I would hear him shout warningly: "Oh God! I won't stand it! Amen. Oh damnation! A-a-men." Sometimes he would ferociously bark a few extra Amens, and then, soothed and satisfied, peacefully go back to sleep . . . And one night in the country, when the caretaker of our house in town telephoned to Father that the rain was pouring in through a hole in the roof, I heard so much noise that I got out of bed and looked over the banisters, and saw Father standing alone in the hall, shaking his fist at the ceiling, and shouting in hot indignation to Heaven, "What next?"

But Father was patient with God after all. If he didn't forgive, he forgot. His wrath didn't last—he had other things to think of—and he was genial at heart. The very next Sunday after an outburst he would be back in church. Not perhaps as a worshiper or a devotee, but at least as a patron.

## II *My Father and His Pastors*

A man who accepts a religion without being religious lets himself in for more hardships than one would suppose. My father persisted most manfully in going to church; and he usually entered its portals at peace with the world and settled himself down contentedly in his end seat: but somehow before very long his expression would darken, as his hopes of hearing a sensible service little by little were dashed; and he came out in an inflamed state of mind that could not have been good for him.

The Episcopal service in general he didn't criticize; it was stately and quiet; but the sermon, being different every Sunday, was a very bad gamble. And once in awhile there would be an impromptu prayer that he would take great offense at. Sometimes he disliked its subject or sentiments—if he chanced to be listening. Sometimes he decided it was too long, or its tone too lugubrious. I remember seeing him so restive during a prayer of that kind, that—although the entire congregation was kneeling in reverence—he suddenly gave a loud snort, sat up straight in his pew, and glared at the minister's back as though planning to kick it.

I glanced over at Mother. She had been sailing along devoutly, as best she could, in the full tide of prayer, with the lovely rapt look that would come at such times on her face; but she had also begun to watch Father out of one eye—for whenever a prayer was longer than usual she feared its effect on him—and now here he was sitting up and she had to stop praying and turn away from God to this obstinate, obstinate man. "Put your head down," she whispered fiercely; and then, when he wouldn't, she felt so furious at him, and so impotent, and so guilty for having such feelings, and so torn between her yearning to sink back again into the sweet peace of prayer and her hot determination to make the bad boy in Father behave, that she sent him a look like a flash of lightning, shooting out through quick tears; indignant to the very roots of her red hair, and as hurt as a child. This sank into him. He never would at any time kneel in church—she had given up struggling for that—but at last with a deep angry growl he once more bent stiffly down.

Toward the latter part of his life Father found a minister whose sermons he liked. This was the Reverend Mr. Henshaw of Rye, where we lived in the summer. Mr. Henshaw wasn't "one of these pious fellows," Father said, with approval—though why piety was so unsuited to the clergy he never explained. And some years before this, one summer on the Hudson near Tarrytown, there was a Mr. Wenke, an earnest young cleric, who also found favor. But this was mostly because one of the vestry, old Mr. John Rutland, was very strict with Mr. Wenke about the length of his sermons. Mr. Rutland had got it into his head that all sermons should end at twelve, sharp; and if he saw Mr. Wenke being carried away by his own eloquence, he would take out his watch and stare ominously, first at him, then at it. Pretty soon Mr. Wenke's roving eye would be caught and held by this sight. He would falter or sometimes almost choke in the midst of his flow, then lamely end his remarks, and get out of the pulpit.

In the city at this same later period Father went to St. Bartholomew's, and there too the various clergymen suited him, though not quite so well. He liked St. Bartholomew's. The church itself was comfortable, and the congregation were all the right sort. There was Mr. Edward J. Stuyvesant, who was president of three different coal mines, and Admiral Prentice who had commanded the Fleet, and old Mr. Johns of the *Times;* and bank directors and doctors and judges—solid men of affairs. The place was like a good club. And the sermon was like a strong editorial in a conservative newspaper. It did not nag at Father, it attacked the opposition instead; it gave all wrong-headed persons a sound trouncing, just the way Father would have.

Mother didn't enjoy these attacks. Denunciations upset her. She took almost all denouncing personally, as directed at her, and it made her feel so full of faults that she trembled inside, though she looked straight back up at the preacher, round-eyed and scared but defiant. She preferred something healing, and restful; some dear old tale from the Bible. But denunciations satisfied Father. He liked something vigorous. And in general he instinctively took to the Established Church pattern—a church managed like a department of a gentleman's Government. He liked such a church's strong tory flavor, and its recognition of castes. He liked its

441

deference to sound able persons who knew how to run things, and its confidence in their integrity and right point of view. In effect, it put such men on their honor, without foolishly saying so. No other approach would have found a way into their hearts.

But nothing is perfect. After Father had made himself at home in this reliable temple, he discovered too late that even here a man wasn't safe. The rector began talking about the need for what he called a New Edifice. He said the church had a leak in the roof, and the neighborhood was changing to business, and that they had received a good offer for the property and had better move elsewhere. This gave Father an unsettled feeling. He wished to stay put. But the rector kept stirring things up until he at last got his way.

Committees were appointed, and active teams of workers were organized, who began to collect large subscriptions from every parishioner. Father paid no attention to all this. It was no plan of his. If they insisted on having better quarters, he would try to enjoy them, but aside from this effort the rest of it was not his affair. It was only when he was made to see that he too would have to subscribe, that Father became roused and startled. This had never occurred to him. He said he might have known it was just a damn scheme to get money.

He was still more upset when Mother told him what sum was expected of him. He had imagined that they would want fifty dollars, or even a hundred; and that was enough to depress him. But she said that since he had bought a good pew they would expect him to give several thousand. This was like an earthquake. Father in fact took it as some wild cataclysm of nature, some unheard-of violent destruction of an honest citizen's peace. After roaring out that the rector and his Christian workers could all go to hell, he barricaded himself every evening in his cyclone cellar—the library—and declared he wouldn't see any callers. This lasted a week. Then when he had cooled down a little, Mother had a long talk with him, and told him who were on the committee—some men whom he liked. She said he would really have to subscribe. He'd at least have to see them.

He waited, fretful and uneasy, for the attack to begin. One night when Mother was sitting in her room, there were sounds of talk in the library. She hurried down the passageway, clutching her needle and mending, and listened at the door. Father was doing all the talking, it seemed. He was stating his sentiments in his usual round tones, strong and full. He got more and more shouty. Mother began to fear the committee mightn't like being scolded. But when she opened the door on a crack and peeked in, there was no one in there but Father. He was in his easy-chair, talking away, with his face all puckered up, and he was thumping his hand with a hammer-like beat on his newspaper. "In ordinary circumstances," he was saying to the imaginary committeemen, "in ordinary circumstances I should have expected to subscribe to this project. But during the past few years my investments" (thump, thump, on the newspaper) "have shown me heavy losses." Here he thought of the New Haven Railroad and groaned. *"Damned* heavy losses!" he roared, and flung the paper aside. "Who the devil's that? Oh, it's you, Vinnie. Come in, dear Vinnie. I'm lonely."

I don't recall how much he gave in the end, but I think it was a thousand dollars. The reason Mother thought that he would probably have to give more, was that our pew was way up in front; it was—so to speak—in a fine section. All our neighbors were prominent. There may have been plenty of ordinary Christians in other parts of the building, but I did not see them. Furthermore this pew, though a small one, had cost Father five thousand dollars, and parishioners were being asked to give as much as the cost of their pews. Father had hated to invest all that money in a mere place to sit, but he could sell out again some day, and meanwhile he had a good pew. He rented the one in Rye for a hundred and twenty dollars a year, but a family that wanted a good pew at St. Bartholomew's in those old days used to buy it. They went to the sexton or somebody, and told him what size and so forth, and after awhile he would negotiate a purchase for them from some other parishioner. Pews were like seats on the stock exchange. Nobody speculated in pews, of course, and they rarely changed hands; but they went up and down in price, naturally, as the demand rose or fell; and after Father had bought his—most unwillingly—from old Mr. Baggs, he used to ask Mother periodically for the current quotation. Mother disliked to get this. It obliged her to ask the sexton, who was dignified, and who didn't like to quote pews; and another objection was that after Father bought they went down in value. When she came home with the news that the last sale had been for thirty-two hundred, Father said she had led him into this against his own better judgment, and now the bottom was dropping out of the market and he never would get his money back. "Old Baggs, *he* knew. He was a shrewd one," he declared. "Egad, yes! He knew when to sell." And he swore that if that damned pew ever went up again he would unload it on somebody.

When the church moved away from its old quarters, Father wouldn't go with them. After having had to help build a New Edifice which he had not wanted, he felt he'd had enough of such experiences and needed a rest; and he stopped going to church altogether, except in the country.

All during my childhood, before our St. Bartholomew period started, we went to a more home-like church that was less rich and fashionable. It was squeezed in between some old houses on Fifth Avenue near Tyson's Market, and it had a choir of men and boys in surplices, who sang mellow chants, and a narrow but high vaulted roof that rang with the organ music, and stained glass with deep colors; and best of all I thought was Mr. Dryden, the sexton, who had extraordinarily long pointed whiskers that waved in the air when he was in a hurry—a pair of thin curly streamers. He nearly always was in a hurry, and I liked attending this church.

Nowadays there is an office-building there, as tall as a dozen such churches, the air is full of gasoline and the avenue is shut in and darkened; and the powerful traffic throbs by with a tense, roaring hum. But when I was a boy the low houses were set back from broad sidewalks, there was fresh air and plenty of room, and window boxes of flowers; and a bit of green here and there, trees or ivy; and a wide field of sky.

I suppose that the reason we went to this church that I speak of, the Church of the Peace Everlasting, was because it stood near our home. Its name, as least so far as Father was concerned, was a mockery, for he suffered most cruelly there. Yet he went there for years. Yes, and he kept right on going without any question of changing. He disliked change more than he did suffering. In the end he burst out and bought his liberty along with Mr. Baggs' pew—so the latter was cheap after all: but he lost the best years of his life at the Peace Everlasting.

The clergyman there was the Reverend Dr. Owen Lloyd Garden. He was a plump, bustling man, very good-hearted and pleasant; though in spite of his good-heartedness and kindness I never felt at ease with him. He never seemed to speak to me personally, but to a thing called My Child. He was more at home speaking to a large audience than to a small boy, however. He had warm and sympathetic feelings toward people en masse. The congregation responded to this quality in him, and liked him; and he not only kept the pews filled but he sometimes attracted such crowds that Mr. Dryden would scurry by with his whiskers flying straight out behind him, putting chairs in the aisle.

Dr. Garden had come over to New York from England, but by descent he was Welsh. He had a broad red face, thick black hair, and a square blue-black beard. His robes were red, black and white. His strong English accent was a point in his favor, in an Episcopal church; it seemed to go well with the service. But owing we understood to his Welsh descent he was very emotional, and he used to plead with us at times in his sermons, in a sort of high mellow howl. My father disliked this. In the first place he heartily detested having anyone plead with him; in the second place Dr. Garden seldom could plead without crying. It wasn't put on at all; he was deeply moved by his own words. The atmosphere became tense and still when he leaned from his pulpit, and stretched out his arms yearningly to us, and sobbed, "Oh, my people." The whole church was hushed. At such moments Father would testily stir in his seat. "The damned Welshman, there he goes sniveling again," he would mutter.

This would horrify Mother. From her end of the pew she would signal him that he must stop. If he didn't notice, she would tell my small brothers to pass word along to me that I must make Father keep still. It was like expecting a boy to make the jungle behave. The most I felt up to was to get him to see Mother's signals, and that meant that I had to pull myself together and poke him. This was nervous work. He was a muscular, full-barreled man; there was nothing soft in him to poke; and he had a fiery way even of sitting still. It was like poking a stallion. When he became aware that he was being prodded, by my small, timid finger, he would turn fiercely upon me and I would hastily gesture toward Mother. Mother would whisper, "Clare! You mustn't!" and he would reply, "Bah!"

"Oh, Clare!"

"I know, Vinnie; but I can't stand that damned—"

"Sh—sh! Oh, hush!"

Another thing he detested was the picture Dr. Garden drew, sometimes, of a business man sitting in his office at the close of his day. Dr. Garden didn't cry over this, to be sure, but he grew gentle and solemn— he spoke as though he himself were standing at that business-man's side, like an unseen Presence, a loving Good Influence, evoking the man's better self. He apparently had only the haziest ideas of a business office, but he drew on his imagination freely to fill in the picture. He would describe how this hard-headed man sat there, surrounded by ledgers, and how after studying them closely and harshly for hours he would chance to look out of his window at the light in God's sky, and then it would come to him that money and ledgers were dross. Whereat, as the gathering twilight spread over the city, this strange wax-work figure of a business-man would bow his head, and with streaming eyes resolve to devote his life to Far Higher Things.

"Oh damn," Father would burst out, so explosively that the man across the aisle jumped, and I would hear old Mrs. Tillotson, in the second pew behind, titter.

Aside from the wild untruth of such pictures of business, from Father's point of view the whole attitude involved was pernicious. Anyone dreamy enough to think of money as "dross" was bound to get himself in hot water; that went without saying; it was a sign both of ignorance of, and of disrespect for, finance. Father had more respect for finance than he had for the church. When he left the financial district behind him to visit the church, he felt as I suppose Moses felt coming down from the moun-tain. Moses found people blind to his mountain and worshiping a calf idiotically, and Father found Dr. Garden capering around something he called Higher Things. Well, let him caper if he wanted to—that was all he was good for. My father was a more charitable Moses who expected no better. But this flighty parson went further—he wanted Moses to join him! Betray finance for this stuff and nonsense! It was enough to make a man sick.

It was Father's custom to put one dollar in the contribution plate weekly, no more and no less. When Mr. Gregg brought the plate to our pew, Father would first pass it on to us, and we boys would each thump in a nickel, trying to produce a loud ringing sound, as though it were a quarter; and Mother would quietly slip in her offering in a tight little roll; more than she could afford to give, probably, and saved up God knows how. Then Father would hand the plate back to Mr. Gregg, who would patiently wait, while Father took out and unfolded a crisp new dollar bill, and drew it through his fingers so as to make a little crease in it, lengthwise, and laid it out flat on top of everything else, large or small.

This dollar was apt to become the subject of a debate, going home. Mother felt there were Sundays when such a sum was not enough. It bothered her dreadfully, after a sermon that had described some great need, to see Father, absolutely unmoved, put in only his dollar.

Father's first gun in reply was that a dollar was a good handsome sum, and that it would be better for Mother if she could learn this. He had a great deal to say on this point. His second gun, which he would then fire off at her with still more enjoyment, was that any money he gave to the church would be wasted—it would be spent by a pack of visionary enthusiasts in some crazy way. "Sending red-flannel weskits and moral pocket-handkerchiefs to the heathen," he quoted.

But after awhile Mother found a counter-argument which actually beat both of his: she made him feel that it was beneath his own dignity not to put in more, sometimes. Even then he didn't surrender; he compromised instead on this method: before starting for church, he put his usual dollar in his right-hand waist-coat pocket, but in the left-hand pocket he put a new five dollar bill; and he stated that from now on he would make a handsome offer to Garden: let him preach a decent sermon for once and he would give him the five.

This made every sermon a sporting event, in our pew. When Dr. Garden entered the pulpit we boys watched with a thrill, as though he were a race-horse at the barrier, jockeying for a good start. He looked rather fat for a race-horse, but he was impressive and confident, and it was kind of awe-inspiring to see him go down every time to defeat. He always either robbed himself of the prize in the very first lap by getting off on the wrong foot—a wrong key of some sort—or else in spite of a blameless beginning he would fail later on: he would as it were run clear off the course that Father had in silence marked out for him, and gallop away steadily and unconsciously in some other direction. It gave a boy a sobering sense of the grimness of fate.

"I don't see what the matter was today," Mother would declare, going home. "You should have given more than a dollar today, Clare. It was a very nice sermon." But Father would merely say with a twinkle that Garden ought to get a new barrelful.

The only time I saw Father tested was one Sunday in Lent. It was remarkable enough that he should have been present that Sunday, for the one thing he always gave up in Lent was going to church. Dr. Garden's flow of grief in that season was more than he could stomach. But on this particular morning, to our surprise, Father went without question. It turned out afterward he didn't know it was Lent—he had "thought the damn thing was over." And as luck would have it, Dr. Garden was absent, ill in bed with a cold; and the substitute clergyman who took his place won Father's approval. He was a man who showed no emotions, he was plain and matter of fact, and his subject was the needs of some lumber country in the northwest. He had worked there, he knew the men, knew the business, and he described it in detail. I listened awhile, but there were no bears in it or cowboys; it was mostly business statistics; and I was studying a picture on the wall of an angel who looked like Mr. Gregg—a large, droopy angel with wrinkled garments, only he had no mustache—when my brother George secretly nudged me and pointed at Father. Father was listening closely. We glued our eyes on him. His face was keen and set; he had his arms folded; he was taking in every word. But we couldn't tell whether he liked it. The sermon went on a few minutes; and then, before we thought the man was half-through, he stopped. He had finished.

The organist began playing the offertory. There was a rustling of skirts; a stray cough. Imagine our excitement as we waited for the plate to come round. It seemed to take Mr. Gregg hours to get up the aisle, he stood so long, stooping and bulgy, at the end of each pew. "He wouldn't even hurry to see a fire-engine," George whispered indignantly. At last he got to the Hamiltons' pew in front of us—and then he stood at ours. We were all watching Father. But he hardly noticed Mr. Gregg, he was thinking about something else, and his thumb and finger slid automatically into his one-dollar pocket.

We let out our breaths and relaxed from the strain, disappointed. But just as we were slumping dejectedly down, Father paused; he put the one-dollar bill back, and decisively took out the five.

We could barely help cheering aloud at that substitute clergyman's triumph. And yet he himself never realized what he had done—he stepped quietly out of the pulpit and went back to obscurity. This man had won a victory that none of his profession had gained but nobody knew it except the Recording Angel and the four little Day boys.

## III  *My Mother's Discovery*

In spite of his warlike behavior in our hours of worship, Father seemed to me one of the mainstays and chiefs of the church. On weekdays he was a layman, struggling violently with his environment—his business, his family, his homelife, the cook and the coffee—and in general with the natural heat of his feelings among all these antagonists. But on Sundays, after breakfast was over, and the coffee and its sins had departed, and Father had peacefully finished his morning cigar, he put on his shining high hat and he marched us to church; and there, on the end of our pew, was a silver plate with his name on it; and the organ music was rolling and solemn, and Father was a pillar of God.

I felt sure that he was a very good pillar too, and better than most. Better than Mr. Gregg, for instance, who was the church treasurer, and who was a devout but slouchy old Christian with an overdressed wife. And as good as Colonel Hamilton—well-groomed, military-looking, patrician—who seemed to a little Episcopalian like me the very essence of Christianity.

But these other pillars were vestrymen, and Father was not. They seemed to "belong" more than he did. Father didn't happen to want to be a vestryman, but he couldn't be anyhow. I don't recall how I became aware of it; but there was an obstacle.

And another thing, there was a mysterious rite called communion, with soft music in it, and a great deal of whispering and murmuring by Dr. Garden; amid which the congregation, a few at a time, left their pews, and crowded irregularly forward and knelt at the altar. Dr. Garden then said something to each of them, and gave each one a drink; a very small drink from a very large goblet of gold. When all of that group had had theirs, they walked back to their seats, and others passed forward and knelt. I could see the soles of their shoes. Colonel Hamilton had his soles blacked, and they looked trim and elegant; but Mr. Gregg's were almost worn-out, and as stubby as mine.

This rite came after the regular service, it was a separate matter, and less than half of the congregation "stayed for communion." Mr. Gregg always stayed. Colonel Hamilton was more independent—he only stayed when he liked. Mother stayed as regularly as Mr. Gregg did. But Father not once.

There was some tension between Father and Mother about this, I felt; but they didn't discuss it before me. She never asked him to stay. She never even asked if he were going to. It was understood that he wasn't. He walked home ahead with us boys, feeling as lively as we did; and Mother arrived twenty minutes later for our one o'clock Sunday dinner. Once in awhile she was half-an-hour later, and Father said "Damn."

The principal course at our Sunday dinners was a great roast of beef, surrounded by fat roasted potatoes and rich Yorkshire pudding. They were all piping hot, and when Father carved the beef it ran juices. We were not allowed to play with our toys on Sundays, and we had to wear our best clothes, but that dinner was some compensation. Afterward we read, or took walks. There were no week-ends out of town in those days, and golf was almost unknown to us. Father usually read Hume and Smollett's History of England, with his head nodding more and more over it, and his cigar going out. I think it must have been on one of those long afternoons, that Mother, when she thought I was old enough, explained about Father.

She said nobody could go to communion who had not been confirmed. Everybody was baptized, as a baby, to make him a Christian; that was the first step; but to be a full member of the church, one had to learn the creed and the catechism, and go up to the altar, and promise to do and believe everything that his godfathers had promised for him. And the bishop would then lay his hands on him, so he could go to communion.

She said she hoped I would be confirmed when I was thirteen or fourteen, but it must be of my own free will and choice, for it was a great step to take. Father hadn't taken it yet, she confided. She didn't say why.

I took Mother's prayer-book upstairs with me and looked up the baptism service, to see what my godfather had committed me to, with his promises. Mr. Currier was my only living godfather. He had gone pretty far. He had renounced the Devil and all his works, on my behalf, and the pomps and vanities of this wicked world, and the sinful lusts of the flesh. Mr. Currier was such a good old man he had probably thought nothing of it; but I wondered whether I would ever feel up to "renouncing" all that.

I asked Mother a great many questions about confirmation, and from what she said I saw that I'd have to be confirmed by and by. I couldn't get out of it. It wouldn't be fair to Mr. Currier for me to refuse, and leave him responsible to God for my sins all my life.

I looked over the catechism. It was long. It would be hard to learn all that by heart. I inquired whether Father knew the catechism. But Mother said not to ask questions.

My head at once felt full of questions, such as who Father's godfather was, and how much longer he'd wait, and whether he didn't ever get cross about Father's delay.

But it made Mother cry when I asked these. She said I would know by and by. She said Father had been very busy and had had to work very hard; and that she hoped he would be confirmed soon, when he had a little more time.

Mother evidently had her heart set on Father's learning the catechism and letting the bishop lay his hands on him; but Father didn't feel like it. And the rest of the story, as I heard it later, was this:

When Mother married Father she had naturally supposed that he was a good churchman. She had asked him what church he belonged to, and he had replied "The Episcopal." But as time went on she found that his association with it was vague.

Father's parents had been so fond of Mother and she had liked them so much, that it hadn't even occurred to her to cross-question them about Father's upbringing. His mother was a saint on earth, sweet and good; everyone loved her. His father was a newspaper publisher; philosophic and humorous. But it turned out that Grandpa's favorite authors were Voltaire and Shakespeare: he read almost nothing else, but his newspaper; and he had no use for religion. He had been brought up so strictly that he had got his fill of it, and had dismissed the whole subject.

Father had accordingly run about and done as he pleased. It was only through one of his schoolboy friends that he happened to go to a Sunday School. This school gave a party of some kind, at which they served cake; it was good cake, and whenever they had it Father went to that Sunday School.

When he grew older and decided that it was the proper thing to go to church sometimes, it seems that he had picked out an Episcopal church for this purpose. Not being a free-thinker, like my grandfather, he had approved of religion. But beyond this he hadn't looked into it. He had seen no necessity.

This rudimentary and semi-automatic approach to the church, as by a kind of molecular attraction, seemed pathetic to Mother. She was maternal, and she was compassionately eager to help Father in, and make him as good a churchman as anyone. But Father had felt he was already in, and to be confirmed was unnecessary. He didn't understand at all clearly what confirmation was anyhow. He declared it was only some folderol. He refused to be bothered with it. This was the root of all those conversations about whether he'd go to Heaven, when Mother said that to be on the safe side he ought to be confirmed first, and Father said that getting him into Heaven was her affair.

But this wasn't the worst. I don't know when Mother found out the whole truth about Father, but I don't think she knew it when she and I had those first talks. If not, it may have been my asking questions that led her to ask more herself, and thus to stumble on a strange and upsetting discovery.

Still, the discovery would have been almost sure to come some day. It was mere luck it hadn't come sooner. Nobody had purposely hidden Father's story from Mother—least of all poor Father himself. He never kept anything from her. Not that he didn't try to; but he was far too un-guarded to have any secrets.

I remember Father once had his pocket picked on the street-car, coming home. As an old New Yorker, born and bred, he was ashamed of this incident. He was also provoked; and when he unlocked the front door and came in, he was swearing to himself in loud whispers. Mother was upstairs in her room. She heard Father talking away to himself in the front hall, as he hung up his coat. "Damned rascals! if I ever catch them—." He flung his cane in the rack. "Not a word. I shan't say a word about it," he went on, to himself. He stamped up the stairs, mutter-ing, "Yes, too much talk in this house." "Well, Vinnie," he said to Mother, and sat himself down by the fire, in what he evidently meant to be an impenetrable and innocent silence.

"Clare!" Mother said sharply.

"What is it?"

"Clare! What's the matter with you? What has happened?"

"Damnation!" Father said. "What's happened? How do you know that it's happened? There's entirely too much talk in this house. A man can't have any privacy in his own home, that's what it comes down to. I had my pocket-book stolen, that's what's happened. Are you satisfied now?"

"Your pocket-book? Oh! Why did you let them?"

"Let them!" said Father. "Good God! They picked my pocket on the street-car, I tell you. I had it when I left the club."

"Oh, Clare dear! How could you! You must be getting old. Did you have the cook's wages in it?"

Father sprang from his chair in a fury and left the room, saying: "I knew you'd ask that. Yes, damn it, I had the cook's wages. I want this prying to stop." And afterwards, when he came down to dinner, he was bursting to tell the whole story—just how a young whipper-snapper had jostled him, and what he had said to the fellow, while a confederate had stolen his money and jumped off the car. He added, with a baffled look at Mother, that he didn't know how she found out things.

"She finds out every damn thing I ever do," I heard him say later, in his bathroom, in honest bewilderment. He usually chose the bathroom at night for his private communings, although an air-shaft connecting with the other bathrooms carried his words through the house.

A man who was so unselfconscious would have betrayed his religious shortcomings completely and promptly, if he himself had known the facts.

Grandpa knew the facts, but they had seemed to him of no importance. So it wasn't until Mother chanced to ask him directly one day what church Father had been baptized at, that Grandpa said Father had never been baptized at all.

I doubt if I can even imagine what a shock this was to Mother. This was in the conventional eighteen-eighties, when women led sheltered lives, and when men in general conformed to religious requirements. Mother must have felt that she could hardly believe her own ears. She had taken it for granted that everyone in a civilized country was baptized as soon as he was born as a matter of course. She had never met or known about any man, woman or child, who had even dreamed of not being baptized. It was simply unheard of. Why, all the poor Indians in Mexico belonged to some church. Even in the wildest lands, anywhere, there were so many missionaries, that every half-naked savage—with any luck at all—seemed to get baptized. Yet here was her own husband—!

Grandpa explained to her that his idea had been to leave Father free: let the boy grow up and decide all such things for himself. As to Grandma, well, she always spoke of Grandpa as Mr. Day, and she was surprised to hear Mother take on so about this. She said to her gently and patiently, "But Vinnie, dear child, that was the way Mr. Day wished it; and he's generally right."

Mother didn't feel this way at all. She thought Grandpa was wrong about lots of things, and she always told him so to his face. Grandpa liked nothing better. She was young and impulsive and pretty, and very direct, and he used to egg her on by arguing with her in the most outrageous ways he could think of.

But this time there wasn't any argument, so far as I ever heard. Mother couldn't wait; she hurried home to Father with her terrible news, supposing that as soon as he heard it he would be baptized at once. There was some excuse for not being confirmed, since not everyone did it, but nobody would defy God to the extent of not at least being baptized. She had her second great shock when he flatly refused. He was dressing for dinner at the moment, and he said she must not interrupt him. Although he was surprised and displeased to hear he hadn't been christened, he at once declared that nothing could be done to correct matters now.

Mother cried when she talked with me about it, and couldn't give me his reasons. She didn't seem to think that he had any. He was just being obstinate. But I was sometimes allowed to be present when they debated the matter, and this gave me a picture—of some sort—of his state of mind.

"I simply can't understand why you won't be baptized," Mother said. "Clare dear, tell me, aren't you a Christian?"

"Why, confound it, of course I am a Christian," Father roundly declared. "A damned good Christian too. A lot better Christian than those psalm-singing donkeys at church."

"Oh hush, Clare!" Mother always was terrified when he bordered on blasphemy.

Now to say "hush" to Father was like pouring kerosene on a fire. I repeatedly saw Mother try to quench his flames in this way, and every such effort only made him blaze higher—far higher. Yet she tried it again the next time. Neither she nor Father seemed to study the other one's nature. They each insisted the other one's nature should work in some way it didn't. I never once saw either of them observe the other in a calm, detached spirit, to see how his or her ego operated, and how to press the right button. Instead they invariably charged at each other full tilt, and learned unwillingly and dimly—if at all—by collisions.

So Mother said "hush" to Father, and the conflagration was on. And Father, being maddened by the kerosene, swore more and more, and declared that there was no need whatever for him to go and get baptized, and that he was quite as good a Christian as Owen Lloyd Garden.

"But if you won't be baptized," Mother wailed, "you aren't a Christian at all."

Father said he would not be baptized, and he would be a Christian. He begged to inform Mother he would be a Christian in his own way.

In her desperation Mother went to Dr. Garden and pledged him to secrecy, and revealed to him the horrible fact that Father had never been baptized. Dr. Garden was greatly astonished, but said he would attend to it. He was still more astonished when he learned that he would not be allowed to.

Mother tried to explain Father's plan of being his own kind of Christian. Dr. Garden was agitated. He didn't seem to know what to make of this. He said it had never been heard of. Not even the Apostles had omitted being baptized, he explained. If Mr. Day was going to set himself above the Holy Apostles—

Mother felt more frightened than ever at this dreadful picture. That would be just like Father, she felt. That was exactly what he would do.

# IV *My Father's Dark Hour*

If we had been living in England, I imagine a rector would have known the right tone to take to get Father's good will. He wouldn't have been weepy, or concerned at all about Father's soul. He would have been firm, but quite casual: "To bad it wasn't done before, of course; but it will only take a few minutes. Better stop in at the church tomorrow morning, and let me attend to it for you. One can't be eccentric in these things. Bad example to others. A person of your position, Mr. Day—." Father might have been open to an approach of that kind.

But the best that Dr. Garden could do was to supply Mother with texts, and to warn her that Father must be baptized before anything happened. The Bible said absolutely you had to be baptized to be saved. If you died first, why then, instead of Heaven, you would land in hell-fire. In short this was a serious situation, and Mr. Day must give in.

Even this, if it had been led up to little by little and presented to Father impressively, might possibly have made him uneasy about the risk he was running. But Mother was an impetuous ambassador: she threw it all at him at once. She began gently enough; but she was emotional, which set Father on edge; and then at his first impatient word she fired off all her guns. There was a turmoil of texts from the Bible and imprecations from Father; and Father came out of it convinced that this was some damned scheme of Garden's.

Mother at once began a campaign to break Father down, and many pitched battles were fought whenever she suddenly felt like it. Father never knew when he would find himself in the midst of a conflict. He might be going to the theatre with Mother, cross, but handsome and glowing; or he might be reading Hume and Smollett peacefully, on a warm afternoon; or they might be playing backgammon by the fire on some winter evening. Suddenly Mother would remember his danger and go at him again, and Father would bellow at baptism, and stamp off to play billiards.

One Sunday he even made a scene on his way out of church. Dr. Garden had preached about men who would not see the light; and after the service was over, and while Father and Mother were moving down the crowded aisles slowly, Mother whispered that she felt sure the sermon had been meant for him. Father snorted at such pulpit impudence. "The damned dissenter!" he said. And the rest of the way down the aisle they had it out, hot and heavy. Father wouldn't lower his voice; and people stared, until Mother felt most embarrassed. "Garden needn't talk to me as though I were a Welsh miner," Father kept saying. "I have never done anything I was ashamed of."

His counter-attacks upon Mother were not all in one tone. He used every possible way to stop her, according to the mood he was in. When he was in a good humor he would tease her about it. Or sometimes he would be grave and dignified, and remind her that he knew best. Again, he would be stern and peremptory: "That's enough, do you hear?" But Mother couldn't stop. She was troubled. Not only did she have a natural desire to have her own way for once, but Dr. Garden had told her how much God would blame her if she didn't bring Father around. She felt that He was blaming her anyhow for all her own faults; and it just seemed intolerable that an additional sin should be hung round her neck, by Father's inexplicable refusal to go through a short ceremony.

He used every possible way to stop her, I said. But he never used argument. He hadn't the patience to explain clearly what he was thinking. Nevertheless, when he was having a violent eruption, remarks would fly out, like heated rocks from a volcano; and these could be analyzed afterward as a clue to his fires.

His general position seemed to be that he didn't object to baptism. It was all right for savages, for instance. But among civilized people it should come only when one was young. Since it hadn't been attended to in his own case, why, let it go, damn it. It would be ridiculous to baptize him now. It was far too late to do anything. He wasn't to blame. He would have been perfectly willing to be baptized as a child, if they had done the thing soon enough. Since they hadn't, it was no fault of his, and he didn't intend to be bothered.

It was useless to try to make him see that being baptized was a rite, and that it involved something holy and essential. He said it was a mere technicality. As to obeying the Bible, there were a lot of damn things in the Bible. A man would be in a pretty fix if he gave all he had to the poor. No, a man had to use his common-sense about obeying the Bible. And everything else. If he had any.

He seemed to imagine that if he ever came to be tried, by his God, he could easily establish the fact that his position was sound. In any event, he wasn't going to be led around by the nose by a parson. He didn't blame

Mother for being upset; she was only a woman; but even she would come to her senses eventually, and see he was right.

At this point I went to Mother and asked her if she would let me help out. It all seemed so simple and plain to me, that I was sure I could make Father see it. I was in that stage between infancy and adolescence when children will do strange things. Besides, I wasn't neutral: it always upset me and shook me to see Mother unhappy; and the strong emotional vortex before me at last drew me in. Mother was pleased by my wanting to help her, and said I might try. Perhaps she thought Father's heart would be touched by the plea of his child. Needless to say, he was not touched at all; he was merely disgusted.

I can see him now, ruddy and strong, and a little too stout, in his evening clothes and bulging white shirt-front. He lit his cigar after dinner, blew out a rich cloud of smoke, and took a sip of his coffee. "God bless my soul," he said, heartily, and tasted his cognac. "A—men!" He looked over at me. "It doesn't count unless you say A—men," he said, with a wink.

I didn't smile back. I was worriedly waiting for an opening, and counting my weapons.

I had been reading a little devotional book. I don't recall ever willingly reading a book of that kind before; but this time it was almost a pleasure, because I wasn't reading it for my own improvement but Father's. The author was a person who wrote in a superior tone, and who seemed to feel bored and condescending when he explained things to groundlings. I immediately planned to use Father as my groundling, if possible, and to talk in such a calm, easy way to him, that he'd feel impressed. This author, for example, declared that baptism was "of course a matter of religious joy to any right-minded Christian." He also said that when we were baptized we were "buried with Christ." He went on to state that "remission of sins" was badly needed by everyone, and "it is absurd to suppose that we can be buried with Christ without receiving remission of sins." Things like that.

I tried, but without any success, to explain all this to Father. I also told him about a man called Nicodemus, who had argued against being baptized; and how he had been sternly refuted, and warned to behave himself.

But Father said he wasn't interested in Thing-a-ma-jig—Nicodemus. And I might have known, myself, that he took small stock in arguments. If he had ever debated things with me he might easily have won me over; but it didn't interest him, usually, to engage in discussion. He didn't care to marshal his reasons or describe the road he had taken. He preferred to begin by stating his conclusion, and by calling yours non-sense, and to end the debate then and there. There was nothing else to be said.

My picture of him, therefore, was that of a man blind and deaf to the anxious and intelligent warnings of Dr. Garden and me.

I was supposed to be a bright boy. I had a high rank at school. But I was so over-receptive and credulous that in effect I was stupid. I had none of a country boy's cautious approach to ideas. I could swallow ideas by the dozen, and did; good and bad. My mind hadn't any of the seasoning or the toughness of Father's. It was so logical that if it had accepted cer-tain premises it would have marched off a precipice. Or at least it would have marched Father off one.

Father was looking quizzically at me. I went at him again. My next weapon was one that I thought would strike fear to his heart: a text that I had picked out as being especially strong and conclusive. It had one weak point, it didn't specifically use the word baptism, and I expected Father to pounce on this as an objection; but when he did I planned to rebuke him for picking at trifles, and for being concerned with its word-ing instead of its spirit. But Father was not a man to niggle at small technicalities, and he instinctively met this attack—like all others—head on. The text was Christ's saying that unless people confessed Him before men, neither would He confess them before His Father in Heaven. When I read this to Father, to my astonishment he was quite unconcerned. He felt that this was the mere empty warning of a meddlesome middleman. Father was going to deal direct with his Maker. Christ wasn't his Maker. Father felt he had just as much right around Heaven as Christ.

In fact, now I think of it, Father was—if there is such a thing—an Old Testament Christian. He permitted the existence of Christ, but disap-proved of all His ideas.

But I was in no mood to philosophise over this then. My emotions swept over me, and I became exalted and ardent. I told Father that al-though we knew he had always been a good man, still he hadn't taken this step that every Christian must take. If he took it, he would go to Heaven and there be received by the angels. If he didn't, I explained to him that he would be cast into Hell. And I cried, and said there would be "weep-ing and gnashing of teeth."

Instead of being moved to tears by this, and getting right down on his knees, Father sat there, beside the dark book-case, fresh and healthy and solid, breathing out a rich odor of Havana cigar smoke and cognac. Every cell in his body seemed to be robustly resisting destruction. I don't recall now what he said to me, but he didn't say much. He reminded me that I was only a little boy. This seemed to me quite irrelevant. What I wanted to know was, how about those arguments; but he merely smiled at my earnestness. A rather grave smile. Perhaps he was wondering how on earth he had produced such a son. At any rate he showed great forbearance, and sent me up to bed; while he got out the cards from the game-box and played solitaire.

His situation looked pretty black to me, as I lay in bed. I pictured to myself how the rest of us would be standing around, up in Heaven, and how very upset we'd all feel to see Father in Hell.

Yet somehow I felt more excitement than grief, at this scene. I must have been deeply impressed by Father's intrepid firmness. True, he was only too plainly shutting himself out of bliss; and ordinarily I'd have felt a great horror at the thought of a loved one in torment. But suppose Father positively refused to go to Hell when they said to? He seemed so remarkably able to fend for himself, that it would probably just be another of his fights. He and Satan.

I began to cool off as a missionary, and go back to my toys. But Mother of course kept right on. And suddenly it seemed for a moment that she might prevail. She had a bad illness, which depressed and worried Father so much, that when she kept begging and begging him to do this thing for her, and told him how happy it would make her, he said that he would.

But when she was well again, and eager to take him around to the font, he wouldn't go. His memory seemed to have got very dim. Mother exclaimed that he had solemnly agreed to be baptized, but he said flatly he had no recollection of it.

I don't know what grounds he may have had for taking this stand. He was never a man to justify, or explain, or excuse his own conduct. He didn't refrain out of dignity; he merely didn't examine it. He took himself, his thoughts and his actions, completely for granted, without introspection or analysis. Perhaps in this instance, in her fever, Mother had misunderstood him. Or perhaps his point of view was that he'd have done anything to help her get well, but now that she had happily got well his end was achieved, so how could she fairly expect him to proceed with his sacrifice? All I know is he seemed entirely satisfied with his behavior.

Mother felt very badly, and told him he was breaking her heart. This did not upset him. He probably guessed that underneath her tears there was more exasperation than heart-break. She hated the feeling of impotence he gave her. There seemed to be no way to manage him. She kept telling him that she simply couldn't believe he would really go back on his Sacred Promise—as she now began calling it. She taunted him with it. She said she had always supposed he was a man of his word. Father was quite unperturbed. Downtown, his lightest word to anybody was binding, of course; but that was in the real world of business. Getting baptized was all poppycock.

But Mother began to feel surer now that she could make Father yield. At least she had got one Sacred Promise out of the obstinate man, and she wouldn't let him do any more forgetting if she could once get another. The more her self-confidence grew, the more her tactics improved. She was quite unconscious, probably, that she had handicapped herself, hitherto, by attacking Father only on religious grounds, where he had no soft spots to strike at. He became more vulnerable at once, when she begged him to do her a favor. They were in love with each other; and he would have done a good deal for Mother—"Anything in reason," he said.

He went into the whole matter as thoroughly as a railroad report. He asked just how wet would a man have to get to be baptized. Would he have to go to the River Jordan to please Mother, and do the thing properly? If not, then exactly what rigmarole would he have to go through. He said if it wasn't too complicated, perhaps he'd consider it.

Mother showed him the baptismal service in the prayer-book for those of riper years; but Father said that by persons of riper years it must mean those who knew better. It was nothing but a lot of prayers anyhow. That was the clergyman's part of it. What he wanted to know was how much trouble he himself would be put to. But when Mother impatiently answered his questions about this, he was startled. He said the thing was even more impracticable than he had supposed. It wasn't as though he could have an accommodating parson trot around to the house and baptize him quietly some morning, after his coffee and eggs; no, he learned that the performance would have to take place in a church; and, worse, there would have to be others present. A congregation, the book said. Father declared that that ended it. He said he certainly wasn't going around to the Peace Everlasting to be made a fool of in that way. He said, damn it, he'd be the laughing-stock of all his friends. Mother said, why, his friends would be proud of him for standing up for his Saviour; but Father said he'd never hear the last of it, around at the club.

# V  *My Father Enters the Church*

The way it ended was simple. Mother's family had lived at one time in a pretty little two-storied house, called "The Cottage," in East Twenty-ninth Street; it had casement windows, set with diamond-shaped panes of leaded glass, and a grass plot in front. On the other side of the street, at Fifth Avenue, stood the church that is now known as the Little Church Around the Corner. The first Dr. Houghton was the rector in those times, and Mother was fond of him. One day Mother heard that a young relative of his, the Reverend Mr. Morley, had taken a far-away parish near what was then Audubon Park, a mile or two north of where in later years they erected Grant's Tomb. This part of the city was so thinly settled that it was like a remote country suburb. There were dirt roads and lanes instead of streets; and thick, quiet old woods. Mother suddenly got the idea that perhaps this would suit Father, since he seemed bent on "confessing God before men" only where no one was looking. Besides, Mother knew young Mr. Morley, and she felt that here was some one she could go to with her curious problem. She asked him to come down and see her. He was sympathetic. He agreed to make everything as easy for Father as possible.

I don't know just why it was, but somehow that was all there was to it. Father still got in a very bad humor whenever the subject was mentioned; but at least Mother wasn't, any longer, asking the impossible of him. It was thoroughly distasteful and he hated it, but he supposed he could go through it sometime. Perhaps he even got to the point of wishing to get the thing over with.

So the day came on which Father had agreed he would enter the church. The only person who had to be reminded of it was Father himself. I remember excitedly looking out of the window at breakfast, and seeing a hired brougham from Ryerson & Brown's in the street. The coachman had on a blue coat with a double row of bright buttons, and on his legs were faded green trousers from some other man's livery. He was looking up at our front door. His horse was as weather-beaten as the horse on the plains of Siberia, in the picture in my Geography; and he too seemed to be looking up at our house and wondering what would come out of it.

I stood out on our front stoop staring down at them, and listening to the sounds in our hallway. Father had come down to breakfast in a good temper that morning, and the bacon and eggs had suited him for once, and the coffee too had found favor. Mother gave a happy, tender look at this soul she was saving. The dining-room seemed full of sunshine, and the whole world light-hearted. But when Mother said it was nearly eight o'clock and the cab would soon be here, Father had demanded what cab. He listened to her answer in horror, and sprang up with a roar.

It was as though an elephant which had been tied up with infinite pains had trumpeted and burst every fetter, after the labor of months. It was all to do over again. Father not only had to be convinced that a day had been set, and that this was the day, but the whole question of baptism had to be reopened and proved. All the religious instruction that had been slowly inscribed on his mind had apparently utterly vanished—the slate was wiped clean. He was back at his original starting-point, that this thing was all folderol—it was nothing but a wild idea of Mother's with which he had no concern.

A woman of less determination would have given up, Father was so indignant. But Mother, though frightened and discouraged and tearful, was angry. She wasn't going to let Father off, after all she had done. At first I thought she surely had lost. He was completely intractable. She stood up to him, armed with God's word and the laws of the church, and also, as she despairingly reminded him, with his own "Sacred Promise," and again she learned that not a one of them was any good. But she had one other weapon: Ryerson & Brown's waiting cab.

There were some things that were unheard of in our family: they simply weren't done. One was wasting money on cabs. When we went to the length of ordering a cab, we did not keep it waiting. And the sight of this cab at the door seemed to hypnotize Father. It stood there like a link in some inevitable chain of events. At first he declared it could go to the devil, he didn't care if there were fifty cabs waiting. But he was by habit and instinct a methodical man. When he helped himself to a portion of anything at the table, for instance, he did his best to finish that portion, whether he liked it or not. He got all the more angry if it didn't taste right, but his code made him eat it. If he began a book he was bound to go on with it, no matter how much it bored him. He went through with any and every program to which he once felt committed. The fact that this cab had been ordered, and now stood at the door, prevailed in those depths of his spirit which God couldn't reach. Where I sat on the steps I could hear him upstairs in his room, banging doors and putting on his overcoat and cursing at fate.

Mother darted out and told the coachman where he was to take us; and then she got in, bonneted and cloaked, to wait for Father to come. The coachman looked puzzled when he found we were going to church. He could see we weren't dressed for a funeral, yet it was hardly a wedding. Perhaps he thought we were a very devout family, seeking for some extra worship.

Then Father came down the steps, blackly. He got in the cab. And the horse and the coachman both jumped as Father slammed the door shut.

The cab bumped along over the cobblestones, with its ironshod wheels. The steady-going rattle and jolting made me dreamy. It was soothing to see the landscape slide by, at five or six miles an hour. Milkmen, ladling milk out of tall cans. Chambermaids polishing door-bells. Ladies, with the tops of their sleeves built up high at each shoulder. Horses straining at street-cars. Flocks of sparrows hopping about, pecking at refuse and dung, and waiting until a horse almost stepped on them before flying off.

We drove up Madison Avenue to the Park, and out at West Seventy-second Street. Then under the Elevated, with its coal-dust sifting down and stray cinders, blackening the pools in the street; and its little locomotives chuff-chuffing along overhead. At the Boulevard, as upper Broadway was then named, we turned northward. Over toward the river were rocky wastelands, old shanties and goats. The skyline along the Boulevard was one of telegraph poles, along bare blocks and rail fences. I liked the looks of this ungraded district; it was all up-and-down and had ponds in it. And it ought to have comforted Father. No members of the club or the stock exchange could be sighted for miles; they probably never set foot in such regions. What more could Father ask?

But Father was glaring about, looking like a caged lion. Apparently he had confidently believed up to this very moment that Heaven would intervene somehow, and spare him this dose. He had never done Heaven any harm; why should it be malignant? His disappointment was increasingly bitter as he saw he was trapped. Another sort of man would have opened the cab door and bolted. But Father was drinking his hemlock. He also was freely expressing his feelings about it. The hardships of marriage had never before impressed him so sharply. A woman's demands on her husband were simply beyond human reckoning. He felt, and he said plainly to Mother, as the cab rattled on, that if he did this thing for her, it must be understood that it was his supreme contribution. No diamond necklace. No other sacrifices of any kind. He must never be asked to do anything more all his life.

Mother tried to point out that he wasn't doing it for her but for God, but Father said: "Pshaw! I won't hear to it." He had never had any trouble with God till Mother appeared on the scene.

Mother quoted Dr. Garden again to him, but Father said "Pish!"

"Oh Clare, you mustn't," said Mother.

"Bah!" Father roared. "Bah! What do you suppose I care for that fellow!"

"But it's in the Bible."

"Pooh! Damn."

Mother shuddered at this. Here was a man who defied even the Bible. She half-expected God to come bursting right out of the sky, and bang his fist down on the Ryerson & Brown cab and all in it.

"Damnation!" Father repeated, consumed by his wrongs.

Mother said, oh how could he talk so, on his way to the font! She drew away from him, and then looked back with awe at this being, whose sense of his powers was so great that he would stand up to Anyone.

We had now come in sight of the church. It stood halfway up a steep hill, which the horse climbed at a walk, although Father said if the cab didn't hurry he wouldn't have time to be baptized—he'd be late at the office.

"What is the name of this confounded place?" he said, as we got out, making a jab at the little House of God with his cane.

"O Clare, dear! Please don't. It's the Church of the Epiphany, I told you."

"Epiphany! Humph," Father grunted. "More gibberish."

Inside it was cold and bare, and it smelled of varnish. The pews were of new yellow pine, and the stained-glass looked cheap. There was nobody present. The sexton had hurried away to fetch the minister, after letting us in.

Father glowered around like a bull in some Plaza del Toro, waiting to charge the reverend toreador and trample upon him. He stood there, boxed up in surroundings where he didn't belong, hurt and outraged and lonely. His whole private life had been pried into, even his babyhood. He had kept decently aloof from the depths of religion, as a gentleman should—he was no emotional tinker like that fellow, John Bunyan—yet here he was, dragged into this damned evangelist orgy, far from his own proper world, in the hands of his wife and a parson.

A footstep was heard.

"Oh, good morning, Mr. Morley," said Mother. "This is Mr. Day."

Mr. Morley was a young man, shy but friendly, with a new-looking beard. He approached our little group trustingly, to shake Father's hand, but he got such a look that he turned to me instead and patted me on the head several times. There was a rich smell of something about him. It wasn't bayrum, such as Father sometimes used after shaving. It was far more delicious to me than any cologne or sachet scent. And besides, it had much more body to it; more satisfaction. But I couldn't identify it. I only knew that it was a magnificent fragrance, and seemed to come from his beard. He led us up to the front of the church and the service began.

It says in the prayer-book that when a person of riper years is to be baptized, he shall be exhorted to prepare himself, with prayers and with fasting. And if he shall be found fit, "then the Godfathers and Godmothers (the People being assembled upon the Sunday or Prayer Day appointed) shall be ready to present him at the font." I suppose that was why I was taken along, so that there would be enough people there for a congregation: Mother and the sexton and me. The sexton, who seemed a nervous man, was skulking in a rear pew; but Mother and I stood just behind Father, to bolster him up. It was a curious situation for a small boy to be in, as I look back on it.

Mr. Morley presently read an address to the three of us, as we stood there before him. (I condense this and the following quotations, from the service in my old prayer-book.) "Dearly beloved," he said to us, "forasmuch as all men are conceived and born in sin, and they who are in the flesh cannot please God, but live in sin; and our Saviour Christ saith, none can enter into the kingdom of God, except he be regenerate and born anew; I beseech you to call upon God that of his bounteous goodness he will grant to this person that which by nature he cannot have; that he may be baptized with Water and the Holy Ghost, and received into Christ's holy Church, and be made a lively member of the same."

Next came a prayer in which Mr. Morley went back to the ark, and spoke of how God saved Noah and his family from perishing by water; and of how God also led the children of Israel safely through the Red Sea; and of how Jesus was baptized in the Jordan. These three incidents were cited as proof that God had sanctified "the element of Water to the mystical washing away of sin."

"We beseech thee," Mr. Morley continued, "that thou wilt mercifully look upon this thy Servant; wash him and sanctify him with the Holy Ghost; that he, being delivered from thy wrath, may be received into the ark of Christ's Church; and being steadfast in faith, joyful through hope, and rooted in charity, may come to the land of everlasting life."

Father was getting restive by this time, but Mr. Morley kept on. He read us a part of the Gospel of John, and a long exhortation and prayer; and after this he bravely turned and spoke as follows to Father:

"Well-beloved, who are come hither desiring to receive holy Baptism, you have heard how the congregation hath prayed that our Lord Jesus Christ would release you of your sins, to give you the kingdom of Heaven, and everlasting life. You have heard also that our Lord hath promised to grant all those things that we have prayed for. Wherefore you must also faithfully, in the presence of these your Witnesses and this whole congregation, promise and answer to the following questions:

"Dost thou renounce the devil and all his works, the vain pomp and glory of the world, with all covetous desires of the same, and the sinful desires of the flesh?"

The answer to this was rather long, and Father of course had not learned it; but Mother whispered the words in his ear, and he repeated some of them impatiently, in a harsh, stony voice. He looked as though he might have been an annoyed Roman general, participating much against his will in a low and barbaric rite.

There were only three more questions, however, and the answers were short.

"O Merciful God," said Mr. Morley, when these were finished, "grant that the old Adam in this person may be so buried, that the new man may be raised up in him. Amen." He had to say this, because it was in the prayer-book; but Father's eyes were on fire, and there was a great deal of the old Adam in him, and it didn't look buried.

Four more little prayers followed, and then came the great moment, when Mr. Morley tried to pour water on Father. Owing to Father's being no longer an infant, the prayer-book didn't require Mr. Morley to take him into his arms for this purpose, and hold him over the font; but he did have to wet him a little. I don't know how he managed it. I remember how Father stood, grim and erect, in his tailed morning-coat; but when I saw Mr. Morley make a pass at Father's forehead, I am sorry to say I shut my eyes tightly at this frightful sacrilege, and whether he actually landed or not I never knew. But he did go on to say, "I baptize thee," and all the rest of it, to Father. "We receive this person into the congregation of Christ's flock," he added; "and do sign him with the sign of the Cross, in token that hereafter he shall not be ashamed to confess the faith of Christ crucified, and manfully to fight under his banner, against sin, the world, and the devil; and to continue Christ's faithful soldier and servant unto his life's end. Amen."

The baptism part was now over. Father started to leave, but we managed somehow to detain him while we knelt and gave thanks. And, to end with, Mr. Morley urged Father to "mortify all his evil affections," and exhorted Mother and me to remember that it was our part and duty to put Father in mind what a solemn vow he had now made, that so he might grow in grace and in the knowledge of Christ, "and live godly, righteously, and soberly, in this present world."

We stood awkwardly still for a moment, but there was nothing else. Mr. Morley started in being chatty, in a more everyday voice. He stood next to me as he talked, and I remember how absorbed I was, again, by his mellow aroma. The odor was so grateful to my senses that it seemed almost nourishing. I sniffed and I sniffed—till all of a sudden I knew what it was. It was cocoa. We seldom had cocoa at our house. It made me feel hungry. I greedily inhaled the last bits of it while Mr. Morley talked on. He said he hoped we'd attend services in this new church of his, sometimes. He began to describe how the bishop had come there to consecrate it.

But Father broke in, saying abruptly, "I shall be late at the office," and strode down the aisle. Mother and I hurried after him. He was muttering such blasphemous things that I heard Mother whisper: "Oh, please, Clare, please; please don't. This poor little church! It'll have to be consecrated all over again."

As we drove off, Mother sank back into her corner of the cab, quite worn out. Father was still seething away, as though his very soul was boiling over. If he could only have known it, long quiet days were ahead, when he and God could go back in peace to their comfortable old ways together; for he was never confirmed, or troubled in any way again by religious demands. But all he could think of, for the moment, were his recent indignities.

He got out at the nearest Elevated station, to take a train for the office, with the air of a man who had thoroughly wasted the morning. He slammed the cab door on us, leaving us to drive home alone. But before he turned away to climb the stairs, he thrust his red face in the window, and with a burning look at Mother said, "I hope to God you are satisfied." Then this new son of the church took out his watch, gave a start, and Mother and I heard him shout "Hell!" as he raced up the steps.

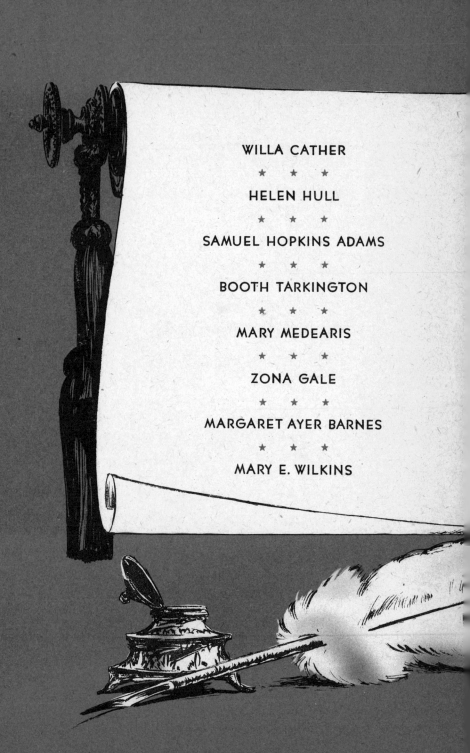

WILLA CATHER

★ ★ ★

HELEN HULL

★ ★ ★

SAMUEL HOPKINS ADAMS

★ ★ ★

BOOTH TARKINGTON

★ ★ ★

MARY MEDEARIS

★ ★ ★

ZONA GALE

★ ★ ★

MARGARET AYER BARNES

★ ★ ★

MARY E. WILKINS